THE GUINNESS BOOK OF SPORTS RECORDS 1994-1995

EDITOR

MARK YOUNG

Facts On File®

AN INFOBASE HOLDINGS COMPANY

THE GUINNESS BOOK OF SPORTS RECORDS 1994–95

Copyright © 1994 by Guinness Publishing Ltd.

Facts On File, Inc.
460 Park Avenue South
New York NY 10016
USA

This book is taken in part from *The Guinness Book of Records* © 1994

Facts On File books are available at special discounts when purchased in bulk quantities for businesses, associations, institutions or sales promotions. Please contact the Special Sales Department of our New York office at 212/683-2244 or 1-800/322-8755.

ISBN 0-8160-2655-6 (hardcover)
ISBN 0-8160-2656-4 (paperback)
ISSN 1054-4178

Text design by Ron Monteleone
Jacket design by Mark Safran
Composition by Catherine Rincon Hyman/Facts On File, Inc.
Illustrations by Sam Moore
Production by Kevin Duffy

Manufactured by R. R. Donnelley & Sons, Inc.
Printed in the United States of America

10 9 8 7 6 5 4 3 2 1

This book is printed on acid-free paper.

CONTENTS

ACKNOWLEDGMENTS

The goal of this book is to provide the most comprehensive and accurate account of the records established in the world of sports. Accumulating such a vast and disparate array of information has required the cooperation, patience and expertise of many organizations and individuals. I would like to thank the media representatives, librarians and historians of the following organizations for their help: National Championship Air Races, U.S. National Archery Assoc., Championship Auto Racing Teams, Indianapolis Motor Speedway, National Assoc. for Stock Car Auto Racing, National Hot Rod Association, U.S. Badminton Assoc., Major League Baseball, The National Baseball Hall of Fame and Museum, Little League Baseball, National Collegiate Athletic Assoc., Naismith Memorial Basketball Hall of Fame, National Basketball Assoc., U.S. Biathlon Assoc., U.S. Bobsled and Skeleton Fed., Professional Bowling Assoc., Ladies Professional Bowling Tour, American Bowling Congress, Women's Int'l Bowling Congress, USA Boxing, U.S. Canoe and Kayak Team, U.S. Croquet Assoc., U.S. Curling Assoc., U.S. Cycling Assoc., Ultra Marathon Cycling Assoc., U.S. Diving, American Horse Shows Assoc., U.S. Fencing Assoc., U.S. Field Hockey Assoc., U.S. Figure Skating Assoc., National Football League, Canadian Football League, World Flying Disc Federation, World Footbag Assoc., PGA Tour, LPGA Tour, European PGA Tour, U.S. Gymnastics Fed., U.S. Hang Gliding Assoc., U.S. Trotting Assoc., National Hockey League, New York Racing Assoc., Oak Tree Racing Assoc., National Horseshoe Pitchers Assoc., U.S. Judo, USA Karate Fed., U.S. Modern Pentathlon Assoc., U.S. Olympic Committee, U.S. Orienteering Fed., U.S. Polo Assoc., Billiard Congress of America, American Powerboat Assoc., American Amateur Racquetball Assoc., Professional Rodeo Cowboys Assoc., U.S. Amateur Confederation of Roller Skating, U.S. Rowing Assoc., National Rifle Assoc., U.S. Skiing, Iditarod Trail Committee, Amateur Softball Assoc., U.S. Int'l Speedskating Assoc., Assoc. of Surfing Professionals, U.S. Swimming, U.S. Synchronized Swimming, U.S. Table Tennis Assoc., U.S. Taekwondo Union, U.S. Team Handball Fed., Women's Tennis Assoc., I.B.M./A.P.T. Tour, The Athletics Congress, New York Road Runners Club, American Trampoline and Tumbling Assoc., Triathlon Fed. USA, World Triathlon Corp., Assoc. of Volleyball Professionals, U.S. Water Polo, American Water Ski Assoc., U.S. Weightlifting, USA Wrestling, America's Cup Organizing Committee.

Regrettably, space prevents me from mentioning all the individuals who have helped me compile this book; however, I must mention certain people whose contributions have added immensely to this project: at Guinness Publishing in Enfield, England, Peter Matthews, Michelle Dunkley McCarthy, Stewart Newport and Debbie Collings. Special thanks is extended to Ken Park, Ken Rosenberg, and Walter Kronenberg for allowing me access to their encyclopedic knowledge of the world of sports records.

As I write in this space each year, publishing, as with sports, requires the efforts of many people to produce the on-field performance. I am once again indebted to the talented and professional team of people who have assisted me in producing this book: Jo Stein, Kevin Duffy, Cathy Hyman, Grace M. Ferrara, Sam Moore, Joe Reilly, Virginia Rubens, Marjorie Bank, and Denise Jack.

Mark C. Young
New York City

AEROBATICS

ORIGINS The first aerobatic "maneuver" is generally considered to be the sustained inverted flight in a Blériot flown by Célestin-Adolphe Pégoud (France), at Buc, France on September 21, 1913. Stunt flying became popular in the United States during the 1920s and 1930s. In the late 1950s aerobatic contests regained popularity at air shows. In 1970 the International Aerobatic Club formed standardized rules for the sport, establishing four categories of competition: unlimited, advanced, intermediate and sportsman.

WORLD CHAMPIONSHIPS First held in 1960, the world championships are a biennial event. The competition consists of three flight programs: known and unknown compulsories and a free program. The judges award scores based on a system devised by Col. José Aresti (Spain).

Most titles (team) The USSR won the men's title a record six times, 1964, 1966, 1976, 1982, 1986, and 1990.

Most titles (individual) Petr Jimus (Czechoslovakia) has won two men's world titles: 1984 and 1986. Betty Stewart (U.S.) has won two women's world titles, 1980 and 1982.

AIR RACING

Air racing, or airplane racing, consists of piloted aircraft racing a specific number of laps over a closed circuit marked by pylons. As with auto racing, the first plane to cross the finish line is the winner. Air races are divided into several catego-

UPSIDE DOWN ☛ THE DURATION RECORD FOR INVERTED FLIGHT IS 4 HOURS 38 MINUTES 10 SECONDS BY JOANN OSTERUD (U.S.). SHE FLEW FROM VANCOUVER TO VANDERHOOF, CANADA ON JULY 24, 1991.

FASTEST SPORT ■ UNLIMITED CLASS AIR RACING IS THE FASTEST ENGINE-POWERED SPORT. THE NCAR RACE RECORD IS 481.618 MPH. (WILLIAM S. ROMANO)

ries, depending on the type of plane and engine. The top level of the sport is the unlimited class.

ORIGINS The first international airplane racing competition, the Bennett Trophy, was held at Rheims, France from August 22–28, 1909.

United States The first international air race staged in the United States was the second Bennett Trophy competition, held at Belmont Park, N.Y. in 1910. Air racing became very popular in the 1920s. Competitions, such as the National Air Races (inaugurated in 1924) and the Thompson Trophy (inaugurated in 1930), drew enormous crowds— 500,000 people attended the 1929 National Air Races in Cleveland, Ohio. Following World War II the popularity of the sport declined. During the mid-1950s, enthusiasts revived the sport, racing smaller World War II military planes. In 1964 Bill Stead staged the first National Championship Air Races (NCAR) at Reno, Nev.; this is now the premier air racing event in the United States.

NATIONAL CHAMPIONSHIP AIR RACES (NCAR)

Staged annually in Reno, Nev., since 1964, the NCAR has been held at its present site, the Reno/Stead Airport, since 1986. Races are staged in four categories: Unlimited class, AT-6 class, Formula One class and Biplane class.

UNLIMITED CLASS In this class the aircraft must use piston engines, be propeller-driven and be capable of pulling six G's. The planes race over a pylon-marked 9.128 mile course.

Most titles Darryl Greenmyer has won seven unlimited NCAR titles: 1965–69, 1971 and 1977.

AT-6 Class Only World War II Advanced Trainers (AT), complying to the original stock configuration, are allowed to compete. Seats can be removed and the engines stripped and reassembled, but the cubic inch displacement of the 650-horsepower 1340-R Pratt & Whitney engine cannot exceed the original level.

Most titles Eddie Van Fossen has won six AT-6 NCAR titles: 1986–88, 1991–93.

Fastest average speed (race) Eddie Van Fossen won the 1992 NCAR title recording the fastest average speed at 234.788 mph in "Miss TNT."

Fastest qualifying speed The one-lap NCAR qualifying record is 235.223 mph, by Eddie Van Fossen in 1992.

Fastest average speed (race) Lyle Shelton won the 1991 NCAR title recording the fastest average speed at 481.618 mph in his "Rare Bear."

Fastest qualifying speed The one-lap NCAR qualifying record is 482.892 mph, by Lyle Shelton in 1992.

ARCHERY

Origins The exact date of the invention of the bow is unknown, but historians agree that it was at least 50,000 years ago. The origins of archery as a compet-

ALL-TIME WINNER ■ EDDIE VAN FOSSEN, PILOTING MISS TNT, WON THE 1993 NCAR AT-6 TITLE, A RECORD SIXTH WIN IN THE EVENT. (WILLIAM S. ROMANO)

FLIGHT SHOOTING WORLD RECORDS

The object in flight shooting is to fire the arrow the greatest distance possible. There are two flight shooting classifications: regular flight and broadhead flight.

Regular Flight

Men

Bow Type	Distance	Archer	Date
Crossbow	2,047 yds 0 ft 2 in	Harry Drake	July 30, 1988
Unlimited Footbow	2,028 yds 0 ft 0 in	Harry Drake	Oct. 24, 1971
Conventional Footbow	1,542 yds 2 ft 10 in	Harry Drake	Oct. 6, 1979
Unlimited Recurve Bow	1,336 yds 1 ft 3 in	Don Brown	Aug. 2, 1987
Unlimited Compound Bow	1,320 yds 1 ft 3 in	Kevin Strother	July 31, 1992
Unlimited Longbow	356 yds 1 ft 2 in	Don Brown	July 29, 1989
Unlimited Primitive Bow	521 yds 0 ft 2 in	Daniel Perry	June 18, 1993

Women

Bow Type	Distance	Archer	Date
Unlimited Recurve Bow	1,039 yds 1 ft 1 in	April Moon	Sept. 13, 1981
Conventional Footbow	1,113 yds 2 ft 6 in	Arlyne Rhode	Sept. 10, 1978
Unlimited Compound Bow	807 yds 1 ft 3 in	April Moon	Aug. 1, 1987
Unlimited Longbow	217 yds 2 ft 3 in	April Moon	July 30, 1989

Broadhead Flight

Men

Bow Type	Distance	Archer	Date
Unlimited Compound Bow	784 yds 2 ft 9 in	Bert McCune Jr.	Aug. 2, 1992
Unlimited Recurve Bow	526 yds 0 ft 5 in	Don Brown	June 26, 1988
Unlimited Longbow	332 yds 2 ft 0 in	Don Brown	Aug. 2, 1992
Unlimited Primitive Bow	244 yds 2 ft 7 in	Daniel Perry	June 24, 1990

Women

Bow Type	Distance	Archer	Date
Unlimited Compound Bow	481 yds 0 ft 7 in	April Moon	June 24, 1989
Unlimited Recurve Bow	364 yds 0 ft 4 in	April Moon	June 28, 1987
Unlimited Longbow	237 yds 2 ft 3 in	April Moon	Aug. 2, 1992
Unlimited Primitive Bow	107 yds 1 ft 5 in	Gwen Perry	June 24, 1990

Source: U.S. National Archery Association

WORLD RECORDS (Single FITA Rounds)

Men

Event	Archer	Country	Points	Year
FITA	Vladimir Esheev	USSR	1,352	1990
90 m	Vladimir Esheev	USSR	330	1990
70 m	Hiroshi Yamamoto	Japan	344	1990
50 m	Rick McKinney	U.S.	345	1982
30 m	Antonio Vazquez Megldo	Spain	358	1992
Final	Vladimir Esheev	USSR	345	1989

Women

Event	Archer	Country	Points	Year
FITA	Cho Youn-Jeong	S. Korea	1,375	1992
70 m	Cho Youn-Jeong	S. Korea	338	1992
60 m	Kim Soo-nyung	S. Korea	347	1989
50 m	Cho Youn-Jeong	S. Korea	338	1992
30 m	Joanne Edens	Great Britain	357	1990
Final	Kim Soo-nyung	S. Korea	346	1990

Source: U.S. National Archery Association

itive sport are also unclear. It is believed that the ancient Olympic Games (776 B.C. to 393 A.D.) featured archery, using tethered doves as targets. The legends of Robin Hood and William Tell indicate that archery prowess was highly regarded in Europe by the 13th century. Archery became an official event in the modern Olympics in 1900. In 1931, the *Fédération Internationale de Tir à l'Arc* (FITA) was founded as the world governing body of the sport.

United States The date of the first use of the bow as a weapon in North America is unknown; however, it is believed that Native American tribes in the eastern part of North America were familiar with the bow by the 11th century. The National Archery Association was founded in 1879 in Crawfordsville, Ind. and is the oldest amateur sports organization in continuous existence in the United States.

TIMEOUT

ON TARGET ☞ ON APRIL 1, 1991 SIMON TARPLEE AND DAVID HATHAWAY (BOTH GREAT BRITAIN) SET THE PAIRS 24-HOURS SCORING RECORD. THEY SCORED 76,158 DURING 70 PORTSMOUTH ROUNDS AT EVESHAM, ENGLAND. TARPLEE ALSO SET THE INDIVIDUAL RECORD OF 38,500.

TARGET ARCHERY

The most widely practiced discipline in archery is Olympic-style target archery (also known as FITA style). Olympic-style target archery competition is based on the Single FITA round system of scoring. A Single FITA round consists of 36 arrows shot from four distances: 90, 70, 50 and 30 meters for men; 70, 60, 50 and 30 for women, for a total of

144 arrows. Scoring ranges from 10 in the center gold circle to 1 in the outer white ring. The maximum possible score for a Single FITA round is 1,440 points. Competition varies from accumulated scores based on two or more Single FITA rounds to single elimination rounds in which each archer's score reverts to zero at each stage of the tournament.

OLYMPIC GAMES Archery made its first appearance in the 1900 Games in Paris, France. It was also featured in 1904, 1908 and 1920, but then was omitted until 1972, when enough countries had adopted FITA standardized rules to allow for a meaningful international competition.

Most gold medals Hubert van Innis (Belgium) has won six gold medals (au cordon dore—33 meters, au chapelet—33 meters, 1900; moving bird target, 28 meters, 33 meters, moving bird target [team], 33 meters, 50 meters, 1920).

Most medals Hubert van Innis has won nine medals in all: six gold (see above), and three silver (au cordon dore—50 meters, 1900; moving bird target, 50 meters, moving bird target [team] 28 meters, 1920).

WORLD CHAMPIONSHIPS Target archery world championships were first held in 1931 in Lvov, Poland. The championships are staged biennially.

Most titles (archer) The most titles won is seven, by Janina Spychajowa-Kurkowska (Poland) in 1931–34, 1936, 1939 and 1947. The most titles won by a man is four, by Hans Deutgen (Sweden) in 1947–50.

Most titles (country) The United States has a record 14 men's (1959–83) and eight women's (1952–77) team titles.

UNITED STATES NATIONAL CHAMPIONSHIPS The U.S. national championships were first held in Chicago, Ill. from August 12–14, 1879, and are staged annually.

Most titles The most archery titles won is 17, by Lida Howell between 1883 and 1907. The most men's titles is nine (three individual, six pairs), by Rick McKinney, 1977, 1979–83, and 1985–87.

AUSTRALIAN RULES FOOTBALL

ORIGINS A cross between soccer and rugby, Australian Rules Football was developed in the mid-19th century by Henry Harrison and Thomas Wills, who helped form the Melbourne Football Club in 1858. In 1877, the Victorian Football Association was founded, from which eight clubs broke away to form the Victorian Football League (VFL). Four more teams had been admitted by 1925, and in 1987 teams from Queensland and Western Australia joined the league, which has since been renamed the Australian Football League.

GRAND FINAL The sports premier event is the Grand Final, played annually since 1897. Staged at the Melbourne Cricket Ground, it had a record attendance of 121,696 in 1970.

Most wins Two teams have won the Grand Final on 15 occasions: Carlton, 1906–08, 1914–15, 1938, 1945, 1947, 1968, 1970, 1972, 1979, 1981–82, 1987; Essendon, 1897, 1901, 1911–12, 1923–24, 1942, 1946, 1949–50, 1962, 1965, 1984–85, 1993.

AUTO RACING

The nationality of the competitors in this section is U.S. unless noted otherwise.

ORIGINS The site of the first automobile race is open to debate. There is a claim that the first race was held in the United States in 1878, from Green Bay to Madison, Wis., won by an Oshkosh steamer. However, France discounts this, claiming that *La Velocipede*, a 19.3-mile race in Paris on April 20, 1887, was the first race. The first organized race did take place in France: 732 miles from Paris to Bordeaux and back, on June 11–14, 1895. The first closed-circuit race was held over five laps of a one-mile dirt track at Narragansett Park, Cranston, R.I. on September 7, 1896. Grand Prix racing started in 1906, also in France. The Indianapolis 500 was first run on May 30, 1911 (see below).

INDIANAPOLIS 500

The first Indianapolis 500 was held on May 30, 1911 at the Indianapolis Motor Speedway, where the event is still run. The Speedway was opened on August 19, 1909. The original track surface was crushed stone and tar, but several accidents during its initial races convinced the owners to install a paved surface, a project that required 3.2 million bricks and was completed by December 1909. In 1937, parts of the track were resurfaced with asphalt, and the track was completely resurfaced in 1976. The race track is a 2½ mile square oval that has two straightaways of 3,300 feet and two of 660 feet, all 50 feet wide. The four turns are each 1,320 feet, all 60 feet wide and banked 9 degrees, 12 minutes. A 36-inch strip of original brick marks the start–finish line.

VICTORY LANE

Most wins Three drivers have won the race four times: A. J. Foyt Jr., in 1961, 1964, 1967 and 1977;

Al Unser, in 1970–71, 1978 and 1987; and Rick Mears, in 1979, 1984, 1988 and 1991.

Fastest win The record time is 2 hours 41 minutes 18.404 seconds (185.981 mph) by Arie Luyendyk (Netherlands) driving a 1990 Lola-Chevrolet on May 27, 1990.

Slowest win The slowest time is 6 hours 42 minutes 8 seconds (74.602 mph) by Ray Harroun in the inaugural race in 1911.

Consecutive wins Four drivers have won the race in consecutive years: Wilbur Shaw, 1939–40; Mauri Rose, 1947–48; Bill Vukovich, 1953–54; and Al Unser, 1970–71.

Oldest winner Al Unser became the oldest winner when he won the 1987 race at age 47 years 11 months.

INDIANAPOLIS 500 WINNERS (1911–1954)

Year	Driver	Av. Speed (mph)	Year	Driver	Av. Speed (mph)
1911	Ray Harroun	74.602	1933	Louis Meyer	104.162
1912	Joe Dawson	78.719	1934	William Cummings	104.863
1913	Jules Goux	75.933	1935	Kelly Petillo	106.240
1914	Rene Thomas	82.474	1936	Louis Meyer	109.069
1915	Ralph DePalma	89.840	1937	Wilbur Shaw	113.580
1916	Dario Resta	84.001	1938	Floyd Roberts	117.200
1917	(not held)		1939	Wilbur Shaw	115.035
1918	(not held)		1940	Wilbur Shaw	114.277
1919	Howard Wilcox	88.050	1941	Floyd Davis & Mauri Rose	115.117
1920	Gaston Chevrolet	88.618	1942	(not held)	
1921	Tommy Milton	89.621	1943	(not held)	
1922	Jimmy Murphy	94.484	1944	(not held)	
1923	Tommy Milton	90.954	1945	(not held)	
1924	L.L. Corum & Joe Boyer	98.234	1946	George Robson	114.820
1925	Peter DePaolo	101.127	1947	Mauri Rose	116.338
1926	Frank Lockhart	95.904	1948	Mauri Rose	119.814
1927	George Souders	97.545	1949	Bill Holland	121.327
1928	Louis Meyer	99.482	1950	Johnnie Parsons	124.002
1929	Ray Keech	97.585	1951	Lee Wallard	126.244
1930	Billy Arnold	100.448	1952	Troy Ruttman	128.922
1931	Louis Schneider	96.629	1953	Bill Vukovich	128.740
1932	Fred Frame	104.144	1954	Bill Vukovich	130.840

Youngest winner Troy Ruttman became the youngest winner when he won the 1952 race at age 22 years 2 months.

Closest finish The closest margin of victory was 0.043 seconds in 1992 when Al Unser Jr. edged Scott Goodyear (Canada).

Lap leader Al Unser has led the race for a cumulative 644 laps during his 27 starts, 1965–93.

Highest earnings The record prize fund is $7,681,300 awarded in 1993. The individual prize record is $1,244,184, by Al Unser Jr. in 1992. Rick Mears leads the field in career earnings at $4,299,392 from 15 starts, 1978–92.

QUALIFYING

Official time trials are held on the two weekends prior to the race to allow entrants to qualify for the 33 starting positions. A completed trial consists of four consecutive laps around the track with the course cleared of all other traffic. Pole position is determined at the "first day" trials. Qualifiers on each subsequent day are lined up behind the qualifiers of previous days. In 1991 Rick Mears gained pole position with an average speed of 224.113 mph, but Gary Bettenhausen recorded the fastest overall average speed of 224.468 mph on the following day, yet only gained a spot on Row 5 of the starting grid. This was the 14th time that this paradox had happened since the introduction of speed time trials in 1915.

Most starts A. J. Foyt Jr. has started a record 35 races (1958–92).

Pole position Rick Mears has gained a record six poles, in 1979, 1982, 1986, 1988–89 and 1991.

INDIANAPOLIS 500 WINNERS (1955–1993)

Year	Driver	Av. Speed (mph)	Year	Driver	Av. Speed (mph)
1955	Bob Sweikert	128.209	1975	Bobby Unser	149.213
1956	Pat Flaherty	128.490	1976	Johnny Rutherford	148.725
1957	Sam Hanks	135.601	1977	A. J. Foyt Jr.	161.331
1958	Jim Bryan	133.791	1978	Al Unser	161.363
1959	Rodger Ward	135.857	1979	Rick Mears	158.899
1960	Jim Rathmann	138.767	1980	Johnny Rutherford	142.862
1961	A. J. Foyt Jr.	139.131	1981	Bobby Unser	139.084
1962	Rodger Ward	140.293	1982	Gordon Johncock	162.029
1963	Parnelli Jones	143.137	1983	Tom Sneva	162.117
1964	A. J. Foyt Jr.	147.350	1984	Rick Mears	163.612
1965	Jim Clark[1]	150.686	1985	Danny Sullivan	152.982
1966	Graham Hill[1]	144.317	1986	Bobby Rahal	170.722
1967	A. J. Foyt Jr.	151.207	1987	Al Unser	162.175
1968	Bobby Unser	152.882	1988	Rick Mears	144.809
1969	Mario Andretti	156.867	1989	Emerson Fittipaldi[2]	167.581
1970	Al Unser	155.749	1990	Arie Luyendyk[3]	185.981
1971	Al Unser	157.735	1991	Rick Mears	176.457
1972	Mark Donohue	162.962	1992	Al Unser Jr.	134.477
1973	Gordon Johncock	159.036	1993	Emerson Fittipaldi[2]	157.207
1974	Johnny Rutherford	158.589			

1—Great Britain; 2—Brazil; 3—Netherlands

Fastest qualifier The record average speed for four laps qualifying is 232.482 mph by Roberto Guerrero (Colombia) in a Lola-Buick on May 9, 1992. On the same day he set the one-lap record of 233.433 mph.

INDY CAR RACING

The first Indy Car Championship was held in 1909 under the sponsorship of the American Automobile Association (AAA). In 1956 the United States Automobile Club (USAC) took over the running of the Indy series. Since 1979, Championship Auto Racing Teams Inc. (CART) has organized the Indy Championship, which has been called the PPG Indy Car World Series Championship since 1979.

VICTORY LANE

Most championships A.J. Foyt Jr. has won seven Indy Car National Championships: 1960–61, 1963–64, 1967, 1975 and 1979.

FASTEST INDY CAR RACES

Distance	Race	Driver	Av. Speed (mph)	Year
100 miles	Ontario 100	Wally Dallenbach	179.910	1973
150 miles	Atlanta 150	Rick Mears	182.094	1979
200 miles	Michigan 200	Rick Mears	182.325	1983
250 miles	Michigan 250	Bobby Rahal	181.701	1986
500 miles	Michigan 500	Al Unser Jr.	189.727	1990

Source: CART

MEAN MACHINES

In the air, on the road or across water, the challenge of pushing machines to their ultimate limit has excited drivers and thrilled fans since the first automobile race in the late 1870's. While engineers have created machines that surpass supersonic speeds, the greatest challenge is to open the throttle in competition. On race day the occupant of the cockpit must reach the highest speed while overcoming his opponents and the risks. These are the men and machines that reached the checkered flag the fastest of all.

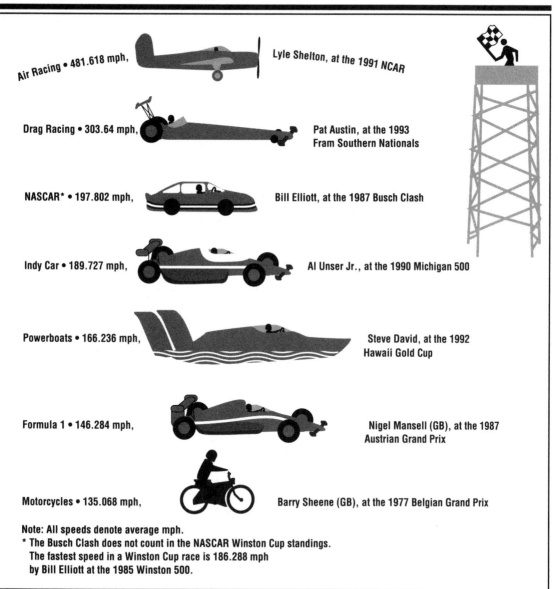

Air Racing • 481.618 mph, Lyle Shelton, at the 1991 NCAR

Drag Racing • 303.64 mph, Pat Austin, at the 1993 Fram Southern Nationals

NASCAR* • 197.802 mph, Bill Elliott, at the 1987 Busch Clash

Indy Car • 189.727 mph, Al Unser Jr., at the 1990 Michigan 500

Powerboats • 166.236 mph, Steve David, at the 1992 Hawaii Gold Cup

Formula 1 • 146.284 mph, Nigel Mansell (GB), at the 1987 Austrian Grand Prix

Motorcycles • 135.068 mph, Barry Sheene (GB), at the 1977 Belgian Grand Prix

Note: All speeds denote average mph.
* The Busch Clash does not count in the NASCAR Winston Cup standings. The fastest speed in a Winston Cup race is 186.288 mph by Bill Elliott at the 1985 Winston 500.

Most consecutive championships Ted Horn won three consecutive national titles from 1946–48.

Most wins (career) A.J. Foyt Jr. has won a career record 67 Indy car races, 1957–92. Foyt's first victory came at the DuQuoin 100 in 1960 and his last at the Pocono 500 in 1981.

Most wins (season) The record for most victories in a season is 10, shared by two drivers: A.J. Foyt Jr. in 1964 and Al Unser in 1970.

Consecutive winning seasons Bobby Unser won at least one race per season for 11 seasons from 1966–76.

Most wins (road course) Mario Andretti has won a record 21 road course races, 1964–93.

Most wins (500-mile races) A. J. Foyt Jr. has won nine 500-mile races: Indianapolis 500 in 1961, 1964, 1967 and 1977; Pocono 500 in 1973, 1975, 1979 and 1981; California 500 in 1975.

Oldest winner On April 4, 1993 Mario Andretti won the Valvoline 200 at the Phoenix International Raceway. At 53 years 52 days Andretti became the oldest driver to win an Indy Car race.

Youngest winner Troy Ruttman's victory in the 1952 Indianapolis 500 at age 22 years 2 months is the youngest age any driver has won an Indy Car race.

Closest races The closest margin of victory in an Indy car race was 0.02 seconds on April 10, 1921 when Ralph DePalma edged Roscoe Sarles to win the Beverly Hills 25. The closest finish in a 500-mile event was Al Unser Jr.'s 0.043-second victory in the 1992 Indianapolis 500. Mario Andretti pulled off the closest finish in an Indy road race, when he won the Portland 200 by 0.07 seconds on June 15, 1986. The loser in this memorable showdown was his son, Michael. (Well, it was Father's Day!)

Highest earnings (season) The single-season record is $2,575,554, set in 1993 by Emerson Fittipaldi.

Highest earnings (career) Through the 1993 season, Bobby Rahal has the highest career earnings for Indy drivers with $12,024,828.

QUALIFYING

Most starts Mario Andretti has made a record 391 starts in Indy car racing, 1964–93.

Most poles (career) Mario Andretti has earned a record 66 pole positions, 1964–93.

Most poles (season) A.J. Foyt Jr. earned 10 poles in 1965.

Most poles (road courses) Mario Andretti has earned 26 poles on road courses.

Most poles (500-mile races) Rick Mears has earned a record 16 poles in 500-mile races.

Fastest qualifiers The fastest qualifying lap ever for an Indy car race was 234.275 mph by Mario Andretti on August 1, 1993 in qualifying for the Marlboro 500.

NASCAR (NATIONAL ASSOCIATION FOR STOCK CAR AUTO RACING)

The National Association for Stock Car Auto Racing, Inc., was founded by Bill France Sr. in 1947. The first NASCAR-sanctioned race was held on February 15, 1948 on Daytona's beach course. The first NASCAR championship, the Grand National series, was held in 1949. Since 1970, the championship series has been called the Winston Cup Championship. The Winston Cup is won by the driver who accumulates the most points during the season series.

VICTORY LANE

Most championships Richard Petty has won a record seven NASCAR titles: 1964, 1967, 1971–72, 1974–75 and 1979.

Most consecutive titles Cale Yarborough is the only driver to "threepeat" as NASCAR champion, winning in 1976–78.

Most wins (career) Richard Petty has won 200 NASCAR Winston Cup races out of 1,185 in which he competed, 1958–92.

Most wins (season) Richard Petty won a record 27 races in 1967.

Fastest average speed The fastest average speed in a Winston Cup race is 186.288 mph, set by Bill Elliott at Talladega Superspeedway, Ala. on May 5, 1985.

Highest earnings (season) Dale Earnhardt earned a record $3,353,789 in 1993.

Highest earnings (career) Dale Earnhardt also holds the career earnings mark at $19,448,571, 1975–93.

DAYTONA 500

The Daytona 500 has been held at the 2½ mile oval Daytona International Speedway in Daytona Beach, Fla. since 1959. The Daytona 500 is the most prestigious event on the NASCAR calendar.

•

DAYTONA 500 WINNERS (1959–1993)

Year	Driver	Av. Speed (mph)	Year	Driver	Av. Speed (mph)
1959	Lee Petty	135.521	1977	Cale Yarborough	153.218
1960	Junior Johnson	124.740	1978	Bobby Allison	159.730
1961	Marvin Panch	149.601	1979	Richard Petty	143.977
1962	Fireball Roberts	152.529	1980	Buddy Baker	177.602
1963	Tiny Lund	151.566	1981	Richard Petty	169.651
1964	Richard Petty	154.334	1982	Bobby Allison	153.991
1965	Fred Lorenzen	141.539	1983	Cale Yarborough	155.979
1966	Richard Petty	160.627	1984	Cale Yarborough	150.994
1967	Mario Andretti	149.926	1985	Bill Elliott	172.265
1968	Cale Yarborough	143.251	1986	Geoff Bodine	148.124
1969	LeeRoy Yarborough	157.950	1987	Bill Elliott	176.263
1970	Pete Hamilton	149.601	1988	Bobby Allison	137.531
1971	Richard Petty	144.462	1989	Darrell Waltrip	148.466
1972	A. J. Foyt Jr.	161.550	1990	Derrike Cope	165.761
1973	Richard Petty	157.205	1991	Ernie Irvan	148.148
1974	Richard Petty	140.894	1992	Davey Allison	160.256
1975	Benny Parsons	153.649	1993	Dale Jarrett	154.972
1976	David Pearson	152.181			

VICTORY LANE

Most wins Richard Petty has won a record seven times: 1964, 1966, 1971, 1973–74, 1979 and 1981.

Consecutive wins Richard Petty and Cale Yarborough are the only drivers to have repeated as Daytona 500 winners in consecutive years. Petty's double was in 1973–74 and Yarborough's in 1983–84.

Oldest winner Bobby Allison became the oldest winner of the race in 1988 at age 50 years 2 months 11 days.

Youngest winner Richard Petty became the youngest winner in 1964, at age 26 years 4 months 18 days.

Fastest win The record average speed for the race is 177.602 mph, by Buddy Baker in 1980.

Slowest win The slowest average speed is 124.740 mph, by Junior Johnson in 1960.

Highest earnings The individual race earnings record is $244,050, by Davey Allison in 1992. The career earnings record is $972,920, by Bill Elliott in 15 races, 1978–93.

QUALIFYING

Most starts Richard Petty competed in 32 Daytona 500 races, 1959–92.

Fastest qualifying time The record average speed for qualifying for the race is 210.364 mph, set by Bill Elliott in 1987.

Most poles Cale Yarborough has earned a record four poles at the Daytona 500, in 1968, 1970, 1978 and 1984.

FORMULA ONE (GRAND PRIX)

The World Drivers' Championship was inaugurated in 1950. Currently the championship is contested over 16 races in 14 different countries worldwide. Points are awarded to the first six finishers in each race; the driver with the most points at the end of the season is the champion.

VICTORY LANE

Most championships Juan-Manuel Fangio (Argentina) has won the drivers' championship five times, 1951 and 1954–57. He also holds the record for consecutive titles with four straight, 1954–57.

Oldest champion Juan-Manuel Fangio is the oldest world champion, winning the 1957 title at age 46 years 41 days.

Youngest champion Emerson Fittipaldi (Brazil) became the youngest champion in 1972, at age 25 years 273 days.

Most wins (career) Alain Prost (France) has won 51 Formula One races, the most of any driver.

Most wins (season) Nigel Mansell (Great Britain) won a record nine races in 1992. His victories came in South Africa, Mexico, Brazil, Spain, San Marino, France, Great Britain, Germany and Portugal.

Oldest winner The oldest driver to win an official race was Luigi Fagioli (Italy), who was 53 years 22 days old when he won the 1951 French Grand Prix.

Youngest winner The youngest driver to win an official race was Troy Ruttman, who was 22 years 2 months old when he won the 1952 Indianapolis 500, which counted in the World Drivers' Championship that year.

Closest finish The narrowest margin of victory in a Formula One race was when Ayrton Senna (Brazil) held off Nigel Mansell by 0.014 seconds to win the Spanish Grand Prix on April 13, 1986.

United States Two Americans have won the Formula One title—Phil Hill in 1961 and Mario Andretti in 1978.

QUALIFYING

Most starts Riccardo Patrese (Italy) has raced in a record 255 Grand Prix races from 1977–93.

Most poles Ayrton Senna has earned a record 62 poles in 158 races, 1985–93.

Fastest qualifying time Keke Rosberg (Finland) set the fastest qualifying lap in Formula One history, when he qualified for the British Grand Prix at Silverstone with an average speed of 160.817 mph on July 20, 1985.

DRAG RACING

Drag racing is an acceleration contest between two cars racing from a standing start over a precisely measured, straight-line, quarter-mile course. Competition is based on two-car elimination heats culminating in a final round. The fastest elapsed time wins the race. Elapsed time is measured over

QUICK OFF THE MARK ■ DON GARLITS HAS WON A CAREER RECORD 35 TOP FUEL RACES. (NHRA)

the distance of the course; the top speed is a measurement of the last 66 feet of the track, where a special speed trap electronically computes the speed of the dragster. There are several classifications in drag racing, based on the engine size, type of fuel and vehicle weight limitations of the car. The most prominent drag racing organization is the National Hot Rod Association (NHRA), which was founded in 1951. The NHRA recognizes 12 categories of racers, with the three main categories being Top Fuel, Funny Car and Pro Stock.

TOP FUEL

Top Fuel dragsters are 4,000-horsepower machines that are powered by nitromethane. The engines are mounted behind the driver, and parachutes are the primary braking system.

SPEED RECORDS

Quickest elapsed time in an NHRA event The quickest elapsed time recorded by a Top Fuel dragster from a standing start for 440 yards is

4.762 seconds by Cory McClenathon at the Sears Craftsman Nationals in Topeka, Kan., on October 3, 1993.

Fastest top speed in an NHRA event The fastest speed recorded in a Top Fuel race is 303.64 mph by Pat Austin on April 24, 1993 at the Fram Southern Nationals at Atlanta, Ga.

VICTORIES

Most wins (career) Don Garlits has won a record 35 Top Fuel races (1975–92).

Most wins (season) Six drivers have won six Top Fuel races in a season: Don Garlits, 1985; Darrel Gwynn, 1988; Gary Ormsby, 1989; Joe Amato, 1990; Kenny Bernstein, 1991; and Eddie Hill, 1993.

FUNNY CAR

A Funny Car is a short-wheelbase version of the Top Fuel dragster. Funny Cars mount a fiberglass replica of a production car with the engine located in front of the driver.

GO-KART GOER ■ ON APRIL 9, 1993, 10-YEAR-OLD ZACK DAWSON DROVE HIS 100CC GO-KART A RECORD 249.117 MILES IN SIX HOURS AT MESA MARIN RACEWAY, BAKERSFIELD, CALIF.

SPEED RECORDS

Quickest elapsed time in an NHRA event The quickest elapsed time recorded in the Funny Car class is 4.996 seconds, by John Force on October 16, 1993 at the Chief Nationals, Dallas, Tex.

Fastest top speed in an NHRA event Jim Epler was timed at 300.40 mph at the Sears Craftsman Finals at Topeka, Kan., on October 3, 1993.

VICTORIES

Most wins (career) Don Prudhomme has won a record 35 Funny Car races (1975–89).

Most wins (season) John Force won a record 11 races in 1993.

PRO STOCK

Pro Stock dragsters look like their oval-racing counterparts, but feature extensive engine modifications. A maximum 500-cubic-inch displacement and a minimum vehicle weight of 2,350 pounds are allowed under NHRA rules.

SPEED RECORDS

Quickest elapsed time in an NHRA event The quickest elapsed time in the Pro Stock class is 7.027 seconds by Warren Johnson on March 6, 1993 at the Slick 50 Nationals, Houston, Tex.

Fastest top speed in an NHRA event The fastest speed in a Pro Stock race is 196.24 mph by Warren Johnson on March 20, 1993 at the Gaternational, Gainesville, Fla.

VICTORIES

Most wins (career) Bob Glidden has won a record 84 races (1972–93), the most victories of any driver in NHRA events.

Most wins (season) Darrell Alderman won a record 11 races in 1991.

NHRA WINSTON DRAG RACING SERIES The NHRA World Championship Series was inaugurated in 1951. Since 1975 the series has been known as the NHRA Winston Drag Racing Series.

MOST TITLES

Top Fuel Joe Amato has won a record five national titles: 1984, 1988 and 1990–92.

Funny Car Two drivers have won a record four national titles: Don Prudhomme, 1975–78, and Kenny Bernstein, 1985–88.

Pro Stock Bob Glidden has won a record 10 national titles, in 1974–75, 1978–80 and 1985–89.

BADMINTON

ORIGINS Badminton is a descendant of the children's game of battledore and shuttlecock. It is believed that a similar game was played in China more than 2,000 years ago. Badminton takes its name from Badminton House in England, where the Duke of Beaufort's family and guests popularized the game in the 19th century. British army officers took the game to India in the 1870s, where the first modern rules were codified in 1876. The world governing body is the International Badminton Federation, formed in 1934.

United States The earliest known reference to badminton in the United States is a description of battledore shuttlecock in the 1864 *American Boy's Book of Sports and Games*. The first badminton club formed in the United States was the Badminton Club of New York, founded in 1878. The game was not organized at the national level until 1935, when the American Badminton Association (ABA) was founded in Boston, Mass. In 1978 the ABA was renamed the United States Badminton Association.

OLYMPIC GAMES Badminton was included in the Olympic Games as an official sport for the first time at the Barcelona Games in 1992. The game was included as a demonstration sport at the Munich Games in 1972.

Most medals No player in Barcelona won more than one medal. The four gold medals awarded were shared equally between players from Indonesia and South Korea.

QUICK SHUTTLE ☞ AT THE 1992 OLYMPIC GAMES, CHRISTINE MAGNUSSON (SWEDEN) DEFEATED MARTINE DE SOUZA (MAURITIUS) 11–1, 11–0 IN 8 MIN 30 SEC. THIS IS THE SHORTEST GAME RECORDED IN INTERNATIONAL COMPETITION.

WORLD CHAMPIONSHIPS The first championships were staged in Malmo, Sweden in 1977. Since 1983 the event has been held biennially.

Most titles (overall) Park Joo-bong (South Korea) has won a record five world titles: men's doubles in 1985 and 1991; mixed doubles in 1985, 1989 and 1991. Three women have won three titles: Lin Ying (China), doubles in 1983, 1987 and 1989; Li Lingwei (China), singles in 1983 and 1989, doubles in 1985; Guan Weizhan (China), doubles in 1987, 1989 and 1991.

Most titles (singles) Yang Yang (China) is the only man to have won two world singles titles, in 1987 and 1989. Two women have won two singles titles: Li Lingwei (China), 1983 and 1989; Han Aiping (China), 1985 and 1987.

UNITED STATES NATIONAL CHAMPIONSHIPS The first competition was held in 1937.

Most titles Judy Hashman (née Devlin) has won a record 31 titles: 12 women's singles, 1954, 1956–63 and 1965–67; 12 women's doubles, 1953–55, 1957–63 and 1966–67 (10 with her sister Susan); and seven mixed doubles, 1956–59, 1961–62 and 1967. David G. Freeman has won a record seven men's singles titles: 1939–42, 1947–48 and 1953.

BASEBALL

ORIGINS In 1907, baseball's national commission appointed a committee to research the history of the game. The report, filed in 1908, concluded that Abner Doubleday had invented the game in 1839 at Cooperstown, N.Y. At the time, the report was viewed with some skepticism because of the friendship between Doubleday and the committee chairman, A. G. Mills; however, in 1939, major league baseball celebrated its centennial and cemented the legend of Doubleday's efforts in American folklore. Sports historians today discount the Doubleday theory, claiming that baseball in North America evolved from such English games as cricket, paddleball and rounders.

Uncontested is that Alexander Cartwright Jr. formulated the rules of the modern game in 1845, and that the first match under these rules was played on June 19, 1846 when the New York Nine defeated the New York Knickerbockers, 23–1, in four innings. On March 17, 1871 the National

Association of Professional Base Ball Players was formed, the first professional league in the United States. Today there are two main professional baseball associations, the National League (organized in 1876) and the American League (organized in 1901, recognized in 1903), which together form the major leagues, along with approximately 20 associations that make up the minor leagues. The champions of the two leagues first played a World Series in 1903 and have played one continuously since 1905. (For further details on World Series history, see page 30.)

MAJOR LEAGUE RECORDS

Records listed in this section are for the all-time major league record. Where an all-time record is dated prior to 1900, the modern record (1900–present) is also listed.

GAMES PLAYED

Career 3,562, by Pete Rose, Cincinnati Reds (NL), 1963–78, 1984–86; Philadelphia Phillies (NL), 1979–83; Montreal Expos (NL), 1984.

Consecutive 2,130, by Lou Gehrig, New York Yankees (AL), June 1, 1925 through April 30, 1939.

BATTING RECORDS

BATTING AVERAGE

Career .367, by Ty Cobb, Detroit Tigers (AL), 1905–26; Philadelphia Athletics (AL), 1927–28. Cobb compiled his record from 4,191 hits in 11,429 at-bats.

Season .438, by Hugh Duffy, Boston Beaneaters (NL) in 1894. Duffy compiled 236 hits in 539 at-bats. The modern record is .424, by Rogers

STRONG ARM ☛ THE GREATEST DISTANCE A REGULATION BASEBALL HAS BEEN THROWN IS 445 FEET 10 INCHES, BY GLEN GORBOUS (CANADA) ON AUGUST 1, 1957.

Hornsby, St. Louis Cardinals (NL), in 1924. Hornsby compiled 227 hits in 536 at-bats.

HITS

Career 4,256, by Pete Rose, Cincinnati Reds (NL), 1963–78, 1984–86; Philadelphia Phillies (NL), 1979–83; Montreal Expos (NL), 1984. Rose compiled his record hits total in 14,053 at-bats.

Season 257, by George Sisler, St. Louis Browns (AL), in 1920, in 631 at-bats.

Game Nine, by John Burnett, Cleveland Indians (AL), during an 18-inning game on July 10, 1932. The record for a nine-inning game is seven hits, by two players: Wilbert Robinson, Baltimore Orioles (NL), on June 10, 1892; Rennie Stennett, Pittsburgh Pirates (NL), on September 16, 1975.

SINGLES

Career 3,215, by Pete Rose, Cincinnati Reds (NL), 1963–78, 1984–86; Philadelphia Phillies, 1979–83, Montreal Expos, 1984.

Season 206, by Wee Willie Keeler, Baltimore Orioles (NL) in 1898. The modern-day record is 198, by Lloyd Waner, Pittsburgh Pirates, in 1927.

Game Seven, by John Burnett, Cleveland Indians (AL), in an 18-inning game on July 10, 1932. In regulation play the record for both the National and American leagues is six hits by several players.

DOUBLES

Career 793, by Tris Speaker, Boston Red Sox (AL), 1907–1915; Cleveland Indians (AL), 1916–1926; Washington Senators (AL), 1927; Philadelphia Athletics (AL), 1928.

Season 67, by Earl Webb, Boston Red Sox (AL), in 1931.

Game Four, by many players in both leagues.

TRIPLES

Career 312, by Sam Crawford, Cincinnati Reds (NL), 1899–1902; Detroit Tigers (AL), 1903–17.

Season 36, by Owen Wilson, Pittsburgh Pirates (NL), in 1912.

Game Four, by two players: George A. Strief, Philadelphia Athletics (American Association) on June 25, 1885; William Joyce, New York Giants (NL) on May 18, 1897. The modern-day record for both leagues is three, achieved by several players.

HOME RUNS

Career 755, by Hank Aaron, Milwaukee/Atlanta Braves (NL), 1954–74; Milwaukee Brewers (AL), 1975–76. Aaron hit his record dingers in 12,364 at-bats.

Season 61, Roger Maris, New York Yankees (AL), in 1961.

Game Four, by 12 players: Bobby Lowe, Boston (NL), May 30, 1894; Ed Delahanty, Philadelphia Phillies (NL), July 13, 1896; Lou Gehrig, New York Yankees (AL), June 3, 1932; Chuck Klein, Philadelphia Phillies (NL), July 10, 1936; Pat Seerey, Chicago White Sox (AL), July 18, 1948; Gil Hodges, Brooklyn Dodgers (NL), August 31, 1950; Joe Adcock, Milwaukee Braves (NL), July 31, 1954; Rocky Colavito, Cleveland Indians (AL), June 10, 1959; Willie Mays, San Francisco Giants (NL), April 30, 1961; Mike Schmidt, Philadelphia Phillies (NL), April 17, 1976; Bob Horner, Atlanta Braves (NL), July 6, 1986; and Mark Whiten, St. Louis Cardinals (NL), September 7, 1993. Klein, Schmidt and Seerey matched the record in extra-inning games.

GRAND SLAMS

Career 23, by Lou Gehrig, New York Yankees (AL), 1923–39.

Season Six, by Don Mattingly, New York Yankees (AL), in 1987.

Game Two, by seven players: Tony Lazzeri, New York Yankees (AL), May 24, 1936; Jim Tabor, Boston Red Sox (AL), July 4, 1939; Rudy York, Boston Red Sox (AL), July 27, 1946; Jim Gentile,

QUITE A PASTIME ■ WAYNE ZUMWALT ATTENDED GAMES AT ALL 28 MAJOR LEAGUE STADIUMS ON 28 CONSECUTIVE DAYS, FROM JUNE 10–JULY 7, 1993. (VAL MAZZENGA)

Baltimore Orioles (AL), May 9, 1961; Tony Cloninger, Atlanta Braves (NL), July 3, 1966; Jim Northrup, Detroit Tigers (AL), June 24, 1968; and Frank Robinson, Baltimore Orioles (AL), June 26, 1970. Cloninger is the only player from the National League to achieve this feat, and he was a pitcher!

RUNS BATTED IN

Career 2,297, by Hank Aaron, Milwaukee/Atlanta Braves (NL), 1954–74; Milwaukee Brewers (AL), 1975–76.

Season 190, by Hack Wilson, Chicago Cubs (NL), in 1930.

Game 12, by two players: Jim Bottomley, St. Louis Cardinals (NL), on September 16, 1924; and Mark Whiten, St. Louis Cardinals (NL), on September 7, 1993.

RUNS SCORED

Career 2,245, by Ty Cobb, Detroit Tigers (AL), 1905–26; Philadelphia Athletics (AL), 1927–28.

Season 196, by Billy Hamilton, Philadelphia Phillies (NL), in 1894. The modern-day record is 177 runs, scored by Babe Ruth, New York Yankees (AL), in 1921.

Game Seven, by Guy Hecker, Louisville Colonels (American Association), on August 15, 1886. The modern-day record is six runs scored, achieved by 12 players, 10 in the National League and two in the American League.

TOTAL BASES

Career 6,856, by Hank Aaron, Milwaukee/Atlanta Braves (NL), 1954–74; Milwaukee Brewers (AL), 1975–76. Aaron's record is comprised of 2,294 singles, 624 doubles, 98 triples and 755 home runs.

Season 457, by Babe Ruth, New York Yankees (AL) in 1921. Ruth's total comprised 85 singles, 44 doubles, 16 triples and 59 home runs.

Game 18, by Joe Adcock, Milwaukee Braves (NL) on July 31, 1954. Adcock hit four home runs and a double.

WALKS

Career 2,056, by Babe Ruth, Boston Red Sox (AL), 1914–19; New York Yankees (AL), 1920–34; Boston Braves (NL), 1935.

Season 170, by Babe Ruth, New York Yankees (AL) in 1923.

ROUND AND ROUND THE BASES ■ IN 1993, KEN GRIFFEY JR. (LEFT) AND MARK WHITEN (RIGHT) TIED MAJOR LEAGUE HOME RUN MARKS. GRIFFEY HIT HOMERS IN EIGHT CONSECUTIVE GAMES IN JULY, AND WHITEN HIT FOUR IN A GAME IN SEPTEMBER. (SEATTLE MARINERS, ALLSPORT/STEPHEN DUNN)

STRIKEOUTS

Career 2,597, by Reggie Jackson, Kansas City/Oakland Athletics (AL), 1967–75, 1987; Baltimore Orioles (AL), 1976; New York Yankees (AL), 1977–81; California Angels (AL), 1982–86.

Season 189, by Bobby Bonds, San Francisco Giants (NL), in 1970.

HIT BY PITCH

Career 267, by Don Baylor, Baltimore Orioles (AL), 1970–75; Oakland Athletics (AL), 1976, 1988; California Angels (AL), 1977–82; New York Yankees (AL), 1983–85; Boston Red Sox (AL), 1986–87; Minnesota Twins (AL), 1987.

Season 50, by Ron Hunt, Montreal Expos (NL) in 1971.

CONSECUTIVE BATTING RECORDS

Hits in a row 12, by two players: Pinky Higgins, Boston Red Sox (AL), over four games, June 19–21, 1938; and Walt (Moose) Droppo, Detroit Tigers (AL), over three games, July 14–15, 1952.

Games batted safely 56, by Joe DiMaggio, New York Yankees (AL), May 15 through July 16, 1941. During the streak, DiMaggio gained 91 hits in 223 at-bats: 56 singles, 16 doubles, 4 triples and 15 home runs.

Home runs in a row Four, by four players: Bobby Lowe, Boston (NL), May 30, 1894; Lou Gehrig, New York Yankees (AL), June 3, 1932; Rocky Colavito, Cleveland Indians (AL), June 10, 1959; and Mike Schmidt, Philadelphia Phillies (NL), April 17, 1976.

Games hitting home runs Eight, by three players: Dale Long, Pittsburgh Pirates (NL), May 19–28, 1956; Don Mattingly, New York Yankees (AL), July 8–18, 1987; and Ken Griffey Jr., Seattle Mariners (AL), July 20–28, 1993.

Walks in a row Seven, by three players: Billy Rogell, Detroit Tigers (AL), August 17–19, 1938; Mel Ott, New York Giants (NL), June 16–18, 1943; Eddie Stanky, New York Giants (NL), August 29–30, 1950.

Games receiving a walk 22, by Roy Cullenbine, Detroit Tigers (AL), July 2 through July 22, 1947.

PITCHING RECORDS

GAMES PLAYED

Career 1,070, by Hoyt Wilhelm, New York Giants (NL), 1952–56; St. Louis Cardinals (NL), 1957; Cleveland Indians (AL), 1957–58; Baltimore Orioles (AL), 1958–62; Chicago White Sox (AL), 1963–68; California Angels (AL), 1969; Atlanta Braves (NL), 1969–70; Chicago Cubs (NL), 1970; Atlanta Braves (NL), 1971; Los Angeles Dodgers (NL), 1971–72.

Season 106, by Mike Marshall, Los Angeles Dodgers (NL), in 1974.

VICTORIES

Career 511, by Cy Young, Cleveland Spiders (NL), 1890–98; St. Louis Cardinals (NL), 1899–1900; Boston Red Sox (AL), 1901–08; Cleveland Indians (AL), 1909–11; Boston Braves (NL), 1911.

Season 60, by "Old Hoss" Radbourn, Providence Grays (NL), in 1884. The modern-day record is 41, by Jack Chesbro, New York Yankees (AL), in 1904.

LOSSES

Career 313, by Cy Young, Cleveland Spiders (NL), 1890–98; St. Louis Cardinals (NL), 1899–1900; Boston Red Sox (AL), 1901–08; Cleveland Indians (AL), 1909–11; Boston Braves (NL), 1911.

Season 48, by John Coleman, Philadelphia Phillies (NL), in 1883. The modern-day record is 29, by Vic Willis, Boston Braves (NL), in 1905.

EARNED RUN AVERAGE (ERA)

Career (min. 2,000 innings) 1.82, by Ed Walsh, Chicago White Sox (AL), 1904–16; Boston Braves (NL), 1917.

Season (min. 200 innings) 1.01, by Dutch Leonard, Boston Red Sox (AL), in 1914.

INNINGS PITCHED

Career 7,356, by Cy Young, Cleveland Spiders (NL), 1890–98; St. Louis Cardinals (NL), 1899–1900; Boston Red Sox (AL), 1901–08; Cleveland Indians (AL), 1909–11; Boston Braves (NL), 1911.

Season 680, by Will White, Cincinnati Reds (NL), in 1879. The modern-day record is 464, by Ed Walsh, Chicago White Sox (AL), in 1908.

NO-HITTERS

On September 4, 1991, baseball's Committee for Statistical Accuracy defined a no-hit game as "one in which a pitcher or pitchers complete a game of

DUBIOUS DISTINCTION ■ NEW YORK METS PITCHER ANTHONY YOUNG LOST 27 CONSECUTIVE GAMES, 1992–93. HE SNAPPED THE UNWANTED STREAK ON JULY 28, 1993 WHEN THE METS DEFEATED THE FLORIDA MARLINS, 5–4. (NEW YORK METS)

nine innings or more without allowing a hit." All previously considered no-hit games that did not fit into this definition—such as rain-shortened games; eight-inning, complete game no-hitters hurled by losing pitchers; and games in which hits were recorded in the tenth inning or later—would be considered "notable achievements," not no-hitters.

The first officially recognized no-hitter was pitched by Joe Borden for Philadelphia of the National Association v. Chicago on July 28, 1875. Through the 1993 season 238 no-hitters have been

pitched. The most no-hitters pitched in one season is seven, on two occasions: 1990 and 1991.

Career Seven, by Nolan Ryan: California Angels v. Kansas City Royals (3–0), on May 15, 1973; California Angels v. Detroit Tigers (6–0), on July 15, 1973; California Angels v. Minnesota Twins (4–0), on September 28, 1974; California Angels v. Baltimore Orioles (1–0), on June 1, 1975; Houston Astros v. Los Angeles Dodgers (5–0), on September 26, 1981; Texas Rangers v. Oakland Athletics (5–0), on June 11, 1990; and Texas Rangers v. Toronto Blue Jays (3–0), on May 1, 1991.

Season Two, by four players: Johnny Vander Meer, Cincinnati Reds (NL), in 1938; Allie Reynolds, New York Yankees (AL), in 1951; Virgil Trucks, Detroit Tigers (AL) in 1952; and Nolan Ryan, California Angels (AL), in 1973.

PERFECT GAMES

In a perfect game, no batter reaches base during a complete game of at least nine innings.

The first officially recognized perfect game was hurled by John Richmond on June 12, 1880 for Worcester v. Cleveland in a National League game. Through the 1993 season there have been 14 perfect games pitched: Richmond (see above); John Ward, Providence v. Buffalo (NL), June 17, 1880; Cy Young, Boston Red Sox v. Philadelphia Athletics (AL), May 5, 1904; Addie Joss, Cleveland Indians v. Chicago White Sox (AL), October 2, 1908; Ernie Shore, Boston Red Sox v. Washington Senators (AL), June 23, 1917; Charlie Robertson, Chicago White Sox v. Detroit Tigers (AL), April 30, 1922; Don Larsen, New York Yankees v. Brooklyn Dodgers (World Series game), October 8, 1956; Jim Bunning, Philadelphia Phillies v. New York Mets (NL), June 21, 1964; Sandy Koufax, Los Angeles Dodgers v. Chicago Cubs (NL), September 9, 1965; Catfish Hunter, Oakland Athletics v. Minnesota Twins (AL), May 8, 1968; Len Barker, Cleveland Indians v. Toronto Blue Jays (AL), May 15, 1981; Mike Witt, California Angels v. Texas Rangers (AL), September 30, 1984; Tom Browning, Cincinnati Reds v. Los Angeles Dodgers (NL), September 16, 1988; and Dennis Martinez, Montreal Expos v. Los Angeles Dodgers (NL), July 28, 1991.

COMPLETE GAMES

Career 750, by Cy Young, Cleveland Spiders (NL), 1890–98; St. Louis Cardinals (NL), 1899–1900; Boston Red Sox (AL), 1901–08; Cleveland

Indians (AL), 1909–11; Boston Braves (NL), 1911. The modern-day record is 531, by Walter Johnson, Washington Senators (AL), 1907–27.

Season 75, by Will White, Cincinnati Reds (NL) in 1879. The modern-day record is 48, by Jack Chesbro, New York Yankees (AL), in 1904.

SHUTOUTS

Career 110, by Walter Johnson, Washington Senators (AL), 1907–27.

Season 16, by two pitchers: George Bradley, St. Louis (NL), in 1876; and Grover Alexander, Philadelphia Phillies (NL), in 1916.

STRIKEOUTS

Career 5,714, by Nolan Ryan, New York Mets (NL), 1966–71; California Angels (AL), 1972–79; Houston Astros (NL), 1980–88; Texas Rangers (AL), 1989–93.

Season 513, by Matt Kilroy, Baltimore (American Association), in 1886. The modern-day record is 383, by Nolan Ryan, California Angels (AL), in 1973.

Game (extra innings) 21, by Tom Cheney, Washington Senators (AL), on September 12, 1962 in a 16-inning game.

Game (nine innings) 20, by Roger Clemens, Boston Red Sox (AL), on April 29, 1986.

WALKS

Career 2,795, by Nolan Ryan, New York Mets (NL), 1966–71; California Angels (AL), 1972–79; Houston Astros (NL), 1980–88; Texas Rangers (AL), 1989–93.

Season 218, by Amos Rusie, New York Giants (NL), in 1893. The modern-day record is 208, by Bob Feller, Cleveland Indians (AL), in 1938.

Game 16, by two pitchers: Bruno Haas, Philadelphia Athletics (AL), on June 23, 1915 in a nine-inning game; Tom Byrne, St. Louis Browns (AL) on August 22, 1951 in a 13-inning game.

SAVES

Career 401, by Lee Smith, Chicago Cubs (NL), 1980–87; Boston Red Sox (AL), 1988–90; St. Louis Cardinals (NL), 1990–93; New York Yankees (AL), 1993.

Season 57, by Bobby Thigpen, Chicago White Sox (AL), in 1990.

CONSECUTIVE PITCHING RECORDS

Games won 24, by Carl Hubbell, New York Giants (NL), 16 in 1936 and eight in 1937.

Starting assignments 544, by Steve Carlton, from May 15, 1971 through 1986 while playing for four teams: St. Louis Cardinals (NL), Philadelphia Phillies (NL), San Francisco Giants (NL), and Chicago White Sox (AL).

Scoreless innings 59, by Orel Hershiser, Los Angeles Dodgers (NL), from sixth inning, August 30 through tenth inning, September 28, 1988.

No-hitters Two, by Johnny Vander Meer, Cincinnati Reds (NL), on June 11 and June 15, 1938.

Shutouts Six, by Don Drysdale, Los Angeles Dodgers (NL), May 14 through June 4, 1968.

Strikeouts 10, by Tom Seaver, New York Mets (NL) on April 22, 1970.

BASERUNNING

STOLEN BASES

Career 1,095, by Rickey Henderson, Oakland Athletics (AL), 1979–84, 1989–93; New York Yankees (AL), 1985–89; Toronto Blue Jays (AL), 1993.

Season 130, by Rickey Henderson, Oakland Athletics (AL), in 1982.

Game Seven, by two players: George Gore, Chicago Cubs (NL), on June 25, 1881; Billy Hamilton, Philadelphia Phillies (NL), on August 31, 1894. The modern-day record is six, by two players: Eddie Collins, Philadelphia Athletics (AL), on September 11, 1912; Otis Nixon, Atlanta Braves (NL), on June 17, 1991.

40/40 Club The only player to steal at least 40 bases and hit at least 40 home runs in one season is Jose Canseco, Oakland Athletics (AL), in 1988, when he stole 40 bases and hit 42 home runs.

FIELDING

HIGHEST FIELDING PERCENTAGE

Career .995, by two players: Wes Parker, Los Angeles Dodgers (NL), 1964–72; and Jim Spencer, California Angels (AL), 1968–73; Texas Rangers (AL), 1973–75; Chicago White Sox (AL), 1976–77; New York Yankees (AL), 1978–81; Oakland Athletics (AL), 1981–82. Parker played 1,108 games at first base and 155 in the outfield.

Spencer played 1,221 games at first base and 24 in the outfield.

ASSISTS

Career 8,133, by Bill Dahlen, Chicago Cubs (NL), 1891–98; Brooklyn Dodgers (NL), 1899–1903, 1910–11; New York Giants (NL), 1904–07; Boston Braves (NL), 1908–09. Dahlen played 2,132 games at shortstop, 223 at third base, 19 at second base and 58 in the outfield.

MANAGERS

Most games managed 7,755, by Connie Mack, Pittsburgh Pirates (NL), 1894–96; Philadelphia Athletics (AL), 1901–50. Mack's career record was 3,731 wins, 3,948 losses, 75 ties and one no-decision.

Most wins 3,731, by Connie Mack, Pittsburgh Pirates (NL), 1894–96; Philadelphia Athletics (AL), 1901–50.

Most losses 3,948, by Connie Mack, Pittsburgh Pirates (NL), 1894–96; Philadelphia Athletics (AL), 1901–50.

Highest winning percentage .615, by Joe McCarthy, Chicago Cubs (NL), 1926–30; New York Yankees (AL), 1931–46; Boston Red Sox (AL), 1948–50. McCarthy's career record was 2,125 wins, 1,333 losses, 26 ties and three no-decisions.

MISCELLANEOUS

Youngest player The youngest major league player of all time was the Cincinnati Reds (AL) pitcher Joe Nuxhall, who played one game in June 1944, at age 15 years 314 days. He did not play again in the National League until 1952.

FAN APPRECIATION ■ THE COLORADO ROCKIES' ROOKIE SEASON ATTRACTED 4,483,350 PEOPLE, SETTING BASEBALL'S HOME ATTENDANCE MARK. (COLORADO ROCKIES/RICH CLARKSON)

Oldest player Satchel Paige pitched for the Kansas City A's (AL) at age 59 years 80 days on September 25, 1965.

Shortest and tallest players The shortest major league player was Eddie Gaedel, a 3-foot-7-inch, 65-pound midget, who pinch-hit for the St. Louis Browns (AL) v. the Detroit Tigers (AL) on August 19, 1951. Wearing number ⅛, the batter with the smallest-ever major league strike zone walked on four pitches. Following the game, major league rules were hastily rewritten to prevent any recurrence. The tallest major leaguers of all time are two 6-foot-10-inch pitchers: Randy Johnson, who played in his first game for the Montreal Expos (NL) on September 15, 1988; and Eric Hillman, who debuted for the New York Mets (NL) on May 18, 1992.

Father and son On August 31, 1990, Ken Griffey Sr. and Ken Griffey Jr., of the Seattle Mariners (AL), became the first father and son to play for the same major league team at the same time. In 1989 the Griffeys had been the first father/son combination to play in the major leagues at the same time. Griffey Sr. played for the Cincinnati Reds (NL) during that season.

Father, son and grandson On August 19, 1992, Bret Boone made his major league debut for the Seattle Mariners (AL), making the Boone family the first three-generation family in major league history. Boone's father Bob Boone played 18 seasons in the majors, 1972–89, and his grandfather Ray Boone played from 1948–60.

Record attendances The all-time season record for attendance for both leagues is

TRIPLE PLAY ■ IN 1993, BARRY BONDS BECAME THE EIGHTH PLAYER TO WIN THREE MVP AWARDS. (SAN FRANCISCO GIANTS/MARTHA JANE STANTON)

70,257,938, set in 1993 (33,333,365 for the 14-team American League, and 36,924,573 for the 14-team

(continued on p. 27)

Most Valuable Player Award (MVP) There have been three different MVP Awards in baseball: the Chalmers Award (1911–14), the League Award (1922–29), and the Baseball Writers' Association of America Award (1931–present).

CHALMERS AWARD (1911–1914)

National League				American League		
Year	Player	Team	Position	Year	Player	Team	Position
1911	Wildfire Schulte	Chicago Cubs	OF	1911	Ty Cobb	Detroit Tigers	OF
1912	Larry Doyle	New York Giants	2B	1912	Tris Speaker	Boston Red Sox	OF
1913	Jake Daubert	Brooklyn Dodgers	1B	1913	Walter Johnson	Washington Senators	P
1914	Johnny Evers	Boston Braves	2B	1914	Eddie Collins	Philadelphia A's	2B

LEAGUE AWARD (1922–1929)

	National League					American League		
Year	Player	Team	Position		Year	Player	Team	Position
1922	no selection				1922	George Sisler	St. Louis Browns	1B
1923	no selection				1923	Babe Ruth	New York Yankees	OF
1924	Dazzy Vance	Brooklyn Dodgers	P		1924	Walter Johnson	Washington Senators	P
1925	Rogers Hornsby	St. Louis Cardinals	2B		1925	Roger Peckinpaugh	Washington Senators	SS
1926	Bob O'Farrell	St. Louis Cardinals	C		1926	George Burns	Cleveland Indians	1B
1927	Paul Waner	Pittsburgh Pirates	OF		1927	Lou Gehrig	New York Yankees	1B
1928	Jim Bottomley	St. Louis Cardinals	1B		1928	Mickey Cochrane	Philadelphia A's	C
1929	Rogers Hornsby	Chicago Cubs	2B		1929	no selection		

BASEBALL WRITERS' AWARD (1931–1948)

Most wins Three, by eight players: Jimmie Foxx, Philadelphia Athletics (AL), 1932–33, 1938; Joe DiMaggio, New York Yankees (AL), 1939, 1941, 1947; Stan Musial, St. Louis Cardinals (NL), 1943, 1946, 1948; Roy Campanella, Brooklyn Dodgers (NL), 1951, 1953, 1955; Yogi Berra, New York Yankees (AL), 1951, 1954–55; Mickey Mantle, New York Yankees (AL), 1956–57, 1962; Mike Schmidt, Philadelphia Phillies (NL), 1980–81, 1986; and Barry Bonds, Pittsburgh Pirates (NL), 1990, 1992, San Francisco Giants (NL), 1993.
Wins, both leagues Frank Robinson, Cincinnati Reds (NL), in 1961; Baltimore Orioles (AL), in 1966.

	National League					American League		
Year	Player	Team	Position		Year	Player	Team	Position
1931	Frankie Frisch	St. Louis Cardinals	2B		1931	Lefty Grove	Philadelphia A's	P
1932	Chuck Klein	Philadelphia Phillies	OF		1932	Jimmie Foxx	Philadelphia A's	1B
1933	Carl Hubbell	New York Giants	P		1933	Jimmie Foxx	Philadelphia A's	1B
1934	Dizzy Dean	St. Louis Cardinals	P		1934	Mickey Cochrane	Detroit Tigers	C
1935	Gabby Hartnett	Chicago Cubs	C		1935	Hank Greenberg	Detroit Tigers	1B
1936	Carl Hubbell	New York Giants	P		1936	Lou Gehrig	New York Yankees	1B
1937	Joe Medwick	St. Louis Cardinals	OF		1937	Charlie Gehringer	Detroit Tigers	2B
1938	Ernie Lombardi	Cincinnati Reds	C		1938	Jimmie Foxx	Boston Red Sox	1B
1939	Bucky Walters	Cincinnati Reds	P		1939	Joe DiMaggio	New York Yankees	OF
1940	Frank McCormick	Cincinnati Reds	1B		1940	Hank Greenberg	Detroit Tigers	OF
1941	Dolf Camilli	Brooklyn Dodgers	1B		1941	Joe DiMaggio	New York Yankees	OF
1942	Mort Cooper	St. Louis Cardinals	P		1942	Joe Gordon	New York Yankees	2B
1943	Stan Musial	St. Louis Cardinals	OF		1943	Spud Chandler	New York Yankees	P
1944	Marty Marion	St. Louis Cardinals	SS		1944	Hal Newhouser	Detroit Tigers	P
1945	Phil Cavarretta	Chicago Cubs	1B		1945	Hal Newhouser	Detroit Tigers	P
1946	Stan Musial	St. Louis Cardinals	1B–OF		1946	Ted Williams	Boston Red Sox	OF
1947	Bob Elliott	Boston Braves	3B		1947	Joe DiMaggio	New York Yankees	OF
1948	Stan Musial	St. Louis Cardinals	OF		1948	Lou Boudreau	Cleveland Indians	SS

BASEBALL WRITERS' AWARD (1949–1982)

National League

Year	Player	Team	Position
1949	Jackie Robinson	Brooklyn Dodgers	2B
1950	Jim Konstanty	Philadelphia Phillies	P
1951	Roy Campanella	Brooklyn Dodgers	C
1952	Hank Sauer	Chicago Cubs	OF
1953	Roy Campanella	Brooklyn Dodgers	C
1954	Willie Mays	New York Giants	OF
1955	Roy Campanella	Brooklyn Dodgers	C
1956	Don Newcombe	Brooklyn Dodgers	P
1957	Hank Aaron	Milwaukee Braves	OF
1958	Ernie Banks	Chicago Cubs	SS
1959	Ernie Banks	Chicago Cubs	SS
1960	Dick Groat	Pittsburgh Pirates	SS
1961	Frank Robinson	Cincinnati Reds	OF
1962	Maury Wills	Los Angeles Dodgers	SS
1963	Sandy Koufax	Los Angeles Dodgers	P
1964	Ken Boyer	St. Louis Cardinals	3B
1965	Willie Mays	San Francisco Giants	OF
1966	Roberto Clemente	Pittsburgh Pirates	OF
1967	Orlando Cepeda	St. Louis Cardinals	1B
1968	Bob Gibson	St. Louis Cardinals	P
1969	Willie McCovey	San Francisco Giants	1B
1970	Johnny Bench	Cincinnati Reds	C
1971	Joe Torre	St. Louis Cardinals	3B
1972	Johnny Bench	Cincinnati Reds	C
1973	Pete Rose	Cincinnati Reds	OF
1974	Steve Garvey	Los Angeles Dodgers	1B
1975	Joe Morgan	Cincinnati Reds	2B
1976	Joe Morgan	Cincinnati Reds	2B
1977	George Foster	Cincinnati Reds	OF
1978	Dave Parker	Pittsburgh Pirates	OF
1979	Willie Stargell	Pittsburgh Pirates	1B*
	Keith Hernandez	St. Louis Cardinals	1B*
1980	Mike Schmidt	Philadelphia Phillies	3B
1981	Mike Schmidt	Philadelphia Phillies	3B
1982	Dale Murphy	Atlanta Braves	OF

American League

Year	Player	Team	Position
1949	Ted Williams	Boston Red Sox	OF
1950	Phil Rizzuto	New York Yankees	SS
1951	Yogi Berra	New York Yankees	C
1952	Bobby Shantz	Philadelphia A's	P
1953	Al Rosen	Cleveland Indians	3B
1954	Yogi Berra	New York Yankees	C
1955	Yogi Berra	New York Yankees	C
1956	Mickey Mantle	New York Yankees	OF
1957	Mickey Mantle	New York Yankees	OF
1958	Jackie Jensen	Boston Red Sox	OF
1959	Nellie Fox	Chicago White Sox	2B
1960	Roger Maris	New York Yankees	OF
1961	Roger Maris	New York Yankees	OF
1962	Mickey Mantle	New York Yankees	OF
1963	Elston Howard	New York Yankees	C
1964	Brooks Robinson	Baltimore Orioles	3B
1965	Zoilo Versalles	Minnesota Twins	SS
1966	Frank Robinson	Baltimore Orioles	OF
1967	Carl Yastrzemski	Boston Red Sox	OF
1968	Denny McLain	Detroit Tigers	P
1969	Harmon Killebrew	Minnesota Twins	1B-3B
1970	Boog Powell	Baltimore Orioles	1B
1971	Vida Blue	Oakland A's	P
1972	Dick Allen	Chicago White Sox	1B
1973	Reggie Jackson	Oakland A's	OF
1974	Jeff Burroughs	Texas Rangers	OF
1975	Fred Lynn	Boston Red Sox	OF
1976	Thurman Munson	New York Yankees	C
1977	Rod Carew	Minnesota Twins	1B
1978	Jim Rice	Boston Red Sox	OF-DH
1979	Don Baylor	California Angels	OF-DH
1980	George Brett	Kansas City Royals	3B
1981	Rollie Fingers	Milwaukee Brewers	P
1982	Robin Yount	Milwaukee Brewers	SS

* Tied vote

BASEBALL WRITERS' AWARD (1983–1993)

National League

Year	Player	Team	Position
1983	Dale Murphy	Atlanta Braves	OF
1984	Ryne Sandberg	Chicago Cubs	2B
1985	Willie McGee	St. Louis Cardinals	OF
1986	Mike Schmidt	Philadelphia Phillies	3B
1987	Andre Dawson	Chicago Cubs	OF
1988	Kirk Gibson	Los Angeles Dodgers	OF
1989	Kevin Mitchell	San Francisco Giants	OF
1990	Barry Bonds	Pittsburgh Pirates	OF
1991	Terry Pendleton	Atlanta Braves	3B
1992	Barry Bonds	Pittsburgh Pirates	OF
1993	Barry Bonds	San Francisco Giants	OF

American League

Year	Player	Team	Position
1983	Cal Ripken Jr.	Baltimore Orioles	SS
1984	Willie Hernandez	Detroit Tigers	P
1985	Don Mattingly	New York Yankees	1B
1986	Roger Clemens	Boston Red Sox	P
1987	George Bell	Toronto Blue Jays	OF
1988	Jose Canseco	Oakland A's	OF
1989	Robin Yount	Milwaukee Brewers	OF
1990	Rickey Henderson	Oakland A's	OF
1991	Cal Ripken Jr.	Baltimore Orioles	SS
1992	Dennis Eckersley	Oakland A's	P
1993	Frank Thomas	Chicago White Sox	1B

CY YOUNG AWARD WINNERS (1956–1973)

Inaugurated in 1956, this award is given to the best pitcher in baseball as judged by the Baseball Writers' Association of America. From 1967 on, separate awards have been given to the best pitcher in each league.

Most wins Four, by Steve Carlton, Philadelphia Phillies, 1972, 1977, 1980 and 1982.

Wins, both leagues The only pitcher to win the Cy Young Award in both leagues is Gaylord Perry: Cleveland Indians (AL), 1972; San Diego Padres (NL), 1978.

Year	Pitcher	Team
1956	Don Newcombe	Brooklyn Dodgers (NL)
1957	Warren Spahn	Milwaukee Braves (NL)
1958	Bob Turley	New York Yankees (AL)
1959	Early Wynn	Chicago White Sox (AL)
1960	Vernon Law	Pittsburgh Pirates (NL)
1961	Whitey Ford	New York Yankees (AL)

Year	Pitcher	Team
1962	Don Drysdale	Los Angeles Dodgers (NL)
1963	Sandy Koufax	Los Angeles Dodgers (NL)
1964	Dean Chance	Los Angeles Angels (AL)
1965	Sandy Koufax	Los Angeles Dodgers (NL)
1966	Sandy Koufax	Los Angeles Dodgers (NL)

National League

Year	Pitcher	Team
1967	Mike McCormick	San Francisco Giants
1968	Bob Gibson	St. Louis Cardinals
1969	Tom Seaver	New York Mets
1970	Bob Gibson	St. Louis Cardinals
1971	Ferguson Jenkins	Chicago Cubs
1972	Steve Carlton	Philadelphia Phillies
1973	Tom Seaver	New York Mets

American League

Year	Pitcher	Team
1967	Jim Lonborg	Boston Red Sox
1968	Denny McLain	Detroit Tigers
1969*	Mike Cuellar / Denny McLain	Baltimore Orioles / Detroit Tigers
1970	Jim Perry	Minnesota Twins
1971	Vida Blue	Oakland Athletics
1972	Gaylord Perry	Cleveland Indians
1973	Jim Palmer	Baltimore Orioles

* Tied vote

CY YOUNG AWARD WINNERS (1974–1993)

National League			American League		
Year	Pitcher	Team	Year	Pitcher	Team
1974	Mike Marshall	Los Angeles Dodgers	1974	"Catfish" Hunter	Oakland Athletics
1975	Tom Seaver	New York Mets	1975	Jim Palmer	Baltimore Orioles
1976	Randy Jones	San Diego Padres	1976	Jim Palmer	Baltimore Orioles
1977	Steve Carlton	Philadelphia Phillies	1977	Sparky Lyle	New York Yankees
1978	Gaylord Perry	San Diego Padres	1978	Ron Guidry	New York Yankees
1979	Bruce Sutter	Chicago Cubs	1979	Mike Flanagan	Baltimore Orioles
1980	Steve Carlton	Philadelphia Phillies	1980	Steve Stone	Baltimore Orioles
1981	Fernando Valenzuela	Los Angeles Dodgers	1981	Rollie Fingers	Milwaukee Brewers
1982	Steve Carlton	Philadelphia Phillies	1982	Pete Vukovich	Milwaukee Brewers
1983	John Denny	Philadelphia Phillies	1983	LaMarr Hoyt	Chicago White Sox
1984	Rick Sutcliffe	Chicago Cubs	1984	Willie Hernandez	Detroit Tigers
1985	Dwight Gooden	New York Mets	1985	Bret Saberhagen	Kansas City Royals
1986	Mike Scott	Houston Astros	1986	Roger Clemens	Boston Red Sox
1987	Steve Bedrosian	Philadelphia Phillies	1987	Roger Clemens	Boston Red Sox
1988	Orel Hershiser	Los Angeles Dodgers	1988	Frank Viola	Minnesota Twins
1989	Mark Davis	San Diego Padres	1989	Bret Saberhagen	Kansas City Royals
1990	Doug Drabek	Pittsburgh Pirates	1990	Bob Welch	Oakland Athletics
1991	Tom Glavine	Atlanta Braves	1991	Roger Clemens	Boston Red Sox
1992	Greg Maddux	Chicago Cubs	1992	Dennis Eckersley	Oakland Athletics
1993	Greg Maddux	Atlanta Braves	1993	Jack McDowell	Chicago White Sox

National League). The American League and National League totals were both league records. The record for home-team attendance is held by the Colorado Rockies (NL) at 4,483,350 in 1993. The American League record is held by the Toronto Blue Jays at 4,057,947 in 1993.

Shortest game The New York Giants (NL) beat the Philadelphia Phillies (NL), 6–1, in nine innings in 51 minutes on September 28, 1919.

Longest games The Brooklyn Dodgers (NL) and the Boston Braves (NL) played to a 1–1 tie after 26 innings on May 1, 1920. The Chicago White Sox (AL) played the longest ballgame in elapsed time—8 hours 6 minutes—before beating the Milwaukee Brewers, 7–6, in the 25th inning on May 9, 1984 in Chicago. The game started on a Tuesday night and was tied at 3–3 when the 1 A.M. curfew caused suspension until Wednesday night.

The actual longest game was a minor league game in 1981 that lasted 33 innings. At the end of nine innings the score was tied, 1–1, with the Rochester (N.Y.) Red Wings battling the home team Pawtucket (R.I.) Red Sox. At the end of 32 innings the score was still 2–2, when the game was suspended. Two months later, play was resumed, and 18 minutes later, Pawtucket scored one run and won.

LEAGUE CHAMPIONSHIP SERIES RECORDS

GAMES PLAYED

Most series played 11, by Reggie Jackson, Oakland Athletics (AL), 1971–75; New York Yankees (AL), 1977–78, 1980–81; California Angels (AL), 1982, 1986.

Most games played 45, by Reggie Jackson, Oakland Athletics (AL), 1971–75; New York Yankees (AL), 1977–78, 1980–81; California Angels (AL), 1982, 1986.

HITTING RECORDS (CAREER)

Batting average (minimum 50 at-bats) .386, by Mickey Rivers, New York Yankees (AL), 1976–78. Rivers collected 22 hits in 57 at-bats in 14 games.

Hits 45, by Pete Rose, Cincinnati Reds (NL), 1970, 1972–73, 1975–76; Philadelphia Phillies (NL), 1980, 1983.

Home runs Nine, by George Brett, Kansas City Royals (AL), 1976–78, 1980, 1984–85.

Runs batted in (RBIs) 21, by Steve Garvey, Los Angeles Dodgers (NL), 1974, 1977–78, 1981; San Diego Padres (NL), 1984.

LEAGUE CHAMPIONSHIP SERIES (1969–1993)

League Championship Series (LCS) playoffs began in 1969 when the American and National Leagues expanded to 12 teams each and created two divisions, East and West. To determine the respective league pennant winners, the division winners played a best-of-five-games series, which was expanded to best-of-seven in 1985.

National League

Year	Winner	Loser	Series
1969	New York Mets (East)	Atlanta Braves (West)	3–0
1970	Cincinnati Reds (West)	Pittsburgh Pirates (East)	3–0
1971	Pittsburgh Pirates (East)	San Francisco Giants (West)	3–1
1972	Cincinnati Reds (West)	Pittsburgh Pirates (East)	3–2
1973	New York Mets (East)	Cincinnati Reds (West)	3–2
1974	Los Angeles Dodgers (West)	Pittsburgh Pirates (East)	3–1
1975	Cincinnati Reds (West)	Pittsburgh Pirates (East)	3–0
1976	Cincinnati Reds (West)	Philadelphia Phillies (East)	3–0
1977	Los Angeles Dodgers (West)	Philadelphia Phillies (East)	3–1
1978	Los Angeles Dodgers (West)	Philadelphia Phillies (East)	3–1
1979	Pittsburgh Pirates (East)	Cincinnati Reds (West)	3–0
1980	Philadelphia Phillies (East)	Houston Astros (West)	3–2
1981	Los Angeles Dodgers (West)	Montreal Expos (East)	3–2
1982	St. Louis Cardinals (East)	Atlanta Braves (West)	3–0
1983	Philadelphia Phillies (East)	Los Angeles Dodgers (West)	3–1
1984	San Diego Padres (West)	Chicago Cubs (East)	3–2
1985	St. Louis Cardinals (East)	Los Angeles Dodgers (West)	4–2
1986	New York Mets (East)	Houston Astros (West)	4–2
1987	St. Louis Cardinals (East)	San Francisco Giants (West)	4–3
1988	Los Angeles Dodgers (West)	New York Mets (East)	4–3
1989	San Francisco Giants (West)	Chicago Cubs (East)	4–1
1990	Cincinnati Reds (West)	Pittsburgh Pirates (East)	4–2
1991	Atlanta Braves (West)	Pittsburgh Pirates (East)	4–3
1992	Atlanta Braves (West)	Pittsburgh Pirates (East)	4–3
1993	Philadelphia Phillies (East)	Atlanta Braves (West)	4–2

Runs scored 22, by George Brett, Kansas City Royals (AL), 1976–78, 1980, 1984–85.

Walks 23, by Joe Morgan, Cincinnati Reds (NL), 1972–73, 1975–76, 1979; Houston Astros (NL), 1980; Philadelphia Phillies (NL), 1983.

Stolen bases 14, by Rickey Henderson, Oakland Athletics (AL), 1981, 1989–90, 1992; Toronto Blue Jays (AL), 1993.

PITCHING RECORDS (CAREER)

Most series pitched Eight, by Bob Welch, Los Angeles Dodgers (NL), 1978, 1981, 1983, 1985; Oakland Athletics (AL), 1988–90, 1992.

Most games pitched 15, by two pitchers: Tug McGraw, New York Mets (NL), 1969, 1973; Philadelphia Phillies (NL), 1976–78, 1980; Dennis Eckersley, Chicago Cubs (NL), 1984; Oakland Athletics (AL), 1988–90, 1992.

Wins Eight, by Dave Stewart, Oakland Athletics (AL), 1988–90, 1992; Toronto Blue Jays (AL), 1993.

Losses Seven, by Jerry Reuss, Pittsburgh Pirates (NL), 1974–75; Los Angeles Dodgers (NL), 1981, 1983, 1985.

LEAGUE CHAMPIONSHIP SERIES (1969–1993)

American League

Year	Winner	Loser	Series
1969	Baltimore Orioles (East)	Minnesota Twins (West)	3–0
1970	Baltimore Orioles (East)	Minnesota Twins (West)	3–0
1971	Baltimore Orioles (East)	Oakland A's (West)	3–0
1972	Oakland A's (West)	Detroit Tigers (East)	3–2
1973	Oakland A's (West)	Baltimore Orioles (East)	3–2
1974	Oakland A's (West)	Baltimore Orioles (East)	3–1
1975	Boston Red Sox (East)	Oakland A's (West)	3–0
1976	New York Yankees (East)	Kansas City Royals (West)	3–2
1977	New York Yankees (East)	Kansas City Royals (West)	3–2
1978	New York Yankees (East)	Kansas City Royals (West)	3–1
1979	Baltimore Orioles (East)	California Angels (West)	3–1
1980	Kansas City Royals (West)	New York Yankees (East)	3–0
1981	New York Yankees (East)	Oakland A's (West)	3–0
1982	Milwaukee Brewers (East)	California Angels (West)	3–2
1983	Baltimore Orioles (East)	Chicago White Sox (West)	3–1
1984	Detroit Tigers (East)	Kansas City Royals (West)	3–0
1985	Kansas City Royals (West)	Toronto Blue Jays (East)	4–3
1986	Boston Red Sox (East)	California Angels (West)	4–3
1987	Minnesota Twins (West)	Detroit Tigers (East)	4–1
1988	Oakland A's (West)	Boston Red Sox (East)	4–0
1989	Oakland A's (West)	Toronto Blue Jays (East)	4–1
1990	Oakland A's (West)	Boston Red Sox (East)	4–0
1991	Minnesota Twins (West)	Toronto Blue Jays (East)	4–1
1992	Toronto Blue Jays (East)	Oakland A's (West)	4–2
1993	Toronto Blue Jays (East)	Chicago White Sox (West)	4–2

OCTOBER ACE ■ IN WINNING THE 1993 ALCS MVP AWARD, DAVE STEWART EXTENDED HIS PLAYOFF WINS RECORD TO EIGHT VICTORIES. (TORONTO BLUE JAYS)

Innings pitched 69⅓, by Jim "Catfish" Hunter, Oakland Athletics (AL), 1971–74, New York Yankees (AL), 1976, 1978.

Complete games Five, by Jim Palmer, Baltimore Orioles (AL), 1969–71, 1973–74, 1979.

Strikeouts 46, by two players: Nolan Ryan, New York Mets (NL), 1969; California Angels (AL), 1979; Houston Astros (NL), 1980, 1986; and Jim Palmer, Baltimore Orioles (AL), 1969–71, 1973–74, 1979.

Saves 10, by Dennis Eckersley, Chicago Cubs (NL), 1984; Oakland Athletics (AL), 1988–90, 1992.

WORLD SERIES

ORIGINS Played annually between the champions of the National League and the American League, the World Series was first staged unofficially in 1903, and officially from 1905 on. On October 20, 1992 the Toronto Blue Jays hosted the first World Series game played outside the United States. The Blue Jays won the 1992 Series, thus becoming the first non-U.S. team to win the fall classic.

WORLD SERIES RECORDS

TEAM RECORDS

Most wins 22, by the New York Yankees (AL), 1923, 1927–28, 1932, 1936–39, 1941, 1943, 1947, 1949–53, 1956, 1958, 1961– 62, 1977–78.

Most appearances 33, by the New York Yankees (AL), 1921–23, 1926–28, 1932, 1936–39, 1941–43, 1947, 1949–53, 1955–58, 1960–64, 1976–78, 1981.

INDIVIDUAL RECORDS

GAMES PLAYED

Most series 14, by Yogi Berra, New York Yankees (AL), 1947, 1949–53, 1955–58, 1960–63.

Most series (pitcher) 11, by Whitey Ford, New York Yankees (AL), 1950, 1953, 1955–58, 1960–64.

Most games 75, by Yogi Berra, New York Yankees (AL), 1947, 1949–53, 1955–58, 1960–63.

Most games (pitcher) 22, by Whitey Ford, New York Yankees (AL), 1950, 1953, 1955–58, 1960–64.

HITTING RECORDS

BATTING AVERAGE

Career (min. 20 games) .391, by Lou Brock, St. Louis Cardinals (NL), 1964, 1967–68. Brock collected 34 hits in 87 at-bats over 21 games.

Series (min. four games) .750, by Billy Hatcher, Cincinnati Reds (NL), in 1990. Hatcher collected nine hits in 12 at-bats in four games.

TIMEOUT

LONGEST GAME ☛ THE LONGEST WORLD SERIES GAME WAS PLAYED ON OCTOBER 20, 1993, LASTING 4 HOURS 14 MINUTES. THE TORONTO BLUE JAYS DEFEATED THE PHILADELPHIA PHILLIES IN PHILADELPHIA, 15–14. THE GAME WAS ALSO THE HIGHEST-SCORING IN SERIES HISTORY, WITH 29 RUNS.

WORLD SERIES (1903–1938)

Year	Winner	Loser	Series
1903	Boston Pilgrims (AL)	Pittsburgh Pirates (NL)	5–3
1904	no series		
1905	New York Giants (NL)	Philadelphia A's (AL)	4–1
1906	Chicago White Sox (AL)	Chicago Cubs (NL)	4–2
1907	Chicago Cubs (NL)	Detroit Tigers (AL)	4–0–1 *
1908	Chicago Cubs (NL)	Detroit Tigers (AL)	4–1
1909	Pittsburgh Pirates (NL)	Detroit Tigers (AL)	4–3
1910	Philadelphia A's (AL)	Chicago Cubs (NL)	4–1
1911	Philadelphia A's (AL)	New York Giants (NL)	4–2
1912	Boston Red Sox (AL)	New York Giants (NL)	4–3–1*
1913	Philadelphia A's (AL)	New York Giants (NL)	4–1
1914	Boston Braves (NL)	Philadelphia A's (AL)	4–0
1915	Boston Red Sox (AL)	Philadelphia Phillies (NL)	4–1
1916	Boston Red Sox (AL)	Brooklyn Robins (NL)	4–1
1917	Chicago White Sox (AL)	New York Giants (NL)	4–2
1918	Boston Red Sox (AL)	Chicago Cubs (NL)	4–2
1919	Cincinnati Reds (NL)	Chicago White Sox (AL)	5–3
1920	Cleveland Indians (AL)	Brooklyn Robins (NL)	5–2
1921	New York Giants (NL)	New York Yankees (AL)	5–3
1922	New York Giants (NL)	New York Yankees (AL)	4–0–1*
1923	New York Yankees (AL)	New York Giants (NL)	4–2
1924	Washington Senators (AL)	New York Giants (NL)	4–3
1925	Pittsburgh Pirates (NL)	Washington Senators (AL)	4–3
1926	St. Louis Cardinals(NL)	New York Yankees (AL)	4–3
1927	New York Yankees (AL)	Pittsburgh Pirates (NL)	4–0
1928	New York Yankees (AL)	St. Louis Cardinals (NL)	4–0
1929	Philadelphia A's (AL)	Chicago Cubs (NL)	4–1
1930	Philadelphia A's (AL)	St. Louis Cardinals (NL)	4–2
1931	St. Louis Cardinals (NL)	Philadelphia A's (AL)	4–3
1932	New York Yankees (AL)	Chicago Cubs (NL)	4–0
1933	New York Giants (NL)	Washington Senators (AL)	4–1
1934	St. Louis Cardinals (NL)	Detroit Tigers (AL)	4–3
1935	Detroit Tigers (AL)	Chicago Cubs (NL)	4–2
1936	New York Yankees (AL)	New York Giants (NL)	4–2
1937	New York Yankees (AL)	New York Giants (NL)	4–1
1938	New York Yankees (AL)	Chicago Cubs (NL)	4–0

* Tied game

WORLD SERIES (1939–1975)

Year	Winner	Loser	Series
1939	New York Yankees (AL)	Cincinnati Reds (NL)	4–0
1940	Cincinnati Reds (NL)	Detroit Tigers (AL)	4–3
1941	New York Yankees (AL)	Brooklyn Dodgers (NL)	4–1
1942	St. Louis Cardinals (NL)	New York Yankees (AL)	4–1
1943	New York Yankees (AL)	St. Louis Cardinals (NL)	4–1
1944	St. Louis Cardinals (NL)	St. Louis Browns (AL)	4–2
1945	Detroit Tigers (AL)	Chicago Cubs (NL)	4–3
1946	St. Louis Cardinals (NL)	Boston Red Sox (AL)	4–3
1947	New York Yankees (AL)	Brooklyn Dodgers (NL)	4–3
1948	Cleveland Indians (AL)	Boston Braves (NL)	4–2
1949	New York Yankees (AL)	Brooklyn Dodgers (NL)	4–1
1950	New York Yankees (AL)	Philadelphia Phillies (NL)	4–0
1951	New York Yankees (AL)	New York Giants (NL)	4–2
1952	New York Yankees (AL)	Brooklyn Dodgers (NL)	4–3
1953	New York Yankees (AL)	Brooklyn Dodgers (NL)	4–2
1954	New York Giants (NL)	Cleveland Indians (AL)	4–0
1955	Brooklyn Dodgers (NL)	New York Yankees (AL)	4–3
1956	New York Yankees (AL)	Brooklyn Dodgers (NL)	4–3
1957	Milwaukee Braves (NL)	New York Yankees (AL)	4–3
1958	New York Yankees (AL)	Milwaukee Braves (NL)	4–3
1959	Los Angeles Dodgers (NL)	Chicago White Sox (AL)	4–2
1960	Pittsburgh Pirates (NL)	New York Yankees (AL)	4–3
1961	New York Yankees (AL)	Cincinnati Reds (NL)	4–1
1962	New York Yankees (AL)	San Francisco Giants (NL)	4–3
1963	Los Angeles Dodgers (NL)	New York Yankees (AL)	4–0
1964	St. Louis Cardinals (NL)	New York Yankees (AL)	4–3
1965	Los Angeles Dodgers (NL)	Minnesota Twins (AL)	4–3
1966	Baltimore Orioles (AL)	Los Angeles Dodgers (NL)	4–0
1967	St. Louis Cardinals (NL)	Boston Red Sox (AL)	4–3
1968	Detroit Tigers (AL)	St. Louis Cardinals (NL)	4–3
1969	New York Mets (NL)	Baltimore Orioles (AL)	4–1
1970	Baltimore Orioles (AL)	Cincinnati Reds (NL)	4–1
1971	Pittsburgh Pirates (NL)	Baltimore Orioles (AL)	4–3
1972	Oakland A's (AL)	Cincinnati Reds (NL)	4–3
1973	Oakland A's (AL)	New York Mets (NL)	4–3
1974	Oakland A's (AL)	Los Angeles Dodgers (NL)	4–1
1975	Cincinnati Reds (NL)	Boston Red Sox (AL)	4–3

WORLD SERIES (1976–1993)

Year	Winner	Loser	Series
1976	Cincinnati Reds (NL)	New York Yankees (AL)	4–0
1977	New York Yankees (AL)	Los Angeles Dodgers (NL)	4–2
1978	New York Yankees (AL)	Los Angeles Dodgers (NL)	4–2
1979	Pittsburgh Pirates(NL)	Baltimore Orioles (AL)	4–3
1980	Philadelphia Phillies (NL)	Kansas City Royals (AL)	4–2
1981	Los Angeles Dodgers (NL)	New York Yankees (AL)	4–2
1982	St. Louis Cardinals (NL)	Milwaukee Brewers (AL)	4–3
1983	Baltimore Orioles (AL)	Philadelphia Phillies (NL)	4–1
1984	Detroit Tigers (AL)	San Diego Padres (NL)	4–1
1985	Kansas City Royals (AL)	St. Louis Cardinals (NL)	4–3
1986	New York Mets (NL)	Boston Red Sox (AL)	4–3
1987	Minnesota Twins (AL)	St. Louis Cardinals (NL)	4–3
1988	Los Angeles Dodgers (NL)	Oakland A's (AL)	4–1
1989	Oakland A's (AL)	San Francisco Giants (NL)	4–0
1990	Cincinnati Reds (NL)	Oakland A's (AL)	4–0
1991	Minnesota Twins (AL)	Atlanta Braves (NL)	4–3
1992	Toronto Blue Jays (AL)	Atlanta Braves (NL)	4–2
1993	Toronto Blue Jays (AL)	Philadelphia Phillies (NL)	4–2

HITS

Career 71, by Yogi Berra, New York Yankees (AL), 1947–63. In 259 at-bats, Berra hit 12 home runs, 10 doubles and 49 singles.

Series 13, by three players: Bobby Richardson, New York Yankees (AL), in 1960; Lou Brock, St. Louis Cardinals (NL), in 1968; Marty Barrett, Boston Red Sox (AL), in 1986.

HOME RUNS

Career 18, by Mickey Mantle, New York Yankees (AL), 1951–53, 1955–58, 1960–64. Mantle hit his record 18 homers in 230 at-bats in 65 games.

Series Five, by Reggie Jackson, New York Yankees (AL), in 1977.

Game Three, by two players: Babe Ruth, New York Yankees (AL), who did it twice: on October 6, 1926 *v.* St. Louis Cardinals, and on October 9, 1928 *v.* St. Louis Cardinals; and Reggie Jackson, New York Yankees (AL), on October 18, 1977 *v.* Los Angeles Dodgers.

RUNS BATTED IN (RBIS)

Career 40, by Mickey Mantle, New York Yankees (AL), 1951–53, 1955–58, 1960–64.

Series 12, by Bobby Richardson, New York Yankees (AL), in 1960.

Game Six, by Bobby Richardson, New York Yankees (AL), on October 8, 1960 *v.* Pittsburgh Pirates.

PITCHING RECORDS

WINS

Career Ten, by Whitey Ford, New York Yankees (AL), in 11 series, 1950–64. Ford's career record was 10 wins, 8 losses in 22 games.

Series Three, by 12 pitchers. Only two pitchers have won three games in a five-game series: Christy Mathewson, New York Giants (NL) in 1905; Jack Coombs, Philadelphia Athletics (AL) in 1910.

STRIKEOUTS

Career 94, by Whitey Ford, New York Yankees (AL), in 11 series, 1950–64.

Series 35, by Bob Gibson, St. Louis Cardinals (NL) in 1968, from seven games.

Game 17, by Bob Gibson, St. Louis Cardinals (NL), on October 2, 1968 *v.* Detroit Tigers.

INNINGS PITCHED

Career 146, by Whitey Ford, New York Yankees (AL), in 11 series, 1950, 1953, 1955–58, 1960–64.

Series 44, by Deacon Phillippe, Pittsburgh Pirates (NL), in 1903 in an eight-game series.

Game 14, by Babe Ruth, Boston Red Sox (AL), on October 9, 1916 *v.* Brooklyn Dodgers.

SAVES

Career Six, by Rollie Fingers, Oakland Athletics (AL), 1972–74.

Series Three, by Kent Tekulve, Pittsburgh Pirates (NL), in 1979 in a seven-game series.

PERFECT GAME The only perfect game in World Series history was hurled by Don Larsen, New York Yankees (AL), on October 8, 1956 *v.* Brooklyn Dodgers.

MOST VALUABLE PLAYER AWARD The World Series MVP award has been won a record two times by three players: Sandy Koufax, Los Angeles Dodgers (NL), 1963 and 1965; Bob Gibson, St. Louis Cardinals (NL), 1964 and 1967; and Reggie Jackson, Oakland Athletics (AL), 1973, New York Yankees (AL), 1977.

MANAGERS

Most series Ten, by Casey Stengel, New York Yankees (AL), 1949–53, 1955–58, 1960. Stengel's record was seven wins, three losses.

Most wins Seven, by two managers: Joe McCarthy, New York Yankees (AL), 1932, 1936–39, 1941, 1943; and Casey Stengel, New York Yankees (AL), 1949–53, 1956, 1958.

Most losses Six, by John McGraw, New York Giants (NL), 1911–13, 1917, 1923–24.

Wins, both leagues The only manager to lead a team from each league to a World Series title is Sparky Anderson, who skippered the Cincinnati Reds (NL) to championships in 1975–76, and the Detroit Tigers (AL) in 1984.

COLLEGE BASEBALL

ORIGINS Various forms of college baseball have been played throughout the 20th century; however, the NCAA did not organize a championship until 1947 and did not begin to keep statistical records until 1957.

(continued on p. 38)

COLLEGE WORLD SERIES (1947–1969)

Year	Winner	Loser	Score	Year	Winner	Loser	Score
1947	California	Yale	2–0 *	1958	Southern Cal.	Missouri	8–7
1948	Southern Cal.	Yale	2–1 *	1959	Oklahoma St.	Arizona	5–3
1949	Texas	Wake Forest	10–3	1960	Minnesota	Southern Cal.	2–1
1950	Texas	Washington St.	3–0	1961	Southern Cal.	Oklahoma St.	1–0
1951	Oklahoma	Tennessee	3–2	1962	Michigan	Santa Clara	5–4
1952	Holy Cross	Missouri	8–4	1963	Southern Cal.	Arizona	5–2
1953	Michigan	Texas	7–5	1964	Minnesota	Missouri	5–1
1954	Missouri	Rollins	4–1	1965	Arizona St.	Ohio St.	2–1
1955	Wake Forest	Western Mich.	7–6	1966	Ohio St.	Oklahoma St.	8–2
1956	Minnesota	Arizona	12–1	1967	Arizona St.	Houston	11–2
1957	California	Penn State	1–0	1968	Southern Cal.	Southern Ill.	4–3
				1969	Arizona St.	Tulsa	10–1

* Series score

OKLA-HOMER! ■ OKLAHOMA STATE SLUGGER PETE INCAVIGLIA HIT AN NCAA RECORD 100 CAREER HOME RUNS, 1983–85. (OKLAHOMA STATE)

COLLEGE WORLD SERIES (1970–1993)

Year	Winner	Loser	Score	Year	Winner	Loser	Score
1970	Southern Cal.	Florida St.	2–1	1982	Miami (Fla.)	Wichita St.	9–3
1971	Southern Cal.	Southern Ill.	7–2	1983	Texas	Alabama	4–3
1972	Southern Cal.	Arizona St.	1–0	1984	Cal. St. Fullerton	Texas	3–1
1973	Southern Cal.	Arizona St.	4–3	1985	Miami (Fla.)	Texas	10–6
1974	Southern Cal.	Miami (Fla.)	7–3	1986	Arizona	Florida St.	10–2
1975	Texas	South Carolina	5–1	1987	Stanford	Oklahoma St.	9–5
1976	Arizona	Eastern Mich.	7–1	1988	Stanford	Arizona St.	9–4
1977	Arizona St.	South Carolina	2–1	1989	Wichita St.	Texas	5–3
1978	Southern Cal.	Arizona St.	10–3	1990	Georgia	Oklahoma St.	2–1
1979	Cal. St. Fullerton	Arkansas	2–1	1991	Louisiana St.	Wichita St.	6–3
1980	Arizona	Hawaii	5–3	1992	Pepperdine	Cal. State Fullerton	3–2
1981	Arizona St.	Oklahoma St.	7–4	1993	Louisiana St.	Wichita St.	8–0

LITTLE LEAGUE BASEBALL WORLD SERIES

Little League Baseball is the world's largest youth sports organization, boasting 2.7 million participants in 77 countries playing on 200,000 teams aided by nearly 1 million volunteers. Founded in 1939 in Williamsport, Pa., by Carl Stotz and George and Bert Bebble, Little League consisted of 12 leagues in Pennsylvania and New Jersey at the time of the first World Series in 1947. By 1950, there were 307 leagues throughout the United States, and Little League Baseball was quickly establishing itself as an American institution. In 1957 Monterrey, Mexico became the first international team to win the title. Teams from 11 states and four countries have won the Little League championship, with teams representing Taiwan claiming the most, 15. Unlike their elder professional counterparts, Little Leaguers can justifiably claim to be champions of the world.

LITTLE LEAGUE WORLD SERIES CHAMPIONSHIP GAME RECORDS

- ○ Most championships — **15,** Taiwan (Chinese Taipei), 1969–92
- ○ Most championships (US state) — **5,** California, 1961–63, 1992–93
- ○ Consecutive championships — **5,** Taiwan (1977–81)
- ○ Most runs (two teams) — **23,** Williamsport 16   Lock Haven 7, 1947
- ○ Most runs (one team) — **21,** Taiwan (*v.* Irvine 1), 1987
- ○ Fewest runs (two teams) — **1,** on two occasions:
    Birmingham 1   Schenectady 0, 1953
    Japan 1   Richmond 0, 1968
- ○ Fewest runs (one team) — **0,** on 18 occasions*
- ○ Perfect game pitched — **1,** Angel Marcias, Monterrey, Mexico, 1957
- ○ No-hitters pitched — **5,** Angel Marcias, Monterrey, Mexico, 1957
    Joe Mormello, Levittown, Pa., 1960
    Ted Campbell, San Jose, Cal., 1962
    Danny Yacarino, Staten Island, NY, 1964
    Dai Han-Chao, Pu-Tzu Town, Taiwan, 1979

*This total does not include the 1992 final. Zamboanga City won that game 15–4, but was subsequently disqualified following the tournament for fielding overage players. The championship game was declared a 6–0 forfeit to Long Beach, Cal.

SIMPLY PERFECT ■ ANGEL MARCIAS THREW A PERFECT GAME TO WIN THE 1957 LITTLE LEAGUE WORLD SERIES. (PUTSEE VANNUCCI)

WORLD SERIES LITTLE LEAGUERS

Five players have played in both the Little League World Series and the World Series.

Players	Years
Jim Barbieri	Schenectady, 1954; Los Angeles Dodgers, 1966
Boog Powell	Colton, 1954; Baltimore Orioles, 1966, 1969–71
Rick Wise	Kankakee, 1958; Boston Red Sox, 1975
Carney Lansford	Santa Clara, 1969; Oakland A's, 1988–90
Derek Bell	Belmont Heights, 1980–81; Toronto Blue Jays, 1992

LITTLE LEAGUER/BIG LEAGUER ■ BOOG POWELL IS ONE OF FIVE PLAYERS TO PLAY IN BOTH THE LITTLE LEAGUE AND WORLD SERIES. HE STARRED FOR COLTON IN 1954 (LEFT) AND FOR THE BALTIMORE ORIOLES IN 1966, 1969–71 (RIGHT). (PUTSEE VANNUCCI/BALTIMORE ORIOLES/MORT TADDER)

Year	Winner	Loser	Score
1947	Maynard, Pa.	Lock Haven, Pa.	16–7
1948	Lock Haven, Pa.	St. Petersburg, Fla.	6–5
1949	Hammonton, NJ	Pensacola, Fla.	5–0
1950	Houston, Tex.	Bridgeport, Conn.	2–1
1951	Stamford, Conn.	North Austin Lions, Tex.	3–0
1952	Norwalk, Conn.	Monongahela, Pa.	4–3
1953	Birmingham, Ala.	Schenectady, NY	1–0
1954	Schenectady, NY	Colton Lions, Cal.	7–5
1955	Morrisville, Pa.	Delaware/Merchantville, NJ	4–3
1956	Rosewell Lions Hondo, NM	Delaware Township, NJ	3–1
1957	Monterrey, Mexico	La Mesa Northern, Cal.	4–0
1958	Monterrey, Mexico	Kankakee, Ill.	10–1
1959	Hamtramck, Mich.	West Auburn, Cal.	12–0
1960	Levittown, Pa.	Fort Worth, Tex.	5–0
1961	El Cajon, Cal.	El Campo, Tex.	4–2
1962	San Jose, Cal.	Kankakee, Ill.	3–0
1963	Granada Hills, Cal.	Stamford, Conn.	2–1
1964	Staten Island, NY	Monterrey, Mexico	4–0
1965	Windsor Locks, Conn.	Stoney Creek, Canada	3–1
1966	Houston, Tex.	West New York, NJ	8–2
1967	Tokyo, Japan	North Roseland, Ill.	4–1
1968	Wakayama, Japan	Tuckahoe, Va.	1–0
1969	Taipei, Taiwan	Briarwood of Santa Clara, Cal.	5–0
1970	Wayne, NJ	Campbell, Cal.	2–0
1971	Tainan, Taiwan	Anderson, Ind.	12–3
1972	Taipei, Taiwan	Edison, Ind.	6–0
1973	Tainan City, Taiwan	Cactus of Tucson, Ariz.	12–0
1974	Kao Hsiung, Taiwan	Red Bluff, Cal.	12–1
1975	Lakewood, NJ	Belmont Heights, Fla.	4–3
1976	Chofu, Japan	Campbell, Cal.	10–3
1977	Li-Teh, Taiwan	El Cajon, Cal.	7–2
1978	Pin-Kuang, Taiwan	Danville, Cal.	11–1
1979	Pu-Tzu Town, Taiwan	Campbell, Cal.	2–1
1980	Long Kuong, Taiwan	Belmont Heights, Fla.	4–3
1981	Tai-Ping, Taiwan	Belmont Heights, Fla.	4–2
1982	Kirkland, Wash.	Pu-Tzu Town, Taiwan	6–0
1983	Marietta, Ga.	Liquito Hernandez, Dom. Rep.	3–1
1984	Seoul, South Korea	Altamonte Springs, Fla.	6–2
1985	Seoul, South Korea	Mexicali, Baja Cal., Mexico	7–1
1986	Tainan Park, Taiwan	Tucson, Ariz.	12–0
1987	Hua Lian, Taiwan	Northwood, Irvine, Cal.	21–1
1988	Tai Ping, Taiwan	Pearl City, Hawaii	10–0
1989	Trumbull, Conn.	Kang-Tu, Taiwan	5–2
1990	San-Hua, Taiwan	Shippensburg, Pa.	9–0
1991	Hsi Nan, Tai Chung, Taiwan	Danville, Cal.	11–0
1992	Long Beach, Cal.	Zamboanga City, Philippines	6–0*
1993	Long Beach, Cal.	Chiriqui, Panama	3–2

*Zamboanga won the game 15–4, but was subsequently disqualified for fielding overage players. The game was declared a 6–0 forfeit.

More than 75 percent of major league baseball players have played Little League Baseball. Of these, so far, only five have been inducted into the Baseball Hall of Fame: Carl Yastrzemski, Jim Palmer, Tom Seaver, Rollie Fingers and Steve Carlton.

CARL YASTRZEMSKI South Fork Little League, Bridgehampton, N.Y., 1949–52; Boston Red Sox, 1961–83; Hall of Fame, 1989. (BOSTON RED SOX)

JIM PALMER Beverly Hills Little League, Calif., 1955–58; Baltimore Orioles, 1965–84; Hall of Fame, 1990. (PUTSEE VANNUCCI)

TOM SEAVER Spartan Little League, Fresno, Calif., 1954–57; New York Mets, 1967–77; Cincinnati Reds, 1977–82; New York Mets, 1983; Chicago White Sox, 1984–86; Boston Red Sox, 1986; Hall of Fame, 1992. (NEW YORK METS)

ROLLIE FINGERS Rancho Cucamonga, Calif., 1958; Oakland Athletics, 1968–80; Milwaukee Brewers, 1981–85; Hall of Fame, 1992. (MILWAUKEE BREWERS/LARRY STOUDT)

STEVE CARLTON North Miami Little League, 1956; St. Louis Cardinals, 1965–71; Philadelphia Phillies, 1972–86; San Francisco Giants, 1986; Chicago White Sox, 1986; Cleveland Indians, 1987; Minnesota Twins, 1987–88; Hall of Fame, 1994. (PHILADELPHIA PHILLIES)

ABOVE AVERAGE ■ MICHAEL JORDAN HOLDS THE NBA RECORD FOR HIGHEST CAREER SCORING AVERAGE AT 32.3 POINTS PER GAME. (CHICAGO BULLS/BILL SMITH)

NCAA DIVISION I

HITTING RECORDS (CAREER)

Home runs 100, by Pete Incaviglia, Oklahoma State, 1983–85.

Hits 418, by Phil Stephenson, Wichita State, 1979–82.

PITCHING RECORDS (CAREER)

Wins 51, by Don Heinkel, Wichita State, 1979–82.

Strikeouts 541, by Derek Tatsumo, University of Hawaii, 1977–79.

COLLEGE WORLD SERIES The first College World Series was played in 1947 at Kalamazoo, Mich. The University of California at Berkeley defeated Yale University in a best-of-three-game series, 2–0. In 1949 the series format was changed to a championship game. Since 1950 the College World Series has been played at Rosenblatt Stadium, Omaha, Neb.

Most championships The most wins is 11, by Southern Cal., in 1948, 1958, 1961, 1963, 1968, 1970–74 and 1978.

HITTING RECORDS (CAREER)

Home runs Four, by five players: Bud Hollowell, Southern Cal., 1963; Pete Incaviglia, Oklahoma State, 1983–85; Ed Sprague, Stanford, 1987–88; Gary Hymel, Louisiana State, 1990–91; and Lyle Mewton, Louisiana State, 1990–91.

Hits 23, by Keith Moreland, Texas, 1973–75.

PITCHING RECORDS (CAREER)

Wins Four, by nine players: Bruce Gardner, Southern Cal., 1958, 1960; Steve Arlin, Ohio State, 1965–66; Bert Hooten, Texas at Austin, 1969–70; Steve Rogers, Tulsa, 1969, 1971; Russ McQueen, Southern Cal., 1972–73; Mark Bull, Southern Cal., 1973–74; Greg Swindell, Texas, 1984–85; Kevin Sheary, Miami (Fla.), 1984–85; Greg Brummett, Wichita State, 1988–89.

Strikeouts 64, by Carl Thomas, Arizona, 1954–56.

BASKETBALL

ORIGINS Basketball was invented by the Canadian-born Dr. James Naismith at the Training School of the International YMCA College at Springfield, Mass. in mid-December 1891. The first game played under modified rules was on January 20, 1892. The International Amateur Basketball Federation (FIBA) was founded in 1932; it has now dropped the word Amateur from its title.

NATIONAL BASKETBALL ASSOCIATION (NBA)

ORIGINS The Amateur Athletic Union (AAU) organized the first national tournament in the United States in 1897. The first professional league was the National Basketball League (NBL), founded in 1898, but this league only lasted two seasons. The American Basketball League was formed in 1925, but declined, and the NBL was refounded in 1937. This organization merged with the Basketball Association of America in 1949 to form the National Basketball Association (NBA).

NBA TEAM RECORDS

SCORING

Most points (one team) 186, by the Detroit Pistons, defeating the Denver Nuggets, 186–184, at Denver, on December 13, 1983 after three overtimes.

Most points, regulation (one team) 173, by two teams: Boston Celtics *v.* Minneapolis Lakers (139 points), at Boston, on February 27, 1959; Phoenix Suns *v.* Denver Nuggets (143 points), at Phoenix, on November 10, 1990.

Highest-scoring game (aggregate) 370 points, Detroit Pistons defeated the Denver Nuggets, 186–184, at Denver, on December 13, 1983 after three overtimes.

Highest-scoring game (aggregate), regulation 320 points, Golden State Warriors defeated the Denver Nuggets, 162–158, at Denver, on November 2, 1990.

Lowest-scoring game (aggregate) 37 points, Fort Wayne Pistons defeated the Minneapolis Lakers, 19–18, at Minneapolis, on November 22, 1950.

Greatest margin of victory 68 points, by the Cleveland Cavaliers, defeating the Miami Heat, 148–80, on December 17, 1991.

WINS AND LOSSES

Most wins (season) 69, by the Los Angeles Lakers in 1971–72.

Most consecutive wins 33, by the Los Angeles Lakers. The Lakers' streak began with a 110–106 victory over the Baltimore Bullets on November 5, 1971 in Los Angeles, and ended on January 9, 1972 when they were beaten 120–104 by the Milwaukee Bucks in Milwaukee.

Most losses (season) 73, by the Philadelphia 76ers in 1972–73.

Most consecutive losses 24, by the Cleveland Cavaliers. The Cavs' undesirable roll started on March 19, 1982 when they lost to the Milwaukee Bucks, 119–97, in Milwaukee, and ended on November 10, 1982 when they defeated the Golden State Warriors 132–120 in overtime on November 10, 1982. During the streak the Cavs lost the last 19 games of the 1981–82 season, and the first five of the 1982–83 season.

(continued on p. 43)

OVERTIME ■ IN A FIVE-OVERTIME GAME ON NOVEMBER 9, 1989, DALE ELLIS PLAYED AN NBA RECORD 69 MINUTES. (SAN ANTONIO SPURS)

TIMEOUT

HALF GAME PRESS ☞ THE MOST POINTS SCORED IN ONE HALF IS 59 BY WILT CHAMBERLAIN (PHILADELPHIA WARRIORS). THE BIG DIPPER SET THE MARK DURING THE 2ND HALF OF HIS RECORD 100-POINT GAME V. THE NEW YORK KNICKS ON MARCH 2, 1962.

NBA INDIVIDUAL RECORDS

Games Played

		Player(s)	Team(s)	Date(s)
Season	88	Walt Bellamy	New York Knicks, Detroit Pistons	1968–69
Career	1,560	Kareem Abdul-Jabbar	Milwaukee Bucks, Los Angeles Lakers	1969–89

Minutes Played

Game	69	Dale Ellis	Seattle SuperSonics v. Milwaukee Bucks	Nov 9, 1989 (5 OT)
Season	3,882	Wilt Chamberlain	Philadelphia Warriors	1961–62
Career	57,446	Kareem Abdul-Jabbar	Milwaukee Bucks, Los Angeles Lakers	1969–89

Points

Game	100	Wilt Chamberlain	Philadelphia Warriors v. New York Knicks	March 2, 1962
Season	4,029	Wilt Chamberlain	Philadelphia Warriors	1961–62
Career	38,387	Kareem Abdul-Jabbar	Milwaukee Bucks, Los Angeles Lakers	1969–89

Field Goals

Game	36	Wilt Chamberlain	Philadelphia Warriors v. New York Knicks	March 2, 1962
Season	1,597	Wilt Chamberlain	Philadelphia Warriors	1961–62
Career	15,837	Kareem Abdul-Jabbar	Milwaukee Bucks, Los Angeles Lakers	1969–89

Three-Point Field Goals

Game	10	Brian Shaw	Miami Heat v. Milwaukee Bucks	April 8, 1993
Season	172	Vernon Maxwell	Houston Rockets	1990–91
Career	941	Dale Ellis	Dallas Mavericks, Seattle Supersonics, Milwaukee Bucks, San Antonio Spurs	1983–94*

Free Throws

Game	28	Wilt Chamberlain Adrian Dantley	Philadelphia Warriors v. New York Knicks Utah Jazz v. Houston Rockets	March 2, 1962 January 4, 1984
Season	840	Jerry West	Los Angeles Lakers	1965–66
Career	8,465	Moses Malone	Buffalo Braves, Houston Rockets, Philadelphia 76ers, Washington Bullets, Atlanta Hawks, Milwaukee Bucks	1976–94*

---

* As of January 11, 1994

Source: NBA

NBA INDIVIDUAL RECORDS

Assists

		Player(s)	Team(s)	Date(s)
Game	30	Scott Skiles	Orlando Magic v. Denver Nuggets	December 30, 1990
Season	1,164	John Stockton	Utah Jazz	1990–91
Career	9,921	Magic Johnson	Los Angeles Lakers	1979–91

Rebounds

Game	55	Wilt Chamberlain	Philadelphia Warriors v. Boston Celtics	November 24, 1960
Season	2,149	Wilt Chamberlain	Philadelphia Warriors	1960–61
Career	23,924	Wilt Chamberlain	Philadelphia/San Francisco Warriors, Philadelphia 76ers, Los Angeles Lakers	1959–73

Steals

Game	11	Larry Kenon	San Antonio Spurs v. Kansas City Kings	December 26, 1976
Season	301	Alvin Robertson	San Antonio Spurs	1985–86
Career	2,310	Maurice Cheeks	Philadelphia 76ers, San Antonio Spurs, New York Knicks, Atlanta Hawks, New Jersey Nets	1978–93

Blocked Shots †

Game	17	Elmore Smith	Los Angeles Lakers v. Portland Trail Blazers	October 28, 1973
Season	456	Mark Eaton	Utah Jazz	1984–85
Career	3,189	Kareem Abdul-Jabbar	Milwaukee Bucks, Los Angeles Lakers	1973–89

Personal Fouls

Game	8	Don Otten	Tri-Cities v. Sheboygan	November 24, 1949
Season	386	Darryl Dawkins	New Jersey Nets	1983–84
Career	4,657	Kareem Abdul-Jabbar	Milwaukee Bucks, Los Angeles Lakers	1969–89

Disqualifications ††

Season	26	Don Meineke	Fort Wayne Pistons	1952–53
Career	127	Vern Mikkelsen	Minneapolis Lakers	1950–59

† Compiled since 1973–74 season.

†† Through January 11, 1994, Moses Malone (Houston Rockets, Philadelphia 76ers, Washington Bullets, Atlanta Hawks, Milwaukee Bucks) has played 1,165 consecutive games without fouling out.

THREE–POINT LAND

Arguably no play in sports has more synonyms than the three–point field goal. Players have delighted in "shooting the trey," "launching from three–point land," and "going downtown," to name just three. The origins of basketball's most rewarding shot are recent. The NBA introduced the three–point field goal for the 1979–80 season. The three–point line was set at 23 feet, 9 inches from the top of the key and 22 feet along the baseline. The dimensions haven't changed and neither has the Larry Bird maxim: "Keep your feet behind the line, and aim for the back rim."

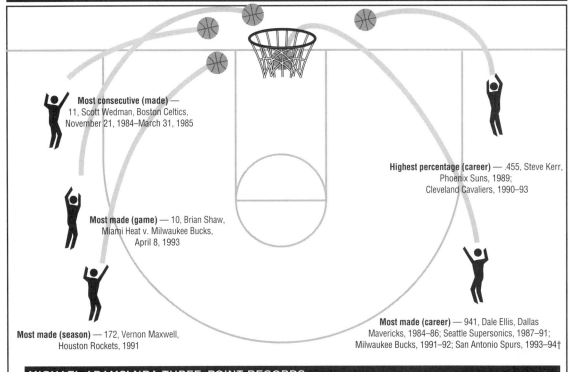

Most consecutive (made) — 11, Scott Wedman, Boston Celtics, November 21, 1984–March 31, 1985

Highest percentage (career) — .455, Steve Kerr, Phoenix Suns, 1989; Cleveland Cavaliers, 1990–93

Most made (game) — 10, Brian Shaw, Miami Heat v. Milwaukee Bucks, April 8, 1993

Most made (season) — 172, Vernon Maxwell, Houston Rockets, 1991

Most made (career) — 941, Dale Ellis, Dallas Mavericks, 1984–86; Seattle Supersonics, 1987–91; Milwaukee Bucks, 1991–92; San Antonio Spurs, 1993–94†

MICHAEL ADAMS' NBA THREE–POINT RECORDS

Michael Adams (Sacramento Kings, 1986; Washington Bullets, 1987; Denver Nuggets, 1988–91; Washington Bullets, 1992–93) might not be the best three–point shooter of all time, but if statistics are to be believed, then he loves shooting from downtown more than any other player. The following are the NBA records Adams held at the end of the 1992–93 season:

Most attempts (career) — 2,544. Adams made 851 of these shots, second highest on the all-time list.

Most attempts (season) — 564 in 1991. Adams made 167 shots, second highest on the all-time list.

Most attempts (game) — 20 on April 12, 1991. Adams was playing for the Denver Nuggets v. Los Angeles Clippers. During this game Adams also set the NBA record for most attempts in a half with 13.

Most attempts, none made (game) — The dubious honor for most missed three-pointers in a game is 8, a feat performed four times: twice by Adams. He was the first to reach this plateau v. Washington Bullets on February 15, 1989. He repeated the 8-miss standard on March 17, 1991 v. Indiana Pacers. Vernon Maxwell and Reggie Miller have since joined Adams in this exclusive club.

MICHAEL ADAMS
(DENVER NUGGETS)

†As of January 11, 1994

LOTS OF XS AND OS ■ BILL FITCH COACHED A RECORD 1,722 NBA GAMES WITH FOUR TEAMS, 1970–79. (NEW JERSEY NETS)

CONSECUTIVE RECORDS (INDIVIDUAL)

Games played 906, by Randy Smith, from February 18, 1972 to March 13, 1983. During his streak, Smith played for the Buffalo Braves, San Diego Clippers (twice), Cleveland Cavaliers, and New York Knicks.

TIMEOUT

$1 MILLION SHOT ☛ DON CALHOUN SANK A 75-FOOT BASKET AT CHICAGO STADIUM ON APRIL 14, 1993 TO WIN A $1 MILLION PRIZE. CALHOUN HAD BEEN RANDOMLY SELECTED FROM THE CROWD TO TRY HIS LUCK AT THE CONTEST DURING HALF-TIME OF A CHICAGO BULLS GAME.

Games scoring 50+ points Seven, by Wilt Chamberlain, Philadelphia Warriors, December 16–29, 1961.

Games scoring 10+ points 787, by Kareem Abdul-Jabbar, Los Angeles Lakers, from December 4, 1977 through December 2, 1987.

Free throws 97, by Micheal Williams, Minnesota Timberwolves, from March 24 through November 9, 1993.

Free throws (game) 23, by Dominique Wilkins, Atlanta Hawks on December 8, 1992.

COACHES

Most wins 938, by Red Auerbach, Washington Capitols (115 wins, 1946–49); Tri-Cities Blackhawks (28 wins, 1949–50); Boston Celtics (795 wins, 1950–66).

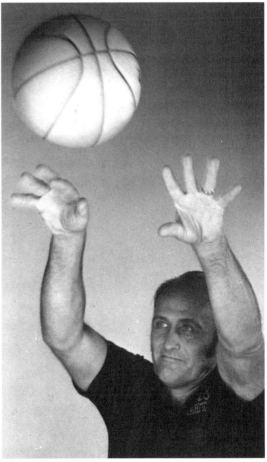

SHARPSHOOTER ■ TED ST. MARTIN SANK 2,036 CONSECUTIVE FREE THROWS ON JUNE 25, 1977. (TED ST. MARTIN)

NBA MOST VALUABLE PLAYER AWARD (1956–1993)

The Maurice Podoloff Trophy was instituted in 1956 to be awarded to the NBA's most valuable player. From 1956 to 1980 the award was decided by a vote of eligible NBA players; since 1980 the winner has been decided by a vote of eligible writers and broadcasters.

Most wins Six, by Kareem Abdul-Jabbar, Milwaukee Bucks, 1971–72, 1974; Los Angeles Lakers, 1976–77, 1980.

Year	Player	Team	Year	Player	Team
1956	Bob Pettit	St. Louis Hawks	1975	Bob McAdoo	Buffalo Braves
1957	Bob Cousy	Boston Celtics	1976	Kareem Abdul-Jabbar	Los Angeles Lakers
1958	Bill Russell	Boston Celtics	1977	Kareem Abdul-Jabbar	Los Angeles Lakers
1959	Bob Pettit	St. Louis Hawks	1978	Bill Walton	Portland Trail Blazers
1960	Wilt Chamberlain	Philadelphia Warriors	1979	Moses Malone	Houston Rockets
1961	Bill Russell	Boston Celtics	1980	Kareem Abdul-Jabbar	Los Angeles Lakers
1962	Bill Russell	Boston Celtics	1981	Julius Erving	Philadelphia 76ers
1963	Bill Russell	Boston Celtics	1982	Moses Malone	Houston Rockets
1964	Oscar Robertson	Cincinnati Royals	1983	Moses Malone	Philadelphia 76ers
1965	Bill Russell	Boston Celtics	1984	Larry Bird	Boston Celtics
1966	Wilt Chamberlain	Philadelphia 76ers	1985	Larry Bird	Boston Celtics
1967	Wilt Chamberlain	Philadelphia 76ers	1986	Larry Bird	Boston Celtics
1968	Wilt Chamberlain	Philadelphia 76ers	1987	Magic Johnson	Los Angeles Lakers
1969	Wes Unseld	Baltimore Bullets	1988	Michael Jordan	Chicago Bulls
1970	Willis Reed	New York Knicks	1989	Magic Johnson	Los Angeles Lakers
1971	Kareem Abdul-Jabbar	Milwaukee Bucks	1990	Magic Johnson	Los Angeles Lakers
1972	Kareem Abdul-Jabbar	Milwaukee Bucks	1991	Michael Jordan	Chicago Bulls
1973	Dave Cowens	Boston Celtics	1992	Michael Jordan	Chicago Bulls
1974	Kareem Abdul-Jabbar	Milwaukee Bucks	1993	Charles Barkley	Phoenix Suns

Highest winning percentage .723, by Pat Riley, Los Angeles Lakers, 1981–90, New York Knicks, 1991–93. Riley's record is 644 wins, 247 losses.

Most games 1,722, by Bill Fitch, Cleveland Cavaliers, 1970–79; Boston Celtics, 1979–83; Houston Rockets, 1983–88; New Jersey Nets, 1989–92. Fitch's career totals are 845 wins, 877 losses.

NBA CHAMPIONSHIP

The NBA recognizes the 1946–47 season as its first championship; however, at that time the league was known as the Basketball Association of America (BAA).

Most titles 16, by the Boston Celtics, 1957, 1959–66, 1968–69, 1974, 1976, 1981, 1984, 1986.

Consecutive titles Eight, by the Boston Celtics, 1959–66.

Most titles (coach) Nine, by Red Auerbach, Boston Celtics, 1957, 1959–66.

NBA CHAMPIONSHIP RECORDS (FINALS SERIES)

INDIVIDUAL RECORDS (GAME)

Most minutes played 62, by Kevin Johnson, Phoenix Suns *v.* Chicago Bulls on June 13, 1993. The game went to three overtimes.

Most points scored 61, by Elgin Baylor, Los Angeles Lakers *v.* Boston Celtics on April 14, 1962 in Boston.

Most field goals made 22, by two players: Elgin Baylor, Los Angeles Lakers *v.* Boston Celtics on April 14, 1962 in Boston; Rick Barry, San Francisco Warriors *v.* Philadelphia 76ers on April 18, 1967 in San Francisco.

Most free throws made 19, by Bob Pettit, St. Louis Hawks *v.* Boston Celtics on April 9, 1958 in Boston.

Most rebounds 40, by Bill Russell, Boston Celtics, who has performed this feat twice: *v.* St. Louis Hawks on March 29, 1960; *v.* Los Angeles Lakers on April 18, 1962, in an overtime game.

Most assists 21, by Magic Johnson, Los Angeles Lakers *v.* Boston Celtics on June 3, 1984.

Most steals Six, by four players: John Havlicek, Boston Celtics *v.* Milwaukee Bucks, May 3, 1974; Steve Mix, Philadelphia 76ers *v.* Portland Trail Blazers, May 22, 1977; Maurice Cheeks, Philadelphia 76ers *v.* Los Angeles Lakers, May 7, 1980; Isiah Thomas, Detroit Pistons *v.* Los Angeles Lakers, June 19, 1988.

Most blocked shots Eight, by two players: Bill Walton, Portland Trail Blazers *v.* Philadelphia 76ers, June 5, 1977; Hakeem Olajuwon, Houston Rockets *v.* Boston Celtics, June 5, 1986.

TEAM RECORDS (GAME)

Most points (one team) 148, by the Boston Celtics *v.* Los Angeles Lakers (114 points) on May 27, 1985.

(continued on p. 47)

NBA CHAMPIONSHIP FINALS (1947–1993)

Year	Winner	Loser	Series	Year	Winner	Loser	Series
1947	Philadelphia Warriors	Chicago Stags	4–1	1971	Milwaukee Bucks	Baltimore Bullets	4–0
1948	Baltimore Bullets	Philadelphia Warriors	4–2	1972	Los Angeles Lakers	New York Knicks	4–1
1949	Minneapolis Lakers	Washington Capitols	4–2	1973	New York Knicks	Los Angeles Lakers	4–1
1950	Minneapolis Lakers	Syracuse Nationals	4–2	1974	Boston Celtics	Milwaukee Bucks	4–3
1951	Rochester Royals	New York Knicks	4–3	1975	Golden State Warriors	Washington Bullets	4–0
1952	Minneapolis Lakers	New York Knicks	4–3	1976	Boston Celtics	Phoenix Suns	4–2
1953	Minneapolis Lakers	New York Knicks	4–1	1977	Portland Trail Blazers	Philadelphia 76ers	4–2
1954	Minneapolis Lakers	Syracuse Nationals	4–3	1978	Washington Bullets	Seattle SuperSonics	4–3
1955	Syracuse Nationals	Fort Wayne Pistons	4–3	1979	Seattle SuperSonics	Washington Bullets	4–1
1956	Philadelphia Warriors	Fort Wayne Pistons	4–1	1980	Los Angeles Lakers	Philadelphia 76ers	4–2
1957	Boston Celtics	St. Louis Hawks	4–3	1981	Boston Celtics	Houston Rockets	4–2
1958	St. Louis Hawks	Boston Celtics	4–2	1982	Los Angeles Lakers	Philadelphia 76ers	4–2
1959	Boston Celtics	Minneapolis Lakers	4–0	1983	Philadelphia 76ers	Los Angeles Lakers	4–0
1960	Boston Celtics	St. Louis Hawks	4–3	1984	Boston Celtics	Los Angeles Lakers	4–3
1961	Boston Celtics	St. Louis Hawks	4–1	1985	Los Angeles Lakers	Boston Celtics	4–2
1962	Boston Celtics	Los Angeles Lakers	4–3	1986	Boston Celtics	Houston Rockets	4–2
1963	Boston Celtics	Los Angeles Lakers	4–2	1987	Los Angeles Lakers	Boston Celtics	4–2
1964	Boston Celtics	San Francisco Warriors	4–1	1988	Los Angeles Lakers	Detroit Pistons	4–3
1965	Boston Celtics	Los Angeles Lakers	4–1	1989	Detroit Pistons	Los Angeles Lakers	4–0
1966	Boston Celtics	Los Angeles Lakers	4–3	1990	Detroit Pistons	Portland Trail Blazers	4–1
1967	Philadelphia 76ers	San Francisco Warriors	4–2	1991	Chicago Bulls	Los Angeles Lakers	4–1
1968	Boston Celtics	Los Angeles Lakers	4–2	1992	Chicago Bulls	Portland Trail Blazers	4–2
1969	Boston Celtics	Los Angeles Lakers	4–3	1993	Chicago Bulls	Phoenix Suns	4–2
1970	New York Knicks	Los Angeles Lakers	4–3				

NBA PLAYOFF RECORDS

Points

		Player(s)	Team(s)	Date(s)
Game	63	Michael Jordan	Chicago Bulls v. Boston Celtics	April 20, 1986 (2 OT)
	61	Elgin Baylor	Los Angeles Lakers v. Boston Celtics	April 14, 1962*
Series	284	Elgin Baylor	Los Angeles Lakers v. Boston Celtics	1962
Career	5,762	Kareem Abdul-Jabbar	Milwaukee Bucks, Los Angeles Lakers	1969–89

Field Goals

Game	24	Wilt Chamberlain	Philadelphia Warriors v. Syracuse Nationals	March 14, 1960
		John Havlicek	Boston Celtics v. Atlanta Hawks	April 1, 1973
		Michael Jordan	Chicago Bulls v. Cleveland Cavaliers	May 1, 1988
Series	113	Wilt Chamberlain	San Francisco Warriors v. St. Louis	1964
Career	2,356	Kareem Abdul-Jabbar	Milwaukee Bucks, Los Angeles Lakers	1970–89

Free Throws

Game	30	Bob Cousy	Boston Celtics v. Syracuse Nationals	March 21, 1953 (4 OT)
	23	Michael Jordan	Chiacgo Bulls v. New York Knicks	May 14, 1989*
Series	86	Jerry West	Los Angeles Lakers v. Baltimore Bullets	1965
Career	1,213	Jerry West	Los Angeles Lakers	1960–74

Assists

Game	24	Magic Johnson	Los Angeles Lakers v. Phoenix Suns	May 15, 1984
		John Stockton	Utah Jazz v. Los Angeles Lakers	May 17, 1988
Series	115	John Stockton	Utah Jazz v. Los Angeles Lakers	1988
Career	2,320	Magic Johnson	Los Angeles Lakers	1979–91

Rebounds

Game	41	Wilt Chamberlain	Philadelphia 76ers v. Boston Celtics	April 5, 1967
Series	220	Wilt Chamberlain	Philadelphia 76ers v. Boston Celtics	1965
Career	4,104	Bill Russell	Boston Celtics	1956–69

Steals

Game	8	Rick Barry	Golden State Warriors v. Seattle SuperSonics	April 14, 1975
		Lionel Hollins	Portland Trail Blazers v. Los Angeles Lakers	May 8, 1977
		Maurice Cheeks	Philadelphia 76ers v. New Jersey Nets	April 11, 1979
		Craig Hodges	Milwaukee Bucks v. Philadelphia 76ers	May 9, 1986
		Tim Hardaway	Golden State Warriors v. Los Angeles Lakers	May 8, 1991
		Tim Hardaway	Golden State Warriors v. Seattle SuperSonics	April 30, 1992
Series	28	John Stockton	Utah Jazz v. Los Angeles Lakers	1988
Career	358	Magic Johnson	Los Angeles Lakers	1979–91

---

* Regulation play
Source: NBA

DEFENSE ■ IN THE 1986 NBA FINALS, HAKEEM OLAJUWON BLOCKED EIGHT SHOTS IN ONE GAME, TIEING BILL WALTON'S MARK. (HOUSTON ROCKETS)

Highest-scoring game (aggregate) 276 points, Philadelphia 76ers defeated the San Francisco Warriors, 141–135, in overtime, on April 14, 1967.

Highest-scoring game, regulation (aggregate) 263 points, Los Angeles Lakers defeated the Boston Celtics, 141–122, on June 4, 1987.

Greatest margin of victory 35 points, Washington Bullets shot down the Seattle SuperSonics, 117–82, on June 4, 1978.

NCAA College Basketball

Men's Basketball (NCAA)

The National Collegiate Athletic Association (NCAA) has compiled statistics for its men's basketball competitions since the 1937–38 season. NCAA men's basketball is classified by three divisions: I, II and III.

NCAA CAREER INDIVIDUAL RECORDS (DIVISIONS I, II, III)

POINTS SCORED

Game 113, by Clarence "Bevo" Francis, Rio Grande (Division II), *v.* Hillsdale on February 2, 1954.

Season 1,381, by Pete Maravich, Louisiana State (Division I) in 1970. Pistol Pete hit 522 field goals and 337 free throws in 31 games.

Career 4,045, by Travis Grant, Kentucky State (Division II), 1969–72.

ASSISTANCE ■ DUKE'S BOBBY HURLEY COMPLETED HIS COLLEGIATE CAREER IN 1993 WITH AN NCAA RECORD 1,076 ASSISTS. (DUKE UNIVERSITY)

FIELD GOALS MADE

Game 41, by Frank Selvy, Furman (Division I), *v.* Newberry on February 13, 1954. Selvy amassed his record total from 66 attempts.

Season 539, by Travis Grant, Kentucky State (Division II) in 1972. Grant's season record was gained from 869 attempts.

Career 1,760, by Travis Grant, Kentucky State (Division II), 1969–72. Grant achieved his career record from 2,759 attempts.

ASSISTS

Game 26, by Robert James, Kean (Division III), *v.* New Jersey Tech on March 11, 1989.

Season 406, by Mark Wade, UNLV (Division I) in 1987. Wade played in 38 games.

Career 1,076, by Bobby Hurley, Duke (Division I), 1990–93. During his record-setting career Hurley played in 140 games.

REBOUNDS

Game 51, by Bill Chambers, William & Mary (Division I), *v.* Virginia on February 14, 1953.

Season 799, by Elmore Smith, Kentucky State (Division II) in 1971. Smith played in 33 games.

Career 2,334, by Jim Smith, Steubenville (Division II), 1955–58. Smith amassed his record total from 112 games.

NCAA TEAM RECORDS (DIVISION I)

Most points scored (one team) 186, by Loyola Marymount (Cal.) *v.* U.S. International (140 points), on January 5, 1991.

Highest-scoring game (aggregate) 331 points, Loyola Marymount (Cal.) defeating U.S. International, 181–150, on January 31, 1989.

Fewest points scored (team) Six, by two teams: Temple *v.* Tennessee (11 points), on December 15, 1973; Arkansas State *v.* Kentucky (75 points), on January 8, 1945.

Lowest-scoring game (aggregate) 17 points, Tennessee defeating Temple, 11–6, on December 15, 1973.

Widest margin of victory 95 points, Oklahoma defeating Northeastern Illinois, 146–51, on December 2, 1989.

(continued on p. 50)

NCAA DIVISION I MEN'S RECORDS

Points

		Player(s)	Team(s)	Date(s)
Game	100	Frank Selvy	Furman v. Newberry	February 13, 1954
	72	Kevin Bradshaw	U.S. International v. Loyola–Marymount	January 5, 1991*
Season	1,381	Pete Maravich	Louisiana State	1970
Career	3,667	Pete Maravich	Lousiana State	1968–70

Field Goals

Game	41	Frank Selvy	Furman v. Newberry	February 13, 1954
Season	522	Pete Maravich	Lousiana State	1970
Career	1,387	Pete Maravich	Lousiana State	1968–70

Free Throws

Game	30	Pete Maravich	Louisiana State v. Oregon State	December 22, 1969
Season	355	Frank Selvy	Furman	1954
Career	905	Dickie Hemric	Wake Forest	1952–55

Assists

Game	22	Tony Fairly	Baptist CS v. Armstrong State	February 9, 1987
		Avery Johnson	Southern-B.R. v. Texas Southern	January 25, 1988
		Sherman Douglas	Syracuse v. Providence	January 28, 1989
Season	406	Mark Wade	UNLV	1987
Career	1,076	Bobby Hurley	Duke	1990–93

Rebounds

Game	51	Bill Chambers	William & Mary v. Virginia	February 14, 1953
Season	734	Walt Dukes	Seton Hall	1953
Career	2,201	Tom Gola	La Salle	1952–55

Blocked Shots

Game	14	David Robinson	Navy v. N.C.–Wilmington	January 4, 1986
		Shawn Bradley	BYU v. Eastern Kentucky	December 7, 1990
Season	207	David Robinson	Navy	1986
Career	453	Alonzo Mourning	Georgetown	1989–92

Steals

Game	13	Mookie Blaylock	Oklahoma v. Centenary	December 12, 1987
		Mookie Blaylock	Oklahoma v. Loyola–Marymount	December 17, 1988
Season	150	Mookie Blaylock	Oklahoma	1988
Career	376	Eric Murdock	Providence	1988–91

* Game between two Division I teams
Source: NCAA

Greatest deficit overcome 29 points, Duke defeating Tulane, 74–72, on December 30, 1950, after trailing 27–56 at half-time.

Most wins (season) 37, by two teams: Duke in 1986 (37 wins, 3 losses); UNLV in 1987 (37 wins, 2 losses).

Most losses (season) 28, by Prairie View in 1992 (0 wins, 28 losses).

CONSECUTIVE RECORDS (INDIVIDUAL, DIVISION I)

Games scoring 10+ points 115, by Lionel Simmons, La Salle, 1987–90.

NCAA DIVISION I CHAMPIONS (1939–1993)

Year	Winner	Loser	Score	Year	Winner	Loser	Score
1939	Oregon	Ohio State	46–33	1967	UCLA	Dayton	79–64
1940	Indiana	Kansas	60–42	1968	UCLA	North Carolina	78–55
1941	Wisconsin	Washington State	39–34	1969	UCLA	Purdue	92–72
1942	Stanford	Dartmouth	53–38	1970	UCLA	Jacksonville	80–69
1943	Wyoming	Georgetown	46–34	1971	UCLA	Villanova*	68–62
1944	Utah	Dartmouth	42–40†	1972	UCLA	Florida State	81–76
1945	Oklahoma State	NYU	49–45	1973	UCLA	Memphis State	87–66
1946	Oklahoma State	North Carolina	43–40	1974	N. Carolina State	Marquette	76–64
1947	Holy Cross	Oklahoma	58–47	1975	UCLA	Kentucky	92–85
1948	Kentucky	Baylor	58–42	1976	Indiana	Michigan	86–68
1949	Kentucky	Oklahoma State	46–36	1977	Marquette	North Carolina	67–59
1950	CCNY	Bradley	71–68	1978	Kentucky	Duke	94–88
1951	Kentucky	Kansas State	68–58	1979	Michigan State	Indiana State	75–64
1952	Kansas	St. John's	80–63	1980	Louisville	UCLA*	59–54
1953	Indiana	Kansas	69–68	1981	Indiana	North Carolina	63–50
1954	LaSalle	Bradley	92–76	1982	North Carolina	Georgetown	63–62
1955	San Francisco	LaSalle	77–63	1983	N. Carolina State	Houston	54–52
1956	San Francisco	Iowa	83–71	1984	Georgetown	Houston	84–75
1957	North Carolina	Kansas	54–53‡	1985	Villanova	Georgetown	66–64
1958	Kentucky	Seattle	84–72	1986	Louisville	Duke	72–69
1959	California	West Virginia	71–70	1987	Indiana	Syracuse	74–73
1960	Ohio State	California	75–55	1988	Kansas	Oklahoma	83–79
1961	Cincinnati	Ohio State	70–65†	1989	Michigan	Seton Hall	80–79†
1962	Cincinnati	Ohio State	71–59	1990	UNLV	Duke	103–73
1963	Loyola (Ill.)	Cincinnati	60–58†	1991	Duke	Kansas	72–65
1964	UCLA	Duke	98–83	1992	Duke	Michigan	71–51
1965	UCLA	Michigan	91–80	1993	North Carolina	Michigan	77–71
1966	UTEP	Kentucky	72–65				

* These teams were disqualified by the NCAA for rules violations uncovered following the completion of the tournament.
† Overtime
‡ Triple overtime

Games scoring 50+ points Three, by Pete Maravich, Louisiana State, February 10 to February 15, 1969.

Field goals 25, by Ray Voelkel, American, over nine games from November 24 through December 16, 1978.

Field goals (game) 16, by Doug Grayson, Kent *v.* North Carolina on December 6, 1967.

Three-point field goals 15, by Todd Leslie, Northwestern, over four games from December 15 through December 28, 1990.

Three-point field goals (game) 11, by Gary Bossert, Niagara *v.* Sienna, January 7, 1987.

Free throws 64, by Joe Dykstra, Western Illinois, over eight games, December 1, 1981 through January 4, 1982.

Free throws (game) 24, by Arlen Clark, Oklahoma State *v.* Colorado, March 7, 1959.

CONSECUTIVE RECORDS (TEAM, DIVISION I)

Wins (regular season) 76, by UCLA, from January 30, 1971 through January 17, 1974. The streak was ended on January 19, 1974 when the Bruins were defeated by Notre Dame, 71–70.

Wins (regular season and playoffs) 88, by UCLA, from January 30, 1971 through January 17, 1974.

Losses 37, by Citadel, from January 16, 1954 through December 12, 1955.

Winning seasons 46, by Louisville, 1945–90.

COACHES (DIVISION I)

Most wins 875, by Adolph Rupp, Kentucky, 1931–72.

Highest winning percentage .837, by Jerry Tarkanian, Long Beach State, 1969–73; UNLV, 1974–

BALL HANDLER ■ **POINT GUARD RUMEAL ROBINSON LED MICHIGAN TO THE 1989 NCAA TITLE WITH A GAME RECORD 11 ASSISTS.** (UNIV. OF MICHIGAN/BOB KALMBACH)

92. The shark's career record was 625 wins, 122 losses.

Most games 1,105, by Henry Iba, Northwest Missouri State, 1930–33; Colorado, 1934; Oklahoma State, 1935–70. Iba's career record was 767 wins, 338 losses.

Most years 48, by Phog Allen, Baker, 1906–08; Kansas, 1908–09; Haskell, 1909, Central Missouri State, 1913–19, Kansas, 1920–56.

NCAA CHAMPIONSHIP TOURNAMENT

The NCAA finals were first contested in 1939 at Northwestern University, Evanston, Ill. The University of Oregon, University of Oklahoma, Villanova University and Ohio State University were the first "final four." Oregon defeated Ohio State 46–33 to win the first NCAA title.

Most wins (team) 10, by UCLA, 1964–65, 1967–73, 1975.

Most wins (coach) 10, by John Wooden. Wooden coached UCLA to each of its NCAA titles.

CHAMPIONSHIP GAME RECORDS (INDIVIDUAL, 1939–1993)

Most points 44, by Bill Walton, UCLA *v*. Memphis State in 1973.

Most field goals 21, by Bill Walton, UCLA *v*. Memphis State in 1973.

Most rebounds 27, by Bill Russell, San Francisco *v*. Iowa in 1956.

Most assists 11, by Rumeal Robinson, Michigan *v*. Seton Hall, 1989.

SWISH ■ SHERYL SWOOPES (22) SCORED A RECORD 47 POINTS IN LEADING TEXAS TECH TO THE 1993 NCAA TITLE. (ALLSPORT/JIM GUND)

WOMEN'S BASKETBALL

ORIGINS Senda Berenson and Clara Baer are generally credited as the pioneers of women's basketball. In 1892, Berenson, a physical education instructor at Smith College, adapted James Naismith's rules of basketball to create a "divided-court" version, which required the players to remain in their assigned sections of the court, making the game less physically demanding and thus, presumably, more suitable for women. Clara Baer introduced women's basketball to Sophie Newcomb Memorial College in her native New Orleans, La., in 1893. Baer also adapted the style of Naismith's game, and published her own set of rules in 1895; these became known as the Newcomb College rules.

The game spread rapidly in the late 19th century, with the first women's collegiate game being played between California and Stanford on April 4, 1896. Women's basketball was unable to sustain its growth in the 20th century, however, due to controversy over whether it was safe for women to play the game. It wasn't until after World War II that attitudes changed and women's basketball began to organize itself on a national level and bring its rules into line with the men's game.

In 1969, Carol Eckman, coach at West Chester University, Pa., organized the first national invitation tournament. Under the auspices of the Association for Intercollegiate Athletics for Women (AIAW) the national tournament was expanded, and in 1982 the NCAA was invited to take over the tournament.

NCAA INDIVIDUAL RECORDS (DIVISIONS I, II, III)

POINTS SCORED

Game 67, by Jackie Givens, Fort Valley State (Division II), *v*. Knoxville on February 22, 1991. Givens hit 19 field goals, six three-point field goals, and 11 free throws.

Season 1,075, by Jackie Givens, Fort Valley State (Division II), in 1991. Givens' record-setting season consisted of 249 field goals, 120 three-point field goals, and 217 free throws in 28 games.

Career 3,171, by Jeannie Demers, Buena Vista (Division III), 1983–87. Demers' career totals are 1,386 field goals and 399 free throws in 105 games.

(continued on p. 54)

NCAA DIVISION I WOMEN'S RECORDS

Points

		Player(s)	Team(s)	Date(s)
Game	60	Cindy Brown	Long Beach State v. San Jose State	February 16, 1987
Season	974	Cindy Brown	Long Beach State	1987
Career	3,122	Patricia Hoskins	Mississippi Valley	1985–89

Field Goals

Game	27	Lorri Bauman	Drake v. Southwest Missouri State	January 6, 1984
Season	392	Barbara Kennedy	Clemson	1982
Career	1,259	Joyce Walker	Louisiana State	1981–84

Free Throws

Game	23	Shaunda Greene	Washington v. Illinois	November 30, 1991
Season	275	Lorri Bauman	Drake	1982
Career	907	Lorri Bauman	Drake	1981–84

Assists

Game	23	Michelle Burden	Kent v. Ball State	February 6, 1991
Season	355	Suzie McConnell	Penn State	1987
Career	1,307	Suzie McConnell	Penn State	1984–88

Rebounds

Game	40	Deborah Temple	Delta State v. Alabama– Birmingham	February 14, 1983
Season	534	Wanda Ford	Drake	1985
Career	1,887	Wanda Ford	Drake	1983–86

Blocked Shots

Game	15	Amy Lundquist	Loyola (Cal.) v. Western Illinois	December 20, 1992
Season	151	Michelle Wilson	Texas Southern	1989
Career	428	Genia Miller	Cal. St. Fullerton	1987–91

Steals

Game	14	Natalie White	Florida A&M v. South Alabama	December 13, 1991
		Heidi Caruso	Lafayette v. Kansas St.	December 5, 1992
Season	168	Heidi Caruso	Lafayette	1993
Career	454	Dawn Staley	Virginia	1988–92

Source: NCAA

FIELD GOALS MADE

Game 28, by Ann Gilbert, Oberlin (Division III), *v.* Allegheny on February 6, 1991.

Season 392, by Barbara Kennedy, Clemson (Division I) in 1982. Kennedy set her record total from 760 attempts.

Career 1,386, by Jeannie Demers, Buena Vista (Division III), 1983–87. Demers made her record total from 2,838 attempts.

ASSISTS

Game 23, by two players: Michelle Burden, Kent (Division I), *v.* Ball State on February 6, 1991; and Selina Bynum, Albany State (Ga.) (Division II), *v.* Moyne-Owen on January 13, 1993.

Season 355, by Suzie McConnell, Penn State (Division I), in 1987.

Career 1,307, by Suzie McConnell, Penn State (Division I), 1984–88.

REBOUNDS

Game 40, by Deborah Temple, Delta State (Division I), *v.* Alabama–Birmingham, on February 14, 1983.

Season 635, by Francine Perry, Quinnipac (Division II), in 1982.

Career 1,887, by Wanda Ford, Drake (Division I), 1983–86.

NCAA TEAM RECORDS (DIVISION I)

Most points scored (one team) 149, by Long Beach State *v.* San Jose State (69 points), on February 16, 1987.

Highest-scoring game (aggregate) 243 points, Virginia defeating North Carolina State, 123–120, after three overtimes on January 12, 1991.

Fewest points scored (one team) 12, by Bennett *v.* North Carolina A&T (85 points), on November 21, 1990.

Lowest-scoring game (aggregate) 72 points, Virginia defeating San Diego State, 38–34, on December 29, 1981.

Most wins (season) 35, by three teams: Texas, 1982; Louisiana Tech, 1982; Tennessee, 1989.

Most losses (season) 28, by Charleston South in 1991.

COACHES (DIVISION I)

Most wins 620, by Jody Conradt, Texas, 1970–93.

Highest winning percentage .885, by Leon Barmore, Louisiana Tech, 1983–92. Barmore's career record through the 1991–92 season is 307 wins, 52 losses.

NCAA CHAMPIONS (1982–1993)

Year	Winner	Loser	Score
1982	Louisiana Tech.	Cheyney	76–62
1983	Southern Cal.	Louisiana Tech.	69–67
1984	Southern Cal.	Tennessee	72–61
1985	Old Dominion	Georgia	70–65
1986	Texas	Southern Cal.	97–81
1987	Tennessee	Louisiana Tech.	67–44
1988	Louisiana Tech.	Auburn	56–54
1989	Tennessee	Auburn	76–60
1990	Stanford	Auburn	88–81
1991	Tennessee	Virginia	70–67*
1992	Stanford	Western Kentucky	78–62
1993	Texas Tech.	Ohio State	84–82

* Overtime

IN A SPIN ■ BRUCE CREVIER DEMONSTRATES HIS RECORD-BREAKING BASKETBALL-SPINNING TECHNIQUE. ON NOVEMBER 18, 1993 HE BALANCED 17 BALLS ACROSS HIS BODY. (BRUCE CREVIER)

TIMEOUT

NCAA CHAMPIONSHIP TOURNAMENT

The NCAA instituted a women's basketball championship in 1982.

Most wins (team) Three, by Tennessee, 1987, 1989 and 1991.

Most wins (coach) Three, by Pat Summitt. Summitt coached Tennessee to all three NCAA titles.

CHAMPIONSHIP GAME RECORDS (INDIVIDUAL)

Most points 47, by Sheryl Swoopes, Texas Tech *v*. Ohio State in 1993.

Most field goals 16, by Sheryl Swoopes, Texas Tech *v*. Ohio State, in 1993.

Most rebounds 20, by Tracy Claxton, Old Dominion *v.* Georgia, in 1985.

Most assists 10, by two players: Kamie Ethridge, Texas *v.* Southern Cal, in 1986; Melissa McCray, Tennessee *v.* Auburn, in 1989.

OLYMPIC GAMES The men's basketball competition was introduced at the Berlin Olympics in 1936. In April 1989, the International Olympic Committee voted to allow professional players to compete in the Games. The women's basketball competition was introduced at the Montreal Olympics in 1976.

Most gold medals (men) The United States has won 10 gold medals in Olympic basketball competition: 1936, 1948, 1952, 1956, 1960, 1964, 1968, 1976, 1984 and 1992.

Most gold medals (women) In the women's basketball tournament the gold medal has been won three times by the USSR/Unified Teams: 1976, 1980 and 1992.

WORLD CHAMPIONSHIPS An official men's world championship was first staged in 1950 in Buenos Aires, Argentina, and has been held quadrennially since. A women's world championship was first staged in 1953 and is now also staged as a quadrennial event.

Most titles (men) Two countries have won the men's title three times: USSR, 1967, 1974 and 1982; Yugoslavia, 1970, 1978 and 1990.

Most titles (women) The USSR has won the women's event a record six times: 1959, 1964, 1967, 1971, 1975 and 1983.

United States The United States has won the women's title five times: 1953, 1957, 1979, 1986 and 1990; and the men's title twice: 1954 and 1986.

BIATHLON

The biathlon is a composite test of cross-country skiing and rifle marksmanship. Competitors ski over a prepared course carrying a small-bore rifle; at designated ranges the skiers stop and complete the shooting assignment for the race. Time penalties are assessed for missed shots; the winner of the event is the one with the fastest time.

ORIGINS The sport reflects one of the earliest techniques of human survival; rock carvings in Roedoey, Norway dating to 3000 B.C. seem to depict hunters stalking their prey on skis. Biathlon as a modern sport evolved from military ski patrol maneuvers, which tested the soldier's ability as a fast skier and accurate marksman. In 1958 the *Union Internationale de Pentathlon Moderne et Biathlon* (UIPMB) was formed as the international governing body of biathlon and modern pentathlon. Biathlon was included in the Olympic Games for the first time in 1960.

United States The 1960 Olympic Games at Squaw Valley, Calif. introduced biathlon to this country. National championships were first held in 1965. The current governing body of the sport is the United States Biathlon Association, founded in 1980 and based in Essex Junction, Vt.

OLYMPIC GAMES "Military patrol," the forerunner to biathlon, was included in the Games of 1924, 1928, 1936 and 1948. Biathlon was included in the Winter Games for the first time at Squaw Valley, Calif. in 1960. Women's events were included for the first time at the 1992 Games at Albertville, France.

Most gold medals Aleksandr Tikhonov (USSR) has won four gold medals as a member of the Soviet relay team that won the 4 x 7,500 meter races in 1968, 1972, 1976 and 1980. Magnar Solberg (Norway) and Franz-Peter Rotsch (East Germany) have both won two gold medals in individual events. Solberg won the 20,000 meters in 1968 and 1972; Rotsch won the 10,000 meters and 20,000 meters in 1988.

Most medals Aleksandr Tikhonov has won a record five medals in Olympic competition. In addition to his four gold medals (see above), he won the silver medal in the 20,000 meters in 1968.

WORLD CHAMPIONSHIPS First held in 1958 for men and in 1984 for women, the world championships are an annual event. In Olympic years, the Games are considered the world championships; therefore, records in this section include results from the Games.

Most titles (overall) Aleksandr Tikhonov (USSR) has won 14 world titles: 10 in the 4 x 7,500 meter relay, 1968–74, 1976–77 and 1980; four individual events, 10,000 meter in 1977 and 20,000 meter in 1969–70 and 1973. In women's events, Kaya Parve (USSR) has won a record six gold medals: four in the 3 x 5,000 meter relay, 1984–86, 1988; two individual titles, the 5,000 meter in 1986 and the 10,000 meter in 1985.

Most titles (individual) Frank Ullrich (East Germany) has won a record six individual titles: 10,000 meter, 1978–81; 20,000 meter, 1982–83.

UNITED STATES NATIONAL CHAMPIONSHIPS In this competition, first held in 1965 in Rosendale, N.Y., men's events have been staged annually. Women's events were included in 1985.

Most titles Lyle Nelson has won seven national championships: five in the 10,000 meter, 1976, 1979, 1981, 1985 and 1987; two in the 20,000 meter, 1977 and 1985. Anna Sonnerup holds the women's record with five titles: two in the 10,000 meter, 1986–87; two in the 15,000 meter, 1989 and 1991; and one in the 7,500 meter in 1989.

BOBSLED AND LUGE

BOBSLED

ORIGINS The earliest known sled is dated c. 6500 B.C. and was found at Heinola, Finland. There are references to sled racing in Norwegian folklore dating from the 15th century. The first tracks built for sled racing were constructed in the mid-18th century in St. Petersburg, Russia. The modern sport of bobsled dates to the late 19th century, when British enthusiasts organ-

ized competitions in Switzerland. The first run built for bobsled racing was constructed in St. Moritz, Switzerland in 1902. The *Federation Internationale de Bobsleigh de Tobagganing* (FIBT) was founded in 1923 and is the world governing body of bobsled racing.

United States The United States Bobsled & Skeleton Federation was founded in 1941 and is still the governing body for the sport in this country.

OLYMPIC GAMES A four-man bob competition was included in the first Winter Games in 1924 at Chamonix, France. Bobsled events have been included in every Games except 1960, when the Squaw Valley organizing committee refused to build a bobsled track.

Four-man bob Switzerland has won a record five Olympic titles: 1924, 1936, 1956, 1972 and 1988.

Two-man bob Switzerland has won a record three Olympic titles: 1948, 1980 and 1992.

Most gold medals Meinhard Nehmer and Bernhard Germeshausen (both East Germany) have both won a record three gold medals. They were both members of the 1976 two-man and four-man winning crews and the 1980 four-man winning crews.

SPEED SLEDDING ■ THE FOUR-MAN BOBSLED EVENT WAS INCLUDED IN THE FIRST WINTER OLYMPICS IN 1924. SWITZERLAND HAS WON FIVE TITLES. (ALLSPORT/MIKE POWELL)

Most medals Eugenio Monti (Italy) has won six medals: two gold, two silver and two bronze, 1956–68.

WORLD CHAMPIONSHIPS A world championship staged independently of the Olympic Games was first held in 1930 for four-man bob, and from 1931 for two-man bob. In Olympic years the Games are considered the world championship; therefore, records in this section include the Games of 1924 and 1928.

Four-man bob Switzerland has won the world title a record 19 times: 1924, 1936, 1939, 1947, 1954–57, 1971–73, 1975, 1982–83 and 1986–90.

Two-man bob Italy has won the world title 14 times: 1954, 1956–63, 1966, 1968–69, 1971 and 1975.

Most titles Eugenio Monti (Italy) has won 11 bobsled world championships: eight in the two-man, 1957–1961, 1963, 1966 and 1968; three in the four-man, 1960–61 and 1968.

LUGE

In luge the rider adopts a supine as opposed to a sitting position.

ORIGINS The first international luge race took place in 1883. Organized by the hotel keepers of Davos, Switzerland to promote their town, the race attracted 21 entrants from seven countries, including the United States. The course was 2½ miles, from St. Wolfgang to Klosters. The FIBT governed luge racing until 1957, when the *Fédération Internationale de Luge* (FIL) was formed.

United States The United States has participated in all Olympic luge events since the sport was sanctioned for the 1964 Games, but there was no organized governing body for the sport in this country until 1979, when the United States Luge Association was formed. The only luge run in the United States accredited for international competition is the refrigerated run used for the Lake Placid Olympics in 1980.

OLYMPIC GAMES One-man skeleton races were included in the 1928 and 1948 Games; however, in skeleton races riders race face down rather than lying on their backs as in luge. Luge was included in the Games for the first time in 1964 in Innsbruck, Austria.

Most gold medals Thomas Kohler, Hans Rinn, Norbert Hahn and Steffi Martin-Walter (all East Germany) have each won two Olympic titles: Kohler won the single-seater in 1964 and the two-seater in 1968; Rinn and Hahn won the two-seater in 1976 and 1980; Martin-Walter won the women's single-seater in 1984 and 1988.

United States No American luger has won a medal at the Olympic Games. In the skeleton sled races held in 1928 and 1948, the United States won one gold and two silvers out of six races. Jennison Heaton was the winner of the 1928 single skeleton sled event.

WORLD CHAMPIONSHIPS First held in 1955, the world championships have been staged biennially since 1981. In Olympic years the Games are considered the world championships; therefore, records in this section include results from the Games.

Most titles Thomas Kohler and Hans Rinn (both East Germany) have both won six world titles: Kohler won the single-seater in 1962, 1964 and 1966–67, and the two-seater in 1967–68; Rinn won the single-seater in 1973 and 1977, and the two-seater in 1976–77 and 1980 (two world championships were held in 1980, with Rinn winning each time). Margit Schumann (East Germany) holds the women's mark with five world titles, 1973–77.

UNITED STATES NATIONAL CHAMPIONSHIPS This competition was inaugurated in 1974.

Most titles Frank Masley has won a record six men's championships: 1979, 1981–83 and 1987–88. Bonny Warner has won a record five women's titles: 1983–84, 1987–88 and 1990.

BOWLING

ORIGINS The ancient German game of nine-pins (*Heidenwerfen*—"knock down pagans") was exported to the United States in the early 17th century. In 1841, the Connecticut state legislature prohibited the game, and other states followed. Eventually a tenth pin was added to evade the ban. The first body to standardize rules was the American Bowling Congress (ABC), established in New York City on September 9, 1895.

PBA TOUR SCORING RECORDS

Games	Score	Bowler	Site	Year
6	1,615	Walter Ray Williams Jr.	Beaumont, Tex.	1991
8	2,165	Billy Hardwick	Tokyo, Japan	1968
12	3,052	Walter Ray Williams Jr.	Beaumont, Tex.	1991
16	4,015	Carmen Salvino	Sterling Heights, Mich.	1980
18	4,515	Earl Anthony	New Orleans, La.	1977
24	5,826	Kelly Coffman	Riverside, Cal.	1993

Source: PBA Tour

PROFESSIONAL BOWLERS ASSOCIATION (PBA)

The PBA was founded in 1958 by Eddie Elias and is based in Akron, Ohio.

Most titles (career) Earl Anthony of Dublin, Calif. has won a career record 41 PBA titles, 1970–83.

Most titles (season) The record number of titles won in one PBA season is eight, by Mark Roth of North Arlington, N.J., in 1978.

TRIPLE CROWN The United States Open, the PBA National Championship and the Firestone Tournament of Champions comprise the Triple Crown of men's professional bowling. No bowler has won all three titles in the same year, and only three have managed to win all three during a career. The first bowler to accumulate the three legs of the triple crown was Billy Hardwick: National Championship (1963); Firestone Tournament of Champions (1965); U.S. Open (1969). Hardwick's feat was matched by Johnny Petraglia: Firestone (1971); U.S. Open (1977); National (1980); and by Pete Weber: Firestone (1987); U.S. Open (1988 and 1991); National (1989).

U.S. OPEN In this tournament, inaugurated in 1942, the most wins is four, by two bowlers: Don Carter in 1953–54 and 1957–58, and Dick Weber in 1962–63 and 1965–66.

PBA NATIONAL CHAMPIONSHIP In this contest, inaugurated in 1960, the most wins is six, by Earl Anthony in 1973–75 and 1981–83.

FIRESTONE TOURNAMENT OF CHAMPIONS In this tournament, inaugurated in 1965, the most wins is three, by Mike Durbin in 1972, 1982 and 1984.

PEFECT GAMES

A total of 210 perfect (300 score) games were bowled in PBA tournaments in 1993, the most ever for one year.

Most perfect games (career) Since 1977, when the PBA began to keep statistics on perfect games, Wayne Webb has bowled 33 in tournament play.

Most perfect games (season) Three bowlers have bowled seven perfect games in one season: Amleto Monacelli, 1989; Walter Ray Williams, Jr., 1993; and Dave Arnold, 1993.

Highest earnings Marshall Holman has won a career record $1,606,961 in PBA competitions through 1993. Mike Aulby of Indianapolis, Ind. set a single-season earnings mark of $298,237 in 1989.

LADIES PROFESSIONAL BOWLERS TOUR (LPBT)

Founded in 1981, the LPBT is based in Rockford, Ill.

Most titles (career) Lisa Wagner has won 28 tournaments in her twelve-year career, 1980–93.

Most titles (season) Patty Costello won a season record seven tournaments in 1976.

PERFECT GAMES

Most bowled (career) Two bowlers have bowled an LPBT-approved record 21 perfect games: Jeanne Naccarato (née Maiden) and Trish Johnson.

Most bowled (season) The record for most perfect games in a season is seven, by Trish Johnson in 1993.

TOP SCORER ■ WALTER RAY WILLIAMS JR. HOLDS THE PBA TOUR RECORDS FOR MOST POINTS SCORED IN SIX GAMES AND IN 12 GAMES. (PBA TOUR)

Highest team score (one game) The all-time ABC-sanctioned two-man single-game record is 600, held jointly by five teams: John Cotta and Steve Larson, May 1, 1981 at Manteca, Calif.; Jeff Mraz and Dave Roney, November 8, 1987 at Canton, Ohio; William Gruner and Dave Conway, February 27, 1990 at Oceanside, Calif.; Scott Williams and Willie Hammar, June 7, 1990 at Utica, N.Y.; Darrell Guertin and George Tignor, February 20, 1993 at Rutland, Vt.

Highest team score (three games) The highest three-game team score is 3,858, by Budweisers of St. Louis on March 12, 1958.

Highest season average The highest season average attained in sanctioned competition is 247.89, by Jeff Phipps of Salem, Ore., in the 1992–93 season.

Juniors Brentt Arcement, at age 16, bowled a three-game series of 888, the highest ever bowled in a league or tournament sanctioned by the Young American Bowling Alliance, which is the national organization serving junior bowlers (age 21 and under). The highest score by a girl is 824 by Cindy Shipman of Endicott, N.Y. during the 1985–86 season.

Consecutive strikes The record for consecutive strikes in sanctioned play is 33, by two bowlers: John Pezzin at Toledo, Ohio on March 4, 1976, and Fred Dusseau at Yuma, Ariz., on March 3, 1992.

TIMEOUT

HIGHEST SCORE IN 24 HOURS ☛ A SIX-MAN TEAM SCORED 212,692 AT STRYKERS PLEASURE BOWL, BUSHBURY, ENGLAND ON JUNE 20–21, 1992. THE INDIVIDUAL RECORD IS 47,566, BY BRIAN LARKINS AT HOLLYWOOD BOWL, BOLTON, ENGLAND ON APRIL 9–10, 1993.

Highest earnings Lisa Wagner has won a career record $543,277 in prize money, 1980–93. Robin Romeo won a season record $113,750 in 1989.

AMERICAN BOWLING CONGRESS (ABC)

SCORING RECORDS

Highest individual score (three games) The highest individual score for three games is 899, by Thomas Jordan at Union, N.J. on March 7, 1989.

PERFECT GAMES

Most bowled (career) The highest number of sanctioned 300 games is 43, by Bob Learn Jr. of Erie, Pa.

Oldest The oldest person to bowl a perfect game is Jerry Wehman of Port St. Lucie, Fla. He performed the feat at St. Lucie Lanes on April 15, 1992 when aged 81 years old.

Youngest The youngest person to bowl a perfect game is Matthew Gilman of Davie, Fla. He achieved perfection on July 17, 1993, aged 11 years 2 months.

Consecutive Two perfect games were rolled back-to-back *twice* by two bowlers: Al Spotts of West Reading, Pa. on March 14, 1982 and again on February 1, 1985, and Jerry Wright of Idaho Falls, Idaho on January 9, 1992 and again on February 26, 1992.

PERFECT YOUTH ■ AT AGE 11 YEARS 2 MONTHS, MATTHEW GILMAN BOWLED A PERFECT GAME ON JULY 17, 1993, BECOMING THE YOUNGEST PERSON TO PERFORM THE FEAT. (SUN-SENTINEL, FORT LAUDERDALE)

WOMEN'S INTERNATIONAL BOWLING CONGRESS (WIBC)

SCORING RECORDS

Highest individual score (three games) The highest individual score for three games is 865, by Anne Marie Duggan at Dallas, Tex., on July 18, 1993.

Highest team score (one game) Pamela Beach and Cindy Fry bowled the all-time two-woman single-game highest score of 578 in Lansing, Mich., on November 21, 1992.

Highest team score (three games) The highest three-game team score is 3,446, by Drug Package Inc. of St. Louis, Mo., on January 5, 1993.

Highest season average The highest season average attained in sanctioned WIBC-competition is 232.0, by Patty Ann of Appleton, Wis., in the 1983–84 season.

Consecutive strikes Jeanne Maiden bowled a record 40 consecutive strikes on November 23, 1986 at Sodon, Ohio.

PERFECT GAMES

Most bowled (career) The highest number of WIBC-sanctioned perfect games (300) is 20, by Jeanne Maiden.

Oldest The oldest woman to bowl a perfect game is Evelyn Culbert of Austin, Minn. She performed the feat at Eden Lanes, Austin, Minn., on April 4, 1993 when aged 66 years old.

Bowled, lowest average Of all the women who have rolled a perfect game, the one with the lowest average was Diane Ponza of Santa Cruz, Calif., who had a 112 average in the 1977–78 season.

BOXING

The nationality of the competitors in this section is U.S. unless stated otherwise.

ORIGINS Boxing with gloves is depicted on a fresco from the Isle of Thera, Greece that has been dated to 1520 B.C. The earliest prize-ring code of rules was formulated in England on August 16, 1743 by the champion pugilist Jack Broughton, who reigned from 1734 to 1750. In 1867, boxing came under the Queensberry Rules, formulated for

John Sholto Douglas, 8th Marquess of Queensberry.

United States New York was the first state to legalize boxing, in 1896. Today professional boxing is regulated in each state by athletic or boxing commissions.

Longest fights The longest recorded fight with gloves was between Andy Bowen and Jack Burke at New Orleans, La. on April 6–7, 1893. It lasted 110 rounds, 7 hours 19 minutes (9:15 P.M.–4:34 A.M.) and was declared a no contest (later changed to a draw). The longest bare-knuckle fight was 6 hours 15 minutes between James Kelly and Jack Smith at Fiery Creek, Dalesford, Victoria, Australia on December 3, 1855.

The greatest number of rounds was 276 in 4 hours 30 minutes when Jack Jones beat Patsy Tunney in Cheshire, England in 1825.

Shortest fights The shortest fight on record appears to be one in a Golden Gloves tournament at Minneapolis, Minn. on November 4, 1947, when Mike Collins floored Pat Brownson with the first punch and the contest was stopped, without a count, 4 seconds after the bell. The World Boxing Council reports that the shortest fight in the history of professional boxing occured on June 19, 1991, when Paul Rees (Australia) scored a technical knockout over Charlie Hansen (Australia) in five seconds in a junior-middleweight bout in Brisbane, Australia.

The shortest world title fight was 20 seconds, when Gerald McClellan beat Jay Bell in a WBC middleweight bout at Bayamon, Puerto Rico on August 7, 1993.

Most fights without loss Of boxers with complete records, Packey McFarland had 97 fights (five draws) from 1905 to 1915 without a defeat.

Consecutive wins Pedro Carrasco (Spain) won 83 consecutive fights from April 22, 1964 to September 3, 1970.

Most knockouts The greatest number of finishes classified as "knockouts" in a career is 145 (129 in professional bouts), by Archie Moore.

Consecutive knockouts The record for consecutive knockouts is 44, by Lamar Clark from 1958 to January 11, 1960.

Attendance The largest paid attendance at any boxing event is 132,274, at the Aztec Stadium, Mexico City on February 20, 1993. The card featured four world title bouts headed by the Julio César Chavez (Mexico) v. Greg Haugen WBC super light-welterweight title fight. Chavez knocked out Haugen in the fifth round.

The largest nonpaying attendance is 135,132, at the Tony Zale v. Billy Pryor bout at Juneau Park, Milwaukee, Wis., on August 16, 1941.

Lowest attendance The smallest crowd at a world heavyweight title fight was 2,434, at the Cassius Clay (Muhammad Ali) v. Sonny Liston fight at Lewiston, Me., on May 25, 1965. Clay knocked out Liston in the first round.

HEAVYWEIGHT DIVISION

Long accepted as the first world heavyweight title fight, with gloves and three-minute rounds, was that between John L. Sullivan and James J. "Gentleman Jim" Corbett in New Orleans, La. on September 7, 1892. Corbett won in 21 rounds.

Longest reign Joe Louis was champion for 11 years 252 days, from June 22, 1937, when he knocked out James J. Braddock in the eighth round at Chicago, Ill., until announcing his retirement on March 1, 1949. During his reign, Louis defended his title a record 25 times.

Shortest reign The shortest reign was 64 days for IBF champion Tony Tucker, May 30–August 1, 1987.

Most recaptures Muhammad Ali is the only man to have regained the heavyweight championship twice. Ali first won the title on February 25, 1964, defeating Sonny Liston. He defeated George Foreman on October 30, 1974, having been stripped of the title by the world boxing authorities on April 28, 1967. He won the WBA title from Leon Spinks on September 15, 1978, having previously lost to him on February 15, 1978.

Undefeated Rocky Marciano is the only world champion at any weight to have won every fight of his entire professional career (1947–56); 43 of his 49 fights were by knockouts or stoppages.

Oldest successful challenger Jersey Joe Walcott was 37 years 168 days when he knocked out Ezzard Charles on July 18, 1951 in Pittsburgh, Pa.

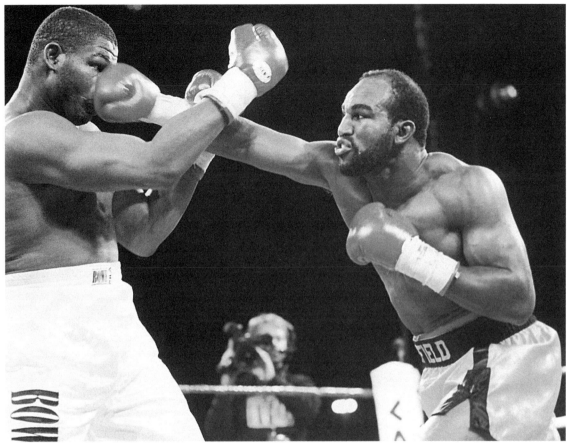

DOUBLE WHAMMY ■ ON NOVEMBER 6, 1993, EVANDER HOLYFIELD BECAME THE THIRD BOXER IN HISTORY TO REGAIN THE HEAVYWEIGHT TITLE, WHEN HE DEFEATED RIDDICK BOWE. (ALLSPORT/HOLLY STEIN)

Youngest champion Mike Tyson was 20 years 144 days when he beat Trevor Berbeck to win the WBC title at Las Vegas, Nev., on Nov. 22, 1986. He became the youngest undisputed champion on August 1, 1987 when he defeated Tony Tucker for the IBF title.

Lightest champion Bob Fitzsimmons (Great Britain) weighed 167 pounds when he won the title by knocking out James J. Corbett at Carson City, Nev. on March 17, 1897.

Heaviest champion Primo Carnera (Italy) weighed in at 270 pounds for the defense of his title *v.* Tommy Loughran on March 1, 1934. Carnera won a unanimous point decision.

MOST KNOCK-DOWNS ☛ VIC TOWEEL (SOUTH AFRICA) HOLDS THE RECORD FOR MOST KNOCK-DOWNS IN A WORLD TITLE FIGHT. HE FLOORED DANNY O'SULLIVAN (GREAT BRITAIN) 14 TIMES IN TEN ROUNDS IN WINNING THEIR BANTAMWEIGHT BOUT ON DECEMBER 2, 1950 AT JOHANNESBURG, SOUTH AFRICA.

Quickest knockout The quickest knockout in a heavyweight title fight was 55 seconds, by James J. Jeffries over Jack Finnegan at Detroit, Mich. on April 6, 1900.

WORLD CHAMPIONS (ANY WEIGHT)

Reign (longest) Joe Louis's heavyweight duration record of 11 years 252 days stands for all divisions.

Reign (shortest) Tony Canzoneri was world light welterweight champion for 33 days, May 21 to June 23, 1933, the shortest period for a boxer to have won and lost the world title in the ring.

Most recaptures The only boxer to win a world title five times at one weight is Sugar Ray Robinson, who beat Carmen Basilio in Chicago Stadium, Ill. on March 25, 1958 to regain the world middleweight title for the fourth time.

Greatest weight difference Primo Carnera (Italy) outweighed his opponent, Tommy Loughran, by 86 pounds (270 pounds to 184 pounds) when they fought for the heavyweight title on March 1, 1934 in Miami, Fla. Surprisingly, the bout went the distance, with Carnera winning on points.

Greatest tonnage The greatest tonnage recorded in any fight is 700 pounds, when Claude "Humphrey" McBride, 340 pounds, knocked out Jimmy Black, 360 pounds, in the third round of their bout at Oklahoma City, Okla. on June 1, 1971. The greatest combined weight for a world title fight is 488¾ pounds, when Primo Carnera (Italy), 259½ pounds, fought Paolino Uzcudun (Spain), 229¼ pounds, in Rome, Italy on October 22, 1933.

AMATEUR

OLYMPIC GAMES Boxing contests were included in the ancient games, and were first included in the modern Games in 1904.

Most gold medals Two boxers have won three gold medals: Laszlo Papp (Hungary) won the middleweight title in 1948, and the light middleweight in 1952 and 1956; Teofilo Stevenson (Cuba) won the heavyweight division in 1972, 1976 and 1980. The only man to win two titles at the same Games was Oliver L. Kirk, who won both the bantamweight and featherweight titles in 1904. It should be noted that Kirk only had to fight one bout in each class.

WORLD CHAMPIONSHIPS The world championships were first staged in 1974, and are held quadrennially.

Most titles Félix Savon (Cuba) has won a record four world titles. Savon won the heavyweight division in 1986, 1989, 1991 and 1993.

UNITED STATES NATIONAL CHAMPIONSHIPS U.S. amateur championships were first staged in 1888.

Most titles The most titles won is five, by middleweight W. Rodenbach, 1900–04.

CANOEING

ORIGINS The most influential pioneer of canoeing as a sport was John MacGregor, a British attorney, who founded the Canoe Club in Surrey, England in 1866. The sport's world governing body is the International Canoe Federation, founded in 1924.

United States The New York Canoe Club, founded in Staten Island, N.Y., in 1871, is the oldest in the United States. The American Canoe Association was formed on August 3, 1880.

OLYMPIC GAMES Canoeing was first included in the Games as a demonstration sport in 1924. At the 1936 Games, canoeing was included as an official Olympic sport for the first time.

Most gold medals Gert Fredriksson (Sweden) won a record six Olympic gold medals: 1,000 meter Kayak Singles (K1), 1948, 1952 and 1956; 10,000 meter K1, 1948 and 1956; 1,000 meter Kayak Pairs (K2), 1960. In women's competition, Birgit Schmidt (née Fischer; East Germany/Germany) has won four golds: 500 meter K1, 1980 and 1992; 500 meter K2, 1988; 500 meter K4, 1988.

WORLD CHAMPIONSHIPS In Olympic years, the Games also serve as the world championship.

Most titles Birgit Schmidt (East Germany/Germany) has won a record 25 titles, 1978–93. The men's record is 13, by three canoeists: Gert Fredriksson (Sweden), 1948–60; Rudiger Helm (East Germany), 1976–83; and Ivan Patzaichin (Romania), 1968–84.

Most titles Marcia Ingram Jones Smoke won 35 national titles from 1962–81. The men's record is 33, by Ernest Riedel from 1930–48.

CRICKET

ORIGINS Cricket originated in England in the Middle Ages. It is impossible to pinpoint its exact origin; however, historians believe that the modern game developed in the mid-16th century. The earliest surviving scorecard is from a match played between England and Kent on June 18, 1744. The Marylebone Cricket Club (MCC) was founded in 1787 and, until 1968, was the world governing body for the sport. The International Cricket Conference (ICC) is responsible for international (Test) cricket, while the MCC remains responsible for the laws of cricket.

INTERNATIONAL (TEST) CRICKET

Test match cricket is the highest level of the sport. The Test playing nations are Australia, England, India, New Zealand, Pakistan, South Africa, Sri Lanka and the West Indies. Test matches are generally played over five days. The result is decided by which team scores the most runs in two full innings (one inning sees all 11 members of a team come to bat; their opponents must achieve 10 outs to end the inning). If, at the end of the allotted time period, one or either team has not completed two full innings, the game is declared a tie. The first Test match was played at Melbourne, Australia on March 15–19, 1877 between Australia and England.

TEST MATCH RECORDS (TEAM)

Most runs (innings) England scored 903 runs (for 7 declared) *v.* Australia at The Oval, London on August 20–22, 1938.

Most runs (total aggregate) In a 10-day match played from March 3–14, 1939 in Durban, South Africa, England and South Africa scored 1,981 runs. South Africa scored 530 runs in the first innings and 481 in the second. England scored 316 runs in the first innings and 654 for 5 in the second. The record for a five-day match (standard for current test matches) is 1,764 runs, Australia (533, 339 for 9) *v.* West Indies (276, 616) at Adelaide, Australia on January 24–29, 1969. Both games ended in stalemate and were declared ties as time ran out.

Fewest runs (innings) New Zealand scored 26 runs *v.* England at Auckland on March 28, 1955.

Fewest runs (two innings) South Africa scored a combined 81 runs (36, 45) *v.* Australia at Melbourne, Australia on February 12–15, 1932. Australia scored 153 runs and won the match by an inning and 72 runs.

Greatest margin of victory England defeated Australia by an inning and 579 runs at The Oval on August 20–24, 1938. Australia scored 201 in its first innings and 123 in the second. In each innings they played with only nine players, two short of a full team.

Tied score matches There have been two tied score matches (both teams' aggregate scores the same at the end of play on the final day) in test cricket history: Australia *v.* West Indies in Brisbane, Australia, December 9–14, 1960; India *v.* Australia, in Madras, India, September 18–22, 1986.

TEST MATCH RECORDS (INDIVIDUAL)

Most runs (game) 365 not out, by Gary Sobers, West Indies *v.* Pakistan at Sabina Park, Jamaica on February 27–March 1, 1958.

Most runs (career) 10,927 runs, by Allan Border, Australia, 1978–93. Border has played in 152 tests for an average of 51.06 runs.

Highest average (career) 99.94 runs, by Donald Bradman, Australia, 1928–48. "The Don" played in 52 tests scoring 6,996 runs.

Most wickets (game) 19, by Jim Laker for England *v.* Australia at Old Trafford, Manchester, from July 27–31, 1956.

Most wickets (career) 432, by Kapil Dev, India, 1978–94. As of February 8, 1994, Kapil had played in 130 tests.

NATIONAL CRICKET CHAMPIONSHIPS

Australia The premier event in Australia is the Sheffield Shield, an interstate competition contested since 1891–92. New South Wales has won the title a record 41 times.

England The major championship in England is the County Championship, an intercounty competition officially recognized since 1890. Yorkshire has won the title a record 30 times.

India The Ranji Trophy is India's premier cricket competition. Established in 1934 in memory of K. S. Ranjitsinhji, it is contested on a zonal basis, culminating in a playoff competition. Bombay has won the tournament a record 30 times.

New Zealand Since 1975, the major championship in New Zealand has been the Shell Trophy. Otago, Wellington and Auckland have each won the competition four times.

WICKETS WONDER ■ TED PRENTIS HAS WON SIX U.S. CROQUET CHAMPIONSHIPS, INCLUDING A RECORD FOUR DOUBLES TITLES. (USCA)

Pakistan Pakistan's national championship is the Quaid-e-Azam Trophy, established in 1953. Karachi has won the trophy a record eight times.

South Africa The Currie Cup, donated by Sir Donald Currie, was first contested in 1889. Transvaal has won the competition a record 28 times.

West Indies The Red Stripe Cup, established in 1966, is the premier prize played for by the association of Caribbean islands (plus Guyana) that form the West Indies Cricket League. Barbados has won the competion a record 13 times.

CROQUET

ORIGINS Its exact beginnings are unknown; however, it is believed that croquet developed from the French game *jeu de mail*. A game resembling croquet was played in Ireland in the 1830s and introduced to England 20 years later. Although croquet was played in the United States for a number of years, a national body was not established until the formation of the United States Croquet Association (USCA) in 1976. The first United States championship was played in 1977.

USCA NATIONAL CHAMPIONSHIPS J. Archie Peck has won the singles title a record four times (1977, 1979–80, 1982). Ted Prentis has won the doubles title four times with three different partners (1978, 1980–81, 1988). The teams of Ted Prentis and Ned Prentis (1980–81) and Dana Dribben and Ray Bell (1985–86) have each won the doubles title twice. The New York Croquet Club has won a record six National Club Championships (1980–83, 1986, 1988).

CROSS-COUNTRY RUNNING

ORIGINS The earliest recorded international cross-country race took place on March 20, 1898 between England and France. The race was staged at Ville d'Avray, near Paris, France over a course 9 miles 18 yards long.

WORLD CHAMPIONSHIPS The first international cross-country championships were staged in Glasgow, Scotland on March 28, 1903. Since 1973 the event has been an official world championship organized by the International Amateur Athletic Federation.

Most titles England has won the men's team event a record 45 times, 1903–14, 1920–21, 1924–25, 1930–38, 1951, 1953–55, 1958–60, 1962, 1964–72, 1976, 1979–80. The women's competition has been won eight times by two countries: United States, 1968–69, 1975, 1979, 1983–85, 1987; USSR, 1976–77, 1980–82, 1988–90.

Most titles (individual) Two women have won five titles: Doris Brown (U.S.), 1967–71, and Grete Waitz (Norway), 1978–81 and 1983. John Ngugi (Kenya) has won the men's title a record five times, 1986–89 and 1992.

UNITED STATES NATIONAL CHAMPIONSHIPS This competition was first staged in 1890 for men, and in 1972 for women.

Most titles Pat Porter has won the men's event a record eight times, 1982–89. Lynn Jennings has won the women's event seven times, 1985, 1987–90 and 1992–93.

NCAA CHAMPIONSHIPS The first NCAA cross-country championship was held in 1938, and was open only to men's teams. A women's event was not staged until 1981.

Most titles (team) In men's competition, Michigan State has won the team title a record eight times: 1939, 1948–49, 1952, 1955–56, 1958–59.

Most titles (individuals) Three athletes have won the men's individual title three times: Gerry Lindgren (Washington State), 1966–67 and 1969; Steve Prefontaine (Oregon), 1970–71 and 1973; Henry Rono (Washington State), 1976–77 and 1979.

Most titles (team) In women's competition, Villanova has won the team title five times, 1989–93.

Most titles (individual) Three runners have won the title twice: Betty Springs (North Carolina State), 1981 and 1983; Sonia O'Sullivan (Villanova), 1990 and 1991; Carole Zajac (Villanova), 1992–93.

CURLING

ORIGINS The traditional home of curling is Scotland; some historians, however, believe that the sport originated in the Netherlands in the 15th century. There is evidence of a curling club in Kilsyth, Scotland in 1716, but the earliest recorded club is the Muthill Curling Club, Tayside, Scotland, formed in 1739, which produced the first known written rules of the game on November 17, 1739. The Grand (later Royal) Caledonian Curling Club was founded in 1838 and was the international governing body of the sport until 1966, when the International Curling Federation was formed; this was renamed the World Curling Federation in 1991.

United States and Canada Scottish immigrants introduced curling to North America in the 18th century. The earliest known club was the Royal Montreal Curling club, founded in 1807. The first international game was between Canada and the United States in 1884—the inaugural Gordon International Medal series. In 1832, Orchard Lake Curling Club, Mich., was founded, the first in the United States. The oldest club in continuous existence in the U.S. is the Milwaukee Curling Club, Wis., formed *c.* 1850. Regional curling associations governed the sport in the U.S. until 1947, when the United States Women's Curling Association was formed, followed in 1958 by the Men's Curling Association. In 1986, the United States Curling Association was formed and is the current governing body for the sport. In Canada, the Dominion Curling Association was formed in 1935, renamed the Canadian Curling Association in 1968.

OLYMPIC GAMES Curling has been a demonstration sport at the Olympic Games of 1924, 1932, 1964, 1988 and 1992.

WORLD CHAMPIONSHIPS First held in 1959, these championships are held annually. Women's competition was introduced in 1979.

Most titles (men) Canada has dominated this event, winning 21 titles: 1959–64, 1966, 1968–72, 1980, 1982–83, 1985–87, 1989–90, and 1993. Ernie Richardson (Canada) has been winning skip a record four times, 1959–60, 1962–63.

Most titles (women) Canada has won seven championships, in 1980, 1984–87, 1989, and 1993. Djordy Nordby (Norway) has been skip of two winning teams, 1990–91.

UNITED STATES NATIONAL CHAMPIONSHIPS A men's tournament was first held in 1957. A women's event was introduced in 1977.

Men Two curlers have been skips on five championship teams: Bud Somerville (Superior Curling Club, Wis. in 1965, 1968–69, 1974 and 1981), and Bruce Roberts (Hibbing Curling Club, Minn. in 1966–67, 1976–77 and 1984).

Women In this competition, Nancy Langley of Seattle, Wash. has been the skip of a record four championship teams: 1979, 1981, 1983 and 1988.

THE LABATT BRIER (FORMERLY THE MACDONALD BRIER 1927–79) The Brier is the Canadian men's curling championship. The competition was first held at the Granite Club, Toronto in 1927. Sponsored by Macdonald Tobacco Inc., it had been known as the Macdonald Brier; since 1980 Labatt Brewery has sponsored the event.

Most titles The most wins is 23, by Manitoba (1928–32, 1934, 1936, 1938, 1940, 1942, 1947, 1949, 1952–53, 1956, 1965, 1970–72, 1979, 1981, 1984 and 1992). Ernie Richardson (Saskatchewan) has been winning skip a record four times (1959–60 and 1962–63).

Perfect game Stu Beagle, of Calgary, Alberta, played a perfect game (48 points) against Nova Scotia in the Canadian Championships (Brier) at Fort William (now Thunder Bay), Ontario on March 8, 1960. Andrew McQuiston skipped the Scotland team to a perfect game *v.* Switzerland at the Uniroyal Junior Men's World Championship at Kitchener, Ontario, Canada in 1980.

Bernice Fekete, of Edmonton, Alberta, Canada, skipped her rink to two consecutive eight-enders on the same ice at the Derrick Club, Edmonton on January 10 and February 6, 1973.

Two eight-enders in one bonspiel were scored at the Parry Sound Curling Club, Ontario, Canada from January 6–8, 1983.

CYCLING

ORIGINS The forerunner of the bicycle, the *celerifere*, was demonstrated in the garden of the Palais Royale, Paris, France in 1791. The velocipede, the first practical pedal-propelled vehicle, was built in March 1861 by Pierre Michaux and his son Ernest and demonstrated in Paris. The first velocipede race occurred on May 31, 1868 at the Parc St. Cloud, Paris, over a distance of 1.24 miles. The first international organization was the International Cyclist Association (ICA), founded in 1892, which launched the first world championships in

---

TRANSCONTINENTAL CYCLING RECORDS

Men's Records (United States Crossing)

Event	Rider(s)	Start/Finish	Days: Hrs: Min	Av. mph	Year
Solo (time)	Michael Secrest	HB–NYC	7:23:16	15.24	1990
Solo (av. mph)	Pete Penseyres	HB–AC	8:09:47	15.40	1986
Tandem	Lon Haldeman & Pete Penseyres	HB–AC	7:14:15	15.97	1987

Men's Records (Canada Crossing)

Event	Rider(s)	Start/Finish	Days: Hrs: Min	Av. mph	Year
Solo	William Narasnek	Van–Hal	13:09:06	11.68	1991

Women's Records (United States Crossing)

Event	Rider(s)	Start/Finish	Days: Hrs: Min	Av. mph	Year
Solo	Susan Notorangelo	CM–NYC	9:09:09	12.93	1989
Tandem	Estelle Grey & Cheryl Marek	SM–NYC	10:22:48	11.32	1984

HB: Huntington Beach Calif.; NYC: New York City; AC: Atlantic City N.J.; Van: Vancouver; Hal: Halifax, Nova Scotia; CM: Costa Mesa, Calif.; SM: Santa Monica, Calif.

Source: Ultra Marathon Cycling Association (UMCA), The Guinness Book of Records, 1993

TOUR DE FRANCE CHAMPIONS (1903–1948)

Year	Winner	Country	Year	Winner	Country
1903	Maurice Garin	France	1926	Lucien Buysse	Belgium
1904	Henri Cornet	France	1927	Nicholas Frantz	Luxembourg
1905	Louis Trousselier	France	1928	Nicholas Frantz	Luxembourg
1906	Rene Pottier	France	1929	Maurice Dewaele	Belgium
1907	Lucien Petit-Breton	France	1930	Andre Leducq	France
1908	Lucien Petit-Breton	France	1931	Antonin Magne	France
1909	Francois Faber	Luxembourg	1932	Andre Leducq	France
1910	Octave Lapize	France	1933	Georges Speicher	France
1911	Gustave Garrigou	France	1934	Antonin Magne	France
1912	Odile Defraye	Belgium	1935	Romain Maes	Belgium
1913	Philippe Thys	Belgium	1936	Sylvere Maes	Belgium
1914	Philippe Thys	Belgium	1937	Roger Lapebie	France
1915	not held		1938	Gino Bartali	Italy
1916	not held		1939	Sylvere Maes	Belgium
1917	not held		1940	not held	
1918	not held		1941	not held	
1919	Firmin Labot	Belgium	1942	not held	
1920	Philippe Thys	Belgium	1943	not held	
1921	Leon Scieur	Belgium	1944	not held	
1922	Firmin Labot	Belgium	1945	not held	
1923	Henri Pelissier	France	1946	Jean Lazarides	France
1924	Ottavio Bottecchia	Italy	1947	Jean Robic	France
1925	Ottavio Bottecchia	Italy	1948	Gino Bartali	Italy

1893. The current governing body, the *Union Cycliste Internationale* (UCI), was founded in 1900.

OLYMPIC GAMES Cycling was included in the first modern Games held in 1896, and has been part of every Games since, with the exception of 1904. Women's events were first staged in 1984.

Most gold medals Four men have won three gold medals: Paul Masson (France), 1,000 meter time-trial, 1,000 meter sprint, 10,000 meter track in 1896; Francesco Verri (Italy), 1,000 meter time-trial, 1,000 meter sprint, 5,000 meter track in 1906; Robert Charpentier (France), individual road race, team road race, 4,000 meter team pursuit in 1936; Daniel Morelon (France), 1,000 meter sprint in 1968 and 1972, 2,000 meter tandem in 1968.

Most medals Daniel Morelon (France) has won five Olympic medals: three gold (see above); one silver, 1,000 meter sprint in 1972; one bronze, 1,000 meter sprint in 1964.

WORLD CHAMPIONSHIPS World championships are contested annually. They were first staged for amateurs in 1893 and for professionals in 1895.

Most titles (one event) The most wins in one event is 10, by Koichi Nakano (Japan), professional sprint 1977–86. The most wins in a men's amateur event is seven, by two cyclists: Daniel Morelon (France), sprint, 1966–67, 1969–71, 1973, 1975; and Leon Meredith (Great Britain), 100 kilometer motor-paced, 1904–05, 1907–09, 1911 and 1913.

TOUR DE FRANCE CHAMPIONS (1949–1993)

Year	Winner	Country	Year	Winner	Country
1949	Fausto Coppi	Italy	1972	Eddy Merckx	Belgium
1950	Ferdinand Kubler	Switzerland	1973	Luis Ocana	Spain
1951	Hugo Koblet	Switzerland	1974	Eddy Merckx	Belgium
1952	Fausto Coppi	Italy	1975	Bernard Thevenet	France
1953	Louison Bobet	France	1976	Lucien van Impe	Belgium
1954	Louison Bobet	France	1977	Bernard Thevenet	France
1955	Louison Bobet	France	1978	Bernard Hinault	France
1956	Roger Walkowiak	France	1979	Bernard Hinault	France
1957	Jacques Anquetil	France	1980	Joop Zoetemilk	Netherlands
1958	Charly Gaul	Luxembourg	1981	Bernard Hinault	France
1959	Federico Bahamontes	Spain	1982	Bernard Hinault	France
1960	Gastone Nencini	Italy	1983	Laurent Fignon	France
1961	Jacques Anquetil	France	1984	Laurent Fignon	France
1962	Jacques Anquetil	France	1985	Bernard Hinault	France
1963	Jacques Anquetil	France	1986	Greg LeMond	U.S.
1964	Jacques Anquetil	France	1987	Stephen Roche	Ireland
1965	Felice Gimondi	Italy	1988	Pedro Delgado	Spain
1966	Lucien Aimar	France	1989	Greg LeMond	U.S.
1967	Roger Pingeon	France	1990	Greg LeMond	U.S.
1968	Jan Janssen	Netherlands	1991	Miguel Indurain	Spain
1969	Eddy Merckx	Belgium	1992	Miguel Indurain	Spain
1970	Eddy Merckx	Belgium	1993	Miguel Indurain	Spain
1971	Eddy Merckx	Belgium			

The most women's titles is eight, by Jeannie Longo (France), pursuit 1986 and 1988–89 and road 1985–87 and 1989–90.

United States The most world titles won by a U.S. cyclist is five, in women's 3 kilometer pursuit by Rebecca Twigg, 1982, 1984–85, 1987, and 1993. The most successful man has been Greg LeMond, winner of the individual road race in 1983 and 1989.

UNITED STATES NATIONAL CHAMPIONSHIPS National cycling championships have been held annually since 1899. Women's events were first included in 1937.

Most titles Leonard Nitz has won 16 titles: five pursuit (1976 and 1980–83); eight team pursuit (1980–84, 1986 and 1988–89); two 1 kilometer time-trial (1982 and 1984); one criterium (1986). Connie Carpenter has won 11 titles in women's events: four road race (1976–77, 1979 and 1981); three pursuit (1976–77 and 1979); two criterium (1982–83); two points (1981–82).

TOUR DE FRANCE

First staged in 1903, the Tour meanders throughout France and sometimes neighboring countries over a four-week period.

Most wins Three riders have each won the event five times: Jacques Anquetil (France), 1957, 1961–64; Eddy Merckx (Belgium), 1969–72, 1974; Bernard Hinault (France), 1978–79, 1981–82, 1985.

Longest race The longest race held was 3,569 miles in 1926.

Closest race The closest race ever was in 1989, when after 2,030 miles over 23 days (July 1–23) Greg LeMond (U.S.), who completed the Tour in 87 hours 38 minutes 35 seconds, beat Laurent Fignon (France) in Paris by only 8 seconds.

Fastest speed The fastest average speed was 24.547 mph by Miguel Indurain (Spain) in 1992.

Longest stage The longest-ever stage was the 486 kilometers (302 miles) from Les Sables d'Olonne to Bayonne in 1919.

Most participants The most participants was 210 starters in 1986.

Most finishers A record 151 riders finished the 1988 race.

Most races Joop Zoetemilk (Netherlands) participated in a record 16 tours, 1970–86. He won the race in 1980 and finished second a record six times.

Most stage wins Eddy Merckx (Belgium) won a record 35 individual stages in just seven races, 1969–75.

United States Greg LeMond became the first American winner in 1986; he returned from serious injury to win again in 1989 and 1990.

RACE ACROSS AMERICA

ORIGINS An annual nonstop transcontinental crossing of the United States from west to east, the Race Across AMerica was first staged in 1982. A women's division was introduced in 1984. The start and finish lines have varied, but currently the race starts in Irvine, Ca., and finishes in Savannah, Ga. The race must travel a minimum distance of 2,900 miles.

Most wins Three cyclists have won two men's titles: Lon Haldeman, 1982–83; Pete Penseyres, 1984, 1986; Bob Fourney, 1990–91. In the women's division two riders have won two titles: Susan Notorangelo, 1985 and 1989; Seana Hogan, 1992–93.

SUPERBIKE ■ CHRIS BOARDMAN CYCLED A WORLD RECORD 52.27 KM IN ONE HOUR ON THE REVOLUTIONARY LOTUS BICYCLE ON JULY 23, 1993. (ALLSPORT/DAVID CANNON)

DARTS SCORING RECORDS (FEWEST THROWN)

Scores of 201 in four darts, 301 in six darts, 401 in seven darts and 501 in nine darts have been achieved on many occasions.

Score	Darts Thrown	Player(s)	Date
1,001	19	Cliff Inglis (England)	Nov. 11, 1975
	19	Jocky Wilson (Scotland)	March 23, 1989
2,001	52	Alan Evans (Wales)	Sept. 3, 1976
3,001	73	Tony Benson (England)	July 12, 1986
100,001	3,732	Alan Downie (Scotland)	Nov. 21, 1986
1,000,001	36,583	Eight-man team (U.S.)*	Oct. 19–20, 1991

* An eight-man team set the record at Buzzy's Pub and Grub in Lynn, Mass.

DARTS

ORIGINS Darts, or dartes (heavily weighted 10-inch throwing arrows) were first used in Ireland in the 16th century, as a weapon for self-defense. The Pilgrims played darts for recreation aboard the *Mayflower* in 1620. The modern game dates to 1896, when Brian Gamlin of Bury, England devised the present board numbering system. The first recorded score of 180, the maximum with three darts, was by John Reader at the Highbury Tavern, Sussex, England in 1902.

WORLD CHAMPIONSHIP This competition was instituted in 1978.

Most titles Eric Bristow of England has won the title a record five times (1980–81, 1984–86).

SCORING RECORDS (HIGHEST SCORES)

10-HOURS SCORES

Individual The pair of Jon Archer and Neil Rankin (Great Britain) scored 465,919, while retrieving their own darts, at the Royal Oak, Cossington, England on November 17, 1990.

Bulls Johnny "Darts" Mielcarek (U.S.) hit 1,200 bulls in 10 hours at the Pete Rose Ballpark Cafe, Boca Raton, Fla., on May 27, 1993.

24-HOURS SCORES

Individual Davy Richardson-Page (Great Britain) scored 518,060 points at Blucher Social Club, Newcastle, England on July 6–7, 1991.

Team (8-man) The Broken Hill Darts Club of New South Wales, Australia scored 1,722,249 points in 24 hours from September 28–29, 1985.

ON TARGET ■ ON MAY 27, 1993, JOHNNY "DARTS" MIELCAREK HIT 1,200 BULLSEYES IN 10 HOURS. (GARY DALLONE)

Team (8-woman) A team representing the Lord Clyde Pub of London, England scored 744,439 points on October 13–14, 1990.

Bulls and 25s (8-man team) The Kent and Canterbury Hospital Sports and Social Club of Canturbury, England hit 510,625 bulls and 25s on October 20–21, 1989.

DIVING

ORIGINS Diving traces its roots to the gymnastics movement that developed in Germany and Sweden in the 17th century. During the summer, gymnasts would train at the beach, and acrobatic techniques would be performed over water as a safety measure. From this activity the sport of diving developed. The world governing body for diving is the *Fédération Internationale de Natation Amateur* (FINA), founded in 1980. FINA is also the governing body for swimming and water polo.

United States Ernst Bransten and Mike Peppe are considered the two main pioneers of diving in the United States. Bransten, a Swede, came to the United States following World War I. He introduced Swedish training methods and diving techniques, which revolutionized the sport in this country. Peppe's highly successful program at Ohio State University, 1931–68, produced several Olympic medalists and helped promote the sport here.

WATER BABY ■ CHINA'S FU MINGXIA IS THE YOUNGEST WOMAN TO WIN A WORLD TITLE. SHE WAS 12 YEARS OLD WHEN SHE WON THE 1991 PLATFORM EVENT. (ALLSPORT/GARY MORTIMORE)

OLYMPIC GAMES Men's diving events were introduced at the 1904 Games, and women's events in 1912.

Most gold medals Two divers have won four gold medals: Pat McCormick (U.S.), who won both the women's springboard and the highboard events in 1952 and 1956; and Greg Louganis (U.S.), who performed the highboard/springboard double in 1984 and 1988.

Most medals Two divers have won five medals: Klaus Dibiasi (Italy), three golds, highboard in 1968, 1972 and 1976, and two silver, highboard in 1964 and springboard in 1968; and Greg Louganis, four golds (see above) and one silver, highboard in 1976.

WORLD CHAMPIONSHIPS Diving events were included in the first world aquatic championships staged in 1973.

TRIPLE PLAY ☛ IN 10 HOURS PAUL TAYLOR (GREAT BRITAIN) HIT 3,056 TRIPLES (INNER RING OF A STANDARD DART BOARD) FROM 7,992 DARTS THROWN ON OCTOBER 19, 1985. TAYLOR PERFORMED THE FEAT AT THE WOODHOUSE TAVERN, LONDON, ENGLAND.

Most titles Greg Louganis (U.S.) has won a record five world titles—highboard in 1978 and the highboard/springboard double in 1982 and 1986. Philip Boggs (U.S.) is the only diver to win three gold medals at one event, springboard, in 1973, 1975 and 1978.

UNITED STATES NATIONAL CHAMPIONSHIPS The Amateur Athletic Union (AAU) organized the first national diving championships in 1909. Since 1981, United States Diving has been the governing body of the sport in this country, and thus responsible for the national championships.

Most titles Greg Louganis has won a record 47 national titles: 17, one-meter springboard; 17, three-meter springboard; 13, platform. In women's competition, Cynthia Potter has won a record 28 titles.

EQUESTRIAN SPORTS

ORIGINS Evidence of horseback riding dates from a Persian engraving dated *c.* 3000 B.C. The three separate equestrian competitions recognized at the Olympic level are show jumping, the three-day event and dressage. The earliest known show jumping competition was in Ireland, when the Royal Dublin Society held its first "Horse Show" on April 15, 1864. Dressage competition derived from the exercises taught at 16th century Italian and French horsemanship academies, while the three-day event developed from cavalry endurance

CARRIAGE DRIVING ☛ THE ONLY MAN TO DRIVE 48 HORSES IN A SINGLE HITCH IS DICK SPARROW (U.S.). THE LEAD HORSES WERE ON REINS 135 FEET LONG. SPARROW PERFORMED THE FEAT MANY TIMES AT COUNTRY FAIRS FROM 1972 THROUGH 1977.

rides. The world governing body for all three disciplines is the *Fédération Equestre Internationale* (FEI), founded in Brussels, Belgium in 1921.

OLYMPIC GAMES In the ancient games, chariot races featured horses, and later riding contests were included. Show jumping was included in the 1900 Games; the three-day event and dressage disciplines were not added until 1912. In 1956 the equestrian events were held in Stockholm, Sweden, separate from the main Games in Melbourne, Australia, because of the strict Australian quarantine laws.

Most medals (all events) Germany has dominated the equestrian events, winning 64 medals overall: 27 gold, 17 silver and 20 bronze.

SHOW JUMPING

OLYMPIC GAMES

Most gold medals (rider) Hans-Gunther Winkler (West Germany) has won five titles, 1956, 1960, 1964 and 1972 in the team competition, and the individual championship in 1956. The only rider to win two individual titles is Pierre Jonqueres d'Oriola (France), in 1952 and 1964.

Most gold medals (horse) The most successful horse is Halla, ridden by Hans-Gunther Winkler during his individual and team wins in 1956, and during the team win in 1960.

Most medals Hans-Gunther Winkler has won a record seven medals: five gold (see above), one silver and one bronze in the team competition in 1976 and 1968.

United States Two American riders have won the individual event: Bill Steinkraus in 1968, and Joe Fargis in 1984. The United States won the team event in 1984.

WORLD CHAMPIONSHIPS The men's world championship was inaugurated in 1953. In 1965, 1970 and 1974 separate women's championships were held. An integrated championship was first held in 1978 and is now held every four years.

Most titles Two riders share the record for most men's championships with two victories: Hans-Gunther Winkler (West Germany), 1954–55, and Raimondo d'Inzeo (Italy), 1956 and 1960. The women's title was won twice by Janou Tissot (née Lefebvre) of France, in 1970 and 1974. No rider has won the integrated competition more than once.

THREE-DAY EVENT

OLYMPIC GAMES

Most gold medals Charles Pahud de Mortanges (Netherlands) has won four gold medals—the individual title in 1928 and 1932, and the team event in 1924 and 1928. Mark Todd (New Zealand) is the only other rider to have won the individual title twice, in 1984 and 1988.

Most medals (rider) Charles Pahud de Mortanges has won five medals: four gold (see above) and one silver in the 1932 team event.

Most gold medals (horse) Marcroix was ridden by Charles Pahud de Mortanges in three of his four medal rounds, 1928–32.

United States The most medals won for the U.S. is six, by J. Michael Plumb: team gold, 1976 and 1984, and four silver medals, team 1964, 1968 and 1972, and individual 1976. Tad Coffin is the only U.S. rider to have won both team and individual gold medals, in 1976.

WORLD CHAMPIONSHIP First held in 1966, the event is held quadrenially and is open to both men and women.

Most titles (rider) Two riders have won three world titles: Bruce Davidson (U.S.), individual title in 1974 and 1978, team title in 1974; and Virginia Leng (Great Britain), individual 1986 and team in 1982 and 1986. Davidson is the only rider to have won two individual championships.

Most titles (country) Great Britain has won the team title a record three times, 1970, 1982 and 1986. The United States won the team event in 1974.

DRESSAGE

OLYMPIC GAMES

Most gold medals (rider) Reiner Klimke (West Germany) has won six gold medals: one individual in 1984, and five team in 1964, 1968, 1976, 1984 and 1988. Henri St. Cyr (Sweden) is the only rider to have won two individual titles, in 1952 and 1956.

Most gold medals (horse) Ahlerich was ridden by Reiner Klimke in three of his gold medal rounds, individual in 1984, and team in 1984 and 1988. Two riders have won the individual title on two occasions: Henri St. Cyr (Sweden), 1952 and 1956; and Nicole Uphoff (Germany), 1988 and 1992.

Most medals Reiner Klimke won eight medals: six gold (see above), and two bronze in the individual event in 1968 and 1976.

United States The United States has never won a gold medal in dressage. In the team event the United States has won one silver, 1948, and three bronze, in 1932, 1976, and 1992. Hiram Tuttle is the only rider to have won an individual medal, earning the bronze in 1932.

WORLD CHAMPIONSHIPS This competition was instituted in 1966.

Most titles (country) West Germany has won a record six times: 1966, 1974, 1978, 1982, 1986 and 1990.

Most titles (rider) Reiner Klimke (West Germany) is the only rider to have won two individual titles, on Mehmed in 1974 and on Ahlerich in 1982.

FENCING

ORIGINS Evidence of swordsmanship can be traced back to Egypt as early as *c.* 1360 B.C., where it was demonstrated during religious ceremonies. Fencing, "fighting with sticks," gained popularity as a sport in Europe in the 16th century.

The modern foil, a light court sword, was introduced in France in the mid-17th century; in the late 19th century, the fencing "arsenal" was expanded to include the épée, a heavier dueling weapon, and the sabre, a light cutting sword.

The *Fédération Internationale d'Escrime* (FIE), the world governing body, was founded in Paris, France in 1913. The first European championships were held in 1921 and were expanded into world championships in 1935.

United States In the United States, the Amateur Fencers League of America (AFLA) was founded on April 22, 1891 in New York City. This group assumed supervision of the sport in the U.S., staging the first national championship in 1892. In June 1981, the AFLA changed its name to the United States Fencing Association (USFA).

OLYMPIC GAMES Fencing was included in the first Olympic Games of the modern era at Athens in 1896, and is one of only six sports to be featured in every Olympiad.

Most gold medals Aladar Gerevich (Hungary) has won a record seven gold medals, all in sabre:

NOT FOILED ■ MICHAEL MARX (LEFT) HAS WON EIGHT U.S. FOIL TITLES. (U.S. FENCING ASSOCIATION)

individual, 1948; team, 1932, 1936, 1948, 1952, 1956 and 1960. In individual events, two fencers have won three titles: Ramon Fonst (cuba), épée, 1900 and 1904, and foil, 1904; Nedo Nadi (Italy), foil, 1912 and 1920, and sabre, 1920. The most golds won by a woman is four, by Yelena Novikova (née Belova; USSR), all in foil: individual, 1968; team, 1968, 1972 and 1976.

Most medals Edoardo Mangiarotti (Italy) has won a record 13 medals in fencing: six gold, five silver and two bronze in foil and épée events from 1936 to 1960.

United States Albertson Van Zo Post is the only American to have won an Olympic title. He won the single sticks competition and teamed with two Cubans to win the team foil title in 1904. In overall competition the United States has won 19 medals (both Cuba and the United States are credited with a gold medal for the 1904 team foil): two gold, six silver and 11 bronze—all in men's events.

WORLD CHAMPIONSHIPS The first world championships were staged in Paris, France in 1937. Foil, épée and sabre events were held for men and just foil for women. In 1989, a women's épée event was added. The tournament is staged annually.

Most titles The greatest number of individual world titles won is five, by Aleksandr Romankov (USSR), at foil, 1974, 1977, 1979, 1982 and 1983. Five women foilists have won three world titles: Hélène Mayer (Germany), 1929, 1931 and 1937; Ilona Schacherer-Elek (Hungary), 1934–35, 1951; Ellen Müller-Preis (Austria), 1947, 1949–50; Cornelia Hanisch (West Germany), 1979, 1981 and 1985; and Anja Fichtel (West Germany), 1986, 1988 and 1990.

UNITED STATES NATIONAL CHAMPIONSHIPS

Most titles The most U.S. titles won at one weapon is 12 at sabre, by Peter Westbrook, in 1974, 1975, 1979–86, 1988 and 1989. The women's record is 10 at foil, by Janice Romary in 1950–51, 1956–57, 1960–61, 1964–66 and 1968.

The most individual foil championships won is eight, by Michael Marx in 1977, 1979, 1982, 1985–87, 1990 and 1993. L. G. Nunes won the most épée championships, with six—1917, 1922, 1924, 1926, 1928 and 1932. Vincent Bradford won a record number of women's épée championships with four in 1982–84 and 1986.

NCAA CHAMPIONSHIP DIVISION I (TEAM) A men's championship was first staged in 1941. A women's championship was not introduced until 1982. In 1990 these two tournaments were replaced by a combined team event. In the now-defunct separate events, New York University won the men's title 12 times, 1947–76; and Wayne State (Mich.), won the women's event three times, 1982, 1988–89.

Most wins Two teams have won two titles: Penn State, 1990–91; and Columbia-Barnard, 1992–93.

Most titles (fencer) Michael Lofton, New York University, has won the most titles in a career, with four victories in the sabre, 1984–87. In women's competition, Caitlin Bilodeaux, Columbia–Barnard, and Molly Sullivan, Notre Dame, have both won the individual title twice: Bilodeaux in 1985 and 1987, and Sullivan in 1986 and 1988.

FIELD HOCKEY

ORIGINS Hitting a ball with a stick is a game that dates back to the origins of the human race. Basreliefs and frescoes discovered in Egypt and Greece depict hockey-like games. A drawing of a "bully" on the walls of a tomb at Beni Hassan in the Nile Valley has been dated to *c*. 2050 B.C. The birthplace of modern hockey is Great Britain, where the first definitive code of rules was established in 1886. The *Fédération Internationale de Hockey* (FIH), the world governing body, was founded on January 7, 1924.

United States The sport was introduced to this country in 1921 by a British teacher, Constance M. K. Applebee. The Field Hockey Association of America (FHAA) was founded in 1928 by Henry Greer. The first game was staged between the Germantown Cricket Club and the Westchester Field Hockey Club, also in 1928.

OLYMPIC GAMES Field hockey was added to the Olympic Games in 1908 and became a permanent feature in 1928; a women's tournament was added in 1980.

Most gold medals (team) In the men's competition, India has won eight gold medals: 1928, 1932, 1936, 1948, 1952, 1956, 1964 and 1980. In the women's competition, no team has won the event more than once.

United States The United States has never won either the men's or women's events; the best result has been a bronze in 1932 (men), and in 1984 (women).

NCAA DIVISION I (WOMEN) The women's championship was inaugurated in 1981.

Most titles Old Dominion has won the most championships, with seven titles: 1982–84, 1988 and 1990–92.

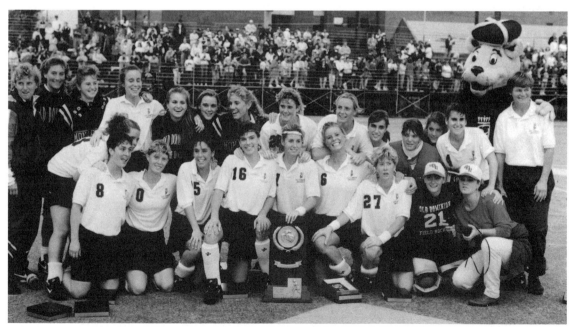

O.D. BUT GOODY ■ OLD DOMINION HAS WON SEVEN NCAA TITLES IN 10 YEARS. (OLD DOMINION)

SCORING RECORDS

Highest score The highest score in an international game was India's 24–1 defeat of the United States at Los Angeles, Calif., in the 1932 Olympic Games. In women's competition, England hammered France 23–0 at Merton, England on February 3, 1923.

Most goals Paul Litjens (Netherlands) holds the record for most goals by one player in international play. He scored 267 goals in 177 games.

Fastest goal The fastest goal scored in an international game was netted only seven seconds after the bully by John French for England *v.* West Germany at Nottingham, England on April 25, 1971.

FIGURE SKATING

ORIGINS The earliest reference to ice skating is in Scandinavian literature dating to the 2nd century A.D. Jackson Haines, a New Yorker, is regarded as the pioneer of the modern concept of figure skating, a composite of skating and dancing. Although his ideas were not initially favored in the United States, Haines moved to Europe in the mid-1860s, where his "International Style of Figure Skating" was warmly received and promoted. The first artificial rink was opened in London, England on January 7, 1876. The world governing body is the International Skating Union (ISU), founded in 1892. The sport functioned informally in the United States until 1921, when the United States Figure Skating Association (USFSA) was formed to oversee skating in this country—a role it still performs.

OLYMPIC GAMES Figure skating was first included in the 1908 Summer Games in London, and has been featured in every Games since 1920. Uniquely, both men's and women's events have been included in the Games from the first introduction of the sport.

Most gold medals Three skaters have won three gold medals: Gillis Grafstrom (Sweden) in 1920, 1924 and 1928; Sonja Henie (Norway) in 1928, 1932 and 1936; Irina Rodnina (USSR), with two different partners, in the pairs in 1972, 1976 and 1980.

United States Dick Button is the only American skater to win two gold medals, in 1948 and 1952.

FIRST QUADS ■ IN 1988 KURT BROWNING (LEFT) WAS THE FIRST SKATER TO COMPLETE A QUADRUPLE JUMP IN COMPETITION. IN 1991 SURUYA BONALY (RIGHT) BECAME THE FIRST FEMALE SKATER TO ACHIEVE THIS FEAT. (ALLSPORT/BOB MARTIN, ALLSPORT/TONY DUFFY)

American skaters have won the men's title six times and the women's five. No American team has won either the pairs or dance titles.

WORLD CHAMPIONSHIPS This competition was first staged in 1896.

Most titles (individual) The greatest number of men's individual world figure skating titles is 10, by Ulrich Salchow (Sweden), in 1901–05 and 1907–11. The women's record (instituted 1906) is also 10 individual titles, by Sonja Henie (Norway) between 1927 and 1936.

Most titles (pairs) Irina Rodnina (USSR) has won 10 pairs titles (instituted 1908), four with Aleksey Ulanov, 1969–72, and six with her husband, Aleksandr Zaitsev, 1973–78.

Most titles (ice dance) The most ice dance titles (instituted 1952) won is six, by Lyudmila Pakhomova and her husband, Aleksandr Gorshkov (USSR), 1970–74 and 1976.

United States Dick Button won five world titles, 1948–52. Five women's world titles were won by Carol Heise, 1956–60.

UNITED STATES NATIONAL CHAMPIONSHIPS The U.S. championships were first held in 1914.

Most titles The most titles won by an individual is nine, by Maribel Y. Vinson, 1928–33 and 1935–37. She also won six pairs titles, and her aggregate of 15 titles is equaled by Therese Blanchard (née Weld), who won six individual and nine pairs titles between 1914 and 1927. The men's individual record is seven, by Roger Turner, 1928–34, and by Dick Button, 1946–52.

BARREL JUMPING AT TERREBONNE, QUEBEC, CANADA, YVON JOLIN CLEARED 18 BARRELS ON JANUARY 25, 1981. THE DISTANCE OF 29 FEET 5 INCHES WAS A RECORD FOR A JUMPER WEARING ICE SKATES.

HIGHEST MARKS The highest tally of maximum six marks awarded in an international championship was 29, to Jayne Torvill and Christopher Dean (Great Britain) in the World Ice Dance Championships at Ottawa, Canada on March 22–24, 1984. They previously gained a perfect set of nine sixes for artistic presentation in the free dance at the 1983 World Championships in Helsinki, Finland and at the 1984 Winter Olympic Games in Sarajevo, Yugoslavia. In their career, Torvill and Dean received a record total of 136 sixes.

The highest tally by a soloist is seven, by Donald Jackson (Canada) in the World Men's Championship at Prague, Czechoslovakia in 1962; and by Midori Ito (Japan) in the World Ladies' Championships at Paris, France in 1989.

FISHING

Oldest existing club The Ellem fishing club was formed by a number of Edinburgh and Berwickshire gentlemen in Scotland in 1829. Its first annual general meeting was held on April 29, 1830.

Largest single catch The largest officially ratified fish ever caught on a rod was a man-eating great white shark (*Carcharodon carcharias*) weighing 2,664 lb and measuring 16 ft 10 in long, caught on a 130–lb test line by Alf Dean at Denial Bay, near Ceduna, South Australia on April 21, 1959. A great white shark weighing 3,388 lb was caught by Clive Green off Albany, Western Australia on April 26, 1976 but will remain unratified, as whale meat was used as bait.

In June 1978, a great white shark measuring 20 ft 4 in in length and weighing more than 5,000 lb was harpooned and landed by fishermen in the harbor of San Miguel, Azores.

The largest marine animal killed by hand harpoon was a blue whale 97 ft in length, by Archer Davidson in Twofold Bay, New South Wales, Australia in 1910. Its tail flukes measured 20 ft across and its jawbone 23 ft 4 in.

Casting The longest freshwater cast ratified under ICF (International Casting Federation) rules is 574 ft 2 in, by Walter Kummerow (West Germany), for the Bait Distance Double-Handed

30 g event held at Lenzerheide, Switzerland in the 1968 Championships.

At the currently contested weight of 17.7 g, the longest Double-Handed cast is 457 ft ½ in by Kevin Carriero (U.S.) at Toronto, Canada on July 24, 1984.

The longest Fly Distance Double-Handed cast is 319 ft 1 in by Wolfgang Feige (West Germany) at Toronto, Canada on July 23, 1984.

WORLD CHAMPIONSHIP (FRESHWATER) The first freshwater world championships were held in 1957. The event is staged annually.

FRESHWATER AND SALT WATER ALL-TACKLE CLASS WORLD RECORDS

A selection of records ratified by the International Game Fish Association to January 1, 1994.

Species	Weight	Caught By	Location	Date
Arawana	10 lb 2 oz	Gilberto Fernandes	Brazil	Feb. 3, 1990
Barracuda, great	83 lb 0 oz	K. Hackett	Nigeria	Jan. 13, 1952
Bass, kelp	14 lb 2 oz	Wes Worthing	Catalina Island, Calif.	Nov. 17, 1992
Bass, largemouth	22 lb 4 oz	George W. Perry	Montgomery Lake, Ga.	June 2, 1932
Bass, smallmouth	11 lb 15 oz	David L. Hayes	Dale Hollow Lake, Ky.	July 9, 1955
Bass, striped	78 lb 8 oz	Albert Reynolds	Atlantic City, N.J.	Sept. 21, 1982
Bluefish	31 lb 12 oz	James M. Hussey	Hatteras, N.C.	Jan. 30, 1972
Carp, common	75 lb 11 oz	Leo van der Gugten	France	May 21, 1987
Carp, grass	62 lb 0 oz	Craig Bass	Pinson, Ala.	May 13, 1991
Catfish, blue	109 lb 4 oz	George A. Lijewski	Moncks Corner, S.C.	March 14, 1991
Chub, Bermuda	11 lb 2 oz	Herman Cross	Fort Pierce, Fla.	Jan. 18, 1993
Cod, Atlantic	98 lb 12 oz	Alphonse Bielevich	Isle of Shoals, N.H.	June 8, 1969
Conger	110 lb 8 oz	Hans Clausen	English Channel	Aug. 20, 1991
Eel, American	8 lb 8 oz	Gerald Lapierre	Brewster, Mass.	May 17, 1992
Flounder, summer	22 lb 7 oz	Charles Nappi	Montauk, N.Y.	Sept. 15, 1975
Geelbek	16 lb 15 oz	Ellen Saunders	South Africa	Oct. 5, 1992
Goldfish	3 lb 0 oz	Kenneth Kinsey	Livingston, Tex.	May 8, 1988
Grouper, black	113 lb 6 oz	Donald Bone	Dry Tortugas, Fla.	Jan. 27, 1990
Grouper, broomtail	83 lb 0 oz	Enrique Weisson	Ecuador	June 28, 1992
Haddock	11 lb 11 oz	Jim Mailea	Ogunquit, Me.	Sept. 12, 1991
Halibut, Atlantic	255 lb 4 oz	Sonny Manley	Gloucester, Mass.	July 28, 1989
Halibut, Pacific	368 lb 0 oz	Celia Dueitt	Gustavus, Alaska	July 5, 1991
Houndfish	14 lb 0 oz	Deborah Dunaway	Costa Rica	July 18, 1992
Mackerel, broad barred	17 lb 10 oz	Glen Walker	Australia	Aug. 6, 1992
Marlin, black	1,560 lb 0 oz	Alfred Glassell Jr.	Peru	Aug. 4, 1953
Marlin, blue (Atlantic)	1,402 lb 2 oz	Roberto A. Amorim	Brazil	Feb. 29, 1992
Marlin, blue (Pacific)	1,376 lb 0 oz	Jay de Beaubien	Kona, Hawaii	May 31, 1982
Perch, Nile	191 lb 8 oz	Andy Davison	Kenya	Sept. 5, 1991
Pike, northern	55 lb 1 oz	Lothar Louis	Germany	Oct. 16, 1986

Most wins (team) France has won the team event 12 times, 1959, 1963–64, 1966, 1968, 1972, 1974–75, 1978–79, 1981 and 1990.

Most wins (individual) Robert Tesse (France) has won the individual title three times, 1959–60 and 1965.

WORLD CHAMPIONSHIP (FLY FISHING) First staged in 1981, this event is held annually.

Most wins (team) Italy has won the team event five times, 1982–84, 1985 and 1992.

Most wins (individual) No fisherman has won the title more than once.

FRESHWATER AND SALT WATER ALL-TACKLE CLASS WORLD RECORDS

A selection of records ratified by the International Game Fish Association to January 1, 1994.

Species	Weight	Caught By	Location	Date
Piranha, black	3 lb 0 oz	Doug Olander	Brazil	Nov. 23, 1991
Quilback	6 lb 8 oz	Mike Berg	Lake Michigan, Ind.	Jan. 15, 1993
Ray, black	82 lb 10 oz	Peter Blondell	Australia	Jan. 20, 1993
Roosterfish	114 lb 0 oz	Abe Sackheim	Mexico	June 1, 1960
Sailfish, Atlantic	135 lb 5 oz	Ron King	Nigeria	Nov. 10, 1991
Sailfish, Pacific	221 lb 0 oz	C.W. Stewart	Ecuador	Feb. 12, 1947
Salmon, Atlantic	79 lb 2 oz	Henrik Henriksen	Norway	1928
Salmon, chinook	97 lb 4 oz	Les Anderson	Kenai River, Alaska	May 17, 1985
Salmon, pink	13 lb 1 oz	Ray Higaki	Canada	Sept. 23, 1992
Samson fish	80 lb 7 oz	Terry Coote	Australia	Jan. 3, 1993
Shad, American	11 lb 4 oz	Bob Thibodo	S. Hadley, Mass.	May 19, 1986
Shark, blue	437 lb 0 oz	Peter Hyde	Australia	Oct. 2, 1976
Shark, Greenland	1,708 lb 9 oz	Terje Nordtvedt	Norway	Oct. 18, 1987
Shark, hammerhead	991 lb 0 oz	Allen Ogle	Sarasota, Fla.	May 30, 1982
Shark, mako	1,115 lb 0 oz	Patrick Guillanton	Mauritius	Nov. 16, 1988
Shark, narrow tooth	533 lb 8 oz	Gaye Harrison-Armstrong	New Zealand	Jan. 9, 1993
Shark, tiger	1,780 lb 0 oz	Walter Maxwell	Cherry Grove, S.C.	June 14, 1964
Shark, white	2,664 lb 0 oz	Alfred Dean	Australia	April 21, 1959
Snapper, red	46 lb 8 oz	E. Lane Nichols	Destin, Fla.	Oct. 1, 1985
Stingray, southern	229 lb 0 oz	David Anderson	Galveston Bay, Tex.	June 2, 1991
Sturgeon, lake	92 lb 4 oz	James DeOtis	Kettle River, Minn.	Sept. 11, 1986
Sturgeon, white	468 lb 0 oz	Joey Pallotta III	Benica, Calif.	July 9, 1983
Swordfish	1,182 lb 0 oz	L. Marron	Chile	May 7, 1953
Tarpon	283 lb 4 oz	Yvon Sebag	Sierra Leone	April 16, 1991
Trout, brook	14 lb 8 oz	W.J. Cook	Canada	July, 1916
Trout, brown	40 lb 4 oz	Howard L. Collins	Heber Springs, Ark.	May 9, 1992
Trout, rainbow	42 lb 2 oz	David White	Bell Island, Alaska	June 22, 1970
Tuna, bluefin	1,496 lb 0 oz	Ken Fraser	Canada	Oct. 26, 1979
Wahoo	155 lb 8 oz	William Bourne	Bahamas	April 3, 1990

FOOTBAG

A footbag is a small, pliable, pellet-filled ball-like object with little or no bounce. The concept of the game is to keep the footbag in the air for the longest possible time. Both the time and the number of consecutive kicks are recorded.

ORIGINS The sport of footbag was invented by Mike Marshall and John Stalberger (U.S.) in 1972. The governing body for the sport is the World Footbag Association, based in Golden, Colo.

CONSECUTIVE RECORDS

Men's singles 51,155 kicks by Ted Martin (U.S.) on May 29, 1993 in Mount Prospect, Ill. Martin kept the footbag aloft for 7 hours 1 minute 42 seconds.

Women's singles 15,458 kicks by Francine Beaudry (Canada) on July 28, 1987 in Golden, Colo. Beaudry kept the footbag aloft for 2 hours 35 minutes 13 seconds.

Men's doubles 83,453 kicks by Andy Linder and Ted Martin (both U.S.) on September 26, 1992 in Mount Prospect, Ill. The pair kept the footbag aloft for 12 hours 39 minutes 15 seconds.

Women's doubles 21,025 kicks by Constance Reed and Marie Elsner (both U.S.) on July 31, 1986. The pair kept the footbag aloft for 3 hours 6 minutes 37 seconds.

TIMEOUT

FRIGID ☛ THE COLDEST TEMPERATURE RECORDED FOR AN NFL GAME IS -60 DEGREES (INCLUDING WINDCHILL). THE "ICE BOWL" WAS PLAYED ON DECEMBER 31, 1967 AT LAMBEAU FIELD, MILWAUKEE, WIS. THE GREEN BAY PACKERS DEFEATED THE DALLAS COWBOYS 21–17 TO WIN THE NFL CHAMPIONSHIP.

"SHARPE" REFLEXES ■ PACKERS WIDE RECEIVER STERLING SHARPE CAUGHT 112 PASSES IN 1993, SETTING THE NFL SEASON MARK. (GREEN BAY PACKERS/JIMMY CRIBB)

FOOTBALL

ORIGINS On November 6, 1869, Princeton and Rutgers staged what is generally regarded as the first intercollegiate football game at New Brunswick, N.J. In October 1873 the Intercollegiate Football Association was formed (Columbia, Princeton, Rutgers and Yale), with the purpose of standardizing rules. At this point football was a modified version of soccer. The first significant move toward today's style of play came when Harvard accepted an invitation to play McGill University (Montreal, Canada) in a series of three challenge matches, the first being in May 1874, under modified rugby rules. Walter Camp is credited with organizing the basic format of the current game. Between 1880 and 1906, Camp sponsored the concepts of scrimmage lines, 11-man teams, reduction in field size, "downs" and "yards to gain" and a new scoring system.

NATIONAL FOOTBALL LEAGUE (NFL)

ORIGINS William (Pudge) Heffelfinger became the first professional player on November 12, 1892, when he was paid $500 by the Allegheny Athletic Association (AAA) to play for them against the Pittsburgh Athletic Club (PAC). In 1893, PAC signed one of its players, believed to have been Grant Dibert, to the first known professional contract. The first game to be played with admitted professionals participating was played at Latrobe, Pa., on August 31, 1895, with Latrobe YMCA defeating the Jeanette Athletic Club 12–0. Professional leagues existed in Pennsylvania and Ohio at the turn of the 20th century; however, the major breakthrough for professional football was the formation of the American Professional Football Association (APFA), founded in Canton, Ohio on September 17, 1920. Reorganized a number of times, the APFA was renamed the National Football League (NFL) on June 24, 1922. Since 1922, several rival leagues have challenged the NFL, the most significant being the All-America Football Conference (AAFL) and the American Football League (AFL). The AAFL began play in 1946 but after four seasons merged with the NFL for the 1950 season. The AFL challenge was stronger and more acrimonious. Formed in 1959, it had its inaugural season in 1960. The AFL–NFL "war" was halted on June 4, 1966, when an agreement to merge the leagues was announced. The leagues finally merged for the 1970 season, but an AFL–NFL championship game, the Super Bowl, was first played in January 1967.

NFL INDIVIDUAL RECORDS (1922–1993)

ENDURANCE

Most games played (career) George Blanda played in a record 340 games in a record 26 seasons in the NFL, for the Chicago Bears (1949, 1950–58), the Baltimore Colts (1950), the Houston Oilers (1960–66), and the Oakland Raiders (1967–75).

Most consecutive games played Jim Marshall played 282 consecutive games from 1960–79 for two teams: the Cleveland Browns, 1960, and the Minnesota Vikings, 1961–79.

LONGEST PLAYS

Run from scrimmage Tony Dorsett, Dallas Cowboys, ran through the Minnesota Vikings defense for a 99-yard touchdown on January 3, 1983.

Pass completion The longest pass completion, all for touchdowns, is 99 yards, performed by six quarterbacks: Frank Filchock (to Andy Farkas), Washington Redskins v. Pittsburgh Steelers, October 15, 1939; George Izo (to Bobby Mitchell), Washington Redskins v. Cleveland Browns, September 15, 1963; Karl Sweetan (to Pat Studstill), Detroit Lions v. Baltimore Colts, October 16, 1966;

(continued on p. 86)

SPECIAL PLAY ■ ON OCTOBER 24, 1993, ERIC METCALF BECAME THE EIGHTH PLAYER TO RETURN TWO PUNTS FOR TOUCHDOWNS IN AN NFL GAME. (CLEVELAND BROWNS)

NFL INDIVIDUAL RECORDS

POINTS SCORED

		Player(s)	Team(s)	Date(s)
Game	40	Ernie Nevers	Chicago Cardinals *v.* Chicago Bears	Nov. 18, 1929
Season	176	Paul Hornung	Green Bay Packers	1960
Career	2,002	George Blanda	Chicago Bears, Baltimore Colts, Houston Oilers, Oakland Raiders	1949–75

TOUCHDOWNS SCORED

Game	6	Ernie Nevers	Chicago Cardinals *v.* Chicago Bears	Nov. 28, 1929
		Dub Jones	Cleveland Browns *v.* Chicago Bears	Nov. 25, 1951
		Gale Sayers	Chicago Bears *v.* San Francisco 49ers	Dec. 12, 1965
Season	24	John Riggins	Washington Redskins	1983
Career	126	Jim Brown	Cleveland Browns	1957–65

PASSING

Yards Gained

Game	554	Norm Van Brocklin	Los Angeles Rams *v.* New York Yankees	Sept. 28, 1951
Season	5,084	Dan Marino	Miami Dolphins	1984
Career	47,003	Fran Tarkenton	Minnesota Vikings, New York Giants	1961–78

Completions

Game	42	Richard Todd	New York Jets *v.* San Francisco 49ers	Sept. 21, 1980
Season	404	Warren Moon	Houston Oilers	1991
Career	3,686	Fran Tarkenton	Minnesota Vikings, New York Giants	1961–78

Attempts

Game	68	George Blanda	Houston Oilers *v.* Buffalo Bills	Nov. 1, 1964
Season	655	Warren Moon	Houston Oilers	1991
Career	6,467	Fran Tarkenton	Minnesota Vikings, New York Giants	1961–78

Touchdowns Thrown

Game	7	Sid Luckman	Chicago Bears *v.* New York Giants	Nov. 14, 1943
		Adrian Burk	Philadelphia Eagles *v.* Washington Redskins	Oct. 17, 1954
		George Blanda	Houston Oilers *v.* New York Titans	Nov. 19, 1961
		Y. A. Tittle	New York Giants *v.* Washington Redskins	Oct. 28, 1962
		Joe Kapp	Minnesota Vikings *v.* Baltimore Colts	Sept. 28, 1969
Season	48	Dan Marino	Miami Dolphins	1984
Career	342	Fran Tarkenton	Minnesota Vikings, New York Giants	1961–78

NFL INDIVIDUAL RECORDS

PASSING (cont.)

Average Yards Gained

		Player(s)	Team(s)	Date(s)
Game (min. 20 attempts)	18.58	Sammy Baugh	Washington Redskins v. Boston Yanks (24–446)	Oct. 31, 1948
Season (qualifiers)	11.17	Tommy O'Connell	Cleveland Browns (110–1,229)	1957
Career (min. 1,500 attempts)	8.63	Otto Graham	Cleveland Browns (1,565–13,499)	1950–55

PASS RECEIVING

Receptions

Game	18	Tom Fears	Los Angeles Rams v. Green Bay Packers	Dec. 3, 1950
Season	112	Sterling Sharpe	Green Bay Packers	1993
Career	888	Art Monk	Washington Redskins	1980–93

Yards Gained

Game	336	Willie Anderson	Los Angeles Rams v. New Orleans Saints	Nov. 26, 1989*
Season	1,746	Charley Hennigan	Houston Oilers	1961
Career	14,020	James Lofton	Green Bay Packers, Los Angeles Raiders, Buffalo Bills, Los Angeles Rams, Philadelphia Eagles	1978–93

Touchdown Receptions

Game	5	Bob Shaw	Chicago Cardinals v. Baltimore Colts	Oct. 2, 1950
		Kellen Winslow	San Diego Chargers v. Oakland Raiders	Nov. 22, 1981
		Jerry Rice	San Francisco 49ers v. Atlanta Falcons	Oct. 14, 1990
Season	22	Jerry Rice	San Francisco 49ers	1987
Career	118	Jerry Rice	San Francisco 49ers	1985–93

Average Yards Gained

Game (min. 3 catches)	60.67	Bill Groman	Houston Oilers v. Denver Broncos (3–182)	Nov. 20, 1960
		Homer Jones	New York Giants v. Washington Redskins (3–182)	Dec. 12, 1965
Season (min. 24 catches)	32.58	Don Currivan	Boston Yanks (24–782)	1947
Career (min. 200 catches)	22.26	Homer Jones	New York Giants, Cleveland Browns (224–4,986)	1964–70

* Overtime

Table continued on page 87

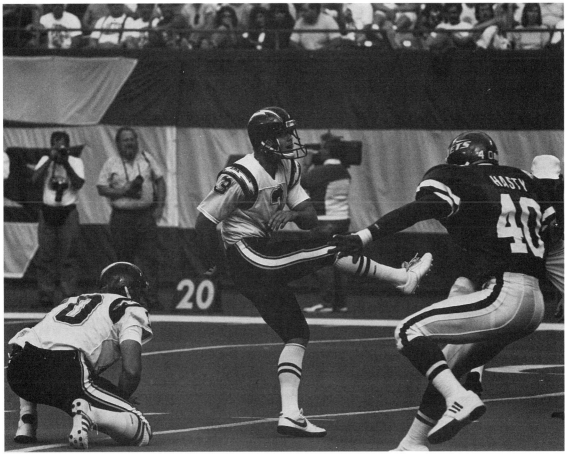

GOOD... AGAIN ■ DURING THE 1993 SEASON CHARGERS KICKER JOHN CARNEY SET THE NFL RECORD FOR CONSECUTIVE FIELD GOALS MADE, AT 29. (SAN DIEGO CHARGERS/ SAM STONE)

Sonny Jurgensen (to Gerry Allen), Washington Redskins *v*. Chicago Bears, September 15, 1968; Jim Plunkett (to Cliff Branch), Los Angeles Raiders *v*. Washington Redskins, October 2, 1983; Ron Jaworski (to Mike Quick), Philadelphia Eagles *v*. Atlanta Falcons, November 10, 1985.

Field goal The longest was 63 yards, by Tom Dempsey, New Orleans Saints *v*. Detroit Lions, on November 8, 1970.

Punt Steve O'Neal, New York Jets, boomed a 98-yard punt on September 21, 1969 *v*. Denver Broncos.

Interception return The longest interception return, both for touchdowns, is 103 yards, by two players: Vencie Glenn, San Diego Chargers *v*. Denver Broncos, November 29, 1987; and Louis Oliver, Miami Dolphins *v*. Buffalo Bills, October 4, 1992.

Kickoff return Three players share the record for a kickoff return at 106 yards: Al Carmichael, Green Bay Packers *v*. Chicago Bears, October 7, 1956; Noland Smith, Kansas City Chiefs *v*. Denver Broncos, December 17, 1967; and Roy Green, St. Louis Cardinals *v*. Dallas Cowboys, October 21, 1979. All three players scored touchdowns.

Missed field goal return Al Nelson, Philadelphia Eagles, returned a Dallas Cowboys' missed field goal 101 yards for a touchdown on September 26, 1971.

(continued on p. 90)

NFL INDIVIDUAL RECORDS

RUSHING

Yards Gained

		Player(s)	Team(s)	Date(s)
Game	275	Walter Payton	Chicago Bears *v.* Minnesota Vikings	Nov. 20, 1977
Season	2,105	Eric Dickerson	Los Angeles Rams	1984
Career	16,726	Walter Payton	Chicago Bears	1975–87

Attempts

Game	45	Jamie Morris	Washington Redskins *v.* Cincinnati Bengals	Dec. 17, 1988*
Season	407	James Wilder	Tampa Bay Buccaneers	1984
Career	3,838	Walter Payton	Chicago Bears	1975–87

Touchdowns Scored

Game	6	Ernie Nevers	Chicago Cardinals *v.* Chicago Bears	Nov. 28, 1929
Season	24	John Riggins	Washington Redskins	1983
Career	110	Walter Payton	Chicago Bears	1975–87

Average Yards Gained

Game (min. 10 attempts)	17.09	Marion Mottley	Cleveland Browns *v.* Pittsburgh Steelers (11–188)	Oct. 29, 1950
Season (qualifiers)	8.44	Beattie Feathers	Chicago Bears (119–1,004)	1934
Career (min. 700 attempts)	5.22	Jim Brown	Cleveland Browns (2,359–12,312)	1957–65

INTERCEPTIONS

Game	4	16 players have achieved this feat.		
Season	14	Dick "Night Train" Lane	Los Angeles Rams	1952
Career	81	Paul Krause	Washington Redskins, Minnesota Vikings	1964–79

Interceptions Returned for Touchdowns

Game	2	18 players have achieved this feat.		
Season	4	Ken Houston	Houston Oilers	1971
		Jim Kearney	Kansas City Chiefs	1972
		Eric Allen	Philadelphia Eagles	1993
Career	9	Ken Houston	Houston Oilers, Washington Redskins	1967–80

---

* Overtime

NFL INDIVIDUAL RECORDS

SACKS
(compiled since 1982)

		Player(s)	Team(s)	Date(s)
Game	7	Derrick Thomas	Kansas City v. Seattle Seahawks	Nov. 11, 1990
Season	22	Mark Gastineau	New York Jets	1984
Career	137	Reggie White	Philadelphia Eagles, Green Bay Packers	1985–93

KICKING

Field Goals

Game	7	Jim Bakken	St. Louis Cardinals v. Pittsburgh Steelers	Sept. 24, 1967
		Rich Karlis	Minnesota Vikings v. Los Angeles Rams	Nov. 5, 1989*
Season	35	Ali Haji-Sheikh	New York Giants	1983
Career	373	Jan Stenerud	Kansas City Chiefs, Green Bay Packers, Minnesota Vikings	1967–85

Highest Percentage

Game	100.00	This has been achieved by many kickers. The most field goals kicked with no misses is 7, by Rich Karlis, Minnesota Vikings v. Los Angeles Rams on Nov. 5, 1989 in an overtime game.		
Season (qualifiers)	100.00	Tony Zendejas	Los Angeles Rams (17–17)	1991
Career (min. 100 field goals)	80.05	Nick Lowery	New England Patriots, Kansas City Chiefs (329–411)	1978, 1980–93

Field Goals 50 or More Yards

Game	2	This record has been achieved 24 times; Nick Lowery, Kansas City Chiefs, is the only kicker to have done it 3 times.		
Season	6	Dean Biasucci	Indianapolis Colts	1988
Career	21	Morten Andersen	New Orleans Saints	1982–92

Points After Touchdown (PATs)

Game	9	Pat Harder	Chicago Cardinals v. New York Giants	Oct. 17, 1948
		Bob Waterfield	Los Angeles Rams v. Baltimore Colts	Oct. 22, 1950
		Charlie Gogolak	Washington Redskins v. New York Giants	Nov. 27, 1966
Season	66	Uwe von Schamann	Miami Dolphins	1984
Career	943	George Blanda	Chicago Bears, Baltimore Colts, Houston Oilers, Oakland Raiders	1949–75

---

* Overtime

NFL INDIVIDUAL RECORDS

PUNTING

Punts

		Player(s)	Team(s)	Date(s)
Game	15	John Teltschik	Philadelphia Eagles v. New York Giants	Dec. 6, 1987*
Season	114	Bob Parsons	Chicago Bears	1981
Career	1,154	Dave Jennings	New York Giants, New York Jets	1974–87

Average Yards Gained

Game (min. 4 punts)	61.75	Bob Cifers	Detroit Lions v. Chicago Bears (4–247)	Nov. 24, 1946
Season (qualifiers)	51.40	Sammy Baugh	Washington Redskins (35–1,799)	1940
Career (min. 300 punts)	45.10	Sammy Baugh	Washington Redskins (338–15,245)	1937–52

SPECIAL TEAMS

Punt Returns for Touchdowns

Game	2	Jack Christiansen	Detroit Lions v. Los Angeles Rams	Oct. 14, 1951
		Jack Christiansen	Detroit Lions v. Green Bay Packers	Nov. 22, 1951
		Dick Christy	New York Titans v. Denver Broncos	Sept. 24, 1961
		Rick Upchurch	Denver Broncos v. Cleveland Browns	Sept. 26, 1976
		LeRoy Irvin	Los Angeles Rams v. Atlanta Falcons	Oct. 11, 1981
		Vai Sikahema	St. Louis Cardinals v. Tampa Bay Buccaneers	Dec. 21, 1986
		Todd Kinchen	Los Angeles Rams v. Atlanta Falcons	Dec. 27, 1992
		Eric Metcalf	Cleveland Browns v. Pittsburgh Steelers	Oct. 24, 1993
Season	4	Jack Christiansen	Detroit Lions	1951
		Rick Upchurch	Denver Broncos	1976
Career	8	Jack Christiansen	Detroit Lions	1951–58
		Rick Upchurch	Denver Broncos	1975–83

Kickoff Returns for Touchdowns

Game	2	Timmy Brown	Philadelphia Eagles v. Dallas Cowboys	Nov. 6, 1966
		Travis Williams	Green Bay Packers v. Cleveland Browns	Nov. 12, 1967
		Ron Brown	Los Angeles Rams v. Green Bay Packers	Nov. 24, 1985
Season	4	Travis Williams	Green Bay Packers	1967
		Cecil Turner	Chicago Bears	1970
Career	6	Ollie Matson	Chicago Cardinals, Los Angeles Rams, Detroit Lions, Philadelphia Eagles	1952–64
		Gale Sayers	Chicago Bears	1965–71
		Travis Williams	Green Bay Packers, Los Angeles Rams	1967–71

* Overtime
Source: NFL

Punt return Four players share the record for the longest punt return at 98 yards: Gil LeFebvre, Cincinnati Reds *v.* Brooklyn Dodgers, December 3, 1933; Charlie West, Minnesota Vikings *v.* Washington Redskins, November 3, 1968; Dennis Morgan, Dallas Cowboys *v.* St. Louis Cardinals, October 13, 1974; Terance Mathis, New York Jets *v.* Dallas Cowboys, November 4, 1990. All four players scored touchdowns.

Fumble return Jack Tatum, Oakland Raiders, returned a Green Bay Packers fumble 104 yards for a touchdown on September 24, 1972.

CONSECUTIVE RECORDS

Scoring (games) 186, Jim Breech, Oakland Raiders, 1979; Cincinnati Bengals, 1980–92.

Scoring touchdowns (games) 18, Lenny Moore, Baltimore Colts, 1963–65.

Points after touchdown (PATs), consecutive kicked 234, Tommy Davis, San Francisco 49ers, 1959–65.

Field goals, consecutive kicked 29, John Carney, San Diego Chargers, 1992–93.

Field goals (games) 31, Fred Cox, Minnesota Vikings, 1968–70.

100+ yards rushing (games) 11, Marcus Allen, Los Angeles Raiders, 1985–86.

200+ yards rushing (games) 2, by two players: O.J. Simpson, Buffalo Bills, 1973, 1976; Earl Campbell, Houston Oilers, 1980.

Touchdown passes (games) 47, Johnny Unitas, Baltimore Colts, 1956–60.

Touchdown rushes (games) 13, by two players: John Riggins, Washington Redskins, 1982–83; George Rogers, Washington Redskins, 1985–86.

FAIR CATCH ☛ THE MOST FAIR CATCHES MADE IN AN NFL CAREER IS 102, BY WILLIE WOOD, GREEN BAY PACKERS, 1960–71.

Touchdown receptions (games) 13, Jerry Rice, San Francisco 49ers, 1986–87.

Passes completed (consecutive) 22, Joe Montana, San Francisco 49ers *v.* Cleveland Browns, November 29, 1987 (5); *v.* Green Bay Packers, December 6, 1987 (17).

300+ yards passing (games) 5, Joe Montana, San Francisco 49ers, 1982.

Four or more touchdown passes (games) 4, Dan Marino, Miami Dolphins, 1984.

Pass receptions (games) 177, Steve Largent, Seattle Seahawks, 1977–89.

NFL TEAM RECORDS

WINS AND LOSSES

Most consecutive games won The Chicago Bears won 17 straight regular-season games, covering the 1933–34 seasons.

Most consecutive games unbeaten The Canton Bulldogs played 25 regular-season games without a defeat, covering the 1921–23 seasons. The Bulldogs won 22 games and tied three.

Most games won in a season Two teams have compiled 15-win seasons: the San Francisco 49ers in 1984, and the Chicago Bears in 1985.

Perfect season The only team to win all its games in one season was the 1972 Miami Dolphins. The Dolphins won 14 regular-season games and then won three playoff games, including Super Bowl VII, to complete the only perfect season in NFL history.

Most consecutive games lost This most undesirable of records is held by the Tampa Bay Buccaneers, who lost 26 straight games from 1976–77.

Most games lost in a season Four teams hold the dubious honor of having lost 15 games in one season: the New Orleans Saints in 1980, the Dallas Cowboys in 1989, the New England Patriots in 1990 and the Indianapolis Colts in 1991.

SCORING

Most points scored, game The Washington Redskins scored 72 points *v.* the New York Giants on November 27, 1966 to set the single-game NFL regular-season record for most points scored by one team.

Highest aggregate score On November 27, 1966, the Washington Redskins defeated the New York Giants 72–41 in Washington, D.C. The Redskins' total was an NFL record for most points (see above).

Largest deficit overcome On January 3, 1993, the Buffalo Bills, playing at home in the AFC Wild Card game, trailed the Houston Oilers 35-3 with 28 minutes remaining. The Bills rallied to score 35 unanswered points and take the lead with 3:08 left. The Bills eventually won the game in overtime, overcoming a deficit of 32 points—the largest in NFL history.

TRADES

Largest in NFL history Based on the number of players and/or draft choices involved, the largest trade in NFL history is 15, which has happened twice. On March 26, 1953 the Baltimore Colts and the Cleveland Browns exchanged 15 players; and on January 28, 1971, the Washington Redskins and the Los Angeles Rams completed the transfer of seven players and eight draft choices.

COACHES

Most seasons 40, George Halas, Decatur/Chicago Staleys/Chicago Bears: 1920–29, 1933–42, 1946–55, 1958–67.

COACHING DON ■ ON NOVEMBER 14, 1993, DON SHULA SURPASSED GEORGE HALAS AS THE ALL-TIME WINNINGEST NFL COACH. AT SEASON'S END HIS CAREER TOTAL WAS **327** WINS. (MIAMI DOLPHINS)

Most wins (including playoffs) 327, by Don Shula, Baltimore Colts, 1963–69; Miami Dolphins, 1970–93.

NFL CHAMPIONSHIP

The first NFL championship was awarded in 1920 to the Akron Pros, as the team with the best record. From 1920 to 1931, the championship was based on regular-season records. The first championship game was played in 1932.

In 1966, the National Football League (NFL) and the American Football League (AFL) agreed to merge their competing leagues to form an expanded NFL. Regular-season play would not begin until 1970, but the two leagues agreed to stage an annual AFL–NFL world championship game beginning in January 1967. The proposed championship game was dubbed the Super Bowl, and in 1969 the NFL officially recognized the title.

Most NFL titles The Green Bay Packers have won 11 NFL championships: 1929– 31, 1936, 1939, 1944, 1961–62, 1965, and Super Bowls I and II (1966 and 1967 seasons).

THE SUPER BOWL

Super Bowl I was played on January 15, 1967, with the Green Bay Packers (NFL) defeating the Kansas City Chiefs (AFL), 35–10.

Most wins Three teams have won the Super Bowl four times: the Pittsburgh Steelers, Super Bowls IX, X, XIII and XIV; the San Francisco 49ers, XVI, XIX, XXIII and XXIV; and the Dallas Cowboys, VI, XII, XXVII, XXVIII.

Consecutive wins Five teams have won Super Bowls in successive years: the Green Bay Packers, I and II; the Miami Dolphins, VII and VIII; the Pittsburgh Steelers (twice), IX and X, and XIII and XIV; the San Francisco 49ers, XXIII and XXIV; and the Dallas Cowboys, XXVII and XXVIII.

Most appearances The Dallas Cowboys have played in seven Super Bowls: V, VI, X, XII, XIII, XXVII, and XXVIII. The Cowboys have won four games and lost three.

SCORING RECORDS

Most points scored The San Francisco 49ers scored 55 points *v.* the Denver Broncos in Super Bowl XXIV.

(continued on p. 96)

NFL CHAMPIONS (1920–1957)

Season	Winner	Loser	Score
1920	Akron Pros	—	—
1921	Chicago Staleys	—	—
1922	Canton Bulldogs	—	—
1923	Canton Bulldogs	—	—
1924	Cleveland Bulldogs	—	—
1925	Chicago Cardinals	—	—
1926	Frankford Yellowjackets	—	—
1927	New York Giants	—	—
1928	Providence Steam Roller	—	—
1929	Green Bay Packers	—	—
1930	Green Bay Packers	—	—
1931	Green Bay Packers	—	—
1932	Chicago Bears	Portsmouth Spartans	9–0
1933	Chicago Bears	New York Giants	23–21
1934	New York Giants	Chicago Bears	30–13
1935	Detroit Lions	New York Giants	26–7
1936	Green Bay Packers	Boston Redskins	21–6
1937	Washington Redskins	Chicago Bears	28–21
1938	New York Giants	Green Bay Packers	23–17
1939	Green Bay Packers	New York Giants	27–0
1940	Chicago Bears	Washington Redskins	73–0
1941	Chicago Bears	New York Giants	37–9
1942	Washington Redskins	Chicago Bears	14–6
1943	Chicago Bears	Washington Redskins	41–21
1944	Green Bay Packers	New York Giants	14–7
1945	Cleveland Rams	Washington Redskins	15–14
1946	Chicago Bears	New York Giants	24–14
1947	Chicago Cardinals	Philadelphia Eagles	28–21
1948	Philadelphia Eagles	Chicago Cardinals	7–0
1949	Philadelphia Eagles	Los Angeles Rams	14–0
1950	Cleveland Browns	Los Angeles Rams	30–28
1951	Los Angeles Rams	Cleveland Browns	24–17
1952	Detroit Lions	Cleveland Browns	17–7
1953	Detroit Lions	Cleveland Browns	17–16
1954	Cleveland Browns	Detroit Lions	56–10
1955	Cleveland Browns	Los Angeles Rams	38–14
1956	New York Giants	Chicago Bears	47–7
1957	Detroit Lions	Cleveland Browns	59–14

NFL CHAMPIONS (1958–1965)

Season	Winner	Loser	Score
1958	Baltimore Colts	New York Giants	23–17*
1959	Baltimore Colts	New York Giants	31–16
1960	Philadelphia Eagles	Green Bay Packers	17–13
1961	Green Bay Packers	New York Giants	37–0
1962	Green Bay Packers	New York Giants	16–7
1963	Chicago Bears	New York Giants	14–10
1964	Cleveland Browns	Baltimore Colts	27–0
1965	Green Bay Packers	Cleveland Browns	23–12

* Overtime

SUPER BOWL RESULTS (1967–1994)

Bowl	Date	Winner	Loser	Score	Site
I	Jan. 15, 1967	Green Bay Packers	Kansas City Chiefs	35–10	Los Angeles, Calif.
II	Jan. 14, 1968	Green Bay Packers	Oakland Raiders	33–14	Miami, Fla.
III	Jan. 12, 1969	New York Jets	Baltimore Colts	16–7	Miami, Fla.
IV	Jan. 11, 1970	Kansas City Chiefs	Minnesota Vikings	23–7	New Orleans, La.
V	Jan. 17, 1971	Baltimore Colts	Dallas Cowboys	16–13	Miami, Fla.
VI	Jan. 16, 1972	Dallas Cowboys	Miami Dolphins	24–3	New Orleans, La.
VII	Jan. 14, 1973	Miami Dolphins	Washington Redskins	14–7	Los Angeles, Calif.
VIII	Jan. 13, 1974	Miami Dolphins	Minnesota Vikings	24–7	Houston, Tex.
IX	Jan. 12, 1975	Pittsburgh Steelers	Minnesota Vikings	16–6	New Orleans, La.
X	Jan. 18, 1976	Pittsburgh Steelers	Dallas Cowboys	21–17	Miami, Fla.
XI	Jan. 9, 1977	Oakland Raiders	Minnesota Vikings	32–14	Pasadena, Calif.
XII	Jan. 15, 1978	Dallas Cowboys	Denver Broncos	27–10	New Orleans, La.
XIII	Jan. 21, 1979	Pittsburgh Steelers	Dallas Cowboys	35–31	Miami, Fla.
XIV	Jan. 20, 1980	Pittsburgh Steelers	Los Angeles Rams	31–19	Pasadena, Calif.
XV	Jan. 25, 1981	Oakland Raiders	Philadelphia Eagles	27–10	New Orleans, La.
XVI	Jan. 24, 1982	San Francisco 49ers	Cincinnati Bengals	26–21	Pontiac, Mich.
XVII	Jan. 30, 1983	Washington Redskins	Miami Dolphins	27–17	Pasadena, Calif.
XVIII	Jan. 22, 1984	Los Angeles Raiders	Washington Redskins	38–9	Tampa, Fla.
XIX	Jan. 20, 1985	San Francisco 49ers	Miami Dolphins	38–16	Stanford. Calif.
XX	Jan. 26, 1986	Chicago Bears	New England Patriots	46–10	New Orleans, La.
XXI	Jan. 25, 1987	New York Giants	Denver Broncos	39–20	Pasadena, Calif.
XXII	Jan. 31, 1988	Washington Redskins	Denver Broncos	42–10	San Diego, Calif.
XXIII	Jan. 22, 1989	San Francisco 49ers	Cincinnati Bengals	20–16	Miami, Fla.
XXIV	Jan. 28, 1990	San Francisco 49ers	Denver Broncos	55–10	New Orleans, La.
XXV	Jan. 27, 1991	New York Giants	Buffalo Bills	20–19	Tampa, Fla.
XXVI	Jan. 25, 1992	Washington Redskins	Buffalo Bills	37–24	Minneapolis, Minn.
XXVII	Jan. 31, 1993	Dallas Cowboys	Buffalo Bills	52–17	Pasadena, Calif.
XXVIII	Jan. 30, 1994	Dallas Cowboys	Buffalo Bills	30–13	Atlanta, Ga.

SUPER BOWL RECORDS

POINTS SCORED

		Player(s)	Team(s)	Super Bowl
Game	18	Roger Craig	San Francisco 49ers	XIX
		Jerry Rice	San Francisco 49ers	XXIV
Career	24	Franco Harris	Pittsburgh Steelers	IX, X, XIII, XIV
		Roger Craig	San Francisco 49ers	XIX, XXIII, XXIV
		Jerry Rice	San Francisco 49ers	XXIII, XXIV
		Thurman Thomas	Buffalo Bills	XXV–XXVIII

TOUCHDOWNS SCORED

Game	3	Roger Craig	San Francisco 49ers	XIX
		Jerry Rice	San Francisco 49ers	XXIV
Career	4	Franco Harris	Pittsburgh Steelers	IX, X, XIII, XIV
		Roger Craig	San Francisco 49ers	XIX, XXIII, XXIV
		Jerry Rice	San Francisco 49ers	XXIII, XXIV
		Thurman Thomas	Buffalo Bills	XXV–XXVIII

PASSING

Yards Gained

Game	357	Joe Montana	San Francisco 49ers	XXIII
Career	1,142	Joe Montana	San Francisco 49ers	XVI, XIX, XXIII, XXIV

Completions

Game	29	Dan Marino	Miami Dolphins	XIX
Career	83	Joe Montana	San Francisco 49ers	XVI, XIX, XXIII, XXIV

Touchdowns Thrown

Game	5	Joe Montana	San Francisco 49ers	XXIV
Career	11	Joe Montana	San Francisco 49ers	XVI, XIX, XXIII, XXIV

Highest Completion Percentage

Game (min. 20 attempts)	88.0	Phil Simms	New York Giants (22–25)	XXI
Career (min. 40 attempts)	68.0	Joe Montana	San Francisco 49ers (83–122)	XVI, XIX, XXIII, XXIV

SUPER BOWL RECORDS
PASS RECEIVING

		Player(s)	Team(s)	Super Bowl

Receptions

		Player(s)	Team(s)	Super Bowl
Game	11	Dan Ross	Cincinnati Bengals	XVI
		Jerry Rice	San Francisco 49ers	XXIII
Career	27	Andre Reed	Buffalo Bills	XXV–XXVIII

Yards Gained

Game	215	Jerry Rice	San Francisco 49ers	XXIII
Career	364	Lynn Swann	Pittsburgh Steelers	IX, X, XIII, XIV

Touchdown Receptions

Game	3	Jerry Rice	San Francisco 49ers	XXIV
Career	4	Jerry Rice	San Francisco 49ers	XXIII, XXIV

RUSHING
Yards Gained

Game	204	Timmy Smith	Washington Redskins	XXII
Career	354	Franco Harris	Pittsburgh Steelers	IX, X, XIII, XIV

Touchdowns Scored

Game	2	This feat has been achieved by 10 players		
Career	4	Franco Harris	Pittsburgh Steelers	IX, X, XIII, XIV
		Thurman Thomas	Buffalo Bills	XXV–XXVIII

Interceptions

Game	3	Rod Martin	Oakland Raiders	XV
Career	3	Chuck Howley	Dallas Cowboys	V, VI
		Rod Martin	Oakland/Los Angeles Raiders	XV, XVIII

FIELD GOALS KICKED

Game	4	Don Chandler	Green Bay Packers	II
		Ray Wersching	San Francisco 49ers	XVI
Career	5	Ray Wersching	San Francisco 49ers	XVI, XIX

LONGEST PLAYS

Run from Scrimmage	74 yards	Marcus Allen	Los Angeles Raiders	XVIII
Pass Completion	80 yards	Jim Plunkett	(to Kenny King) Oakland Raiders	XV
		Doug Williams	(to Ricky Sanders) Washington Redskins	XXII
Field Goal	54 yards	Steve Christie	Buffalo Bills	XXVIII
Punt	63 yards	Lee Johnson	Cincinnati Bengals	XXIII

Source: NFL

Highest aggregate score The highest aggregate score is 69 points when the Dallas Cowboys beat the Buffalo Bills 52–17 in Super Bowl XXVII.

Greatest margin of victory The greatest margin of victory is 45 points, set by the San Francisco 49ers when they defeated the Denver Broncos 55–10 in Super Bowl XXIV.

Most MVP awards Joe Montana, quarterback of the San Francisco 49ers, has been voted the Super Bowl MVP on a record three occasions, XVI, XIX, XXIV.

COACHES

Most wins Chuck Noll led the Pittsburgh Steelers to four Super Bowl titles, IX, X, XIII and XIV.

Most appearances Don Shula has been the head coach of six Super Bowl teams: the Baltimore Colts, III; the Miami Dolphins, VI, VII, VIII, XVII and XIX. He won two games and lost four.

COLLEGE FOOTBALL (NCAA)

ORIGINS At the turn of the 20th century, football's popularity was rising rapidly; however, with the increased participation came a rise in serious injuries and even some deaths. Many institutions, alarmed at the violent nature of the game, called for controls to be established.

In December 1905, 13 universities, led by Chancellor Henry M. MacCracken of New York University, outlined a plan to establish an organization to standardize playing rules. On December 28, the Intercollegiate Athletic Association of the United States (IAAUS) was founded in New York City with 62 charter members. The IAAUS was officially constituted on March 31, 1906, and was renamed the National Collegiate Athletic Association (NCAA) in 1910.

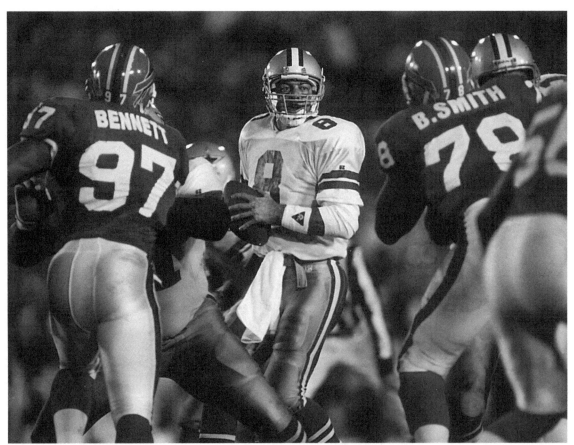

SUPER SCORING ■ SUPER BOWL XXVII WAS THE HIGHEST-SCORING GAME IN SUPER BOWL HISTORY. THE DALLAS COWBOYS DEFEATED THE BUFFALO BILLS, 52–17. (ALLSPORT/RICK STEWART)

The NCAA first began to keep statistics for football in 1937, and the records in this section date from that time. In 1973, the NCAA introduced a classification system creating Divisions I, II, and III to identify levels of college play. In 1978, Division I was subdivided into I-A and I-AA.

INDIVIDUAL RECORDS

NCAA OVERALL CAREER RECORDS (DIVISIONS I-A, I-AA, II AND III)

POINTS SCORED

Game Three players have scored 48 points in an NCAA game: Junior Wolf, Panhandle State (Div. II), set the mark on November 8, 1958 *v.* St. Mary's (Kans.); Paul Zaeske, North Park (Div. II), tied the record on October 12, 1968 *v.* North Central; Howard Griffith, Illinois (Div I-A), created a triumvirate on September 22, 1990.

Season The most points scored in a season is 234, by Barry Sanders, Oklahoma State (Div. I-A) in 1988, all from touchdowns, 37 rushing and two receptions.

Career The career record for most points scored is 474, by Joe Dudek, Plymouth State (Div. III), 1982–85. Dudek scored 79 touchdowns, 76 rushing and three receptions.

RUSHING (YARDS GAINED)

Game Carey Bender, Coe College (Div. III) rushed for an NCAA single-game record 417 yards, *v.* Grinnell on October 9, 1993.

Season The most yards gained in a season is 2,628, by Barry Sanders, Oklahoma State (Div. I-A), in 1988. Sanders played in 11 games and

HOME COOKING ☞ THE LONGEST HOME WINNING STREAK IN NCAA FOOTBALL IS **57**, BY ALABAMA. THE CRIMSON TIDE PUSHED BACK ALL VISITORS FROM 1963–82.

ROUTE RUNNER ■ PACIFIC RECEIVER AARON TURNER SETS NCAA CAREER MARKS FOR MOST CATCHES AND MOST YARDS GAINED. (PACIFIC)

carried the ball 344 times for an average gain of 7.64 yards per carry.

Career The career record for most yards gained is 6,320, by Johnny Bailey, Texas A&I (Div. II), 1986–89. Bailey carried the ball 885 times for an average gain of 7.14 yards per carry.

PASSING (YARDS GAINED)

Game David Klingler, Houston (Div. I-A) threw for an NCAA single-game record 716 yards *v.* Arizona State on December 2, 1990.

Season The single-season NCAA mark is held by Ty Detmer, BYU, who threw for 5,188 yards in 1990.

Career The career passing record is 15,031 yards, set by Ty Detmer, BYU (Div. I-A).

RECEIVING (YARDS GAINED)

Game The most yards gained from pass receptions in a single game is 370, by two players: Barry Wagner, Alabama A&M (Div. II), *v.* Clark Atlanta

(continued on p. 102)

NCAA DIVISION I–A RECORDS

SCORING

Points Scored

		Player(s)	Team(s)	Date(s)
Game	48	Howard Griffith	Illinois v. Southern Illinois (8 TDs)	Sept. 22, 1990
Season	234	Barry Sanders	Oklahoma State (39 TDs)	1988
Career	423	Roman Anderson	Houston (70 FGs, 213 PATs)	1988–91

Touchdowns Scored

Game	8	Howard Griffith	Illinois v. Southern Illinois (all rushing)	Sept. 22, 1990
Season	39	Barry Sanders	Oklahoma State	1988
Career	65	Anthony Thompson	Indiana (64 rushing, 1 reception)	1986–89

2-Point Conversions

Game	6	Jim Pilot	New Mexico State v. Hardin-Simmons	Nov. 25, 1961
Season	6	Pat McCarthy	Holy Cross	1960
		Jim Pilot	New Mexico State	1961
		Howard Twilley	Tulsa	1964
Career	13	Pat McCarthy	Holy Cross	1960–62

PASSING

Touchdown Passes

Game	11	David Klingler	Houston v. Eastern Washington	Nov. 17, 1990
Season	54	David Klingler	Houston	1990
Career	121	Ty Detmer	BYU	1988–91

Yards Gained

Game	716	David Klingler	Houston v. Arizona State	Dec. 1, 1990
Season	5,188	Ty Detmer	BYU	1990
Career	15,031	Ty Detmer	BYU	1988–91

Completions

Game	48	David Klingler	Houston v. SMU	Oct. 20, 1990
Season	374	David Klingler	Houston	1990
Career	958	Ty Detmer	BYU	1988–91

Attempts

Game	79	Matt Vogler	TCU v. Houston	Nov. 3, 1990
Season	643	David Klingler	Houston	1990
Career	1,530	Ty Detmer	BYU	1988–91

NCAA DIVISION I-A RECORDS

PASSING (cont.)

Average Yards Gained per Attempt

		Player(s)	Team(s)	Date(s)
Game (min. 40 attempts)	14.07	John Walsh	BYU v. Utah State (44 for 619 yards)	Oct. 30, 1993
Season (min. 400 attempts)	11.07	Ty Detmer	BYU (412 for 4,560 yards)	1989
Career (min. 1,000 attempts)	9.82	Ty Detmer	BYU (1,530 for 15,031 yards)	1988–91

PASS RECEIVING

Touchdown Receptions

Game	6	Tim Delaney	San Diego State v. New Mexico State	Nov. 15, 1969
Season	22	Emmanuel Hazard	Houston	1989
Career	43	Aaron Turner	Pacific (Cal.)	1989–92

Receptions

Game	22	Jay Miller	BYU v. New Mexico	Nov. 3, 1973
Season	142	Emmanuel Hazard	Houston	1989
Career	266	Aaron Turner	Pacific (Cal.)	1989–92

Yards Gained

Game	349	Chuck Hughes	UTEP v. North Texas	Sept. 18, 1965
Season	1,779	Howard Twilley	Tulsa	1965
Career	4,345	Aaron Turner	Pacific (Cal.)	1989–92

Average Yards Gained per Reception

Game (min. 5 catches)	52.6	Alexander Wright	Auburn v. Pacific (5 for 263 yards)	Sept. 9, 1989
Season (min. 50 catches)	24.4	Henry Ellard	Fresno State (62 for 1,510 yards)	1982
Career (min. 105 catches)	22.0	Herman Moore	Virginia (114 for 2,504 yards)	1988–90

NCAA DIVISION I–A RECORDS

RUSHING

Yards Gained

		Player(s)	Team(s)	Date(s)
Game	396	Tony Sands	Kansas v. Missouri	Nov. 23, 1991
Season	2,628	Barry Sanders	Oklahoma State	1988
Career	6,082	Tony Dorsett	Pittsburgh	1973–76

Attempts

Game	58	Tony Sands	Kansas v. Missouri	Nov. 23, 1991
Season	403	Marcus Allen	Southern Cal.	1981
Career	1,215	Steve Bartalo	Colorado State	1983–86

Average Yards Gained per Attempt

Game (min. 15 rushes)	21.40	Tony Jeffery	TCU v. Tulane (16 for 343 yards)	Sept. 13, 1986
Season (min. 250 rushes)	7.81	Mike Rozier	Nebraska (275 for 2,148 yards)	1983
Career (min. 600 rushes)	7.16	Mike Rozier	Nebraska (668 for 4,780 yards)	1981–83

Touchdowns Scored

Game	8	Howard Griffith	Illinois v. Southern Illinois	Sept. 22, 1990
Season	37	Barry Sanders	Oklahoma State	1988
Career	64	Anthony Thompson	Indiana	1986–89

TOTAL OFFENSE (Rushing plus Passing)

Yards Gained

Game	732	David Klingler	Houston v. Arizona State (716 passing, 16 rushing)	Dec. 2, 1990
Season	5,221	David Klingler	Houston (81 rushing, 5,140 passing)	1990
Career	14,665	Ty Detmer	BYU (–366 rushing, 15,031 passing)	1988–91

Interceptions

Game	5	Lee Cook	Oklahoma State v. Detroit	Nov. 28, 1942
		Walt Pastuszak	Brown v. Rhode Island	Oct. 8, 1949
		Byron Beaver	Houston v. Baylor	Sept. 22, 1962
		Dan Rebsch	Miami (Ohio) v. Western Michigan	Nov. 4, 1972
Season	14	Al Worley	Washington	1968
Career	29	Al Brosky	Illinois	1950–52

NCAA DIVISION I–A RECORDS

KICKING

Field Goals Kicked

		Player(s)	Team(s)	Date(s)
Game	7	Mike Prindle	Western Michigan v. Marshall	Sept. 29, 1984
		Dale Klein	Nebraska v. Missouri	Oct. 19, 1985
Season	29	John Lee	UCLA	1984
Career	80	Jeff Jaeger	Washington	1983–86

Points Scored

Game	24	Mike Prindle	Western Michigan v. Marshall (7 FGs, 3 PATSs)	Sept. 29, 1984
Season	131	Roman Anderson	Houston (22 FGs, 65 PATs)	1989
Career	423	Roman Anderson	Houston (70 FGs, 213 PATs)	1988–91

Points After Touchdown (PATs)

Game	13	Terry Leiweke	Houston v. Tulsa	Nov. 23, 1968
		Derek Mahoney	Fresno State v. New Mexico	Oct. 5, 1991
Season	67	Cary Blanchard	Oklahoma State	1988
Career	216	Derek Mahoney	Fresno State	1990–93

PUNTING

Most Punts

Game	36	Charlie Calhoun	Texas Tech v. Centenary	Nov. 11, 1939
Season	101	Jim Bailey	Virginia Military	1969
Career	320	Cameron Young	TCU	1976–79

Average Yards Gained

Game (min. 5 punts)	60.4	Lee Johnson	BYU v. Wyoming (5 for 302 yds)	Oct. 8, 1983
Season (min. 50 punts)	48.2	Ricky Anderson	Vanderbilt (58 for 2,793)	1984
Career (min. 200 punts)	44.7	Ray Guy	Southern Mississippi (200 for 8,934)	1970–72

Yards Gained

Game	1,318	Charlie Calhoun	Texas Tech v. Centenary	Nov. 11, 1939
Season	4,138	Johnny Pingel	Michigan State	1938
Career	12,947	Cameron Young	TCU	1976–79

Source: NCAA

on November 4, 1989; Michael Lerch, Princeton (Div. 1-AA), *v.* Brown on October 12, 1991.

Season The single-season NCAA record is 1,812 yards, by two players: Barry Wagner, Alabama A&M (Div. II). Wagner caught 106 passes for an average gain of 17.1 yards.

Career The all-time NCAA mark is held by Jerry Rice, Mississippi Valley (Div. I-AA), 1981–84. He gained 4,693 yards on 301 catches (also an NCAA career record), for an average gain of 15.6 yards.

FIELD GOALS (MOST MADE)

Game Goran Lingmerth, Northern Arizona (Div. I-AA) booted 8 out of 8 field goals *v.* Idaho on October 25, 1986. The distances were 39, 18, 20, 33, 46, 27, 22 and 35 yards each.

Season The most kicks made in a season is 29, by John Lee, UCLA (Div. I-A) from 33 attempts in 1984.

YARDAGE ■ CORNHUSKER RUNNING BACK MIKE ROZIER SET NCAA SEASON AND CAREER RECORDS FOR AVERAGE YARDS GAINED. (UNIV. OF NEBRASKA)

NCAA DIVISION I–A NATIONAL CHAMPIONS (1936–1963)

In 1936 the Associated Press introduced the AP poll, a ranking of college teams by a vote of sportswriters and broadcasters. In 1950 the United Press, later UPI, introduced a coaches' poll. The AP and UPI polls were still used as the basis for declaring the national college football champion until 1991. In 1992 the CNN/USA Today poll joined the AP as the main arbitrator of the National Championship. The polls have chosen different champions on nine occasions: 1954, 1957, 1965, 1970, 1973, 1974, 1978, 1990, and 1991. Notre Dame has been voted national champion a record eight times: 1943, 1946–47, 1949, 1966, 1973, 1977 and 1988.

Year	Team	Record	Year	Team	Record
1936	Minnesota	7–1–0	1951	Tennessee	10–0–0
1937	Pittsburgh	9–0–1	1952	Michigan State	9–0–0
1938	TCU	11–0–0	1953	Maryland	10–1–0
1939	Texas A&M	11–0–0	1954	Ohio State (AP)	10–0–0
1940	Minnesota	8–0–0		UCLA (UPI)	9–0–0
1941	Minnesota	8–0–0	1955	Oklahoma	11–0–0
1942	Ohio State	9–1–0	1956	Oklahoma	10–0–0
1943	Notre Dame	9–1–0	1957	Auburn (AP)	10–0–0
1944	Army	9–0–0		Ohio State (UPI)	9–1–0
1945	Army	9–0–0	1958	LSU	11–0–0
1946	Notre Dame	8–0–1	1959	Syracuse	11–0–0
1947	Notre Dame	9–0–0	1960	Minnesota	8–2–0
1948	Michigan	9–0–0	1961	Alabama	11–0–0
1949	Notre Dame	10–0–0	1962	Southern Cal.	11–0–0
1950	Oklahoma	10–1–0	1963	Texas	11–0–0

Career The NCAA all-time career record is 80, by Jeff Jaeger, Washington (Div. I-A) from 99 attempts, 1983–86.

LONGEST PLAYS (DIVISION I-A)

Run from scrimmage 99 yards, by four players: Gale Sayers (Kansas *v.* Nebraska), 1963; Max Anderson (Arizona State *v.* Wyoming), 1967; Ralph Thompson (West Texas State *v.* Wichita State), 1970; Kelsey Finch (Tennessee *v.* Florida), 1977.

Pass completion 99 yards, on eight occasions, performed by seven players (Terry Peel and Robert Ford did it twice): Fred Owens (to Jack Ford), Portland *v.* St. Mary's, Calif., 1947; Bo Burris (to Warren McVea), Houston *v.* Washington State, 1966; Colin Clapton (to Eddie Jenkins), Holy Cross *v.* Boston U, 1970; Terry Peel (to Robert Ford), Houston *v.* Syracuse, 1970; Terry Peel (to Robert Ford), Houston *v.* San Diego State, 1972; Cris Collingsworth (to Derrick Gaffney), Florida *v.* Rice, 1977; Scott Ankrom (to James Maness), TCU *v.* Rice, 1984; Gino Torretta (to Horace Copeland), Miami *v.* Arkansas, 1991.

Field goal 67 yards, by three players: Russell Erxleben (Texas *v.* Rice), 1977; Steve Little (Arkansas *v.* Texas), 1977; Joe Williams (Wichita State *v.* Southern Illinois), 1978.

Punt 99 yards, by Pat Brady, Nevada–Reno *v.* Loyola, Calif. in 1950.

CONSECUTIVE RECORDS

REGULAR SEASON (INDIVIDUAL—DIVISION I-A)

Scoring touchdowns (games) 23, by Bill Burnett, Arkansas. Burnett amassed 47 touchdowns during his 23-game streak, which ran from October 5, 1968–October 31, 1970.

Touchdown passes (games) 35, Ty Detmer, BYU, September 7, 1989–November 23, 1991.

NCAA DIVISION I–A NATIONAL CHAMPIONS (1964–1993)

Year	Team	Record	Year	Team	Record
1964	Alabama	10–1–0		Southern Cal. (UPI)	12–1–0
1965	Alabama (AP)	9–1–1	1979	Alabama	12–0–0
	Michigan State (UPI)	10–1–0	1980	Georgia	12–0–0
1966	Notre Dame	9–0–1	1981	Clemson	12–0–0
1967	Southern Cal.	10–1–0	1982	Penn State	11–1–0
1968	Ohio State	10–0–0	1983	Miami, Fla.	11–1–0
1969	Texas	11–0–0	1984	BYU	13–0–0
1970	Nebraska (AP)	11–0–1	1985	Oklahoma	11–1–0
	Texas (UPI)	10–1–0	1986	Penn State	12–0–0
1971	Nebraska	13–0–0	1987	Miami, Fla.	12–0–0
1972	Southern Cal.	12–0–0	1988	Notre Dame	12–0–0
1973	Notre Dame (AP)	11–0–0	1989	Miami, Fla.	11–1–0
	Alabama (UPI)	11–1–0	1990	Colorado (AP)	11–1–1
1974	Oklahoma (AP)	11–0–0		Georgia Tech (UPI)	11–0–1
	Southern Cal. (UPI)	10–1–1	1991	Miami, Fla. (AP)	12–0–0
1975	Oklahoma	11–1–0		Washington (UPI)	12–0–0
1976	Pittsburgh	12–0–0	1992	Alabama	13–0–0
1977	Notre Dame	11–1–0	1993	Florida State	12–1–0
1978	Alabama (AP)	11–1–0			

Touchdown passes (consecutive) 6, by Brooks Dawson, UTEP *v.* New Mexico, October 28, 1967. Dawson completed his first 6 passes for touchdowns, which must rank as the greatest start to a game ever!

Passes completed 22, shared by two players: Steve Young, BYU *v.* Utah State, October 30, 1982, *v.* Wyoming, November 6, 1982; Chuck Long, Iowa *v.* Indiana, October 27, 1984.

100 yards+ rushing (games) 31, by Archie Griffin, Ohio State, September 15, 1973–November 22, 1975.

200 yards+ rushing (games) 5, shared by two players: Marcus Allen, Southern Calif., 1981; Barry Sanders, Oklahoma State, 1988.

Touchdown receptions (games) 12, by two players: Desmond Howard, Michigan, 1990–91; Aaron Turner, Pacific (Cal.), 1990–91.

Pass receptions (caught for touchdowns) 6, by two players: Carlos Carson, Louisiana State, 1977—Carlson scored touchdowns on his last five receptions *v.* Rice on September 24, 1977, and from his first reception *v.* Florida on October 1, 1977 (amaz-ingly, these were the first six receptions of his collegiate career!)—and Gerald Armstrong, Nebraska, 1992. Armstrong caught six touchdown passes over five games, September 5–November 7.

Pass receptions (games) 46, by Carl Winston, New Mexico, 1990–93.

Field goals (consecutive) 30, by Chuck Nelson, Washington, 1981–82. Nelson converted his last five kicks of the season *v.* Southern Cal on November 14, 1981, and then booted the first 25 of the 1982 season, missing an attempt *v.* Washington State on November 20, 1982.

Field goals (games) 19, shared by two players: Larry Roach, Oklahoma State (1983–84); Gary Gussman, Miami (Ohio) (1986–87).

TEAM RECORDS (DIVISION I-A)

Most wins Michigan has won 739 games out of 1,017 played, 1879–1993.

Highest winning percentage The highest winning percentage in college football history is .762 by Notre Dame. The Fighting Irish have won 723, lost 211 and tied 41 out of 975 games played, 1887–1993.

HEISMAN TROPHY WINNERS (1935–1960)

Awarded annually since 1935 by the Downtown Athletic Club of New York to the top college football player as determined by a poll of journalists. Most wins (player), 2, Archie Griffin, Ohio State, 1974–75. Most wins (college), 7, Notre Dame, 1943, 1947, 1949, 1953, 1956, 1964, 1987.

Year	Player	Team	Year	Player	Team
1935	Jay Berwanger	Chicago	1948	Doak Walker	SMU
1936	Larry Kelley	Yale	1949	Leon Hart	Notre Dame
1937	Clint Frank	Yale	1950	Vic Janowicz	Ohio State
1938	Davey O'Brien	TCU	1951	Dick Kazmaier	Princeton
1939	Nile Kinnick	Iowa	1952	Billy Vessels	Oklahoma
1940	Tom Harmon	Michigan	1953	Johnny Lattner	Notre Dame
1941	Bruce Smith	Minnesota	1954	Alan Ameche	Wisconsin
1942	Frank Sinkwich	Georgia	1955	Howard Cassady	Ohio State
1943	Angelo Bertelli	Notre Dame	1956	Paul Hornung	Notre Dame
1944	Les Horvath	Ohio State	1957	John David Crow	Texas A&M
1945	Doc Blanchard	Army	1958	Pete Dawkins	Army
1946	Glenn Davis	Army	1959	Billy Cannon	LSU
1947	Johnny Lujack	Notre Dame	1960	Joe Bellino	Navy

Longest winning streak The longest winning streak in Division I-A football, including bowl games, is 47 games by Oklahoma from 1953–57. Oklahoma's streak was stopped on November 16, 1957, when Notre Dame defeated them 7–0 in Norman.

Longest undefeated streak Including bowl games, Washington played 63 games, 1907–17, without losing a game. California ended the streak with a 27–0 victory on November 3, 1917. Washington's record during the streak was 59 wins and 4 ties.

Longest losing streak The most consecutive losses in Division I-A football is 34 games, by Northwestern. This undesirable streak started on September 22, 1979 and was finally snapped three years later on September 25, 1982 when Northern Illinois succumbed to the Wildcats 31–6.

Most points scored Wyoming crushed Northern Colorado 103–0 on November 5, 1949 to set the Division I-A mark for most points scored by one team in a single game. The Cowboys scored 15 touchdowns and converted 13 PATs.

Highest-scoring game The most points scored in a Division I-A game is 124, when Oklahoma defeated Colorado 82–42 on October 4, 1980.

Highest-scoring tie game BYU and San Diego State played a 52–52 tie on November 16, 1991.

BOWL GAMES

The oldest college bowl game is the Rose Bowl. It was first played on January 1, 1902 at Tournament Park, Pasadena, Calif., where Michigan defeated Stanford 49–0. The other three bowl games that make up the "big four" are the Orange Bowl, initiated in 1935; the Sugar Bowl, 1935; and the Cotton Bowl, 1937.

ROSE BOWL In the first game, played on January 1, 1902, Michigan blanked Stanford 49–0.

Most wins Southern Cal. has won the Rose Bowl 19 times: 1923, 1930, 1932–33, 1939–40, 1944–45, 1953, 1963, 1968, 1970, 1973, 1975, 1977, 1979–80, 1985, 1990.

HEISMAN TROPHY WINNERS (1961–1993)

Year	Player	Team	Year	Player	Team
1961	Ernie Davis	Syracuse	1978	Billy Sims	Oklahoma
1962	Terry Baker	Oregon State	1979	Charles White	Southern Cal.
1963	Roger Staubach	Navy	1980	George Rogers	South Carolina
1964	John Huarte	Notre Dame	1981	Marcus Allen	Southern Cal.
1965	Mike Garrett	Southern Cal.	1982	Herschel Walker	Georgia
1966	Steve Spurrier	Florida	1983	Mike Rozier	Nebraska
1967	Gary Beban	UCLA	1984	Doug Flutie	Boston College
1968	O. J. Simpson	Southern Cal.	1985	Bo Jackson	Auburn
1969	Steve Owens	Oklahoma	1986	Vinny Testaverde	Miami, Fla.
1970	Jim Plunkett	Stanford	1987	Tim Brown	Notre Dame
1971	Pat Sullivan	Auburn	1988	Barry Sanders	Oklahoma State
1972	Johnny Rodgers	Nebraska	1989	Andre Ware	Houston
1973	John Cappelletti	Penn State	1990	Ty Detmer	BYU
1974	Archie Griffin	Ohio State	1991	Desmond Howard	Michigan
1975	Archie Griffin	Ohio State	1992	Gino Torretta	Miami, Fla.
1976	Tony Dorsett	Pittsburgh	1993	Charlie Ward	Florida State
1977	Earl Campbell	Texas			

WINNING STREAKS

The most famous streak in American sports is Joe DiMaggio's 56–game hitting streak. While fans may argue the difficulties of consecutive home runs, successive games tossing touchdowns or back–to–back shutouts there is no questioning the most important streak: a winning streak. Highlighted are some of the most impressive team and individual winning streaks (no ties) in a variety of sports.

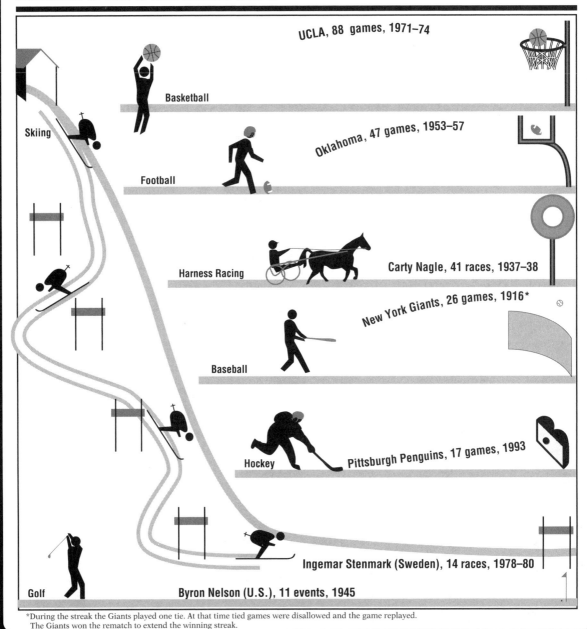

UCLA, 88 games, 1971–74

Basketball

Skiing

Oklahoma, 47 games, 1953–57

Football

Harness Racing — Carty Nagle, 41 races, 1937–38

New York Giants, 26 games, 1916*

Baseball

Hockey — Pittsburgh Penguins, 17 games, 1993

Ingemar Stenmark (Sweden), 14 races, 1978–80

Golf — Byron Nelson (U.S.), 11 events, 1945

*During the streak the Giants played one tie. At that time tied games were disallowed and the game replayed. The Giants won the rematch to extend the winning streak.

Most appearances Southern Cal. has played in the Rose Bowl 27 times, with a record of 19 wins and 8 losses.

ORANGE BOWL In the first game, played on January 1, 1935, Bucknell shut out Miami (Fla.) 26–0.

Most wins Oklahoma has won the Orange Bowl 11 times: 1954, 1956, 1958–59, 1968, 1976, 1979–81, 1986–87.

Most appearances Oklahoma has played in the Orange Bowl 16 times, with a record of 11 wins and 5 losses.

SUGAR BOWL In the first game, played on January 1, 1935, Tulane defeated Temple 20–14.

Most wins Alabama has won the Sugar Bowl eight times: 1962, 1964, 1967, 1975, 1978–80, 1992.

Most appearances Alabama has played in the Sugar Bowl 12 times, with a record of 8 wins and 4 losses.

COTTON BOWL In the first game, played on January 1, 1937, Texas Christian defeated Marquette 16–6.

Most wins Texas has won the Cotton Bowl nine times: 1943, 1946, 1953, 1962, 1964, 1969–70, 1973, 1982.

Most appearances Texas has played in the Cotton Bowl 18 times, with a record of 9 wins, 8 losses and 1 tie.

BOWL GAME RECORDS Alabama, Georgia, Georgia Tech and Notre Dame are the only four teams to have won each of the "big four" bowl games.

Most wins Alabama has won a record 26 bowl games: Sugar Bowl, eight times, 1962, 1964, 1967, 1975, 1978–80, 1992; Rose Bowl, four times, 1926, 1931, 1935, 1946; Orange Bowl, four times, 1943, 1953, 1963, 1966; Sun Bowl (now John Hancock Bowl), three times, 1983, 1986, 1988; Cotton Bowl, twice, 1942, 1981; Liberty Bowl, twice, 1976, 1982; Aloha Bowl, once, 1985; Blockbuster Bowl, once, 1991; Gator Bowl, once, 1993.

Consecutive seasons UCLA won a bowl game for seven consecutive seasons: Rose Bowl, 1983–84; Fiesta Bowl, 1985; Rose Bowl, 1986; Freedom Bowl, 1986; Aloha Bowl, 1987; Cotton Bowl, 1989.

22 IN A ROW ■ STEVE YOUNG (LEFT) THREW 22 CONSECUTIVE PASS COMPLETIONS OVER TWO GAMES TO SET THE NCAA MARK IN 1982. IN A SINGLE GAME ON OCTOBER 27, 1984, CHUCK LONG (ABOVE) MATCHED YOUNG'S MARK. (BYU, UNIV. OF IOWA)

Bowl game appearances Alabama has played in 46 bowl games.

COACHES

Wins (Division I-A) In Division I-A competition, Paul "Bear" Bryant has won more games than any other coach, with 323 victories over 38 years. Bryant coached four teams: Maryland, 1945 (6–2–1); Kentucky, 1956–53 (60–23–5); Texas A&M, 1954–57 (25–14–2); and Alabama, 1958–82 (232–46–9). His completed record was 323 wins–85 losses–17 ties, for a .780 winning percentage.

Wins (all divisions) In overall NCAA competition, Eddie Robinson, Grambling (Division I-AA) holds the mark for most victories with 388.

Highest winning percentage (Division I-A) The highest winning percentage in Division I-A competition is .881, held by Knute Rockne of Notre Dame. Rockne coached the Irish from 1918 to 1930, for a record of 105 wins–12 losses–5 tied.

ATTENDANCES

Single game It has been estimated that crowds of 120,000 were present for two Notre Dame games played at Soldier Field, Chicago, Ill.: v. Southern Cal. (November 26, 1927); v. Navy (October 13, 1928). Official attendance records have been kept by the NCAA since 1948. The highest official crowd for a regular-season NCAA game was 106,851 Wolverine fans at Michigan Football Stadium, Ann Arbor, Mich., on September 11, 1993 for the Michigan v. Notre Dame game. As Michigan lost 27–23, a record may have been set for the greatest number of depressed people at a football game!

Bowl game The record attendance for a bowl game is 106,869 people at the 1973 Rose Bowl, where Southern Cal. defeated Ohio State 42–17.

Season average The highest average attendance for home games is 105,651 for the six games played by Michigan in 1993.

CANADIAN FOOTBALL LEAGUE (CFL)

ORIGINS The earliest recorded football game in Canada was an intramural contest between students of the University of Toronto on November 9, 1861. As with football in the U.S., the development of the game in Canada dates from a contest between two universities—McGill and Harvard, played in May 1874.

Canadian football differs in many ways from its counterpart in the U.S. The major distinctions are the number of players (CFL–12, NFL–11); size of field (CFL–110 yards x 65 yards, NFL–100 yards x 53 yards); number of downs (CFL–3, NFL–4); and a completely different system for scoring and penalties.

The current CFL is comprised of nine teams in two divisions, the Western and Eastern. The divisional playoff champions meet in the Grey Cup to decide the CFL champion.

CFL TEAM RECORDS

Longest winning streak The Calgary Stampeders won 22 consecutive games between August 25, 1948 and October 22, 1949 to set the CFL mark.

Longest winless streak The Hamilton Tiger-Cats hold the dubious distinction of being the CFL's most futile team, amassing a 20-game winless streak (0–19–1), from September 28, 1948 to September 2, 1950.

Highest-scoring game The Toronto Argonauts defeated the B.C. Lions 68–43 on September 1, 1990 to set a CFL combined score record of 111 points.

Highest score by one team The Montreal Alouettes rolled over the Hamilton Tiger-Cats 82–14 on October 20, 1956 to set the CFL highest-score mark.

THE GREY CUP

In 1909, Lord Earl Grey, the governor general of Canada, donated a trophy that was to be awarded to the Canadian Rugby Football champion. The competition for the Grey Cup evolved during the first half of the 20th century from an open competition for amateurs, college teams and hybrid rugby teams to the championship of the professional Canadian Football League that was formed in 1958.

Most wins 12, Toronto Argonauts: 1914, 1921, 1933, 1937–38, 1945–47, 1950, 1952, 1983, 1991.

Most consecutive wins Five, Edmonton Eskimos: 1978–83.

CFL INDIVIDUAL RECORDS

Games Played

		Player(s)	Team(s)	Date(s)
Most	288	Ron Lancaster	Ottawa/Saskatchewan Roughriders	1960–78
Consecutive	253	Dave Cutler	Edmonton Eskimos	1969–84

Points Scored

Game	36	Bob McNamara	Winnipeg Blue Bombers v. B.C. Lions	Oct. 13, 1956
Season	236	Lance Chomyc	Toronto Argonauts	1991
Career	2,829	Lui Passaglia	B.C. Lions	1976–93

Touchdowns Scored

Game	6	Eddie James	Winnipegs v. Winnipeg St. Johns	Sept. 28, 1932
		Bob McNamara	Winnipeg Blue Bombers v. B.C. Lions	Oct. 13, 1956
Season	20	Pat Abbruzzi	Montreal Alouettes	1956
		Darrell K. Smith	Toronto Argonauts	1990
		Blake Marshall	Edmonton Eskimos	1991
		Jon Volpe	B.C. Lions	1991
Career	137	George Reed	Saskatchewan Roughriders	1963–75

PASSING

Yards Gained

Game	601	Danny Barrett	B.C. Lions v. Toronto Argonauts	Aug. 12, 1993
Season	6,619	Doug Flutie	B.C. Lions	1991
Career	50,535	Ron Lancaster	Ottawa Roughriders/Saskatchewan Roughriders	1960–78

Touchdowns Thrown

Game	8	Joe Zuger	Hamilton Tiger-Cats	Oct. 15, 1962
Season	44	Doug Flutie	Calgary Stampeders	1993
Career	333	Ron Lancaster	Ottawa/Saskatchewan Roughriders	1960–78

Completions

Game	41	Dieter Brock	Winnipeg Blue Bombers v. Ottawa Roughriders	Oct. 3, 1981
		Kent Austin	Saskatchewan Roughriders v. Toronto Argonauts	Oct. 31, 1993
Season	466	Doug Flutie	B.C. Lions	1991
Career	3,384	Ron Lancaster	Ottawa Roughriders/Saskatchewan Roughriders	1960–78

CFL INDIVIDUAL RECORDS

PASS RECEIVING

Receptions

		Player(s)	Team(s)	Date(s)
Game	16	Terry Greer	Toronto Argonauts v. Ottawa Roughriders	Aug. 19, 1983
		Brian Wiggins	Calgary Stampeders v. Saskatchewan Roughriders	Oct. 23, 1993
Season	118	Allen Pitts	Calgary Stampeders	1991
Career	706	Rocky DiPietro	Hamilton Tiger-Cats	1978–91

Yards Gained

Game	338	Hal Patterson	Montreal Alouettes v. Hamilton Tiger-Cats	Sept. 29, 1956
Season	2,003	Terry Greer	Toronto Argonauts	1983
Career	11,186	Ray Elgaard	Saskatchewan Roughriders	1983–93

Touchdown Receptions

Game	5	Ernie Pitts	Winnipeg Blue Bombers v. Saskatchewan Roughriders	Aug. 29, 1959
Season	20	Darrell K. Smith	Toronto Argonauts	1990
Career	97	Brian Kelly	Edmonton Eskimos	1979–87

RUSHING

Yards Gained

Game	287	Ron Stewart	Ottawa Roughriders v. Montreal Alouettes	Oct. 10, 1960
Season	1,896	Willie Burden	Calgary Stampeders	1975
Career	16,116	George Reed	Saskatchewan Roughriders	1963–75

Touchdowns Scored

Game	5	Earl Lunsford	Calgary Stampeders v. Edmonton Eskimos	Sept. 3, 1962
Season	18	Gerry James	Winnipeg Blue Bombers	1957
		Jim Germany	Edmonton Eskimos	1981
Career	134	George Reed	Saskatchewan Roughriders	1963–75

Longest Plays (Yards)

Rushing	109	George Dixon	Montreal Alouettes	Sept. 2, 1963
		Willie Fleming	B.C. Lions	Oct. 17, 1964
Pass Completion	109	Sam Etcheverry to Hal Patterson	Montreal Alouettes	Sept. 22, 1956
		Jerry Keeling to Terry Evanshen	Calgary Stampeders	Sept. 27, 1966
Field Goal	60	Dave Ridgway	Saskatchewan Roughriders	Sept. 6, 1987
Punt	108	Zenon Andrusyshyn	Toronto Argonauts	Oct. 23, 1977

Source: CFL

GREY CUP RESULTS (1909–1944)

Year	Winner	Loser	Score
1909	University of Toronto	Toronto Parkdale	26–6
1910	University of Toronto	Hamilton Tigers	16–7
1911	University of Toronto	Toronto Argonauts	14–7
1912	Hamilton Alerts	Toronto Argonauts	11–4
1913	Hamilton Tigers	Toronto Parkdale	44–2
1914	Toronto Argonauts	University of Toronto	14–2
1915	Hamilton Tigers	Toronto Rowing	13–7
1916	not held		
1917	not held		
1918	not held		
1919	not held		
1920	University of Toronto	Toronto Argonauts	16–3
1921	Toronto Argonauts	Edmonton Eskimos	23–0
1922	Queen's University	Edmonton Elks	13–1
1923	Queen's University	Regina Roughriders	54–0
1924	Queen's University	Toronto Balmy Beach	11–3
1925	Ottawa Senators	Winnipeg Tammany Tigers	24–1
1926	Ottawa Senators	University of Toronto	10–7
1927	Toronto Balmy Beach	Hamilton Tigers	9–6
1928	Hamilton Tigers	Regina Roughriders	30–0
1929	Hamilton Tigers	Regina Roughriders	14–3
1930	Toronto Balmy Beach	Regina Roughriders	11–6
1931	Montreal AAA Winged Wheelers	Regina Roughriders	22–0
1932	Hamilton Tigers	Regina Roughriders	25–6
1933	Toronto Argonauts	Sarnia Imperials	4–3
1934	Sarnia Imperials	Regina Roughriders	20–12
1935	Winnipeg	Hamilton Tigers	18–12
1936	Sarnia Imperials	Ottawa Rough Riders	26–20
1937	Toronto Argonauts	Winnipeg Blue Bombers	4–3
1938	Toronto Argonauts	Winnipeg Blue Bombers	30–7
1939	Winnipeg Blue Bombers	Ottawa Rough Riders	8–7
1940 (Nov.)	Ottawa Rough Riders	Toronto Balmy Beach	8–2
1940 (Dec.)	Ottawa Rough Riders	Toronto Balmy Beach	12–5
1941	Winnipeg Blue Bombers	Ottawa Rough Riders	18–16
1942	Toronto Hurricanes	Winnipeg Bombers	8–5
1943	Hamilton Flying Wildcats	Winnipeg Bombers	23–14
1944	St. Hyacinthe-Donnacona Navy	Hamilton Wildcats	7–6

GREY CUP RESULTS (1945–1980)

Year	Winner	Loser	Score
1945	Toronto Argonauts	Winnipeg Blue Bombers	35–0
1946	Toronto Argonauts	Winnipeg Blue Bombers	28–6
1947	Toronto Argonauts	Winnipeg Blue Bombers	10–9
1948	Calgary Stampeders	Ottawa Rough Riders	12–7
1949	Montreal Alouettes	Calgary Stampeders	28–15
1950	Toronto Argonauts	Winnipeg Blue Bombers	13–0
1951	Ottawa Rough Riders	Saskatchewan Roughriders	21–14
1952	Toronto Argonauts	Edmonton Eskimos	21–11
1953	Hamilton Tiger-Cats	Winnipeg Blue Bombers	12–6
1954	Edmonton Eskimos	Montreal Alouettes	26–25
1955	Edmonton Eskimos	Montreal Alouettes	34–19
1956	Edmonton Eskimos	Montreal Alouettes	50–27
1957	Hamilton Tiger-Cats	Winnipeg Blue Bombers	32–7
1958	Winnipeg Blue Bombers	Hamilton Tiger-Cats	35–28
1959	Winnipeg Blue Bombers	Hamilton Tiger-Cats	21–7
1960	Ottawa Senators	Edmonton Eskimos	16–6
1961	Winnipeg Blue Bombers	Hamilton Tiger-Cats	21–14*
1962	Winnipeg Blue Bombers	Hamilton Tiger-Cats	28–27†
1963	Hamilton Tiger-Cats	B.C. Lions	21–10
1964	B.C. Lions	Hamilton Tiger-Cats	34–24
1965	Hamilton Tiger-Cats	Winnipeg Blue Bombers	22–16
1966	Saskatchewan Roughriders	Ottawa Senators	29–14
1967	Hamilton Tiger-Cats	Saskatchewan Roughriders	24–1
1968	Ottawa Rough Riders	Calgary Stampeders	24–21
1969	Ottawa Rough Riders	Saskatchewan Roughriders	29–11
1970	Montreal Alouettes	Calgary Stampeders	23–10
1971	Calgary Stampeders	Toronto Argonauts	14–11
1972	Hamilton Tiger-Cats	Saskatchewan Roughriders	13–10
1973	Ottawa Rough Riders	Edmonton Eskimos	22–18
1974	Montreal Alouettes	Edmonton Eskimos	20–7
1975	Edmonton Eskimos	Montreal Alouettes	9–8
1976	Ottawa Rough Riders	Saskatchewan Roughriders	23–20
1977	Montreal Alouettes	Edmonton Eskimos	41–6
1978	Edmonton Eskimos	Montreal Alouettes	20–13
1979	Edmonton Eskimos	Montreal Alouettes	17–9
1980	Edmonton Eskimos	Hamilton Tiger-Cats	48–10

* Overtime.   † Halted by fog. The remaining 9:29 was played the following day.

GREY CUP RESULTS (1981–1993)

Year	Winner	Loser	Score
1981	Edmonton Eskimos	Ottawa Senators	26–23
1982	Edmonton Eskimos	Toronto Argonauts	32–16
1983	Toronto Argonauts	B.C. Lions	18–17
1984	Winnipeg Blue Bombers	Hamilton Tiger-Cats	47–17
1985	B.C. Lions	Hamilton Tiger-Cats	37–24
1986	Hamilton Tiger-Cats	Edmonton Eskimos	39–15
1987	Edmonton Eskimos	Toronto Argonauts	38–36
1988	Winnipeg Blue Bombers	B.C. Lions	22–21
1989	Saskatchewan Roughriders	Hamilton Tiger-Cats	43–40
1990	Winnipeg Blue Bombers	Edmonton Eskimos	50–11
1991	Toronto Argonauts	Calgary Stampeders	36–21
1992	Calgary Stampeders	Winnipeg Blue Bombers	24–10
1993	Edmonton Eskimos	Winnipeg Blue Bombers	33–23

FRISBEE (FLYING DISC THROWING)

ORIGINS The design of a carved plastic flying disc was patented in the United States by Fred Morrison in 1948. In 1957 Wham-O Inc. of San Gabriel, Calif. bought Morrison's patent and trademarked the name *FRISBEE* in 1958. In 1968 Wham-O helped form the International FRISBEE Association (IFA) as a vehicle for organizing the *FRISBEE* craze that had swept across the United States. The IFA folded in 1982 and it wasn't until 1986 that the World Flying Disc Federation was formed to organize and standardize rules for the sport.

FLYING DISC RECORDS

Distance thrown Sam Ferrans (U.S.) set the flying disc distance record at 623 feet 7 inches on July 2, 1988 at La Habra, Calif. The women's record is 426 feet 9½ inches by Amy Bekken (U.S.) on June 25, 1990 at La Habra, Calif.

Throw, run, catch Hiroshi Oshima (Japan) set the throw, run, catch distance record at 303 feet 11 inches on July 20, 1988 at San Francisco, Calif. The women's record is 196 feet 11 inches by Judy Horowitz (U.S.) on June 29, 1985 at La Mirada, Calif.

Time aloft The record for maximum time aloft is 16.72 seconds, by Don Cain (U.S.) on May 26, 1984 at Philadelphia, Pa. The women's record is 11.81 seconds, by Amy Bekken (U.S.) on August 1, 1991.

24-hour distance (pairs) Leonard Muise and Gabe Ontiveros (both U.S.) threw a *FRISBEE* 362.40 miles on September 20–21, 1988 at Carson, Calif. The women's record is 115.65 miles by Jo Cahow and Amy Berard (both U.S.) on December 30–31, 1979 at Pasadena, Calif.

GOLF

The nationality of the competitors in this section is U.S. unless stated otherwise.

ORIGINS The Chinese Nationalist Golf Association claims that golf (*ch'ui wan*—"the ball-hitting game") was played in China in the 3rd or 2nd century B.C. There is evidence that a game resembling golf was played in the Low Countries (present-day Belgium, Holland and northern France) in the Middle Ages. Scotland, however, is generally regarded as the home of the modern game. The oldest club of which there is written evidence is the Honourable Company of Edinburgh Golfers, Scotland, founded in 1744. The Royal & Ancient Club of St. Andrews (R&A), has been in existence since 1754. The R&A is credited with formulating the rules of golf upon which the modern game is based. Gutta percha balls succeeded feather balls in 1848. In 1899 Coburn Haskell (U.S.) invented rubber-cored balls. Steal shafts were authorized in the United States in 1925.

United States There are claims that golf was played in this country as early as the 18th century in North Carolina and Virginia. The oldest recognized club in North America is the Royal Montreal Golf Club, Canada, formed on November 4, 1873. Two clubs claim to be the first established in the U.S.: the Foxberg Golf Club, Clarion County, Pa. (1887), and St. Andrews Golf Club of Yonkers, N.Y. (1888). The United States Golf Association (USGA) was founded in 1894 as the governing body of golf in the United States.

PROFESSIONAL GOLF (MEN)

GRAND SLAM CHAMPIONSHIPS (THE MAJORS)

GRAND SLAM In 1930, Bobby Jones won the U.S. and British Open Championships and the U.S. and British Amateur Championships. This feat was christened the "Grand Slam." In 1960, the professional Grand Slam (the Masters, U.S. Open, British Open, and Professional Golfers Association [PGA] Championships) gained recognition when Arnold Palmer won the first two legs, the Masters and the U.S. Open. However, he did not complete the set of titles, and the Grand Slam has still not been attained. Ben Hogan came the closest in 1951, when he won the first three legs, but didn't return to the U.S. from Great Britain in time for the PGA Championship.

Most grand slam titles Jack Nicklaus has won the most majors, with 18 professional titles (six Masters, four U.S. Opens, three British Opens, five PGA Championships).

THE MASTERS Inaugurated in 1934, this event is held annually at the 6,980-yd Augusta National Golf Club, Augusta, GA.

Most wins Jack Nicklaus has won the coveted green jacket a record six times (1963, 1965–66, 1972, 1975, 1986).

Consecutive wins Jack Nicklaus (1965–66) and Nick Faldo (1989–90) are the only two players to have won back-to-back Masters.

MASTERS CHAMPIONS (1934–1993)

Year	Champion	Year	Champion	Year	Champion	Year	Champion
1934	Horton Smith	1949	Sam Snead	1964	Arnold Palmer	1979	Fuzzy Zoeller
1935	Gene Sarazen	1950	Jimmy Demaret	1965	Jack Nicklaus	1980	Seve Ballesteros[2]
1936	Horton Smith	1951	Ben Hogan	1966	Jack Nicklaus	1981	Tom Watson
1937	Byron Nelson	1952	Sam Snead	1967	Jay Brewer	1982	Craig Stadler
1938	Henry Picard	1953	Ben Hogan	1968	Bob Goalby	1983	Seve Ballesteros
1939	Ralph Guldahl	1954	Sam Snead	1969	George Archer	1984	Ben Crenshaw
1940	Jimmy Demaret	1955	Cary Middlecoff	1970	Billy Casper	1985	Bernhard Langer[3]
1941	Craig Wood	1956	Jack Burke Jr.	1971	Charles Coody	1986	Jack Nicklaus
1942	Byron Nelson	1957	Doug Ford	1972	Jack Nicklaus	1987	Larry Mize
1943	not held	1958	Arnold Palmer	1973	Tommy Aaron	1988	Sandy Lyle[4]
1944	not held	1959	Art Wall Jr.	1974	Gary Player	1989	Nick Faldo[4]
1945	not held	1960	Arnold Palmer	1975	Jack Nicklaus	1990	Nick Faldo
1946	Herman Keiser	1961	Gary Player[1]	1976	Raymond Floyd	1991	Ian Woosnam[4]
1947	Jimmy Demaret	1962	Arnold Palmer	1977	Tom Watson	1992	Fred Couples
1948	Claude Harmon	1963	Jack Nicklaus	1978	Gary Player	1993	Bernhard Langer

Nationalities: 1—South Africa, 2—Spain, 3—Germany, 4—Great Britain

Lowest 18-hole total (any round) 63, by Nick Price (Zimbabwe) in 1986.

Lowest 72-hole total 271, by Jack Nicklaus (67, 71, 64, 69) in 1965; and Raymond Floyd (65, 66, 70, 70) in 1976.

Oldest champion 46 years 81 days, Jack Nicklaus (1986).

Youngest champion 23 years 2 days, Severiano Ballesteros (1980).

THE UNITED STATES OPEN Inaugurated in 1895, this event is held on a different course each year. The Open was expanded from a three-day, 36-hole Saturday finish to four days of 18 holes of play in 1965.

Most wins Four players have won the title four times: Willie Anderson (1901, 1903–05); Bobby Jones (1923, 1926, 1929–30); Ben Hogan (1948, 1950–51, 1953); Jack Nicklaus (1962, 1967, 1972, 1980).

Most consecutive wins Three, by Willie Anderson (1903–05).

Lowest 18-hole total (any round) 63, by three players: Johnny Miller at Oakmont Country Club, Pa., on June 17, 1973; Jack Nicklaus and Tom

---

U.S. OPEN CHAMPIONS (1895–1993)

Year	Champion	Year	Champion	Year	Champion	Year	Champion
1895	Horace Rawlins	1920	Edward Ray[1]	1945	not held	1970	Tony Jacklin[1]
1896	James Foulis	1921	Jim Barnes	1946	Lloyd Mangrum	1971	Lee Trevino
1897	Joe Lloyd	1922	Gene Sarazen	1947	Lew Worsham	1972	Jack Nicklaus
1898	Fred Herd	1923	Bobby Jones	1948	Ben Hogan	1973	Johnny Miller
1899	Willie Smith	1924	Cyril Walker	1949	Cary Middlecoff	1974	Hale Irwin
1900	Harry Vardon[1]	1925	Willie MacFarlane	1950	Ben Hogan	1975	Lou Graham
1901	Willie Anderson	1926	Bobby Jones	1951	Ben Hogan	1976	Jerry Pate
1902	Laurie Auchterlonie	1927	Tommy Armour	1952	Julius Boros	1977	Hubert Green
1903	Willie Anderson	1928	Johnny Farrell	1953	Ben Hogan	1978	Andy North
1904	Willie Anderson	1929	Bobby Jones	1954	Ed Furgol	1979	Hale Irwin
1905	Willie Anderson	1930	Bobby Jones	1955	Jack Fleck	1980	Jack Nicklaus
1906	Alex Smith	1931	Billy Burke	1956	Cary Middlecoff	1981	David Graham[3]
1907	Alex Ross	1932	Gene Sarazen	1957	Dick Mayer	1982	Tom Watson
1908	Fred McLeod	1933	Johnny Goodman	1958	Tommy Bolt	1983	Larry Nelson
1909	George Sargent	1934	Olin Dutra	1959	Billy Casper	1984	Fuzzy Zoeller
1910	Alex Smith	1935	Sam Parks Jr.	1960	Arnold Palmer	1985	Andy North
1911	John McDermott	1936	Tony Manero	1961	Gene Littler	1986	Raymond Floyd
1912	John McDermott	1937	Ralph Guldahl	1962	Jack Nicklaus	1987	Scott Simpson
1913	Francis Ouimet	1938	Ralph Guldahl	1963	Julius Boros	1988	Curtis Strange
1914	Walter Hagen	1939	Byron Nelson	1964	Ken Venturi	1989	Curtis Strange
1915	Jerome Travers	1940	Lawson Little	1965	Gary Player[2]	1990	Hale Irwin
1916	Charles Evans Jr.	1941	Craig Wood	1966	Billy Casper	1991	Payne Stewart
1917	not held	1942	not held	1967	Jack Nicklaus	1992	Tom Kite
1918	not held	1943	not held	1968	Lee Trevino	1993	Lee Janzen
1919	Walter Hagen	1944	not held	1969	Orville Moody		

Nationalities: 1—Great Britain, 2—South Africa, 3—Australia

SHARK ATTACK ■ GREG NORMAN SHOT A FOURTH ROUND 64 TO WIN THE 1993 BRITISH OPEN. HIS 72-HOLE TOTAL OF 267 WAS A RECORD FOR THE EVENT. (WILLIAM S. ROMANO)

LONGEST DRIVE ☞ NILES LIED (AUSTRALIA) DROVE A GOLF BALL 2,640 YARDS (1½ MILES) ACROSS AN ICE CAP AT MAWSON BASE, ANTARCTICA IN 1962.

Weiskopf, both at Baltusrol Country Club, Springfield, N.J., on June 12, 1980.

Lowest 72-hole total 272, by two players: Jack Nicklaus (63, 71, 70, 68), at Baltusrol Country Club, Springfield, N.J., in 1980; and Lee Janzen (67, 67, 69, 69), also at Baltusrol, in 1993.

Oldest champion 45 years 15 days, Hale Irwin (1990).

Youngest champion 19 years 317 days, John J. McDermott (1911).

THE BRITISH OPEN In this event, inaugurated in 1860, the first dozen tournaments were staged at Prestwick, Scotland. Since 1873, the locations have varied, but all venues are coastal links courses.

Most wins Harry Vardon won a record six titles, in 1896, 1898–99, 1903, 1911, 1914.

Most consecutive wins Four, Tom Morris Jr. (1868–70, 1872; the event was not held in 1871).

Lowest 18-hole total (any round) 63, by five players: Mark Hayes at Turnberry, Scotland, on July 7, 1977; Isao Aoki (Japan) at Muirfield, Scotland, on July 19, 1980; Greg Norman (Australia) at Turnberry, Scotland, on July 18, 1986; Paul Broadhurst (Great Britain) at St. Andrews, Scotland, on July 21, 1990; Jodie Mudd at Royal Birkdale, England, on July 21, 1991.

Lowest 72-hole total 267 (66, 68, 69, 64) by Greg Norman (Australia) at Royal St. George's, England in 1993.

Oldest champion 46 years 99 days, Tom Morris Sr. (Great Britain) (1867).

Youngest champion 17 years 249 days, Tom Morris Jr. (Great Britain) (1868).

THE PROFESSIONAL GOLFERS ASSOCIATION (PGA) CHAMPIONSHIP Inaugurated in 1916, the tournament was a match-play event, but switched to a 72-hole stroke-play event in 1958.

Most wins Two players have won the title five times: Walter Hagen (1921, 1924–27); and Jack Nicklaus (1963, 1971, 1973, 1975, 1980).

Most consecutive wins Four, by Walter Hagen (1924–27).

Lowest 18-hole total (any round) 63, by three players: Bruce Crampton (Australia) at Firestone Country Club, Akron, Ohio, in 1975; Ray

(continued on p. 118)

BRITISH OPEN CHAMPIONS (1860–1967)

Year	Champion	Year	Champion	Year	Champion
1860	Willie Park Sr.[1]	1896	Harry Vardon[1]	1932	Gene Sarazen
1861	Tom Morris Sr.[1]	1897	Harold H. Hilton	1933	Densmore Shute
1862	Tom Morris Sr.	1898	Harry Vardon	1934	Henry Cotton[1]
1863	Willie Park Sr.	1899	Harry Vardon	1935	Alfred Perry[1]
1864	Tom Morris Sr.	1900	John H. Taylor	1936	Alfred Padgham[1]
1865	Andrew Strath[1]	1901	James Braid[1]	1937	Henry Cotton
1866	Willie Park Sr.	1902	Sandy Herd[1]	1938	Reg Whitcombe[1]
1867	Tom Morris Sr.	1903	Harry Vardon	1939	Dick Burton[1]
1868	Tom Morris Jr.[1]	1904	Jack White[1]	1940	not held
1869	Tom Morris Jr.	1905	James Braid	1941	not held
1870	Tom Morris Jr.	1906	James Braid	1942	not held
1871	not held	1907	Arnaud Massy[2]	1943	not held
1872	Tom Morris Jr.	1908	James Braid	1944	not held
1873	Tom Kidd[1]	1909	John H. Taylor	1945	not held
1874	Mungo Park[1]	1910	James Braid	1946	Sam Snead
1875	Willie Park Sr.	1911	Harry Vardon	1947	Fred Daly[1]
1876	Bob Martin[1]	1912	Edward Ray[1]	1948	Henry Cotton
1877	Jamie Anderson[1]	1913	John H. Taylor	1949	Bobby Locke[3]
1878	Jamie Anderson	1914	Harry Vardon	1950	Bobby Locke
1879	Jamie Anderson	1915	not held	1951	Max Faulkner[1]
1880	Robert Ferguson[1]	1916	not held	1952	Bobby Locke
1881	Robert Ferguson	1917	not held	1953	Ben Hogan
1882	Robert Ferguson	1918	not held	1954	Peter Thomson[4]
1883	Willie Fernie[1]	1919	not held	1955	Peter Thomson
1884	Jack Simpson[1]	1920	George Duncan[1]	1956	Peter Thomson
1885	Bob Martin[1]	1921	Jock Hutchinson	1957	Bobby Locke
1886	David Brown[1]	1922	Walter Hagen	1958	Peter Thomson
1887	Willie Park Jr.[1]	1923	Arthur Havers[1]	1959	Gary Player[3]
1888	Jack Burns[1]	1924	Walter Hagen	1960	Kel Nagle[4]
1889	Willie Park Jr.	1925	Jim Barnes	1961	Arnold Palmer
1890	John Ball[1]	1926	Bobby Jones	1962	Arnold Palmer
1891	Hugh Kirkaldy[1]	1927	Bobby Jones	1963	Bob Charles[5]
1892	Harold H. Hilton[1]	1928	Walter Hagen	1964	Tony Lema
1893	William Auchterlonie[1]	1929	Walter Hagen	1965	Peter Thomson
1894	John H. Taylor[1]	1930	Bobby Jones	1966	Jack Nicklaus
1895	John H. Taylor	1931	Tommy Armour	1967	Roberto de Vicenzo[6]

Nationalities: 1—Great Britain, 2—France, 3—South Africa, 4—Australia, 5—New Zealand, 6—Argentina

BRITISH OPEN CHAMPIONS (1968–1993)

Year	Champion	Year	Champion	Year	Champion
1968	Gary Player	1977	Tom Watson	1986	Greg Norman[4]
1969	Tony Jacklin[1]	1978	Jack Nicklaus	1987	Nick Faldo[1]
1970	Jack Nicklaus	1979	Seve Ballesteros[7]	1988	Seve Ballesteros
1971	Lee Trevino	1980	Tom Watson	1989	Mark Calcavecchia
1972	Lee Trevino	1981	Bill Rogers	1990	Nick Faldo
1973	Tom Weiskopf	1982	Tom Watson	1991	Ian Baker-Finch[4]
1974	Gary Player	1983	Tom Watson	1992	Nick Faldo
1975	Tom Watson	1984	Seve Ballesteros	1993	Greg Norman
1976	Johnny Miller	1985	Sandy Lyle[1]		

Nationalities: 7—Spain

ZINGED ■ 1993 PGA WINNER PAUL AZINGER AN-CHORED THE U.S. TEAM TO A RECORD 23RD RYDER CUP WIN. (WILLIAM S. ROMANO)

Floyd at Southern Hills, Tulsa, Okla., in 1982; Vijay Singh (Fiji) at the Inverness Club, Toledo, Ohio in 1993.

Lowest 72-hole total 271 (64, 71, 69, 67), by Bobby Nichols at Columbus Country Club, Ohio in 1964.

Oldest champion 48 years 140 days, Julius Boros (1968).

Youngest champion 20 years 173 days, Gene Sarazen (1922).

PROFESSIONAL GOLFERS ASSOCIATION (PGA) TOUR RECORDS

Most wins (season) Byron Nelson won a record 18 tournaments in 1945.

Most wins (career) Sam Snead won 81 official PGA tour events from 1936–65.

Most consecutive wins 11, Byron Nelson, 1945.

Most wins (same event) Sam Snead won the Greater Greensboro Open eight times to set the individual tournament win mark. His victories came in 1938, 1946, 1949–50, 1955–56, 1960, 1965.

Most consecutive wins (same event) Four, by Walter Hagen, PGA Championship, 1924–27.

Oldest winner 52 years 10 months, Sam Snead, 1965 Greater Greensboro Open.

Youngest winner 19 years 10 months, Johnny McDermott, 1911 U.S. Open.

Widest winning margin 16 strokes, by Bobby Locke (South Africa), 1948 Chicago Victory National Championship.

LOWEST SCORES

Nine holes 27, by two players: Mike Souchak at the Brackenridge Park Golf Course, San Antonio, Texas, on the back nine of the first round of the 1955 Texas Open; Andy North at the En-Joie Golf Club, Endicott, N.Y., on the back nine of the first round of the 1975 B.C. Open.

18 holes 59, by two players: Al Geiberger at the Colonial Country Club, Memphis, Tenn., during the second round of the 1977 Danny Thomas Memphis Classic; Chip Beck at the Sunrise Golf Club, Las Vegas, Nev., during the third round of the 1991 Las Vegas Invitational.

36 holes 125, by three players: Gay Brewer at the Pensacola Country Club, Pensacola, Fla., during the second and third rounds of the 1967 Pensacola Open; Ron Streck at the Oak Hills Country Club, San Antonio, Tex., during the

---

PGA CHAMPIONS (1916–1993)

Year	Champion	Year	Champion	Year	Champion
1916	Jim Barnes	1942	Sam Snead	1968	Julius Boros
1917	not held	1943	not held	1969	Raymond Floyd
1918	not held	1944	Bob Hamilton	1970	Dave Stockton
1919	Jim Barnes	1945	Byron Nelson	1971	Jack Nicklaus
1920	Jock Hutchinson	1946	Ben Hogan	1972	Gary Player[1]
1921	Walter Hagen	1947	Jim Ferrier	1973	Jack Nicklaus
1922	Gene Sarazen	1948	Ben Hogan	1974	Lee Trevino
1923	Gene Sarazen	1949	Sam Snead	1975	Jack Nicklaus
1924	Walter Hagen	1950	Chandler Harper	1976	Dave Stockton
1925	Walter Hagen	1951	Sam Snead	1977	Lanny Wadkins
1926	Walter Hagen	1952	Jim Turnesa	1978	John Mahaffey
1927	Walter Hagen	1953	Walter Burkemo	1979	David Graham[2]
1928	Leo Diegel	1954	Chick Harbert	1980	Jack Nicklaus
1929	Leo Diegel	1955	Doug Ford	1981	Larry Nelson
1930	Tommy Armour	1956	Jack Burke Jr.	1982	Raymond Floyd
1931	Tom Creavy	1957	Lionel Hebert	1983	Hal Sutton
1932	Olin Dutra	1958	Dow Finsterwald	1984	Lee Trevino
1933	Gene Sarazen	1959	Bob Rosburg	1985	Hubert Green
1934	Paul Runyan	1960	Jay Herbert	1986	Bob Tway
1935	Johnny Revolta	1961	Jerry Barber	1987	Larry Nelson
1936	Densmore Shute	1962	Gary Player[1]	1988	Jeff Sluman
1937	Densmore Shute	1963	Jack Nicklaus	1989	Payne Stewart
1938	Paul Runyan	1964	Bobby Nichols	1990	Wayne Grady[2]
1939	Henry Picard	1965	Dave Marr	1991	John Daly
1940	Byron Nelson	1966	Al Geiberger	1992	Nick Price[3]
1941	Vic Ghezzi	1967	Don January	1993	Paul Azinger

Nationalities: 1—South Africa, 2—Australia, 3—Zimbabwe

LONG DAY ■ DOUG WERT PLAYED A RECORD 440 HOLES IN 12 HOURS ON THE 6,044-YARD TPC EAGLE TRACE COURSE IN CORAL SPRINGS, FLA., ON JUNE 7, 1993. (DOUG WERT)

third and fourth rounds of the 1978 Texas Open; Blaine McCallister at the Oakwood Country Club, Coal Valley, Ill., during the second and third rounds of the 1988 Hardee's Golf Classic.

54 holes 189, by Chandler Harper at the Brackenridge Park Golf Course, San Antonio, Tex., during the last three rounds of the 1954 Texas Open.

72 holes 257, by Mike Souchak at the Brackenridge Park Golf Course, San Antonio, Tex., at the 1955 Texas Open.

TIMEOUT

TARGET GOLF ☞ THE MOST BALLS DRIVEN IN ONE HOUR, OVER 100 YARDS AND INTO A TARGET AREA, IS 1,536 BY NOEL HUNT. HE PERFORMED THE FEAT AT SHRIGLEY HALL, ENGLAND ON MAY 2, 1990.

90 holes 325, by Tim Kite at four courses, La Quinta, Calif., at the 1993 Bob Hope Chrysler Classic.

Most shots under par 35, by Tom Kite at the 90-hole 1993 Bob Hope Chrysler Classic. The most shots under par in a 72-hole tournament is 27, shared by two players: Mike Souchak, at the 1955 Texas Open; and Ben Hogan, at the 1945 Portland Invitational.

HIGHEST EARNINGS

Season Nick Price (Zimbabwe), $1,478,557 in 1993.

Career As of February 7, 1994 Tom Kite has career earnings of $8,585,164.

Most times leading money winner Eight, Jack Nicklaus, 1964–65, 1967, 1971–73, 1975–76.

SENIOR PGA TOUR

The Senior PGA tour was established in 1982. Players 50 years and older are eligible to compete on the tour. Tournaments vary between 54- and 72-hole stroke-play.

Most wins 24, by Miller Barber (1981–92).

Most wins (season) Nine, by Peter Thomson, 1985.

Most consecutive wins Three, by two players: Bob Charles and Chi Chi Rodriguez, both in 1987.

Senior Tour / Regular Tour win Ray Floyd (U.S.) is the only player to win a Senior Tour event and a PGA Tour event in the same year. He won the Doral Open PGA event in March 1992, and won his first Senior event, the GTE Northern, in September 1992.

HIGHEST EARNINGS

Season $1,190,518, Lee Trevino in 1990.

Career As of February 7, 1994 Bob Charles (New Zealand) has career earnings of $4,766,168.

THE PGA EUROPEAN TOUR

Most wins (season) Seven, by two players: Norman von Nida (Australia), 1947; and Flory van Donck (Belgium), 1953.

Most wins (career) 51, by Severiano Ballesteros (Spain), 1976–93.

HIGHEST EARNINGS

Season £871,777, by Nick Faldo (Great Britain) in 1992.

Career £4,222,421 by Nick Faldo, 1976–93.

Most times leading money winner Six, Severiano Ballesteros, 1976–78, 1986, 1988, 1991.

RYDER CUP A biennial match-play competition between professional representative teams of the United States and Europe (Great Britain and Ireland prior to 1979), this event was launched in 1927. The U.S. leads the series 23–5, with two ties.

Most individual wins Arnold Palmer has won the most matches in Ryder Cup competition with 22 victories out of 32 played.

Most selections Christy O'Connor Sr. (Great Britain and Ireland) has played in the most contests, with 10 selections 1955–73. Three players have played eight times for the United States team: Billy Casper, 1961–75; Ray Floyd, 1969–93; and Lanny Wadkins, 1977–93.

PROFESSIONAL GOLF (WOMEN)

GRAND SLAM CHAMPIONSHIPS

GRAND SLAM A Grand Slam in ladies' professional golf has been recognized since 1955. From 1955–66, the United States Open, Ladies Professional Golf Association (LPGA) Championship, Western Open and Titleholders Championship served as the "majors." From 1967–82 the Grand Slam events changed, as first the Western Open (1967) and then the Titleholders Championship (1972) were discontinued. Since 1983, the U.S. Open, LPGA Championship, du Maurier Classic and Nabisco Dinah Shore have comprised the Grand Slam events.

Most grand slam titles Patty Berg has won the most majors, with 15 titles (one U.S. Open, seven Titleholders, seven Western Open).

THE UNITED STATES OPEN In this competition, inaugurated in 1946, the first event was played as a match-play tournament; however, since 1947, the 72-hole stroke-play format has been used.

Most wins Two players have won the title four times: Betsy Rawls (1951, 1953, 1957, 1960); Mickey Wright (1958–59, 1961, 1964).

Most consecutive wins Two, by five players: Mickey Wright (1958–59); Donna Caponi (1969–

U.S. OPEN CHAMPIONS (1946–1993)

Year	Champion	Year	Champion	Year	Champion
1946	Patty Berg	1962	Murle Lindstrom	1978	Hollis Stacy
1947	Betty Jameson	1963	Mary Mills	1979	Jerilyn Britz
1948	Babe Zaharias	1964	Mickey Wright	1980	Amy Alcott
1949	Louise Suggs	1965	Carol Mann	1981	Pat Bradley
1950	Babe Zaharias	1966	Sandra Spuzich	1982	Janet Anderson
1951	Betsy Rawls	1967	Catherine Lacoste[1]	1983	Jan Stephenson
1952	Louise Suggs	1968	Susie Berning	1984	Hollis Stacy
1953	Betsy Rawls	1969	Donna Caponi	1985	Kathy Baker
1954	Babe Zaharias	1970	Donna Caponi	1986	Jane Geddes
1955	Fay Crocker	1971	JoAnne Carner	1987	Laura Davies[2]
1956	Kathy Cornelius	1972	Susie Berning	1988	Liselotte Neumann[3]
1957	Betsy Rawls	1973	Susie Berning	1989	Betsy King
1958	Mickey Wright	1974	Sandra Haynie	1990	Betsy King
1959	Mickey Wright	1975	Sandra Palmer	1991	Meg Mallon
1960	Betsy Rawls	1976	JoAnne Carner	1992	Patty Sheehan
1961	Mickey Wright	1977	Hollis Stacy	1993	Laurie Merten

1—France, 2—Great Britain, 3—Sweden

LPGA CHAMPIONS (1955–1993)

Year	Champion	Year	Champion	Year	Champion
1955	Beverly Hanson	1968	Sandra Post	1981	Donna Caponi
1956	Marlene Hagge	1969	Betsy Rawls	1982	Jan Stephenson
1957	Louise Suggs	1970	Shirley Englehorn	1983	Patty Sheehan
1958	Mickey Wright	1971	Kathy Whitworth	1984	Patty Sheehan
1959	Betsy Rawls	1972	Kathy Ahem	1985	Nancy Lopez
1960	Mickey Wright	1973	Mary Mills	1986	Pat Bradley
1961	Mickey Wright	1974	Sandra Haynie	1987	Jane Geddes
1962	Judy Kimball	1975	Kathy Whitworth	1988	Sherri Turner
1963	Mickey Wright	1976	Betty Burfeindt	1989	Nancy Lopez
1964	Mary Mills	1977	Chako Higuchi	1990	Beth Daniel
1965	Sandra Haynie	1978	Nancy Lopez	1991	Meg Mallon
1966	Gloria Ehret	1979	Donna Caponi	1992	Betsy King
1967	Kathy Whitworth	1980	Sally Little	1993	Patty Sheehan

HALL OF FAMER ■ 1993 LPGA HALL OF FAME IN-
DUCTEE PATTY SHEEHAN WON HER RECORD THIRD
LPGA CHAMPIONSHIP IN 1993. (LPGA/JEFF HORNBACK)

70); Susie Berning (1972–73); Hollis Stacy (1977–78); Betsy King (1989–90).

Lowest 18-hole total 65, by three players: Sally Little at Country Club of Indianapolis, Ind., in 1978; Judy Dickinson at Baltusrol Golf Club, Springfield, N.J., in 1985; Ayako Okamoto (Japan) at Indian Wood Golf and Country Club, Lake Orion, Mich., in 1989.

Lowest 72-hole total 277, by Liselotte Neumann (Sweden) at Baltimore Country Club, Md., in 1988.

Oldest champion 40 years 11 months, Fay Croker (1955).

Youngest champion 22 years 5 days, Catherine Lacoste (France; 1967).

LPGA CHAMPIONSHIP This event was inaugurated in 1955; since 1987, it has been officially called the Mazda LPGA Championship.

Most wins Mickey Wright has won the LPGA a record four times: 1958, 1960–61, 1963.

Most consecutive wins Two, by two players: Mickey Wright (1960–61); Patty Sheehan (1983–84).

Lowest 18-hole total 64, by Patty Sheehan at the Jack Nicklaus Sports Center, Kings Island, Ohio, in 1984.

Lowest 72-hole total 267, by Betsy King at the Bethesda Country Club, Md., in 1992.

Nabisco Dinah Shore Inaugurated in 1972, this event was formerly called the Colgate-Dinah Shore (1972–82). The event was designated a "major" in 1983. Mission Hills Country Club, Rancho Mirage, Calif. is the permanent site.

Most wins Amy Alcott has won the title three times: 1983, 1988 and 1991.

Most consecutive wins Two, by Sandra Post (1978–79).

Lowest 18-hole total 64, by two players: Nancy Lopez in 1981; Sally Little in 1982.

Lowest 72-hole total 273, by Amy Alcott in 1991.

du Maurier Classic Inaugurated in 1973, this event was formerly known as La Canadienne (1973) and the Peter Jackson Classic (1974–82). Granted "major" status in 1979, the tournament is held annually at different sites in Canada.

Most wins Pat Bradley has won this event a record three times, 1980, 1985–86.

Most consecutive wins Two, by Pat Bradley (1985–86).

Lowest 18-hole total 64, by three players: Jo-Anne Carner at St. George's Country Club, Toronto in 1978; Jane Geddes at Beaconsfield Country Club, Montreal, Canada in 1985; Dawn Coe-Jones at London Hunt and Country Club, Ontario in 1993.

Lowest 72-hole total 276, by three players. Pat Bradley and Ayako Okamato (Japan) tied in regulation play in 1986 at the Board of Trade Country Club, Toronto. Bradley defeated Okamoto for the title in a sudden-death playoff. Cathy

NABISCO DINAH SHORE CHAMPIONS (1972–1993)

Year	Champion	Year	Champion
1972	Jane Blalock	1983	Amy Alcott
1973	Mickey Wright	1984	Juli Inkster
1974	Jo Ann Prentice	1985	Alice Miller
1975	Sandra Palmer	1986	Pat Bradley
1976	Judy Rankin	1987	Betsy King
1977	Kathy Whitworth	1988	Amy Alcott
1978	Sandra Post	1989	Juli Inkster
1979	Sandra Post	1990	Betsy King
1980	Donna Caponi	1991	Amy Alcott
1981	Nancy Lopez	1992	Dottie Mochrie
1982	Sally Little	1993	Helen Alfredsson[1]

1—Sweden

Johnston matched Bradley and Okamato in 1990 at Westmont Golf and Country Club, Kitchener, Ontario.

LADIES PROFESSIONAL GOLF ASSOCIATION (LPGA) TOUR

Origins In 1944, three women golfers, Hope Seignious, Betty Hicks and Ellen Griffin, launched the Women's Professional Golf Association (WPGA). By 1947 the WPGA was unable to sustain the tour at the level that was hoped, and it seemed certain that women's professional golf would fade away. However, Wilson Sporting Goods stepped in, over-

DU MAURIER CLASSIC CHAMPIONS (1973–1993)

Year	Champion	Year	Champion	Year	Champion
1973	Jocelyne Bourassa	1980	Pat Bradley	1987	Jody Rosenthal
1974	Carole Jo Skala	1981	Jan Stephenson	1988	Sally Little
1975	JoAnne Carner	1982	Sandra Haynie	1989	Tammie Green
1976	Donna Caponi	1983	Hollis Stacy	1990	Cathy Johnston
1977	Judy Rankin	1984	Juli Inkster	1991	Nancy Scranton
1978	JoAnne Carner	1985	Pat Bradley	1992	Sherri Steinhauer
1979	Amy Alcott	1986	Pat Bradley	1993	Brandie Burton

LOW ROUND ■ HOLLIS STACEY'S 62 AT THE 1992 SAFECO CLASSIC TIED THE LPGA TOUR RECORD FOR LOWEST 18-HOLE SCORE. SHE SHARES THE RECORD WITH THREE OTHER PLAYERS. (LPGA)

hauled the tour and called it the Ladies Professional Golf Association. In 1950, the LPGA received its official charter.

Most wins (career) 88, by Kathy Whitworth, 1962–85.

Most wins (season) 13, by Mickey Wright, in 1963.

Most consecutive wins (scheduled events) Four, by two players: Mickey Wright, on two occasions, 1962, 1963; Kathy Whitworth, 1969.

Most consecutive wins (in events participated in) Five, by Nancy Lopez between May and June 1978.

Most wins (same event) Seven, by Patty Berg, who won two tournaments, the Titleholders Championship and the Western Open, both now defunct, on seven occasions during her illustrious career. She won the Titleholders in 1937–39, 1948, 1953, 1955, 1957; and the Western in 1941, 1943, 1948, 1951, 1955, 1957–58.

Oldest winner 46 years 5 months 9 days, JoAnne Carner at the 1985 Safeco Classic.

Youngest winner 18 years 14 days, Marlene Hagge at the 1952 Sarasota Open.

Widest margin of victory 14 strokes, by two players: Louise Suggs in the 1949 U.S. Open; Cindy Mackey in the 1986 Mastercard International.

HIGHEST EARNINGS

Season $863,578, by Beth Daniel in 1990.

Career $4,535,841, by Pat Bradley, 1974–93.

Most times leading money winner Eight, Kathy Whitworth, 1965–68, 1970–73.

LOWEST SCORES

Nine holes 28, by four players: Mary Beth Zimmerman at the Rail Golf Club, Springfield, Ill., during the 1984 Rail Charity Golf Classic; Pat Bradley at the Green Gables Country Club, Denver, Colo., during the 1984 Columbia Savings Classic; Muffin Spencer-Devlin at the Knollwood Country Club, Elmsford, N.Y., during the 1985 MasterCard International Pro-Am; Peggy Kirsch at the Squaw-Creek Country Club, Vienna, Ohio during the 1991 Phar-Mar in Youngstown.

18 holes 62, by four players: Mickey Wright at Hogan Park Golf Club, Midland, Tex., in the first round of the 1964 Tall City Open; Vicki Fergon at Alamaden Golf & Country Club, San Jose, Calif., in the second round of the 1984 San Jose Classic; Laura Davies (Great Britain) at the Rail Golf Club, Springfield, Ill., during the 1991 Rail Charity Golf Classic; and Hollis Stacy at the Meridian Valley

TIMEOUT

OLDEST ACE ☞ THE OLDEST GOLFER TO HAVE SHOT A HOLE IN ONE IS OTTO BUCHER (SWITZERLAND). HE WAS 99 YEARS 244 DAYS OLD WHEN HE ACED THE 130-YARD 12TH HOLE AT LA MANGA GOLF CLUB, SPAIN ON JANUARY 13, 1985.

Country Club, Seattle, Wash., during the 1992 Safeco Classic.

36 holes 129, by Judy Dickinson at Pasadena Yacht & Country Club, St. Petersburg, Fla., during the 1985 S&H Golf Classic.

54 holes 197, by Pat Bradley at the Rail Golf Club, Springfield, Ill., in the 1991 Rail Charity Golf Classic.

72 holes 267, by Betsy King at the Bethesda Country Club, Md., in the 1992 Mazda LPGA Championship.

AMATEUR GOLF (MEN)

UNITED STATES AMATEUR CHAMPIONSHIP Inaugurated in 1895, the initial format was match-play competition. In 1965, the format was changed to stroke-play; however, since 1972, the event has been played under the original match-play format.

Most wins Five, by Bobby Jones, 1924–25, 1927–28, 1930.

Lowest score (stroke-play) 279, Lanny Wadkins, 1970.

Biggest winning margin (match-play: final) 12 & 11, Charles Macdonald, 1895.

NCAA CHAMPIONSHIP The men's championship was initiated in 1897 as a match-play championship. In 1967 the format was switched to stroke-play.

Most titles (team) Yale has won the most team championships with 21 victories (1897–98, 1902, 1905–13, 1915, 1924–26, 1931–33, 1936, 1943).

Most titles (individual) Two golfers have won three individual titles: Ben Crenshaw (Texas), 1971–73, Phil Mickelson (Arizona State), 1989–90, 1992.

GYMNASTICS

ORIGINS The ancient Greeks and Romans were exponents of gymnastics, as shown by demonstration programs in the ancient Olympic Games (776 B.C. to A.D. 393). Modern training techniques were developed in Germany toward the end of the 18th century. Johann Friedrich Simon was the first teacher of the modern methods, at Basedow's School, Dessau, Germany in 1776. Friedrich Jahn, who founded the Turnverein in Berlin, Germany

in 1811, is regarded as the most influential of the gymnastics pioneers. The International Gymnastics Federation (IGF) was formed in 1891.

United States Gymnastics was introduced to the United States in the 19th century. With the advent of the modern Olympic Games, interest in the sport grew in this country, and in 1920 the United States entered its first gymnastics team in the Games. The sport was governed by the Amateur Athletic Union (AAU) and then by the National Collegiate Athletic Association (NCAA) until 1963, when the United States Gymnastics Federation (USGF) was formed. The USGF is still the governing body for the sport, and has its headquarters in Indianapolis, Ind.

OLYMPIC GAMES Gymnastics was included in the first modern Olympic Games in 1896; however, women's competition was not included until 1928.

Most gold medals Larissa Latynina (USSR) has won nine gold medals: six individual—all-around title, 1956 and 1960; floor exercise, 1956, 1960 and 1964; vault, 1956; and three team titles—1956, 1960 and 1964. In men's competition, Sawao Kato (Japan) has won eight gold medals: five individual—all-around title, 1968 and 1972; floor exercise, 1968; and parallel bars, 1972 and 1976; and three team titles—1968, 1972 and 1976.

Vera Caslavska (Czechoslovakia) has won a record seven individual gold medals: all-around title, 1964 and 1968; uneven bars, 1968; beam, 1964; floor exercise, 1968; and vault, 1964 and 1968. In men's competition, Boris Shakhlin and Nikolai Andrianov (both USSR) have each won six individual titles. Shakhlin won the all-around title, 1960; parallel bars, 1960; pommel horse, 1956, 1960; horizontal bar, 1964; vault, 1960. Andrianov won the all-around title, 1976; floor exercise, 1972, 1976; pommel horse, 1976; and vault, 1976 and 1980.

Most medals Larissa Latynina (USSR) has won 18 medals, the most of any athlete in any sport. She has won nine gold (six in individual events [see above] and one team event, 1980); five silver—all-around title, 1964; uneven bars, 1956 and 1960; beam, 1960; vault, 1964; and four bronze—uneven bars, 1964; beam, 1964; vault, 1964; and the portable apparatus team event (now discontinued) in 1956. Nikolai Andrianov holds the men's record at 15, which is the most by any male athlete in any sport. He won seven gold (six in individual events [see above] and one team event, 1980); five silver—team event, 1972 and 1976; all-around title, 1980; floor exercise, 1980; parallel bars, 1976; and three bronze—pommel horse, 1976; horizontal bar, 1980; and vault, 1972.

WORLD CHAMPIONSHIPS First held in Antwerp, Belgium in 1903, the championships were discontinued in 1913. Reintroduced in 1922, the event was held quadrenially until 1979, when the format became biennial. Until 1979 the Olympic Games served as the world championships, and results from Olympic competition are included in world championship statistics.

Most titles Larissa Latynina (USSR) won 17 world titles: five team and 12 individual, 1956–64. In men's competition, Boris Shakhlin (USSR) has won 13 titles: three team and 10 individual, 1954–64.

United States Three Americans gymnasts have won three gold medals: Kurt Thomas, floor exercise, 1978 and 1979, horizontal bar, 1979; Kim Zmeskal, all-around, 1991, beam and floor exercise, 1992; Shannon Miller, all-around, floor exercise, uneven bars, 1993.

UNITED STATES NATIONAL CHAMPIONSHIPS

Most titles Alfred A. Jochim won a record seven men's all-around U.S. titles, 1925–30 and 1933, and a total of 34 at all exercises between 1923 and 1934. The women's record is six all-around, 1945–46 and 1949–52, and 39 at all exercises, including 11 in succession at balance beam, 1941–51, by Clara Marie Schroth Lomady.

LARGEST AEROBICS DISPLAY ☞ THE LARGEST NUMBER OF PARTICIPANTS IN AN AEROBICS DISPLAY IS 15,017 AT THE 1993 BOOTS AEROBATHON IN LONDON, ENGLAND ON MAY 9, 1993.

CAREER LEADER ■ MISSY MARLOWE HAS WON FIVE NCAA TITLES, INCLUDING THE 1992 ALL-AROUND TITLE. (UNIV. OF UTAH)

NCAA CHAMPIONSHIPS (MEN) The men's competition was first held in 1932.

Most team titles The most team championships won is nine, by two colleges: Illinois, 1939–42, 1950, 1955–56, 1958, 1989; Penn State, 1948, 1953–54, 1957, 1959–61, 1965, 1976.

INDIVIDUAL RECORDS

Most titles (one year) Four, by two gymnasts: Jean Cronstedt, Penn State, won the all-around title, parallel bar, horizontal bar and floor exercise in 1954; Robert Lynn, Southern Cal., won the all-around title, parallel bar, horizontal bar and floor exercise in 1962.

Most titles (career) Seven, by two gymnasts: Joe Giallombardo, Illinois, won the tumbling, 1938–40, all-around title, 1938–40; and floor exercise, 1938; Jim Hartung, Nebraska, won the all-around title, 1980–81; rings, 1980–82; and parallel bar, 1981–82.

NCAA CHAMPIONSHIPS (WOMEN) The women's competition was first held in 1982.

Most team titles The most team championships won is seven, by Utah, 1982–86, 1990, 1992.

INDIVIDUAL RECORDS

Most titles (one year) Four, by Missy Marlowe, Utah, who won the all-around, balance beam, uneven bars and floor exercise in 1992.

Most titles (career) Five, by Missy Marlowe, Utah. She won the balance beam, 1991–92, all-around, 1992, uneven bars, 1992, and floor exercise, 1992.

MODERN RHYTHMIC GYMNASTICS

Modern rhythmic gymnastics involves complex body movements combined with handling of apparatus such as ropes, hoops, balls, clubs and ribbons. The performance must include required elements, and the choreography must cover the entire floor area and include elements such as jumps, pivots and leaps.

ORIGINS In 1962 the International Gymnastics Federation (IGF) officially recognized rhythmic gymnastics as a distinct sport. The first world championships were held in 1963 and the sport was included in the Olympic Games in 1984.

OLYMPIC GAMES No gymnast has won more than one medal in Olympic competition. Marina Lobach (USSR) won the 1988 Olympic title with perfect scores of 60.00 points in each of her events.

WORLD CHAMPIONSHIPS

Most titles (individual) Maria Gigova (Bulgaria) has won three individual world championships in 1969, 1971 and 1973 (tied).

Most titles (country) Bulgaria has won eight team championships: 1969, 1971, 1973, 1981, 1983, 1985, 1987 and 1989 (tie).

GYMNASTICS EXERCISES

Records listed are for the most repetitions of the following activities within the given time span.

Exercise	Total	Time	Gymnast	Date
Burpees	1,822	1 hr	Paddy Doyle (Great Britain	Feb. 6, 1993
Dips	3,726	1 hr	Kim Yang-Ki (South Korea)	Nov. 28, 1991
Squats	4,289	1 hr	Paul Wai Man Chung (Hong Kong)	Apr. 5, 1993
Push-ups	46,001	24 hrs	Charles Servizio (U.S.)	Apr. 24–25, 1993
Sit-ups	70,715	24 hrs	Lou Scripa Jr. (U.S.)	Dec. 1–2, 1992
Push-ups	1,500,230	1 yr	Paddy Doyle (Great Britain)	1988–89

HANG GLIDING

ORIGINS In the 11th century the monk Eilmer is reported to have flown from the 60-foot tower of Malmesbury Abbey, Wiltshire, England. The earliest modern pioneer was Otto Lilienthal (Germany), with about 2,500 flights in gliders of his own construction between 1891 and 1896. In the 1950s, Professor Francis Rogallo of the National Space Agency developed a flexible "wing" from his space capsule reentry research.

WORLD RECORDS The *Fédération Aéronautique Internationale* recognizes world records for flexible-wing, rigid-wing, and multiplace flexible-wing.

FLEXIBLE WING—SINGLE PLACE DISTANCE RECORDS (MEN)

Straight line Larry Tudor (U.S.) piloted a Wills Wing HPAT 158 for a straight-line distance of 303.36 miles, from Hobbs, N. Mex. to Elkhart, Kans., on July 3, 1990.

Single turnpoint Christian Durif (France) piloted a La Mouette Compact 15 a single-turnpoint record 158.94 miles over Owens Valley, Calif. on July 3, 1990.

Triangular course James Lee Jr. (U.S.) piloted a Willis Wing HPAT 158 for a triangular course record 121.82 miles over Garcia, Colo. on July 4, 1991.

Out and return The out and return goal distance record is 192.818 miles, set by two pilots on the same day, July 26, 1988, over Lone Pine, Calif.: Larry Tudor, Wills Wing HPAT 158; Geoffrey Loyns (Great Britain), Enterprise Wings.

Altitude gain Larry Tudor set a height gain record of 14,250.69 feet flying a G2-155 over Horseshoe Meadows, Calif. on August 4, 1985.

FLEXIBLE WING—SINGLE PLACE DISTANCE RECORDS (WOMEN)

Straight line Kari Castle (U.S.) piloted a Wills Wing AT 145 a straight-line distance of 208.63 miles over Lone Pine, Calif. on July 22, 1991.

Single turnpoint Kari Castle piloted a Pacific Airwave Magic Kiss a single-turnpoint distance of 181.47 miles over Hobbs, N.Mex. on July 1, 1990.

Triangular course Judy Leden (Great Britain) flew a triangular course record 70.173 miles over Austria on June 22, 1991.

Out and return The out and return goal distance record is 81.99 miles, set by Tover Buas-Hansen (Norway), piloting an International Axis over Owens Valley, Calif. on July 6, 1989.

Altitude gain Tover Buas-Hansen set an altitude gain record of 11,998.62 feet, piloting an International Axis over Bishop Airport, Calif. on July 6, 1989.

RIGID WING—SINGLE PLACE DISTANCE RECORDS (MEN)

Straight line The straight-line distance record is 139.07 miles, set by William Reynolds (U.S), piloting a Wills Wing over Lone Pine, Calif. on June 27, 1988.

Out and return The out and return goal distance is 47.46 miles, set by Randy Bergum (U.S.), piloting an Easy Riser over Big Pine, Calif. on July 12, 1988.

Altitude gain Rainer Scholl (South Africa) set an altitude gain record of 12,532.80 feet on May 8, 1985.

FLEXIBLE WING—MULTIPLACE DISTANCE RECORDS (MEN)

Straight line The straight line distance record is 100.60 miles, set by Larry Tudor and Eri Fujita, flying a Comet II-185 on July 12, 1985.

Out and return The out and return goal distance record is 81.99 miles, set by Kevin and Tom Klinefelter (U.S.) on July 6, 1989.

Altitude gain Tom and Kevin Klinefelter set an altitude record of 10,997.30 feet on July 6, 1989 over Bishop Airport, Calif. flying a Moyes Delta Glider.

HARNESS RACING

Harness racing involves two styles of racing: trotting and pacing. The distinction between trotters and pacers is in the gait of the horses. The trotting gait requires the simultaneous use of the diagonally opposite legs, while pacers thrust out their fore and hind legs simultaneously on one side.

ORIGINS Trotting races are known to have been held in Valkenburg, the Netherlands in 1554. There is also evidence of trotting races in England in the late 16th century.

United States Harness racing became popular in the United States in the mid-19th century. The National Trotting Association was founded, originally as the National Association for the Promotion of the Interests of the Trotting Turf, in 1870, and is still the governing body for the sport in the United States.

AMONG THE BIRDS ■ IN THE 1950s, NASA ENGINEER FRANCIS ROGALLO DEVELOPED A "FLEXIBLE WING" THAT ICARUS-WANNABEES USED TO CREATE THE SPORT OF HANG GLIDING. (SKIP BROWN)

WELL PACED ■ THE ALL-TIME CAREER EARNINGS FOR A PACER IS $3,225,653 BY NIHILATOR, 1984–85. (U.S. TROTTING ASSOC.)

TROTTING

HORSES' RECORDS

VICTORIES

Career Goldsmith Maid won an all-time record 350 races (including dashes and heats) from 1864 through 1877.

Season Make Believe won a record 53 races in 1949.

HIGHEST EARNINGS

Career The greatest career earnings for any harness horse is $4,907,307, by Peace Corps, 1988–92.

Season The single-season earnings record for a trotter is $1,610,608, by Prakas in 1985.

Race The richest race in the trotting calendar is the Hambletonian. The richest Hambletonian was the 1992 event, with a total purse of $1,380,000. The record first-place prize was $673,000 for the 1990 race, won by Harmonious.

INDIVIDUAL RACES

THE TRIPLE CROWN The Triple Crown for trotters consists of three races: Hambletonian, Kentucky Futurity and Yonkers Trot. Six trotters have won the Triple Crown.

TRIPLE CROWN WINNERS—TROTTERS

Year	Horse	Driver
1955	Scott Frost	Joe O'Brien
1963	Speedy Scot	Ralph Baldwin
1964	Ayres	John Simpson Sr.
1968	Nevele Pride	Stanley Dancer
1969	Lindy's Pride	Howard Beissinger
1972	Super Bowl	Stanley Dancer

HAMBLETONIAN The most famous race in North American harness racing, the Hambletonian, was first run in 1926. The Hambletonian has been run at six venues: New York State Fairgrounds, Syracuse, N.Y. (1926 and 1928); The Red Mile, Lexington, Ky. (1927 and 1929); Good Time Park, Goshen, N.Y. (1930–42, 1944–56); Empire City, Yonkers, N.Y. (1943); Du Quoin State Fair, Du Quoin, Ill. (1957–80); and The Meadowlands, N.J. (1981–present). The Hambletonian is open to three-year-olds and is run over one mile.

Fastest time The fastest time is 1 minute 53$\frac{2}{5}$ seconds, by American Winner, driven by Ron Pierce, in 1993.

Most wins (driver) Three drivers have won the Hambletonian four times: Ben White, 1933, 1936, 1942 and 1943; Stanley Dancer, 1968, 1972, 1975 and 1983; William Haughton, 1974, 1976–77 and 1980.

KENTUCKY FUTURITY First held in 1893, the Kentucky Futurity is a one-mile race for three-year-olds, raced at The Red Mile, Lexington, Ky.

Fastest time The fastest time is 1 minute 52$\frac{3}{5}$ seconds, by Pine Chip, driven by John Campbell, in 1993.

Most wins (driver) Ben White has driven the winning trotter seven times: 1916, 1922, 1924–25, 1933, 1936–37.

YONKERS TROT First run in 1955, when it was known as "The Yonkers," this race has been known since 1975 as the Yonkers Trot. Run over one mile for three-year-olds, the race is currently staged at Yonkers Raceway, N.Y.

Fastest time The fastest time is 1 minute 56$\frac{2}{5}$ seconds, by American Winner, driven by Ron Pierce, in 1993.

Most wins (driver) Stanley Dancer has driven the winning trotter six times: 1959, 1965, 1968, 1971–72 and 1975.

PACERS

HORSES' RECORDS

VICTORIES

Career Single G won 262 races (including dashes and heats), 1918–26.

Career (modern record) Symbol Allen won 241 races from 1943 through 1958.

Season Victory Hy won a record 65 races in 1950.

Consecutive wins Carty Nagle won 41 consecutuve races from 1937 through 1938.

HIGHEST EARNINGS

Career The all-time earnings record for a pacer is $3,225,653, by Nihilator, 1984–85.

Season The single-season record for a pacer is $2,222,166, by Presidential Ball in 1993.

Race The richest race in harness racing history was the 1984 Woodrow Wilson, which carried a total purse of $2,161,000. The winner, Nihilator, earned a record $1,080,500.

INDIVIDUAL RACES

THE TRIPLE CROWN The Triple Crown for pacers consists of three races: Cane Pace, Little Brown Jug and Messenger Stakes. Seven horses have won the Triple Crown.

TRIPLE CROWN WINNERS—PACERS

Year	Horse	Driver
1959	Adios Butler	Clint Hodgins
1965	Bret Hanover	Frank Ervin
1966	Romeo Hanover	Jerry Silverman
1968	Rum Customer	William Haughton
1970	Most Happy Fella	Stanley Dancer
1980	Niatross	Clint Galbraith
1983	Ralph Hanover	Ron Waples

CANE PACE First run in 1955, this race was originally known as the Cane Futurity. Since 1975, it has been called the Cane Pace. Run over one mile, the race is open to three-year-olds, and is run at Yonkers Raceway, N.Y.

Fastest time The fastest time is 1 minute 51$\frac{2}{5}$ seconds, by Riyadh, driven by Jim Morrill, Jr., in 1993.

Most wins (driver) Stanley Dancer has driven the winning pacer four times: 1964, 1970–71 and 1976.

LITTLE BROWN JUG First run in 1946, the Jug is raced annually at Delaware County Fair, Delaware, Ohio. The race is for three-year-olds and is run over one mile.

Fastest time The fastest time is 1 minute 52 seconds, by Life Sign, driven by John Campbell, in 1993.

Most wins (driver) William Haughton has driven five winning pacers, in 1955, 1964, 1968–69 and 1974.

MESSENGER STAKES First run in 1956, this race has been staged at various locations during its history. The race is run over one mile and is open to three-year-olds only.

Fastest time The fastest time is 1 minute 51⅕ seconds, by Die Laughing, driven by Richard Silverman, in 1991.

Most wins (drivers) William Haughton has driven the winning pacer seven times, in 1956, 1967–68, 1972 and 1974–76.

DRIVERS' RECORDS

Most wins (career) Herve Filion (Canada) has won 14,109 harness races as of February 7, 1994.

Most wins (season) Walter Case won a record 843 races in 1992.

Most wins (day) Mike Lachance won 12 races at Yonkers Raceway, N.Y. on June 23, 1987.

HIGHEST EARNINGS

Career John Campbell has won a career record $119,502,188 in prize money, 1972–February 7, 1994.

Season John Campbell won a season record $11,620,878 in 1990, when he won 543 races.

HOCKEY

ORIGINS There is pictorial evidence that a hockey-like game (*kalv*) was played on ice in the early 16th century in the Netherlands. The game was probably first played in North America on December 25, 1855 at Kingston, Ontario, Canada, but Halifax also lays claim to priority. The International Ice Hockey Federation was founded in 1908.

NATIONAL HOCKEY LEAGUE (NHL)

ORIGINS The National Hockey League (NHL) was founded on November 22, 1917 in Montreal, Canada. The formation of the NHL was precipitated by the collapse of the National Hockey Association of Canada (NHA). Four teams formed the original league: the Montreal Canadiens, Montreal Wanderers, Ottawa Senators and Quebec Bulldogs. The Toronto Arenas were admitted as a fifth team, but the Bulldogs were unable to operate, and the league began as a four-team competition. The first NHL game was played on December 19, 1917. The NHL is now comprised of 26 teams, eight from Canada and 18 from the United States, divided into two divisions within two conferences: Northeast and Atlantic Divisions in the Eastern Conference; Pacific and Central Division in the Western Conference. At the end of the regular season, 16 teams compete in the Stanley Cup playoffs to decide the NHL Championship. (For further details of the Stanley Cup, see pages 137–145.)

TEAM RECORDS

Most wins (season) The Montreal Canadiens won 60 games during the 1976–77 season. In 80 games, "the Habs" won 60, lost 8 and tied 12.

Highest winning percentage (season) The 1929–30 Boston Bruins set an NHL record .875 winning percentage. The Bruins' record was 38 wins, 5 losses and 1 tie.

Most points (season) The Montreal Canadiens accumulated 132 points during their record-setting campaign of 1976–77, when they won a record 60 games.

Most losses (season) The Washington Capitals hold the unenviable record of having lost the most games in one season. During the 1974–75 season, the first for the franchise, the Capitals lost 67 of 80 games played.

Most goals (game) The NHL record for goals in one game is 21, which has occurred on two occasions. The mark was set on January 10, 1920, when the Montreal Canadiens defeated the Toronto St. Patricks, 14–7, at Montreal. This record was matched on December 11, 1985, when the Edmonton Oilers beat the Chicago Blackhawks, 12–9, at Chicago.

Most goals (game—one team) The Montreal Canadiens pounded the Quebec Bulldogs 16–3 on March 3, 1920 to set the single-game scoring record. To make matters worse for Quebec, it was on home ice!

Most goals (season) The Edmonton Oilers scored 446 goals in 80 games during the 1983–84 season.

NATIONAL HOCKEY LEAGUE RECORDS

Goals

		Player(s)	Team(s)	Date(s)
Period	4	Busher Jackson	Toronto Maple Leafs v. St. Louis Eagles	November 20, 1934
		Max Bentley	Chicago Blackhawks v. New York Rangers	January 28, 1943
		Clint Smith	Chicago Blackhawks v. Montreal Canadiens	March 4, 1945
		Red Berenson	St. Louis Blues v. Philadelphia Flyers	November 7, 1968
		Wayne Gretzky	Edmonton Oilers v. St. Louis Blues	February 18, 1981
		Grant Mulvey	Chicago Blackhawks v. St. Louis Blues	February 3, 1982
		Bryan Trottier	New York Islanders v. Philadelphia Flyers	February 13, 1982
		Al Secord	Chicago Blackhawks v. Toronto Maple Leafs	January 7, 1987
		Joe Nieuwendyk	Calgary Flames v. Winnipeg Jets	January 11, 1989
Game	7	Joe Malone	Quebec Bulldogs v. Toronto St. Patricks	January 31, 1920
Season	92	Wayne Gretzky	Edmonton Oilers	1981–82
Career	801	Gordie Howe	Detroit Red Wings, Hartford Whalers	1946–71, 1979–80

Assists

		Player(s)	Team(s)	Date(s)
Period	5	Dale Hawerchuk	Winnipeg Jets v. Los Angeles Kings	March 6, 1984
Game	7	Billy Taylor	Detroit Red Wings v. Chicago Blackhawks	March 16, 1947
		Wayne Gretzky	Edmonton Oilers v. Washington Capitals	February 15, 1980
		Wayne Gretzky	Edmonton Oilers v. Chicago Blackhawks	December 11, 1985
		Wayne Gretzky	Edmonton Oilers v. Quebec Nordiques	February 14, 1986
Season	163	Wayne Gretzky	Edmonton Oilers	1985–86
Career	1,629	Wayne Gretzky	Edmonton Oilers, Los Angeles Kings	1979–94*

Points

		Player(s)	Team(s)	Date(s)
Period	6	Bryan Trottier	New York Islanders v. New York Rangers	December 23, 1978
Game	10	Darryl Sittler	Toronto Maple Leafs v. Boston Bruins	February 7, 1976
Season	215	Wayne Gretzky	Edmonton Oilers	1985–86
Career	2,420	Wayne Gretzky	Edmonton Oilers, Los Angeles Kings	1979–94*

Goaltenders
Shutouts

		Player(s)	Team(s)	Date(s)
Season	22	George Hainsworth	Montreal Canadiens	1928–29
Career	103	Terry Sawchuk	Detroit Red Wings, Boston Bruins, Toronto Maple Leafs, Los Angeles Kings, New York Rangers	1949–70

Wins

		Player(s)	Team(s)	Date(s)
Season	47	Bernie Parent	Philadelphia Flyers	1973–74
Career	435	Terry Sawchuk	Detroit Red Wings, Boston Bruins, Toronto Maple Leafs, Los Angeles Kings, New York Rangers	1949–70

---

* As of February 6, 1994
Source: NHL

Most assists (season) The Edmonton Oilers recorded 737 assists during the 1985–86 season.

Most points (season) The Edmonton Oilers amassed 1,182 points (446 goals, 736 assists) during the 1983–84 season.

Most power-play goals scored (season) The Pittsburgh Penguins scored 119 power-play goals during the 1988–89 season.

Most shorthand goals scored (season) The Edmonton Oilers scored 36 shorthand goals during the 1983–84 season.

Most penalty minutes in one game At the Boston Garden on February 26, 1981, the Boston Bruins and the Minnesota North Stars received a combined 406 penalty minutes, a record for one game. The Bruins received 20 minors, 13 majors, three 10-minute misconducts and six game misconducts for a total of 195 penalty minutes; the North Stars received 18 minors, 13 majors, four 10-minute misconducts and seven game misconducts for a total of 211 penalty minutes. It is also

QUICK OFF THE MARK ■ THE SABRES' ALEXANDER MOGILNY IS ONE OF A TRIO OF NHL PLAYERS TO HAVE SCORED A GOAL FIVE SECONDS INTO THE GAME. (BUFFALO SABRES/BILL WIPPERT)

reported that a hockey game broke out between the fights, which the Bruins won 5–1.

Longest winning streak The Pittsburgh Penguins won 17 consecutive games from March 9–April 10, 1993.

Longest undefeated streak The longest undefeated streak in one season is 35 games by the Philadelphia Flyers. The Flyers won 25 games and tied 10 from October 14, 1979–January 6, 1980.

Longest losing streak Two teams share the unwanted honor of losing 17 consecutive games: Washington Capitals from February 18–March 26, 1975; San Jose Sharks from January 4–February 12, 1993.

Longest winless streak The Winnipeg Jets set the mark for the longest winless streak at 30 games. From October 19 to December 20, 1980, the Jets lost 23 games and tied seven.

Longest game The longest game was played between the Detroit Red Wings and the Montreal Maroons at the Forum Montreal and lasted 2 hours 56 minutes 30 seconds. The Red Wings won when Mud Bruneteau scored the only goal of the game in the sixth period of overtime at 2:25 A.M. on March 25, 1936. Norm Smith, the Red Wings goaltender, turned aside 92 shots for the NHL's longest shutout.

INDIVIDUAL RECORDS

Most games played Gordie Howe played 1,767 games over a record 26 seasons for the Detroit Red Wings (1946–71) and Hartford Whalers (1979–80). The most games played by a goaltender is 971, by Terry Sawchuk, who played 21 seasons for five teams: Detroit Red Wings, Boston Bruins, Toronto Maple Leafs, Los Angeles Kings and New York Rangers (1949–70).

Most consecutive games played Doug Jarvis played 964 consecutive games from October 8, 1975 to October 10, 1987. During the streak, Jarvis played for three teams: the Montreal Canadiens, Washington Capitals and Hartford Whalers.

Fastest goal The fastest goal from the start of a game is 5 seconds, a feat performed by three players: Doug Smail (Winnipeg Jets) v. St. Louis Blues at Winnipeg on December 20, 1981; Bryan Trottier (New York Islanders) v. Boston Bruins at Boston on March 22, 1984; and Alexander Mogilny (Buffalo Sabres) v. Toronto Maple Leafs at To-

TOP SCORER ■ PAUL COFFEY (77) HOLDS THE NHL CAREER RECORDS FOR ASSISTS, POINTS AND GOALS SCORED BY A DEFENSEMAN. (DETROIT RED WINGS/JIM MACKEY)

ronto on December 21, 1991. The fastest goal from the start of any period was after 4 seconds achieved by two players: Claude Provost (Montreal Canadiens) *v.* Boston Bruins in the second period at Montreal on November 9, 1957, and by Denis Savard (Chicago Blackhawks) *v.* Hartford Whalers in the third period at Chicago on January 12, 1986.

Most hat tricks The most hat tricks (three or more goals in a game) in a career is 49, by Wayne Gretzky for the Edmonton Oilers and Los Angeles Kings in 13 seasons (1979–92). "The Great One" has recorded 36 three-goal games, nine four-goal games and four five-goal games. Gretzky also holds the record for most hat tricks in a season, 10, in both the 1981–82 and 1983–84 seasons for the Edmonton Oilers.

Longest consecutive goal-scoring streak The most consecutive games scoring at least one goal in a game is 16, by Harry (Punch) Broadbent (Ottawa Senators) in the 1921–22 season. Broadbent scored 25 goals during the streak.

Longest consecutive assist-scoring streak The record for most consecutive games recording at least one assist is 23 games, by Wayne Gretzky (Los Angeles Kings) in 1990–91. Gretzky was credited with 48 assists during the streak.

Most consecutive 50-or-more-goal seasons Mike Bossy (New York Islanders) scored at least 50 goals in nine consecutive seasons from 1977–78 through 1985–86.

Longest consecutive point-scoring streak The most consecutive games scoring at least one point is 51, by Wayne Gretzky (Edmonton Oilers) between October 5, 1983 and January 27, 1984. During the streak, Gretzky scored 61 goals, 92 assists for 153 points.

Longest shutout sequence by a goaltender Alex Connell (Ottawa Senators) played 461 minutes, 29 seconds without conceding a goal in the 1927–28 season.

Longest undefeated streak by a goaltender Gerry Cheevers (Boston Bruins) went 32 games (24 wins, 8 ties) undefeated during the 1971–72 season.

HART MEMORIAL TROPHY WINNERS (1924–1993)

The Hart Trophy has been awarded annually since the 1923–24 season by the Professional Hockey Writers Association to the Most Valuable Player of the NHL. Wayne Gretzky has won the award a record nine times, 1980–87 and 1989.

Year	Player	Team	Year	Player	Team
1924	Frank Nighbor	Ottawa Senators	1959	Andy Bathgate	New York Rangers
1925	Billy Burch	Hamilton Tigers	1960	Gordie Howe	Detroit Red Wings
1926	Nels Stewart	Montreal Maroons	1961	Bernie Geoffrion	Montreal Canadiens
1927	Herb Gardiner	Montreal Canadiens	1962	Jacques Plante	Montreal Canadiens
1928	Howie Morenz	Montreal Canadiens	1963	Gordie Howe	Detroit Red Wings
1929	Roy Worters	New York Americans	1964	Jean Beliveau	Montreal Canadiens
1930	Nels Stewart	Montreal Maroons	1965	Bobby Hull	Chicago Blackhawks
1931	Howie Morenz	Montreal Canadiens	1966	Bobby Hull	Chicago Blackhawks
1932	Howie Morenz	Montreal Canadiens	1967	Stan Mikita	Chicago Blackhawks
1933	Eddie Shore	Boston Bruins	1968	Stan Mikita	Chicago Blackhawks
1934	Aurel Joliat	Montreal Canadiens	1969	Phil Esposito	Boston Bruins
1935	Eddie Shore	Boston Bruins	1970	Bobby Orr	Boston Bruins
1936	Eddie Shore	Boston Bruins	1971	Bobby Orr	Boston Bruins
1937	Babe Siebert	Montreal Canadiens	1972	Bobby Orr	Boston Bruins
1938	Eddie Shore	Boston Bruins	1973	Bobby Clarke	Philadelphia Flyers
1939	Toe Blake	Montreal Canadiens	1974	Phil Esposito	Boston Bruins
1940	Ebbie Goodfellow	Detroit Red Wings	1975	Bobby Clarke	Philadelphia Flyers
1941	Bill Cowley	Boston Bruins	1976	Bobby Clarke	Philadelphia Flyers
1942	Tom Anderson	Brooklyn Americans	1977	Guy Lafleur	Montreal Canadiens
1943	Bill Cowley	Boston Bruins	1978	Guy Lafleur	Montreal Canadiens
1944	Babe Pratt	Toronto Maple Leafs	1979	Bryan Trottier	New York Islanders
1945	Elmer Lach	Montreal Canadiens	1980	Wayne Gretzky	Edmonton Oilers
1946	Max Bentley	Chicago Blackhawks	1981	Wayne Gretzky	Edmonton Oilers
1947	Maurice Richard	Montreal Canadiens	1982	Wayne Gretzky	Edmonton Oilers
1948	Buddy O'Connor	New York Rangers	1983	Wayne Gretzky	Edmonton Oilers
1949	Sid Abel	Detroit Red Wings	1984	Wayne Gretzky	Edmonton Oilers
1950	Charlie Rayner	New York Rangers	1985	Wayne Gretzky	Edmonton Oilers
1951	Milt Schmidt	Boston Bruins	1986	Wayne Gretzky	Edmonton Oilers
1952	Gordie Howe	Detroit Red Wings	1987	Wayne Gretzky	Edmonton Oilers
1953	Gordie Howe	Detroit Red Wings	1988	Mario Lemieux	Pittsburgh Penguins
1954	Al Rollins	Chicago Blackhawks	1989	Wayne Gretzky	Los Angeles Kings
1955	Ted Kennedy	Toronto Maple Leafs	1990	Mark Messier	Edmonton Oilers
1956	Jean Beliveau	Montreal Canadiens	1991	Brett Hull	St. Louis Blues
1957	Gordie Howe	Detroit Red Wings	1992	Mark Messier	New York Rangers
1958	Gordie Howe	Detroit Red Wings	1993	Mario Lemieux	Pittsburgh Penguins

Defensemen Paul Coffey (Edmonton Oilers, 1980–87; Pittsburgh Penguins, 1987–91; Los Angeles Kings, 1991–93; Detroit Red Wings, 1993) holds the all-time records for goals, assists and points by a defenseman. As of February 6, 1994, Coffey's career marks were 339 goals, 911 assists and 1,250 points. Coffey also holds the single-season record for goals scored by a defenseman, 48, which he scored in 1985–86 when he played for the Edmonton Oilers. Bobby Orr (Boston Bruins) holds the single-season marks for assists (102) and points (139), both of which were set in 1970–71.

COACHES

Most wins As of February 6, 1994, Scotty Bowman has coached his teams to 864 victories (110 wins, St. Louis Blues, 1967–71; 419 wins, Montreal Canadiens, 1971–79; 210 wins, Buffalo Sabres, 1979–87; 95 wins, Pittsburgh Penguins, 1991–93; 30 wins, Detroit Red Wings, 1993–94).

Most games coached As of February 6, 1994, Al Arbour has coached a record 1,573 games with two teams: St. Louis Blues, 1970–73; New York Islanders, 1973–86, 1988–94. Arbour's career record is 764 wins, 567 losses, 242 ties.

STANLEY CUP

The Stanley Cup is currently the oldest competition in North American professional sports. The cup was donated to the Canadian Amateur Hockey Association (AHA) by Sir Frederick Arthur Stanley, Lord Stanley of Preston in 1893.

STANLEY CUP CHAMPIONS (1893–1904)

Year	Champion	Loser	Series
1893	Montreal A.A.A.	(no challenger)	——
1894	Montreal A.A.A.	Ottawa Generals	3–1*
1895	Montreal Victorias	(no challenger)	——
1896	Winnipeg Victorias (February)	Montreal Victorias	2–0*
	Montreal Victorias (December)	Winnipeg Victorias	6–5*
1897	Montreal Victorias	Ottawa Capitals	15–2*
1898	Montreal Victorias	(no challenger)	——
1899	Montreal Victorias (February)	Winnipeg Victorias	2–0
	Montreal Shamrocks (March)	Queen's University	6–2*
1900	Montreal Shamrocks	Halifax Crescents	**
		Winnipeg Victorias	
1901	Winnipeg Victorias	Montreal Shamrocks	2–0
1902	Winnipeg Victorias (January)	Toronto Wellingtons	2–0
	Montreal A.A.A. (March)	Winnipeg Victorias	2–1
1903	Montreal A.A.A. (February)	Winnipeg Victorias	2–1
	Ottawa Silver Seven (March)	Rat Portage Thistles	**
		Montreal Victorias	
1904	Ottawa Silver Seven	Brandon Wheat Kings	**
		Montreal Wanderers	
		Toronto Marlboros	
		Winnipeg Rowing Club	

* Final score of single challenge game.

** Multiple challenger series.

STANLEY CUP CHAMPIONS (1905–1926)

Year	Champion	Loser	Series
1905	Ottawa Silver Seven	Rat Portage Thistles Dawson City Nuggets	**
1906	Ottawa Silver Seven (February)	Queen's Unversity Smith's Falls	**
	Montreal Wanderers (March)	New Glasgow Clubs Ottawa Silver Seven	**
1907	Kenora Thistles (January) Montreal Wanderers (March)	Montreal Wanderers Kenora Thistles	2–0 1–1†
1908	Montreal Wanderers	Edmonton Eskimos Toronto Maple Leafs Winnipeg Maple Leafs Ottawa Victorias	**
1909	Ottawa Senators	(no challenger)	
1910	Ottawa Senators (January)	Galt Edmonton Eskimos	**
	Montreal Wanderers (March)	Berlin (Kitchener)	7–3*
1911	Ottawa Senators	Galt Port Arthur	**
1912	Quebec Bulldogs	Moncton Victorias	2–0
1913	Quebec Bulldogs	Sydney Miners	2–0
1914	Toronto Blueshirts	Victoria Cougars Montreal Canadiens	**
1915	Vancouver Millionaires	Ottawa Senators	3–0
1916	Montreal Canadiens	Portland Rosebuds	3–2
1917	Seattle Metropolitans	Montreal Canadiens	3–1
1918	Toronto Arenas	Vancouver Millionaires	3–2
1919	no decision		‡
1920	Ottawa Senators	Seattle Metropolitans	3–2
1921	Ottawa Senators	Vancouver Millionaires	3–2
1922	Toronto St. Patricks	Vancouver Millionaires	3–2
1923	Ottawa Senators	Vancouver Maroons Edmonton Eskimos	**
1924	Montreal Canadiens	Vancouver Maroons Calgary Tigers	**
1925	Victoria Cougars	Montreal Canadiens	3–1
1926	Montreal Maroons	Victoria Cougars	3–1

* Final score of single challenge game.

** Multiple challenger series.

† Series decided on total goals scored.

‡ Due to an influenza epidemic in Seattle the final series between the Montreal Canadiens and the Seattle Metropolitans was cancelled. The series was tied 2–2–1 in games.

STANLEY CUP CHAMPIONS (1927–1964)

Year	Champion	Loser	Series
1927	Ottawa Senators	Boston Bruins	2–0
1928	New York Rangers	Montreal Maroons	3–2
1929	Boston Bruins	New York Rangers	2–0
1930	Montreal Canadiens	Boston Bruins	2–0
1931	Montreal Canadiens	Chicago Blackhawks	3–2
1932	Toronto Maple Leafs	New York Rangers	3–0
1933	New York Rangers	Toronto Maple Leafs	3–1
1934	Chicago Blackhawks	Detroit Red Wings	3–1
1935	Montreal Maroons	Toronto Maple Leafs	3–0
1936	Detroit Red Wings	Toronto Maple Leafs	3–1
1937	Detroit Red Wings	New York Rangers	3–2
1938	Chicago Blackhawks	Toronto Maple Leafs	3–1
1939	Boston Bruins	Toronto Maple Leafs	4–1
1940	New York Rangers	Toronto Maple Leafs	4–2
1941	Boston Bruins	Detroit Red Wings	4–0
1942	Toronto Maple Leafs	Detroit Red Wings	4–3
1943	Detroit Red Wings	Boston Bruins	4–0
1944	Montreal Canadiens	Chicago Blackhawks	4–0
1945	Toronto Maple Leafs	Detroit Red Wings	4–3
1946	Montreal Canadiens	Boston Bruins	4–1
1947	Toronto Maple Leafs	Montreal Canadiens	4–2
1948	Toronto Maple Leafs	Detroit Red Wings	4–0
1949	Toronto Maple Leafs	Detroit Red Wings	4–0
1950	Detroit Red Wings	New York Rangers	4–3
1951	Toronto Maple Leafs	Montreal Canadiens	4–1
1952	Detroit Red Wings	Montreal Canadiens	4–0
1953	Montreal Canadiens	Boston Bruins	4–1
1954	Detroit Red Wings	Montreal Canadiens	4–3
1955	Detroit Red Wings	Montreal Canadiens	4–3
1956	Montreal Canadiens	Detroit Red Wings	4–1
1957	Montreal Canadiens	Boston Bruins	4–1
1958	Montreal Canadiens	Boston Bruins	4–2
1959	Montreal Canadiens	Toronto Maple Leafs	4–1
1960	Montreal Canadiens	Toronto Maple Leafs	4–0
1961	Chicago Blackhawks	Detroit Red Wings	4–2
1962	Toronto Maple Leafs	Chicago Blackhawks	4–2
1963	Toronto Maple Leafs	Detroit Red Wings	4–1
1964	Toronto Maple Leafs	Detroit Red Wings	4–3

STANLEY CUP CHAMPIONS (1965–1993)

Year	Champion	Loser	Series
1965	Montreal Canadiens	Chicago Blackhawks	4–3
1966	Montreal Canadiens	Detroit Red Wings	4–2
1967	Toronto Maple Leafs	Montreal Canadiens	4–2
1968	Montreal Canadiens	St. Louis Blues	4–0
1969	Montreal Canadiens	St. Louis Blues	4–0
1970	Boston Bruins	St. Louis Blues	4–0
1971	Montreal Canadiens	Chicago Blackhawks	4–3
1972	Boston Bruins	New York Rangers	4–2
1973	Montreal Canadiens	Chicago Blackhawks	4–2
1974	Philadelphia Flyers	Boston Bruins	4–2
1975	Philadelphia Flyers	Buffalo Sabres	4–2
1976	Montreal Canadiens	Philadelphia Flyers	4–0
1977	Montreal Canadiens	Boston Bruins	4–0
1978	Montreal Canadiens	Boston Bruins	4–2
1979	Montreal Canadiens	New York Rangers	4–1
1980	New York Islanders	Philadelphia Flyers	4–2
1981	New York Islanders	Minnesota North Stars	4–1
1982	New York Islanders	Vancouver Canucks	4–0
1983	New York Islanders	Edmonton Oilers	4–0
1984	Edmonton Oilers	New York Islanders	4–1
1985	Edmonton Oilers	Philadelphia Flyers	4–1
1986	Montreal Canadiens	Calgary Flames	4–1
1987	Edmonton Oilers	Philadelphia Flyers	4–3
1988	Edmonton Oilers	Boston Bruins	4–0
1989	Calgary Flames	Montreal Canadiens	4–2
1990	Edmonton Oilers	Boston Bruins	4–1
1991	Pittsburgh Penguins	Minnesota North Stars	4–2
1992	Pittsburgh Penguins	Chicago Blackhawks	4–0
1993	Montreal Canadiens	Los Angeles Kings	4–1

The inaugural championship was presented to the AHA champion, but since 1894 there has always been a playoff. The playoff format underwent several changes until 1926, when the National Hockey League (NHL) playoffs became the permanent forum to decide the Stanley Cup champion.

Most championships The Montreal Canadiens have won the Stanley Cup a record 24 times: 1916, 1924, 1930–31, 1944, 1946, 1953, 1956–60, 1965–66, 1968–69, 1971, 1973, 1976–79, 1986, 1993.

Most consecutive wins The Montreal Canadiens won the Stanley Cup for five consecutive years, 1956–60.

Most games played Larry Robinson has played in 227 Stanley Cup playoff games for the Montreal Canadiens (1973–89, 203 games) and the Los Angeles Kings (1990–92, 24 games).

STANLEY CUP INDIVIDUAL RECORDS

Records in this section are listed only from the formation of the National Hockey League in 1917.

Goals Scored

		Player(s)	Team(s)	Date(s)
Period	4	Tim Kerr	Philadelphia Flyers *v.* New York Rangers	April 13, 1985
		Mario Lemieux	Pittsburgh Penguins *v.* New York Rangers	April 25, 1989
Game	5	Newsy Lalonde	Montreal Canadiens *v.* Ottawa Senators	March 1, 1919
		Maurice Richard	Montreal Canadiens *v.* Toronto Maple Leafs	March 23, 1944
		Darryl Sittler	Toronto Maple Leafs *v.* Philadelphia Flyers	April 22, 1976
		Reggie Leach	Philadelphia Flyers *v.* Boston Bruins	May 6, 1976
		Mario Lemieux	Pittsburgh Penguins *v.* Philadelphia Flyers	April 25, 1989
Series (any round)	12	Jari Kurri	Edmonton Oilers *v.* Chicago Blackhawks	1985
Series (final)	9	Babe Dye	Toronto St. Patricks *v.* Vancouver Millionaires	1922
Season	19	Reggie Leach	Philadelphia Flyers	1976
		Jari Kurri	Edmonton Oilers	1985
Career	110	Wayne Gretzky	Edmonton Oilers, Los Angeles Kings	1979–93

Power-Play Goals Scored

Period	3	Tim Kerr	Philadelphia Flyers *v.* New York Rangers	April 13, 1985
Series	6	Chris Kontos	Los Angeles Kings *v.* Edmonton Oilers	1989
Season	9	Mike Bossy	New York Islanders	1981
		Cam Neely	Boston Bruins	1991
Career	35	Mike Bossy	New York Islanders	1977–87

Points Scored

Period	4	Maurice Richard	Montreal Canadiens *v.* Toronto Maple Leafs	March 29, 1945
		Dickie Moore	Montreal Canadiens *v.* Boston Bruins	March 25, 1954
		Barry Pederson	Boston Bruins *v.* Buffalo Sabres	April 8, 1982
		Peter McNab	Boston Bruins *v.* Buffalo Sabres	April 11, 1982
		Tim Kerr	Philadelphia Flyers *v.* New York Rangers	April 13, 1985
		Ken Linseman	Boston Bruins *v.* Montreal Canadiens	April 14, 1985
		Wayne Gretzky	Edmonton Oilers *v.* Los Angeles Kings	April 12, 1987
		Glenn Anderson	Edmonton Oilers *v.* Winnipeg Jets	April 6, 1988
		Mario Lemieux	Pittsburgh Penguins *v.* Philadelphia Flyers	April 25, 1989
		Dave Gagner	Minnesota North Stars *v.* Chicago Blackhawks	April 8, 1991
		Mario Lemieux	Pittsburgh Penguins *v.* Washington Capitals	April 23, 1992
Game	8	Patrik Sundstrom	New Jersey Devils *v.* Washington Capitals	April 22, 1988
		Mario Lemieux	Pittsburgh Penguins *v.* Philadelphia Flyers	April 25, 1989
Series (any round)	19	Rick Middleton	Boston Bruins *v.* Buffalo Sabres	1983
Series (final)	13	Wayne Gretzky	Edmonton Oilers *v.* Boston Bruins	1988
Season	47	Wayne Gretzky	Edmonton Oilers	1985
Career	346	Wayne Gretzky	Edmonton Oilers, Los Angeles Kings	1979–93

STANLEY CUP INDIVIDUAL RECORDS

Assists

		Player(s)	Team(s)	Date(s)
Period	3	This feat has been achieved 58 times.		
Game	6	Mikko Leinonen	New York Rangers v. Philadelphia Flyers	April 8, 1982
		Wayne Gretzky	Edmonton Oilers v. Los Angeles Kings	April 9, 1987
Series	14	Rick Middleton	Boston Bruins v. Buffalo Sabres	1983
(any round)		Wayne Gretzky	Edmonton Oilers v. Chicago Blackhawks	1985
Series (final)	10	Wayne Gretzky	Edmonton Oilers v. Boston Bruins	1988
Season	31	Wayne Gretzky	Edmonton Oilers	1988
Career	236	Wayne Gretzky	Edmonton Oilers, Los Angeles Kings	1979–93

Goaltenders

Shutouts

Season	4	Clint Benedict	Montreal Maroons	1926
		Clint Benedict	Montreal Maroons	1928
		Dave Kerr	New York Rangers	1937
		Frank McCool	Toronto Maple Leafs	1945
		Terry Sawchuk	Detroit Tigers	1952
		Bernie Parent	Philadelphia Flyers	1975
		Ken Dyrden	Montreal Canadiens	1977
Career	15	Clint Benedict	Ottawa Senators, Montreal Maroons	1917–30

Minutes Played

Season	1,540	Ron Hextall	Philadelphia Flyers	1987
Career	7,645	Billy Smith	New York Islanders	1971–89

Wins

Season	16	Grant Fuhr	Edmonton Oilers	1988
		Mike Vernon	Calgary Flames	1989
		Bill Ranford	Edmonton Oilers	1990
		Tom Barrasso	Pittsburgh Penguins	1992
Career	88	Billy Smith	New York Islanders	1975–88

Penalty Minutes

Game	42	Dave Schultz	Philadelphia Flyers v. Toronto Maple Leafs	April 22, 1976
Career	599	Dale Hunter	Quebec Nordiques, Washington Capitals	1980–93

Source: NHL

GOAL SCORING RECORDS

Fastest goal The fastest goal from the start of any playoff game was scored by Don Kozak (Los Angeles Kings) past Gerry Cheevers (Boston Bruins) with 6 seconds elapsed. The Kings went on to win 7–4; the game was played on April 17, 1977. Kozak's goal shares the mark for fastest goal from the start of any period with one scored by Pelle Eklund (Philadelphia Flyers). Eklund scored in the second period of a game against the Pittsburgh Penguins in Pittsburgh on April 25, 1989; his effort was in vain, however, as the Penguins won 10–7.

SHORTHANDED GOALS SCORED

Period The most shorthanded goals scored in a single period is two, shared by three players. Bryan Trottier was the first player to perform this feat, on April 8, 1990 for the New York Islanders *v.* the Los Angeles Kings. His goals came in the second period of an 8–1 Islanders victory. Bobby Lalonde (Boston Bruins) matched Trottier on April 11, 1981. His double came in the third period of a Bruins 6–3 loss to the Minnesota North Stars. Jari Kurri (Edmonton Oilers) joined this club on April 24, 1983. His goals came in the third period of an Oilers 8–4 win over the Chicago Blackhawks.

Series The record for most shorthanded goals in a playoff series is three, shared by two players: Bill Barber (Philadelphia Flyers) in a Flyers 4–1 series victory over the Minnesota North Stars in 1980; and Wayne Presley (Chicago Blackhawks) in a series *v.* the Detroit Red Wings in 1989.

Season The record for shorthanded goals in one season is three, shared by five players: Derek Sanderson (Boston Bruins) in 1969; Bill Barber (Philadelphia Flyers) in 1980; Lorne Henning (New York Islanders) in 1980; Wayne Gretzky (Edmonton Oilers) in 1983; and Wayne Presley (Chicago Blackhawks) in 1989.

Career Mark Messier (Edmonton Oilers, New York Rangers) holds the mark for career playoff goals at 13 in 156 games (1979–92).

DEFENSEMEN RECORDS

GOAL SCORING

Game The most goals scored by a defenseman in a playoff game is three, by seven players: Bobby Orr, Boston Bruins *v.* Montreal Canadiens, April 11, 1971; Dick Redmond, Chicago Blackhawks *v.*

PERIOD PIECE ■ MARIO LEMIEUX SHARES THE PLAYOFF RECORD FOR MOST GOALS SCORED IN ONE PERIOD. HIS FOUR GOALS IN A 1989 GAME TIED TIM KERR'S MARK. (PITTSBURGH PENGUINS)

St. Louis Blues, April 4, 1973; Denis Potvin, New York Islanders *v.* Edmonton Oilers, April 17, 1981; Paul Reinhart, Calgary Flames, who performed the feat twice, *v.* Edmonton Oilers, April 14, 1983; *v.* Vancouver Canucks, April 8, 1984; Doug Halward, Vancouver Canucks *v.* Calgary Flames, April 7, 1984; Al Ioufrate, Washington Capitals *v.* New York Islanders, April 26, 1993; and Eric DesJardins, Montreal Canadiens *v.* Los Angeles Kings, June 3, 1993.

Season Paul Coffey (Edmonton Oilers) scored 12 goals in 18 games during the 1985 playoffs.

Career Denis Potvin (New York Islanders, 1973–88) has scored a playoff record 56 goals.

ASSISTS

Game The most assists in a game is five by two players: Paul Coffey, Edmonton Oilers *v.* Chicago Blackhawks on May 14, 1985; and Risto Siltanen, Quebec Nordiques *v.* Hartford Whalers on April 14, 1987.

STANLEY STREAK ■ ED BELFOUR (LEFT) AND TOM BARRASSO (RIGHT) BOTH WON A RECORD 11 STRAIGHT PLAYOFF GAMES IN 1992. (CHICAGO BLACKHAWKS/RAY GRABOWSKI, PITTSBURGH PENGUINS)

Season The most assists in one playoff year is 25 by Paul Coffey, Edmonton Oilers in 1985. Coffey played in 18 games.

Career The most assists by a defenseman in a career is 108 by Denis Potvin (New York Islanders, 1983–88). Potvin played in 185 games.

POINT SCORING

Game Paul Coffey earned a record six points on one goal and five assists, for the Edmonton Oilers *v.* the Chicago Blackhawks on May 14, 1985.

Season Paul Coffey also holds the record for most points by a defenseman in a season, with 37 in 1985 for the Edmonton Oilers. Coffey's total comprised 12 goals and 25 assists in 18 games.

Career Denis Potvin (New York Islanders, 1973–88) has scored a playoff record 164 points. Potvin scored 56 goals and 108 assists in 185 games.

CONSECUTIVE RECORDS

Point-scoring streak Bryan Trottier (New York Islanders) scored a point in 27 consecutive playoff games over three seasons (1980–82), scoring 16 goals and 26 assists for 42 points.

Goal-scoring streak Reggie Leach (Philadelphia Flyers) scored at least one goal in nine consecutive playoff games in 1976. The streak started on April 17 *v.* the Toronto Maple Leafs, and ended on May 9 when he was shut out by the Montreal Canadiens. Overall, Leach scored 14 goals during his record-setting run.

Consecutive wins by a goaltender Two goalies have won 11 straight playoff games: Ed Belfour (Chickago Blackhawks), and Tom Barrasso (Pittsburgh Penguins), both in 1992.

Longest shutout sequence In the 1936 semifinal contest between the Detroit Red Wings and the Montreal Maroons, Norm Smith, the Red Wings goaltender, shut out the Maroons for 248 minutes, 32 seconds. The Maroons failed to score in the first two games (the second game lasted 116 minutes, 30 seconds, the longest overtime game in playoff history), and finally breached Smith's defenses at 12:02 of the first period in game three. After such a stellar performance, it is no surprise that the Red Wings swept the series 3–0.

COACHES

Most championships Toe Blake coached the Montreal Canadiens to eight Stanley Cups, 1956–60, 1965–66, 1968.

Most playoff wins Through the 1992–93 season the record for playoff wins is 137 games by Scotty Bowman, St. Louis Blues, 1967–71 (26 wins), Montreal Canadiens, 1971–79 (70 wins), Buffalo Sabres, 1979–87 (18 wins), Pittsburgh Penguins, 1992–93 (23 wins).

Most games Scotty Bowman holds the mark for most games coached, at 219 with four teams: St. Louis Blues, 1967–71; Montreal Canadiens, 1971–79; Buffalo Sabres, 1979–87; Pittsburgh Penguins, 1992–93.

OLYMPIC GAMES

Hockey was included in the 1920 Summer Olympics in Antwerp, Belgium, and has been an integral part of the Winter Olympics since its introduction in 1924.

Most gold medals (country) The USSR/Unified Team has won eight Olympic titles, in 1956, 1964, 1968, 1972, 1976, 1984, 1988 and 1992.

WORLD CHAMPIONSHIPS (MEN) The world championships were first held in 1920 in conjunction with the Olympic Games. Since 1930, the world championships have been held annually. Through the 1964 Olympics, the Games were considered the world championships, and records for those Games are included in this section. Since 1977, the championships have been open to professionals.

Most titles The USSR has won the world championship 22 times: 1954, 1956, 1963–71, 1973–75, 1978–79, 1981–83, 1986, 1989–90.

PLAYOFF WINS ■ SCOTTY BOWMAN HAS WON A RECORD 137 PLAYOFF GAMES OUT OF A RECORD 219 COACHED. (DETROIT RED WINGS)

TRIPLE CROWN WINNERS

Year	Horse	Jockey	Trainer	Owner
1919	Sir Barton	Johnny Loftus	H. Guy Bedwell	J. K. L. Ross
1930	Gallant Fox	Earl Sande	J. E. Fitzsimmons	Belair Stud
1935	Omaha	Willie Saunders	J. E. Fitzsimmons	Belair Stud
1937	War Admiral	Chas. Kurtsinger	George Conway	Samuel Riddle
1941	Whirlaway	Eddie Arcaro	Ben A. Jones	Calumet Farm
1943	Count Fleet	Johnny Longden	Don Cameron	Mrs. J. D. Hertz
1946	Assault	Warren Mehrtens	Max Hirsch	King Ranch
1948	Citation	Eddie Arcaro	Ben A. Jones	Calumet Farm
1973	Secretariat	Ron Turcotte	Lucien Laurin	Meadow Stable
1977	Seattle Slew	Jean Cruguet	Billy Turner	Karen Taylor
1978	Affirmed	Steve Cauthen	Laz Barrera	Harbor View Farm

Jim Fitzsimmons and Ben Jones are the only trainers to have trained two Triple Crown winners. Eddie Arcaro is the only jockey to have ridden two Triple Crown winners.

Most consecutive titles The USSR won nine consecutive championships from 1963–71.

WORLD CHAMPIONSHIPS (WOMEN) The inaugural tournament was held in 1990. Canada won the inaugural event, defeating the United States 5–2 in the final, staged in Ottawa, Canada on March 24, 1990.

NCAA CHAMPIONSHIPS A men's Division I hockey championship was first staged in 1948, and has been held annually since.

Most wins Michigan has won the title seven times: 1948, 1951–53, 1955–56 and 1964.

HORSE RACING

ORIGINS Horsemanship was an important part of the Hittite culture of Anatolia, Turkey, dating from 1400 B.C. The 33rd ancient Olympic Games of 648 B.C. in Greece featured horse racing. Horse races can be traced in England from the 3rd century. The first sweepstakes race was originated by the 12th Earl of Derby at his estate in Epsom in 1780. The Epsom Derby is still run today and is the classic race of the English flat racing season.

United States Horses were introduced to the North American continent from Spain by Cortéz in 1519. In colonial America, horse racing was common. Colonel Richard Nicholls, commander of English forces in New York, is believed to have staged the first organized race at Salisbury Plain, Long Island, N.Y. in 1665. The first Jockey Club to be founded was at Charleston, S.C. in 1734. Thoroughbred racing was first staged at Saratoga Springs, N.Y. in 1863.

RACING RECORDS (UNITED STATES)

HORSES

CAREER RECORDS

Most wins The most wins in a racing career is 89, by Kingston, from 138 starts, 1886–94.

Most wins (graded stakes races) John Henry won 25 graded stakes races, including 16 Grade I races, 1978–84.

HIGHEST EARNINGS

Career The career record for earnings is $6,679,242, by Alysheba, 1986–88. Alysheba's career record was 11 wins, eight seconds and two thirds from 26 races.

Season The single-season earnings record is $4,578,454, by Sunday Silence, in 1989, from nine starts (seven wins and two seconds).

KENTUCKY DERBY WINNERS (1875–1993)

This event is held on the first Saturday in May at Churchill Downs, Louisville, Ky. The first race was run in 1875 over 1½ miles; the distance was shortened to 1¼ miles in 1896 and is still run at that length.

Most Wins
Jockey Five, by two jockeys: Eddie Arcaro (1938, 1941, 1945, 1948, 1952); Bill Hartack (1957, 1960, 1962, 1964, 1969).

Trainer Six, by Ben Jones (1938, 1941, 1944, 1948–49, 1952).

Owner Eight, by Calumet Farm (1941, 1944, 1948–49, 1952, 1957–58, 1968).

Fastest time 1 minute 59⅖ seconds, by Secretariat, 1973.

Largest field 23 horses in 1974.

Year	Horse	Year	Horse	Year	Horse	Year	Horse
1875	Aristides	1905	Agile	1935	Omaha	1965	Lucky Debonair
1876	Vagrant	1906	Sir Huon	1936	Bold Venture	1966	Kauai King
1877	Baden-Baden	1907	Pink Star	1937	War Admiral	1967	Proud Clarion
1878	Day Star	1908	Stone Street	1938	Lawrin	1968	Forward Pass
1879	Lord Murphy	1909	Wintergreen	1939	Johnstown	1969	Majestic Prince
1880	Fonso	1910	Donau	1940	Gallahadian	1970	Dust Commander
1881	Hindoo	1911	Meridian	1941	Whirlaway	1971	Canonero II
1882	Apollo	1912	Worth	1942	Shut Out	1972	Riva Ridge
1883	Leonatus	1913	Donerail	1943	Count Fleet	1973	Secretariat
1884	Buchanan	1914	Old Rosebud	1944	Pensive	1974	Cannonade
1885	Joe Cotton	1915	Regret	1945	Hoop Jr.	1975	Foolish Pleasure
1886	Ben Ali	1916	George Smith	1946	Assault	1976	Bold Forbes
1887	Montrose	1917	Omar Khayyam	1947	Jet Pilot	1977	Seattle Slew
1888	Macbeth II	1918	Exterminator	1948	Citation	1978	Affirmed
1889	Spokane	1919	Sir Barton	1949	Ponder	1979	Spectacular Bid
1890	Riley	1920	Paul Jones	1950	Middleground	1980	Genuine Risk
1891	Kingman	1921	Behave Yourself	1951	Count Turf	1981	Pleasant Colony
1892	Azra	1922	Morvich	1952	Hill Gail	1982	Gato Del Sol
1893	Lookout	1923	Zev	1953	Dark Star	1983	Sunny's Halo
1894	Chant	1924	Black Gold	1954	Determine	1984	Swale
1895	Halma	1925	Flying Ebony	1955	Swaps	1985	Spend a Buck
1896	Ben Brush	1926	Bubbling Over	1956	Needles	1986	Ferdinand
1897	Typhoon II	1927	Whiskery	1957	Iron Liege	1987	Alysheba
1898	Plaudit	1928	Reigh Count	1958	Tim Tam	1988	Winning Colors
1899	Manuel	1929	Clyde Van Dusen	1959	Tomy Lee	1989	Sunday Silence
1900	Lieut. Gibson	1930	Gallant Fox	1960	Venetian Way	1990	Unbridled
1901	His Eminence	1931	Twenty Grand	1961	Carry Back	1991	Strike the Gold
1902	Alan-a-Dale	1932	Burgoo King	1962	Decidedly	1992	Lil E. Tee
1903	Judge Himes	1933	Brokers Tip	1963	Chateaugay	1993	Sea Hero
1904	Elwood	1934	Cavalcade	1964	Northern Dancer		

PREAKNESS STAKES WINNERS (1873–1993)

Inaugurated in 1873, this event is held annually at Pimlico Race Course, Baltimore, Md. Originally run at 1½ miles, the distance was changed several times before being settled at the current length of 1³⁄₁₆ miles in 1925.

Most Wins
Jockey Six, by Eddie Arcaro (1941, 1948, 1950–51, 1955, 1957).

Trainer Seven, by Robert Wyndham Walden (1875, 1878–82, 1888).

Owner Five, by George Lorillard (1878–82).

Fastest time 1 minute 53⅕ seconds, by Tank's Prospect, 1985.

Largest field 18 horses in 1928.

Year	Horse	Year	Horse	Year	Horse	Year	Horse
1873	Survivor	1903	Flocarline	1932	Burgoo King	1963	Candy Spots
1874	Culpepper	1904	Bryn Mawr	1933	Head Play	1964	Northern Dancer
1875	Tom Ochiltree	1905	Cairngorm	1934	High Quest	1965	Tom Rolfe
1876	Shirley	1906	Whimsical	1935	Omaha	1966	Kauai King
1877	Cloverbrook	1907	Don Enrique	1936	Bold Venture	1967	Damascus
1878	Duke of Magenta	1908	Royal Tourist	1937	War Admiral	1968	Forward Pass
1879	Harold	1909	Effendi	1938	Dauber	1969	Majestic Prince
1880	Grenada	1910	Layminister	1939	Challedon	1970	Personality
1881	Saunterer	1911	Watervale	1940	Bimelech	1971	Canonero II
1882	Vanguard	1912	Colonel Holloway	1941	Whirlaway	1972	Bee Bee Bee
1883	Jacobus	1913	Buskin	1942	Alsab	1973	Secretariat
1884	Knight of Ellerslie	1914	Holiday	1943	Count Fleet	1974	Little Current
1885	Tecumseh	1915	Rhine Maiden	1944	Pensive	1975	Master Derby
1886	The Bard	1916	Damrosch	1945	Polynesian	1976	Elocutionist
1887	Dunboyne	1917	Kalitan	1946	Assault	1977	Seattle Slew
1888	Refund	1918	War Cloud*	1947	Faultless	1978	Affirmed
1889	Buddhist	1918	Jack Hare Jr.*	1948	Citation	1979	Spectacular Bid
1890	Montague	1919	Sir Barton	1949	Capot	1980	Codex
1891	not held	1920	Man o'War	1950	Hill Prince	1981	Pleasant Colony
1892	not held	1921	Broomspun	1951	Bold	1982	Aloma's Ruler
1893	not held	1922	Pillory	1952	Blue Man	1983	Deputed Testamony
1894	Assignee	1923	Vigil	1953	Native Dancer	1984	Gate Dancer
1895	Belmar	1924	Nellie Morse	1954	Hasty Road	1985	Tank's Prospect
1896	Margrave	1925	Coventry	1955	Nashua	1986	Snow Chief
1897	Paul Kauvar	1926	Display	1956	Fabius	1987	Alysheba
1898	Sly Fox	1927	Bostonian	1957	Bold Ruler	1988	Risen Star
1899	Half Time	1928	Victorian	1958	Tim Tam	1989	Sunday Silence
1900	Hindus	1929	Dr. Freeland	1959	Royal Orbit	1990	Summer Squall
1901	The Parader	1930	Gallant Fox	1960	Bally Ache	1991	Hansel
1902	Old England	1931	Mate	1961	Carry Back	1992	Pine Bluff
				1962	Greek Money	1993	Prairie Bayou

* The 1918 race was run in two divisions.

BELMONT STAKES WINNERS (1867–1993)

This race is the third leg of the Triple Crown, first run in 1867 at Jerome Park, N.Y. Since 1905 the race has been staged at Belmont Park, N.Y. Originally run over 1 mile 5 furlongs, the current distance of 1½ miles has been set since 1926.

Most Wins

Jockey Six, by two jockeys: Jim McLaughlin (1882–84, 1886–88); Eddie Arcaro (1941–42, 1945, 1948, 1952, 1955).

Trainer Eight, by James Rowe Sr. (1883–84, 1901, 1904, 1907–08, 1910, 1913).

Owner Six, by three owners: Belmont Family (1869, 1896, 1902, 1916–17, 1983); James R. Keene (1879, 1901, 1904, 1907–08, 1910); Belair Stud (1930, 1932, 1935–36, 1939, 1955).

Fastest time 2 minutes 24 seconds, by Secretariat, 1973.

Largest field 15 horses, in 1983.

Year	Horse	Year	Horse	Year	Horse	Year	Horse
1867	Ruthless	1899	Jean Bereaud	1931	Twenty Grand	1963	Chateaugay
1868	General Duke	1900	Ildrim	1932	Faireno	1964	Quadrangle
1869	Fenian	1901	Commando	1933	Hurryoff	1965	Hail to All
1870	Kingfisher	1902	Masterman	1934	Peace Chance	1966	Amberoid
1871	Harry Bassett	1903	Africander	1935	Omaha	1967	Damascus
1872	Joe Daniels	1904	Delhi	1936	Granville	1968	Stage Door Johnny
1873	Springbok	1905	Tanya	1937	War Admiral	1969	Arts and Letters
1874	Saxon	1906	Burgomaster	1938	Pasteurized	1970	High Echelon
1875	Calvin	1907	Peter Pan	1939	Johnstown	1971	Pass Catcher
1876	Algerine	1908	Colin	1940	Bimelech	1972	Riva Ridge
1877	Cloverbrook	1909	Joe Madden	1941	Whirlaway	1973	Secretariat
1878	Duke of Magenta	1910	Sweep	1942	Shut Out	1974	Little Current
1879	Spendthrift	1911	not held	1943	Count Fleet	1975	Avatar
1880	Grenada	1912	not held	1944	Bounding Home	1976	Bold Forbes
1881	Saunterer	1913	Prince Eugene	1945	Pavot	1977	Seattle Slew
1882	Forester	1914	Luke McLuke	1946	Assault	1978	Affirmed
1883	George Kinney	1915	The Finn	1947	Phalanx	1979	Coastal
1884	Panique	1916	Friar Rock	1948	Citation	1980	Temperence Hill
1885	Tyrant	1917	Hourless	1949	Capot	1981	Summing
1886	Inspector B.	1918	Johren	1950	Middleground	1982	Conquistador Cielo
1887	Hanover	1919	Sir Barton	1951	Counterpoint	1983	Caveat
1888	Sir Dixon	1920	Man o'War	1952	One Count	1984	Swale
1889	Eric	1921	Grey Lag	1953	Native Dancer	1985	Creme Fraiche
1890	Burlington	1922	Pillory	1954	High Gun	1986	Danzig Connection
1891	Foxford	1923	Zev	1955	Nashua	1987	Bet Twice
1892	Patron	1924	Mad Play	1956	Needles	1988	Risen Star
1893	Commanche	1925	American Flag	1957	Gallant Man	1989	Easy Goer
1894	Henry of Navarre	1926	Crusader	1958	Cavan	1990	Go and Go
1895	Belmar	1927	Chance Shot	1959	Sword Dancer	1991	Hansel
1896	Hastings	1928	Vito	1960	Celtic Ash	1992	A.P. Indy
1897	Scottish Chieftain	1929	Blue Larkspur	1961	Sherluck	1993	Colonial Affair
1898	Bowling Brook	1930	Gallant Fox	1962	Jaipur		

OUTSTANDING SEASON ■ THE GREATEST PRIZE MONEY EARNED IN A SINGLE SEASON BY A JOCKEY IS $14,877,298, BY JOSE SANTOS IN 1988. (NYRA)

TIMEOUT

WORST DISASTER 🐎 IN RECENT HISTORY, THE WORST SPORTS DISASTER OCCURRED AT THE HONG KONG JOCKEY CLUB RACECOURSE ON FEBRUARY 26, 1918. THE MAIN STAND COLLAPSED AND CAUGHT FIRE, KILLING 604 PEOPLE. IT IS REPORTED THAT 1,112 PEOPLE PERISHED WHEN THE UPPER TIERS OF THE CIRCUS MAXIMUS COLLAPSED DURING A GLADIATORIAL CONTEST. THE DATE OF THAT TRAGEDY IS UNKNOWN.

Single race The richest race in the United States is the Breeders' Cup Classic, which carries a purse of $3 million, with first-place prize money of $1,560,000 to the winner.

JOCKEYS

CAREER RECORDS

Most wins Bill Shoemaker rode a record 8,833 winners from 40,350 mounts. "The Shoe" made his debut aboard Waxahachie on March 19, 1949, and raced for the last time on Patchy Groundfog on February 3, 1990. His first victory came on April 20, 1949 aboard Shafter V, his last on January 20, 1990 aboard Beau Genius at Gulfstream Park, Fla.

SEASON RECORDS

Most wins Kent Desormeaux rode a season record 598 winners, from 2,312 mounts, in 1989.

Most wins (stakes races) Mike Smith rode a season record 62 stakes race winners in 1993.

DAILY RECORDS

Most wins (single day) The most winners ridden in one day is nine, by Chris Antley on October 31, 1987. Antley rode four winners in the afternoon at Aqueduct, N.Y. and five in the evening at The Meadowlands, N.J.

Most wins (one card) The most winners ridden on one card is eight, achieved by four jockeys: Hubert Jones, from 13 rides, at Caliente, Calif., on June 11, 1944; Dave Gall, from 10 rides, at Cahokia Downs, East St. Louis, Ill., on October 18, 1978; Robert Williams, from 10 rides, at Lincoln, Neb., on September 29, 1984; and Pat Day, from nine rides, at Arlington, Ill., on September 13, 1989.

Consecutive wins The longest consecutive winning streak by a jockey is nine races, by Albert Adams, at Marlboro Racetrack, Md., over three days, September 10–12, 1930. He won the last two races on September 10, all six races on September 11, and the first race on September 12; and Tony Black, July 30–31, 1993. Black won three races at Atlantic City Racecourse on July 30, two at Philadelphia Park on July 31 and four at Atlantic City on July 31.

HIGHEST EARNINGS

Career Laffit Pincay Jr. has won a career record $177,069,620 from 1964 through December 31, 1993.

Season The greatest prize money earned in a single season is $14,877,298, by Jose Santos in 1988.

JOCKEYS (WOMEN)

Most wins Julie Krone has won a record 2,766 races from 1980 through 1993.

TRIPLE FIRST ■ JULIE KRONE BECAME THE FIRST WOMAN TO WIN A TRIPLE CROWN RACE WHEN SHE RODE COLONIAL AFFAIR TO WIN THE 1993 BELMONT STAKES. (NYRA)

Highest earnings Julie Krone has won a record $53,922,226 from 1980 through 1993.

THE TRIPLE CROWN The races that make up the Triple Crown are the Kentucky Derby, the Preakness Stakes and the Belmont Stakes. The Triple Crown is for three-year-olds only and has been achieved by 11 horses.

BREEDERS' CUP CHAMPIONSHIP

The Breeders' Cup Championship has been staged annually since 1984. It was devised by John R. Gaines, a leading thoroughbred owner and breeder, to provide a season-ending championship for each division of thoroughbred racing. The Breeders' Cup Championship consists of seven races: Juvenile, Juvenile Fillies, Sprint, Mile, Distaff, Turf and the Classic, with a record purse of $10 million.

CHAMPIONSHIP RECORDS

HORSES

Most wins Three horses have won two Breeders' Cup races: Bayakoa, which won the Distaff in 1989

and 1990; Miesque, which won the Mile in 1987 and 1988; and Lure, which won the Mile in 1992 and 1993.

Highest earnings Alysheba has won a record $2,133,000 in Breeders' Cup races, from three starts, 1986–88.

JOCKEYS

Most wins Two jockeys have ridden seven winners in the Breeders' Cup Championship: Laffit Pincay Jr., Juvenile (1985, 1986, 1988), Classic (1986), Distaff (1989, 1990), Juvenile Fillies (1993); and Eddie Delahoussaye, Distaff (1984, 1993), Turf (1989), Juvenile Fillies (1991), Sprint (1992, 1993).

Highest earnings Pat Day has won a record $9,551,000 in Breeders' Cup racing, 1984–93.

BREEDERS' CUP CLASSIC This race, the principal event of the Breeders' Cup Championship, is run over 1¼ miles. The Classic offers a single-race record $3 million purse, with $1,560,000 to the winner.

LONGEST SHOT ■ PRICED AT 133–1, ARCANGUES WON THE 1993 BREEDER'S CUP CLASSIC, BECOMING THE LONGEST LONG SHOT TO WIN THE BREEDERS' CUP CLASSIC. (ALLSPORT/STEPHEN DUNN)

Most wins (horse) The Classic has been won by a different horse on each occasion.

Most wins (jockey) Three jockeys have won the Classic twice: Pat Day, 1984 and 1990; Chris Mc-Carron, 1988 and 1989; and Jerry Bailey, 1991 and 1993.

INTERNATIONAL RACES

VRC Melbourne Cup This contest, Australia's most prestigious classic race, has been staged annually since 1861. The race is run almost two miles at the Flemington Racetrack, Victoria.

Fastest time The fastest time is 3 minutes 16.3 seconds, by Kingston Rule, ridden by Darren Beadman in 1990.

Most wins (jockeys) Two jockeys have won the race four times: Bobby Lewis, 1902, 1915, 1919 and 1927; Harry White, 1974–75 and 1978–79.

Derby England's most prestigious classic race has been staged annually since 1780. The race is contested over 1 mile 4 furlongs at Epsom Downs, Surrey.

Fastest time The fastest time is 2 minutes 33.8 seconds, by Mahmoud, ridden by Charlie Smirke, in 1936. Kahyasi, ridden by Ray Cochrane, won the 1988 Derby in an electronically timed 2 minutes 33.84 seconds.

Most wins (jockey) Lester Piggott has won the Derby a record nine times: 1954, 1957, 1960, 1968, 1970, 1972, 1976–77 and 1983.

Grand National England's most famous steeplechase race, and most beloved sporting event, has been staged annually since 1839. The race is contested over a 4½ mile course of 30 fences at Aintree, Liverpool.

Fastest time The fastest time is 8 minutes 47.8 seconds, by Mr. Frisk, ridden by Marcus Armytage, in 1990.

Most wins (jockey) George Stevens won the National five times: 1856, 1863–64 and 1869–70.

Prix de l'Arc de Triomphe France's most prestigious classic race, and Europe's richest thoroughbred race, has been staged annually since 1920. The race is contested over 1 mile 864 yards at Longchamps, Paris.

Fastest time The fastest time is 2 minutes 26.3 seconds, by Trempolino, ridden by Pat Eddery, in 1987.

Most wins (jockey) Four jockeys have won the Arc four times: Jacques Doyasbere, 1942, 1944, 1950–51; Freddy Head, 1966, 1972, 1976, 1979; Yves Saint-Martin, 1970, 1974, 1982, 1984; Pat Eddery, 1980, 1985–87.

Irish Derby Ireland's most prestigious classic race has been staged annually since 1866. The race is contested over 1½ miles at The Curragh, County Kildare.

Fastest time The fastest time is 2 minutes 25.6 seconds, by St. Jovite, ridden by Christie Roche in 1992.

Most wins (jockey) Morny Wing has won the Irish Derby a record six times: 1921, 1923, 1930, 1938, 1942 and 1946.

HORSESHOE PITCHING

The object of the game of horseshoes is to toss a horseshoe over an iron stake so that it "comes to rest encircling the stake." The playing area, the horseshoe court, requires two stakes to be securely grounded 40 feet apart within a six-foot-square pitcher's box. Each contestant pitches two shoes in succession from the pitcher's box to the stake at the opposite end of the court. The pitching distance is 40 feet for men, and 30 feet for women. The winner is determined by a point system based on the shoe that is pitched closest

A SHOE-IN ☛ AT THE 1968 WORLD CHAMPIONSHIP, ELMER HOHL (CANADA) THREW 56 CONSECUTIVE RINGERS. THIS WAS THE LONGEST PERFECT GAME EVER IN A HORSESHOE-PITCHING CONTEST.

to the stake. The pitcher with the most points wins the contest.

ORIGINS Historians claim that a variation of horseshoe pitching was first played by Roman soldiers to relieve the monotony of guard duty. Horseshoes was introduced to North America by the first settlers, and every town had its own horseshoe courts and competitions. The game was a popular pastime for soldiers during the Revolutionary War, and the famed British officer the Duke of Wellington wrote in his memoirs that "The War was won by pitchers of horse hardware!" The modern sport of horseshoes dates to the formation of the National Horseshoe Pitcher's Association (NHPA) in 1914.

WORLD CHAMPIONSHIPS First staged in 1909, the tournament was staged intermittently until 1946; since then it has been an annual event.

Most titles (men) Ted Allen (U.S.) has won 10 world titles: 1933–35, 1940, 1946, 1953, 1955–57 and 1959.

Most titles (women) Vicki Winston (née Chappelle) has won a record 10 women's titles: 1956, 1958–59, 1961, 1963, 1966–67, 1969, 1975 and 1981.

Perfect game A perfect game consists of amassing 40 points throwing only ringers. In world championship play only three pitchers have thrown perfect games: Guy Zimmerman (U.S.) in 1948; Elmer Hohl (Canada) in 1968; and Jim Walters (U.S.) in 1993.

JUDO

ORIGINS Judo is a modern combat sport that developed from an amalgam of several old Japanese martial arts, the most popular of which was jujitsu (jiujitsu), which is thought to be of Chinese origin. Judo has developed greatly since 1882, when it was first devised by Dr. Jigoro Kano. The International Judo Federation was founded in 1951.

Highest grades The efficiency grades in judo are divided into pupil (*kyu*) and master (*dan*) grades. The highest grade awarded is the extremely rare red belt *judan* (10th dan), given to only 13 men so far. The judo protocol provides for an 11th dan (*juichidan*) who also would wear a red belt, a 12th dan (*junidan*) who would wear a white belt twice as wide as an ordinary belt, and the highest of all, *shihan* (doctor), but these have never been bestowed, save for the 12th dan, to the founder of the sport, Dr. Jigoro Kano.

OLYMPIC GAMES Judo was first included in the Games in 1964 in Tokyo, Japan, and has been included in every Games since 1972. Women's events were first included as official events at the Barcelona Games in 1992.

IMPORTANT MATTERS ■ DR. JIGORO KANO DEVISED JUDO IN 1882, BUT WORLD CHAMPIONSHIPS WERE FIRST STAGED IN 1956. THE 1993 TOURNEY (SHOWN HERE) WAS HELD IN ONTARIO, CANADA. (ALLSPORT/GRAY MORTIMORE))

Most gold medals Four men have won two gold medals: Willem Ruska (Netherlands), open class and over 93 kilograms class, in 1972; Hiroshi Saito (Japan), over 95 kilograms class, in 1984 and 1988; Peter Seisenbacher (Austria), up to 86 kilograms class, in 1984 and 1988; and Waldemar Legien (Poland), up to 78 kilograms class, in 1988 and up to 86 kilograms class, in 1992.

Most medals (individual) Angelo Parisi has won a record four Olympic medals, while representing two countries. In 1972 Parisi won a bronze medal in the open class, representing Great Britain. In 1980 Parisi represented France and won a gold, over 95 kilograms class, and a silver, open class; and won a second silver in the open class in 1984.

WORLD CHAMPIONSHIPS The first men's world championships were held in Tokyo, Japan in 1956. The event has been staged biennially since 1965. A world championship for women was first staged in New York City in 1980.

Most titles (men) Three men have won four world titles: Yasuhiro Yamashita (Japan), open class, 1981; over 95 kilograms class, 1979, 1981, 1983; Shozo Fujii (Japan), under 80 kilograms class, 1971, 1973, 1975; under 78 kilograms class, 1979; and Naoya Ogawa (Japan), open class, 1987, 1989, 1991 and over 95 kilograms class, 1989.

Most titles (women) Ingrid Berghmans (Belgium) has won a record six world titles: open class, 1980, 1982, 1984 and 1986; under 72 kilograms class, 1984 and 1989.

JUDO THROWS ☛ LEE FINNEY AND GARY FOSTER (BOTH GREAT BRITAIN) COMPLETED 27,083 THROWING MOVES IN 10 HOURS AT THE FOREST JUDO CLUB, LEICESTER, ENGLAND ON SEPTEMBER 25, 1993.

KARATE

ORIGINS Karate is a martial art developed in Japan. Karate (empty hand) techniques evolved from the Chinese art of shoalin boxing, known as kempo, which was popularized in Okinawa in the 16th century as a means of self-defense, and became known as Tang Hand. Tang Hand was introduced to Japan by Funakoshi Gichin in the 1920s, and the name karate was coined in the 1930s. Gichin's style of karate, known as shotokan, is one of five major styles adapted for competition, the others being wado-ryu, gojuryu, shito-ryu and kyokushinkai. Each style places different emphasis on the elements of technique, speed and power. Karate's popularity grew in the West in the late 1950s.

WORLD CHAMPIONSHIPS The first men's world championships were staged in Tokyo, Japan in 1970; a women's competition was first staged in 1980. Both tournaments are now staged biennially. The competition consists of two types: kumite, in which combatants fight each other, and kata events, in which contestants perform routines.

KUMITE CHAMPIONSHIPS (MEN)

Most titles (team) Great Britain has won six kumite world team titles, in 1975, 1982, 1984, 1986, 1988 and 1990.

Most titles (individual) Four men have won two individual world titles: Pat McKay (Great Britain) in the under 80 kilograms class, 1982, 1984; Emmanuel Pinda (France), in the open class, 1984, and the over 80 kilograms class, 1988; Theirry Masci (France), in the under 70 kilograms class, 1986, 1988; Jose Manuel Egea (Spain), in the under 80 kilograms class, 1990, 1992.

KATA CHAMPIONSHIPS (MEN)

Most titles (team) Japan has won two kata world team titles, in 1986 and 1988.

Most titles (individual) Tsuguo Sakumoto (Japan) has won three world titles, in 1984, 1986 and 1988.

KUMITE CHAMPIONSHIPS (WOMEN)

Most titles (individual) Guus van Mourik (Netherlands) has won four world titles in the over 60 kilograms class, in 1982, 1984, 1986 and 1988.

KATA CHAMPIONSHIPS (WOMEN)

Most titles (individual) Mie Nakayama (Japan) has won three world titles, in 1982, 1984 and 1986.

LACROSSE

LACROSSE (MEN)

ORIGINS The sport is of Native American origin, derived from the intertribal game of *baggataway*, which has been recorded as being played by Iroquois tribes as early as 1492. French settlers in North America coined the name "La Crosse" (the French word for a crozier or staff). The National Lacrosse Association was formed in Canada in 1867. The United States Amateur Lacrosse Association was founded in 1879. The International Federation of Amateur Lacrosse (IFAL) was founded in 1928.

WORLD CHAMPIONSHIPS The men's world championships were first staged in Toronto, Canada in 1967.

Most titles The United States has won five world titles, in 1967, 1974, 1982, 1986 and 1990.

NCAA CHAMPIONSHIPS (DIVISION I) The men's NCAA championship was first staged in 1971.

Most titles Johns Hopkins has won seven lacrosse titles, in 1974, 1978–80, 1984–85 and 1987.

LACROSSE (WOMEN)

ORIGINS Women were first reported to have played lacrosse in 1886. The women's game evolved separately from the men's, developing different rules; thus two distinct games were created: the women's game features 12-a-side and six-a-side games, while men's games field 10-a-side teams.

WORLD CHAMPIONSHIPS A women's world championship was first held in 1969. Since 1982 the world championships have been known as the World Cup.

Most titles The United States has won four world titles, in 1974, 1982, 1989, and 1993.

NCAA CHAMPIONSHIPS (DIVISION I) The NCAA first staged a women's national championship in 1982.

Most titles Three teams have won two titles: Temple, 1984 and 1988; Penn State, 1987 and 1989; and Maryland, 1986 and 1992.

MODERN PENTATHLON

ORIGINS The modern pentathalon is comprised of five activities: fencing, horseback riding, pistol shooting, swimming and cross-country running. The sport derives from military training in the 19th century, which was based on a messenger's being able to travel across country on horseback, fighting his way through with sword and pistol, and being prepared to swim across rivers and complete his journey on foot. Each event is scored on points, determined either against other contestants or against scoring tables. There is no standard course; therefore, point totals are not comparable. *L'Union Internationale de Pentathlon Moderne* (UIPM) was formed in 1948 and expanded to include the administration of the biathlon in 1957. (For further information on the biathlon, see pages 56–57.)

United States The United States Modern Pentathlon and Biathlon Association was established in 1971, but this body was split to create the U.S. Modern Pentathlon Association in 1978.

OLYMPIC GAMES Modern pentathlon was first included in the 1912 Games held in Stockholm, Sweden, and has been part of every Olympic program since.

Most gold medals Andras Balczo (Hungary) has won three gold medals in Olympic competition: team event, 1960 and 1968; individual title, 1972.

Most gold medals (team event) Two countries have won the team event four times: Hungary, 1952, 1960, 1968 and 1988; USSR, 1956, 1964, 1972 and 1980.

Most medals (individual) Pavel Lednev (USSR) has won a record seven medals in Olympic competition: two gold—team event, 1972 and 1980; two silver—team event, 1968; individual event, 1976; and three bronze—individual event, 1968, 1972 and 1980.

WORLD CHAMPIONSHIPS An official men's world championship was first staged in 1949, and has been held annually since. In Olympic years the Games are considered the world championships, and results from those events are included in world championship statistics. A women's world championship was inaugurated in 1981.

MEN'S CHAMPIONSHIP

Most titles (overall) Andras Balczo (Hungary) has won a record 13 world titles, including a record six individual titles: seven team, 1960, 1963, 1965–68 and 1970; six individual, 1963, 1965–67, 1969 and 1972.

Most titles (team event) The USSR has won 17 world championships: 1956–59, 1961–62, 1964, 1969, 1971–74, 1980, 1982–83, 1985 and 1991.

United States The United States won its only team world title in 1979, when Bob Nieman became the first American athlete, and so far the only man, to win an individual world championship.

WOMEN'S CHAMPIONSHIP

Most titles (individual event) Eva Fjellerup (Denmark) is the only woman to win the individual title three times, in 1990, 1991 and 1993.

Most titles (team event) Poland has won five world titles: 1985, 1988–91.

United States The best result for the U.S. in the team event is second place, which has been achieved twice, in 1981 and 1989. Lori Norwood won the individual championship in 1989.

UNITED STATES NATIONAL CHAMPIONSHIPS The men's championship was inaugurated in 1955, and the women's in 1977.

Most titles (men) Mike Burley has won four men's titles, in 1977, 1979, 1981 and 1985.

Most titles (women) Kim Arata (née Dunlop) has won nine titles, in 1979–80, 1984–89 and 1991.

MOTORCYCLE RACING

ORIGINS The first recorded motorcycle race took place in France on September 20, 1896, when eight riders took part in a 139-mile race from Paris to Nantes and back. The winner was M. Chevalier on a Michelin-Dion tricycle; he covered the course in 4 hours 10 minutes 37 seconds. The first race for two-wheeled motorcycles was held on a one-mile oval track at Sheen House, Richmond, England on November 29, 1897. The *Fédération Internationale Motorcycliste* (FIM) was founded in 1904 and is the world governing body.

WORLD CHAMPIONSHIPS The FIM instituted world championships in 1949 for 125, 250, 350 and 500cc classes. In 1962, a 50cc class was intro-

WORLD CHAMPION ■ THE MOST WORLD MOTORCYCLE TITLES WON BY AN AMERICAN RACER IS FOUR, BY EDDIE LAWSON. (ALLSPORT/VANDYSTADT)

duced, which was upgraded to 80cc in 1983. In 1982, the 350cc class was discontinued.

Most Championships

Overall 15, by Giacomo Agostini (Italy): 7—350cc (1968–74); 8—500cc (1966–72, 1975).

50cc 6, by Angel Nieto (Spain), 1969–70, 1972, 1975–77.

80cc 3, by Jorge Martinez (Spain), 1986–88.

125cc 7, by Angel Nieto (Spain), 1971–72, 1979, 1981–84.

250cc 4, by Phil Read (Great Britain), 1964–65, 1968, 1971.

350cc 7, by Giacomo Agostini (Italy), 1968–74.

500cc 8, by Giacomo Agostini (Italy), 1966–72, 1975.

Multiple titles The only rider to win more than one world championship in one year is Freddie Spencer (U.S.), who won the 250cc and 500cc titles in 1985.

United States The most world titles won by an American rider is four, by Eddie Lawson at 500cc in 1984, 1986, 1988–89.

Most Grand Prix Wins

Overall 122, by Giacomo Agostini (Italy): 54—350cc; 68—500cc.

50cc 27, by Angel Nieto (Spain).

80cc 21, by Jorge Martinez (Spain).

125cc 62, by Angel Nieto (Spain).

250cc 33, by Anton Mang (West Germany).

350cc 54, by Giacomo Agostini (Italy).

500cc 68, by Giacomo Agostini (Italy).

Most successful machines Japanese Yamaha machines won 45 world championships between 1964 and 1993.

Fastest circuits The highest average lap speed attained on any closed circuit is 160.288 mph, by Yvon du Hamel (Canada) on a modified 903cc four-cylinder Kawasaki Z1 at the 31-degree banked 2.5 mile Daytona International Speedway, Fla. in March 1973. His lap time was 56.149 seconds.

The fastest road circuit was the Francorchamps circuit near Spa, Belgium, then 8.74 miles long. It was lapped in 3 minutes 50.3 seconds (average speed 137.150 mph) by Barry Sheene (Great Britain) on a 495cc four-cylinder Suzuki during the Belgian Grand Prix on July 3, 1977. On that occasion he set a record time for this 10-lap (87.74-mile) race of 38 minutes 58.5 seconds (average speed 135.068 mph).

OLYMPIC GAMES

Records in this section include results from the Intercalated Games staged in 1906.

ORIGINS The exact date of the first Olympic Games is uncertain. The earliest date for which there is documented evidence is July 776 B.C. By order of Theodosius I, emperor of Rome, the Games were prohibited in A.D. 394. The revival of the Olympic Games is credited to Pierre de Fredi, Baron de Coubertin, a French aristocrat, who was commissioned by his government to form a universal sports association in 1889. Coubertin presented his proposals for a modern Games on November 25, 1892 in Paris; this led to the formation of the International Olympic Committee (IOC) in 1894 and thence to the staging of the first modern Olympic Games, which were opened in Athens, Greece on April 6, 1896. In 1906, the IOC organized the Intercalated Games in Athens, to celebrate the 10th anniversary of the revival of the Games. In 1924, the first Winter Olympics were held in Chamonix, France.

OLYMPIC GAMES MEDAL RECORDS

INDIVIDUAL RECORDS

Most gold medals Ray Ewry (U.S.) has won 10 gold medals in Olympic competition: standing high jump, 1900, 1904, 1906 and 1908; standing long jump, 1900, 1904, 1906 and 1908; standing triple jump, 1900 and 1904. The most gold medals won by a woman is nine, by gymnast Larissa Latynina (USSR): all-around, 1956 and 1960; vault, 1956; floor exercise, 1956, 1960 and 1964; team title, 1956, 1960 and 1964.

Most medals Gymnast Larissa Latynina (USSR) has won 18 medals (nine gold, five silver and four bronze), 1956–64. The most medals won by a man is 15 (seven gold, five silver and three bronze), by gymnast Nikolai Andrianov (USSR), 1972–80.

Most gold medals at one Olympics Swimmer Mark Spitz (U.S.) won a record seven gold medals at Munich in 1972. His victories came in the 100-meter freestyle, 200-meter freestyle, 100-meter butterfly, 200-meter butterfly, and three relay events. The most gold medals won at one Games by a woman athlete is six, by swimmer Kristin Otto (East Germany), who won six gold medals at the 1988 Games. Her victories came in the 50-meter freestyle, 100-meter freestyle, 100-meter backstroke, 100-meter butterfly, and two relay events. The most individual events won at one Games is five, by speed skater Eric Heiden (U.S.) in 1980. Heiden won the 500 meters, 1,000 meters, 1,500 meters, 5,000 meters, and 10,000 meters.

Most medals at one Olympics Gymnast Aleksandr Dityatin (USSR) won eight medals (three gold, four silver and one bronze) at Moscow, USSR in 1980. The most medals won by a woman athlete is seven (two gold and five silver), by gymnast Maria Gorokhovskaya (USSR) in 1952.

Most consecutive gold medals (same event) Al Oerter (U.S.) is the only athlete to win the same event, the discus, at four consecutive Games, 1956–68. Yachtsman Paul Elvstrom (Denmark) won four successive golds at monotype events, 1948–60, but there was a class change: Firefly in 1948; Finn class, 1952–60. Including the Intercalated Games of 1906, Ray Ewry (U.S.) won four consecutive gold medals in two events: standing high jump, 1900–1908; standing long jump, 1900–1908.

Oldest gold medalist Oscar Swahn (Sweden) was aged 64 years 258 days when he won an Olympic gold medal in 1912 as a member of the team that won the running deer shooting single-shot title. The oldest woman to win a gold medal was Queenie Newall

(Great Britain), who won the 1908 national round archery event at age 53 years 275 days.

Youngest gold medalist The youngest-ever winner was an unnamed French boy who coxed the Netherlands pair to victory in the 1900 rowing event. He was believed to be 7–10 years old. The youngest-ever woman champion was Marjorie Gestring (U.S.), who at age 13 years 268 days won the 1936 women's springboard diving event.

Most Games Three Olympians have competed in eight Games: show jumper Raimondo d'Inzeo (Italy), 1948–76; yachtsman Paul Elvstrom (Den-

mark), 1948–60, 1968–72, 1984–88; yachtsman Durwood Knowles (Great Britain/Bahamas), 1948–72, 1988. The most appearances by a woman is seven, by fencer Kerstin Palm (Sweden), 1964–88.

Summer/Winter Games gold medalist The only person to have won gold medals in both Summer and Winter Olympiads is Edward Eagan (U.S.), who won the 1920 light-heavyweight boxing title and was a member of the 1932 winning four-man bobsled team.

Summer/Winter Games medalist (same year) The only athlete to have won medals at both the Winter and Summer Games held in the same year is

SUMMER OLYMPIC GAMES MEDAL WINNERS (1896–1992)

Country	Gold	Silver	Bronze	Total	Country	Gold	Silver	Bronze	Total
United States	789	603	518	1,910	Greece	24	40	39	103
USSR[1]	442	361	333	1,136	South Korea	31	27	41	99
Germany[2]	186	227	236	649	Yugoslavia[5]	26	30	30	86
Great Britain	177	224	218	619	Cuba	36	25	23	84
France	161	175	191	527	Austria	19	29	33	81
Sweden	133	149	171	453	New Zealand	27	10	28	65
East Germany[3]	154	131	126	411	South Africa	16	17	20	53
Italy	153	126	131	410	Turkey	26	15	12	53
Hungary	136	124	144	404	Argentina	13	19	15	47
Finland	98	77	112	287	Spain	17	19	10	46
Japan	90	83	93	266	Mexico	9	13	18	40
Australia	78	76	98	252	Brazil	9	10	21	40
Romania	59	70	90	219	Kenya	13	13	13	39
Poland	43	62	105	210	Iran	4	12	17	33
Canada	45	67	80	192	Jamaica	4	13	9	26
Netherlands	45	52	72	169	Estonia[6]	7	6	10	23
Switzerland	42	63	58	163	North Korea[7]	6	5	10	21
Bulgaria	38	69	55	162	Egypt	6	6	6	18
Czechoslovakia[4]	49	50	49	148	Ireland	5	5	5	15
Denmark	26	51	53	130	India	8	3	3	14
Belgium	35	47	44	126	Portugal	2	4	7	13
China	36	41	37	114	Mongolia	0	5	8	13
Norway	43	37	34	114	Ethiopia	6	1	6	13

[1] Includes Czarist Russia; Unified Team (1992)
[2] Germany 1896–1964, 1992; West Germany 1968–88
[3] 1968–88
[4] Includes Bohemia
[5] Includes I.O.P. (1992)
[6] Estonia and Latvia up to 1936
[7] North Korea from 1964

Christa Rothenburger-Luding (East Germany). At the 1988 Winter Games in Calgary, Canada, Rothenburger-Luding won two speed skating medals: gold medal, 1,000 meters, and silver medal, 500 meters; and at the Seoul Games that summer she won a silver medal in the women's sprint cycling event.

UNITED STATES RECORDS

Most gold medals The records for most gold medals overall and at one Games are both held by American athletes (see above). The most gold medals won by an American woman is four, by three athletes: Patricia McCormick (née Keller), diving, 1952–1956; Evelyn Ashford, track and field, 1984–92; Janet Evans, swimming, 1988–92.

Most medals The most medals won by an American Olympian is 11, by three athletes: Carl Osburn, shooting—five gold, four silver and two bronze (1912–24); Mark Spitz, swimming—nine gold, one silver and one bronze (1968–72); Matt Biondi, swimming—eight golds, two silver and one bronze (1984–92). The most medals won by an

SUMMER OLYMPIC GAMES MEDAL WINNERS (1896–1992) (cont.)

Country	Gold	Silver	Bronze	Total	Country	Gold	Silver	Bronze	Total
Pakistan	3	3	4	10	Tanzania	0	2	0	2
Morocco	4	2	3	9	Cameroon	0	1	1	2
Uruguay	2	1	6	9	Haiti	0	1	1	2
Venezuela	1	2	5	8	Iceland	0	1	1	2
Chile	0	6	2	8	Israel	0	1	1	2
Nigeria	0	4	4	8	Panama	0	0	2	2
Philippines	0	1	7	8	Slovenia	0	0	2	2
Trinidad	1	2	4	7	Zimbabwe	1	0	0	1
Indonesia	2	3	1	6	Costa Rica	0	1	0	1
Latvia[8]	0	4	2	6	Ivory Coast	0	1	0	1
Colombia	0	2	4	6	Netherlands Antilles	0	1	0	1
Uganda	1	3	1	5	Senegal	0	1	0	1
Puerto Rico	0	1	4	5	Singapore	0	1	0	1
Tunisia	1	2	2	5	Sri Lanka	0	1	0	1
Peru	1	3	0	4	Syria	0	1	0	1
Algeria	1	0	3	4	Virgin Islands	0	1	0	1
Lebanon	0	2	2	4	Barbados	0	0	1	1
Taipei (Taiwan)	0	2	2	4	Bermuda	0	0	1	1
Ghana	0	1	3	4	Djibouti	0	0	1	1
Thailand	0	1	3	4	Dominican Republic	0	0	1	1
Bahamas	1	0	2	3	Guyana	0	0	1	1
Croatia	0	1	2	3	Iraq	0	0	1	1
Luxembourg	1	1	0	2	Malaysia	0	0	1	1
Lithuania	1	0	1	2	Niger	0	0	1	1
Suriname	1	0	1	2	Qatar	0	0	1	1
Namibia	0	2	0	2	Zambia	0	0	1	1

[8] Estonia and Latvia up to 1936

American woman is eight, by Shirley Babashoff, swimming—two gold and six silver (1972–76).

Oldest gold medalist The oldest U.S. Olympic champion was Galen Spencer, who won a gold medal in the Team Round archery event in 1904, at age 64 years 2 days.

Youngest gold medalist The youngest gold medalist was Jackie Fields, who won the 1924 featherweight boxing title at age 16 years 162 days.

Oldest medalist The oldest U.S. medalist was Samuel Duvall, who was a member of the 1904 silver-medal-winning team in the team round archery event, at age 68 years 194 days.

Youngest medalist The youngest American medal winner, and the youngest-ever participant, was Dorothy Poynton, who won a silver medal in springboard diving at the 1928 Games at age 13 years 23 days. The youngest men's medalist was Donald Douglas Jr., who won a silver medal at six-meter yachting in 1932, at age 15 years 40 days.

Most games Equestrian Michael Plumb has participated in seven Olympics, 1960–76, 1984 and 1992. He was selected for the 1980 team, but the Moscow Games were boycotted by the U.S. Fencer Janice Romary has appeared in six Games, 1948–68, the most for an American woman.

WINTER GAMES MEDAL RECORDS

INDIVIDUAL RECORDS

Most gold medals Speed skater Lydia Skoblikova (USSR) has won six gold medals in Winter Games competition: 500 meters, 1964; 1,000 meters, 1964; 1,500 meters, 1960–64; 3,000 meters, 1960–64. The most gold medals won by a man is five, by two speed skaters: Clas Thunberg (Finland), 500 meters, 1928; 1,500 meters, 1924–28; 5,000 meters, 1924; all-around title, 1924; Eric Heiden (U.S.), 500, 1,000, 1,500, 5,000 and 10,000 meters, all in 1980.

Most medals Cross-country skier Raisa Smetanina (USSR/Unified Team) has won 10 medals (four gold, five silver and one bronze), 1976–92. The most medals won by a man is nine (four gold, three silver and two bronze), by cross-country skier Sixten Jernberg (Sweden), 1956–64.

Oldest gold medalist Jay O'Brien (U.S.) was aged 48 years 359 days when he won an Olympic gold medal in 1932 in the 4-man bobsled event. The oldest woman to win a gold medal was Raisa Smetanina (Unified Team), who was a member of the 1992 4 x 5 km relay team at age 39 years 352 days.

Youngest gold medalist Maxi Herber (Germany) was aged 15 years 128 days when she won the 1936 figure skating title. The youngest-ever men's champion was Toni Neiminen (Finland), who at age 16 years 259 days was a member of the winning ski jumping team in 1992.

WINTER OLYMPIC GAMES MEDAL WINNERS (1924–1992)

Country	Gold	Silver	Bronze	Total
USSR[1]	88	63	67	218
Norway	63	66	59	188
United States	47	50	37	134
Austria	34	45	40	119
Finland	36	44	37	117
East Germany[2]	39	36	35	110
Germany[3]	36	36	29	101
Sweden	37	25	34	96
Switzerland	24	25	27	76
Canada	16	15	20	51
France	16	15	17	48
Italy	18	16	13	47
Netherlands	14	18	14	46
Czechoslovakia[4]	2	8	16	26
Great Britain	7	4	10	21
Japan	2	6	6	14
Liechtenstein	2	2	5	9
Hungary	0	2	4	6
South Korea	2	1	1	4
Belgium	1	1	2	4
Poland	1	1	2	4
Yugoslavia	0	3	1	4
China	0	3	0	3
Spain	1	0	1	2
Luxembourg	0	2	0	2
North Korea[5]	0	1	1	2
New Zealand	0	1	0	1
Bulgaria	0	0	1	1
Romania	0	0	1	1

[1] Includes Unified Team (1992)

[2] 1968–82

[3] Germany 1924–64, 1992, West Germany from 1968–88

[4] Includes Bohemia

[5] North Korea from 1964

ORIENTEERING

Orienteering combines cross-country running with compass and map navigation. The object of the sport is for the competitor to navigate across a set course in the fastest time possible using a topographical map and a compass. The course contains designated locations called controls, identified by orange and white markers, which the runner must find and identify on a punch card that is handed to the official timer at the end of the race.

ORIGINS Orienteering can be traced to Scandinavia at the turn of the 20th century. Major Ernst Killander (Sweden) is regarded as the father of the sport, having organized the first large race in Saltsjobaden, Sweden in 1919. The Swedish federation, *Svenska Orienteringsforbundet*, was founded in 1936. The International Orienteering Federation was established in 1961.

United States Orienteering was introduced to the U.S. in the 1940s. The first U.S. Orienteering Championships were held on October 17, 1970. The U.S. Orienteering Federation (USOF) was founded on August 1, 1971.

WORLD CHAMPIONSHIPS The world championships were first held in 1966 in Fiskars, Finland, and are held biennially.

Most titles (relay) The men's relay has been won a record seven times by Norway—1970, 1978, 1981, 1983, 1985, 1987 and 1989. Sweden has won the women's relay 10 times—1966, 1970, 1974, 1976, 1981, 1983, 1985, 1989, 1991, and 1993.

YOUNGEST CHAMPION ■ IN 1992 SKI JUMPER TONI NEIMINEN BECAME THE YOUNGEST MEN'S CHAMPION IN WINTER GAMES HISTORY. (ALLSPORT)

BALANCED INDIVIDUALS

Hand–eye coordination, stamina, courage and quick wits are just a few of the qualities required by an outstanding athlete. Another essential attribute is an innate sense of balance. Highlighted here are some activities that require physical balancing skills.

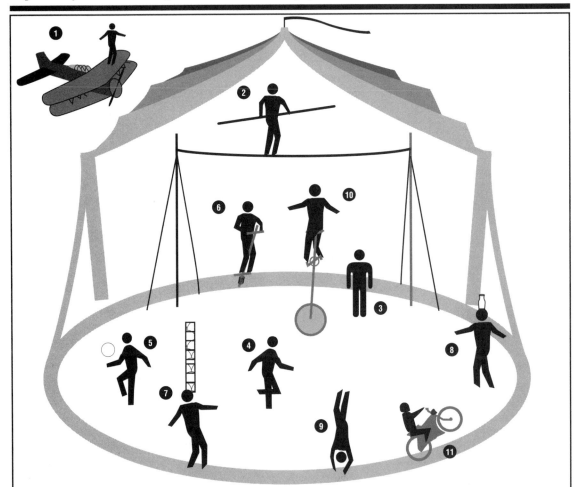

1. Wing-walking • Roy Castle (G.B.) flew on the wing of a Boeing Stearman biplane for 3 hrs 23 min on August 2, 1990. Castle flew from London, England to Paris, France. *2. Tightrope walking* • In Orlando, Fl., Jorge Ojeda–Guzman (U.S.) stayed on a tightrope continuously for 205 days from January 1–July 25, 1993. The 36-foot-long tightrope was strung 35 feet above the ground. *3. Standing still* • Antonio Gomes dos Santos (Portugal) stood motionless for 15 hrs 2 min 55 sec at the Amoreiras Shopping Centre, Lisbon, Portugal on July 30, 1988. *4. Balancing on one foot* • Girish Sharma (India) balanced on one foot for 55 hrs 35 min at Deori, India from October 2–4, 1992. *5. Soccer ball juggling* • Huh Nam Jin (South Korea) juggled a soccer ball for 17 hrs 10 min 57 sec non-stop without the ball touching the ground at Seoul, South Korea on May 24, 1991. *6. Pogo stick jumping* • The greatest number of jumps achieved is 177,737 by Gary Stewart (U.S.) at Huntington Beach, Ca., on May 25–26, 1992. *7. Milk crate balancing* • Terry Cole (G.B.) balanced 25 crates on his chin for 10.3 seconds in London, England on July 28, 1991. *8. Milk bottle balancing* • The greatest distance walked balancing a milk bottle on the head is 70 miles by Ashrita Furman (U.S.) on July 20, 1993 in New York City. *9. Walking on hands* • Shin Don-mok (South Korea) completed the 50 meter dash, walking on his hands, in 17.44 seconds on November 14, 1986. *10. Tallest unicycle* • Steve McPeak (U.S.) rode a 101 foot 9 inch tall unicycle 376 feet at Las Vegas, Nv., in October 1980.* *11. Longest wheelie* • The longest wheelie ever performed is 205.7 miles by Yasuyuki Kudoh (Japan) on a Honda TLM220R motorcycle at Tsukuba, Japan on May 5, 1991.

*This feat was performed while wearing a safety harness.

Most titles (individual) Three women's individual titles have been won by Annichen Kringstad (Sweden), in 1981, 1983 and 1985. The men's title has been won twice by three men: Age Hadler (Norway), in 1966 and 1972; Egil Johansen (Norway), in 1976 and 1978; and Oyvin Thon (Norway), in 1979 and 1981.

UNITED STATES NATIONAL CHAMPIONSHIPS First held on October 17, 1970, the nationals are held annually.

Most titles Sharon Crawford, New England Orienteering Club, has won a record 11 overall women's titles: 1977–82, 1984–87, and 1989. The men's title has been won six times by Mikell Platt, Blue Star Komplex Orienteering Club, 1986, 1988–92.

PARACHUTING

ORIGINS The sport of parachuting traces its origins to the early 20th century, when daredevils performed parachute stunts at fairs and carnivals across America. Target jumping contests were first organized in the 1930s. In 1952 the sport was organized internationally by the *Federation Aeronautique Internationale*. The sport is now contested in two main formats: target jumping and display formation.

WORLD CHAMPIONSHIPS

Most wins (team) The USSR won seven men's world titles, 1954, 1958, 1960, 1966, 1972, 1976 and 1980; and six women's world titles, 1956, 1958, 1966, 1968, 1972, 1976.

YOU ARE NEVER TOO OLD ☞ THE OLDEST PERSON TO PARACHUTE JUMP IS GEORGE SAYLER. ON JUNE 18, 1992, AT AGE 91 YEARS, HE PERFORMED A TANDEM PARACHUTE JUMP OVER SNOHOMISH, WASH.

Most wins (individual) Nikolay Ushamyev (USSR) is the only jumper to have won two world titles, 1974 and 1980.

POLO

The object of the game is to score in the opponent's goals, the goalposts being eight yards wide, with the team scoring the most goals winning the game. Each side fields a team of four players; the game is played over six periods of seven minutes' duration each. A period is known as a chukka, and players must change their mount after each chukka.

ORIGINS Polo originated in Central Asia, possibly as early as 3100 B.C., in the state of Manipur. The name is derived from the Tibetan word *pulu*. The modern era began in India in the 1850s when British army officers were introduced to the game. The Cachar Club, Assam, India was founded in 1859, and is believed to be the first polo club of the modern era. The game was introduced in England in 1869. The world governing body, the Hurlingham Polo Association, was founded in London, England in 1874 and drew up the laws of the game in 1875.

United States Polo was introduced to the U.S. by James Gordon Bennett in 1876, when he arranged for the first indoor game at Dickel's Riding Academy, N.Y. The first game played outdoors was held on May 13, 1876 at the Jerome Park Racetrack in Westchester County, N.Y. The oldest existing polo club in the United States is Meadow Brook Polo Club, Jericho, N.Y., founded in 1879. The United States Polo Association was formed on March 21, 1890.

UNITED STATES OPEN POLO CHAMPIONSHIP The U.S. Open was first staged in 1904 and is an annual event.

Most wins The Meadow Brook Polo Club, Jericho, N.Y. has won the U.S. Open 28 times: 1916, 1920, 1923–41, 1946–51, and 1953.

Highest score The highest aggregate number of goals scored in an international match is 30, when Argentina beat the U.S. 21–9 at Meadowbrook, Long Island, N.Y. in September 1936.

Highest handicap Polo players are assigned handicaps based on their skill, with a 10 handicap being the highest level of play. Only 56 players have been awarded the 10 goal handicap.

40-goal games There have only been three games staged between two 40-goal handicap teams. These games were staged in Argentina in 1975, United States in 1990 and Australia in 1991.

POOL

ORIGINS Pool traces its ancestry to billiards, an English game introduced in Virginia in the late 17th century. During the 19th century the game evolved from one in which a mace was used to push balls around a table, to a game of precise skill using a cue, with the aim of pocketing numbered balls. The original form of pool in the United States was known as pyramid pool, with the object being to pocket eight out of the 15 balls on the table. From this game, "61-pool" evolved: each of the 15 balls was worth points equal to its numerical value; the first player to score 61 points was the winner. In 1878 the first world championship was staged under the rules of 61-pool. In 1910, Jerome Keogh suggested that the rules be adjusted to make the game faster and more attractive; he proposed that the last ball be left free on the table to be used as a target on the next rack; the result was 14.1 continuous pool (also known as American straight pool). The game of 14.1 was adopted as the championship form of pool from 1912 onwards. In the last 20 years, nine-ball pool and eight-ball pool have surpassed 14.1 in popularity. In 1990 the World Pool Billiard Association inaugurated the nine-ball world championship.

14.1 CONTINUOUS POOL (ALSO KNOWN AS AMERICAN STRAIGHT POOL)

WORLD CHAMPIONSHIPS The first official world championship was held in April 1912 and was won by Edward Ralph (U.S.).

Most titles Two players have won the world title six times: Ralph Greenleaf (U.S.) and Willie Mosconi (U.S.). From 1919–37, Greenleaf won the title six times and defended it 13 times. Between 1941 and 1956, Mosconi also won the title six times and defended it 13 times.

Longest consecutive run The longest consecutive run in 14.1 recognized by the Billiard Con-

gress of America (BCA) is 526 balls, by Willie Mosconi in March 1954 during an exhibition in Springfield, Ohio. Michael Eufemia is reported to have pocketed 625 balls at Logan's Billiard Academy in Brooklyn, N.Y. on February 2, 1960; however, this run has never been ratified by the BCA.

NINE-BALL POOL

WORLD CHAMPIONSHIP In this competition, inaugurated in 1990, Earl Strickland (U.S.) has won the men's title twice, 1990–1991. Robin Bell (U.S.) has won the women's title twice, 1990–91.

POWERBOAT RACING

ORIGINS A gasoline engine was first installed in a boat by Jean Lenoir on the River Seine, Paris, France in 1865. Organized powerboat races were first run at the turn of the 20th century. The first major international competition was the Harnsworth Trophy, launched in 1903. Modern powerboat racing is broken down into two main types: circuit racing in sheltered waterways, and offshore racing. Offshore events were initially for displacement (nonplaning) cruisers, but in 1958 the 170-mile Miami, Fla.-to-Nassau, Bahamas race was staged for planing cruisers.

United States The American Power Boat Association (APBA) was founded on April 22, 1903 in New York City. In 1913 the APBA issued the "Racing Commission" rules, which created its powers for governing the sport in North America. In 1924 the APBA set rules for boats propelled by outboard detachable motors and became the governing body for both inboard and outboard racing in North America. The APBA is currently based in Eastpointe, Mich.

APBA GOLD CUP The APBA held its first Gold Cup race at the Columbia Yacht Club on the Hudson River, N.Y. in 1904, when the winner was *Standard*, piloted by C. C. Riotto at an average speed of 23.6 mph.

Most wins (driver) The most wins is nine, by Chip Hanauer, 1982–88 and 1992–93.

Most wins (boat) The most successful boat has been *Miss Budweiser* with nine wins, driven by Bill Sterett Sr. in 1969; by Dean Chenoweth in 1970,

FULL THROTTLE ■ CHIP HANAUER'S 1993 APBA GOLD CUP WIN WAS HIS RECORD NINTH TRIUMPH IN THE EVENT. (ALLSPORT/CARYN LEVY)

POWERBOAT SPEED RECORDS

The following is a selection of speed records recognized by the APBA as of January 1, 1994.

Distance: One Kilometer

Type	Class	Speed (mph)	Driver	Location	Year
Inboard	GP	170.024	Kent MacPhail	Decatur, Ill.	1989
Inboard	KRR	146.649	Gordon Jennings	Lincoln City, Ore.	1989
Offshore	Super Boat	148.238	Thomas Gentry	New Orleans, La.	1987
Offshore	Open	138.512	Al Copeland	New Orleans, La.	1987
PR Outboard	500ccH	121.940	Daniel Kirts	Moore Haven, Fla.	1987
PR Outboard	700ccH	118.769	Billy Rucker Jr.	Waterford, Calif.	1992
Performance	Champ Boat	131.963	Jim Merten	Kaukauna, Wis.	1978
Performance	Mod U	142.968	Bob Wartinger	Moore Haven, Fla.	1989
Special Event	Formula 1	165.338	Robert Hering	Parker, Ariz.	1986
Special Event	Jet	317.600	Ken Warby	Tumut, Australia	1976

Unlimited in Competition

Type	Distance	Speed (mph)	Driver	Location	Year
Qual. Lap	2 miles	165.975	Chip Hanauer	Evansville, Ind.	1992
Lap	2 miles	156.713	Chip Hanauer	Evansville, Ind.	1992
Qual. Lap	2.5 miles	168.935	Chip Hanauer	Evansville, Ind.	1992
Lap	2.5 miles	166.296	Steve David	Honolulu, Hawaii	1992
Lap	3 miles	155.682	Mark Tate	San Diego, Calif.	1991

Source: APBA

AGAINST THE WALL ■ MICHELLE GILMAN-GOULD HAS WON A RECORD FIVE U.S. TITLES. (VANDERSCHUIT STUDIO)

1973 and 1980–81; by Tom D'Eath in 1989–90; and by Chip Hanauer in 1992–93.

Consecutive wins Chip Hanauer has won a record seven successive victories, 1982–88.

Fastest winner The highest average speed for the race is 143.176 mph by Tom D'Eath, piloting *Miss Budweiser* in 1990.

RACQUETBALL

ORIGINS Racquetball, using a 40-foot x 20-foot court, was invented in 1950 by Joe Sobek at the Greenwich YMCA, Greenwich, Conn. Sobek designed a "strung paddle racquet" and combined the rules of squash and handball to form the game of "paddle rackets." The International Racquetball Association (IRA) was founded in 1960 by Bob Kendler, and was renamed the American Amateur Racquetball Association (AARA) in 1979. The International Amateur Racquetball Federation (IARF) was founded in 1979 and staged its first world championship in 1981.

WORLD CHAMPIONSHIPS First held in 1981, the IARF world championships have been held biennially since 1984.

Most titles (team) The United States has won all six team titles, in 1981, 1984, 1986 (tie with Canada), 1988, 1990 and 1992.

Most titles (men) Egan Inoue (U.S.) has won two singles titles, in 1986 and 1990.

Most titles (women) Two women have won two world titles: Cindy Baxter (U.S.), 1981 and 1986; and Heather Stupp (Canada), 1988 and 1990.

UNITED STATES NATIONAL CHAMPIONSHIPS The first championships were held in 1968.

Most titles Michelle Gilman-Gould of Idaho has won a record five women's titles, 1989–93. Four men's open titles have been won by Ed Andrews of California, 1980–81 and 1985–86.

RODEO

ORIGINS Rodeo originated in Mexico, developing from 18th century fiestas, and moved north to the United States and Canada with the expansion of the North American cattle industry in the 18th and 19th centuries. There are several claims to the earliest organized rodeo. The Professional Rodeo Cowboys Association (PRCA) sanctions the West of the Pecos Rodeo, Pecos, Tex. as the oldest; it was first held in 1883. The development of rodeo as a regulated national sport can be traced to the formation of the Cowboys' Turtle Association in 1936. In 1945 the Turtles became the Rodeo Cowboy Association, which in 1975 was renamed the Professional Rodeo Cowboys Association (PRCA). The PRCA is recognized as the oldest and largest rodeo-governing body in the world.

Rodeo events are divided into two groups: roughstock and timed.

Roughstock The roughstock events are saddle bronc riding, bareback riding, and bull riding. In these events the cowboy is required to ride the mount for eight seconds to receive a score. The cowboy must use only one hand to grip the "rigging" (a handhold secured to the animal), and is disqualified if the free hand touches the animal or equipment during the round. The performance is judged on the cowboy's technique and the animal's bucking efforts.

Timed The timed events are calf roping, steer roping, team roping, and steer wrestling. In these events the cowboy chases the calf or steer, riding a registered quarter horse, catches up to the animal, and then captures the animal performing the required feat. The cowboy's performance is timed, with the fastest time winning the event.

WORLD CHAMPIONSHIPS The Rodeo Association of America organized the first world championships in 1929. The championship has been organized under several different formats and sponsored by several different groups throughout its existence. The current championship is a season-long competition based on PRCA earnings. The PRCA has organized the championship since 1945 (as the Rodeo Cowboy Association through 1975).

Most titles (overall) Jim Shoulders has won 16 rodeo world championship events: all-around, 1949, 1956–59; bareback riding, 1950, 1956–58; bull riding, 1951, 1954–59.

INDIVIDUAL EVENTS

All-around Two cowboys have won six all-around titles: Larry Mahan, 1966–70, 1973; Tom Ferguson, 1974–79.

Saddle bronc riding Casey Tibbs won six saddle bronc titles, in 1949, 1951–54 and 1959.

Bareback riding Two cowboys have won five titles: Joe Alexander, 1971–75; Bruce Ford, 1979–80, 1982–83, 1987.

Bull riding Don Gay has won eight bullriding titles: 1975–81 and 1984.

Calf roping Dean Oliver has won eight titles: 1955, 1958, 1960–64 and 1969.

Steer roping Everett Shaw has won six titles: 1945–46, 1948, 1951, 1959 and 1962.

TEAM ROPING ■ JAKE BARNES AND CLAY O'BRIEN COOPER HAVE WON A RECORD FIVE PRCA TEAM ROPING TITLES. (PRCA)

Steer wrestling Homer Pettigrew has won six titles: 1940, 1942–45 and 1948.

Team roping The team of Jake Barnes and Clay O'Brien Cooper has won five titles, 1985–89.

Women's barrel racing Charmayne Rodman has won 10 titles, 1984–93.

Oldest world champion Ike Rude won the 1953 steer roping title at age 59 to became the oldest rodeo titleholder.

Youngest world champion Jim Rodriguez Jr. won the 1959 team roping title at age 18 to become the youngest rodeo titleholder.

RODEO RICHES ■ THE ALL-TIME PRCA EARNINGS LEADER IS ROY COOPER. HE HAS WON $1,476,107 IN PRIZE MONEY. (PRCA)

HIGHEST SCORES (MAXIMUM POSSIBLE: 100 POINTS)

Bull riding Wade Leslie scored 100 points riding Wolfman Skoal at Central Point, Ore. in 1991.

Saddle bronc riding Doug Vold scored 95 points riding Transport at Meadow Lake, Saskatchewan, Canada in 1979.

Bareback riding Joe Alexander scored 93 points riding Marlboro at Cheyenne, Wyo. in 1974.

FASTEST TIMES

Calf roping The fastest time in this event is 5.7 seconds, by Lee Phillips at Assinobia, Saskatchewan, Canada in 1978.

Steer wrestling Without a barrier, the fastest time is reported to have been 2.2 seconds by Oral Zumwalt in the 1930s. With a barrier, the record time is 2.4 seconds, achieved by three cowboys: Jim Bynum at Marietta, Okla. in 1955; Gene Melton at Pecatonia, Ill. in 1976; and Carl Deaton at Tulsa, Okla. in 1976.

Team roping The team of Bob Harris and Tee Woolman performed this feat in a record 3.7 seconds at Spanish Fork, Utah in 1986.

Steer roping The fastest time in this event is 8.4 seconds, by Guy Allen at Garden City, Kan. in 1991.

HIGHEST EARNINGS

Career Roy Cooper holds the career PRCA earnings mark at $1,476,107, 1976–93.

Season The single-season PRCA mark is $297,896 by Ty Murray in 1993.

ROLLER SKATING

ORIGINS Roller skates were invented by Joseph Merlin of Belgium. He demonstrated his new mode of transport at a masquerade party in London in 1760, with disastrous consequences—he was unable to stop and crashed into a large mirror, receiving near-fatal wounds. In 1863, James L. Plimpton of Medfield, Mass. patented the modern four-wheeled roller skate. In 1866, he opened the first public roller skating rink in the United States in Newport, R.I. The *Federation Internationale de Roller Skating* was founded in 1924 and is now headquartered in Spain. The Roller Skating Rink

Operators' Association staged the first U.S. National Championship in 1937. Since 1973 the United States Amateur Confederation of Roller Skating has been the governing body of the sport in the United States. Three distinct sports have derived from roller skating: speed skating, artistic skating, and roller hockey.

SPEED SKATING

International speed skating events are divided into two categories: road racing and track racing. World championships are staged in alternate years for each discipline.

WORLD CHAMPIONSHIPS The first world championships were held in Monza, Italy in 1937. A women's championship was first staged in 1953.

Most titles Alberta Vianello (Italy) has won a record 19 world titles—eight track and 11 road—1953–65. Marco Cantarella (Italy) has won 15 men's titles—seven track and eight road—1964–80.

UNITED STATES NATIONAL CHAMPIONSHIPS The first U.S. championships were staged in 1937 for indoor competition, and contests have been held annually since. In 1985 a separate outdoor championship was initiated, and this is also staged annually.

Most titles Dante Muse has won seven men's overall titles—four indoors, 1986, 1990, 1992–93; three outdoors, 1987, 1989 and 1990. Mary Merrell has won a record six overall champion titles, 1959–61, 1964, and 1966–67 (all indoors).

ARTISTIC SKATING

WORLD CHAMPIONSHIPS The first world championships were held in Washington D.C. in 1947. The championships have been held annually since 1970.

Most titles Scott Cohen (U.S.) has won five men's free-skating titles, 1985–86 and 1989–91. Sandro Guerra (Italy) has won five men's combined titles, 1987–89, 1991–92. Rafaella del Vinaccio (Italy) has won five free-skating and five combined women's titles, 1988–92.

UNITED STATES NATIONAL CHAMPIONSHIPS The first U.S. championships were staged in 1939, and contests are now held annually.

Most titles Michael Jacques has won seven free-skating titles, 1966–72. Laurene Anselmi has won seven women's titles—three figure skating, 1951, 1953–54; four free-skating, 1951–54.

ROLLER HOCKEY

Roller hockey is played by two five-man teams over two twenty-minute periods.

WORLD CHAMPIONSHIPS First held in Stuttgart, Germany in 1936, the world championships have been held under several formats, both annual and biennial. Currently the tournament is an annual event.

Most titles Portugal has won 14 world titles: 1947–50, 1952, 1956, 1958, 1960, 1962, 1968, 1974, 1982, 1991 and 1993.

ROWING

ORIGINS Forms of rowing can be traced back to ancient Egypt; however, the modern sport of rowing dates to 1715, when the Doggett's Coat and Badge scull race was established in London, England. Types of regattas are believed to have taken place in Venice, Italy in 1300, but the modern regatta can also be traced to England, where races were staged in 1775 on the River Thames at Ranleigh Gardens, Putney. The world governing body is the *Federation Internationale des Sociétés d'Aviron* (FISA), founded in 1892. Rowing has been part of the Olympic Games since 1900.

United States The first organized boat races in the United States were reportedly races staged between boatmen in New York harbor in the late 18th century. The first rowing club formed in the United States was the Castle Garden Amateur Boat

LIMBO ON ROLLERSKATES ☞
SYAMALA GOWRI SET A NEW LIMBO ON ROLLER SKATES RECORD OF 4.7 INCHES AT HYDERABAD, INDIA ON MAY 10, 1993.

Club Association, New York City, in 1834. The oldest active boat club is the Detroit Boat Club, founded in 1839. The first and oldest collegiate boat club was formed at Yale University in 1843. The National Association of Amateur Oarsmen (NAAO) was formed in 1872. The NAAO merged with the National Women's Rowing Association in 1982 to form the United States Rowing Association.

OLYMPIC GAMES Men's rowing events have been included in the Olympic Games since 1900. In 1976 women's events were included.

Most gold medals Seven oarsmen have won three gold medals: John Kelly (U.S.), single sculls, 1920, double sculls, 1920 and 1924; Paul Costello (U.S.), double sculls, 1920, 1924 and 1928; Jack Beresford (Great Britain), single sculls, 1924, coxless fours, 1932, double sculls, 1936; Vyacheslav Ivanov (USSR), single sculls, 1956, 1960 and 1964; Siegfried Brietzke (East Germany), coxless pairs, 1972, coxless fours, 1976 and 1980; Pertti Karppinen (Finland), single sculls, 1976, 1980 and 1984; Steven Redgrave (Great Britain), coxed fours, 1984, coxless pairs, 1988 and 1992.

Most medals Jack Beresford (Great Britain) won five medals in rowing competition: three gold (see above) and two silver (single sculls, 1920, and eights, 1928).

WORLD CHAMPIONSHIPS World rowing championships staged separately from the Olympic Games were first held in 1962. Since 1974 the championships have been staged annually. In Olympic years the Games are considered the world championships, and results from the Olympics are included in this section.

Most titles Giuseppe and Carmine Abbagnale (both Italy) have won nine coxed pairs titles, 1981–82, 1984–85 and 1987–91. Jutta Behrendt (née Hampe; East Germany) has won six titles: three single sculls, 1983, 1986 and 1988; three quadruple sculls, 1985, 1987 and 1989.

Single sculls Three oarsmen have won five single sculls titles: Peter-Michael Kolbe (West Germany), 1975, 1978, 1981, 1983 and 1986; Pertti Karppinen (Finland), 1976, 1979–80 and 1984–85; and Thomas Lange (Germany), 1988–92. Christine Hahn (née Scheiblich; East Germany) has won five women's titles, 1974–78.

Eights Since 1962, East German crews have won seven men's eights titles—1970, 1975–80. In women's competition the USSR has won seven titles—1978–79, 1981–83, 1985–86.

COLLEGIATE CHAMPIONSHIPS Harvard and Yale staged the first intercollegiate boat race in 1852. The Intercollegiate Rowing Association was formed in 1895, and in 1898 inaugurated the Varsity Challenge Cup, which was recognized as the national championship. In 1979 the United States Rowing Association introduced the women's National Collegiate Championship, which was extended to men's competition in 1982, supplanting the Varsity Cup as the men's national title.

Most wins (men) Cornell has won 24 titles: 1896–97 (includes two wins in 1897), 1901–03, 1905–07, 1909–12, 1915, 1930, 1955–58, 1962–63, 1971, 1977, and 1981. Since 1982, Harvard has won six titles, 1983, 1985, 1987–89, and 1992.

Most wins (women) Washington has won seven titles—1981–85, 1987–88.

Fastest speed The fastest recorded speed on nontidal water for 2,000 meters is by an American eight, in 5 minutes 27.14 seconds (13.68 mph) at Lucerne, Switzerland on June 17, 1984. A crew from Penn AC was timed in 5 minutes 18.8 seconds (14.03 mph) in the FISA Championships on the River Meuse, Liège, Belgium on August 17, 1930.

RUGBY

ORIGINS As with baseball in the United States, the origins of rugby are obscure—but a traditional "history" has become so embedded in the national psyche, in this case that of Great Britain, that any historical revision is either ignored or derided. The tradition is that the game began when William Webb Ellis picked up the ball during a soccer game at Rugby School in November 1823 and ran with it. Whether or not there is any truth to this legend, the "new" handling code of soccer developed, and the game was played at Cambridge University in 1839. The first rugby club was formed at Guy's Hospital, London, England in 1843, and the Rugby Football Union (RFU) was founded in January 1871. The International Rugby Football Board (IRFB) was founded in 1886.

OLYMPIC GAMES Rugby was played at four Games from 1900 to 1924. The only double gold medalist was the U.S., which won in 1920 and 1924.

WORLD CUP The World Cup is staged every four years and is the world championship for rugby. The first World Cup was hosted by Australia and New Zealand in 1987.

Most wins New Zealand won the first World Cup in 1987, and Australia won the second tournament in 1991.

WORLD CUP SCORING RECORDS

TEAM RECORDS

Most points (game) The most points in World Cup play is 74, scored by New Zealand against Fiji

FASTEST TRY THE FASTEST TRY IN RUGBY HISTORY WAS SCORED BY ANDREW BROWN (GREAT BRITAIN) IN 8 SECONDS AFTER THE KICKOFF. BROWN SCORED FOR WIDDEN OLD BOYS V. OLD ASHTONIANS AT GLOUCESTER, ENGLAND ON NOVEMBER 22, 1990.

(13 points) at Christchurch, New Zealand on May 27, 1987.

Most points (game, aggregate score) The highest aggregate score in World Cup competition is 87 points, New Zealand defeating Fiji 74–13 (see above).

INDIVIDUAL RECORDS

Most points (game) Didier Camberabero (France) scored 30 points (three tries and nine conversions) v. Zimbabwe at Auckland, New Zealand on June 2, 1987.

Most points (tournament) Grant Fox (New Zealand) scored 126 points in 1987.

Most points (career) Grant Fox (New Zealand) scored 170 points in 1987 and 1991.

INTERNATIONAL RUGBY RECORDS

Highest score The highest score by a team in a full international game is 106 points, which has occurred twice: New Zealand 106, Japan 4, at Tokyo, Japan on November 1, 1987; France 106, Paraguay 12, at Asunción, Paraguay on June 28, 1988.

INDIVIDUAL RECORDS

Game

Most points Phil Bennett (Wales) scored 34 points (two tries, 10 conversions, two penalty goals) v. Japan at Tokyo on September 24, 1975.

Most tries Patrice Lagisquet (France) scored seven tries v. Paraguay at Asunción, Paraguay on June 28, 1988.

Most penalty goals Mark Wyatt (Canada) kicked eight penalty goals v. Scotland at St. John, New Brunswick on May 25, 1991.

Career

Most points Michael Lynagh (Australia) has scored a record 789 points in international rugby competition, 1984–93.

Most tries David Campese (Australia) is the leading try scorer in international competition with 57 tries, 1982–93.

Most internationals Philippe Sella (France) has played a record 94 international matches, 1982–94.

Consecutive internationals Two players played in 53 consecutive games: Gareth Edwards (Wales), 1967–78; Willie John McBride (Ireland), 1962–75.

SHOOTING—INDIVIDUAL WORLD RECORDS

In 1986 the International Shooting Union introduced new regulations for determining major championships and world records. Now the leading competitors undertake an additional round with a target subdivided to tenths of a point for rifle and pistol shooting and an extra 25 shots for trap and skeet. The table below shows the world records for the 13 Olympic shooting disciplines, giving in parentheses the score for the number of shots specified plus the score in the additional round.

Men

Event	Points	Marksman (Country)	Date
Free rifle 50 m 3 x 40 shots	1,287.9 (1,186 + 101.9)	Rajmond Debevec (Slovenia)	August 29,1992
Free rifle 50 m 60 shots prone	703.5 (599 + 104.5)	Jens Harskov (Denmark)	June 6, 1991
Air rifle 10 m 60 shots	699.4 (596 + 103.4)	Rajmond Debevec (Yugoslavia)	June 7, 1990
Free pistol 50 m 60 shots	672.5 (575 + 97.5)	Sergey Pyzhyanov (USSR)	June 15, 1993
Rapid-fire pistol 25 m 60 shots	689 (593 +96)	Vladimir Vokhmianin (Kazakhstan)	June 2, 1993
Air pistol 10 m 60 shots	695.1 (593 + 102.1)	Sergey Pyzhyanov (USSR)	October 3, 1989
Running target 10 m 30 + 30 shots	679 (582 + 97)	Lubos Racansky (Czechoslovakia)	May 30, 1991
Trap 150 targets	148 (124 + 24)	Giovanni Pellielo (Italy)	June 9, 1993
	149 (124 + 25)	Marco Venturini (Italy)	June 15, 1993
Skeet 150 targets	149 (124 + 25)	Dean Clark (U.S.)	June 20, 1993

Women

Event	Points	Markswoman (Country)	Date
Standard rifle 50 m 3 x 20 shots	689.3 (590 + 99.3)	Vessela Letcheva (Bulgaria)	August 28, 1992
Air rifle 10 m 40 shots	500.8 (399 + 101.8)	Valentina Cherkasova (Georgia)	May 8, 1993
Sport pistol 25 m 60 shots	693.8 (591 + 102.8)	Nino Salukvadse (USSR)	July 13, 1989
Air pistol 10 m 40 shots	492.4 (392 + 100.4)	Lieselotte Breker (West Germany)	May 18, 1989

The first world record by a woman at any sport for a category in direct and measurable competition with men was by Margaret Murdock (née Thompson; U.S.), who set a world record for smallbore rifle (kneeling position) of 391 in 1967.

SHOOTING

The National Rifle Association recognizes four categories of shooting competition: conventional, international, silhouette, and action pistol. This section reports records only for international style shooting—the shooting discipline used at the Olympic Games.

ORIGINS The earliest recorded shooting club is the Lucerne Shooting Guild (Switzerland), formed c. 1466. The first known shooting competition was held at Zurich, Switzerland in 1472.

The international governing body, the *Union International de Tir* (UIT), was formed in Zurich in 1907.

United States The National Rifle Association (NRA) was founded in 1871, and is designated as the national governing body for shooting sports in the United States by the U.S. Olympic Committee.

INTERNATIONAL STYLE SHOOTING

International or Olympic-style shooting is comprised of four disciplines: rifle, pistol, running target, and shotgun. Running target events are limited to male competitors. Shotgun shooting (also known as trap and skeet) requires the competitor to hit clay targets released from a skeet.

OLYMPIC GAMES Shooting has been part of the Olympic program since the first modern Games in 1896. Women were allowed to compete against men at the 1968 Games, and separate women's events were included in 1984.

Most gold medals Seven marksmen have won five gold medals: Konrad Staheli (Switzerland), 1900–1906; Louis Richardet (Switzerland), 1900–06; Alfred Lane (U.S.), 1912–20; Carl Osburn (U.S.), 1912–24; Ole Lilloe-Olsen (Norway), 1920–24; Morris Fisher (U.S.), 1920–24; and Willis Lee (U.S.), 1920. Marina Logvinenko (Unified Team) is the only woman to win two gold medals: sport pistol and air pistol, both in 1992.

Most medals Carl Osburn (U.S.) has won 11 medals: five gold, four silver and two bronze. The greatest tally by a woman competitor is three medals, by Jasna Sekaric (Yugoslavia/Independent Olympic Participant). She won one gold and one bronze in 1988, and one silver in 1992.

NCAA CHAMPIONSHIPS A combined NCAA rifle championship was inaugurated in 1980, and the contest is now held annually.

Most titles (team) West Virginia has won nine NCAA team titles, 1983–84, 1986, and 1988–93.

Most titles (individual) Seven competitors have won two individual titles: Rod Fitz-Randolph, Tennessee Tech, smallbore and air rifle, 1980; Kurt Fitz-Randolph, Tennessee Tech, smallbore, 1981–82; John Rost, West Virginia, air rifle, 1981–82; Pat Spurgin, Murray State, air

rifle, 1984, smallbore, 1985; Web Wright, West Virginia, smallbore, 1987–88; Michelle Scarborough, South Florida, air rifle, 1989, smallbore, 1990; Ann-Marie Pfiffner, West Virginia, air rifle, 1991–92.

SKIING

ORIGINS Skiing traces its history to Scandinavia; *ski* is the Norwegian word for snowshoe. A ski discovered in a peat bog in Hoting, Sweden dates to *c.* 2500 B.C., and records note the use of skis at the Battle of Isen, Norway in A.D. 1200. The first ski races were held in Norway and Australia in the 1850s and 1860s. Two men stand out as pioneers of the development of skiing in the 19th century: Sondre Nordheim, a Norwegian, who designed equipment and developed skiing techniques; and Mathias Zdarsky, an Austrian, who pioneered Alpine skiing. The first national governing body was that of Norway, formed in 1833. The International Ski Commission was founded in 1910 and was succeeded as the world governing body in 1924 by the International Ski Federation (FIS).

United States The first ski club in the United States was formed at Berlin, N.H. in January 1872. The United States Ski Association was originally founded as the National Ski Association in 1905; in 1962, it was renamed the United States Ski Association, and in 1990 it was renamed U.S. Skiing.

In the modern era, skiing has evolved into two main categories, Alpine and Nordic. Alpine skiing encompasses downhill and slalom racing. Nordic skiing covers ski jumping events and cross-country racing.

ALPINE SKIING

OLYMPIC GAMES Downhill and slalom events were first included at the 1936 Olympic Games.

Most gold medals In men's competition, the most gold medals won is three, by three skiers: Anton Sailer (Austria), who won all three events, downhill, slalom and giant slalom, in 1956; Jean-Claude Killy (France), who matched Sailer's feat in 1968; and Alberto Tomba (Italy), who won the slalom and giant slalom in 1988 and the giant slalom in 1992. For women the

FASTEST SKIER THE OFFICIAL WORLD RECORD FOR A SKIER IS 145.161 MPH, BY PHILIPPE GOITSCHEL (FRANCE) ON APRIL 21, 1993.

LONGEST RIDE ■ THE BROMLEY ALPINE SLIDE IN PERU, VT., IS THE WORLD'S LONGEST SLIDE. IT IS 4,000 FEET LONG AND HAS A VERTICAL DROP OF 700 FEET. (BROMLEY MOUNTAIN)

TIMEOUT

24-HOUR CROSS-COUNTRY ☞ SEPPO-JUHANI SAVOLAINEN SKIED 258.2 MILES AT SAARISELKÄ, FINLAND ON APRIL 8–9, 1988.

record is two golds, achieved by seven skiers: Andrea Mead-Lawrence (U.S.), slalom, giant slalom, 1952; Marielle Goitschel (France), giant slalom 1964, slalom, 1968; Marie-Therese Nadig (Switzerland), downhill, giant slalom, 1972; Rosi Mittermaier (West Germany), downhill, slalom, 1976; Hanni Wenzel (Liechtenstein), giant slalom, slalom, 1980; Vareni Schneider (Switzerland), giant slalom, slalom, 1988; and Petra Kronberger (Austria), giant slalom and combined, 1992.

Most medals Hanni Wenzel (Liechtenstein) has won four Olympic medals: two gold, one silver and one bronze, 1976–80. The most medals won by a male skier is also four, by Alberto Tomba (Italy)—three golds and one silver, 1988–92.

WORLD CHAMPIONSHIPS This competition was inaugurated in 1931 at Murren, Switzerland. From 1931–39 the championships were held annually; from 1950 they were held biennially. Up to 1980, the Olympic Games were considered the world championships, except in 1936. In 1985, the championship schedule was changed so as not to coincide with an Olympic year.

Most gold medals Christel Cranz (Germany) won a record 12 titles: four slalom, 1934, 1937–39; three downhill, 1935, 1937, 1939; five combined, 1934–35, 1937–39. Anton Sailer (Austria) holds the men's record with seven titles: one slalom, 1956; two giant slalom, 1956, 1958; two downhill, 1956, 1958; two combined, 1956, 1958.

World Cup Contested annually since 1967, the World Cup is a circuit of races where points are earned during the season, with the champion being the skier with the most points at the end of the season.

Individual Racing Records

Most wins (men) Ingemar Stenmark (Sweden) won a record 86 races (46 giant slalom, 40 slalom) from 287 contested, 1974–89.

Most wins (women) Annemarie Moser-Pröll (Austria) won a record 62 races, 1970–79.

Most wins (season) Ingemar Stenmark (Sweden) won 13 races in 1978–79 to set the men's mark. Vreni Schneider (Switzerland) won 13 races in 1988–89 to set the women's mark.

Consecutive wins Ingemar Stenmark (Sweden) won 14 successive giant slalom races from March 18, 1978 to January 21, 1980. The women's record is 11 wins by Annemarie Moser-Pröll (Austria) in the downhill from December 1972 to January 1974.

United States National Championships

Most titles Tamara McKinney won seven slalom titles, 1982–84, 1986–89—the most by any skier in one discipline. Phil Mahre won five giant slalom titles, 1975, 1977–79, 1981—the most by a male skier in one event.

NCAA Championships The NCAA skiing championship was introduced in 1954. Teams compete in both Alpine and cross-country events, with cumulative point totals determining the national champion. Teams are comprised of both men and women.

Most titles (team) Denver has won 14 titles, 1954–57, 1961–67, and 1969–71.

Most titles (individual) Chiharu Igaya of Dartmouth won a record six NCAA titles: Alpine, 1955–56; downhill, 1955; slalom, 1955–57.

Nordic Skiing

Cross-Country Skiing

Olympic Games Cross-country racing has been included in every Winter Olympic Games.

Most gold medals In men's competition, three skiers have each won four gold medals: Sixten Jernberg (Sweden), 50 km, 1956; 30 km, 1960; 50 km and 4 x 10 km relay, 1964; Gunde Svan (Sweden), 15 km and 4 x 10 km relay, 1984; 50 km and 4 x 10 km relay, 1988; Thomas Wassberg (Swe-

Swiss Success ■ Vreni Schneider won 13 World Cup races during the 1988–89 season, matching Ingemar Stenmark's record. (ALLSPORT/VANDYSTADT)

den), 15 km, 1980; 50 km and 4 x 10 km relay, 1984; 4 x 10 km relay, 1988. The women's record is also four golds, won by two skiers: Galina Kulakova (USSR), 5 km, 10 km and 3 x 5 km relay, 1972; 4 x 5 km relay, 1976; Raisa Smetanina (USSR/Unified Team), 10 km and 4 x 5 km relay, 1976; 5 km, 1980; 4 x 5 km, 1992.

Most medals The most medals won in Nordic events is 10, by Raisa Smetanina (four gold, five silver and one bronze, 1976–92). Sixten Jernberg (Sweden) holds the men's record with nine (four gold, three silver, two bronze, 1956–64).

WORLD CUP A season series of World Cup races was instituted in 1981.

Most titles Gunde Svan (Sweden) has won five overall cross-country skiing titles, 1984–86 and 1988–89. Two women have won three overall titles: Marjo Matikainen (Finland), 1986–88; Yelena Vialbe (USSR/Russia), 1989, 1991–92.

UNITED STATES NATIONAL CHAMPIONSHIPS

Most titles Martha Rockwell has won a record 14 national titles, 1969–75. The record in men's competition is 12, by Audun Endestad, 1984–90.

SKI JUMPING

OLYMPIC GAMES Ski jumping has been included in every Winter Games.

Most gold medals Matti Nykanen (Finland) has won four gold medals: 70-meter hill, 1988; 90-meter hill, 1984 and 1988; 90-meter team, 1988.

Most medals Matti Nykanen has won five medals in Olympic competition: four gold (see above) and one silver, 70-meter hill, 1984.

WORLD CUP A season series of ski jumping events was instituted in 1981.

Most titles Matti Nykanen (Finland) has won four World Cup titles, 1983, 1985–86 and 1988.

UNITED STATES NATIONAL CHAMPIONSHIPS

Most titles Lars Haugen has won seven ski jumping titles, 1912–28.

FREESTYLE SKIING

Freestyle skiing is composed of three skiing disciplines: aerials, ballet and moguls. Moguls was included as an Olympic event for the first time at the 1992 Games.

MOGULS

Skiers race down a slope marked with small snow hills (moguls). The skiers are required to perform two jumps during the run. The score is calculated by combining the speed of the run and marks awarded for performance.

OLYMPIC GAMES Moguls was a full medal sport for the first time at the 1992 Games. Edgar Grospiron (France) won the men's event; Donna Weinbrecht (U.S.) won the women's event.

WORLD CHAMPIONSHIP First staged in 1986, the event has been staged biennially since 1989.

Most wins (men) Edgar Grispiron (France) has won the event twice, 1989 and 1991.

Most wins (women) Raphaelle Monod (France) has won the event twice, 1989 and 1991.

AERIALS

WORLD CHAMPIONSHIP

Most wins (men) Lloyd Langlois (Canada) has won the title twice, 1986 and 1989.

Most wins (women) No skier has won this event more than once.

BALLET

WORLD CHAMPIONSHIP

Most wins (men) No skier has won the event more than once.

Most wins (women) Jan Bucher (U.S.) has won the event twice, 1986 and 1989.

TIMEOUT

LONGEST SLED DOG TRAIN ☞ ON FEBRUARY 8, 1988 THE REV. DONALD MCEWEN (CANADA) DROVE A 76-DOG SLED FOR 2 MILES SINGLE-HANDEDLY ON THE ICE AND AROUND THE SHORE OF LINGHAM LAKE, ONTARIO.

SLED DOG RACING

ORIGINS Racing between harnessed dog teams (usually huskies) is believed to have been practiced by Inuits in North America, and also by the peoples of Scandinavia, long before the first recorded formal race, the All-America Sweepstakes, which took place in 1908. Sled dog racing was a demonstration sport at the 1932 Olympic Games. The best known race is the Iditarod Trail Sled Dog Race, first run in 1973.

IDITAROD TRAIL SLED DOG RACE

The annual race from Anchorage to Nome, Alaska commemorates the 1925 midwinter emergency mission to get medical supplies to Nome during a diphtheria epidemic. Raced over alternate courses, the northern and southern trails, the Iditarod was first run in 1973.

IDITAROD WINNERS

Year	Musher	Elapsed Time
1973	Dick Wilmarth	20 days, 00:49:41
1974	Carl Huntington	20 days, 15:02:07
1975	Emmitt Peters	14 days, 14:43:45
1976	Gerald Riley	18 days, 22:58:17
1977	Rick Swenson	16 days, 16:27:13
1978	Rick Mackey	14 days, 18:52:24
1979	Rick Swenson	15 days, 10:37:47
1980	Joe May	14 days, 07:11:51
1981	Rick Swenson	12 days, 08:45:02
1982	Rick Swenson	16 days, 04:40:10
1983	Rick Mackey	12 days, 14:10:44
1984	Dean Osmar	12 days, 15:07:33
1985	Libby Riddles	18 days, 00:20:17
1986	Susan Butcher	11 days, 15:06:00
1987	Susan Butcher	11 days, 02:05:13
1988	Susan Butcher	11 days, 11:41:40
1989	Joe Runyan	11 days, 05:24:34
1990	Susan Butcher	11 days, 01:53:23
1991	Rick Swenson	12 days, 16:34:39
1992	Martin Buser	10 days, 19:36:17
1993	Jeff King	10 days, 15:38:17

NO PLACE LIKE HOME ■ 1993 IDITAROD WINNER JEFF KING WON THE RACE IN A RECORD TIME OF 10 DAYS, 15:38:17. (IDITAROD TRAIL COMMITTEE)

Most wins Rick Swenson has won the event five times: 1977, 1979, 1981–82, 1991.

Record time The fastest recorded time is 10 days, 15 hours, 38 minutes, 17 seconds, by Jeff King (U.S.) in 1993.

SNOOKER

ORIGINS Neville Chamberlain, a British army officer, is credited with inventing the game in Jubbulpore, India in 1875. Snooker is a hybrid of pool and pyramids. Chamberlain added a set of colored balls to the 15 red ones used in pyramids and devised a scoring system based on pocketing the balls in sequence: red, color, red, color until all the reds have been cleared, leaving the colored balls to be pocketed in numerical order. The modern scoring system (a red ball is worth one point, yellow—2, green—3, brown—4, blue—5, pink—6 and black—7) was adopted in England in 1891. The sequence of pocketing the balls is called a break, the maximum possible being 147. The name *snooker* comes from the term coined for new recruits at the Woolwich Military Academy and was Chamberlain's label for anyone who lost at his game.

WORLD PROFESSIONAL CHAMPIONSHIPS This competition was first organized in 1927.

Most titles Joe Davis (England) won the title on the first 15 occasions it was contested, and this still stands as the all-time record for victories.

Maximum break Two players have scored the 147 "maximum break" in world championship competition: Cliff Thorburn (Canada), 1983; Jimmy White (England), 1992.

SOARING

ORIGINS Research by Isadore William Deiches has shown evidence of the use of gliders in ancient Egypt *c.* 2500–1500 B.C. Emanuel Swedenborg of Sweden made sketches of gliders *c.* 1714. The earliest human-carrying glider was designed by Sir George Cayley and carried his coachman (possibly John Appleby) about 500 yards across a valley in Brompton Dale, North Yorkshire, England in the summer of 1853.

WORLD CHAMPIONSHIPS World championships were instituted in 1937.

Most individual titles The most individual titles won is four, by Ingo Renner (Australia) in 1976 (Standard class), 1983, 1985 and 1987 (Open).

United States The most titles won by an American pilot is two, by George Moffat, in the Open category, 1970 and 1974.

SOARING WORLD RECORDS (SINGLE-SEATERS)

DISTANCE AND HEIGHT

Straight distance 907.7 miles, Hans-Werner Grosse (Germany), Lubeck, Germany to Biarritz, France, April 25, 1972.

Declared goal distance 779.4 miles, by three pilots: Bruce Drake, David Speight and Dick Georgeson (all New Zealand), who each flew from Te Anau to Te Araroa, New Zealand, January 14, 1978.

Goal and return 1,023.2 miles, Tom Knauff (U.S.), Williamsport, Pa. to Knoxville, Tenn., April 25, 1983.

Absolute altitude 49,009 feet, Robert R. Harris (U.S.), over California, February 17, 1986. The women's record is 41,449 feet, by Sabrina Jackintell (U.S.) on February 14, 1979.

Height gain 42,303 feet, Paul Bikle (U.S.), Mojave, Calif., February 25, 1961. The women's record is

33,506 feet, by Yvonne Loader (New Zealand) at Omarama, New Zealand on January 12, 1988.

SPEED OVER TRIANGULAR COURSE

100 km 121.35 mph, Ingo Renner (Australia), December 14, 1982.

300 km 105.32 mph, Jean-Paul Castel (France), November 15, 1986.

500 km 105.67 mph, Beat Bunzli (Switzerland), January 9, 1988.

750 km 98.43 mph, Hans-Werner Grosse (Germany), January 8, 1985.

1,000 km 90.32 mph, Hans-Werner Grosse (Germany), January 3, 1979.

1,250 km 82.79 mph, Hans-Werner Grosse (Germany), January 9, 1980.

SOCCER

ORIGINS A game called *tsu chu* ("to kick a ball of stuffed leather") was played in China more than 2,500 years ago. However, the ancestry of the modern game is traced to England. In 1314, King Edward II prohibited the game because of excessive noise. Three subsequent monarchs also banned the game. Nevertheless, soccer continued its development in England. In 1848, the first rules were drawn up at Cambridge University; in 1863, the Football Association (FA) was founded in England. The sport grew in popularity worldwide, and the *Fédération Internationale de Football Association* (FIFA), the world governing body, was formed in Paris, France in 1904. FIFA currently has more than 160 members.

WORLD CUP (See pp. 182–183)

EUROPEAN CHAMPIONSHIP Staged every four years, the European Championships were the brainchild of Frenchman Henri Delaunay. First held in 1960, the competition was known as the European Nations Cup. In 1968 the tournament was renamed the European Championship.

Most wins West Germany has won the tournament twice, 1972 and 1980.

SOUTH AMERICAN CHAMPIONSHIP The South American Championship was first staged in 1916. By the mid-1960s the tournament had lost popularity and was abandoned in 1967. In 1975 the tournament was revived as the Copa America. Since 1987 the tournament has been staged every two years.

Most wins Argentina has won the tournament 14 times, 1921, 1925, 1927, 1929, 1937, 1941, 1945–47, 1955, 1957, 1959, 1991 and 1993.

AFRICAN NATIONS CUP First staged in 1957, the tournament is played biennially.

Most wins Ghana has won the tournament four times, 1963, 1965, 1978 and 1982.

WORLD CLUB CHAMPIONSHIP Originally designed as a two-game home-and-away series between the European and South American champions, the first World Club Championship was held in 1960. Violence marred many of the games, and European teams often refused invitations to play. In 1980 the format was changed to a one-match playoff staged in Tokyo, Japan, between the winner of the European Champions Cup and the Copa Libertadores.

Most wins Three teams have won the title three times: Penarol (Uruguay), 1961, 1966, 1982; Nacional (Uruguay), 1971, 1980, 1988; A.C. Milan (Italy), 1969, 1989–90.

EUROPEAN CHAMPIONS CUP Known as the European Cup, the competition is an annual playoff competition for the league champions of all UEFA-affiliated countries. The competition was devised by French newspaperman Gabriel Hanot and was first staged in 1956.

Most wins Real Madrid (Spain) has won the competition six times, 1956–60, 1966.

SOUTH AMERICAN CUP First contested in 1960 as the South American Champion Clubs' Cup, the tournament was expanded in 1965 to include two teams from each South American country. At that time the competition was renamed the Copa Libertadores de America.

Most wins Independiente (Argentina) has won the competition seven times, 1964–65, 1972–75, 1984.

INDIVIDUAL SCORING RECORDS

Most goals (game) 16, by Stephan Stanis for Racing Club Lens (*v.* Aubry-Asturies) on December 13, 1942.

Most goals (game, international) 10, by two players: Sofus Nielsen for Denmark (*v.* France) in 1908; Gottfried Fuchs for Germany (*v.* Russia) in 1912.

Most goals (career) 1,329, by Artur Friedenreich, who played for six teams (Germania, CA Ipiranga, Americano, CA Paulistano, Sao Paulo, Flamengo) from 1909–35.

Most goals (career, internationals) 97, by Pele for Brazil in 111 internationals, 1957–70.

Most hat-tricks (career) 92, by Pele, 1956–77.

NCAA DIVISION I CHAMPIONSHIPS The NCAA Division I men's championship was first staged in 1959. A women's tournament was introduced in 1982.

Most titles (men) The University of St. Louis has won the most Division I titles with 10 victories, which includes one tie: 1959–60, 1962–63, 1965, 1967, 1969–70, 1972–73.

Most titles (women) The University of North Carolina has won a record 10 Division I titles. Its victories came in 1982–84 and 1986–92.

MOST RED CARDS ☞ ON JUNE 1, 1993 IN A PARAGUAY LEAGUE SOCCER GAME BETWEEN SPORTIVO AMELIANO AND GENERAL CABALLERO, 20 OUT OF A POSSIBLE 22 PLAYERS WERE EJECTED FROM THE GAME. REFEREE WILLIAM WEILER'S EJECTION OF TWO SPORTIVO PLAYERS SPARKED A 10-MINUTE MASS BRAWL. WEILER DISMISSED A FURTHER 18 PLAYERS, INCLUDING THE REST OF THE SPORTIVO TEAM. THE GAME WAS THEN ABANDONED.

THE WORLD CUP

The first World Cup was held in Uruguay in 1930, and is staged quadrennially. The first World Cup attracted only seven countries, but the success of the event sparked interest worldwide. Since World War II the Finals have outstripped the Olympic Games as the most widely watched sports event in the world. The 1990 Finals, staged in Italy, attracted a record global television audience, estimated at 26.5 billion viewers. The 15th Finals tournament will be staged in the United States from June 17–July 17, 1994. The final will be staged at the Rose Bowl on July 17, 1994.

WORLD CUP FINALS RECORDS

INDIVIDUAL

Most Tournaments • 5, Antonio Carbajal (Mexico, 1950–66)
Most games • 21, by two players: Uwe Seeler (West Germany, 1958–70); Wladyslaw Zmuda (Poland, 1974–86)
Most goals (all-time) • 14, Gerd Muller (West Germany, 1970–74)
Most goals (tournament) • 13, Just Fontaine (France, 1958)
Most goals (game) • 4, by nine players‡
Oldest player§ • 41, Pat Jennings (N. Ireland, 1986)
Youngest player§ • 17, Norman Whiteside (N. Ireland, 1982)

TEAM

Most championships • 3, three teams: Brazil (1958, 1962, 1970); Italy (1934, 1938, 1982); (West) Germany (1954, 1974, 1990)
Most wins (games) • 44, Brazil
Most defeats • 17, Mexico
Most defeats (no wins) • 10, Bulgaria
Most goals (all-time) • 148, Brazil
Most goals (tournament) • 27, Hungary
Most goals (game) • 10, Hungary (v. El Salvador 1, 1982)
Most goals (two teams) • 12, Austria 7, Switzerland 5, 1954

‡Gustav Wetterstrom (Sweden, 1938); Leonidas (Brazil, 1938); Ernest Willimowski (Poland, 1938); Ademir (Brazil, 1950); Juan Schiaffino (Uruguay, 1950); Sandor Kocsis (Hungary, 1954); Just Fontaine (France, 1958); Eusebio (Portugal, 1966); Emilio Butragueno (Spain, 1986).
§ Jennings set the record on his 41st birthday, June 12, 1986 v. Brazil. Whiteside was 17 years 41 days old, June 17, 1982 v. Yugoslavia.

ON TARGET ■ GERD MULLER (LEFT) HAS SCORED A RECORD 14 GOALS IN FINALS PLAY. PAUL BREITNER (RIGHT) IS ONE OF THREE PLAYERS TO SCORE IN TWO DIFFERENT CHAMPIONSHIP GAMES. (ALLSPORT)

QUALIFICATION

24 teams will compete in the 1994 World Cup Finals tournament. Germany, as holders, and the U.S., as hosts, gained automatic berths. 139 countries competed for the remaining 22 spots in a series of regional round–robin tournaments staged over two years. Including USA '94, 61 countries† have gained qualification to the Finals. Brazil is the only nation to qualify for each of them.

* 2 Finals: Algeria, Bolivia, Egypt, El Salvador, Ireland, Norway, Portugal; 1 Final: Australia, Canada, Costa Rica, Cuba, Denmark, Dutch East Indies, East Germany, Greece, Haiti, Honduras, Iran, Iraq, Israel, Kuwait, New Zealand, Nigeria, North Korea, Saudi Arabia, Tunisia, Turkey, United Arab Emirates, Wales, Zaire.
†USSR/Russia counted as one country.

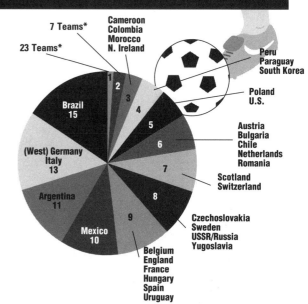

7 Teams*
Cameroon
Colombia
Morocco
N. Ireland

23 Teams*

Peru
Paraguay
South Korea

Poland
U.S.

Austria
Bulgaria
Chile
Netherlands
Romania

Scotland
Switzerland

Czechoslovakia
Sweden
USSR/Russia
Yugoslavia

Belgium
England
France
Hungary
Spain
Uruguay

Brazil 15
(West) Germany Italy 13
Argentina 11
Mexico 10

WORLD CUP WINNERS (1930–90)

Year	Winner	Loser	Score	Venue
1930	Uruguay	Argentina	4–2	Uruguay
1934	Italy	Czechoslovakia	2–1*	Italy
1938	Italy	Hungary	4–2	France
1950	Uruguay	Brazil	2–1†	Brazil
1954	W. Germany	Hungary	3–2	Switzerland
1958	Brazil	Sweden	5–2	Sweden
1962	Brazil	Czechoslovakia	3–1	Chile
1966	England	W. Germany	4–2*	England
1970	Brazil	Italy	4–1	Mexico
1974	W. Germany	Netherlands	2–1	W. Germany
1978	Argentina	Netherlands	3–1*	Argentina
1982	Italy	W. Germany	3–1	Spain
1986	Argentina	W. Germany	3–2	Mexico
1990	W. Germany	Argentina	1–0	Italy

*Overtime
†The 1950 finals concluded with a round-robin format. The Brazil v. Uruguay game was the last game of the series. Through good fortune the game also decided the tournament, and has thus always been considered as the championship game.

CHAMPIONSHIP GAME GOALSCORING RECORDS

One of the oldest clichés in soccer is "goals win games." As there is no bigger soccer game than the World Cup Final, the following is a listing of the record-breakers that have won soccer's most coveted prize.

Most goals (game) • 3, Geoff Hurst, England, 1966

Most goals (career) • 3, Vava, Brazil, 1958, 1962
Pele, Brazil, 1958, 1970
Geoff Hurst, England, 1966

Most games • 2, Vava, Brazil, 1958, 1962
Pele, Brazil, 1958, 1970
Paul Breitner, West Germany, 1974, 1982

Penalty kicks • 1, Johann Neeskens, Netherlands, 1974
Paul Breitner, West Germany, 1974
Andreas Breheme, West Germany, 1990

HAT-TRICK ■ GEOFF HURST IS THE ONLY PLAYER TO SCORE A HAT-TRICK IN THE WORLD CUP FINAL. HERE HE PIVOTS TO SCORE HIS SECOND GOAL IN ENGLAND'S 4–2 TRIUMPH OVER WEST GERMANY IN 1966. (ALLSPORT)

SOFTBALL

ORIGINS Softball, a derivative of baseball, was invented by George Hancock at the Farragut Boat Club, Chicago, Ill. in 1887. Rules were first codified in Minneapolis, Minn. in 1895 under the name kitten ball. The name softball was introduced by Walter Hakanson at a meeting of the National Recreation Congress in 1926. The name was adopted throughout the United States in 1930. Rules were formalized in 1933 by the International Joint Rules Committee for Softball and adopted by the Amateur Softball Association of America. The International Softball Federation was formed in 1950 as governing body for both fast pitch and slow pitch.

FAST PITCH SOFTBALL

WORLD CHAMPIONSHIPS A women's fast pitch world championship was first staged in 1965, and a men's tournament in 1966. Both tournaments are held quadrennially.

Most titles (men) The United States has won five world titles: 1966, 1968, 1976 (tied), 1980 and 1988.

Most titles (women) The United States has won four world titles: 1974, 1978, 1986, and 1990.

AMATEUR SOFTBALL ASSOCIATION NATIONAL CHAMPIONSHIP The first ASA national championship was staged in 1933 for both men's and women's teams.

Most titles (men) The Clearwater Bombers (Florida) won 10 championships between 1950 and 1973.

Most titles (women) The Raybestos Brakettes (Stratford, Conn.) have won 23 women's fast pitch titles from 1958 through 1992.

NCAA CHAMPIONSHIPS The first NCAA Division I women's championship was staged in 1982.

Most titles UCLA has won seven titles: 1982, 1984–85, 1988–90, and 1992.

SLOW PITCH SOFTBALL

WORLD CHAMPIONSHIPS A slow pitch world championship was staged for men's teams in 1987. The United States team won this event. So far a second tournament has not been scheduled. No world championship has been staged for women's teams.

AMATEUR SOFTBALL ASSOCIATION NATIONAL CHAMPIONSHIP The first men's ASA national championship was staged in 1953. The first women's event was staged in 1962.

Most titles (men—major slow pitch) Two teams have won three major slow pitch championships: Skip Hogan A.C. (Pittsburgh, Pa.), 1962, 1964–65; Joe Gatliff Auto Sales (Newport, Ky.), 1956–57, 1963.

Most titles (men—super slow pitch) Two teams have won three super slow pitch titles: Howard's Western Steer (Denver, Colo.), 1981, 1983–84; Steele's Silver Bullets (Grafton, Ohio), 1985–87.

Most titles (women) The Dots of Miami (Fla.) have won five major slow pitch titles, 1969, 1974–75, 1978–79.

SPEED SKATING

ORIGINS The world's longest skating race, the 124-mile "Elfstedentocht" ("Tour of the Eleven Towns"), is said to commemorate a similar race staged in the Netherlands in the 17th century. The first recorded skating race was staged in 1763, from Wisbech to Whittlesey, England. The International Skating Union (ISU) was founded at Scheveningen, Netherlands in 1892 and is the governing body for both speed skating and figure skating.

OLYMPIC GAMES Men's speed skating events have been included in the Olympic Games since 1924. Women's events were first staged in 1960.

Most gold medals Lidiya Skoblikova (USSR) has won six gold medals: 500-meter, 1964; 1,000-meter, 1964; 1,500-meter, 1960, 1964; 3,000-meter, 1960, 1964. The men's record is five, shared by two skaters: Clas Thunberg (Finland), 500-meter, 1928; 1,500-meter, 1924, 1928; 5,000-meter, 1924; all-around title, 1924; and Eric Heiden (U.S.), 500-meter, 1,000-meter, 1,500-meter, 5,000-meter, and 10,000-meter, all in 1980.

WORLD CHAMPIONSHIPS Speed skating world championships were first staged in 1893.

Most titles Oscar Mathisen (Norway) and Clas Thunberg (Finland) have won a record five overall world titles. Mathisen won titles in 1908–09 and 1912–14; Thunberg won in 1923, 1925, 1928–29 and 1931. Karin Enke-Kania (East Germany) holds the women's mark, also at five. She won in 1982, 1984 and 1986–88.

UNITED STATES Eric Heiden won three overall world titles, 1977–79, the most by any U.S. skater. His sister Beth became the only American woman to win an overall championship in 1979.

SHORT TRACK SPEED SKATING

ORIGINS An indoor version of the more familiar outdoor speed skating races, short track speed skating was developed in North America in the 1960s. Besides being held indoors and on a shorter circuit, short track racing also differs from the longer version in that there are usually a pack of four skaters in a race, and a certain amount of bumping between the competitors as allowed. World championships were first staged unofficially in 1978, and the sport gained offical Olympic status at the 1992 Games.

WORLD CHAMPIONSHIP Unofficial world championships were first staged in 1978. Since 1981 the championships have been recognized by the ISU. The event is staged annually. Two championships were staged in 1987.

Most wins (men) Three skaters have won two titles: Guy Daigneault (Canada), 1982 and 1984;

SPEED SKATING WORLD RECORDS

Men

Event	Time	Skater (Country)	Date
500 meters	35.76	Dan Jansen (U.S.)	January 30, 1994
1,000 meters	1:12.54	Kevin Scott (Canada)	December 17, 1993
1,500 meters	1:51.60	Rintje Ritsma (Netherlands)	January 8, 1994
5,000 meters	6:35.53	Johann Olav Koss (Norway)	December 4, 1993
10,000 meters	13:43.54	Johann Olav Koss (Norway)	February 10, 1991

Women

Event	Time	Skater (Country)	Date
500 meters	39.10	Bonnie Blair (U.S.)	February 22, 1988
1,000 meters	1:17.65	Christa Rothenburger (East Germany)	February 26, 1988
1,500 meters	1:59.30	Karin Kania (East Germany)	March 22, 1986
3,000 meters	4:10.80	Gunda Kleemann (Germany)	December 9, 1990
5,000 meters	7:13.29	Gunda Niemann (Germany)	December 6, 1993

Source: United States International Speedskating Association

NEVER CRESTFALLEN ■ SURFER WENDY BOTHA HAS WON THE WOMEN'S WORLD SURFING TITLE FOUR TIMES, A RECORD SHE SHARES WITH FRIEDA ZAMBA. (ALLSPORT/ROB BROWN)

Toshinobu Kawai (Japan), 1985 and 1987; Michel Daignault (Canada), 1987, 1989.

Most wins (women) Sylvie Daigle (Canada) has won four world titles, 1979, 1983, 1989–90.

Olympic Games Short track speed skating was included as a demonstration sport at the 1988 Calgary Games, and gained official status at the 1992 Games in Albertville.

Most gold medals Kim Ki-hoon (South Korea) won two gold medals at the 1992 Games: 1,000 meters and 5,000 meter relay.

SQUASH

ORIGINS Squash is an offshoot of rackets and is believed to have been first played at Harrow School, London, England in 1817. The International Squash Rackets Federation (ISRF) was founded in 1967. The Women's International Squash Rackets Federation was formed in 1976.

United States The U.S. Squash Racquets Association was formed in 1907, and staged the first U.S. amateur championships that year.

WORLD OPEN CHAMPIONSHIPS Both the men's and women's events were first held in 1976. The men's competition is an annual event, but the women's

tournament was biennial until 1989, when it switched to the same system as the men's event. There was no championship in 1978.

Most titles Jahangir Khan (Pakistan) has won six titles, 1981–85 and 1988. Susan Devoy (New Zealand) holds the mark in the women's event with five victories, 1985, 1987, 1990–92.

UNITED STATES AMATEUR CHAMPIONSHIPS The U.S. Amateur Championships were first held for men in 1907, and for women in 1928.

Most titles G. Diehl Mateer won 11 men's doubles titles between 1949 and 1966 with five different partners. Joyce Davenport won eight women's doubles titles between 1969 and 1990 with two different partners.

Most titles (singles) Alicia McConnell has won seven women's singles titles, 1982–88. Stanley Pearson won a record six men's titles, 1915–17, 1921–23.

SURFING

ORIGINS The Polynesian sport of surfing in a canoe (*ehorooe*) was first recorded by the British explorer Captain James Cook in December 1771 during his exploration of Tahiti. The modern sport developed in Hawaii, California and Australia in the mid-1950s. Although Hawaii is one of the 50 states, it is allowed to compete separately from the U.S. in international surfing competition.

WORLD AMATEUR CHAMPIONSHIPS First held in May 1964 in Sydney, Australia, the open championship is the most prestigious event in both men's and women's competition.

Most titles In the women's division the title has been won twice by two surfers: Joyce Hoffman (U.S.), 1965–66; and Sharon Weber (Hawaii), 1970 and 1972. The men's title has been won by different surfers on each occasion.

WORLD PROFESSIONAL CHAMPIONSHIPS First held in 1970, the World Championship has been organized by the Association of Surfing Professionals (ASP) since 1976. The World Championship is a circuit of events held throughout the year; the winning surfer is the one who gains the most points over the course of the year.

Most titles The most titles won by a professional surfer is five, by Mark Richards (Australia), 1975, 1979–82. The women's record is four, by two surfers: Frieda Zamba (U.S.), 1984–86, 1988; Wendy Botha (Australia), 1987, 1989, 1991–92.

SWIMMING

ORIGINS The earliest references to swimming races were in Japan in 36 B.C. The first national swimming association, the Metropolitan Swimming Clubs Association, was founded in England in 1791. The international governing body for swimming, diving and water polo—the *Fédération Internationale de Natation Amateur* (FINA)—was founded in 1908.

OLYMPIC GAMES Swimming events were included in the first modern Games in 1896 and have been included in every Games since.

Most gold medals The greatest number of Olympic gold medals won is nine, by Mark Spitz (U.S.): 100-meter and 200-meter freestyle, 1972; 100-meter and 200-meter butterfly, 1972; 4 x 100-meter freestyle, 1968 and 1972; 4 x 200-meter freestyle, 1968 and 1972; 4 x 100-meter medley, 1972. The record number of gold medals won by a woman is six, by Kristin Otto (East

Germany) at Seoul, South Korea in 1988: 100-meter freestyle, backstroke and butterfly, 50-meter freestyle, 4 x 100-meter freestyle and 4 x 100-meter medley.

Most medals The most medals won by a swimmer is 11, by two competitors: Mark Spitz (U.S.): nine gold (see above), one silver and one bronze, 1968–72; and Matt Biondi (U.S.), eight gold, two silver and one bronze, 1984–92. The most medals won by a woman is eight, by three swimmers: Dawn Fraser (Australia), four gold, four silver, 1956–64; Kornelia Ender (East Germany), four gold, four silver, 1972–76; Shirley Babashoff (U.S.), two gold, six silver, 1972–76.

Most medals (one Games) The most medals won at one Games is seven, by two swimmers: Mark Spitz (U.S.), seven golds in 1972; and Matt Biondi (U.S.), five gold, one silver and one bronze in 1988. Kristin Otto (East Germany) won six gold medals at the 1988 Games, the most for a woman swimmer.

WORLD CHAMPIONSHIPS The first world swimming championships were held in Belgrade, Yugoslavia in 1973. The championships have been held quadrennially since 1978.

Most gold medals Kornelia Ender (East Germany) won eight gold medals, 1973–75. Jim Montgomery (U.S.) won six gold medals, 1973–75, the most by a male swimmer.

Most medals Michael Gross (West Germany) has won 13 medals: five gold, five silver and three bronze, 1982–90. The most medals won by a female swimmer is 10, by Kornelia Ender, who won eight gold and two silver, 1973–75.

Most medals (one championship) Matt Biondi (U.S.) won seven medals—three gold, one silver and three bronze—in 1986 at Madrid, Spain. Three swimmers share the women's record of six medals: Tracy Caulkins (U.S.), five gold, one silver in 1978; Kristin Otto (East Germany), four gold, two silver in 1986; Mary T. Meagher (U.S.), one gold, three silver, two bronze in 1986.

UNITED STATES NATIONAL CHAMPIONSHIPS The first United States swimming championships were staged by the Amateur Athletic Union on August 25, 1888.

SWIMMING—MEN'S WORLD RECORDS (set in 50-meter pools)

Freestyle

Event	Time	Swimmer (Country)	Date
50 meters	21.81	Tom Jager (U.S.)	March 24, 1990
100 meters	48.42	Matt Biondi (U.S.)	August 10, 1988
200 meters	1:46.69	Giorgio Lamberti (Italy)	August 15, 1989
400 meters	3:45.00	Yevgeni Sadovyi (Unified Team)	July 29, 1992
800 meters	7:46.60	Kieren Perkins (Australia)	February 14, 1992
1,500 meters	14:43.48	Kieren Perkins (Australia)	July 31, 1992
4 x 100-meter relay	3:16.53	U.S. (Chris Jacobs, Troy Dalbey, Tom Jager, Matt Biondi)	September 25, 1988
4 x 200-meter relay	7:11.95	Unified Team (Dmitri Lepikov, Vladimir Pychenko, Veniamin Taianovitch, Yevgeni Sadovyi)	July 27, 1992

Breaststroke

Event	Time	Swimmer (Country)	Date
100 meters	1:00.95	Karolyi Guttler (Hungary)	August 5, 1993
200 meters	2:10.16	Michael Barrowman (U.S.)	July 29, 1992

Butterfly

Event	Time	Swimmer (Country)	Date
100 meters	52.84	Pablo Morales (U.S.)	June 23, 1986
200 meters	1:55.69	Melvin Stewart (U.S.)	January 12, 1991

Backstroke

Event	Time	Swimmer (Country)	Date
100 meters	53.86	Jeff Rouse (U.S.)	July 31, 1992
200 meters	1:56.57	Martin Zubero (Spain)	November 23, 1991

Individual Medley

Event	Time	Swimmer (Country)	Date
200 meters	1:59.36	Tamás Darnyi (Hungary)	January 13, 1991
400 meters	4:12.36	Tamás Darnyi (Hungary)	January 8, 1991
4 x 100-meter relay	3:36.93	U.S. (David Berkoff, Rich Schroeder, Matt Biondi, Chris Jacobs)	September 23, 1988
	3.36.93	U.S. (Jeff Rouse, Nelson Diebel, Pablo Morales, Jon Olsen)	July 31, 1992

Source: USA Swimming

TIMEOUT

MANHATTAN SWIM ☛ THE FASTEST SWIM AROUND MANHATTAN ISLAND IN NEW YORK CITY WAS 5 HOURS 53 MINUTES 57 SECONDS, BY KRIS RUTFORD (U.S.) ON AUGUST 29, 1992.

Most titles Tracy Caulkins has won a record 48 national swimming titles, 1977–84. The most titles for a male swimmer is 36, by Johnny Weissmuller, 1921–28.

Fastest swimmer In a 25-yard pool, Tom Jager (U.S.) achieved an average speed of 5.37 mph, swimming 50 yards in 19.05 seconds at Nashville, Tenn. on March 23, 1990. The women's fastest time is 4.48 mph, by Yang Wenyi (China) in her 50-meter world record (see World Records table, page 189).

SWIMMING—WOMEN'S WORLD RECORDS (set in 50-meter pools)

Freestyle

Event	Time	Swimmer (Country)	Date
50 meters	24.98	Yang Wenyi (China)	April 11, 1988
100 meters	54.48	Jenny Thompson (U.S.)	March 1, 1992
200 meters	1:57.55	Heike Freidrich (East Germany)	June 18, 1986
400 meters	4:03.85	Janet Evans (U.S.)	September 22, 1988
800 meters	8:16.22	Janet Evans (U.S.)	August 20, 1989
1,500 meters	15:52.10	Janet Evans (U.S.)	March 26, 1988
4 x 100-meter relay	3:39.46	U.S. (Nicole Haislett, Dara Torres, Angel Martino, Jenny Thompson)	July 28, 1992
4 x 200-meter relay	7:55.47	East Germany (Manuella Stellmach, Astrid Strauss, Anke Möhring, Heike Freidrich)	August 18, 1987

Breaststroke

100 meters	1:07.91	Silke Hörner (East Germany)	August 21, 1987
200 meters	2:25.35	Anita Nall (U.S.)	March 2, 1992

Butterfly

100 meters	57.93	Mary T. Meagher (U.S.)	August 16, 1981
200 meters	2:05.97	Mary T. Meagher (U.S.)	August 13, 1981

Backstroke

100 meters	1:00.31	Kristina Egerszegi (Hungary)	August 20, 1991
200 meters	2:06.82	Kristina Egerszegi (Hungary)	August 26, 1991

Individual Medley

200 meters	2:11.65	Lin Li (China)	July 30, 1992
400 meters	4:36.10	Petra Schneider (East Germany)	August 1, 1982
4 x 100-meter relay	4:02.54	U.S. (Lea Loveless, Anita Nall, Crissy Ahmann-Leighton, Jenny Thompson)	July 30, 1992

Source: USA Swimming

MASS RELAY ■ THE MOST PARTICIPANTS IN A ONE-DAY SWIM RELAY IS 2,305, EACH SWIMMING ONE LENGTH OF THE POOL. THIS RECORD RELAY WAS HELD AT THE AUBURN (NY) YMCA-WEIU ON MARCH 5–6, 1993.
(AUBURN YMCA-WEIU)

GOLDEN SWIM ■ ON AUGUST 11, 1993 ANDREW PINETTI BECAME THE YOUNGEST MALE TO SWIM ACROSS THE 1.25 MILE GOLDEN GATE, FROM SAN FRANCISCO TO MARIN. TEN-YEAR-OLD PINETTI COMPLETED THE SWIM IN 31 MINUTES 26 SECONDS.
(STEPHEN PINETTI)

SYNCHRONIZED SWIMMING

In international competition, synchronized swimmers compete in two disciplines: solo and duet. In both disciplines the swimmers perform to music a series of moves that are judged for technical skills and musical interpretation. In solo events the swimmer has to be synchronized with the music; in duet events the swimmers have to be synchronized with each other as well as with the music.

ORIGINS Annette Kellerman and Kay Curtis are considered the pioneers of synchronized swimming in the United States. Kellerman's water ballet performances drew widespread attention throughout the U.S. at the beginning of the 20th century. Curtis was responsible for establishing synchronized swimming as part of the physical education program at the University of Wisconsin. In the 1940s, film star Esther Williams again drew attention to the sport, and in 1945 the Amateur Athletic Union recognized the sport. In 1973 the first world championship was staged, and in 1984 synchronized swimming was recognized as an official Olympic sport. The governing body for the sport in this country is United States Synchronized Swimming, formed in 1978.

OLYMPIC GAMES Synchronized swimming was first staged as an official sport at the 1984 Games.

Most gold medals Two swimmers have won two gold medals: Tracie Ruiz-Conforto (U.S.), solo and duet, 1984; Carolyn Waldo (Canada), solo and duet, 1988.

Most medals Two swimmers have won three medals: Tracie Ruiz-Conforto (U.S.), two gold and one silver, 1984–88; Carolyn Waldo (Canada), two gold and one silver, 1984–88.

WORLD CHAMPIONSHIPS The world championships were first held in 1973, and have been held quadrennially since 1978.

Most titles The solo title has been won by a different swimmer on each occasion.

Most titles (team) The United States has won four team titles, 1973, 1975, 1978 and 1991.

UNITED STATES NATIONAL CHAMPIONSHIPS The first national championships were staged in 1946, and the competition is now an annual event.

Most titles Gail Johnson has won 11 national titles: six solo (two indoors, four outdoors), 1972–75; and five duet (two indoors, three outdoors), 1972–74.

Most titles (duet) The team of Karen and Sarah Josephson has won five national duet titles, 1985–88, and 1990.

ENGLISH CHANNEL SWIM ☞ THE OFFICIAL RECORD FOR SWIMMING THE ENGLISH CHANNEL IS 7 HOURS 40 MINUTES, BY PENNY DEAN (U.S.). SHE SWAM FROM SHAKESPEARE'S BAY, ENGLAND TO CAP GRIS-NEZ, FRANCE ON JULY 29, 1978.

TABLE TENNIS

ORIGINS The earliest evidence relating to a game resembling table tennis has been found in the catalogs of London sporting goods manufacturers in the 1880s. The International Table Tennis Federation (ITTF) was founded in 1926.

United States The United States Table Tennis Association was established in 1933. In 1971, a U.S. table tennis team was invited to play in the People's Republic of China, thereby initiating the first officially sanctioned Chinese-American cultural exchange in almost 20 years.

OLYMPIC GAMES Table tennis was included in the Olympic Games in 1988 for the first time.

Most medals Yoo Nam-Kyu (South Korea) has won three medals in Olympic competition: one gold, two bronze, 1988–92. Chin Jing (China) is the only woman to win two medals, one gold, one silver, in 1988.

WORLD CHAMPIONSHIPS The ITTF instituted European championships in 1926 and later designated this event the world championship. The tournament was staged annually until 1957, when the event became biennial.

SWAYTHLING CUP The men's team championship is named after Lady Swaythling, who donated the trophy in 1926.

Most titles The most wins is 12, by Hungary (1926, 1928–31, 1933 [two events were held that year, with Hungary winning both times], 1935, 1938, 1949, 1952, 1979).

PING, PING, PING ☞ THE RECORD NUMBER OF HITS IN 60 SECONDS IS 173, BY JACKIE BELLINGER AND LISA LOMAS (BOTH GREAT BRITAIN) AT NORTHGATE SPORTS CENTER, IPSWICH, ENGLAND ON FEBRUARY 7, 1993.

CORBILLON CUP The women's team championship is named after M. Marcel Corbillon, president of the French Table Tennis Association, who donated the trophy in 1934.

Most titles China has won the most titles, with nine wins (1965, 1975, 1977, 1979, 1981, 1983, 1985, 1987, 1989).

Men's singles The most victories in singles is five, by Viktor Barna (Hungary), 1931, 1932–35.

Women's singles The most victories is six, by Angelica Rozeanu (Romania), 1950–55.

Men's doubles The most victories is eight, by Viktor Barna (Hungary), 1929–35, 1939. The partnership that has won the most titles is Viktor Barna and Miklos Szabados (Hungary), 1929–33, 1935.

Women's doubles The most victories is seven, by Maria Mednyanszky (Hungary), 1928, 1930–35. The team that has won the most titles is Maria Mednyanszky and Anna Sipos (Hungary), 1930–35.

Mixed doubles Maria Mednyanszky (Hungary) has won a record six mixed doubles titles: 1927–28, 1930–31, 1933 (twice). The pairing of Miklos Szabados and Maria Mednyanszky (Hungary) won the title a record three times: 1930–31, 1933.

UNITED STATES NATIONAL CHAMPIONSHIPS U.S. national championships were first held in 1931.

Most titles Leah Neuberger (née Thall) won a record 21 titles between 1941 and 1961: nine women's singles, 12 women's doubles. Richard Mills won a record 10 men's singles titles between 1945 and 1962.

TAEKWONDO

ORIGINS Taekwondo is a martial art, with all activities based on defensive spirit, developed over 20 centuries in Korea. It was officially recognized as part of Korean tradition and culture on April 11, 1955. The first World Taekwondo Championships were organized by the Korean Taekwondo Association and were held at Seoul, South Korea in 1973. The World Taekwondo Federation was then formed and has organized biennial championships.

United States The United States Taekwondo Union was founded in 1974.

OLYMPIC GAMES Taekwondo was included as a demonstration sport at the 1988 and 1992 Games.

WORLD CHAMPIONSHIPS These biennial championships were first held in Seoul, South Korea in 1973, when they were staged by the Korean Taekwondo Association. Women's events were first staged unofficially in 1983 and have been officially recognized since 1987.

Most titles Chung Kook-hyun (South Korea) has won a record four world titles: light middleweight, 1982–83; welterweight 1985, 1987. The women's record is two titles, achieved by three athletes: Kim So-young (South Korea), 1987 and 1989; Lee Eun-young (South Korea), 1987 and 1989; Lynette Love (U.S.), 1987 and 1991.

TEAM HANDBALL

ORIGINS Team handball developed around the turn of the 20th century. It evolved from a game devised by soccer players in northern Germany and Denmark designed to keep them fit during the winter months. An outdoors version of the game

MARTIAL ART ■ LYNETTE LOVE IS ONE OF THREE ATHLETES TO WIN TWO WOMEN'S TAEKWONDO WORLD TITLES. (LYNETTE LOVE)

was included in the 1936 Olympic Games as a demonstration sport. In 1946 the International Handball Federation (IHF) was formed. The growth of team handball has been rapid since its reintroduction into the Olympic Games in 1972 as an indoor game with seven players on each side. The IHF claims 4.2 million members from 88 countries, second only to soccer in terms of worldwide membership.

United States Team handball was first introduced to the United States in the 1920s, and a national team entered the 1936 Olympic demonstration competition. In 1959 the United States Team Handball Federation (USTHF) was formed, and it still governs the sport in this country.

OLYMPIC GAMES

Most wins In men's competition the USSR/Unified Team has won the Olympic gold medal three times—1976, 1988 and 1992. In women's competition, introduced in 1976, two countries have won the gold medal twice: the USSR in 1976 and 1980; and South Korea in 1988 and 1992.

WORLD CHAMPIONSHIP This competition was instituted in 1938.

Most titles (country) Romania has won four men's and three women's titles (two outdoor, one indoor) from 1956 to 1974. East Germany has also won three women's titles, in 1971, 1975 and 1978.

TENNIS

ORIGINS The modern game evolved from the indoor sport of real tennis. There is an account of a game called "field tennis" in an English sports periodical dated September 29, 1793; however, the "father" of lawn tennis is considered to be Major Walter Wingfield, who patented a type of tennis called "sphairistike" in 1874. The Marylebone Cricket Club, England revised Wingfield's initial rules in 1877, and the famed All-England Croquet Club (home of the Wimbledon Championships) added the name Lawn Tennis to its title in 1877. The "open" era of tennis, when amateurs were permitted to play with and against professionals, was introduced in 1968.

GRAND SLAM

The grand slam is achieved by winning all four grand slam events—the Australian Open, French Open, Wimbledon and U.S. Open—in one calendar year.

GRAND SLAM WINNERS

Singles Don Budge (U.S.) was the first player to achieve the grand slam when he won all four events in 1938. The only player to have won the grand slam twice is Rod Laver (Australia), who accomplished this in 1962 and 1969. Three women have completed the grand slam: Maureen Connolly (U.S.), in 1953; Margaret Court (née Smith; Australia), in 1970; and Steffi Graf (West Germany), in 1988.

Doubles The only men to win the grand slam for doubles were Frank Sedgman and Ken McGregor (Australia) in 1951. Three women have won the grand slam: Maria Bueno (Brazil) in 1960; Martina Navratilova and Pam Shriver (U.S.) in 1984. Navratilova and Shriver won eight consecutive doubles titles from 1983–85.

Mixed doubles Ken Fletcher and Margaret Court (Australia) won all four legs of the grand slam in 1963. Owen Davidson (Australia) won all four events, with two partners, in 1967.

MOST GRAND SLAM TITLES

Singles The most singles championships won in grand slam tournaments is 24, by Margaret Court (née Smith; Australia): 11 Australian, five French, three Wimbledon, five U.S. Open between 1960

SLAM STATS ■ 1994 AUSTRALIAN OPEN CHAMPIONS STEFFI GRAF (LEFT) AND PETE SAMPRAS (RIGHT) BOTH HOLD GRAND SLAM RECORDS. IN 1988 GRAF BECAME THE ONLY PLAYER TO WIN THE GOLDEN SLAM OF TENNIS: THE OLYMPIC TITLE AND THE FOUR PROFESSIONAL GRAND SLAM EVENTS. IN 1990 SAMPRAS BECAME THE YOUNGEST MEN'S CHAMPION AT THE U.S. OPEN. (WILLIAM S. ROMANO, IBM/ATP TOUR/RUSS ADAMS)

and 1973. The men's record is 12, by Roy Emerson (Australia): six Australian, two French, two Wimbledon, two U.S. Open between 1961 and 1967.

Doubles The most wins by a doubles partnership is 20, by two teams: Louise Brough (U.S.) and Margaret Du Pont (U.S.), who won three French, five Wimbledon and 12 U.S. Opens, 1942–57; and by Martina Navratilova (U.S.) and Pam Shriver (U.S.). They won seven Australian, four French, five Wimbledon, four U.S. Opens, 1981–89.

AUSTRALIAN OPEN CHAMPIONSHIPS

The first Australasian championships were held in 1905, with New Zealand hosting the event in 1906 and 1912. A women's championship was not introduced until 1922. The tournament was changed to the Australian Open in 1925 and is counted as a grand slam event from that year. There were two championships in 1977 because the event was moved from early season (January) to December. It reverted to a January date in 1987, which meant

---

AUSTRALIAN OPEN CHAMPIONS (1905–1952)

Men's Singles				Women's Singles			
Year	Player	Year	Player	Year	Player	Year	Player
1905	Rodney Heath	1929	John Gregory	1905	no event	1929	Daphne Akhurst
1906	Tony Wilding	1930	Gar Moon	1906	no event	1930	Daphne Akhurst
1907	Horace Rice	1931	Jack Crawford	1907	no event	1931	Coral Buttsworth
1908	Fred Alexander	1932	Jack Crawford	1908	no event	1932	Coral Buttsworth
1909	Tony Wilding	1933	Jack Crawford	1909	no event	1933	Joan Hartigan
1910	Rodney Heath	1934	Fred Perry	1910	no event	1934	Joan Hartigan
1911	Norman Brookes	1935	Jack Crawford	1911	no event	1935	Dorothy Round
1912	J. Cecil Parke	1936	Adrian Quist	1912	no event	1936	Joan Hartigan
1913	E. F. Parker	1937	V. B. McGrath	1913	no event	1937	Nancye Wynne
1914	Pat O'Hara Wood	1938	Don Budge	1914	no event	1938	Dorothy M. Bundy
1915	Francis Lowe	1939	John Bromwich	1915	no event	1939	Emily Westacott
1916	not held	1940	Adrian Quist	1916	not held	1940	Nancye Wynne
1917	not held	1941	not held	1917	not held	1941	not held
1918	not held	1942	not held	1918	not held	1942	not held
1919	A. Kingscote	1943	not held	1919	no event	1943	not held
1920	Pat O'Hara Wood	1944	not held	1920	no event	1944	not held
1921	Rhys Gemmell	1945	not held	1921	no event	1945	not held
1922	Pat O'Hara Wood	1946	John Bromwich	1922	Margaret Molesworth	1946	Nancye Bolton[1]
1923	Pat O'Hara Wood	1947	Dinny Pails	1923	Margaret Molesworth	1947	Nancye Bolton
1924	James Anderson	1948	Adrian Quist	1924	Sylvia Lance	1948	Nancye Bolton
1925	James Anderson	1949	Frank Sedgman	1925	Daphne Akhurst	1949	Doris Hart
1926	John Hawkes	1950	Frank Sedgman	1926	Daphne Akhurst	1950	Louise Brough
1927	Gerald Patterson	1951	Dick Savitt	1927	Esna Boyd	1951	Nancye Bolton
1928	Jean Borotra	1952	Ken McGregor	1928	Daphne Akhurst	1952	Thelma Long

1– Nancye Bolton (née Wynne)

---

there was no championship in 1986. Currently the tournament is held at the Australian Tennis Center in Melbourne and is the first leg of the grand slam.

Most wins (men) The most wins is six, by Roy Emerson (Australia), 1961, 1963–67.

Most wins (women) The most wins is 11, by Margaret Court (née Smith) of Australia, 1960–66, 1969–71, 1973.

Men's doubles The most wins by one pair is eight, by John Bromwich and Adrian Quist (Aus-

tralia), 1938–40, 1946–50. In addition, Quist holds the record for most wins by one player with 10, winning in 1936–37 with Don Turnbull, to add to his triumphs with Bromwich.

Women's doubles The most wins by one pair is 10, by Nancye Bolton (née Wynne) and Thelma Long (née Coyne), both Australian. Their victories came in 1936–40, 1947–49, 1951–52. Long also holds the record for most wins with 12, winning in 1956 and 1958 with Mary Hawton.

(continued on p. 197)

AUSTRALIAN OPEN CHAMPIONS (1953–1994)

	Men's Singles				Women's Singles		
Year	**Player**	**Year**	**Player**	**Year**	**Player**	**Year**	**Player**
1953	Ken Rosewall	1975	John Newcombe	1953	Maureen Connolly	1975	Evonne Goolagong
1954	Mervyn Rose	1976	Mark Edmondson	1954	Thelma Long	1976	Evonne Cawley[3]
1955	Ken Rosewall	1977	Roscoe Tanner*	1955	Beryl Penrose	1977	Kerry Reid*
1956	Lew Hoad	1977	Vitas Gerulaitis*	1956	Mary Carter	1977	Evonne Cawley*
1957	Ashley Cooper	1978	Guillermo Vilas	1957	Shirley Fry	1978	Christine O'Neill
1958	Ashley Cooper	1979	Guillermo Vilas	1958	Angela Mortimer	1979	Barbara Jordan
1959	Alex Olmedo	1980	Brian Teacher	1959	Mary Reitano[1]	1980	Hana Mandlikova
1960	Rod Laver	1981	Johan Kriek	1960	Margaret Smith	1981	Martina Navratilova
1961	Roy Emerson	1982	Johan Kriek	1961	Margaret Smith	1982	Chris Evert
1962	Rod Laver	1983	Mats Wilander	1962	Margaret Smith	1983	Martina Navratilova
1963	Roy Emerson	1984	Mats Wilander	1963	Margaret Smith	1984	Chris Evert
1964	Roy Emerson	1985	Stefan Edberg	1964	Margaret Smith	1985	Martina Navratilova
1965	Roy Emerson	1986	not held	1965	Margaret Smith	1986	not held
1966	Roy Emerson	1987	Stefan Edberg	1966	Margaret Smith	1987	Hana Mandlikova
1967	Roy Emerson	1988	Mats Wilander	1967	Nancy Richey	1988	Steffi Graf
1968	Bill Bowrey	1989	Ivan Lendl	1968	Billie Jean King	1989	Steffi Graf
1969	Rod Laver	1990	Ivan Lendl	1969	Margaret Court[2]	1990	Steffi Graf
1970	Arthur Ashe	1991	Boris Becker	1970	Margaret Court[2]	1991	Monica Seles
1971	Ken Rosewall	1992	Jim Courier	1971	Margaret Court[2]	1992	Monica Seles
1972	Ken Rosewall	1993	Jim Courier	1972	Virginia Wade	1993	Monica Seles
1973	John Newcombe	1994	Pete Sampras	1973	Margaret Court[2]	1994	Steffi Graf
1974	Jimmy Connors			1974	Evonne Goolagong		

1–Mary Reitano (née Carter)   2–Margaret Court (née Smith)   3–Evonne Cawley (née Goolagong)
* There were two championships in 1977 because the event was moved from early season (January) to December.

FRENCH OPEN CHAMPIONS (1925–1993)

Men's Singles

Year	Player	Year	Player
1925	Rene Lacoste	1960	Nicola Pietrangeli
1926	Henri Cochet	1961	Manuel Santana
1927	Rene Lacoste	1962	Rod Laver
1928	Henri Cochet	1963	Roy Emerson
1929	Rene Lacoste	1964	Manuel Santana
1930	Henri Cochet	1965	Fred Stolle
1931	Jean Borotra	1966	Tony Roche
1932	Henri Cochet	1967	Roy Emerson
1933	Jack Crawford	1968	Ken Rosewall
1934	Gottfried Von Cramm	1969	Rod Laver
1935	Fred Perry	1970	Jan Kodes
1936	Gottfried Von Cramm	1971	Jan Kodes
1937	Henner Henkel	1972	Andres Gimeno
1938	Don Budge	1973	Ilie Nastase
1939	Donald McNeil	1974	Bjorn Borg
1940	not held	1975	Bjorn Borg
1941	Bernard Destremau*	1976	Adriano Panatta
1942	Bernard Destremau*	1977	Guillermo Vilas
1943	Yvon Petra*	1978	Bjorn Borg
1944	Yvon Petra*	1979	Bjorn Borg
1945	Yvon Petra*	1980	Bjorn Borg
1946	Marcel Bernard	1981	Bjorn Borg
1947	Jozsef Asboth	1982	Mats Wilander
1948	Frank Parker	1983	Yannick Noah
1949	Frank Parker	1984	Ivan Lendl
1950	Budge Patty	1985	Mats Wilander
1951	Jaroslav Drobny	1986	Ivan Lendl
1952	Jaroslav Drobny	1987	Ivan Lendl
1953	Ken Rosewall	1988	Mats Wilander
1954	Tony Trabert	1989	Michael Chang
1955	Tony Trabert	1990	Andres Gomez
1956	Lew Hoad	1991	Jim Courier
1957	Sven Davidson	1992	Jim Courier
1958	Mervyn Rose	1993	Sergei Bruguera
1959	Nicola Pietrangeli		

Women's Singles

Year	Player	Year	Player
1925	Suzanne Lenglen	1960	Darlene Hard
1926	Suzanne Lenglen	1961	Ann Haydon
1927	Kea Bouman	1962	Margaret Smith
1928	Helen Moody[1]	1963	Lesley Turner
1929	Helen Moody	1964	Margaret Smith
1930	Helen Moody	1965	Lesley Turner
1931	Cilly Aussem	1966	Ann Jones[3]
1932	Helen Moody	1967	Francoise Durr
1933	Margaret Scriven	1968	Nancy Richey
1934	Margaret Scriven	1969	Margaret Court[4]
1935	Hilde Sperling	1970	Margaret Court
1936	Hilde Sperling	1971	Evonne Goolagong
1937	Hilde Sperling	1972	Billie Jean King
1938	Simone Mathieu	1973	Margaret Court
1939	Simone Mathieu	1974	Chris Evert
1940	not held	1975	Chris Evert
1941	not held	1976	Sue Barker
1942	not held	1977	Mima Jausovec
1943	not held	1978	Virginia Ruzici
1944	not held	1979	Chris Evert
1945	not held	1980	Chris Evert
1946	Margaret Osborne	1981	Hana Mandlikova
1947	Pat Todd	1982	Martina Navratilova
1948	Nelly Landry	1983	Chris Evert
1949	Margaret Du Pont[2]	1984	Martina Navratilova
1950	Doris Hart	1985	Chris Evert
1951	Shirley Fry	1986	Chris Evert
1952	Doris Hart	1987	Steffi Graf
1953	Maureen Connolly	1988	Steffi Graf
1954	Maureen Connolly	1989	Arantxa Sanchez Vicario
1955	Angela Mortimer		
1956	Althea Gibson	1990	Monica Seles
1957	Shirley Bloomer	1991	Monica Seles
1958	Zsuzsi Kormoczy	1992	Monica Seles
1959	Christine Truman	1993	Steffi Graf

1 – Helen Moody (née Wills)   2 – Margaret Du Pont (née Osborne)   3 – Ann Jones (née Haydon)   4 – Margaret Court (née Smith)
* From 1941–45 the event was called Tournoi de France and was open only to French citizens.

Mixed doubles The most wins by one pair is four, by two teams: Harry Hopman and Nell Hopman (née Hall; Australia), 1930, 1936–37, 1939; Colin Long and Nancye Bolton (née Wynne; Australia), 1940, 1946–48.

Most titles (overall) Margaret Court (née Smith) has won a record 21 Australian Open titles between 1960 and 1973—11 singles, eight doubles and two mixed doubles.

Youngest champions The youngest women's singles champion was Monica Seles, Yugoslavia, who won the 1991 event at age 17 years 55 days.

FRENCH OPEN CHAMPIONSHIPS

The first French championships were held in 1891; however, entry was restricted to members of French clubs until 1925. Grand slam records include the French Open only from 1925. This event has been staged at the Stade Roland Garros since 1928 and currently is the second leg of the grand slam.

Most wins (men) Bjorn Borg (Sweden) has won the French title a record six times: 1974–75, 1978–81.

Most wins (women) Chris Evert has won a record seven French titles: 1974–75, 1979–80, 1983, 1985–86.

Men's doubles Roy Emerson (Australia) has won the men's doubles a record six times, 1960–65, with five different partners.

Women's doubles The pair of Martina Navratilova and Pam Shriver (both U.S.) have won the doubles title a record four times, 1984–85, 1987–88. The most wins by an individual player is seven, by Martina Navratilova—four times with Pam Shriver, 1984–85, 1987–88; and with three other players, in 1975, 1982 and 1986.

Mixed doubles Two teams have won the mixed title three times: Ken Fletcher and Margaret Smith (Australia), 1963–65; Jean-Claude Barclay and Francoise Durr (France), 1968, 1971, 1973. Margaret Court (née Smith) has won the title the most times, with four wins, winning with Marty Riessen (U.S.) in 1969, in addition to her three wins with Fletcher. Fletcher and Barclay share the men's record of three wins.

Most titles (overall) Margaret Court (née Smith) has won a record 13 French Open titles, 1962–73: five singles, four doubles and four mixed doubles.

Youngest champions The youngest singles champion at the French Open was Monica Seles (Yugoslavia) in 1990, at 16 years 169 days. The youngest men's winner is Michael Chang (U.S.), who was 17 years 109 days when he won the 1989 title.

WIMBLEDON CHAMPIONSHIPS

The "Lawn Tennis Championships" at the All-England Club, Wimbledon are generally regarded as the most prestigious in tennis and currently form the third leg of the grand slam events. They were first held in 1877 and, until 1922, were organized on a challenge round system (the defending champion automatically qualifies for the following year's final and plays the winner of the challenger event). Wimbledon became an open championship (professionals could compete) in 1968.

Most titles (men) Overall, the most titles is seven, by William Renshaw (Great Britain), 1881–86, 1889. Since the abolition of the Challenge Round in 1922, the most wins is five, by Bjorn Borg (Sweden), 1976–80.

Most titles (women) Martina Navratilova has won a record nine titles: 1978–79, 1982–87, 1990.

Men's doubles Lawrence and Reginald Doherty (Great Britain) won the doubles title a record eight times: 1897–1901, 1903–05.

Women's doubles Suzanne Lenglen (France) and Elizabeth Ryan (U.S.) won the doubles a record six times: 1919–23, 1925. Elizabeth Ryan was a winning partner on a record 12 occasions: 1914, 1919–23, 1925–27, 1930, 1933–34.

Mixed doubles The team of Ken Fletcher and Margaret Court (née Smith), both of Australia, won the mixed doubles a record four times: 1963, 1965–66, 1968. Fletcher's four victories tie him for the men's record for wins, which is shared by two other players: Vic Seixas (U.S.), 1953–56; Owen Davidson (Australia), 1967, 1971, 1973–74. Elizabeth Ryan (U.S.) holds the women's record with seven wins: 1919, 1921, 1923, 1927–28, 1930, 1932.

Most titles (overall) Billie Jean King (U.S.) won a record 20 Wimbledon titles from 1961–79: six singles, 10 doubles and four mixed doubles.

WIMBLEDON CHAMPIONS (1877–1933)

Men's Singles

Year	Player	Year	Player
1877	Spencer Gore	1907	Norman Brookes
1878	Frank Hadlow	1908	Arthur Gore
1879	Rev. John Hartley	1909	Arthur Gore
1880	Rev. John Hartley	1910	Tony Wilding
1881	William Renshaw	1911	Tony Wilding
1882	William Renshaw	1912	Tony Wilding
1883	William Renshaw	1913	Tony Wilding
1884	William Renshaw	1914	Norman Brookes
1885	William Renshaw	1915	not held
1886	William Renshaw	1916	not held
1887	Herbert Lawford	1917	not held
1888	Ernest Renshaw	1918	not held
1889	William Renshaw	1919	Gerald Patterson
1890	Willoughby Hamilton	1920	Bill Tilden
1891	Wilfred Baddeley	1921	Bill Tilden
1892	Wilfred Baddeley	1922	Gerald Patterson
1893	Joshua Pim	1923	William Johnston
1894	Joshua Pim	1924	Jean Borotra
1895	Wilfred Baddeley	1925	Rene Lacoste
1896	Harold Mahoney	1926	Jean Borotra
1897	Reginald Doherty	1927	Henri Cochet
1898	Reginald Doherty	1928	Rene Lacoste
1899	Reginald Doherty	1929	Henri Cochet
1900	Reginald Doherty	1930	Bill Tilden
1901	Arthur Gore	1931	Sidney Wood
1902	Lawrence Doherty	1932	Ellsworth Vines
1903	Lawrence Doherty	1933	Jack Crawford
1904	Lawrence Doherty		
1905	Lawrence Doherty		
1906	Lawrence Doherty		

Women's Singles

Year	Player	Year	Player
1877	no event	1907	May Sutton
1878	no event	1908	Charlotte Sterry
1879	no event	1909	Dora Boothby
1880	no event	1910	Dorothea Lambert-Chambers[3]
1881	no event	1911	Dorothea Lambert-Chambers
1882	no event	1912	Ethel Larcombe
1883	no event	1913	Dorothea Lambert-Chambers
1884	Maud Watson	1914	Dorothea Lambert-Chambers
1885	Maud Watson	1915	not held
1886	Blanche Bingley	1916	not held
1887	Lottie Dod	1917	not held
1888	Lottie Dod	1918	not held
1889	Blanche Hillyard[1]	1919	Suzanne Lenglen
1890	Helene Rice	1920	Suzanne Lenglen
1891	Lottie Dod	1921	Suzanne Lenglen
1892	Lottie Dod	1922	Suzanne Lenglen
1893	Lottie Dod	1923	Suzanne Lenglen
1894	Blanche Hillyard	1924	Kathleen McKane
1895	Charlotte Cooper	1925	Suzanne Lenglen
1896	Charlotte Cooper	1926	Kathleen Godfree[4]
1897	Blanche Hillyard	1927	Helen Wills
1898	Charlotte Cooper	1928	Helen Wills
1899	Blanche Hillyard	1929	Helen Wills
1900	Blanche Hillyard	1930	Helen Moody[5]
1901	Charlotte Sterry[2]	1931	Cilly Aussem
1902	Muriel Robb	1932	Helen Moody
1903	Dorothea Douglass	1933	Helen Moody
1904	Dorothea Douglass		
1905	May Sutton		
1906	Dorothea Douglass		

1–Blanche Hillyard (née Bingley)   2–Charlotte Sterry (née Cooper)   3–Dorothea Lambert-Chambers (née Douglass)   4–Kathleen Godfree (née McKane)

5–Helen Moody (née Wills)

Youngest champions The youngest champion was Lottie Dod (Great Britain), who was 15 years 285 days when she won in 1887. The youngest men's champion was Boris Becker (Germany), who was 17 years 227 days when he won in 1985.

WIMBLEDON CHAMPIONS (1934–1993)

Men's Singles				Women's Singles			
Year	Player	Year	Player	Year	Player	Year	Player
1934	Fred Perry	1964	Roy Emerson	1934	Dorothy Round	1964	Maria Bueno
1935	Fred Perry	1965	Roy Emerson	1935	Helen Moody[5]	1965	Margaret Smith
1936	Fred Perry	1966	Manuel Santana	1936	Helen Jacobs	1966	Billie Jean King
1937	Don Budge	1967	John Newcombe	1937	Dorothy Round	1967	Billie Jean King
1938	Don Budge	1968	Rod Laver	1938	Helen Moody	1968	Billie Jean King
1939	Bobby Riggs	1969	Rod Laver	1939	Alice Marble	1969	Ann Jones
1940	not held	1970	John Newcombe	1940	not held	1970	Margaret Court[6]
1941	not held	1971	John Newcombe	1941	not held	1971	Evonne Goolagong
1942	not held	1972	Stan Smith	1942	not held	1972	Billie Jean King
1943	not held	1973	Jan Kodes	1943	not held	1973	Billie Jean King
1944	not held	1974	Jimmy Connors	1944	not held	1974	Chris Evert
1945	not held	1975	Arthur Ashe	1945	not held	1975	Billie Jean King
1946	Yvon Petra	1976	Bjorn Borg	1946	Pauline Betz	1976	Chris Evert
1947	Jack Kramer	1977	Bjorn Borg	1947	Margaret Osborne	1977	Virginia Wade
1948	Bob Falkenburg	1978	Bjorn Borg	1948	Louise Brough	1978	Martina Navratilova
1949	Ted Schroeder	1979	Bjorn Borg	1949	Louise Brough	1979	Martina Navratilova
1950	Budge Patty	1980	Bjorn Borg	1950	Louise Brough	1980	Evonne Cawley[7]
1951	Dick Savitt	1981	John McEnroe	1951	Doris Hart	1981	Chris Evert
1952	Frank Sedgman	1982	Jimmy Connors	1952	Maureen Connolly	1982	Martina Navratilova
1953	Vic Seixas	1983	John McEnroe	1953	Maureen Connolly	1983	Martina Navratilova
1954	Jaroslav Drobny	1984	John McEnroe	1954	Maureen Connolly	1984	Martina Navratilova
1955	Tony Trabert	1985	Boris Becker	1955	Louise Brough	1985	Martina Navratilova
1956	Lew Hoad	1986	Boris Becker	1956	Shirley Fry	1986	Martina Navratilova
1957	Lew Hoad	1987	Pat Cash	1957	Althea Gibson	1987	Martina Navratilova
1958	Ashley Cooper	1988	Stefan Edberg	1958	Althea Gibson	1988	Steffi Graf
1959	Alex Olmedo	1989	Boris Becker	1959	Maria Bueno	1989	Steffi Graf
1960	Neale Fraser	1990	Stefan Edberg	1960	Maria Bueno	1990	Martina Navratilova
1961	Rod Laver	1991	Michael Stich	1961	Angela Mortimer	1991	Steffi Graf
1962	Rod Laver	1992	Andre Agassi	1962	Karen Susman	1992	Steffi Graf
1963	Chuck McKinley	1993	Pete Sampras	1963	Margaret Smith	1993	Steffi Graf

5 – Helen Moody (née Wills)   6 – Margaret Court (née Smith)   7 – Evonne Cawley (née Goolagong)

UNITED STATES OPEN CHAMPIONSHIPS

The first official U.S. championships were staged in 1881. From 1884 to 1911, the contest was based on a challenger format. In 1968 and 1969, separate amateur and professional events were held. Since 1970, there has been only an Open competition.

On the current schedule the U.S. Open is the fourth and final leg of the grand slam and is played at the U.S. National Tennis Center, Flushing Meadows, N.Y.

Most titles (men) The most wins is seven, by three players: Richard Sears (U.S.), 1881–87; William

U.S. OPEN CHAMPIONS (1881–1938)

Men's Singles

Year	Player	Year	Player
1881	Richard Sears	1910	William Larned
1882	Richard Sears	1911	William Larned
1883	Richard Sears	1912	Maurice McLoughlin
1884	Richard Sears	1913	Maurice McLoughlin
1885	Richard Sears	1914	Richard Williams
1886	Richard Sears	1915	William Johnston
1887	Richard Sears	1916	Richard Williams
1888	Henry Slocum Jr.	1917	Lindley Murray
1889	Henry Slocum Jr.	1918	Lindley Murray
1890	Oliver Campbell	1919	William Johnston
1891	Oliver Campbell	1920	Bill Tilden
1892	Oliver Campbell	1921	Bill Tilden
1893	Robert Wrenn	1922	Bill Tilden
1894	Robert Wrenn	1923	Bill Tilden
1895	Fred Hovey	1924	Bill Tilden
1896	Robert Wrenn	1925	Bill Tilden
1897	Robert Wrenn	1926	Rene Lacoste
1898	Malcolm Whitman	1927	Rene Lacoste
1899	Malcolm Whitman	1928	Henri Cochet
1900	Malcolm Whitman	1929	Bill Tilden
1901	William Larned	1930	John Doeg
1902	William Larned	1931	Ellsworth Vines
1903	Lawrence Doherty	1932	Ellsworth Vines
1904	Holcombe Ward	1933	Fred Perry
1905	Beals Wright	1934	Fred Perry
1906	William Clothier	1935	Wilmer Allison
1907	William Larned	1936	Fred Perry
1908	William Larned	1937	Don Budge
1909	William Larned	1938	Don Budge

Women's Singles

Year	Player	Year	Player
1881	no event	1910	Hazel Hotchkiss
1882	no event	1911	Hazel Hotchkiss
1883	no event	1912	Mary Browne
1884	no event	1913	Mary Browne
1885	no event	1914	Mary Browne
1886	no event	1915	Molla Bjurstedt
1887	Ellen Hansell	1916	Molla Bjurstedt
1888	Bertha Townsend	1917	Molla Bjurstedt
1889	Bertha Townsend	1918	Molla Bjurstedt
1890	Ellen Roosevelt	1919	Hazel Wightman[1]
1891	Mabel Cahill	1920	Molla Mallory[2]
1892	Mabel Cahill	1921	Molla Mallory
1893	Aline Terry	1922	Molla Mallory
1894	Helen Helwig	1923	Helen Wills
1895	Juliette Atkinson	1924	Helen Wills
1896	Elisabeth Moore	1925	Helen Wills
1897	Juliette Atkinson	1926	Molla Mallory
1898	Juliette Atkinson	1927	Helen Wills
1899	Marion Jones	1928	Helen Wills
1900	Myrtle McAteer	1929	Helen Wills
1901	Elisabeth Moore	1930	Betty Nuthall
1902	Marion Jones	1931	Helen Moody[3]
1903	Elisabeth Moore	1932	Helen Jacobs
1904	May Sutton	1933	Helen Jacobs
1905	Elisabeth Moore	1934	Helen Jacobs
1906	Helen Homans	1935	Helen Jacobs
1907	Evelyn Sears	1936	Alice Marble
1908	Maud Bargar-Wallach	1937	Anita Lizana
1909	Hazel Hotchkiss	1938	Alice Marble

1 – Hazel Wightman (née Hotchkiss)   2 – Molla Mallory (née Bjurstedt)   3 – Helen Moody (née Wills)

Larned (U.S.), 1901–02, 1907–11; Bill Tilden (U.S.), 1920–25, 1929.

Most titles (women) Molla Mallory (née Bjurstedt; U.S.) won a record eight titles: 1915–18, 1920–22, 1926.

Men's doubles The most wins by one pair is five, by Richard Sears and James Dwight (U.S.),

1882–84, 1886–87. The most wins by an individual player is six, by two players: Richard Sears, 1882–84, 1886–87 (with Dwight) and 1885 (with Joseph Clark); Holcombe Ward, 1899–1901 (with Dwight Davis), 1904–06 (with Beals Wright).

U.S. OPEN CHAMPIONS (1939–1993)

Men's Singles

Year	Player	Year	Player
1939	Bobby Riggs	1968	Arthur Ashe*
1940	Donald McNeil	1968	Arthur Ashe†
1941	Bobby Riggs	1969	Stan Smith*
1942	Ted Schroeder	1969	Rod Laver†
1943	Joseph Hunt	1970	Ken Rosewall
1944	Frank Parker	1971	Stan Smith
1945	Frank Parker	1972	Ilie Nastase
1946	Jack Kramer	1973	John Newcombe
1947	Jack Kramer	1974	Jimmy Connors
1948	Pancho Gonzalez	1975	Manuel Orantes
1949	Pancho Gonzalez	1976	Jimmy Connors
1950	Arthur Larsen	1977	Guillermo Vilas
1951	Frank Sedgman	1978	Jimmy Connors
1952	Frank Sedgman	1979	John McEnroe
1953	Tony Trabert	1980	John McEnroe
1954	Vic Seixas	1981	John McEnroe
1955	Tony Trabert	1982	Jimmy Connors
1956	Ken Rosewall	1983	Jimmy Connors
1957	Malcolm Anderson	1984	John McEnroe
1958	Ashley Cooper	1985	Ivan Lendl
1959	Neale Fraser	1986	Ivan Lendl
1960	Neale Fraser	1987	Ivan Lendl
1961	Roy Emerson	1988	Mats Wilander
1962	Rod Laver	1989	Boris Becker
1963	Raphael Osuna	1990	Pete Sampras
1964	Roy Emerson	1991	Stefan Edberg
1965	Manuel Santana	1992	Stefan Edberg
1966	Fred Stolle	1993	Pete Sampras
1967	John Newcombe		

Women's Singles

Year	Player	Year	Player
1939	Alice Marble	1968	Margaret Court*4
1940	Alice Marble	1968	Virginia Wade†
1941	Sarah Cooke	1969	Margaret Court*
1942	Pauline Betz	1969	Margaret Court†
1943	Pauline Betz	1970	Margaret Court
1944	Pauline Betz	1971	Billie Jean King
1945	Sarah Cooke	1972	Billie Jean King
1946	Pauline Betz	1973	Margaret Court
1947	Louise Brough	1974	Billie Jean King
1948	Margaret Du Pont	1975	Chris Evert
1949	Margaret Du Pont	1976	Chris Evert
1950	Margaret Du Pont	1977	Chris Evert
1951	Maureen Connolly	1978	Chris Evert
1952	Maureen Connolly	1979	Tracy Austin
1953	Maureen Connolly	1980	Chris Evert
1954	Doris Hart	1981	Tracy Austin
1955	Doris Hart	1982	Chris Evert
1956	Shirley Fry	1983	Martina Navratilova
1957	Althea Gibson	1984	Martina Navratilova
1958	Althea Gibson	1985	Hanna Mandlikova
1959	Maria Bueno	1986	Martina Navratilova
1960	Darlene Hard	1987	Martina Navratilova
1961	Darlene Hard	1988	Steffi Graf
1962	Margaret Smith	1989	Steffi Graf
1963	Maria Bueno	1990	Gabriela Sabatini
1964	Maria Bueno	1991	Monica Seles
1965	Margaret Smith	1992	Monica Seles
1966	Maria Bueno	1993	Steffi Graf
1967	Billie Jean King		

4– Margaret Court (née Smith)   * Amateur championship   † Open championship

Women's doubles The most wins by a pair is 12, by Louise Brough and Margaret Du Pont (née Osborne), both of the U.S.. They won in 1942–50 and in 1955–57. Margaret Du Pont holds the record for an individual player with 13 wins; adding to her victories with Brough was the 1941 title with Sarah Cooke.

Mixed doubles The most wins by one pair is four, by William Talbert and Margaret Osborne (U.S.), who won in 1943–46. The most titles won by any individual is nine, by Margaret Du Pont (née Osborne). She won in 1943–46, 1950, 1956, 1958–60. The most titles won by a man is four, accomplished by six players: Edwin Fischer (U.S.), 1894–96, 1898; Wallace Johnson (U.S.), 1907, 1909, 1911, 1920; Bill Tilden (U.S.), 1913–14, 1922–23; William Talbert (U.S.), 1943–46; Owen Davidson (Australia), 1966–67, 1971, 1973; and Marty Riessen (U.S.), 1969–70, 1972, 1980.

Most titles (overall) Margaret Du Pont (née Osborne) won a record 25 U.S. Open titles from 1941–60—three singles, 13 doubles, and nine mixed doubles.

Youngest champions The youngest singles champion was Tracy Austin (U.S.), who was 16 years 271 days when she won the women's singles in 1979. The youngest men's champion was Pete Sampras (U.S.), who was 19 years 28 days when he won the 1990 title.

OLYMPIC GAMES Tennis was reintroduced to the Olympic Games in 1988, having originally been included at the Games from 1896 to 1924. It was also a demonstration sport in 1968 and 1984.

Most gold medals Max Decugis (France) won four gold medals: men's singles, 1906; men's doubles, 1906; mixed doubles, 1906 and 1920.

Most medals Max Decugis (France) won a record six medals in Olympic competition: four gold (see above), one silver and one bronze, 1900–1920. Kitty McKane (Great Britain) won a women's record five medals: one gold, two silver and two bronze, 1920–24.

DAVIS CUP The Davis Cup, the men's international team championship, was first held in 1900, and is held annually.

Most wins The U.S. team has won the Davis Cup a record 30 times, 1900–92.

Most matches (career) Nicola Pietrangeli (Italy) played a record 163 matches (66 ties), 1954 to 1972, winning 120. He played 109 singles (winning 78) and 54 doubles (winning 42).

Most matches (season) Ilie Nastase (Romania) set a singles season mark of 18 wins (with 2 losses) in 1971.

UNITED STATES TEAM RECORDS

Most selections John McEnroe has played for the U.S. team on 31 occasions, 1978–92.

Most wins John McEnroe has won 60 matches in Davis Cup competition—41 singles and 19 doubles.

FEDERATION CUP The Federation Cup, the women's international team championship, was first held in 1963 and is an annual event.

Most wins The United States has won the Federation Cup a record 14 times.

MEN'S PROFESSIONAL TOUR RECORDS

Most singles titles (career) Jimmy Connors (U.S.) has won 109 singles titles, 1972–89.

MOST TITLES ■ FROM 1972–89 JIMMY CONNORS WON 109 EVENTS, THE MOST OF ANY MALE PLAYER. (ATP TOUR)

TOP EARNER ■ MARTINA NAVRATILOVA HAS WON A RECORD $19,432,645 DURING HER LEGENDARY CAREER. (WILLIAM S. ROMANO)

Most singles titles (season) Three players have won 15 titles in one season: Jimmy Connors (U.S.), 1977; Guillermo Vilas (Argentina), 1977; Ivan Lendl (Czechoslovakia), 1982.

Most doubles titles (career) Tom Okker (Netherlands) has won 78 doubles titles, 1968–79.

Most doubles titles (season) John McEnroe (U.S.) won 17 doubles titles in 1979.

Most consecutive match wins Guillermo Vilas (Argentina) won 46 consecutive matches, 1977–78.

Most weeks ranked number one Jimmy Connors (U.S.) held the number one ranking on the ATP computer from July 29, 1974 to August 16, 1977, a total of 159 weeks—the longest streak in tour history.

Highest earnings (career) Ivan Lendl (Czechoslovakia) has won a career record $20,248,503, 1978–93.

Highest earnings (season) Pete Sampras (U.S.) earned a season record $3,648,075 in 1993.

WOMEN'S PROFESSIONAL TOUR RECORDS

Most singles titles (career) Martina Navratilova (U.S.) has won 166 titles, 1975–93.

Most singles titles (season) Martina Navratilova won 16 titles in 1983.

Most consecutive matches won Martina Navratilova won 74 consecutive matches in 1984.

Most consecutive weeks ranked number one Steffi Graf (Germany) held the number one computer ranking from August 17, 1987 to March 11, 1991, a total of 186 weeks.

Highest earnings (career) Martina Navratilova (U.S.) has won a career record $19,432,645 in prize money, 1972–93.

Highest earnings (season) Steffi Graf (Germany) won a season record of $2,821,337 in 1993.

TRACK AND FIELD

ORIGINS Competition in running, jumping and throwing must have occurred from the earliest days of humankind. The earliest evidence of organized running is from 3800 B.C. in Egypt. The ancient Olympic Games were cultural festivals that highlighted the ancient Greek ideal of perfection of mind and body. The first modern Olympic Games, staged in 1896, focused on athletic achievement and the spirit of competition, and the

(*continued on p. 206*)

BACKWARDS RUNNING ☛ TIMOTHY "BUD" BADYANA (U.S.) RAN THE FASTEST BACKWARDS MARATHON IN 4 HOURS 15 SECONDS AT COLUMBUS, OHIO ON NOVEMBER 10, 1991.

OVERCOMING OBSTACLES ■ IN 1993 COLIN JACK-SON (ABOVE) WON THE 110 METER HURDLES WORLD TITLE IN A RECORD 12.91 SECONDS. IN 1992 MI-CHAEL HOUT (RIGHT) SET A WORLD RECORD OF 20 SECONDS FOR THE SAME DISTANCE WHILE JUGGLING THREE BALLS. (ALLSPORT/MIKE POWELL, DON BENNETT)

TIMEOUT

24-HOUR RELAY ☛ THE GREATEST DISTANCE COVERED IN 24 HOURS BY A TEAM OF TEN IS 280.232 MILES, BY OXFORD STRIDERS RC AT EAST LONDON, SOUTH AFRICA ON OCTOBER 5–6, 1990.

WORLD RECORDS—MEN

World records are for the men's events scheduled by the International Amateur Athletic Federation. Full automatic electronic timing is mandatory for events up to 400 meters.

Event	Time	Athlete (Country)	Place	Date
100 meters	9.86	Carl Lewis (U.S.)	Tokyo, Japan	Aug. 25, 1991
200 meters	19.72	Pietro Mennea (Italy)	Mexico City, Mexico	Sept. 12, 1979
400 meters	43.29	Butch Reynolds (U.S.)	Zürich, Switzerland	Aug. 17, 1988
800 meters	1:41.73	Sebastian Coe (Great Britain)	Florence, Italy	June 10, 1981
1,500 meters	3:28.86	Noureddine Morceli (Algeria)	Rieti, Italy	Sept. 6, 1992
1 mile	3:44.39	Noureddine Morcelli (Algeria)	Rietti, Italy	Sept. 5, 1993
5,000 meters	12:58.39	Saïd Aouita (Morocco)	Rome, Italy	July 22, 1987
10,000 meters	26:58.38	Yobes Ondieki (Kenya)	Oslo, Norway	July 10, 1993
110 meter hurdles	12.91	Colin Jackson (Great Britain)	Stuttgart, Germany	Aug. 20, 1993
400 meter hurdles	46.78	Kevin Young (U.S.)	Barcelona, Spain	Aug. 6, 1992
3,000-meter steeplechase	8:02.08	Moses Kiptanui (Kenya)	Zürich, Switzerland	Aug. 19, 1992
4 x 100 meters	37.40	United States (Mike Marsh, Leroy Burrell, Dennis Mitchell, Carl Lewis)	Barcelona, Spain	Aug. 8, 1992
	37.40	United States (John Drummond, Andre Cason, Dennis Mitchell, Leroy Burrell)	Stuttgart, Germany	Aug. 21, 1993
4 x 400 meters	2:54.29	United States (Andrew Valmon, Quincy Watts, Butch Reynolds, Michael Johnson)	Stuttgart, Germany	Aug. 22, 1993

Distance

Event	Distance	Athlete (Country)	Place	Date
High jump	8' ½"	Javier Sotomayor (Cuba)	Salamanca, Spain	July 27, 1993
Pole vault	20' 1½"	Sergey Bubka (Ukraine)	Tokyo, Japan	Sept. 19, 1992
Long jump	29' 4½"	Mike Powell (U.S.)	Tokyo, Japan	Aug. 30, 1991
Triple jump	58' 11½"	Willie Banks (U.S.)	Indianapolis, Ind.	June 16, 1985
Shot	75' 10¼"	Randy Barnes (U.S.)	Los Angeles, Calif.	May 20, 1990
Discus	243' 0"	Jürgen Schult (East Germany)	Neubrandenburg, Germany	June 6, 1986
Hammer	284' 7"	Yuriy Sedykh (USSR)	Stuttgart, Germany	Aug. 30, 1986
Javelin	313' 10"	Jan Zelezny (Czech Republic)	Sheffield, England	Aug. 29, 1993

Decathlon

8,891 points	Dan O'Brien (U.S.) (1st day: 100m 10.43 sec, Long jump 26' 6¼", Shot put 54' 9¼", High jump 6' 9½", 400 m 48.51 sec), (2nd day: 110 m hurdles 13.98 sec, Discus 159' 4", Pole vault 16' 4¾", Javelin 205' 4", 1,500 m 4:42.10 sec), Talence, France, Sept. 4–5, 1992

Walking

Event	Time	Athlete (Country)	Place	Date
20 km	1:18.35.2	Stefan Johansson (Sweden)	Fana, Norway	May 15, 1992
50 km	3:41.38.4	Raul Gonzales (Mexico)	Bergen, Norway	May 27, 1979

Games have provided the focus for track and field as a sport ever since. In 1983, a separate world championship was introduced.

OLYMPIC GAMES The first modern Olympic Games were staged in Athens, Greece, April 6–15, 1896. Fifty-nine athletes from 10 nations competed; women's events were not added until 1928.

Most gold medals Ray Ewry (U.S.) holds the all-time record for most appearances atop the winners' podium, with 10 gold medals: standing high jump (1900, 1904, 1906, 1908); standing long jump (1900, 1904, 1906, 1908); standing triple jump (1900, 1904). The women's record is four, shared by four athletes: Fanny Blankers-Koen (Netherlands): 100 m, 200 m, 80 m hurdles and 4 x 100 m relay in 1948; Betty Cuthbert (Australia): 100 m, 200 m, 4 x 100 m relay in 1956, and 400 m in 1964; Barbel Wockel (née Eckert; East Germany): 200 m and 4 x 100 m relay in both 1976 and 1980; Evelyn Ashford (U.S.): 100 m and 4 x 100 m relay in 1984, 4 x 100 m relay in 1988, 4 x 100 m relay in 1992.

Most gold medals (one Games) Paavo Nurmi (Finland) won five gold medals at the 1924 Games. His victories came in the 1,500 m, 5,000 m, 10,000 m cross-country, 3,000 m team, and cross-country team. The most wins at individual events (not including relay or other team races) is four, by Alvin Kraenzlein (U.S.) in 1900 at 60 m, 110 m hurdles, 200 m hurdles and the long jump.

Most medals won Paavo Nurmi (Finland) won a record 12 medals (nine gold, three silver) in the Games of 1920, 1924 and 1928. The women's record is seven, shared by two athletes: Shirley de la

Hunty (Australia), three gold, one silver, three bronze in the 1948, 1952 and 1956 Games; Irena Szewinska (Poland), three gold, two silver, two bronze in the 1964, 1968, 1972 and 1976 Games.

INDIVIDUAL RECORDS (U.S. ATHLETES)

Most medals Ray Ewry's 10 gold medals are the most won by any U.S. athlete (see above). Florence Griffith-Joyner has won a women's record five medals in track and field—three golds, two silver in the 1984 and 1988 Games.

Most gold medals Ray Ewry holds the Olympic mark for most golds (see above). The women's record for gold medals is four, by Evelyn Ashford—100m and 4 x 100 m relay in 1984, 4 x 100 m relay in 1988, 4 x 100 m relay in 1992.

Most gold medals (one Games) The most gold medals won at one Olympics is four, by three men: Alvin Kraenzlein (see above); Jesse Owens, 100 m, 200 m, long jump and 4 x 100 m relay in 1936; Carl Lewis, 100 m, 200 m, long jump and 4 x 100 m relay in 1984. The women's record is three golds, held by Wilma Rudolph, Valerie Brisco and Florence Griffith-Joyner (see above).

WORLD CHAMPIONSHIPS Quadriennial world championships distinct from the Olympic Games were first held in 1983 at Helsinki, Finland.

Most medals The most medals won is ten by two athletes: seven gold, two silver, one bronze by Carl Lewis (U.S.), 1983–93; and two gold, two silver, six bronze by Merlene Ottey (Jamaica), 1983–93.

Most consecutive titles Sergei Bubka (USSR/Ukraine) is the only athlete to win four consecutive world titles, winning the pole vault, 1983, 1987, 1991 and 1993.

UNITED STATES NATIONAL CHAMPIONSHIPS

Most titles The most American national titles won at all events, indoors and out, is 65, by Ronald Owen Laird at various walking events between 1958 and 1976. Excluding the walks, the record is 41, by Stella Walsh (née Walasiewicz), who won 41 women's events between 1930 and 1954: 33 outdoors and eight indoors.

Longest winning sequence Iolanda Balas (Romania) won a record 140 consecutive competitions at high jump from 1956 to 1967. The record at a track event was 122, at 400 meter hurdles, by Edwin Moses (U.S.)

(continued on p. 208)

WORLD RECORDS—WOMEN

World records are for the women's events scheduled by the International Amateur Athletic Federation. The same stipulation about automatically timed events applies in the six events up to 400 meters as in the men's list.

Event	Time	Athlete (Country)	Place	Date
100 meters	10.49	Florence Griffith-Joyner (U.S.)	Indianapolis, Ind.	July 16, 1988
200 meters	21.34	Florence Griffith-Joyner (U.S.)	Seoul, South Korea	Sept. 29, 1988
400 meters	47.60	Marita Koch (East Germany)	Canberra, Australia	Oct. 6, 1985
800 meters	1:53.28	Jarmila Kratochvilová (Czechoslovakia)	Münich, Germany	July 26, 1983
1,500 meters	3:50.46	Qu Yunxia (China)	Beijing, China	Sept. 11, 1993
1 mile	4:15.61	Paula Ivan (Romania)	Nice, France	July 10, 1989
3,000 meters	8:06.11	Wang Junxia (China)	Beijing, China	Sept. 13, 1993
5,000 meters	14:37.33	Ingrid Kristiansen (Norway)	Stockholm, Sweden	Aug. 5, 1986
10,000 meters	29:31.78	Wang Junxia (China)	Beijing, China	Sept. 8, 1993
100 meter hurdles	12.21	Yordanka Donkova (Bulgaria)	Stara Zagora, Bulgaria	Aug. 20, 1988
400 meter hurdles	52.74	Sally Gunnell (Great Britain)	Stuttgart, Germany	Aug. 19, 1993
4 x 100 meters	41.37	East Germany (Silke Gladisch, Sabine Rieger, Ingrid Auerswald, Marlies Göhr)	Canberra, Australia	Oct. 6, 1985
4 x 400 meters	3:15.17	USSR (Tatyana Ledovskaya, Olga Nazarova, Maria Pinigina, Olga Bryzgina)	Seoul, South Korea	Oct. 1, 1988

Distance

Event	Time	Athlete (Country)	Place	Date
High jump	6' 10¼"	Stefka Kostadinova (Bulgaria)	Rome, Italy	Aug. 30, 1987
Long jump	24' 8¼"	Galina Chistyakova (USSR)	Leningrad, USSR	June 11, 1988
Triple jump	49' 6¼"	Ana Biryukova (Russia)	Stuttgart, Germany	Aug. 19, 1993
Shot	74' 3"	Natalya Lisovskaya (USSR)	Moscow, USSR	June 7, 1987
Discus	252' 0"	Gabriele Reinsch (East Germany)	Neubrandenburg, Germany	July 9, 1988
Javelin	262' 5"	Petra Felke (East Germany)	Potsdam, Germany	Sept. 9, 1988

Heptathlon

7,291 points   Jacqueline Joyner-Kersee (U.S.) (100 m hurdles 12.69 sec; High jump 6' 1¼"; Shot put 51' 10"; 200 m 22.56 sec; Long jump 23' 10 "; Javelin 149' 9"; 800 m 2:08.51 sec), Seoul, South Korea, Sept. 23–24, 1988

Walking

Event	Time	Athlete (Country)	Place	Date
5 km	20:07.52	Beate Anders (East Germany)	Rostock, Germany	June 23, 1990
10 km	41:56.23	Nadezhda Ryashkina (USSR)	Seattle, Wash.	July 24, 1990

between his loss to Harald Schmid (West Germany) at Berlin, Germany on August 26, 1977 and that to Danny Harris (U.S.) at Madrid, Spain on June 4, 1987.

ROAD RUNNING

MARATHON

The marathon is run over a distance of 26 miles 385 yards. This distance was the one used for the race at the 1908 Olympic Games, run from Windsor to the White City stadium, London, England, and it became standard from 1924 on. The marathon was introduced at the 1896 Olympic Games to commemorate the legendary run of Pheidippides (or Philippides) from the battlefield of Marathon to Athens in 490 B.C. The 1896 Olympic marathon was preceded by trial races that year. The first Boston Marathon, the world's oldest annual marathon race, was held on April 19, 1897 at 24 miles 1,232 yards, and the first national marathon championship was that of Norway in 1897.

The first championship marathon for women was organized by the Road Runners Club of America on September 27, 1970.

WORLD RECORDS There are as yet no official records for the marathon, and it should be noted that courses may vary in severity. The following are the best times recorded, all on courses with verified distances: for men, 2 hours 6 minutes 50 seconds, by Belayneh Dinsamo (Ethiopia) at Rotterdam, Netherlands on April 17, 1988; for women, 2 hours 21 minutes 6 seconds, by Ingrid Kristiansen (née Christensen; Norway) at London, England on April 21, 1985.

United States The Athletics Congress recognizes the following U.S. records: for men, Pat Peterson, 2 hours 10 minutes 4 seconds, at London, England on April 23, 1989; for women, Joan Benoit Samuelson, 2 hours 21 minutes 21 seconds, at Chicago, Ill., on October 20, 1985.

OLYMPIC GAMES The marathon has been run at every Olympic Games of the modern era; however, a women's race wasn't included in the Games until 1984.

RECORD BREAKERS ■ SALLY GUNNELL (LEFT) WON THE 1993 400 METER HURDLE WORLD TITLE IN A RECORD 52.74 SECONDS. ON SEPTEMBER 13, 1993, WANG JUNXIA (RIGHT) SMASHED THE 3,000 METER RECORD IN 8:06:11. (ALLSPORT/TONY DUFFY, ALLSPORT/GARY M. PRIOR)

Most gold medals The record for most wins in the men's race is two, by two marathoners: Abebe Bikila (Ethiopia), 1960 and 1964; Waldemar Cierpinski (East Germany), 1976 and 1980. The women's event has been run twice, with different winners.

WORLD CHAMPIONSHIP The marathon has been included as part of both the men's and women's programs at every World Track and Field championship.

Most wins No athlete in either the men's or women's division has won the world title more than once.

BOSTON MARATHON The world's oldest annual running race, the Boston Marathon was first staged on April 19, 1897.

Most wins Clarence De Mar (U.S.) has won the race seven times—1911, 1922–24, 1927–28, 1930. Rosa Mota (Portugal) has won the women's division three times—1987–88, 1990.

Fastest time The course record for men is 2 hours 7 minutes 51 seconds, by Rob de Castella (Australia) in 1986. The women's record is 2 hours 22 minutes 43 seconds, by Joan Benoit (now Samuelson; U.S.) in 1983.

NEW YORK CITY MARATHON The race was run in Central Park each year from 1970 to 1976, when, to celebrate the U.S. Bicentennial, the course was changed to a route through all five boroughs of the city. From that year, when there were 2,090 runners, the race has become one of the world's great sporting occasions; in 1992 there were a record 27,797 finishers.

Most wins Grete Waitz (Norway) has won nine times—1978–80, 1982–86 and 1988. Bill Rodgers has a men's record four wins—1976–79.

Fastest time The course record for men is 2 hours 8 minutes 1 second, by Juma Ikangaa (Tanzania), and for women, 2 hours 25 minutes 30 seconds, by Ingrid Kristiansen (Norway), both set in 1989. On a course subsequently remeasured as about 170 yards short, Grete Waitz was the 1981 women's winner in 2 hours 25 minutes 29 seconds.

LONG-DISTANCE RUNNING RECORDS

Longest race (distance) The longest races ever staged were the 1928 (3,422 miles) and 1929 (3,665 miles) transcontinental races from New York City to Los Angeles, Calif. Johnny Salo (U.S.) was the winner in 1929 in 79 days, from March 31 to June 18. His elapsed time of 525 hours 57 minutes 20 seconds (averaging 6.97 mph) left him only 2 minutes 47 seconds ahead of Englishman Peter Gavuzzi.

MARATHON EVENT ■ IN 1992 A RECORD 27,797 RUNNERS FINISHED THE NEW YORK MARATHON. AMONG THEM WAS THE EVENT'S FOUNDER, FRED LEBOW, AND ITS MOST SUCCESSFUL COMPETITOR, NINE-TIME WINNER GRETE WAITZ. (NEW YORK ROAD RUNNERS CLUB)

The longest race staged annually is Australia's Westfield Run from Paramatta, New South Wales to Doncaster, Victoria (Sydney to Melbourne). The distance run has varied slightly, but the record is by Yiannis Kouros (Greece) in 5 days 2 hours 27 minutes 27 seconds in 1989, when the distance was 658 miles.

Longest runs The longest run by an individual is one of 11,134 miles around the United States, by Sarah Covington-Fulcher (U.S.), starting and finishing in Los Angeles, Calif., between July 21, 1987 and October 2, 1988. Robert J. Sweetgall (U.S.) ran 10,608 miles around the perimeter of the United States, starting and finishing in Washington D.C., between October 1982 and July 15, 1983.

MIND YOUR BACK ■ ON JULY 25, 1991 FERDIE ADOBOE RAN THE 100 METER BACKWARDS IN A RECORD TIME OF 12.7 SECONDS. (FERDIE ADOBOE)

WALKING

OLYMPIC GAMES Walking races have been included in the Olympic events since 1906.

Most gold medals The only walker to win three gold medals has been Ugo Frigerio (Italy), with the 3,000 meter in 1920, and the 10,000 meter in 1920 and 1924.

Most medals The record for most medals is four, by two walkers: Ugo Frigerio (Italy), three gold, one bronze, 1920–32; Vladimir Golubnichiy (USSR), two gold medals, one silver and one bronze, 1960–68.

WORLD CHAMPIONSHIP Walking races have been included in every World Track and Field championship.

Most medals Maurizio Damilano (Italy) is the only walker to win two world titles, for the 20 km walk in 1987 and 1991.

TRAMPOLINING

ORIGINS Trampolining has been part of circus acts for many years. The sport of trampolining dates from 1936, when the prototype "T" model trampoline was designed by George Nissen of the United States. The first official tournament took place in 1947.

WORLD CHAMPIONSHIPS Instituted in 1964, championships have been staged biennially since 1968. The world championships recognize champions, both men and women, in four events: individual, synchronized pairs, tumbling, and double mini trampoline.

Most titles Judy Wills (U.S.) has won a record five individual world titles, 1964–68. The men's record is two, shared by six trampolinists: Wayne Miller (U.S.), 1966 and 1970; Dave Jacobs (U.S.), 1967–68; Richard Tisson (France), 1974 and 1976; Yevgeniy Yanes (USSR), 1976 and 1978; Lionel Pioline (France), 1984 and 1986; and Alexander Maskalenko (USSR/Russia), 1990 and 1992.

UNITED STATES NATIONAL CHAMPIONSHIPS The American Trampoline & Tumbling Association staged the first national championship in 1947. The inaugural event was open only to men; a women's event was introduced in 1961.

Most titles Stuart Ransom has won a record 12 national titles: six individual, 1975–76, 1978–80, 1982; three synchronized, 1975, 1979–80; three double mini-tramp, 1979–80, 1982. Leigh Hennessy has won a record 10 women's titles: one individual, 1978; eight synchronized, 1972–73, 1976–78, 1980–82; one double mini-tramp, 1978.

TRIATHLON

ORIGINS The triathlon combines long distance swimming, cycling, and running. The sport was developed by a group of dedicated athletes who founded the Hawaii "Ironman" in 1974. After a series of unsuccessful attempts to create a world governing body, *L'Union Internationale de Triathlon* (UIT) was founded in Avignon, France in 1989. The UIT staged the first official world championships in Avignon on August 6, 1989.

WORLD CHAMPIONSHIPS An unofficial world championship has been held in Nice, France since 1982. The three legs comprise a 3,200 meter swim

(4,000 meter since 1988), 120 kilometer bike ride, and 32 kilometer run.

Most titles Mark Allen (U.S.) has won a record eight times, 1982–86, 1989–91. Paula Newby-Fraser (Zimbabwe) has won a record three women's titles, 1989–91.

Fastest times The men's record is 5 hours 46 minutes 10 seconds, by Mark Allen (U.S.) in 1988. The women's record is 6 hours 27 minutes 6 seconds, by Erin Baker (New Zealand) in 1988.

HAWAII IRONMAN This is the first, and best known, of the triathlons. Instituted on February 18, 1978, the first race was contested by 15 athletes. The Ironman grew rapidly in popularity, and 1,000 athletes entered the 1984 race. Contestants must first swim 2.4 miles, then cycle 112 miles, and finally run a full marathon of 26 miles 385 yards.

Most titles Dave Scott (U.S.) has won the Ironman a record six times, 1980, 1982–84, 1986–87.

The women's event has been won a record six times by Paula Newby-Fraser (Zimbabwe) in 1986, 1988–89, and 1991–93.

Fastest times Mark Allen (U.S.) holds the course record at 8 hours 7 minutes 45 seconds in 1993. Paula Newby-Fraser holds the women's record at 8 hours 55 seconds in 1992.

Fastest time The fastest time ever recorded over the Ironman distances is 8 hours 1 minute 32 seconds, by Dave Scott (U.S.) at Lake Biwas, Japan on July 30, 1989.

Largest field The most competitors to finish a triathlon race were the 3,888 who completed the 1987 Bud Lite U.S. Triathlon in Chicago, Ill.

TUG-OF-WAR

ORIGINS Tug-of-War, a trial of strength and skill, involving two teams of eight pulling against each other on opposite ends of a long, thick rope, gained its name in England in the 19th century. The actual test of strength that the sport is based on dates to antiquity.

OLYMPIC GAMES Tug-of-War was an Olympic event from 1900–20.

Most wins Great Britain won the event twice, 1908 and 1920.

WORLD CHAMPIONSHIPS A men's tournament was first staged in 1975 and a women's was added in 1986.

HEAVE ■ THE LONGEST TUG-OF-WAR IS THE 1.616 MILE SUPERTUG ACROSS LITTLE TRAVERSE BAY, LAKE MICHIGAN. (DUDLEY MARVIN)

LONGEST TUG ☛ THE DURATION RECORD FOR A TUG-OF-WAR CONTEST IS 2 HOURS 41 MINUTES. "H" COMPANY DEFEATED "E" COMPANY OF THE 2ND BATTALION OF THE SHERWOOD FORESTERS (DERBYSHIRE REGIMENT) AT JUBBULPORE, INDIA ON AUGUST 12, 1889.

Most wins (men) England has won 15 titles in all weight categories, 1975–90.

Most wins (women) Sweden has won five titles: 520 kg, 1986, 1988; 560 kg, 1986, 1988, 1990.

VOLLEYBALL

ORIGINS The game was invented as *mintonette* in 1895 by William G. Morgan at the YMCA gymnasium at Holyoke, Mass. The International Volleyball Association (IVA) was formed in Paris, France in April 1947. The United States Volleyball Association was founded in 1922 and is the governing body for the sport in this country. The United States National Championships were inaugurated for men in 1928, and for women in 1949.

OLYMPIC GAMES Volleyball became an official Olympic sport in 1964, when both men's and women's tournaments were staged in Tokyo, Japan.

Most gold medals (country) The USSR has won three men's titles, 1964, 1968 and 1980; and four women's titles, 1968, 1972, 1980 and 1988.

Most medals (individual) Inna Ryskal (USSR) has won four medals in Olympic competition: two gold, 1968, 1972; and two silver, 1964, 1976. The men's record is three, won by three players: Yuriy Poyarkov (USSR), two golds, 1964 and 1968, one bronze, 1972; Katsutoshi Nekoda (Japan), one gold, 1972, one silver, 1968, and one bronze, 1964; and Steve Timmons (U.S.), two gold, 1984 and 1988, and one bronze, 1992.

WORLD CHAMPIONSHIPS World championships were instituted in 1949 for men and in 1952 for women.

Most titles The USSR has won six men's titles, 1949, 1952, 1960, 1962, 1978 and 1982, and five women's titles, 1952, 1956, 1960, 1970 and 1990.

BEACH VOLLEYBALL

In professional beach volleyball the court dimensions are the same as in the indoor game: 30 feet x 60 feet, or 30 feet x 30 feet on each side, with the net set at a height of eight feet. In beach volleyball, teams play two-a-side, as opposed to six-a-side for the indoor game.

ORIGINS Beach volleyball originated in California in the 1940s. The sport grew rapidly in the 1960s, and the first world championships were staged in

1976. In 1981 the Association of Volleyball Professionals was founded, and the AVP/Miller Lite Tour was formed that year.

AVP/MILLER LITE TOUR RECORDS

Most tour wins Sinjin Smith has won 135 tour events, 1977–93.

Highest earnings Randy Stoklos has earned a career record $1,278,963, 1982–93.

WATER POLO

ORIGINS This game was originally played in England as "water soccer" in 1869. The first rules were drafted in 1876. Water polo has been an Olympic event since 1900. In 1908, FINA (see Swimming) became the governing body for water polo. The first world championships were held in 1973.

OLYMPIC GAMES Water polo was first included at the 1900 Games, and has been included in every Games since.

Most gold medals (country) Hungary has won six Olympic titles, 1932, 1936, 1952, 1956, 1964 and 1976.

Most gold medals (players) Five players have won three gold medals: George Wilkinson (Great Britain), 1900, 1908, 1912; Paul Radmilovic (Great Britain), 1908, 1912, 1920; Charles Smith (Great Britain), 1908, 1912, 1920; Deszo Gyarmati (Hungary), 1952, 1956, 1964; Gyorgy Karpati (Hungary), 1952, 1956, 1964.

WORLD CHAMPIONSHIPS A competition was first held at the World Swimming Championships in 1973. A women's event was included from 1986.

Most titles Two countries have won two men's titles: USSR, 1975 and 1982; Yugoslavia, 1986 and 1991. The women's competition was won by Australia in 1986, and by the Netherlands in 1991.

UNITED STATES NATIONAL CHAMPIONSHIPS The first men's national championship was held in 1891. A women's tournament was first held in 1926.

Most titles The New York Athletic Club has won 25 men's titles: 1892–96, 1903–04, 1906–08, 1922, 1929–31, 1933–35, 1937–39, 1954, 1956, 1960–61, and 1971. The Industry Hills Athletic Club (Calif.) has won nine women's titles: 1980–81 and 1984–88 (outdoors), 1987–88 (indoors).

AT THE BEACH

The recent growth in popularity in beach volleyball's AVP Tour has resulted in the emergence in the national sports psyche of such outstanding players as Karch Kiraly, Randy Stoklos and Sinjin Smith. The success of beach volleyball begs the question: What is the next growth beach sport? Sand yachting, paragliding, kite flying and stone skipping may seem unlikely contenders, but records are already recognized in each of these activities. A selection of exceptional shoreline successes from a variety of beach activities is highlighted below.

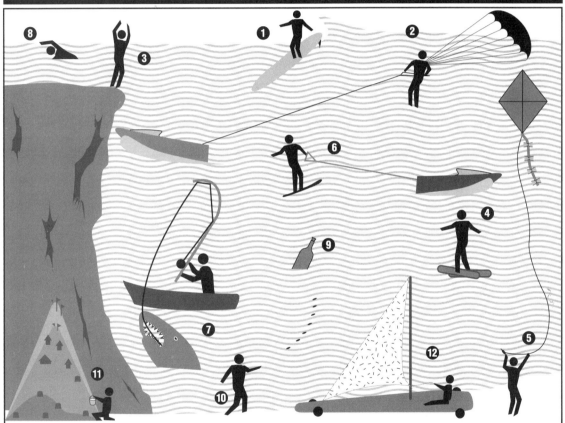

1. Longest wave • Surfer's paradise may well be Matanchan Bay near San Blas, Mexico. Four to six times a year mother nature creates waves that make it possible to ride 5,700 feet. *2. Paragliding* • The greatest distance flown is 174.9 miles by Alex Lowe (South Africa) from Kuruman, South Africa on December 31, 1992. *3. Highest dive* • The greatest height from which head-first dives are performed is 87 1/2 feet at La Quebrada, Acapulco, Mexico. *4. Walking on water* • Rémy Bricka (France) walked across the Atlantic Ocean from the Canary Islands to Trinidad from April 2 to May 21, 1988. Bricka walked a distance of 3,502 miles. *5. Longest kite* • The longest kite flown measured 3,394 feet. Built by a team led by Michel Trouillet (France), they flew the kite at Nîmes, France on November 18, 1990. *6. Longest water ski run* • The greatest distance traveled on water skis is 1,327.65 miles by Leonard Bonacci (U.S.). He performed the feat at Ox Bow Lake, Tunkhannock, Pa., on June 21–24, 1993. *7. Biggest catch* • The largest fish caught on a hook and line is a 2,662-lb great white shark. It was hooked by Alf Dean (Australia) at Denial Bay, Australia on April 21, 1959. *8. Fastest channel swim* • On July 29, 1978, Penny Dean (U.S.) swam across the English Channel in a record time of 7 hours 40 minutes. She swam from Dover, England to Cap Gris–Nez, France. *9. Message in a bottle* • The longest interval between drop and pickup is 73 years. A message thrown from the SS *Arawatta* off Australia on June 9, 1910 was found on Moreton Island, Queensland on June 6, 1983. *10. Stone skipping* • The most skips achieved stone skipping (verified by video) is 38. Jerdone "Jerry" McGhee performed the feat at Wimberley, Tex. on October 20, 1992. *11. Tallest sandcastle* • The tallest sandcastle built by hand using only buckets and shovels is 24 feet 3 5/8 inches high. It was built by Sand Sculptures International in Roanoke, Va. from April 15–29, 1993. *12. Fastest sand yacht* • The official world speed record for a sand yacht is 66.48 mph set by Christian Yves Nau (France) at Le Touquet, France on March 22, 1981.

WATERSKIING WORLD RECORDS

Slalom

Men

Buoys	Line	Skier	Location	Date
3.5	10.25m	Andrew Mapple (Great Britain)	Miami, Fla.	October 6, 1991

Women

1	10.75m	Susi Graham (Canada)	West Palm Beach, Fla.	October 13, 1990
1	10.75m	Deena Mapple (U.S.)	West Palm Beach, Fla.	October 13, 1990
1	10.75m	Kristi Overton (U.S.)	Shreveport, La.	July 25, 1992

Tricks

Men

Points	Skier	Location	Date
11,150	Cory Pickos (U.S.)	Mulberry, Fla.	September 27, 1992

Women

8,580	Tawn Larsen (U.S.)	Groveland, Fla.	July 4, 1991

Jumping

Men

Distance	Skier	Location	Date
208 feet	Sammy Duvall (U.S.)	Shreveport, La.	July 24, 1992

Women

156 feet	Deena Mapple (U.S.)	Charlotte, N.C.	July 9, 1988

WATERSKIING

ORIGINS Modern waterskiing was pioneered in the 1920s. Ralph Samuelson, who skied on Lake Pepin, Minn. in 1922 using two curved pine boards, is generally credited as being the father of the sport. Forms of skiing on water can be traced back centuries to people attempting to walk on water with planks. The development of the motorboat to tow skiers was the largest factor in the sport's growth. The world governing body is the World Water Ski Union (WWSU), which succeeded the *Union Internationale de Ski Nautique* that had been formed in Geneva, Switzerland in 1946. The American Water Ski Association was founded in 1939 and held the first national championships that year.

WORLD CHAMPIONSHIPS The first world championships were held in 1949.

Most titles Sammy Duvall (U.S.) has won four overall titles, in 1981, 1983, 1985 and 1987. Two women have won three overall titles: Willa Mc-

WALKING ON WATER ☞ RÉMY BRICKA (FRANCE) "WALKED" ACROSS THE ATLANTIC OCEAN ON WATERSKIS 13 FEET 9 INCHES LONG IN 1988. HE DEPARTED FROM TENERIFE, CANARY ISLANDS ON APRIL 2, 1988, ARRIVING IN TRINIDAD 3,502 MILES LATER ON MAY 31, 1988.

Guire (née Worthington; U.S.), 1949–50 and 1955; Liz Allan-Shetter (U.S.), 1965, 1969 and 1975.

Most individual titles Liz Allan-Shetter has won a record eight individual championship events and is the only person to win all four titles—slalom, jumping, tricks, and overall in one year, at Copenhagen, Denmark in 1969. Patrice Martin (France) has won a men's record seven titles: three overall, 1989, 1991, 1993, and four tricks, 1979, 1985, 1987 and 1991.

POWERLIFTING ☞ LAMAR GANT (U.S.) WAS THE FIRST MAN TO DEADLIFT FIVE TIMES HIS OWN BODY WEIGHT. HE RAISED A 661 LB BAR WHEN WEIGHING 132 LB IN 1985.

UNITED STATES NATIONAL CHAMPIONSHIPS National championships were first held at Marine Stadium, Jones Beach State Park, Long Island, N.Y. on July 22, 1939.

Most titles The most overall titles is eight, by Willa Worthington McGuire, 1946–51 and 1954–55, and by Liz Allan-Shetter, 1968–75. The men's record is six titles, by Chuck Stearns, 1957–58, 1960, 1962, 1965 and 1967.

WEIGHTLIFTING

There are two standard lifts in weightlifting: the "snatch" and the "clean and jerk." Totals of the two lifts determine competition results. The "press," which had been a standard lift, was abolished in 1972.

ORIGINS Competitions for lifting weights of stone were held at the ancient Olympic Games. In the 19th century, weightlifting consisted of professional exhibitions in which some of the advertised poundages were open to doubt. The *Fédération Internationale Haltérophile et Culturiste*, now the International Weightlifting Federation (IWF), was established in

WORLD WEIGHTLIFTING RECORDS (MEN)
Bantamweight 56 kg (123¼ lb)

Event	Weight	Lifter (Country)	Date
Snatch	135.0 kg	Liu Shoubin (China)	September 28, 1991
Jerk	171.0 kg	Neno Terziiski (Bulgaria)	September 6, 1987
Total	300.0 kg	Naim Suleimanov (Bulgaria)	May 11, 1984

Featherweight 60 kg (132¼ lb)

Snatch	152.5 kg	Naim Suleymanoglü (Turkey)*	September 20, 1988
Jerk	190.0 kg	Naim Suleymanoglü (Turkey)*	September 20, 1988
Total	342.5 kg	Naim Suleymanoglü (Turkey)*	September 20, 1988

Lightweight 67.5 kg (148¾ lb)

Snatch	160.0 kg	Israil Militosyan (USSR)	September 18, 1989
Jerk	200.5 kg	Mikhail Petrov (Bulgaria)	September 8, 1987
Total	355.0 kg	Mikhail Petrov (Bulgaria)	December 5, 1987

Middleweight 75 kg (165¼ lb)

Snatch	170.0 kg	Angel Guenchev (Bulgaria)	December 11, 1987
Jerk	215.5 kg	Aleksandr Varbanov (Bulgaria)	December 5, 1987
Total	382.5 kg	Aleksandr Varbanov (Bulgaria)	February 20, 1988

Light-Heavyweight 82.5 kg (181¾ lb)

Snatch	183.0 kg	Asen Zlatev (Bulgaria)	December 7, 1986
Jerk	225.0 kg	Asen Zlatev (Bulgaria)	November 12, 1986
Total	405.0 kg	Yuri Vardanyan (USSR)	September 14, 1984

Middle-Heavyweight 90 kg (198¼ lb)

Snatch	195.5 kg	Blagoi Blagoyev (Bulgaria)	May 1, 1983
Jerk	235.0 kg	Anatoliy Khrapatliy (USSR)	April 29, 1988
Total	422.5 kg	Viktor Solodov (USSR)	September 15, 1984

First-Heavyweight 100 kg (220¼ lb)

Snatch	200.5 kg	Nicu Vlad (Romania)	November 14, 1986
Jerk	242.5 kg	Aleksandr Popov (USSR)	March 5, 1988
Total	440.0 kg	Yuriy Zakharevich (USSR)	March 4, 1983

Heavyweight 110 kg (242½ lb)

Snatch	210.0 kg	Yuriy Zakharevich (USSR)	September 27, 1988
Jerk	250.5 kg	Yuriy Zakharevich (USSR)	April 30, 1988
Total	455.0 kg	Yuriy Zakharevich (USSR)	September 27, 1988

Super-Heavyweight—over 110 kg (242½ lb)

Snatch	216.0 kg	Antonio Krastev (Bulgaria)	September 13, 1987
Jerk	266.0 kg	Leonid Taranenko (USSR)	November 26, 1988
Total	475.0 kg	Leonid Taranenko (USSR)	November 26, 1988

* Formerly Naim Suleimanov or Neum Shalamanov of Bulgaria

1905, and its first official championships were held in Tallinn, Estonia on April 29–30, 1922.

OLYMPIC GAMES Weightlifting events were included in the first modern Games in 1896.

Most gold medals Four lifters have won two gold medals: John Davis Jr. (U.S.), heavyweight, 1942 and 1952; Tommy Kono (U.S.), lightweight, 1952, light heavyweight, 1956; Chuck Vinci Jr. (U.S.), bantamweight, 1956 and 1960; and Naim Suleymanoglü (Turkey), featherweight, 1988 and 1992.

Most medals Norbert Schemansky (U.S.) has won four medals: one gold, one silver and two bronze, 1960–64.

WORLD CHAMPIONSHIPS The IWF held its first world championships at Tallinn, Estonia in 1922, but has subsequently recognized 18 championships held in Vienna, Austria between 1898 and 1920. The championships have been held annually since 1946, with the Olympic Games recognized as world championships in the year of the Games until 1988, when a championship separate from the Olympics was staged. A women's championship was introduced in 1987.

Most titles The record for most titles is eight, held by three lifters: John Davis (U.S.), 1938, 1946–52; Tommy Kono (U.S.), 1952–59; and Vasiliy Alekseyev (USSR), 1970–77.

UNITED STATES NATIONAL CHAMPIONSHIPS

Most titles The most titles won is 13, by Anthony Terlazzo at 137 pounds, 1932 and 1936, and at 148 pounds, 1933, 1935, 1937–45.

WRESTLING

ORIGINS Wrestling was the most popular sport in the ancient Olympic Games; wall drawings dating to *c.* 2600 B.C. show that the sport was popular long before the Greeks. Wrestling was included in the first modern Games. The International Amateur Wrestling Association (FILA) was founded in 1912. There are two forms of wrestling at the international level: freestyle and Greco-Roman. The use of the legs and holds below the waist are prohibited in Greco-Roman.

OLYMPIC GAMES Wrestling events have been included in all the Games since 1896.

Most gold medals Three wrestlers have won three Olympic titles: Carl Westergren (Sweden) in 1920, 1924 and 1932; Ivar Johansson (Sweden) in 1932 (two) and 1936; and Aleksandr Medved (USSR) in 1964, 1968 and 1972.

Most medals (individual) Wilfried Dietrich (Germany) has won five medals in Olympic competition: one gold, two silver and two bronze, 1956–68.

WORLD CHAMPIONSHIPS

Most titles The freestyler Aleksandr Medved (USSR) won a record 10 world championships, 1962–64 and 1966–72, in three weight categories. The most world titles won by any U.S. wrestler is six by the freestyler John Smith, 1987–92.

NCAA DIVISION I CHAMPIONSHIP Oklahoma State University was the first unofficial national champion, in 1928.

Most titles Including five unofficial titles, Oklahoma State has won a record 29 NCAA titles, in 1928–31, 1933–35, 1937–42, 1946, 1948–49, 1954–56, 1958–59, 1961–62, 1964, 1966, 1968, 1971, 1989–90.

SIZEABLE SUMO ■ THE LARGEST-EVER RIKISHI WAS 580 LB SAMOAN-BORN KONISHIKI. (ALLSPORT/ VANDYSTADT)

Consecutive titles The University of Iowa has won the most consecutive titles, with nine championships from 1978–86.

SUMO WRESTLING

Sumo bouts are fought between two wrestlers (*rikishi*) inside a 14.9-foot-diameter earthen circle (*dohyo*), covered by a roof, symbolizing a Shinto shrine. The wrestlers try to knock each other out of the ring or to the ground. The wrestler who steps out of the dohyo or touches the ground with any part of his body except the soles of his feet loses the contest. Sumo wrestlers are ranked according to their skills; the highest rank is *Yokozuna* (Grand Champion).

ORIGINS Sumo wrestling traces its origins to the development of the Shinto religion in Japan in the eighth century A.D. Sumo matches were staged at Shinto shrines to honor the divine spirits (known as *kami*) during planting and harvesting ceremonies. During the Edo era (1600–1868) sumo wrestling became a professional sport. Currently, sumo wrestling is governed by Nihon Sumo Kyokai (Japan Sumo Association), which stages six 15-day tournaments (*basho*) throughout the year.

Most wins (bouts) Kenji Hatano, known as Oshio, won a record 1,107 bouts in 1,891 contests, 1962–88.

Highest winning percentage Tameemon Torokichi, known as Raiden, compiled a .961 winning percentage—244 wins in 154 bouts—from 1789 to 1810.

YACHTING

ORIGINS Sailing as a sport dates from the 17th century. Originating in the Netherlands, it was introduced to England by Charles II, who participated in a 23 mile race along the River Thames in 1661. The oldest yacht club in the world is the Royal Cork Yacht Club, which claims descent from the Cork Harbor Water Club, founded in Ireland in 1720. The oldest continuously existing yacht club in the United States is the New York Yacht Club, founded in 1844.

AMERICA'S CUP The America's Cup was originally won as an outright prize by the schooner *America* on August 22, 1851 at Cowes, England and was later offered by the New York Yacht Club as a challenge trophy. On August 8, 1870, J. Ashbury's *Cambria* (Great Britain) failed to capture the trophy from *Magic*, owned by F. Osgood (U.S.). The Cup has been challenged 27 times.

SMALLEST BOAT ■ IN SEPTEMBER 1993 HUGO VILHEN ARRIVED IN FALMOUTH, ENGLAND ABOARD HIS 5-FOOT 4-INCH BOAT, FATHER'S DAY, THE SMALLEST BOAT EVER TO HAVE CROSSED THE ATLANTIC OCEAN. (KEVIN WISNIEWSKI)

The U.S. was undefeated until 1983, when *Australia II*, skippered by John Bertrand and owned by a Perth syndicate headed by Alan Bond, beat *Liberty* 4–3, the narrowest series victory, at Newport, R.I.

Most wins (skipper) Three skippers have won the cup three times: Charlie Barr (U.S.), who defended in 1899, 1901 and 1903; Harold S. Vanderbilt (U.S.), who defended in 1930, 1934 and 1937; and Dennis Conner (U.S.), who defended in 1980, challenged in 1987, and defended in 1988.

Largest yacht The largest yacht to have competed in the America's Cup was the 1903 defender, the gaff-rigged cutter *Reliance*, with an overall length of 144 feet, a record sail area of 16,160 square feet and a rig 175 feet high.

OLYMPIC GAMES Bad weather caused the abandonment of yachting events at the first modern Games in 1896. However, the weather has stayed "fair" ever since, and yachting has been part of every Games.

Most gold medals Paul Elvstrom (Denmark) won a record four gold medals in yachting, and in the process became the first competitor in Olympic history to win individual gold medals in four successive Games. Elvstrom's titles came in the Firefly class in 1948, and in the Finn class in 1952, 1956 and 1960.

Most medals Paul Elvstrom's four gold medals are also the most medals won by any Olympic yachtsman.

ROUND-THE-WORLD RACING

Longest race (nonstop) The world's longest nonstop sailing race is the Vendée Globe Challenge, the first of which started from Les Sables

AMERICA'S CUP WINNERS (1851–1992)

Year	Cup Winner	Skipper	Challenger	Series
1851	America	Richard Brown	—	—
1870	Magic	Andrew Comstock	Cambria (England)	—
1871	Columbia	Nelson Comstock	Livonia (England)	4–1
1876	Madeleine	Josephus Williams	Countess of Dufferin (Canada)	2–0
1881	Mischief	Nathaniel Cook	Atalanta (Canada)	2–0
1885	Puritan	Aubrey Crocker	Genesta (England)	2–0
1886	Mayflower	Martin Stone	Galatea (England)	2–0
1887	Volunteer	Henry Haff	Thistle (Scotland)	2–0
1893	Vigilant	William Hansen	Valkyrie II (England)	3–0
1895	Defender	Henry Haff	Valkyrie III (England)	3–0
1899	Columbia	Charlie Barr	Shamrock I (England)	3–0
1901	Columbia	Charlie Barr	Shamrock II (England)	3–0
1903	Reliance	Charlie Barr	Shamrock III (England)	3–0
1920	Resolute	Charles Adams	Shamrock IV (England)	3–2
1930	Enterprise	Harold Vanderbilt	Shamrock V (England)	4–0
1934	Rainbow	Harold Vanderbilt	Endeavour (England)	4–2
1937	Ranger	Harold Vanderbilt	Endeavour II (England)	4–0
1958	Columbia	Briggs Cunningham	Sceptre (England)	4–0
1962	Weatherly	Emil Mosbacher Jr.	Gretel (Australia)	4–1
1964	Constellation	Bob Bavier Jr.	Sovereign (England)	4–0
1967	Intrepid	Emil Mosbacher Jr.	Dame Pattie (Australia)	4–0
1970	Intrepid	Bill Fricker	Gretel II (Australia)	4–1
1974	Courageous	Ted Hood	Southern Cross (Australia)	4–0
1977	Courageous	Ted Turner	Australia (Australia)	4–0
1980	Freedom	Dennis Conner	Australia (Australia)	4–1
1983	Australia II	John Bertrand	Liberty (U.S.)	4–3
1987	Stars & Stripes	Dennis Conner	Kookaburra III (Australia)	4–0
1988	Stars & Stripes	Dennis Conner	New Zealand (New Zealand)	2–0
1992	America[3]	Bill Koch	Il Moro di Venezia (Italy)	4–1

d'Olonne, France on November 26, 1989. The distance circumnavigated without stopping was 22,500 nautical miles. The race is for boats between 50–60 feet, sailed single-handed. The record time on the course is 109 days 8 hours 48 minutes 50 seconds, by Titouan Lamazou (France) in the sloop *Ecureuil d'Aquitaine*, which finished at Les Sables on March 19, 1990.

Longest race (total distance) The longest and oldest regular sailing race around the world is the quadrennial Whitbread Round the World race (instituted August 1973), organized by the Royal Naval Sailing Association (Great Britain). It starts in England, and the course around the world and the number of legs with stops at specified ports are varied from race to race. The distance for 1989–90 was 32,000 nautical miles from Southampton, England and return, with stops and restarts at Punta del Este, Uruguay; Fremantle, Australia; Auckland, New Zealand; Punta del Este, Uruguay, and Fort Lauderdale, Fla.

A selective listing of world champions, national champions, tournament winners and leading money winners of the 1993 sports year.

Country abbreviation codes:

ALG	Algeria	**LAT**	Latvia
ARG	Argentina	**LUX**	Luxembourg
ARM	Armenia	**MEX**	Mexico
AUS	Australia	**MOR**	Morocco
AUT	Austria	**MOZ**	Mozambique
BEL	Belgium	**NAM**	Namibia
BLS	Belarus	**NET**	Netherlands
BRA	Brazil	**NKO**	North Korea
BUL	Bulgaria	**NOR**	Norway
CAN	Canada	**NZL**	New Zealand
CHI	China	**PAN**	Panama
CHL	Chile	**PAR**	Paraguay
COL	Colombia	**PER**	Peru
CRO	Croatia	**POL**	Poland
CUB	Cuba	**PUR**	Puerto Rico
CZE	Czechoslovakia	**ROM**	Romania
DEN	Denmark	**RUS**	Russia
EST	Estonia	**SAF**	South Africa
ETH	Ethiopia	**SKO**	South Korea
FIJ	Fiji	**SPA**	Spain
FIN	Finland	**SUR**	Surinam
FRA	France	**SWE**	Sweden
GBR	Great Britain	**SWI**	Switzerland
GER	Germany	**THA**	Thailand
GHA	Ghana	**TKM**	Turkmenistan
GRE	Greece	**TUR**	Turkey
HUN	Hungary	**UKR**	Ukraine
INA	Indonesia	**USA**	United States
IRA	Iran		of America
IRE	Ireland	**UZB**	Uzbekistan
ISR	Israel	**VEN**	Venezuela
ITA	Italy	**YUG**	Yugoslavia
JAM	Jamaica	**ZAM**	Zambia
JAP	Japan	**ZIM**	Zimbabwe
KEN	Kenya		

AIR RACING

NATIONAL CHAMPIONSHIP AIR RACES STAGED AT RENO/STEAD AIRPORT, NEV., SEPTEMBER 16–19

CHAMPIONS

Unlimited ■ Bill Destefani (Strega); AT-6 ■ Eddie Van Fossen (Miss TNT); Fomula 1 ■ Jon Sharp (Nemesis); Biplane ■ Patti Johnson-Nelson (Full Tilt Boogie).

ARCHERY

WORLD TARGET ARCHERY CHAMPIONSHIPS STAGED AT ANTALYA, TURKEY, SEPTEMBER 8–12

Men's champion ■ Kyung Mo Park, SKO; Men's team ■ France; Women's champion ■ Hyo Jung Kim, SKO; Women's team ■ South Korea

UNITED STATES NATIONAL OUTDOOR CHAMPIONSHIPS STAGED AT OXFORD, OHIO, AUGUST 1–6

Men's champion ■ Jay Barrs; Women's champion ■ Denise Parker

UNITED STATES NATIONAL FLIGHT CHAMPIONSHIPS STAGED AT WENDOVER, UTAH, JUNE 18–20

REGULAR FLIGHT (MEN)

Unlimited Compound Bow ■ Kevin Strother; Compund Bow ■ Buddy DeConnick; Unlimited Primitive Bow ■ Daniel Perry

BROADHEAD FLIGHT (MEN)

Compound Bow ■ Arian Reynolds; Unlimited Compound Bow ■ Kevin Strother

AUTO RACING

CART PPG-INDY CAR WORLD SERIES

Champion ■ Nigel Mansell (GBR), 191 points

RACE WINNERS

Australian Grand Prix ■ Nigel Mansell; Valvoline 200 ■ Mario Andretti; Toyota Grand Prix of Long Beach ■ Paul Tracy (CAN); Indianapolis 500 ■ Emerson Fittipaldi (BRA); Miller 200 ■ Nigel Mansell; Detroit Grand Prix ■ Danny Sullivan; Budweiser/G.I. Joe's 200 ■ Emerson Fittipaldi; Budweiser Cleveland Grand Prix ■ Paul Tracy; Molson Indy Toronto ■ Paul Tracy; Marlboro 500 ■ Nigel Mansell; New England 200 ■ Nigel Mansell; Texaco-Havoline 200 ■ Paul Tracy; Molson

INDY CAR CHAMP ■ BRITISH DRIVER NIGEL MANSELL WON THE 1993 INDY CAR SERIES. (INDY CAR)

Indy Vancouver ■ Al Unser Jr.; Pioneer 200 ■ Emerson Fittipaldi; Bosch Spark Plug Grand Prix ■ Nigel Mansell; Toyota Monterey Grand Prix ■ Paul Tracy.

NASCAR WINSTON CUP CHAMPIONSHIP

Champion ■ Dale Earnhardt, 4,526 points

RACE WINNERS

Daytona 500 ■ Dale Jarrett; Goodwrench 500 ■ Rusty Wallace; Pontiac Excitement 400 ■ Davey Allison; Motorcraft 500 ■ Morgan Shepherd; Trans-South 500 ■ Dale Earnhardt; Food City 500 ■ Rusty Wallace; First Union 400 ■ Rusty Wallace; Hanes 500 ■ Rusty Wallace; Winston 500 ■ Ernie Irvan; Save Mart 300 ■ Geoff Bodine; The Winston ■ Dale Earnhardt; Coca-Cola 600 ■ Dale Earnhardt; Budweiser 500 ■ Dale Earnhardt; Champion Spark Plug 500 ■ Kyle Petty; Miller 400 ■ Ricky Rudd; Pepsi 400 ■ Dale Earnhardt; Slick 50 300 ■ Rusty Wallace; Miller 500 ■ Dale Earnhardt; Diehard 500 ■ Dale Earnhardt; The Bud at the Glen ■ Mark Martin; Champion Spark Plug 400 ■ Mark Martin; Bud 500 ■ Mark Martin; Southern 500 ■ Mark Martin; Miller 400 ■ Rusty Wallace; Splitfire Spark Plug 500 ■ Rusty Wallace; Goody's 500 ■ Ernie Irvan; Tyson Holly Farms 500 ■ Rusty Wallace; Mello Yellow 500 ■ Ernie Irvan; AC Delco 500 ■ Rusty Wallace; Slick 50 500 ■ Mark Martin; Hooters 500 ■ Rusty Wallace.

FORMULA ONE DRIVERS CHAMPIONSHIP

Champion ■ Alain Prost (FRA), 99 points

GRAND PRIX WINNERS

South Africa ■ Alain Prost; Brazil ■ Ayrton Senna (BRA); European ■ Ayrton Senna; San Marino ■ Alain Prost; Spain ■ Alain Prost; Monaco ■ Ayrton Senna; Canada ■ Alain Prost; France ■ Alain Prost; Great Britain ■ Alain Prost; Germany ■ Alain Prost; Hungary ■ Damion Hill (GBR); Belgium ■ Damion Hill; Italy ■ Damian Hill; Portugal ■ Michael Schumacher (GER); Japan ■ Ayrton Senna; Australia ■ Ayrton Senna

NHRA WINSTON CUP CHAMPIONSHIP

Top Fuel Champion ■ Eddie Hill, 12,789 points; Funny Car Champion ■ John Force, 18,074 points; Pro Stock Champion ■ Warren Johnson, 17,008 points

ENDURANCE RACES

Rolex 24 Hours of Daytona ■ P.J. Jones/Rocky Moran/ Mark Dismore; Camel 12 Hours of Sebring ■ Juan Manuel Fangio II (ARG)/Andy Wallace (GBR); 24 Hours of Le Mans ■ Geoff Brabham (AUS)/Christophe Bouchot (FRA)/Eric Helary (FRA)

BASEBALL

MAJOR LEAGUES (For playoff results see page 223.)

1993 FINAL STANDINGS

AMERICAN LEAGUE EAST

Team	W	L	Pct.	GB
Toronto	95	67	.586	—
New York	88	74	.543	7
Baltimore	85	77	.525	10
Detroit	85	77	.525	10
Boston	80	82	.494	15
Cleveland	76	86	.469	19
Milwaukee	69	93	.426	26

NATIONAL LEAGUE EAST

Team	W	L	Pct.	GB
Philadelphia	97	65	.599	—
Montreal	94	68	.580	3
St. Louis	87	75	.537	10
Chicago	84	78	.519	13
Pittsburgh	75	87	.463	22
Florida	64	98	.395	33
New York	59	103	.364	38

AMERICAN LEAGUE WEST

Team	W	L	Pct.	GB
Chicago	94	68	.580	—
Texas	86	76	.531	8
Kansas City	84	78	.519	10
Seattle	82	80	.506	12
California	71	91	.438	23
Minnesota	71	91	.438	23
Oakland	68	94	.420	26

NATIONAL LEAGUE WEST

Team	W	L	Pct.	GB
Atlanta	104	58	.642	—
San Francisco	103	59	.636	1
Houston	85	77	.525	19
Los Angeles	81	81	.500	23
Cincinnati	73	89	.451	31
Colorado	67	95	.414	37
San Diego	61	101	.377	43

1993 STATISTICAL LEADERS

AMERICAN LEAGUE

Batting Average	.363	John Olerud, Toronto
Runs Batted In	129	Albert Belle, Cleveland
Home Runs	46	Juan Gonzales, Texas
Triples	14	Lance Johnson, Chicago
Doubles	54	John Olerud, Toronto
Hits	211	Paul Molitor, Toronto
Runs Scored	124	Rafael Palmeiro, Texas
Stolen Bases	70	Kenny Lofton, Cleveland
Earned Run Average	2.56	Kevin Appier, Kansas City
Victories	22	Jack McDowell, Chicago (22–10)
Strikeouts	308	Randy Johnson, Seattle
Saves	45	Jeff Montgomery, Kansas City Duane Ward, Toronto

NATIONAL LEAGUE

Batting Average	.370	Andres Galarrage, Colorado
Runs Batted In	123	Barry Bonds, San Francisco
Home Runs	46	Barry Bonds, San Francisco
Triples	13	Steve Finley, Houston
Doubles	45	Charlie Hayes, Colorado
Hits	194	Lenny Dykstra, Philadelphia
Runs Scored	143	Lenny Dykstra, Philadelphia
Stolen Bases	58	Chuck Carr, Florida
Earned Run Average	2.36	Greg Maddux, Atlanta
Victories	22	Tom Glavine, Atlanta (22–6)
	22	John Burkett, San Francisco (22–7)
Strikeouts	227	Jose Rijo, Cincinnati
Saves	53	Randy Myers, Chicago

AWARDS

AMERICAN LEAGUE

Most Valuable Player	Frank Thomas, Chicago
Cy Young Award	Jack McDowell, Chicago
Rookie of the Year	Tim Salmon, California
Manager of the Year	Gene Lamont, Chicago

NATIONAL LEAGUE

Most Valuable Player	Barry Bonds, San Francisco
Cy Young Award	Greg Maddux, Atlanta
Rookie of the Year	Mike Piazza, Los Angeles
Manager of the Year	Dusty Baker, San Francisco

BADMINTON

WORLD CHAMPIONSHIPS STAGED AT BIRMINGHAM, ENGLAND, MAY 12–26

Men's Singles ■ Joko Suprianto (INA); Women's Singles ■ Susi Susanti (INA); Men's Doubles ■ Ricky Subagja/Rudy Gunawan (INA); Women's Doubles ■ Nong Qunhua/Zhou Lei (CHI); Mixed Doubles ■ Thomas Lund (DEN)/Catrine Bengtsson (SWE)

UNITED STATES NATIONAL CHAMPIONSHIPS STAGED AT COLORADO SPRINGS, COLO., APRIL 18–21

Men's Singles ■ Andy Chong; Women's Singles ■ Andrea Andersson; Men's Doubles ■ Tom Reidy/Ben Lee; Women's Doubles ■ Andrea Andersson/Traci Britton; Mixed Doubles ■ Andy Chong/Linda French

BASEBALL

(For Regular Season standings see page 222.)

1993 PLAYOFFS

AMERICAN LEAGUE CHAMPIONSHIP SERIES
Toronto Blue Jays 4   Chicago White Sox 2

Game 1 (at Chicago)	Toronto 7 Chicago 3
Game 2 (at Chicago)	Toronto 3 Chicago 1
Game 3 (at Toronto)	Chicago 6 Toronto 1
Game 4 (at Toronto)	Chicago 7 Toronto 4
Game 5 (at Toronto)	Toronto 5 Chicago 3
Game 6 (at Chicago)	Toronto 6 Chicago 3

Most Valuable Player ■ Dave Stewart (Toronto)

NATIONAL LEAGUE CHAMPIONSHIP SERIES
Philadelphia Phillies 4   Atlanta Braves 2

Game 1 (at Philadelphia)	Philadelphia 4 Atlanta 3*
Game 2 (at Philadelphia)	Atlanta 14 Philadelphia 3
Game 3 (at Atlanta)	Atlanta 9 Philadelphia 4
Game 4 (at Atlanta)	Philadelphia 2 Atlanta 1
Game 5 (at Atlanta)	Philadelphia 4 Atlanta 3*
Game 6 (at Philadelphia)	Philadelphia 6 Atlanta 3

*10 innings

Most Valuable Player ■ Curt Schilling (Philadelphia)

WORLD SERIES
Toronto Blue Jays 4   Philadelphia Phillies 2

Game 1 (at Toronto)	Toronto 8 Philadelphia 5
Game 2 (at Toronto)	Philadelphia 6 Toronto 4
Game 3 (at Philadelphia)	Toronto 10 Philadelphia 3
Game 4 (at Philadelphia)	Toronto 15 Philadelphia 14
Game 5 (at Philadelphia)	Philadelphia 2 Toronto 0
Game 6 (at Toronto)	Toronto 8 Philadelphia 6

Most Valuable Player ■ Paul Molitor (Toronto)

ALL-STAR GAME AT ORIOLE PARK AT CAMDEN YARDS, BALTIMORE, MD., JULY 13

American League 9 National League 3
Most Valuable Player ■ Kirby Puckett

COLLEGE BASEBALL

COLLEGE WORLD SERIES (AT ROSENBLATT STADIUM, OMAHA, NEB.)

Louisiana State 8 Wichita State 0

NCAA DIVISION II CHAMPIONSHIP AT PATERSON STADIUM, MONTGOMERY, ALA.

Tampa 7 Cal-Poly San Luis Obispo 5

NCAA DIVISION III CHAMPIONSHIP AT BATTLE CREEK, MICH.

Montclair State 3 Wisconsin-Oshkosh 1

LITTLE LEAGUE WORLD SERIES AT WILLIAMSPORT, PA.

Long Beach (Calif.) 3 Chiriqui (Panama) 2

BASKETBALL

NATIONAL BASKETBALL ASSOCIATION (NBA)

1992–93 FINAL STANDINGS
See page 224.

1993 PLAYOFFS
See page 225.

NBA CHAMPIONSHIP FINALS

Chicago Bulls 4   Phoenix Suns 2

Game 1 (at Phoenix)	Chicago 100 Phoenix 92
Game 2 (at Phoenix)	Chicago 111 Phoenix 108
Game 3 (at Chicago)	Phoenix 129 Chicago 121*
Game 4 (at Chicago)	Chicago 111 Phoenix 105
Game 5 (at Chicago)	Phoenix 108 Chicago 98
Game 6 (at Phoenix)	Chicago 99 Phoenix 98

*Triple overtime

NBA Finals MVP ■ Michael Jordan, Chicago

BASKETBALL

NATIONAL BASKETBALL ASSOCIATION (NBA)

1992–93 FINAL STANDINGS

EASTERN CONFERENCE
Atlantic Division

Team	W	L	Pct.	GB
New York	60	22	.732	—*
Boston	48	34	.585	12*
New Jersey	43	39	.524	17*
Orlando	41	41	.500	19
Miami	36	46	.439	24
Philadelphia	26	56	.317	34
Washington	22	60	.268	38

*In Playoffs

WESTERN CONFERENCE
Midwest Division

Team	W	L	Pct.	GB
Houston	55	27	.671	—*
San Antonio	49	33	.598	6*
Utah	47	35	.573	8*
Denver	36	46	.439	19
Minnesota	19	63	.232	36
Dallas	11	71	.134	44

*In Playoffs

Central Division

Team	W	L	Pct.	GB
Chicago	57	25	.695	—*
Cleveland	54	28	.659	3*
Charlotte	44	38	.537	13*
Atlanta	43	39	.524	14*
Indiana	41	41	.500	16
Detroit	40	42	.488	17
Milwaukee	28	54	.341	29

*In Playoffs

Pacific Division

Team	W	L	Pct.	GB
Phoenix	62	20	.756	—*
Seattle	55	27	.671	7*
Portland	51	31	.622	11*
LA Clippers	41	41	.500	21*
LA Lakers	39	43	.476	23*
Golden State	34	48	.415	28
Sacramento	25	57	.305	37

*In Playoffs

1993 STATISTICAL LEADERS

Category	Total	Average	Player
Scoring	2,541 pts	32.6 pts	Michael Jordan, Chicago
Assists	987	12.0	John Stockton, Utah
Rebounds	1,132	18.3	Dennis Rodman, Detroit
Steals	221	2.83	Michael Jordan, Chicago
Blocked Shots	342	4.17	Hakeem Olajuwon, Houston

AWARDS

Most Valuable Player ■ Charles Barkley, Phoenix

Coach of the Year ■ Pat Riley, New York

Rookie of the Year ■ Shaquille O'Neil, Orlando

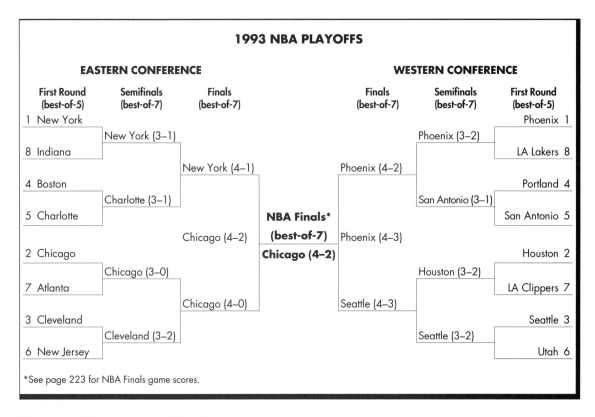

1993 NBA PLAYOFFS

EASTERN CONFERENCE

First Round (best-of-5)	Semifinals (best-of-7)	Finals (best-of-7)				
1 New York						
	New York (3–1)					
8 Indiana		New York (4–1)				
4 Boston						
	Charlotte (3–1)					
5 Charlotte						
		Chicago (4–2)				
2 Chicago						
	Chicago (3–0)					
7 Atlanta		Chicago (4–0)				
3 Cleveland						
	Cleveland (3–2)					
6 New Jersey						

NBA Finals*
(best-of-7)
Chicago (4–2)

WESTERN CONFERENCE

Finals (best-of-7)	Semifinals (best-of-7)	First Round (best-of-5)
		Phoenix 1
	Phoenix (3–2)	
		LA Lakers 8
Phoenix (4–2)		Portland 4
	San Antonio (3–1)	
		San Antonio 5
Phoenix (4–3)		Houston 2
	Houston (3–2)	
		LA Clippers 7
Seattle (4–3)		Seattle 3
	Seattle (3–2)	
		Utah 6

*See page 223 for NBA Finals game scores.

COLLEGE BASKETBALL (MEN)

NCAA DIVISION I

1992–93 CONFERENCE WINNERS

Conference	Season	Tournament
Atlantic Coast	North Carolina	Georgia Tech
Atlantic 10	Massachusetts	Massachusetts
Big East	Seton Hall	Seton Hall
Big Eight	Kansas	Missouri
Big Sky	Idaho	Boise State
Big South	Towson State	Coastal Carolina
Big Ten	Indiana	None played
Big West	New Mexico State	Long Beach State
Colonial	James Madison*	East Carolina
	Old Dominion*	
Great Midwest	Cincinnati	Cincinnati
Ivy Group	Pennsylvania	
Metropolitan	Louisville	Louisville
Metro Atlantic	Manhattan	Manhattan
Mid-American	Ball State*	Ball State
	Miami (Ohio)*	
Mid-Continent	Cleveland State	Wright State
Mid-Eastern	Coppin State	Coppin State
Midwestern	Xavier (Ohio)*	Evansville
	Evansville*	
Missouri Valley	Illinois State	Southern Illinois
North Atlantic	Drexel*	Delaware
	Northeastern*	
Northeast	Rider	Rider
Ohio Valley	Tennessee State	Tennessee State
Pacific-10	Arizona	No tournament
Patriot League	Bucknell	Holy Cross
Southeastern (East)		
Southeastern	Vanderbilt†	Kentucky
	Arkansas‡	
Southern	Tenn-Chattanooga	Tenn-Chattanooga
Southland	NE Louisiana	NE Louisiana

† Eastern division champions
‡ Western division champions

(continued on p. 227)

1993 NCAA DIVISION I MEN'S BASKETBALL CHAMPIONSHIP

First Round March 18–19	Second Round March 20–21	Regionals March 25–28	Semifinals April 3	National Championship April 5	Semifinals April 3	Regionals March 25–28	Second Round March 20–21	First Round March 18–19

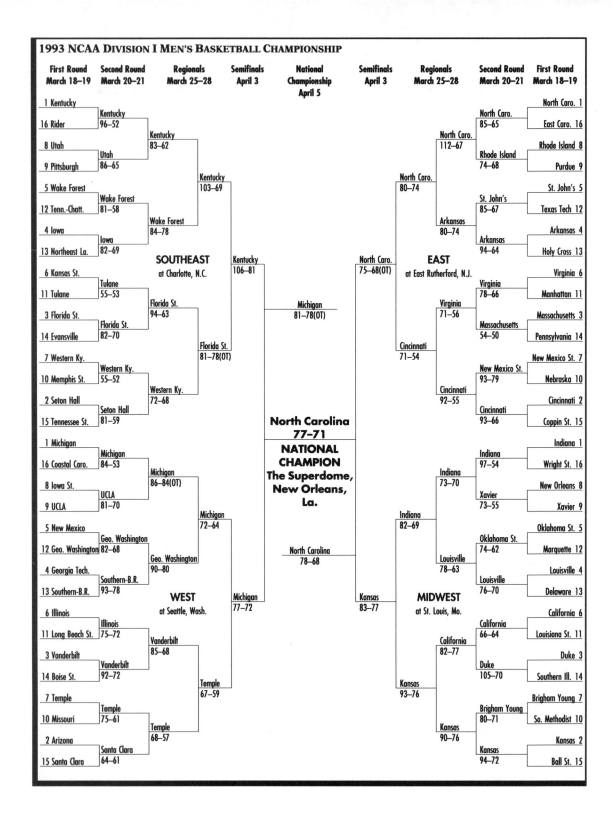

SOUTHEAST at Charlotte, N.C.

1 Kentucky
16 Rider — Kentucky 96–52
8 Utah
9 Pittsburgh — Utah 86–65
Kentucky 83–62
5 Wake Forest
12 Tenn.-Chatt. — Wake Forest 81–58
4 Iowa
13 Northeast La. — Iowa 82–69
Wake Forest 84–78
Kentucky 103–69
6 Kansas St.
11 Tulane — Tulane 55–53
3 Florida St.
14 Evansville — Florida St. 82–70
Florida St. 94–63
7 Western Ky.
10 Memphis St. — Western Ky. 55–52
2 Seton Hall
15 Tennessee St. — Seton Hall 81–59
Western Ky. 72–68
Florida St. 81–78(OT)
Kentucky 106–81

WEST at Seattle, Wash.

1 Michigan
16 Coastal Caro. — Michigan 84–53
8 Iowa St.
9 UCLA — UCLA 81–70
Michigan 86–84(OT)
5 New Mexico
12 Geo. Washington — Geo. Washington 82–68
4 Georgia Tech.
13 Southern-B.R. — Southern-B.R. 93–78
Geo. Washington 90–80
Michigan 72–64
6 Illinois
11 Long Beach St. — Illinois 75–72
3 Vanderbilt
14 Boise St. — Vanderbilt 92–72
Vanderbilt 85–68
7 Temple
10 Missouri — Temple 75–61
2 Arizona
15 Santa Clara — Santa Clara 64–61
Temple 68–57
Temple 67–59
Michigan 77–72

Michigan 81–78(OT)

North Carolina 77–71 NATIONAL CHAMPION The Superdome, New Orleans, La.

North Carolina 78–68

North Carolina 75–68(OT)

Kansas 83–77

EAST at East Rutherford, N.J.

North Caro. 1
East Caro. 16 — North Caro. 85–65
Rhode Island 8
Purdue 9 — Rhode Island 74–68
North Caro. 112–67
St. John's 5
Texas Tech 12 — St. John's 85–67
Arkansas 4
Holy Cross 13 — Arkansas 94–64
Arkansas 80–74
North Caro. 80–74
Virginia 6
Manhattan 11 — Virginia 78–66
Massachusetts 3
Pennsylvania 14 — Massachusetts 54–50
Virginia 71–56
New Mexico St. 7
Nebraska 10 — New Mexico St. 93–79
Cincinnati 2
Coppin St. 15 — Cincinnati 93–66
Cincinnati 92–55
Cincinnati 71–54
North Caro. 75–68(OT)

MIDWEST at St. Louis, Mo.

Indiana 1
Wright St. 16 — Indiana 97–54
New Orleans 8
Xavier 9 — Xavier 73–55
Indiana 73–70
Oklahoma St. 5
Marquette 12 — Oklahoma St. 74–62
Louisville 4
Delaware 13 — Louisville 76–70
Louisville 78–63
Indiana 82–69
California 6
Louisiana St. 11 — California 66–64
Duke 3
Southern Ill. 14 — Duke 105–70
California 82–77
Brigham Young 7
So. Methodist 10 — Brigham Young 80–71
Kansas 2
Ball St. 15 — Kansas 94–72
Kansas 90–76
California 82–77
Kansas 93–76

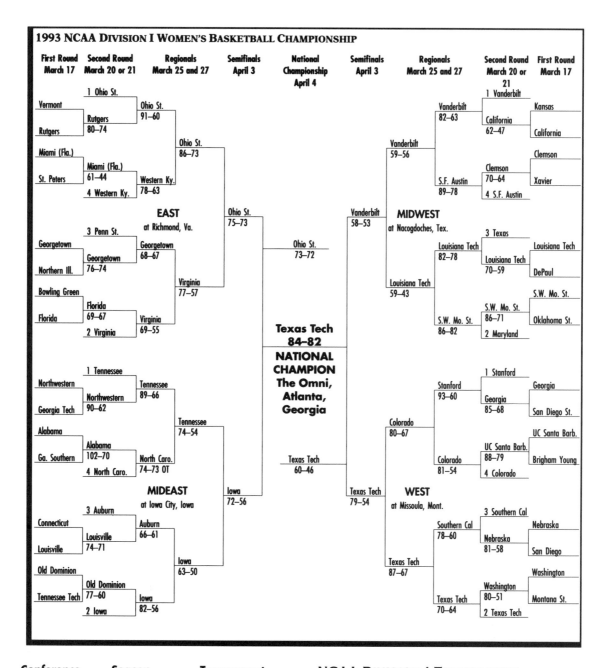

1993 NCAA DIVISION I WOMEN'S BASKETBALL CHAMPIONSHIP

| First Round March 17 | Second Round March 20 or 21 | Regionals March 25 and 27 | Semifinals April 3 | National Championship April 4 | Semifinals April 3 | Regionals March 25 and 27 | Second Round March 20 or 21 | First Round March 17 |

1 Ohio St.

Vermont

Rutgers 80–74 — Rutgers

Ohio St. 91–60

Miami (Fla.)

Miami (Fla.) 61–44 — St. Peters

Ohio St. 86–73

Western Ky. 78–63

4 Western Ky.

EAST at Richmond, Va.

Ohio St. 75–73

3 Penn St.

Georgetown

Georgetown 76–74 — Northern Ill.

Georgetown 68–67

Ohio St. 73–72

Bowling Green

Florida 69–67 — Florida

Virginia 77–57

Virginia 69–55

2 Virginia

Texas Tech 84–82 NATIONAL CHAMPION The Omni, Atlanta, Georgia

1 Tennessee

Northwestern

Northwestern 90–62 — Georgia Tech

Tennessee 89–66

Tennessee 74–54

Alabama

Alabama 102–70 — Ga. Southern

North Caro. 74–73 OT

4 North Caro.

MIDEAST at Iowa City, Iowa

Iowa 72–56

3 Auburn

Connecticut

Louisville 74–71 — Louisville

Auburn 66–61

Texas Tech 60–46

Old Dominion

Old Dominion 77–60 — Tennessee Tech

Iowa 63–50

Iowa 82–56

2 Iowa

---

1 Vanderbilt

Vanderbilt 82–63

Kansas

California 62–47 — California

Vanderbilt 59–56

Clemson

Clemson 70–64 — Xavier

S.F. Austin 89–78

4 S.F. Austin

MIDWEST at Nacogdoches, Tex.

Vanderbilt 58–53

3 Texas

Louisiana Tech 82–78

Louisiana Tech

Louisiana Tech 70–59 — DePaul

Vanderbilt 58–53

Louisiana Tech 59–43

S.W. Mo. St.

S.W. Mo. St. 86–71 — Oklahoma St.

S.W. Mo. St. 86–82

2 Maryland

1 Stanford

Stanford 93–60

Georgia

Georgia 85–68 — San Diego St.

Colorado 80–67

UC Santa Barb.

UC Santa Barb. 88–79 — Brigham Young

Texas Tech 79–54

Colorado 81–54

4 Colorado

WEST at Missoula, Mont.

Texas Tech 79–54

3 Southern Cal

Southern Cal 78–60

Nebraska

Nebraska 81–58 — San Diego

Texas Tech 87–67

Washington

Washington 80–51 — Montana St.

Texas Tech 70–64

2 Texas Tech

Conference	Season	Tournament
Southwest	Southern Methodist	Texas Tech
Southwestern	Jackson State	Southern-Baton Rouge
Sun Belt	New Orleans	Western Kentucky
Trans America	Florida Int'l	Florida Int'l
West Coast	Pepperdine	Santa Clara
Western	Brigham Young	New Mexico

NCAA DIVISION I TOURNAMENT
See page 226

NCAA DIVISION II CHAMPIONSHIP AT
SPRINGFIELD, MASS., MARCH 27

Cal State Bakersfield 85 Troy State 72

NCAA DIVISION III CHAMPIONSHIP AT BUFFALO, N.Y., MARCH 20

Ohio Northern 71 Augustana (Ill.) 68

COLLEGE BASKETBALL (WOMEN)

NCAA DIVISION I TOURNAMENT

See page 227

NCAA DIVISION II CHAMPIONSHIP AT WALTHAM, MASS.

North Dakota State 95 Delta State 63

NCAA DIVISION III CHAMPIONSHIP AT PELLA, IOWA

Central (Iowa) 71 Capital (Ohio) 63

BOXING

WORLD CHAMPIONS (AS OF FEBRUARY 7, 1994)

WORLD BOXING ASSOCIATION (WBA)

Heavyweight ■ Evander Holyfield (USA); Cruiserweight ■ Orlin Norris (USA); Light-Heavyweight ■ Virgil Hill (USA); Super-Middleweight ■ Michael Nunn (USA); Middleweight ■ John Jackson (USA); Super-Welterweight ■ Julio César Vazquez (ARG); Welterweight ■ Crisanto Espana (VEN); Super-Lightweight ■ Juan Martin Coggi (ARG); Lightweight ■ Olzubek Nazarov (RUS); Super-Featherweight ■ Genaro Hernandez (USA); Featherweight ■ Park Young-kyun (SKO); Super-Bantamweight ■ Wilfredo Vasquez (PUR); Bantamweight ■ Junior Jones (USA); Super-Flyweight ■ Katsuya Onizuka (JAP); Flyweight ■ David Griman (VEN); Light-Flyweight ■ Leo Gomez (VEN)

WORLD BOXING COUNCIL (WBC)

Heavyweight ■ Lennox Lewis (GBR); Cruiserweight ■ Anaclet Wamba (FRA); Light-Heavyweight ■ Jeff Harding (AUS); Super-Middleweight ■ Nigel Benn (GBR); Middleweight ■ Gerald McClellan (USA); Super-Welterweight ■ Simon Brown (USA); Welterweight ■ Pernell Whitaker (USA); Super-Lightweight ■ Frankie Randall (USA); Lightweight ■ Miguel Angel Gonzalez (MEX); Super-Featherweight ■ Azumah Nelson (GHA); Featherweight ■ Kevin Kelly (USA); Super-Bantamweight ■ Tracy Patterson (USA); Bantamweight ■ Yasuei Yakushiji (JAP); Super-Flyweight ■ Moon Sung-kil (SKO); Flyweight ■ Yuriy Arbachkov (RUS); Light-Flyweight ■ Michael Carbajal (USA)

INTERNATIONAL BOXING FEDERATION (IBF)

Heavyweight ■ Evander Holyfield (USA); Cruiserweight ■ Alfred Cole (USA); Light-Heavyweight ■ Henry Maske (GER); Super-Middleweight ■ James Toney (USA); Middleweight ■ Roy Jones (USA); Super-Welterweight ■ Gianfranco Rosi (ITA); Welterweight ■ Felix Trinidad (PUR); Super-Lightweight ■ Charles Murray (USA); Lightweight ■ Freddie Pendleton (USA); Super-Featherweight ■ John Molina (PUR); Featherweight ■ Tom Johnson (USA); Super-Bantamweight ■ Kennedy McKinney (USA); Bantamweight ■ Orlando Canizales (USA); Super-Flyweight ■ Julio César Barboa (MEX); Flyweight ■ Pichit Sitbangprachan (THA); Light-Flyweight ■ Michael Carbajal (USA)

CANOEING

WORLD CHAMPIONSHIPS STAGED AT COPENHAGEN, DENMARK, AUGUST 25–29

MEN'S RESULTS

Canadian (C1) 500m ■ Nikolay Buhalov (BUL), 1,000m ■ Ivan Klementjev (LAT); (C2) 500m ■ Hungary, 1,000m ■ Denmark; (C4) 500m ■ Hungary, 1,000m ■ Hungary; Kayak (K1) 500m ■ Mikko Kolehmainen (FIN), 1,000m ■ Knut Holman (NOR); (K2) 500m ■ Germany, 1,000m ■ Germany; (K4) 500m ■ Russia, 1,000m ■ Germany

WOMEN'S RESULTS

Kayak (K1) 500m ■ Birgit Schmidt (GER); (K2) 500m ■ Sweden; (K4) 500m ■ Germany

CROSS-COUNTRY RUNNING

WORLD CHAMPIONSHIP STAGED AT AMOREBIETA, SPAIN, MARCH 28

Individual (men) ■ William Sigel (KEN), Team (men) ■ Kenya; Individual (women) ■ Albertina Dias (POR); Team (women) ■ Kenya

UNITED STATES NATIONAL CHAMPIONSHIPS STAGED AT MISSOULA, MONT., NOVEMBER 27

Men's Champion ■ Todd Williams

Women's Champion ■ Lynn Jennings

NCAA DIVISION I CHAMPIONSHIPS STAGED AT LEHIGH UNIVERSITY, NOVEMBER 22

Team (men) ■ Arkansas, Individual (men) ■ Josephat Kapkory (Washington State); Team (women) ■ Villanova, Individual (women) ■ Carole Zajac (Villanova)

CURLING

WORLD CHAMPIONSHIP STAGED AT GENEVA, SWITZERLAND, MARCH 28–APRIL 4

Team (men) ■ Canada, Russ Howard (skip), Team (women) ■ Canada, Sandra Petersen (skip)

UNITED STATES CHAMPIONSHIPS STAGED AT ST. PAUL, MINN., FEBRUARY 21–27

Team (men) ■ Bemidji (Minn.), Scott Baird (skip), Team (women) ■ Denver (Colo.), Bev Behnke (skip)

THE LABATT BRIER

Men's team ■ Ontario, Russ Howard (skip)

CYCLING

PROFESSIONAL EVENTS

TOUR DE FRANCE (2,311 MILES)

Winner ■ Miguel Indurain (SPA), 95 hours, 57 minutes, 9 seconds

OTHER MAJOR TOUR RACE RESULTS

Tour Du Pont ■ Raul Acala (USA); Tour of Italy ■ Miguel Indurain; Tour of Spain ■ Tony Rominger (SWI); Milk Race ■ Conor Henry (IRE); Tour of Switzerland ■ Giorgio Furlan (ITA); Tour of Catalan ■ Miguel Indurain

WORLD CHAMPIONSHIPS STAGED AT OSLO, NORWAY, AUGUST 17–29

MEN'S RESULTS

Time Trial ■ Florian Rousseau (FRA); Team Time Trial ■ Italy; Sprint ■ Gary Neiwand (AUS); Team Pursuit ■ Australia; Individual Pursuit ■ Graeme Obree (GBR); Road Race (Pro) ■ Lance Armstrong (USA); Points Race ■ Etienne De Wilde (BEL); Keirin ■ Gary Neiwand; Motor Pace ■ Jens Veggerby (DEN)

WOMEN'S RESULTS

Individual Pursuit ■ Rebecca Twigg (USA); Point Race ■ Ingrid Haringa (NET); Team Time Trial ■ Russia; Road Race ■ Leontien Van Moorsel (NET); Sprint ■ Tanya Dubnicoff (CAN)

RACE ACROSS AMERICA

2,915 miles, Irvine, Ca. to Savannah, Ga. Started July 28–August 1

Men's Champion ■ Gerry Tatrai (AUS)

Women's Champion ■ Seana Hogan (USA)

DARTS

WORLD CHAMPIONSHIPS STAGED AT FRIMLEY GREEN, ENGLAND

Champion ■ Phil Taylor (ENG)

UNITED STATES CHAMPIONSHIPS

Men's Champion ■ Dave Kelly; Women's Champion ■ Stacy Bromberg

DIVING

FINA WORLD CUP STAGED AT BEIJING, CHINA, MAY 28–JUNE 2

MEN'S RESULTS

1-meter springboard ■ Lan Wei (CHI); 3-meter springboard ■ Yu Zhuocheng (CHI); Platform ■ Xiong Ni (CHI)

WOMEN'S RESULTS

1-meter springboard ■ Tan Shuping (CHI); 3-meter springboard ■ Tan Shuping (CHI); Platform ■ Chi Bin (CHI)

UNITED STATES INDOOR CHAMPIONSHIP STAGED AT AUSTIN, TEX., APRIL 14–18

MEN'S RESULTS

1-meter springboard ■ Dean Panaro; 3-meter springboard ■ Mark Bradshaw; Platform ■ Russ Bertram

WOMEN'S RESULTS

1-meter springboard ■ Carrie Zarse; 3-meter springboard ■ Veronica Ribot-Canales; Platform ■ Mary Ellen Clark

UNITED STATES OUTDOOR CHAMPIONSHIP STAGED AT LOS ANGELES, CALIF., AUGUST 11–15

MEN'S RESULTS

1-meter springboard ■ Mark Lenzi; 3-meter springboard ■ Mark Bradshaw; Platform ■ Patrick Jeffrey

WOMEN'S RESULTS

1-meter springboard ■ Carrie Zarse; 3-meter springboard ■ Eileen Richetelli; Platform ■ Mary Ellen Clark

EQUESTRIAN SPORTS

VOLVO SHOW JUMPING WORLD CUP FINALS STAGED AT GOTHENBURG, SWEDEN, APRIL 7–12

Champion ■ Almox Retina Z, Ludger Beerbaum (GER)

DRESSAGE WORLD CUP STAGED AT S'HERTOGENBOSCH, NETHERLANDS, MARCH 25–28

Champion ■ Ganimedes Tecrent, Monica Theodorescu (GER)

FENCING

WORLD CHAMPIONSHIPS STAGED AT ESSEN, GERMANY, JULY 1–10

MEN'S RESULTS

Epee ■ Pavel Kolobkov (RUS); Epee (team) ■ Italy; Sabre ■ Grigory Kirienko (RUS); Sabre (team) ■ Hungary; Foil ■ Alexander Koch (GER); Foil (team) ■ Germany

WOMEN'S RESULTS

Epee ■ Oksana Jermakova (EST); Epee (team) ■ Hungary; Foil ■ Francesca Bortolozzi (ITA); Foil (team) ■ Germany

UNITED STATES FENCING ASSOCIATION CHAMPIONSHIPS STAGED AT FORT MYERS, FLA., JUNE 5–13

MEN'S RESULTS

Foil ■ Michael Marx; Epee ■ Benjamin Atkins; Sabre ■ David Mandell

WOMEN'S RESULTS

Foil ■ Felicia Zimmerman; Epee ■ Leslie Marx

NCAA CHAMPIONSHIPS STAGED AT WAYNE STATE, MICH.

MEN'S RESULTS

Team ■ Columbia/Columbia-Barnard; Foil ■ Nick Bravin, Stanford; Epee ■ Ben Atkins, Columbia; Sabre ■ Tom Strzalkowski, Penn State

WOMEN'S RESULTS

Foil ■ Olga Kalinovskaya, Penn State

FIELD HOCKEY

NCAA CHAMPIONSHIPS

Champion ■ Old Dominion

FIGURE SKATING

WORLD CHAMPIONSHIPS STAGED AT PRAGUE, CZECH REPUBLIC, MARCH 9–14

Men ■ Kurt Browning (CAN); Women ■ Oksana Baiul (UKR); Pairs ■ Isabelle Brasseur & Lloyd Eisler (CAN); Dance ■ Maia Usova & Alexandr Zhulin (RUS)

UNITED STATES NATIONAL CHAMPIONSHIPS STAGED AT PHOENIX, ARIZ., JANUARY 17–24

Men ■ Scott Davis; Women ■ Nancy Kerrigan; Pairs ■ Calla Ubanski/Rocky Marval; Dance ■ Renee Roca & Gorsha Sur

FOOTBALL

NATIONAL FOOTBALL LEAGUE (NFL)

1993 NFL FINAL STANDINGS

AMERICAN CONFERENCE
Eastern Division

Team	W	L	Pct.
Buffalo	12	4	.750*
Miami	9	7	.563
NY Jets	8	8	.500
New England	5	11	.313
Indianapolis	4	12	.250

Central Division

Team	W	L	Pct.
Houston	12	4	.750*
Pittsburgh	9	7	.563*
Cleveland	7	9	.438
Cincinnati	3	13	.188

Western Division

Team	W	L	Pct.
Kansas City	11	5	.688*
LA Raiders	10	6	.625*
Denver	9	7	.563*
San Diego	8	8	.500
Seattle	6	10	.375

*Qualified for playoffs

NATIONAL CONFERENCE

Eastern Division

Team	W	L	Pct.
Dallas	12	4	.750*
NY Giants	11	5	.688*
Philadelphia	8	8	.500
Phoenix	7	9	.438
Washington	4	12	.250

Central Division

Team	W	L	Pct.
Detroit	10	6	.625*
Minnesota	9	7	.563*
Green Bay	9	7	.563*
Chicago	7	9	.438
Tampa Bay	5	11	.313

Western Division

Team	W	L	Pct.
San Francisco	10	6	.625*
New Orleans	8	8	.500
Atlanta	6	10	.375
LA Rams	5	11	.313

*Qualified for playoffs

NFL 1993 STATISTICAL LEADERS

Passing yardage	4,030	John Elway, Denver
Rushing yardage	1,486	Emmitt Smith, Dallas
Total yardage	1,900	Emmitt Smith, Dallas
Points scored	132	Jeff Jaeger, LA Raiders
Touchdowns scored	16	Jerry Rice, San Francisco
Touchdowns thrown	29	Steve Young, San Francisco
Quarterback rating	99.9	Steve Young San Francisco
Receptions	112	Sterline Sharpe, Green Bay
Sacks	15	Neil Smith, Kansas City
Interceptions	9	Nate Odomes, Buffalo
	9	Eugene Robinson, Seattle

SUPER BOWL XXVIII PLAYOFFS

AMERICAN CONFERENCE

Wildcard Games

Kansas City 27 Pittsburgh 24 (OT)

LA Raiders 42 Denver 24

Second Round

Buffalo 29 LA Raiders 23

Houston 20 Kansas City 28

A.F.C. CHAMPIONSHIP GAME

Buffalo 30 Kansas City 13

NATIONAL CONFERENCE

Wildcard Games

Detroit 24 Green Bay 28

NY Giants 17 Minnesota 10

Second Round

San Francisco 44 NY Giants 3

Dallas 27 Green Bay 17

N.F.C. CHAMPIONSHIP GAME

Dallas 38 San Francisco 21

SUPER BOWL XXVIII AT THE GEORGIA DOME, ATLANTA, GA.

Dallas 30 Buffalo 13

Super Bowl MVP ■ Emmitt Smith, Dallas

COLLEGE FOOTBALL

NCAA DIVISION I-A

1993 FINAL NATIONAL POLLS

Poll	No. 1 Ranked	Record
A.P.	Florida State	12-1-0
USA Today/CNN	Florida State	12-1-0

BOWL GAME RESULTS (1993 SEASON)

BIG FOUR

Orange ■ Florida State 18 Nebraska 16

Rose ■ Wisconsin 21 UCLA 16

Sugar ■ Florida 41 West Virginia 7

Cotton ■ Notre Dame 24 Texas A&M 21

OTHER BOWL RESULTS

Alamo ■ California 37 Iowa 3

Aloha ■ Colorado 41 Fresno State 30

Blue-Gray Classic ■ Gray 17 Blue 10

Carquest ■ Boston College 31 Virginia 13

Citrus ■ Penn State 31 Tennessee 13

Copper ■ Kansas State 52 Wyoming 17

Fiesta ■ Arizona 29 Miami 0

Freedom ■ Southern Cal 28 Utah 21

Gator ■ Alabama 24 North Carolina 10

Hall of Fame ■ Michigan 42 North Carolina State 7

Heritage ■ Southern 11 South Carolina State 0

Holiday ■ Ohio State 28 Brigham Young 21

Independence ■ Virginia Tech 45 Indiana 20

John Hancock ■ Oklahoma 41 Texas Tech 10

Las Vegas ■ Utah State 42 Ball State 33

Liberty ■ Louisville 18 Michigan State 7

Peach ■ Clemson 14 Kentucky 13

AWARDS

Heisman Trophy ■ Charles Ward, Florida State

Lombardi Trophy ■ Aaron Taylor, Notre Dame

Outland Trophy ■ Rob Waldrop, Arizona State

NCAA DIVISION I-AA CHAMPIONSHIP

Youngstown State 17 Marshall 5

NCAA DIVISION II CHAMPIONSHIP GAME

North Alabama 41 Indiana (Pa.) 34

NCAA DIVISION III CHAMPIONSHIP GAME

Mount Union (Ohio) 34 Rowan (NJ) 24

CANADIAN FOOTBALL LEAGUE (CFL)

1993 CFL FINAL STANDINGS

EASTERN DIVISION

Team	W	L	Pct.
Winnipeg	14	4	.778*
Hamilton	6	12	.333*
Ottawa	4	14	.222*
Toronto	3	15	.187

*Qualified for playoffs

WESTERN DIVISION

Team	W	L	Pct.
Calgary	15	3	.833*
Edmonton	12	6	.667*
Saskatchewan	11	7	.611*
B.C. Lions	10	8	.556*
Sacramento	6	12	.333

*Qualified for playoffs

1993 GREY CUP PLAYOFFS

EASTERN DIVISION

Semifinal

Hamilton Tiger-Cats 21 Ottawa Rough Riders 10

Final

Winnipeg Blue Bombers 20 Hamilton Tiger-Cats 19

WESTERN DIVISION

Semifinal

Calgary Stampeders 17 B.C. Lions 9

Edmonton Eskimos 29 Saskatchewan Roughriders 13

Final

Edmonton Eskimos 29 Calgary Stampeders 15

GREY CUP FINAL (at Calgary, November 28)

Edmonton Eskimos 33 Winnipeg Blue Bombers 23

Grey Cup MVP ■ Damon Allen, Edmonton

GOLF

PGA TOUR

GRAND SLAM RESULTS

The Masters ■ Bernhard Langer (GER); U.S. Open ■ Lee Janzen (USA); British Open ■ Greg Norman (AUS); P.G.A. Championship ■ Paul Azinger (USA)

1993 PGA TOUR WINNERS

Tournament of Champions ■ Davis Love III; Hawaiian Open ■ Howard Twitty; Northern Telecom Open ■ Larry Mize; Phoenix Open ■ Lee Janzen; Pebble Beach National Pro-Am ■ Brett Ogle (AUS); Bob Hope Chrysler Classic ■ Tom Kite; Buick Invitational of California ■ Phil Mickelson; Nissan Los Angeles Open ■ Tom Kite; Doral Ryder Open ■ Greg Norman (AUS); Honda Classic ■ Fred Couples; Nestle Invitational ■ Ben Crenshaw; Players Championship ■ Nick Price (ZIM); Freeport McMoran Classic ■ Mike Standly; The Masters ■ Bernhard Langer (GER); Deposit Guaranty Classic ■ Greg Kraft; MCI Heritage Classic ■ David Edwards; KMart Greater Greensboro Open ■ Rocco Mediate; Shell Houston Open ■ Jim McGovern; Bellsouth Classic ■ Nolan Henke; GTE Byron Nelson Classic ■ Scott Simpson; Kemper Open ■ Grant Waite; Southwestern Bell Colonial ■ Fulton Allem (SAF); The Memorial ■ Paul Azinger; Buick Classic ■ Vijay Singh (FIJ); U.S. Open ■ Lee Janzen; Canon Greater Hartford Open ■ Nick Price; Sprint Western

Open ■ Nick Price; Anheuser-Busch Classic ■ Jim Gallagher Jr.; New England Classic ■ Paul Azinger; Federal Express St. Jude Classic ■ Nick Price; Buick Open ■ Larry Mize; The International ■ Phil Mickelson; NEC World Series of Golf ■ Fulton Allem; Greater Milwaukee Open ■ Billy Mayfair; Canadian Open ■ David Frost (SAF); Hardees Golf Classic ■ David Frost; B.C. Open ■ Blaine McCallister; Buick Southern Open ■ John Inman; Walt Disney World/Oldsmobile Classic ■ Jeff Maggert; H.E.B. Texas Open ■ Jay Haas; Las Vegas Invitational ■ Davis Love III; The Tour Championship ■ Jim Gallagher Jr.

Leading Money Winner ■ Nick Price (ZIM), $1,478,557

OTHER TOURNAMENT RESULTS

The Dunhill Cup ■ United States; Lincoln Mercury Kapalua Invitational ■ Fred Couples; World Cup of Golf ■ USA; The Grand Slam of Golf ■ Greg Norman (AUS); The Skins Game ■ Payne Stewart; JC Penney Classic ■ Melissa McNamara & Mike Springer; Johnnie Walker Championship ■ Larry Mize

LPGA TOUR

GRAND SLAM RESULTS

Nabisco Dinah Shore ■ Helen Alfredsson (SWE); LPGA Championship ■ Patty Sheehan (USA); U.S. Open ■ Lauri Merten (USA); du Maurier Classic ■ Brandie Burton (USA)

1993 LPGA TOUR WINNERS

Healthsouth Palm Beach Classic ■ Tammie Green; Itoki Hawaiian Open ■ Lisa Walters; Ping/Welch's Championship ■ Meg Mallon; Standard Register Ping ■ Patty Sheehan; Nabisco Dinah Shore ■ Helen Alfredsson; Las Vegas LPGA at Canyon Gate ■ Trish Johnson (GBR); Atlanta Women's Championship ■ Trish Johnson; Sprint Classic ■ Kristi Albers; Sara Lee Classic ■ Meg Mallon; McDonald's Championship ■ Laura Davies (GBR); Lady Keystone Open ■ Val Skinner; LPGA Corning Classic ■ Kelly Robbins; Oldsmobile Classic ■ Jane Geddes; Mazda LPGA Championship ■ Patty Sheehan; Rochester International ■ Tammie Green; ShopRite LPGA Classic ■ Shelley Hamlin; Jamie Farr Classic ■ Brandie Burton; Youngstown-Warren LPGA Classic ■ Nancy Lopez;

JAL Big Apple Classic ■ Hiromi Kobayashi (JAP); U.S. Women's Open ■ Lauri Merten; Ping/Welch's Championship ■ Missie Berteotti; McCalls LPGA Classic ■ Dana Lofland-Dormann; Sun-Times Challenge ■ Cindy Schreyer; Minnesota LPGA Classic ■ Hiromi Kobayashi; du Maurier Classic ■ Brandie Burton; State Farm Rail Classic ■ Helen Dobson; Ping-Cellular One LPGA Golf Championship ■ Donna Andrews; Safeco Classic ■ Brandie Burton; Kyocera Inamori Classic ■ Kris Monaghan; World Championship of Women's Golf ■ Dottie Mochrie; Toray Japan Queens Cup ■ Betsy King

Leading Money Winner ■ Betsy King, $595,992

OTHER TOURNAMENT RESULTS

JC Penney/Skins Game ■ Betsy King; Nichirei International ■ United States; JC Penney Classic ■ Melissa McNamara & Mike Springer

PGA SENIOR TOUR

SENIOR SLAM

The Tradition ■ Tom Shaw; PGA Seniors Championship ■ Tom Wargo; Ford Senior Players Championship ■ Jim Colbert; U.S. Senior Open ■ Jack Nicklaus

Leading Money Winner ■ Dick Stockton, $1,175,944

SENIOR PGA TOUR RESULTS

Infiniti Snr. Tournament of Champions ■ Al Geiberger; Royal Caribbean Classic ■ Jim Colbert; Better Homes & Gardens Real Estate Challenge ■ Mike Hill; GTE Suncoast Classic ■ Jim Albus; GTE West Classic ■ Al Geiberger; Vantage at the Dominion ■ J.C. Snead; Gulfstream Aerospace Invitational ■ Raymond Floyd; Doug Sanders Celebrity Classic ■ Bob Charles; Fuji Grandslam ■ Lee Trevino; The Tradition ■ Tom Shaw; PGA Seniors Championship ■ Tom Wargo; Muratec Reunion Pro-Am ■ Dave Stockton; Las Vegas Senior Classic ■ Gibby Gilbert; Liberty Mutual Legends of Golf ■ Harold Henning; Painewebber Invitational ■ Mike Hill; Bell Atlantic Classic ■ Bob Charles (NZL); Cadillac NFL Golf Classic ■ Lee Trevino; NYNEX Commemorative ■ Bob Wynn; Southwestern Bell Classic ■ Dave Stockton; Burnett Senior Classic ■ Chi Chi Rodriguez; Ford Senior Players Championship ■ Jim Colbert; Kroger Senior Classic ■ Simon Hobday (ZIM); U.S. Senior Open ■ Jack Nicklaus; Ameritech Senior Open ■ George

Archer; First of America Classic ■ George Archer; Northville Long Island Classic ■ Raymond Floyd; Bank of Boston Senior Golf Classic ■ Bob Betley; Franklin Quest Championship ■ Dave Stockton; GTE Northwest Classic ■ Dave Stockton; Bruno's Memorial Classic ■ Bob Murphy; Quicksilver Classic ■ Bob Charles; GTE North Classic ■ Bob Murphy; Bank One Classic ■ Gary Player (SAF); Nationwide Championship ■ Lee Trevino; The Transamerica ■ Dave Stockton; Raley's Senior Gold Rush ■ George Archer; Ralph's Senior Classic ■ Dale Douglass; Kaanapali Classic ■ George Archer; Hyatt Senior Tour Championship ■ Simon Holoday (SAF)

OTHER TOURNAMENT RESULTS

Senior Skins Game ■ Arnold Palmer; Chrysler Cup ■ United States; Du Pont Cup ■ United States

AMATEUR GOLF

U.S. Amateur (men) ■ John Harris; U.S. Amateur (women) ■ Jill McGill; NCAA (individual, men) ■ Todd Demsey, Arizona State; NCAA (team, men) ■ Florida; NCAA (individual, women) ■ Charlotta Sorenstam, Texas; NCAA (team, women) ■ Arizona State

GYMNASTICS

WORLD CHAMPIONSHIPS STAGED AT BIRMINGHAM, ENGLAND, APRIL 12–18

MEN'S RESULTS

All-Around ■ Vitaliy Scherbo (BLR); Floor Exercise ■ Grigori Misutin (RUS); Rings ■ Yuri Chechi (ITA); Pommel Horse ■ Pae Gil Su (NKO); Vault ■ Vitaliy Scherbo (BLR); Parallel Bars ■ Vitaliy Scherbo (BLR); Horizontal Bar ■ Sergei Charkov (RUS)

WOMEN'S RESULTS

All-Around ■ Shannon Miller (USA); Vault ■ Yelena Piskoun (BLR) Floor Exercise ■ Shannon Miller (USA); Uneven Bars ■ Shannon Miller (USA); Balance Beam ■ Lavinia Milosovici (ROM)

UNITED STATES CHAMPIONSHIPS STAGED AT SALT LAKE CITY, UTAH, AUGUST 26–29

MEN'S RESULTS

All-Around ■ John Roethlisberger; Floor Exercise ■ Kerry Huston; Rings ■ John Roethlisberger; Pommel Horse ■ Chris Waller; Vault ■ Bill Roth; Parallel Bars ■ Chainey Umphrey; Horizontal Bar ■ Steve McCain

WOMEN'S RESULTS

All-Around ■ Shannon Miller; Vault ■ Dominique Dawes; Floor Exercise ■ Shannon Miller; Uneven Bars ■ Shannon Miller; Balance Beam ■ Dominique Dawes

NCAA CHAMPIONSHIPS (MEN) STAGED AT LINCOLN, NEB.

All-Around ■ John Roethlisberger, Minnesota; Team ■ Stanford

NCAA CHAMPIONSHIPS (WOMEN) STAGED AT CORVALLIS, ORE.

All-Around ■ Jenny Hansen, Kentucky; Team ■ Georgia

HARNESS RACING

TRIPLE CROWN WINNERS

TROTTERS

Yonkers Trot ■ American Winner, Ron Pierce; Hambletonian ■ American Winner, Ron Pierce; Kentucky Futurity ■ Pine Chip, John Campbell

PACERS

Cane Pace ■ Riyadh, Jim Morrill Jr.; Little Brown Jug ■ Life Sign, John Campbell; Messenger Stakes ■ Riyadh, Jim Morrill, Jr.

LEADING MONEY WINNERS

Trotter ■ Pine Chip, $1,363,483

Pacer ■ Presidential Ball, $2,222,166

HOCKEY

NATIONAL HOCKEY LEAGUE (NHL)

1992–93 FINAL STANDINGS
WALES CONFERENCE
Adams Division

Team	W	L	T	Pts.
Boston*	51	26	7	109
Quebec*	47	27	10	104
Montreal*	48	30	6	102
Buffalo*	38	36	10	86

	W	L	T	Pts.
Hartford	26	52	6	58
Ottawa	10	70	4	24

*In Playoffs

Patrick Division

Team	W	L	T	Pts.
Pittsburgh*	56	21	7	119
Washington*	43	34	7	93
NY Islanders*	40	37	7	87
New Jersey*	40	37	7	87
Philadelphia	36	37	11	83
NY Rangers	34	39	11	79

*In Playoffs

CAMPBELL CONFERENCE

Norris Division

Team	W	L	T	Pts.
Chicago*	47	25	12	106
Detroit*	47	28	9	103
Toronto*	44	29	11	99
St. Louis*	37	36	11	85
Minnesota	36	38	10	82
Tampa Bay	23	54	7	53

*In Playoffs

Smythe Division

Team	W	L	T	Pts.
Vancouver*	46	29	9	101
Calgary*	43	30	11	97
Los Angeles*	39	35	10	88
Winnipeg*	40	37	7	87
Edmonton	26	50	8	60
San Jose	11	71	2	24

*In Playoffs

NHL 1992–93 STATISTICAL LEADERS

Points	160	Mario Lemieux, Pittsburgh
Goals	76	Alexander Moligny, Buffalo
	76	Teemu Selanne, Winnipeg
Assists	97	Adam Oates, Boston
Wins	43	Tom Barrasso, Pittsburgh
Shutouts	7	Ed Belfour, Chicago

AWARDS

Hart Trophy (MVP) ■ Mario Lemieux, Pittsburgh; Ross Trophy (Top Scorer) ■ Mario Lemieux, Pittsburgh; Norris Trophy (Top Defenseman) ■ Chris Chelios, Chicago; Vezina Trophy (Top Goaltender) ■ Ed Belfour, Chicago; Calder Trophy (Top Rookie) ■ Teemu Selanne, Winnipeg

ANOTHER CUP ■ THE MONTREAL CANADIENS WON THE STANLEY CUP FOR A RECORD 24TH TIME IN 1993. (BRUCE BENNETT STUDIOS)

STANLEY CUP PLAYOFFS 1993

Playoffs (see p. 236)

STANLEY CUP FINALS

Montreal Canadiens 4 Los Angeles Kings 1

Game 1 (at Montreal)	Los Angeles 4 Montreal 1
Game 2 (at Montreal)	Montreal 3 Los Angeles 2
Game 3 (at Los Angeles)	Montreal 4 Los Angeles 3
Game 4 (at Los Angeles)	Montreal 3 Los Angeles 2
Game 5 (at Montreal)	Montreal 4 Los Angeles 1

Conn Smythe Trophy (Playoffs MVP) ■ Patrick Roy (Montreal)

WORLD CHAMPIONSHIP STAGED AT MUNICH, GERMANY, APRIL 18–MAY 5

Final ■ Russia 3 Sweden 1

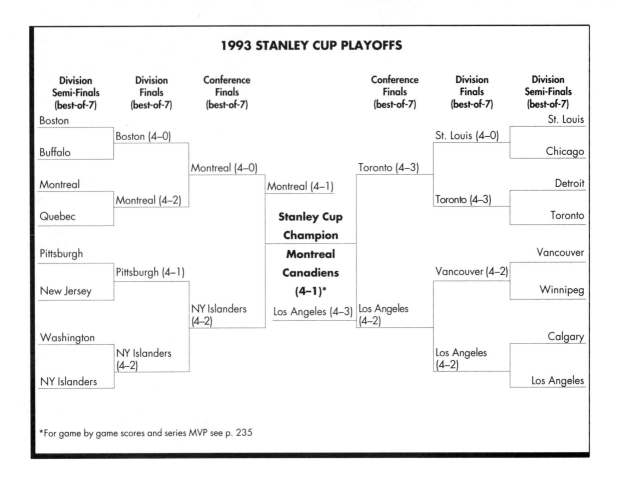

1993 STANLEY CUP PLAYOFFS

Division Semi-Finals (best-of-7)	Division Finals (best-of-7)	Conference Finals (best-of-7)		Conference Finals (best-of-7)	Division Finals (best-of-7)	Division Semi-Finals (best-of-7)
Boston	Boston (4–0)				St. Louis (4–0)	St. Louis
Buffalo		Montreal (4–0)		Toronto (4–3)		Chicago
Montreal	Montreal (4–2)				Toronto (4–3)	Detroit
Quebec			Montreal (4–1)			Toronto
Pittsburgh	Pittsburgh (4–1)		**Stanley Cup Champion Montreal Canadiens (4–1)***		Vancouver (4–2)	Vancouver
New Jersey		NY Islanders (4–2)	Los Angeles (4–3)	Los Angeles (4–2)		Winnipeg
Washington	NY Islanders (4–2)				Los Angeles (4–2)	Calgary
NY Islanders						Los Angeles

*For game by game scores and series MVP see p. 235

NCAA DIVISION I CHAMPIONSHIP (STAGED AT MILWAUKEE, WIS.)

Maine 5 Lake Superior State 4

HORSE RACING

TRIPLE CROWN WINNERS

Kentucky Derby ■ Sea Hero, Jerry Bailey; The Preakness ■ Prairie Bayou, Mike Smith; Belmont Stakes ■ Colonial Affair, Julie Krone; Triple Crown Bonus ■ Sea Hero

THE BREEDERS' CUP WINNERS

Sprint ■ Cardmania, Eddie Delahoussaye; Juvenile Fillies ■ Bone Chatter, Laffit Pincay, Jr.; Distaff ■ Hollywood Wildcat, Eddie Delahoussaye; Mile ■ Lure, Mike Smith; Juvenile ■ Brocco, Gary Stevens; Turf ■ Kotoshaan, Kent Desormeaux; Classic ■ Arcangues, Jerry Bailey

INTERNATIONAL RACES

Prix de l'Arc de Triomphe (France) ■ Urban Sea, Eric Saint-Martin; Epsom Derby (England) ■ Commander in Chief, Michael Kinane; The Grand National (England) ■ *; Melbourne Cup (Australia) ■ Vintage Crop, Michael Kinane

*The race was declared void after 30 horses failed to return to the starting line after a false start.

HORSESHOE PITCHING

WORLD CHAMPIONSHIPS STAGED AT SPEARFISH, S.D., JULY 19–AUGUST 1

Men's Champion ■ Alan Francis (USA); Women's Champion ■ Cathy Carter (USA)

JUDO

MEN'S RESULTS

60 kg ■ Ryuji Sonoda (JAP); 65 kg ■ Nakamura (JAP); 71 kg ■ Yung Chung-hoon (SKO); 78 kg ■ Chun Ki-yong (SKO); 86 kg ■ Yoshio Nakamura (JAP); 95 kg ■ Antal Kovacs (HUN); Over 95 kg ■ David Douillet (FRA); Open ■ Rafal Kubicki (POL)

WOMEN'S RESULTS

48 kg ■ Ryoko Tamura (JAP); 52 kg ■ Legna Verdicia (ITA); 56 kg ■ Nicola Fairbrother (GBR); Gella van de Cavaye (BEL); 66 kg Cho Min-sun (SKO); 72 kg ■ Leng Chenhui (CHI); Over 75 kg J. Hagn (GER); Open ■ Beata Maksymov (POL)

LACROSSE

NCAA Division I (men) ■ Syracuse 13 North Carolina 12
NCAA Division I (women) ■ Virginia 8 Princeton 6

MODERN PENTATHLON

WORLD CHAMPIONSHIPS STAGED AT DARMSTADT, GERMANY, AUGUST 2–8

MEN'S RESULTS

Individual ■ Richard Phelps (GB); Team ■ Hungary

WOMEN'S RESULTS

Individual ■ Eva Fjellerup (DEN); Team ■ Russia

UNITED STATES NATIONAL CHAMPIONSHIPS STAGED AT SAN ANTONIO, TEX., JUNE 19–21

Men's Champion ■ Mike Gostigian; Women's Champion ■ Vanessa Richey

MOTORCYCLE RACING

WORLD CHAMPIONS

125 cc ■ Pedro Tragter (NET); 250 cc ■ Greg Albertyn (SAF); 500 cc ■ Jacky Martens (BEL)

OLYMPIC GAMES

For a complete listing of medal winners from the 1994 Winter Games see pages 245–246.

ORIENTEERING

WORLD CHAMPIONSHIPS STAGED AT HARRIMAN STATE PARK, N.Y., OCTOBER 16–17

MEN'S RESULTS

Classic (15km) ■ Allan Mogensen (DEN); Short (5 km) ■ Petter Thoresen (NOR); Relay ■ Switzerland

WOMEN'S RESULTS

Classic (9 km) ■ Marita Skogum (SWE); Short (4 km) ■ Anna Bogren (SWE); Relay ■ Sweden

UNITED STATES STAGED AT FAHNESTOCK STATE PARK/HARRIMAN STATE PARK, N.Y., SEPTEMBER 11–12

Men's Champion ■ Mikell Platt; Women's Champion ■ Kristin Federer

POLO

U.S. OPEN CHAMPIONSHIP STAGED AT LEXINGTON, KY., OCTOBER 31

Gehache 11 Fish Creek 10

POWERBOAT RACING

APBA GOLD CUP STAGED AT DETROIT, MICH.

Champion ■ Chip Hanauer, *Miss Budweiser*

RACQUETBALL

U.S. CHAMPIONSHIPS STAGED AT HOUSTON, TEX., MAY 26–31

Men's Champion ■ John Ellis
Women's Champion ■ Michelle Gilman-Gould

RODEO

PRCA All-Around Champion ■ Ty Murray

PRCA Individual Event Winners

Saddle bronc riding ■ Dan Mortensen; Bareback riding ■ Deb Greenough; Bull riding ■ Ty Murray; Calf roping ■ Joe Beaver; Steer roping ■ Guy Allen; Steer wrestling ■ Steve Duhon; Team roping ■ Bobby Hurley; Women's barrel racing ■ Charmayne Rodman

ROWING

WORLD CHAMPIONSHIPS STAGED AT PRAGUE, CZECH REPUBLIC, AUGUST 30–SEPTEMBER 5

MEN'S RESULTS

Single Sculls ■ Derek Porter (CAN); Double Sculls ■ Yves Lamarque/Samuel Barathay (FRA); Coxless Pairs ■ Steven Redgrave/Matthew Pinsett (GBR); Coxed Pairs ■ Great Britain; Coxless Fours ■ France; Coxed Fours ■ Romania; Quadruple Sculls ■ Germany; Eights ■ Germany

WOMEN'S RESULTS

Single Sculls ■ Jana Thieme (GER); Double Sculls ■ Philippa Baker/Brenda Lawson (NZL); Coxless Pairs ■ Helene Cortin/Christine Gosse (FRA); Quadruple Sculls ■ China; Coxless Fours ■ China; Eights ■ Romania

SKIING

WORLD ALPINE SKIING CHAMPIONSHIPS STAGED AT MORIOKA, JAPAN, FEBRUARY 3–14

MEN'S RESULTS

Downhill ■ Urs Lehmann (SWI); Slalom ■ Kjetil Andre Aamodt (NOR); Giant Slalom ■ Kjetil Andre Aamodt (NOR); Men's Combined ■ Lasse Kjus (NOR)

WOMEN'S RESULTS

Downhill ■ Kate Pace (CAN); Slalom ■ Karin Buder (AUT); Giant Slalom ■ Carole Merle (FRA); Super G ■ Katja Seizinger (GER); Combined ■ Miriam Vogt (GER)

1992–93 WORLD CUP (ALPINE) FINAL STANDINGS

MEN'S RESULTS

Overall Champion ■ Marc Giradelli (LUX); Downhill ■ Franz Heinzer (SWI); Slalom ■ Tomas Fogdoe (SWE); Giant Slalom ■ Kjetil Andre Aamodt (NOR); Super G ■ Kjetil Andre Aamodt (NOR)

WOMEN'S RESULTS

Overall Champion ■ Anita Wachter (AUT); Downhill ■ Katja Seizinger (GER); Slalom ■ Vreni Schneider (SWI); Giant Slalom ■ Carole Merle (FRA); Super G ■ Katja Seizinger (GER)

NORDIC WORLD CHAMPIONSHIPS STAGED AT FALUN, SWEDEN, FEBRUARY 18–28

MEN'S RESULTS (CROSS-COUNTRY)

10km Classical ■ Sture Sivertsen (NOR); 30km Classical ■ Bjorn Daehlie (NOR); Pursuit ■ Bjorn Daehlie (NOR); 50km Freestyle ■ Torgny Mogren (SWE); Relay (4 x 10km) ■ Norway

WOMEN'S RESULTS (CROSS-COUNTRY)

5km Classical ■ Larissa Lazutina (RUS); 15km Classical ■ Elena Vaelbe (RUS); 30km Freestyle ■ Stefanie Belmondo (ITA); Pursuit ■ Stefanie Belmondo (ITA); Relay (4 x 5km) ■ Russia

SKI-JUMPING RESULTS

Large Hill ■ Espen Bredesen (NOR); Normal Hill ■ Mashiko Harada (JAP); Large Hill (Team) ■ Norway; Nordic Combined ■ Kenki Ogiwera (JAP)

1992–93 WORLD CUP (NORDIC) FINAL STANDINGS

CROSS-COUNTRY RESULTS

Men's Champion ■ Bjorn Daehlie (NOR); Women's Champion ■ Ljubov Egorova (RUS)

SKI-JUMPING RESULTS

Jumping Champion ■ Andreas Goldberger (AUT); Nordic Combined ■ Kenji Ogiwara (JAP)

FREESTYLE WORLD CHAMPIONSHIPS STAGED AT ALTENMARKT, AUSTRIA, MARCH 9–14

MEN'S RESULTS

Aerials ■ Philippe LaRoche (CAN); Moguls ■ Jean-Luc Brassard (CAN); Ballet ■ Fabrice Becker (FRA); Combined ■ Sergei Shupletsov (RUS)

WOMEN'S RESULTS

Aerials ■ Lina Tcherjazova (UZB); Ballet ■ Ellen Breen (USA); Moguls ■ Stine Lisa Hattestad (NOR); Combined ■ Katherina Kubenk (CAN)

1993 FREESTYLE WORLD CUP FINAL STANDINGS

MEN'S RESULTS

Overall Champion ■ Trace Worthington (USA); Aerials ■ Lloyd Langlois (CAN); Moguls ■ Jean-Luc Brassard (CAN); Ballet ■ Rune Kristiansen (NOR); Combined ■ Trace Worthington (CAN)

WOMEN'S RESULTS

Overall Champion ■ Katharina Kubenk (CAN); Aerials ■ Lina Cherjazova (UZB); Moguls ■ Stine Lisa Hattestad (NOR); Ballet ■ Ellen Breen (USA); Combined ■ Katherina Kubenk (CAN)

SLED DOG RACING

THE IDITAROD

Winner ■ Jeff King (USA)

SOARING

WORLD CHAMPIONSHIPS STAGED AT BORLANGE, SWEDEN, JUNE 13–26

CHAMPIONS

Open Class ■ Janusz Centka (POL); 15-meter ■ Gilbert Gerbaud (FRA)*, Eric Napoleon (FRA)*; Standard ■ Andy Davis (GBR)
* Tie

SOCCER

INTERNATIONAL TOURNAMENTS

INTERNATIONAL CLUB TEAM COMPETITIONS

TOYOTA WORLD CUP CHAMPIONSHIP STAGED AT TOKYO, JAPAN, DECEMBER 11

Sao Paulo (BRA) 3 AC Milan (ITA) 2

EUROPEAN CUP FINAL STAGED AT MUNICH, GERMANY, MAY 26

Marseilles (FRA) 1 AC Milan (ITA) 0

EUROPEAN CUP WINNERS CUP FINAL STAGED AT LONDON, ENGLAND, MAY 12

Parma (ITA) 3 Royal Antwerp (BEL) 1

UEFA CUP (2-GAME/AGGREGATE GOALS SERIES)

Borussia Dortmund (GER) 1 Juventus (ITA) 3

Juventus 3 Borussia Dortmund 0

(Juventus won 6–1 on aggregate)

NCAA CHAMPIONSHIPS

DIVISION I (MEN) STAGED AT DAVIDSON, N.C., DECEMBER 9

Virginia 2 South Carolina 0

DIVISION 1 (WOMEN) STAGED AT CHAPEL HILL, N.C., NOVEMBER 21

North Carolina 6 George Mason 0

SOFTBALL

AMERICAN SOFTBALL ASSOCIATION CHAMPIONS

MEN'S CHAMPIONS

Major Fast Pitch ■ Nat'l Health Care Discount, Sioux City, Iowa; Major Modified Pitch ■ Craft Tech, Secaucus, N.J.; Super Slow Pitch ■ Ritch's/Superior, Windsor Locks, Conn.; Major Slow Pitch ■ Back Porch/Destin Roofing, Destin, Fla.

WOMEN'S CHAMPIONS

Major Fast Pitch ■ Redding Rebels, Redding, Calif.; Major Modified Pitch ■ PA Club, Methuen, Mass.; Major Slow Pitch ■ UPI, Cookeville, Tenn.

SPEED SKATING

WORLD CHAMPIONSHIPS (WOMEN) STAGED AT BERLIN, GERMANY, FEBRUARY 6–7

500 meters ■ Qiaobo Ye (CHI); 1,500 meters ■ Gunda Niemann (GER); 3,000 meters ■ Gunda Niemann (GER); 5,000 meters ■ Gunda Niemann (GER)

WORLD CHAMPIONSHIPS (MEN) STAGED AT HAMAR, NORWAY, FEBRUARY 13–14

500 meters ■ Chen Song (CHI); 1,500 meters ■ Johann Olav Koss (NOR); 5,000 meters ■ Falko Zandstra (NET); 10,000 meters ■ Bart Veldkamp (NET)

SHORT TRACK WORLD CHAMPIONSHIPS STAGED AT BEIJING, CHINA, MARCH 26–28

MEN'S RESULTS

500 meters ■ Zmirko Vuillermin (ITA); 1,000 meters ■ Marc Gagnon (CAN); 1,500 meters ■ Marc Gagnon (CAN); 3,000 meters ■ Ji-Hoon Chae (SKO); Relay (5,000 m) ■ New Zealand

WOMEN'S RESULTS

500 meters ■ Yanmei Zhang (CHI); 1,000 meters ■ Nathalie Lambert (CAN); 1,500 meters ■ Nathalie Lambert (CAN); 3,000 meters ■ Nathalie Lambert (CAN); Relay (3,000 m) ■ Canada

SWIMMING

NCAA CHAMPIONSHIPS (MEN) STAGED AT INDIANAPOLIS, IND.

Men's Team ■ Stanford

NCAA CHAMPIONSHIPS (WOMEN) STAGED AT MINNEAPOLIS, MINNESOTA

Women's Team ■ Stanford

TABLE TENNIS

WORLD CHAMPIONSHIPS STAGED AT GOTHENBURG, SWEDEN, MAY 11–23

Men's Singles ■ Jean-Philippe Gatien (FRA); Women's Singles ■ Hyun Jung-hwa (SKO); Men's Doubles ■ Wang Tao/Lu Lin (CHI); Women's Doubles ■ Liu Wei/Qiao Yunping (CHI); Mixed Doubles ■ Wang Tao/Liu Wei (CHI); Men's Team* ■ Sweden; Women's Team† ■ China

*Swaythling Cup

†Corbillon Cup

TAEKWONDO

WORLD CHAMPIONSHIPS STAGED IN NEW YORK CITY, AUGUST 19–21

MEN'S RESULTS

Finweight ■ Seung Tae Jin (SKO); Flyweight ■ Javier Argudo (SPA); Bantamweight ■ Kyoung Kim (SKO); Featherweight ■ Byong Cheol Kim (SKO); Lightweight ■ Se Jin Park (SKO); Welterweight ■ Young Ho Lim (SKO); Middleweight ■ Mikkael Meloul (France); Heavyweight ■ Je Kyoung Kim (SKO)

WOMEN'S RESULTS

Finweight ■ Isabel Cruzado (SPA); Flyweight ■ Su Mi You (SKO); Bantamweight ■ Hui-Wen Tang (TAI); Featherweight ■ Seung Min Lee (SKO); Lightweight ■ Ma Jesus Santolaria (SPA); Welterweight ■ Mi Young Kim (SKO); Middleweight ■ Eun Sun Park (SKO); Heavyweight ■ Myung Suk Jung (SKO)

TENNIS

GRAND SLAM EVENTS

AUSTRALIAN OPEN

Men's Singles ■ Jim Courier (USA); Women's Singles ■ Monica Seles (YUG); Men's Doubles ■ Danie Visser (SAF)/Laurie Warder (AUS); Women's Doubles ■ Natalya Zvereva (BLR)/Gigi Fernandez (USA); Mixed Doubles ■ Arantxa Sanchez-Vicario (SPA)/Todd Woodbridge (AUS)

FRENCH OPEN

Men's Singles ■ Sergi Bruguera (SPA); Women's Singles ■ Steffi Graf (GER); Men's Doubles ■ Luke Jensen/Murphy Jensen (USA); Women's Doubles ■ Natalya Zvereva (BLR)/Gigi Fernandez (USA); Mixed Doubles ■ Eugenia Maniokova/Andrei Olhovskiy (RUS)

WIMBLEDON

Men's Singles ■ Pete Sampras (USA); Women's Singles ■ Steffi Graf (GER); Men's Doubles ■ Mark Woodforde/Todd Woodbridge (AUS); Women's Doubles ■ Natalya Zvereva (BRS)/Gigi Fernandez (USA); Mixed Doubles ■ Martina Navratilova (USA)/Mark Woodforde (AUS)

U.S. Open

Men's Singles ■ Pete Sampras (USA); Women's Singles ■ Steffi Graf (GER); Men's Doubles ■ Ken Flach/Rick Leach (USA); Women's Doubles ■ Helena Sukova (CZE)/Arantxa Sanchez Vicario (SPA); Mixed Doubles ■ Helena Sukova (CZE)/Todd Woodbridge (AUS)

I.B.M./APT Tour Winners

Australian Hardcourts ■ Nicklas Kulti (SWE); Qatar Open ■ Boris Becker (GER); Malaysian Open ■ Richey Reneberg (USA); Benson & Hedges Open ■ Alexander Volkov (RUS); New South Wales Open ■ Pete Sampras (USA); Indonesian Open ■ Michael Chang (USA); Australian Open ■ Jim Courier (USA); The Dubai Duty Free BMW Open ■ Karel Novacek (CZE); Volvo San Francisco ■ Andrei Agassi (USA); Marseille Open ■ Marc Rosset (SWI); The International Indoor ■ Jim Courier; Muratti Time Indoor ■ Boris Becker; U.S. Pro Indoor ■ Mark Woodforde (AUS); Eurocard Open ■ Michael Stich (GER); Rotterdam Open ■ Anders Jarryd (SWE); Purex Tennis Championships ■ Andre Agassi; Mexico City Open ■ Thomas Muster (AUT); Newsweek Champions Cup ■ Jim Courier; Copenhagen Open ■ Andrei Olhovskiy (RUS); Cuidad de Zaragoza ■ Karel Novacek (CZE); Lipton International ■ Pete Sampras; Grand Prix Hassan II ■ Guillermo Perez-Roldan (ARG); South African Open ■ Aaron Krickstein (USA); Estoril Open ■ Andrei Medvedev (UKR); Japan Open ■ Michael Chang; Conde De Godo ■ Andrei Medvedev; Seiko Super Tennis ■ Pete Sampras; Nice Open ■ Marc Goellner (GER); Salem Open ■ Pete Sampras; USTA Clay Court Championships ■ Horacio de la Pena (ARG); Monte Carlo Open ■ Sergi Bruguera (SPA); KAL Cup ■ Chuck Adams (USA); City of Madrid ■ Stefan Edberg (SWE); AT&T Challenge ■ Jacco Eltingh (NET); BMW Open ■ Ivan Lendl (USA); Panasonic German Open ■ Michael Stich; USTA Men's Clay Courts of Tampa ■ Jaime Yzaga (PER); Italian Open ■ Jim Courier; Match Point World Series ■ Todd Martin (USA); Peugeot ATP World Team Cup ■ United States; Bologna Open ■ Jordi Burillo (SPA); French Open ■ Sergi Bruguera; City of Florence ■ Thomas Muster; Stella Artois ■ Michael Stich; The Continental Grass Court Championships ■ Arnaud Boetsch (FRA); Int'l Grass Court ■ Henri Leconte (FRA); Direct Line Insurance Open ■ Jason Stoltenberg (AUS); IP Cup ■ Thomas Muster; Wimbledon ■ Pete Sampras; Swedish Open ■ Sergi Bruguera; Hall of Fame ■ Greg Rusedski (CAN); Swiss Open ■ Sergi Bruguera; Stuttgart Grand Prix ■ Magnus Gustaffsson (SWE); Washington Tennis Classic ■ Amos Mansdorf (ISR); Players International ■ Mikael Pernfors (SWE); Dutch Open ■ Carlos Costa (SPA); Philips Head Cup ■ Thomas Muster; Skoda Czech Open ■ Sergi Bruguera; Volvo of Los Angeles ■ Richard Krajicek (NET); ATP Championship ■ Michael Chang; San Marino Open ■ Thomas Muster; Volvo International ■ Petr Korda (CZE); RCA US Men's Hardcourt Championships ■ Jim Courier; Hamlet Cup ■ Michael Chang; Croatia Open ■ Thomas Muster; OTB Interntional ■ Thomas Enqvist (SWE); U.S. Open ■ Pete Sampras; Bucharest Open ■ Goran Ivanisevic (CRO); Grand Prix Passing Shot Bordeaux ■ Sergi Bruguera; Swiss Indoors ■ Michael Stich; Campionati Internazionale di Sicilia ■ Thomas Muster; Kuala Lumpur Open ■ Michael Chang; Australian Indoors ■ Jaime Yzage (PER); Grand Prix de Toulouse ■ Arnaud Boetsch; Athens International ■ Jordi Arrese (SPA); Seiko Super Tennis ■ Ivan Lendl; Bolzano Open ■ Johnathan Stark (USA); Riklis Israel Tennis Classic ■ Stefano Pescosolido (ITA); Grand Prix de Lyon ■ Pete Sampras; CA Tennis Trophy ■ Goran Ivanisevic; Beijing Open ■ Michael Chang; Stockholm Open ■ Michael Stich; Santiago Open ■ Javier Frana (ARG); Paris Open ■ Goran Ivanisevic; Antwerp Open ■ Pete Sampras; Bayer Kremlin Cup ■ Marc Rosset (SWI); Buenos Aires Open ■ Carlos Costa (SPA); IBM/ATP Championship ■ Michael Stich

Leading Money Winner ■ Pete Sampras (USA), $3,648,075

Kraft General Foods World Tour Winners

Australian Women's Hardcourts ■ Concita Martinez (SPA); New South Wales Open ■ Jenifer Capriati (USA); Sunsmart Victorian Women's Open ■ Amanda Coetzer (SAF); Australian Open ■ Monica Seles (YUG); Nutri-Metics Bendon Classic ■ Elna Reinach (SAF); Toray Pan Pacific Open ■ Martina Navratilova (USA); Virginia Slims of Chicago ■ Monica Seles (YUG); World Ladies in Osaka ■ Jana Novotna (CZE); Open Gaz de France ■ Martina Navratilova (USA); Virginia Slims of Oklahoma ■ Zina Garrison Jackson; Matrix Essentials Evert Cup ■ Mary Joe Fernandez (USA); Australian Indoors ■ Manuela Maleeva-Fragniere (SWI); Virginia Slims of Florida ■ Steffi Graf (GER); Lipton International ■ Arantxa Sanchez-Vicario (SPA); Virginia Slims of Houston ■ Concita Martinez (SPA); Family Circle Cup ■ Steffi Graf

(GER); Bausch & Lomb ■ Arantxa Sanchez-Vicario (SPA); Suntory Japan Open ■ Kimiko Date (JAP); Volvo Women's Open ■ Yayuk Basuki (INA); Malaysian Women's Open ■ Nicole Provis (AUS); Int'l Championships of Spain ■ Arantxa Sanchez-Vicario (SPA); Citizen's Cup ■ Arantxa Sanchez Vicario (SPA); Indonesian Women's Tennis Championships ■ Yayuk Basuki (INA); Ilva Trophy ■ Brenda Schultz (NET); Italian Open ■ Concita Martinez (SPA); Belgian Ladies Open ■ Radka Bobkova (CZE); German Open ■ Steffi Graf (GER); Internationaux de Strasbourg ■ Naoko Sawamatsu (JAP); European Open ■ Lindsay Davenport (USA); French Open ■ Steffi Graf (GER); DFS Classic ■ Lori McNeil (USA); Volkswagen Cup ■ Martina Navratilova (USA); Wimbledon ■ Steffi Graf (GER); Torneo Int'l Femminile di Palermo ■ Radka Bobkova (CZE); Citroen Cup ■ Anke Huber (GER); BW Prague Open ■ Natalia Medvedeva (UKR); Acura U.S. Hardcourts ■ Conchita Martinez (SPA); Puerto Rico Open ■ Linda Harvey-Wild (USA); Mazda Tennis Classic ■ Steffi Graf (USA); Virginia Slims of Los Angeles ■ Martina Navratilova (USA); Matinee Ltd., Int'l-Canadian Open ■ Steffi Graf (GER); OTB International ■ Larisa Neiland (UKR); U.S. Open ■ Steffi Graf (GER); Digital Open ■ Shi-ting Wang (TAI); Nichirei Int'l Championships ■ Amanda Coetzer (SAF); Volkswagen Cup ■ Steffi Graf (GER); Sapporo Ladies Open ■ Manuela Maleeva-Fragniere (SWI); P&G Taiwan Women's Open ■ Shi-ting Wang (TAI); Porsche Grand Prix ■ Mary Pierce (FRA); Budapest Ladies Open ■ Zina Garrison Jackson (USA); Autoglass Classic ■ Jana Novotna (CZE); Nokia Grand Prix ■ Natalia Medvedeva (UKR); Bancesa Classic ■ Sabine Hack (GER); Bank of the West Classic ■ Martina Navratilova (USA); Bell Challenge ■ Nathalie Tauziat (FRA); Virginia Slims of Philadelphia ■ Concita Martinez (SPA); Virginia Slims Championship ■ Steffi Graf (GER)

Leading Money Winner ■ Steffi Graf (GER), $2,821,337

TEAM COMPETITIONS

DAVIS CUP FINAL AT DUSSELDORF, GERMANY, DECEMBER 3–5

Germany 4 Australia 1

FEDERATION CUP FINAL AT FRANKFURT, GERMANY, JULY 25

Spain 2 Australia 0

NCAA CHAMPIONSHIPS (MEN) STAGED AT ATHENS, GA.

Team ■ Southern Cal; Singles ■ Chris Woodruff (Tenn)

NCAA CHAMPIONSHIPS (WOMEN) STAGED AT STANFORD, CALIF.

Team ■ Texas; Singles ■ Lisa Raymond (Florida)

TRACK AND FIELD

WORLD CHAMPIONSHIPS STAGED AT STUTTGART, GERMANY, AUGUST 13–22

MEN'S RESULTS

100 meters ■ Linford Christie (GBR); 200 meters ■ Frank Fredericks (NAM); 400 meters ■ Michael Johnson (USA); 800 meters ■ Paul Ruto (KEN); 1,500 meters ■ Noureddine Morceli (ALG); 5,000 meters ■ Ismael Kirui (KEN); 10,000 meters ■ Haile Gebresilasie (ETH); Marathon ■ Mark Plaatjes (USA); 110 meter hurdles ■ Colin Jackson (GBR); 400 meter hurdles ■ Kevin Young (USA); Steeplechase ■ Moses Kiptanui (KEN); 4 x 100 meter relay ■ United States; 4 x 400 meter relay ■ United States; 20 km walk ■ Valentin Massana (SPA); 50 km walk ■ Jesus Angel Garcia (SPA); High Jump ■ Javier Sotomayor (CUB); Pole Vault ■ Sergei Bubka (UKR); Long Jump ■ Mike Powell (USA); Triple Jump ■ Mike Conley (USA); Shot Put ■ Werner Guenthor (SWI); Discus ■ Lars Riedel (GER); Javelin ■ Jan Zelezny (CZE); Decathlon ■ Dan O'Brien (USA)

WOMEN'S RESULTS

100 meters ■ Gail Devers (USA); 200 meters ■ Merlene Ottey (JAM); 400 meters ■ Jearl Miles (USA); 800 meters ■ Maria Mutola (MOZ); 1,500 meters ■ Liu Dong (CHI); 3,000 meters ■ Qu Junxia (CHI); 10,000 meters ■ Wang Junxia (CHI); Marathon ■ Junko Asari (JAP); 100 meter hurdles ■ Gail Devers (USA); 400 meter hurdles ■ Sally Gunnell (GBR); 4 x 100 meter relay ■ Russia; 4 x 400 meter relay ■ USA; 10 km walk ■ Sari Essayah (FIN); High Jump ■ Ioamnet Quintero (CUB); Long Jump ■ Heike Dreschler (GER); Triple Jump ■ Ana Biryukova (RUS); Shot Put ■ Zhihong Huang (CHI); Discus ■ Olga Burova (RUS); Javelin ■ Trine Hattestad (NOR); Heptathlon ■ Jackie Joyner-Kersee (USA)

MAJOR MARATHONS

MEN'S RESULTS

Boston ■ Cosmos N'Deti (KEN); New York ■ Andres Espinosa (MEX); Los Angeles ■ Joselido Rocha (BRA); Rotterdam ■ Dionicio Ceron (MEX); London ■ Eamonn Martin (GBR)

WOMEN'S RESULTS

Boston ■ Olga Markova (RUS); New York ■ Uta Pippig (GER); Los Angeles ■ Lubov Klochko (UKR); Rotterdam ■ Anne van Schuppen (NET); London ■ Katrin Dorre (GER)

TRIATHLON

IRONMAN CHAMPIONSHIP STAGED AT KONA BEACH, HAWAII, OCTOBER 30

Men's Champion ■ Mark Allen (USA); Women's Champion ■ Paula Newby-Fraser (ZIM)

ITU WORLD CHAMPIONSHIP STAGED AT MANCHESTER, ENGLAND, AUGUST 22

Men's Champion ■ Spencer Smith (GB); Women's Champion ■ Michelle Jones (AUS)

VOLLEYBALL

AVP TOUR RESULTS

Miller Lite Open (MLO) at Honolulu ■ Karch Kiraly/Kent Steffes; Evian Indoors ■ Karch Kiraly/Kent Steffes; MLO at Ft. Myers ■ Sinjin Smith/Randy Stoklos; MLO at Pensacola Beach ■ Karch Kiraly/Kent Steffes; MLO at Phoenix ■ Mike Dodd/Tim Hovland; Jose Cuervo Gold Crown (JCGC) at Clearwater ■ Karch Kiraly/Kent Steffes; MLO at Austin ■ Karch Kiraly/Kent Steffes; MLO at San Antonio ■ Adam Johnson/Bruk Vandeweghe; MLO at Ft. Worth ■ Karch Kiraly/Kent Steffes; MLO at San Diego ■ Karch Kiraly/Kent Steffes; JCGC at Boulder ■ Karch Kiraly/Kent Steffes; MLO at Cleveland ■ Karch Kiraly/Kent Steffes; MLO at Seaside Heights ■ Karch Kiraly/Kent Steffes; MLO at Chicago ■ Brian Lewis/Randy Stoklos; MLO at Ocean City ■ Karch Kiraly/Kent Steffes; Killer Loop Open ■ Karch Kiraly/Kent Steffes; MLO at Cape Cod ■ Karch Kiraly/Kent Steffes; MLO at Belmar ■ Karch Kiraly/Kent Steffes; MLO at Grand Haven ■ Karch Kiraly/Kent Steffes; MLO at Seal Beach ■ Mike Dodd/Mike Whitmarsh; JCGC at Santa Cruz ■ Karch Kiraly/Kent Steffes; U.S. Championships ■ Karch Kiraly/Kent Steffes; Old Spice Tournament of Champions ■ Karch Kiraly/Kent Steffes; Old Spice King of the Beach ■ Karch Kiraly.

Leading Money Winner ■ Karch Kiraly, $467,877.50

Number One Ranking ■ Karch Kiraly/Kent Steffes, 3,957.02 points

WATERSKIING

WORLD CHAMPIONSHIPS STAGED AT SINGAPORE, SEPTEMBER 6–12

MEN'S RESULTS

Overall ■ Patrice Martin (FRA); Slalom ■ Brett Thurley (AUS); Tricks ■ Tory Baggiano (USA); Jump ■ Andrea Alessi (ITA)

WOMEN'S RESULTS

Overall ■ Natalya Rumyantseva (RUS); Slalom ■ Helena Kjellander (SWE); Tricks ■ Britt Larsen (USA); Jump ■ Kim De Macedo (CAN)

WEIGHTLIFTING

WORLD CHAMPIONSHIPS STAGED AT MELBOURNE, AUSTRALIA, NOVEMBER 12–21

CHAMPIONS (MEN)

54 kg ■ Ivan Ivanov (BUL); 59 kg ■ Nikolai Pershalov (BUL); 64 kg ■ Naim Suleymanoglu (TUR); 70 kg ■ Yoto Yotov (BUL); 76 kg ■ Altym Orazdurdiev (TKM); 83 kg ■ Pyrros Dimas (GRE); 91 kg ■ Ivan Tchakarov (BUL); 99 kg ■ Victor Tregubov (RUS); 108 kg ■ Timur Taimazov (UKR); +108 kg ■ Ronnie Weller (GER)

CHAMPIONS (WOMEN)

46 kg ■ Mei Chu-Nan (TAI); 50 kg ■ Liu Xiuhua (CHI); 54 kg ■ Chen Xiaomin (CHI); 59 kg ■ Caiyan Sun (CHI); 64 kg ■ Li Hongyun (CHI); 70 kg ■ Milena Trendafilova (BUL); 76 kg ■ Ju Hua (CHI); 83 kg ■ Shu-Chih Chen (TAI); +83 kg ■ Yajuan Li (CHI)

WRESTLING

FREESTYLE WORLD CHAMPIONSHIPS STAGED AT TORONTO, CANADA, AUGUST 25–28

CHAMPIONS

48 kg ■ Alexis Vila (CUB); 52 kg ■ Valentin Jordanov (BUL); 57 kg ■ Terry Brands (USA); 68 kg ■ Ali Akhbar Fallah (IRA); 74 kg ■ Park Jang-Soon (SKO); 82 kg ■ Sebahattin Ozturk (TUR); 90 kg ■ Abbas Jadidi (IRA); 100 kg ■ Leri Khabelov (RUS); 130 kg ■ Bruce Baumgartner (USA); Team ■ United States

GRECO-ROMAN WORLD CHAMPIONSHIPS STAGED AT STOCKHOLM, SWEDEN, SEPTEMBER 16–19

CHAMPIONS

48 kg ■ Wilber Sanchez (CUB); 52 kg ■ Raul Martinez (CUB); 57 kg ■ Agazi Manukjan (ARM); 62 kg ■ Sergei Martinov (RUS); 69 kg ■ Islam Duguchiev (BUL); 74 kg ■ Nestor Alamanza (CUB); 82 kg ■ Mamza Yerlikaya (TUR); 90 kg ■ Gogi Koguchavilli (RUS); 100 kg ■ Mikael Ljungberg (SWE); 130 kg ■ Alexander Karelin (RUS); Team ■ Russia

FASTEST CIRCUMNAVIGATION ■ COMMODORE EXPLORER, SKIPPERED BY BRUNO PEYRON, CIR-CUMNAVIGATED THE GLOBE IN A RECORD 79 DAYS 6 HOURS 6 MINUTES. (ALLSPORT)

NCAA CHAMPIONSHIPS

Team ■ Iowa

YACHTING

Jules Verne Trophy ■ *Commodore Explorer*, Bruno Peyron: 79 days, 6 hours 6 minutes

Country Abbreviation Codes: AUS, Australia; AUT, Austria; BEL, Belarus; CAN, Canada; CHN, China; FIN, Finland; FRA, France; GBR, Great Britain; GER, Germany; ITA, Italy; JPN, Japan; KAZ, Kazakhstan; NET, Netherlands; NOR, Norway; RUS, Russia; SKO, South Korea; SLO, Slovenia; SWE, Sweden; SWI, Switzerland; UKR, Ukraine; USA, United States of America; UZK, Uzbekistan.

EVENT	GOLD	SILVER	BRONZE
		ALPINE SKIING (men)	
Downhill	Tommy Moe (USA)	Kjetil Andre Aamodt (NOR)	Ed Podvinsky (CAN)
Slalom	Thomas Stangassinger (AUT)	Alberto Tomba (ITA)	Jure Kosir (SLO)
Giant Slalom	Markus Wasmeier (GER)	Urs Kaelin (SWI)	Christian Mayer (AUT)
Super-G	Markus Wasmeier (GER)	Tommy Moe (USA)	Kjetil Andre Aamodt (NOR) (NOR)
Combined	Lasse Kjus (NOR)	Kjetil Andre Aamodt (NOR)	Harald Nilsen (NOR)
		ALPINE SKIING (women)	
Downhill	Katja Seizinger (GER)	Picabo Street (USA)	Isolde Kostner (ITA)
Slalom	Vreni Schneider (SWI)	Elffe Eder (AUT)	Katja Koren (SLO)
Giant Slalom	Deborah Compagnoni (ITA)	Martina Ertl (GER)	Vreni Schneider (SWI)
Super-G	Diann Roffe-Steinrotter (USA)	Svetlana Gladischeva (RUS)	Isolde Kostner (ITA)
Combined	Pernilla Wiberg (SWE)	Vreni Schneider (SWI)	Alenka Dovzan (SLO)
		BIATHLON (men)	
10 km	Sergei Chepikov (RUS)	Ricco Gross (GER)	Sergei Tarasov (RUS)
20 km	Sergei Tarasov (RUS)	Frank Luck (GER)	Sven Fischer (GER)
4 x 7.5 km Relay	Germany	Russia	France
		BIATHLON (women)	
7.5 km	Myriam Bedard (CAN)	Svetlana Paramygina (BEL)	Valentyna Tserbe (UKR)
15 km	Myriam Bedard (CAN)	Anne Briand (FRA)	Ursula Disl (GER)
4 x 7.5 km Relay	Russia	Germany	France
		BOBSLED	
2–man	Gustav Weder & Donat Acklin (SWI)	Reto Goetschi & Guido Acklin (SWI)	Gunther Huber & Stefano Ticci (ITA)
4–man	Germany II	Switzerland I	Germany I
		CROSS-COUNTRY SKIING (men)	
10 km	Bjorn Dahlie (NOR)	Vladimir Smirnov (KAZ)	Marco Albarello (ITA)
15 km	Bjorn Dahlie (NOR)	Vladimir Smirnov (KAZ)	Silvio Fauner (ITA)
30 km	Thomas Alsgaard (NOR)	Bjorn Dahlie (NOR)	Mika Myllylae (FIN)
50 km	Vladimir Smirnov (KAZ)	Mika Myllylae (FIN)	Sture Sivertsen (NOR)
4 x 10 km Relay	Italy	Norway	Finland
		CROSS-COUNTRY SKIING (women)	
5 km	Lyubov Egorova (RUS)	Manuela Di Centa (ITA)	Marja-Liisa Kirvesniemi (FIN)
10 km	Lyubov Egorova (RUS)	Manuela Di Centa (ITA)	Stefania Belmondo (ITA)
15 km	Manuela Di Centa (ITA)	Lyubov Egorova (RUS)	Nina Gavriluk (RUS)
30 km	Manuela Di Centa (ITA)	Marit Wold (NOR)	Marja-Liisa Kirvesniemi (FIN)
4 x 5 km Relay	Russia	Norway	Italy
		FIGURE SKATING	
Men	Alexei Urmanov (RUS)	Elvis Stojko (CAN)	Philippe Candeloro (FRA)
Women	Oksana Baiul (UKR)	Nancy Kerrigan (USA)	Chen Lu (CHN)
Pairs	Yekaterina Gordeyeva & Sergei Grinkov (RUS)	Natalia Mishkutienok & Artur Dmitriev (RUS)	Isabelle Brasseur & Lloyd Eisler (CAN)
Ice Dance	Oksana Grichtchuk & Evgeni Platov (RUS)	Maya Usova & Aleksandr Zhulin (RUS)	Jayne Torvill & Christopher Dean (GBR)
		FREESTYLE SKIING (aerials)	
Men	Andreas Schonbachler (SWI)	Philippe Laroche (CAN)	Lloyd Langlois (CAN)
Women	Lina Cheryazova (UZB)	Marie Lindgren (SWE)	Hilde Synnoeve Lid (NOR)
		FREESTYLE SKIING (moguls)	
Men	Jean-Luc Brassard (CAN)	Sergei Shoupletsov (RUS)	Edgar Grospiron (FRA)
Women	Stine Lise Hattestad (NOR)	Liz McIntyre (USA)	Yelizaveta Kojevnikova (RUS)
		HOCKEY	
Team	Sweden	Canada	Finland
		LUGE (men)	
Singles	Georg Hackl (GER)	Markus Prock (AUT)	Armin Zoggeler (ITA)
2–man	Kurt Brugger & Wilfried Huber (ITA)	Hans Raffl & Norbert Huber (ITA)	Stefan Krausse & Jan Behrendt (GER)

EVENT	GOLD	SILVER	BRONZE
		LUGE (women)	
Singles	Gerda Weissensteiner (ITA)	Susi Erdmann (GER)	Andrea Tagwerker (AUT)
		NORDIC COMBINED	
Individual	Fred-Barre Lundberg	Takanori Kono (JPN)	Bjart-Engen Vik (NOR)
Team	Japan	Norway	Switzerland
		SHORT TRACK (men)	
500 m	Chae Ji-Hoon (SKO)	Mirko Vuillermin (ITA)	Nick Gooch (GBR)
1,000 m	Ki-Hoon Kim (SKO)	Gi-Hoon Chae (SKO)	Marc Gagnon (CAN)
5,000 m Relay	Italy	United States	Australia
		SHORT TRACK (women)	
500 m	Cathy Turner (USA)	Zhang Yanmei (CHN)	Amy Peterson (USA)
1,000 m	Chung Lee-Kyung (SKO)	Nathalie Lambert (CAN)	Kim So-Hee (SKO)
3,000 m Relay	South Korea	Canada	United States
		SKI JUMPING	
Normal Hill	Espen Bredesen (NOR)	Lasse Ottesen (NOR)	Dieter Thoma (GER)
Large Hill	Jens Weissflog (GER)	Espen Bredesen (NOR)	Andreas Goldberger (AUT)
Team	Germany	Japan	Austria
		SPEED SKATING (men)	
500 m	Aleksandr Golubev (RUS)	Sergei Klevchenya (RUS)	Manabu Horii (JPN)
1,000 m	Dan Jansen (USA)	Igor Zhelezovsky (BEL)	Sergei Klevchenya (RUS)
1,500 m	Johann Olav Koss (NOR)	Rintje Ritsma (NET)	Falko Zandstra (NET)
5,000 m	Johann Olav Koss (NOR)	Kjell Storelid (NOR)	Rintje Ritsma (NET)
10,000 m	Johann Olav Koss (NOR)	Kjell Storelid (NOR)	Bart Veldkamp (NET)
		SPEED SKATING (women)	
500 m	Bonnie Blair (USA)	Susan Auch (CAN)	Franziska Schenk (GER)
1,000 m	Bonnie Blair (USA)	Anke Baier (GER)	Ye Qiabo (CHN)
1,500 m	Emese Hunyady (AUT)	Svetlana Fedotkina (RUS)	Gunda Niemann (GER)
3,000 m	Svetlana Bazhanova (RUS)	Emese Hunyady (AUT)	Claudia Pechstein (GER)
5,000 m	Claudia Pechstein (GER)	Gunda Niemann (GER)	Hiromi Yamamoto (JPN)

1994 WINTER GAMES MEDAL TABLE

COUNTRY	GOLD	SILVER	BRONZE	TOTAL	COUNTRY	GOLD	SILVER	BRONZE	TOTAL
Norway	10	11	5	26	France	0	1	4	5
Germany	9	7	8	24	Netherlands	0	1	3	4
Russia	11	8	4	23	Sweden	2	1	0	3
Italy	7	5	8	20	Kazakhstan	1	2	0	3
United States	6	5	2	13	China	0	1	2	3
Canada	3	6	4	13	Slovenia	0	0	3	3
Switzerland	3	4	2	9	Ukraine	1	0	1	2
Austria	2	3	4	9	Belarus	0	2	0	2
South Korea	4	1	1	6	Great Britain	0	0	2	2
Finland	0	1	5	6	Uzbekistan	1	0	0	1
Japan	1	2	2	5	Australia	0	0	1	1

OLYMPIC RECORDS SET AT LILLEHAMMER

Most gold medals (career) Nordic skier Lyubov Egorova (RUS) won three gold medals at Lillehammer. She extended her career tally to six, tying Lydia Skoblokova's all-time Winter Games mark.

Most gold medals (U.S.) Speed skater Bonnie Blair's Lillehammer double extended her career total to five gold medals, setting the record for most gold medals won by an American female athlete.

WORLD RECORDS SET AT LILLEHAMMER

Speedskating (men) 1,000 meters ■ Dan Jansen (USA), 1:12.43, February 18, 1994; 1,500 meters ■ Johann Olav Koss (NOR), 1:51.29, February 16, 1994; 5,000 meters ■ Johann Olav Koss (NOR), 6:34.96, February 13, 1994; 10,000 meters ■ Johann Olav Koss (NOR), 13:30.55, February 20, 1994.

Speedskating (women) 5,000 meters ■ Claudie Pechstein (GER), 7:14.37, February 25, 1994.

Special thanks to Jeffrey, Carol, Andrew, Ruth and Sarah for technical assistance in compiling this section.

INDEX

Boldface type indicates main subjects. *Italic* page numbers indicate "Timeout" features. *t* following the page number indicates tables; *c* indicates photo captions. Names of sports figures appear only in the main body of the text.

1350

Economics of State Aid to Education

Economics of State Aid to Education

Elchanan Cohn
The Pennsylvania State University

Assisted by
Stephen D. Millman
Maryland State Board for
Community Colleges

Lexington Books
D.C. Heath and Company
Lexington, Massachusetts
Toronto   London

Library of Congress Cataloging in Publication Data

Cohn, Elchanan.
    Economics of state aid to education.

    Bibliography: p.
    1. State aid to education—United States. 2. Education—United States—
.Finance. I. Millman, Stephen D., joint author. II. Title.
LB2825.C583   379'.122'0973   73-19746
ISBN 0-669-84756-9

Copyright © 1974 by D.C. Heath and Company.

Published simultaneously in Canada.

Printed in the United States of America.

International Standard Book Number: 0-669-84756-9

Library of Congress Catalog Card Number: 73-19746

Contents

List of Figures

List of Tables

Preface

Education is the largest single industry in the United States. Total educational expenditures in the public elementary and secondary schools have increased rapidly over past years and are estimated to be $44.4 billion for the 1971-72 school year. Current expenditures per pupil have risen from $375 in 1959-60 to $870 in 1971-72.[1] Since nearly 50 percent of these expenditures are financed by local revenue, and since institutional-legal constraints restrict the taxing powers of local governments, the potential for increased local revenues for the support of public schools is extremely limited. Moreover, the majority of revenues collected by local governments are obtained through property taxation. Because of adverse allocative and distributive aspects of the property tax,[2] the principal tax base for the collection of local educational revenues has come under severe attack. Although alternative proposals for alleviating the fiscal problems of local governments have been suggested in recent years,[3] it appears that state aid will assume an increasingly important role in the financing of public education.

Recent court decisions in Texas, California, Minnesota, New Jersey, and other states reflect a deep and widespread dissatisfaction with the present systems of providing state aid to local districts. The very recent decision by the U.S. Supreme Court has, for the time being, reduced, if not eliminated, the importance of the federal courts in determining legally acceptable state aid systems. Nevertheless, dissatisfaction with the current systems remains, and it is likely that the battlefield will move from the courts to the state legislatures or the U.S. Congress rather than fade away.[4]

The current state of affairs in educational financing is extremely complicated. Not only is the field in flux, but there is much variation among existing state aid schemes and many of the schemes are very intricate. An attempt will be made here to compare and contrast the various plans and to suggest the general principles under which state aid is given to local districts.

By far, most of the attention in educational finance literature has been concentrated on the issue of equity, that is, whether existing or proposed state aid schemes should strive to equalize resources, "needs," outputs, and so forth. The main focus has been directed at the concept of "equalization." What has

---

1. See Simon and Fullam (1969) and Foster and Barr (1972).

2. For excellent summaries of the economic aspects of the property tax, consult Due and Friedlaender (1973), Chapter 18, and Netzer (1966, 1970).

3. For a discussion of some recent suggestions, see Riew (1971, 1973).

4. For a similar view, see Shannon (1973). It should also be pointed out that the U.S. Supreme Court's decision has no effect on litigation in state courts on the basis of the various states' constitutions. In a recent symposium on state school finance reform, sponsored by the U.S. Office of Education (held in Silver Spring, Maryland, November 26-27, 1973), Stephen Browning, of the Lawyers' Committee for Civil Rights Under Law, indicated that numerous cases are pending before state courts, and that judicial solutions are still actively pursued.

been left out of the analysis is the impact of various aid schemes on the incentives districts have to operate efficiently.

One of the main purposes of this study is, therefore, to focus attention on the relationship between state aid and incentives for the efficient allocation of resources. The study approaches this objective from two angles. First, an empirical analysis is conducted to study the discernible impact of state aid on average school size, per pupil expenditures, rates of enrollment in nonpublic schools, per pupil bond issues, and per pupil local revenues. State and county data have been gathered for this purpose.

Second, the study describes the development of incentive features that could be incorporated into state aid schemes. The incentive features are divided into two groups: incentives for scale effects and output incentives. The scale incentives are designed to highlight the potential for cost savings through scale adjustment. The incentive features are designed to provide a stimulus for districts to reorganize schools in such a manner that they will be able to make maximum use of scale effects.

The analysis of output incentives considers two possible goals: the attainment of maximum output, regardless of cost, and the attainment of maximum output per dollar of cost (maximum efficiency). Incentive features are developed for each of these goals. It is also pointed out that incentive features may be used to attain a combination of these two goals.

The discussion of the economic effects of state aid to education and the analysis of incentive features is preceded by a thorough analysis of the historical and current manifestations of state aid. The origins and development of the state-aid formulas are discussed in Chapter 2, followed by a discussion of the theory and practice of equalization in Chapter 3 and a brief description of current state-aid formulas in Chapter 4.

The economic effects of state aid are analyzed in Chapter 5, followed by a discussion of scale incentives in Chapter 6 and output incentives in Chapter 7. Chapter 8 traces recent developments in higher education and presents a brief discussion of the role of state aid in that domain. The book concludes with a brief summary in Chapter 9.

This volume is based in part on a report to the National Institute of Education entitled *An Economic Analysis of State Aid to Education*. The study was supported by a grant from the National Institute of Education, U.S. Department of Health, Education, and Welfare. Points of view or opinions stated herein do not necessarily represent official National Institute of Education position or policy.

Stephen D. Millman had a major share in the writing of Chapters 2, 3, 4, and 8. Robert W. Clyde gathered most of the data for Chapter 5 and assisted in the writing of Chapter 2. A portion of Chapter 5 is based on his master's essay.

I would like to thank, without implicating, G. Alan Hickrod, Teh-wei Hu, and Gary P. Johnson for valuable comments on a previous draft of this book. I also wish to express my gratitude to Thomas L. Johns of the Task Force on School Finance, U.S. Office of Education, for providing invaluable material on the current status of state aid to education, and Richard Barr of the National Center for Educational Statistics, for current information on educational statistics. The National Education Finance Project was cooperative in providing valuable material for the research.

The staff of the Institute for Research on Human Resources and the Department of Economics at the Pennsylvania State University provided computer, clerical, typing, and editorial assistance. I would like to mention Alice Beamesderfer for her editorial assistance, Patricia Armagast and Sue Dixon for preparing the final manuscript, and Maureen C. Gallagher for preparing the computer runs for Chapter 5.

It goes without saying that the moral support, patience, and understanding throughout the production of this work provided so generously by my wife was indispensible to the successful completion of the study.

Elchanan Cohn
University Park, Pa.
October 1973

1

The Role of Government from an Economic Perspective

It is a well-known fact that government is heavily involved in education. The involvement ranges from regulation through subsidization to production of educational services. Furthermore, it appears that in recent years the degree of governmental intervention in educational affairs has increased considerably. Moreover, government activity in education has shifted from a predominant role by local governments to an ever-increasing role assumed by state and federal governments.

Some of these basic trends may be discerned by observing the data in Table 1-1 concerning educational expenditures by source of funds. For all levels of education, both public and nonpublic, the percentage of educational funds supplied by local governments has decreased from 42.9 percent in 1955-56 to 32.4 percent in 1971-72. At the same time, the federal share has increased from 5.9 percent to 11.2 percent, whereas the share of the states remained relatively stable, increasing from 28.8 percent in 1955-56 to 29.7 percent in 1971-72. The intergovernmental shift in support of public elementary and secondary education is characteristic of this general trend. The local share has decreased from 62.6 percent in 1955-56 to 54.3 percent in 1971-72. The share of the state governments increased from 33.1 to 36.7 percent, whereas the federal share rose from 4.3 to 8.8 percent during the same period.

But is there a compelling rationale for such a massive governmental subsidization of education? Is there justification for *public* operation of educational institutions? And once it is agreed that some form of government involvement is justified, what roles should be played by the various hierarchies of government? In what follows we shall attempt to provide a framework which could be employed in attempting to provide answers to such crucial questions.

We will begin with a theoretical statement of the role of government in the economy. Here we shall closely follow the analysis presented in Musgrave's classic treatise on public finance.[1] In general, it will be shown that government intervention in any economic matter is justified if the intervention (1) will improve the allocation of resources in the economy, (2) will be used to reallocate resources so that society's preferences concerning the distribution of income will be satisfied, and (3) is used to promote economic growth and stability.

In the next section, a discussion of intergovernmental relations is presented in which we will attempt to delineate the appropriate role that each level of

---

1. See Musgrave (1959), Chapter 1, and Friedman (1962), Chapter VI.

Table 1-1

Estimated Expenditures of Educational Institutions, by Source of Funds: United States, 1955-56, 1965-66, and 1971-72[a] (Amounts in Billions of Dollars)

Source of Funds, by Level of Institution and Type of Control	1955-56		1965-66		1971-72	
	Amount	Percent	Amount	Percent	Amount	Percent
1	2	3	4	5	6	7
All Levels						
Total public and nonpublic	$17.0	100.0	$45.5	100.0	$85.1	100.0
Federal	1.0	5.9	5.1	11.2	9.5	11.2
State	4.9	28.8	13.1	28.8	25.3	29.7
Local	7.3	42.9	15.0	33.0	27.6	32.4
All other	3.8	22.4	12.3	27.0	22.7	26.7
Total public	13.9	100.0	35.3	100.0	68.9	100.0
Federal	.8	5.8	3.7	10.5	7.4	10.7
State	4.9	35.2	13.0	36.8	25.2	36.6
Local	7.3	52.5	15.0	42.5	27.5	39.9
All other	.9	6.5	3.6	10.2	8.8	12.8
Total nonpublic	3.1	100.0	10.2	100.0	16.2	100.0
Federal	.2	6.5	1.4	13.7	2.1	13.0
State	b	c	.1	1.0	.1	.6
Local	b	c	b	c	.1	.6
All other	2.9	93.5	8.7	85.3	13.9	85.8
Elementary and Secondary Schools[d]						
Total public and nonpublic	$12.8	100.0	$30.3	100.0	$54.1	100.0
Federal	.5	3.9	2.2	7.2	4.3	7.9
State	3.8	29.7	9.6	31.7	17.9	33.1
Local	7.2	56.2	14.6	48.2	26.5	49.0
All other	1.3	10.2	3.9	12.9	5.4	10.0
Total public	11.5	100.0	26.5	100.0	48.8	100.0
Federal	.5	4.3	2.2	8.0	4.3	8.8
State	3.8	33.1	9.6	36.3	17.9	36.7
Local	7.2	62.6	14.6	55.2	26.5	54.3
All other	.....	.....	.1	.5	.1	.2
Total nonpublic	1.3	100.0	3.8	100.0	5.3	100.0
Federal	.....	.....	.....	.....	.....	.....
State	.....	.....	.....	.....	.....	.....
Local	.....	.....	.....	.....	.....	.....
All other	1.3	100.0	3.8	100.0	5.3	100.0
Institutions of Higher Education						
Total public and nonpublic	$ 4.2	100.0	$15.2	100.0	$31.0	100.0
Federal	.5	12.1	2.9	19.1	5.2	16.8
State	1.1	26.5	3.5	23.0	7.4	23.9

Table 1-1 (cont.)

Source of Funds, by Level of Institution and Type of Control	1955-56		1965-66		1971-72	
	Amount	Percent	Amount	Percent	Amount	Percent
1	2	3	4	5	6	7
Local	.1	3.0	.4	2.6	1.1	3.5
All other	2.5	58.4	8.4	55.3	17.3	55.8
Total public	2.4	100.0	8.8	100.0	20.1	100.0
Federal	.3	11.5	1.5	17.6	3.1	15.7
State	1.1	45.6	3.4	38.4	7.3	36.2
Local	.1	5.1	.4	4.1	1.0	4.9
All other	.9	37.8	3.5	39.9	8.7	43.2
Total nonpublic	1.8	100.0	6.4	100.0	10.9	100.0
Federal	.2	12.8	1.4	22.1	2.1	19.7
State	b	1.6	.1	1.5	.1	1.3
Local	b	.2	b	.1	.1	.5
All other	1.6	85.4	4.9	76.3	8.6	78.5

aData in columns 2 and 3 are for estimated receipts, not expenditures.

bLess than $50 million.

cLess than 0.05 percent.

dIn addition to regular schools, figures include other elementary and secondary schools such as residential schools for exceptional children, federal schools for Indians, federally operated elementary and secondary schools on posts, and subcollegiate departments of colleges.

Note: For original data sources, definitions, and methods of data presentation, consult the sources.

Sources: Columns 2 and 3 are from Simon and Fullam (1968), Table 1; columns 4-7 from Simon and Grant (1972), Table 23.

government should play in educational finance. Another issue to be discussed is the *type* of governmental intervention that would be needed to justify government involvement in education.

The Role of Government in Education

As noted earlier, three main categories for intervention are recognized: (1) allocation of resources, (2) distribution of income, and (3) economic growth and stability. These will be discussed in turn.

Allocation of Resources

In a system of a perfectly competitive economy, with perfect knowledge, perfect foresight, no external economies or diseconomies, and no imperfections in the market whatever, economic theory maintains that allocation by the market will lead to the best possible results—such that no other allocation could improve anyone's economic position without, at the same time, rendering someone else's economic position worse.[2] But the existence of a perfectly competitive market in education is obviously a fiction. Therefore, it could be argued that certain actions by government (taxation, regulation, and direct production) would, in some cases, improve the general welfare of society. A brief exposition of some such cases which are particularly relevant to education are presented below.

Externalities.[3] One of the most important reasons for governmental intervention in education is the alleged existence of externalities. External effects may be positive (external economies) or negative (external diseconomies). On the positive side, external economies exist whenever the actions of any one economic unit (households, firms, etc.) benefit other economic units where the economic units receiving the external benefits are not required to pay for the benefits received. Such externalities accrue to the student himself, to his family, his associates, his employers (present and future), his neighbors, and to society as a whole. That some such benefits are provided by the discovery of new scientific inventions by a select group of students in the natural sciences has been recognized for many years (Becker [1960]). But this select group of individuals is not exclusively responsible for external benefits of education.

One argument, used in many introductory public finance textbooks, to justify the interference of government in the educational market is that the education of one's children will spill over some benefits on his neighbors, his own family, and the community as a whole.[4] First, an educated person's mode of behavior might be better in terms of the norms of society than that of an uneducated (or less educated) person. Also, such an educated person is more likely to participate in civic and cultural activities. The larger the number of such educated people in the community, the greater the likelihood of considerably more pleasant neighborhoods.

Second, the student's family stands to gain as well. The mother, for example, is relieved of baby-sitting duties and as such can go to work without sustaining the expense of hiring a sitter or enjoy a range of activities not possible (or considerably more expensive) when the children are at home. Such a benefit could presumably be calculated by the computation of the potential cost of baby-sitters for all mothers who would require such services in the absence of schooling. Further, those women who prefer to stay home even though their

2. For a discussion of perfect competition consult, for example, Scitovsky (1971), Chapters 21 and 25.

3. There is a voluminous literature on externalities. Probably the first to treat this subject matter was Pigou (1920). Other references include Bator (1958), Buchanan and Stubblebine (1962), McKean (1958), and Scitovsky (1971), Chapter 14.

4. See, for example, Buchanan (1965), Due and Friedlaender (1973), Haveman (1970), Herber (1971), and Sharp and Sliger (1970).

children are at school profit insofar as they can substitute other (presumably more rewarding) activities inside or outside the home for childcaring. A calculation akin to this argument was carried out by Burton A. Weisbrod. Despite whatever difficulties that may beset such calculations, Weisbrod's figures indicate that such effects are quite important:

In March, 1956, there were 3.5 million working mothers in the United States with children six to eleven years of age. Assuming that as few as one million of these mothers would not work except for the schools (the others being willing to let their children stay with hired persons or simply care for themselves), and assuming $2,000 as the earnings of each mother during the school year, the value of the child-care services of elementary school may be estimated as roughly $2 billion per year. Estimating total resource costs (excluding capital outlays but including implicit interest and depreciation) of public and private elementary schools in 1956 at $7.8 billion, we reach the startling conclusion that elementary school support provided a return of 25 percent of cost in the by-product form of child-care services alone. This disregards the value of these services to mothers who do not choose to work; since the value is certainly greater than zero, the total value of the child-care is even more than 25 percent of cost (Weisbrod [1962], p. 117).

Third, there are benefits associated with employment accruing to employer and employee alike. Beginning with the latter, there are likely to be substantial benefits to other employees from increased education of any one employee. Typically, the productivity of one employee depends on that of the others. It is therefore inevitable that education will benefit not only the student but also his associates. Regarding the employer, even if compensation of employees is based upon the marginal productivity theory, increased productivity by one employee, due to education, will bring about increased returns to the employer, too.[5] Also, an entrepreneur who succeeds in recruiting educated personnel is likely to establish a reputation which produces "good will." So we could expect that external educational benefits accrue to both the employer and the other employees (present and future).

Fourth, the student himself—together with the rest of the community—is quite likely to further benefit from the educational investment in the form of lower law-enforcement costs (perhaps also lower insurance rates, etc.) since crime and education are likely to be negatively correlated.[6]

Finally, as Weisbrod suggests, society in general stands to gain from more education. For example, the more people who are literate and educated, the more the demand for books, checking accounts, and so forth. As products and services of this type are typically subject to significant economies of scale,

5. For a discussion of the marginal productivity theory consult, for example, Ferguson (1972), Chapters 13 and 14, and Stigler (1966), Chapter 14.

6. A study by Spiegelman (1968) indicated that "a strong correlation was found between being a high-school dropout and being arrested for participation in juvenile crime" (p. 451).

increased demand will lead to mass production and distribution of these products and services resulting in lower prices. Also, as mentioned above, the more people engaged in research, the more the benefits to society in the form of inventions and innovations for which the inventor cannot generally collect all the fruits of his labor. These types of external benefits, while not exhausting the list, quite clearly demonstrate the wide variety of external benefits associated with education.[7]

It should also be pointed out that governmental intervention is justified to prevent or offset the possible occurrence of negative external effects (external diseconomies). For instance, vocational shops may create water or air pollution; noise from schools might affect the peace and tranquility of a neighborhood; or an extensive use of drugs in schools might affect the general well-being of students and other individuals in the community.

Risk and Time Preferences. Since education provides not only uncertain benefits but, in addition, these benefits accrue over a long time span, time preferences become important determinants of educational investment. To the extent that social time preferences differ from private ones,[8] some government intervention is indicated. Further, measures to reduce risk and uncertainty—such as long-term guaranteed loans, insurance policies, and so forth—could be justified on the basis of the divergence between individual and social risk.

Joint Consumption. Certain aspects of educational services approach the definition of "social wants," that is, services that are jointly consumed by all citizens. To the extent that joint consumption is coupled with nonexcludability, that is, the supplier of the service cannot preclude anyone from enjoying the service even if he refuses to pay for it, we have the situation of a "public good," whose supply must be forthcoming through some type of governmental intervention. Education is only a semipublic good. First, nonexcludability is clearly absent from all but a small number of educational endeavors. Second, while there is some joint consumption—when one student listens to a lecture, another may do the same without reducing the consumption of the first—there is clearly a limit to the degree of joint consumption in education—for example, when I borrow a book from the library, another person may not borrow the *same* book at the *same time*. But the fact that some degree of joint consumption exists is a further justification for governmental involvement in education.

Other Allocative Criteria. Two additional allocative reasons for government intervention may be mentioned. One is the possible existence of monopoly power and control. This may stem from the very nature of the educational

---

7. For further discussions of external benefits of education, consult Weisbrod (1962, 1964), Ribich (1968), pp. 119-22, Spiegelman (1968), and Davis (1970).

8. A discussion of this issue is presented in Eckstein (1961) and Henderson (1968).

service such as the need for accreditation and the fact that school operations are likely to be characterized by significant scale economies.[9]

Further, if scale economies exist, then private production at optimum levels would not be feasible without government subsidization or operation.[10]

Distribution of Income

Even if resources are allocated in an optimal manner, the resulting distribution of income may not be desirable from social, ethical, and economic viewpoints. Further intervention by government to achieve an optimal distribution of income is clearly justified.

The role of government in education, in an effort to achieve a more equitable distribution of income, is a matter of considerable controversy. First, it is far from clear whether we seek to achieve "equality of opportunity," "equality of income," or "equality of economic welfare." Given that individuals have different capacities to enjoy income, equality of income is not necessarily identical to equality of economic welfare. And policies to promote equality of opportunity may conflict with a goal to achieve income equality—and vice versa.

Second, while certain educational policies may be recommended to achieve a greater degree of "equality of opportunity," these policies may conflict with a desire to achieve an optimum in resource allocation. To the extent that income transfers could be used to achieve the desired distribution of income, it is generally agreed that redistributional considerations should not be used to justify or otherwise influence government intervention in education. But it must be conceded that when political, economic, or other constraints hinder the possible application of income transfers to achieve the desired distribution of income, there is a justification for government intervention in education on this score. It should be reemphasized, at the same time, that intervention due to income distributional considerations should be examined in light of its effects on the allocation of resources.[11]

Economic Stability and Growth

The goals of full employment, price stability, and economic growth have for a long time been considered as the prime responsibility of government. Justifi-

---

9. Studies of economies of scale in education include Cohn (1968), Cohn and Hu (1973), Hettich (1968), Maynard (1971), Riew (1966), and Sabulao and Hickrod (1971).

10. See Scitovsky (1971), Chapter 12.

11. The relationship between educational expenditures and the distribution of income is discussed in Ribich (1968, 1970). For a study of the distributional effects of higher education subsidies, consult Hansen and Weisbrod (1969). A discussion of the Hansen-Weisbrod analysis is contained in Cohn (1970), Sharkansky (1970), Pechman (1970), and Hansen and Weisbrod (1971).

cation for government intervention in the economy is clearly established once these goals are considered to be prime social ends.[12] These goals, furthermore, may be considered not merely on the national scale, but also from the point of view of local and regional employment and growth. Thus it may be argued that government should support certain educational programs, in certain locations, not merely because of their inherent social worth but also due to their expected impact on local economic conditions.

Who Should Pay for Educational Programs?

Once it is conceded that government should intervene in the financing and/or provision of educational services, the question remains: Which branch of government should be responsible for a given educational program? For example, who should shoulder the burdens of private and public elementary education, vocational education in high schools, community colleges, and undergraduate higher education?

From a theoretical point of view, answers to such questions are possible, although it must be recognized that the answers will not be simple. To illustrate, consider the case of secondary education. It is recognized by most writers that universal secondary education is highly desirable; that is, we consider secondary education to be associated with substantial external benefits. But since the benefits of secondary education are in the main local, or state-wide, it may be argued that government involvement should be limited to state and local branches of government. This conclusion is based, in part, on data that show that the vast majority of persons receiving only secondary education are likely to remain in the state following graduation from high school. Interstate migration is far more common among persons who have had some college education. But the complexity of the issue becomes apparent even when it is assumed that the federal government has no role in secondary education. For it is far from clear how much of the burden should fall on the local and how much should fall on the state government. The determination of the role of each branch would include: an examination of the extent and direction of externalities and intrastate migration in the resource allocation category; fiscal capabilities, tax structures, and so forth in the distributional category; and employment and other economic conditions in the economic stability category. Moreover, since some of the educational effects are nationwide in scope, some federal involve-

---

12. The relationship between education and economic growth has been documented by Denison (1962, 1964), and Schultz (1961). See also Bowman (1970). A critical view on the value of economic growth is provided by Mishan (1970).

ment is justified. The desired extent of federal, state, and local involvement is obviously not easy to determine.[13]

Forms of Government Intervention

There would be few, if any, who would reject the notion that a combination of factors mentioned above would justify some sort of governmental intervention. What *form* government involvement should take in different cases is, usually, a matter of considerable controversy.

Where the "national interest" precludes private production and distribution—such as in matters of national security—it is almost universally agreed that production or provision by the government is indicated. Yet even in such cases, utilization of the market system may be desirable for purchases that do not involve confidential production. For example, the military could, and should, procure food, clothing, housing, and other supplies through the free-market system whenever possible.

Where national security is not involved, the form of government intervention is more difficult to determine. Should the government operate public schools? Should the government subsidize accredited private schools? Or should the government give educational vouchers to *parents*, who could then use them in an accredited school of their choice?

Answers to such questions are far from simple. They involve, in addition to dispassionate economic rationale, value judgments concerning the appropriate role of government.

But from the reasons that have been described above to justify government involvement in education, one could also provide a case for particular forms of involvement. For example, the existence of external economies would indicate the desirability of government *subsidization*. The same would be true for the scale economies argument. On the other hand, if there is a reason to believe that a particular educational activity is largely characterized by joint consumption, government provision would be indicated. The more limited such joint consumption appears to be, the weaker the argument in favor of direct public provision.

Again, the argument of the existence of risk and a differential between private and social rates of time preference would indicate the desirability of establishing loan programs (such as the proposed Educational Opportunity Bank) and subsidization, respectively.[14] The existence of monopoly power

13. For a detailed discussion of this issue, consult Brazer (1970). For evidence concerning intercommunity spillovers of educational expenditures, consult Hirsch, Segelhorst, and Marcus (1964), Hirsch and Marcus (1969), and Weisbrod (1964).

14. The Educational Opportunity Bank (EOB) is described in Zacharias (1969). Further analysis of the EOB proposal is contained in Shell et al. (1968) and Shell (1970). Other proposals for student loans include Van Den Haag (1956), Vickrey (1962), and Bowen (1969). See also Danière (1969).

would indicate the desirability of government regulations to insure efficient production and pricing.

Conclusion

The role of the states in education is, therefore, dependent upon the nature of the educational system and the economic position of the local communities. Pure economic analysis can only suggest the relevant *areas* of responsibility, the economic reasons for intervention, and the general types of intervention consistent therewith. The following chapters demonstrate that the interpretation of these principles by educational experts and state governments in the United States have varied considerably over time and space. But it should be recognized that legislation concerning the role of the states in education has taken into account a mixture of economic, political, religious, and other factors.

This book is divided into four main parts. The first seeks to identify the sources of educational philosophy concerning the role of the states in education and to describe the current status of state aid to education. The second part discusses empirical attempts to isolate the effect of state aid on revenues, expenditures, and other variables. The third part is concerned with possible modifications of current state-aid programs to provide incentives for greater efficiency in school operations. The final part contains a brief chapter on the financing of higher education.

2

Origins and Development of American Educational Finance

It is the intent of this chapter to direct the reader's attention to the origins, development, and general patterns of current programs of school finance. Detailed information in regard to many of the topics introduced in this chapter is contained in later sections of this volume; however, the purpose here is to provide a general framework and to sketch gross contours for what is to follow.

The study of educational finance has profited from the input of professionals representing many disciplines. While this state of affairs may be expected to result in a more comprehensive view, the impact of scholars operating from different perspectives and using different analytical tools can appear to represent a veritable Tower of Babel. For this reason, if no other, it is essential to provide a common background upon which to foster comprehension of the present study.

Persons familiar with the historical development of educational finance and related issues may wish to proceed directly to other sections of the analysis. However, this chapter provides capsule information for those individuals more interested in a total view.

The Present: A Perspective

When the history of our times is written, it may designate the two decades following World War II as the golden age of American education. Never before was education more highly valued. Never before was so much of it so readily available to so many. Never before had it been supported so generously. Never before was so much expected of it.

But in this eighth decade of the twentieth century, public education in this country appears to be in trouble. Taxpayers are revolting against skyrocketing costs of education. Schools are being denied the funds they need for quality of education (Ebel [1972], p. 3).

As stated above by the president of the American Educational Research Association, it is increasingly evident that public education, which has recently enjoyed so much favor, may now be facing difficult days. Also clearly apparent is the fact—alluded to above—that much of the malaise, directly or indirectly, has to do with issues of educational finance. As a report of the Rockefeller Brothers Fund (1958) pointed out, "All the problems of the schools lead us back sooner or later to one basic problem—financing" (p. 38).

11

Current disenchantment notwithstanding, education in America is a formidable enterprise, the dimensions of which are often not fully appreciated. It might therefore be worthwhile to briefly note the size of the terrain being explored. In its most recent survey of the schools, the National Education Association (1972) reports:

In Fall 1971, 60.5 million pupils were enrolled in the regular schools, public and private, at all grade levels. All full- and part-time workers in the schools were estimated at 6.4 million, 4.0 million of which were teachers, administrators, or other professional staff. The total expenditures of the regular schools are $83.1 billion for the school year 1971-72 (p. 5).

Available data indicate that although funds for the schools are still increasing, the increase is at a decreasing rate. Educators and others are concerned, therefore, that allocation of resources is not keeping pace with increasing demands or increasing costs of existing demands. Conditions would thus suggest the need for more systematic analysis of public support for education.

Taking a Longer View

Even within the context of current debate regarding the level of support for education, there is basic agreement on the perspective of education as a public responsibility. While such a view seems so natural as to be taken for granted, it is worth noting that such a belief has not always existed in this country. Less than a century and a half ago, debate raged in this nation—as in many others—about whether education was a private or public concern. As Meyer (1967) indicates: "The idea that education was a function of the state obtained in only one western nation—the kingdom of Prussia. . . . In America, meanwhile, education [in the 18th century] continued to be regarded as a private or semi-private enterprise, a responsibility left by government to the church and the parents" (p. 121).

The Prussian approach to education was generally adopted by the remainder of the Germanic states and by France. However, the British—from whom most of our educational traditions were adopted—held resolutely, during this period, to the view of education as a private matter.

Walsh and Walsh (1930) note that when the matter was seriously taken up in the state of Pennsylvania, the two opposing views were clearly evident:

On the one hand was the state-supported and state-controlled systems of Germany and France, and on the other, the privately controlled, individualistic, decentralized plan of England. The former was best known and best advertised in America, and it was the one adopted, with modifications, by Massachusetts and other states, but the English plan was most attractive to the decentralized, homogeneous individualistic people of Pennsylvania. This was the most German of the states, but it was also the most decentralized, and even the German settlers had no desire to go back to the Prussian centralization from which many of them had escaped (p. 321).

Public cognizance and support for the needs of "the common schools" began to coalesce firmly during the 1820s and 1830s. Under the leadership of such educational visionaries as Horace Mann, Gordon Carter, Henry Barnard, and others, the public was aroused by what has been called "the free-school movement." The issues were not solved instantly, but great forward movement was initiated. In Meyer's words,

The same issues and the same contestants sprang up everywhere. Now the controversy ignited over the educational powers of the state authority; now over the government's right to lay school taxes; now over its right to conscript children to learn their ABCs. Some apostles cried out for better teachers, better methods, better books; others bawled for more and better buildings (Meyer [1967], p. 185).

At first, schools had been funded exclusively from receipts of tuition for students enrolled, so-called fees and rate bills. As the free-school movement gained momentum, various approaches were attempted to finance the schools. Two quite popular and relatively effective means in the short run were (1) issuing of scrip as proceeds from past or future land sales and (2) instituting state lotteries for education.

As the number of schools and number of students grew, however, the need for increased funds also became evident. Since a personal income tax was not a practicable proposition during this period, most localities turned to what seemed to be the most feasible and equitable source of revenue—a tax on real property.

Subsidiarity and Federalism

Coons, Clune, and Sugarman (1970) state their belief that an understanding of the historical application of the concept of "subsidiarity" is essential to an understanding of the funding and control of American education. Specifically, subsidiarity refers to the philosophical position that decisions should be made at the level closest to the decision situation. This is to say that decisions which can reasonably and expeditiously be made by the family should not be made by government. And situations which can be handled sufficiently by local government should not be taken up by state or federal government.

All other things being equal, there is much intuitive merit to this principle. Coons, Clune, and Sugarman posit that it was this concept, the pervasive embodiment of which is called "federalism," that inspired the framers of

American government. Coons, Clune, and Sugarman describe this distinctly American state of affairs as

that slightly eccentric emphasis upon local government which is the scandal of foreign visitors and the pride of the pioneer. There is no adequate name for it. 'Federalism' is a label for what is merely one domestic example of the principle; the terms 'provincialism' and 'localism' both overemphasize the whimsical aspects. . . . There is nothing simpleminded or bizarre about the principle that government should ordinarily leave decision-making and administration to the smallest unit of society competent to handle them (p. 14).

By whatever name, the principle of local initiative has been particularly evident in American education. An understanding of current issues of control and finance can not proceed without consideration of the historical role of the three levels of government in the operation of public education. In general, matters have been left with the lowest level of government unless a determination is made that considerations of equity or quality demand action by a higher authority. In this way, states and the federal government have been successively brought into the operation of public education.

The history thus far reviewed has dealt primarily with the practical consequences of American educational traditions. What follows is intended to be an analysis of the input made by theorists of educational finance. The form of presentation is to discuss the successive development of various approaches through the ideas of the major scholars in this area. Emphasis is placed on the impact of these theories on the development and adoption of the particular plans by the states.[1]

The Philosophy and Practice of State Aid in Retrospect

Elwood P. Cubberley: Formulating
Basic Concepts of State School
Financing

Elwood P. Cubberley was a student at Teachers College, Columbia University, at the beginning of the twentieth century. His doctoral dissertation, "School Funds and Their Apportionment" (Cubberley [1905]), set down basic values and goals for the distribution of school funds by the states. Of particular concern to Cubberley was the fact that considerable disparities existed in fiscal capacity and tax effort among local school districts within the same state. Cubberley saw that expenditures per pupil in neighboring school districts were often very different.

---

1. Additional information on the history of the development of educational finance can be found in Benson (1968), Johns and Morphet (1969), and Johns (1971).

This observation stimulated the simple but far-reaching conceptualization of what he believed to be the state's responsibility in apportioning state school funds:

Theoretically, all the children of the State are equally important and are entitled to have the same advantages; practically this can never be quite true. The duty of the State is to secure for all as high a minimum of good instruction as is possible, but not to reduce all to this minimum; to place a premium on those local efforts which will enable local communities to rise above the legal minimum as far as possible; and to encourage communities to extend their educational energies to new and desirable undertakings (Cubberley [1905], p. 17).

In the early 1900s much emphasis was being placed on what were known as "stimulation grants," the purpose of which was to encourage the adoption and development of particular innovations in the school curriculum such as industrial education, trade schools, evening and vocational schools, physical training, and farm schools. Cubberley was in favor of extending the range of educational programs and was interested in seeing the day come when secondary education was the rule rather than the exception. He favored the use of state aid as a reward for those districts which took the initiative to pioneer in providing such special services. Cubberley's idea was to stimulate the adoption of such programs so as to get the diffusion process to the point where the programs could be made a part of the state's mandated minimum requirement (Benson [1968]). The rewards would go to those districts which, through innovation, played a part in upgrading the standards of education.

Cubberley's research enabled him to become aware of the inequities existing in the quality of education among school districts within individual states. The obvious reason for this differential was the fact that local financial capability to support schools varied greatly from one district to another. Therefore, educational expenditures and financial capability to support education were positively correlated, and Cubberley noted that the method of distributing state funds, at that time, merely aggravated this situation.

Cubberley's work was successful in exposing what the American public had long preferred not to think about. Satisfied that he had presented a strong case for state aid in general, he directed his attention to the form that this state aid should take. The following is a list of what Cubberley saw as the alternative criteria for the apportionment of state funds for public education:

1. The amount of taxes levied by the district
2. The total population of the district
3. The school census of the district
4. The average membership (enrollment) of the district
5. The average or aggregate daily attendance of the district
6. The number of teachers employed by the district

Cubberley believed that criteria 1 and 2 were both relatively inferior. Criterion 1, which may be described as a shared tax, was inadequate because it had no equalizing effects and would tend to favor city districts over rural districts (the cities in the early twentieth century generally had more wealth than did the rural areas). Criterion 2 would also be biased in favor of those districts whose age distributions were such that the percentage of population of school age was relatively less than that of other districts. Cubberley saw alternatives 3 and 4 to be slightly more desirable but still not adequate to reflect differing local needs. Alternative 5 was considered even more favorable but not without its inequities in that it favored city over rural schools (the former were able to stay open for a greater number of days in a year). Cubberley concluded that the best of the alternatives was 6, the criterion of number of teachers employed, in combination with the criterion of average daily attendance (ADA). The distribution of funds based on these criteria would not discriminate against rural districts, which tended to have a relatively lower teacher-pupil ratio, and could therefore stimulate the adoption of special training programs in that aid would be distributed according to the number of teachers employed regardless of the program in which they were involved. By including the ADA criterion, there would be no reason for the school districts to reduce the number of days in the school year. Cubberley believed that if these criteria were used, then his principal objective—that aid be apportioned on the bases of effort and need—would be achieved.

Cubberley also added a safety valve to his plan. He advocated the distribution of equalizing grants, in addition to general aid, to those school districts which were unable to meet the minimum standards of quality education (set by the state) when it had already taxed itself at the maximum rate permitted by law.

A benchmark from which future plans would evolve, Cubberley's approach was based on concepts and principles which are highly relevant to the discussions and debates on educational finance even today. Cubberley was thus the early proponent of the Flat Grant Plan. Several researchers who succeeded Cubberley in this field argued that Cubberley's plan, although based on commendable objectives, might fail to realize his objectives. It was, in fact, questioned whether Cubberley's plan might not have a disequalizing effect.

Consider two districts of equal size but of unequal wealth. The wealthy district, in an effort to improve the quality of its school, hires more teachers and consequently gets some part of this added cost paid for by the state according to the "teachers-employed" criterion. The poorer district probably would not be able to do the same because that portion of the added cost, not covered by the state, of hiring more teachers would be more burdensome to the poorer district. Hence, the wealthier district gets subsidized out of state tax monies which come from not only the wealthy districts but from the poorer districts as well. The result is a greater degree of inequality, a result, no doubt, that Cubberley either did not consider or believed was too insignificant.[2]

2. Additional insight into Cubberley's views can be found in Cubberley (1919).

Strayer and Haig: Emphasizing the
Equalization of Educational Opportunity

George D. Strayer and Robert M. Haig, two educational finance theorists who followed Cubberley, believed that the two main objectives held by Cubberley, for example, equalization of educational opportunity and the reward for local effort, were mutually inconsistent. As James S. Coleman (1970) points out:

The history of education since the industrial revolution shows a continual struggle between two forces: the desire by members of society to have educational opportunity for all children, and the desire of each family to provide the best education it can afford for its own children. Neither of these desires is to be despised; they both lead to investment by the older generation in the younger. But they can lead to quite different concrete actions (p. vii).

New York State was using Cubberley's Flat Grant Plan at a time when Strayer and Haig were noting the plan's inequities. Giving primary emphasis to equalization of educational opportunity as the objective of state aid, Strayer and Haig had this to say about New York's Flat Grant Plan (one which followed Cubberley's teachers-employed criterion):

Approximately one-half of the state aid is entirely unaffected by the richness of the local economic resources back of the teacher, and the portion which is so affected is allocated in a manner which favors both the very rich and the very poor localities at the expense of those which are moderately well off (Strayer and Haig [1923], p. 162).

Strayer and Haig were thus emphasizing financial considerations as opposed to the "human needs" considerations emphasized by Cubberley (in terms of the number of teachers employed by a school district).

Strayer and Haig then formulated their own plan for a state's distribution of school funds which embodied their main objective of equal opportunity (based on fiscal considerations). This approach, which has come to be known as the Strayer-Haig Minimum Foundation Plan, can be operationalized as follows:

1. The state determines the cost per pupil of a satisfactory minimum educational program.
2. The property tax rate which the wealthiest district in the state would have to levy in order to finance this satisfactory minimum is computed.
3. Each district in the state is required to tax at the rate needed in the wealthiest district to finance this minimum offering.
4. The state grants to each local district a sum equal to the difference between the amount raised locally at the mandatory tax rate and the amount required to finance the satisfactory minimum offering (Jones [1971], p. 9).

The Strayer-Haig formula considers not only the number of pupils in the district but also the local tax base. (Note that the minimum foundation plan would still allow local school districts to raise their tax rate above the required minimum if they so desired.) It is obvious that wealthy districts would be able to raise additional funds by taxing themselves a few mills above the minimum, while a poorer district would realize less additional money by raising their tax rate the same number of mills. The question to be asked is, What, exactly, did Strayer and Haig mean by "equalization of educational opportunity"? Thomas Jones suggests that it is not *equal* educational opportunity at all, but rather *minimum* educational opportunity. "The Strayer-Haig Foundation Plan equalizes local taxes and expenditures only up to a minimum level" (Jones [1971], pp. 9-10).

The Minimum Foundation Plan will be discussed in more detail in a subsequent chapter.

Paul R. Mort: Developing the
Minimum Foundation Program Plan

Paul R. Mort conducted many studies which enabled a large number of states to implement variants of the Strayer-Haig Minimum Foundation Plan. His major ideas can be found in Mort (1933) and Mort, Reusser, and Polley (1960).

The "Mort studies" were made by Paul R. Mort of Teachers College, Columbia University, who proposed more refined measures to determine the financial needs of the school districts, defined and outlined a minimum program of state support, and developed his weighted pupil technique (Cowle [1968], p. 15).

As Johns (1971) puts it, Mort was a disseminator rather than a theorist, and it was his efforts which are primarily responsible for the widespread use of the Minimum Foundation Program Plan.

Like Cubberley, Mort thought that it was extremely important that innovation in education rank high on our list of priorities. Mort considered "adaptability," or the propensity to change with the times—new courses of study, expanded extracurricular activities, and so forth—to be crucial. "Unless local districts are allowed substantial tax leeway, innovations are less likely to occur" (Jones [1971], p. 18).

Jones has narrowed Mort's main ideas down to the following six phases:

Phase 1. A given level of educational service and a given level of state school support are in existence.

Phase 2. One or more local school districts perceive a need to provide some new educational service beyond the state minimum. If necessary, they tax themselves above the amount required by the state to provide this educational service.

Phase 3. The adaptation developed in the lighthouse districts is disseminated to other localities. They too raise their local tax rates to institute the adaptation.

Phase 4. The adaptation gradually becomes accepted practice throughout the state. Eventually, the state provides for the adaptation in all local districts, possibly through the institution of a categorical state grant for the purpose.

Phase 5. The adaptation is required by state law, and state financial support for the adaptation is incorporated into the Strayer-Haig Minimum Foundation Program.

Phase 6. The extra state support allows the original lighthouse districts to reduce their tax burdens; hence, they become more receptive to the possibility of still newer adaptations (Jones [1971], pp. 19-20).

Harlan Updegraff: Justifying the
Rewards for Local Effort on the
Basis of Efficiency

During the years of 1921 and 1922, Harlan Updegraff surveyed the fiscal policies of the states of New York and Pennsylvania in terms of their support of public schools. Updegraff accepted, for the most part, the values and goals set down by Cubberley but placed relatively greater emphasis on the concept of local effort. To Updegraff, efficiency was of primary concern and was his justification for the rewarding of local effort by state governments. R.L. Johns (1971) summarizes Updegraff's views on efficiency as follows:

The efficient participation of citizens in the responsibility of citizenship should be promoted by making the extent of the state's contribution dependent upon local action. . . . Efficiency in the conduct of schools should be promoted by increasing the state grant whenever the true tax rate is increased and by lowering it whenever the local tax is decreased (pp. 6-7).

Today, several states follow Updegraff's basic principle in what is called the "percentage equalizing grant" (sometimes referred to as the variable level foundation program). This is a plan in which the state government shares the burden of supplying funds for local school district expenditures. These present-day plans, however, justify the rewarding of local effort not so much for the sake of efficiency as for the sake of reducing variation in per pupil expenditures among school districts.

Updegraff had one main complaint about the Strayer-Haig Minimum Foundation Program Plan. He believed that the minimum was often too low and that the wealthier districts were sometimes able to spend two and three times as much as the poorer districts. He suggested that even the raising of the minimum would not achieve an equal level of education for children in the poorer districts.

Thus Updegraff wanted local government to control the educational enterprise and thought that the state's primary role was to help local school districts provide the educational service desired by the localities. The desired level of educational service would then be reflected by the effort which the localities made themselves (effort in terms of a higher tax rate). So, Updegraff, unlike Strayer and Haig, did not see the state and local governments as equal partners in the educational scene but rather gave the dominant position to the local districts.

Updegraff introduced two ideas to help implement his basic plan. First, he introduced the idea of the "teacher unit" as a basis for the state's distribution of funds as opposed to Cubberley's teachers-employed criterion. A *teacher unit* would be a standard number of pupils per teacher which could vary for different types of classes. Second, he proposed a sliding scale that would allocate increasing amounts of aid (per teacher unit) for each increase of one-half mill of school taxes which the local school district levied, ranging from three and one-half to nine mills (districts with a lower property value per teacher unit would receive proportionately more aid). Updegraff wanted to help the schools in the poorer communities but maintained the "help those who help themselves" type of attitude:

General aid seeks to give aid to local districts in accordance with a combination of two factors, one of which is the ability of the district to support schools as measured by its equalized value per teacher . . . and the other, the effort which the district makes to support a school as measured by its tax rate. . . . The sound policy would be to grant aid only to those local districts that had made a reasonable effort to support schools (Cowle [1968], p. 13).

Henry C. Morrison: Advocating That
the State Become the Sole Unit of
Taxation and Administrator of
Public Schools

In 1930, a time when great emphasis was being placed on local initiative and home rule in the educational enterprise, Henry C. Morrison, a professor at the University of Chicago, advocated a unified state-wide system of education and full state funding of education. Morrison believed that the purpose of publicly supported education was to train the young people of the state to be good citizens and not to pursue local interests. Benson sums up Morrison's views on the purpose of public education as follows:

It is thus necessary to place limits on the expenditures of rich districts in order that public funds shall not be diverted into "private schools," as distinct from citizenship education. Taxes for schools are to be collected where taxable income can be found in the state, and school resources are to be distributed in accordance with local requirements to provide a uniform standard of citizenship training (Benson [1968], p. 165).

Morrison's primary objective was the equalization of educational opportunity. He saw that great inequities in wealth had caused great inequities in the quality of education and that previous attempts to achieve equality in this area through equalization funds and other means had failed. Morrison had this to say about these past plans:

We have a childish faith in "plans." When the inevitable disillusionment comes, we conclude that the plan "did not work," and look for another. In the case of equalization schemes, the disillusionment is prone to come at a time when the original plan has been forgotten and inequality is discovered all over again (Morrison [1930], p. 194).

There is much dissatisfaction today with the local property taxes as a means of funding education on the local level. Morrison was aware of this disenchantment when he was doing his research, and therefore, along with his proposal of full state funding, he advocated the use of a state income tax for the purpose of state school support.

Today, Hawaii is the only state which has established a complete state-wide system of education with no local school districts, and a few other states have maintained high percentages of state support.

More Recent Additions: Power
Equalizing and Educational Vouchers

Although a number of theorists discussed thus far are relatively contemporary, and some have continued to write up to the present, two relatively major departures from the historical mainstream have aroused much current attention. The new approaches are generally referred to as power equalizing plans and the establishment of educational vouchers. Very often, these approaches are considered in tandem since they draw upon the same philosophical base. Here, for the sake of clarity, they will be considered separately. When added to the concept of full state funding, which is actually an old idea originated by Morrison, these three possibilities must be considered to currently occupy center stage in regard to alternative programs of educational finance.

The concept of power equalizing, developed by Professor Coons and associates (Coons, Clune, and Sugarman [1970]), proposes that the amount of state assistance to particular school districts be a function solely of the *rate* at which citizens of that district are willing to tax themselves for education. That is to say, programs of financial subvention would not be a function of wealth of the community but rather of the tax effort the community makes. Regardless of the different tax bases in different communities, those willing to tax at a specified rate would be guaranteed a fixed total amount available for the schooling of each child.

Because Coons and associates have also written extensively on the concept of educational voucher programs, such an approach is sometimes associated with the program just described. Both place an emphasis on a determination by parents of how much education should be provided and at what price.

The voucher plan, as originally proposed by Milton Friedman, provides that each family would be given a chit for each school-age child, to be used by the family at an educational institution of its choice. All subsidies to education would thus be funneled through the family rather than directly to the school. The aim is to apply the mechanics of supply and demand in a free marketplace to the issues of educational finance. Early thoughts on educational vouchers are contained in Friedman (1955); later modifications are included in Friedman (1962).

Erickson describes the Friedman plan as follows:

Each voucher would represent a child's share of the state's investment in general education and would be redeemable by any approved school that the parents might decide to patronize. Among the advantages that Friedman saw in the approach, two seem particularly pertinent to the present discussion: (1) programs would be more precisely matched to parental wishes, and (2) individual families would have more power to determine how much money was spent on the schooling of their young (Erickson [1970], p. 109).

Because of the distinct advantages (as well as disadvantages) that such a plan would entail, the topic has become highly controversial. The ability of the public sector to do any long-range planning in such a fluid situation has been of particular concern. Issues of educational hucksterism, social policy, social integration, and aid to sectarian institutions are also involved and show no simple resolution.

Under the sponsorship of the Office of Economic Opportunity, a rather large-scale trial of the voucher plan is currently under way in the Alum Rock Union School District of California. Located in a racially-mixed suburb of San Jose, the experiment provides each parent with a voucher for $680 (elementary) or $970 (secondary) which can be redeemed in any *public* school in the district. Private schools are not included because California law precludes financial assistance to such institutions. Approximately half of the students have also been issued "compensatory vouchers" for additional funds due to educational deficiency. This was done both to encourage innovative programs for these students and to transform the least desirable pupils into the most desirable because they bring more money to the schools.

Although the study is still in an early stage and findings must be considered tentative, evidence would seem to debunk some of the most serious objections to such a plan. The racial composition of the individual schools is roughly the same as it was prior to the inception of the experiment. As a matter of fact, only a small number of students are attending schools other than the ones they would have attended otherwise. In regard to innovative curricular developments, it is difficult to determine whether the limited number of programs would have been initiated in any case.[3]

As indicated, the full state assumption of educational costs is derived from Morrison and has received the recent backing of many prestigious groups.[4] Hawaii is the only state operating such a system, and no other states currently show movement in that direction.

Concluding Remarks

This chapter has described the evolution of strategies for school finance up to the present. The various plans, as well as the context in which they emerged, have been discussed.

Relatively early, most states implemented programs whose ostensible purpose was to provide a minimum educational experience for all members of the school-age population. A partnership has been created—on paper at the very least—between the states and their constituent school districts whereby the state variously supplements the resources of the community in providing adequate schooling.

As will be indicated in Chapter 3, however, the actual impact of state programs of educational finance is less clear than their stated purposes would suggest. The structure, funding, or encumbering provisions of the various legislative acts in the states often serve to dilute or distort effectiveness of the programs as originally conceived. The present chapter, however, serves as a base upon which to evaluate reality as described in the next chapter.

---

3. For additional discussion, both pro and con, of the voucher issue, see, for example, Friedman (1955, 1962); Jencks (1971); Carr and Hayward (1970); Glennan (1971); Special issue of *Phi Delta Kappan* (1970).

4. See, for example, Thomas (1970), Wise and Thomas (1973), and Conant (1972). The Superintendent's Advisory Committee on school finance for the state of Illinois has recently recommended, by a majority vote, a full state funding program. See Hickrod et al. (1973). However, the recommendation was *not* adopted by the legislature.

3

Theory and Practice of Equalization

While the previous chapter presented an overview of the entire area of educational finance as it has developed in America, the present chapter concentrates on the concept and practice of equalization in education. Concern for the quality and quantity of education in this country remains an important issue, but the educational community has increasingly focused its attention on matters of equity. This chapter first defines equalization, then discusses theoretical and practical difficulties in conceptualization, and concludes with an examination of the impact of various equalization programs in the various states.

Equality in education, although conceptually related to the general call for social equality in other sectors of society, has a special significance and urgency of its own. There are two reasons for the distinction: (1) equality of education can serve as a base upon which equality in other areas can be accomplished more easily, and (2) the financial support for education is under the control of the state and not a *de facto* condition occurring in its own right. This latter point, which may warrant some additional explanation, is discussed by Coons, Clune, and Sugarman (1970):

There is, however, an important difference between discrimination in public education and most of the other social ills we tend to associate with poverty. Crime, slum housing, illness, and bad nutrition are not the anticipated consequence of government planning. Discrimination in education, on the other hand, is precisely the anticipated consequence of the legislated structure of public education.... Such a system bears the appearance of calculated unfairness (p. 7).

Equalization: Its Meaning

When individuals speak of equity considerations in education, attention most commonly turns to the process through which funds are directed from federal and/or state sources to the school districts and thus to the schools. What, then, constitutes an equalization plan? Roe L. Johns and Richard G. Salmon (1971) framed the following goals of equalization for the National Educational Finance Project:

Financial equalization is most nearly accomplished when the following two factors are met: (1) the varying educational needs of the student population are

25

taken into consideration before the allocations are made, and (2) the variation of the ability of the local school districts to support education is reduced or eliminated through the utilization of state resources (p. 120).

An equalizing approach to educational finance, thus, must be concerned with two conditions: the educational achievement (or deficiency) of the students and the financial capacity of the school district to provide necessary services. Most states have programs of financial assistance to school districts which are labeled "equalizing," but the extent to which these programs are actually equalizing varies greatly, depending, in part, on the following factors: (1) consideration of educational needs; (2) absolute number of dollars devoted to equalization; (3) the existence of flat grants, general grants, and categorical grants; (4) encumbering ceiling, minimum, and save-harmless provisions. These will be discussed in a later section.

In line with the above distinctions, Alexander, Hamilton, and Forth (1971) identify five basic patterns which characterize state programs of finance to public education. The first they label "circumscribed"; this includes categorical and discretionary funds not administered uniformly. The second type is called "uniform," wherein each district receives a flat amount per classroom or student unit. In the third type, "fiscal-modified," the financial capability of the community is considered, but not the educational needs. In type four, the "client-modified" pattern, the varying educational needs of localities are accounted for, but not financial capacity. In the final form, both fiscal and client needs are taken into account in the formulas.

Neither financial capability nor educational need can be determined in particular cases without difficulties of definition and measurement. Figure 3-1 splits the determinants of equalization from the grossest level to the most minute. Starting at the left side of the page, one can take any path to the right side, and this is what most analyses have done. It is increasingly important, however, to evaluate movement along all paths simultaneously.

Various specific plans to accomplish the goal of educational equalization have wide currency and are presently in use in the various states. Before these can be discussed, however, two very fundamental questions must be asked. The first is: What is to be equalized? The second is: Among which units is equalization to occur?[1]

The answers to these questions are not subject to wide agreement, either in academic or judicial discourse. In regard to the first matter (equalization of what?), a wide number of possibilities present themselves. Some of the alternatives concern inputs, others outputs. They are arrayed in these two categories below:

---

1. This section draws heavily from Hickrod (1972).

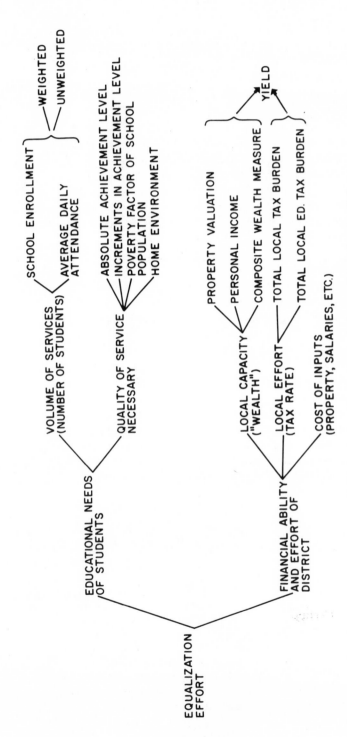

Figure 3-1. Critical Issues in Evaluation of Equalization Effort

INPUTS
Equalization of resources
Equalization of "educational opportunity"
Equalization of tax effort per educational expenditure
Equalization of program options

OUTPUTS
Equalization of student achievement
Equalization of student economic/noneconomic benefits
Equalization of societal economic/noneconomic benefits

Parallel to, but distinct from, the problem of what to equalize is the quandary about the units among which equalization is to occur. Possible alternative answers include the following:

Equalization among states
Equalization among districts within each state
Equalization among schools within each district
Equalization among families (in regard to educational expense)

Figures 3-2 and 3-3 indicate graphically the relationships in the questions of (1) equalization of what? and (2) equalization among which units? At any level of the second question, we may be concerned with equity of inputs, outputs, or outputs as a function of inputs.

Once attention has been drawn to the matter of what is to be equalized, we may begin to ask whether we are concerned successively with equity among families, among schools, among school districts within a state, or among states. Whereas the *Serrano* action concerned equity among school districts, the *Hobson vs. Hansen* judgment dealt with schools within a given school district. Because of

Inputs	*Transformation*	*Outputs*
Dollars	Program Options	Amount of Knowledge
Staff	Techniques	Type of Job Held
Facilities		Income Difference
		Societal Benefits (Externalities)

Figure 3-2. Equalization of What?
Note: In attempting to "equalize" educational opportunity, one must first decide whether to attempt to equalize inputs, transformation (throughout), or outputs. It then becomes necessary to decide which dimensions within these elements are to be equalized. Representative dimensions are given as examples above.

29

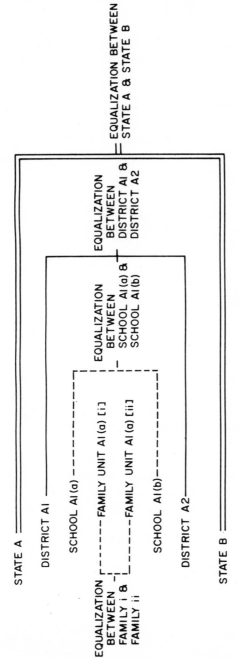

Figure 3-3. Equalization Among Whom?

the lack of clear constitutional issue, the extremes listed above—equalization among families and equalization among states—have not been considered in major judicial action to date.

A final point should be made about Figure 3-2. From this diagram, one might assume that there is some substantive agreement on exactly what constitutes the inputs, transformation process, and outputs of education. Such an assumption would appear to be unwarranted at present, and this serves to add additional ambiguity to an already unclear situation.

Recent court actions have dealt with many of these issues with less than unanimity and with a degree of befuddlement in regard to the complexity of the factors involved. The opinion of Judge Skelly Wright in the case of *Hobson vs. Hansen* (cited in Clune [1972]) serves as a commentary on the situation.

Plaintiff's motion for an amended decree and for further enforcement has now been argued and reargued . . . for one full year. During this time the unfortunate if inevitable tendency has been to lose sight of the disadvantaged young students, on whose behalf this suit was first brought, in an overgrown garden of numbers and charts and jargon like "standard deviation of the variable," "statistical significance," and "Pearson produce moment correlations." The reports by the experts . . . are less helpful than they might have been for the simple reason that they do not begin from a common data base, disagree over crucial statistical assumptions, and reach different conclusions. . . . This court has been forced back to its own common sense approach to a problem, which, though admittedly complex, has certainly been made more obscure than was necessary.

As indicated by Hickrod (1972), judicially acceptable standards of equalization efforts have differed markedly. The differences are of degree as well as of kind. Hickrod suggests that the following possibilities have variously received favorable judicial reaction: (1) "permissible variance," (2) "inverse allocation," (3) "fiscal neutrality," and (4) "fiscal intervention." These are explained below.

The principle of permissible variance is that there may be allowed to exist only a specified variation in the funds allocated per student to individual schools. Exactly how much variation is permissible has not been determined, although suggestions have included a percentage variation of as much as 50 percent and as little as 5 percent. The principle seeks equalization of expenditure irrespective of need.

Through inverse allocation, one attempts to supply additional resources in inverse relation to the wealth of the local community. In theory, most present state aid formulas are of this type, while in practice, they do not seem to meet this standard in a very satisfactory fashion. Many believe that through procedural modifications, however, such an approach can be made workable and is the most viable solution.

The concept of "fiscal neutrality," as explained by Hickrod, would seem to suggest very large flat grants from the state with little or no local contribution.[2] In point of fact, full state funding of educational costs has received increasing attention, and support for such an approach has been voiced by such prestigious groups as the Advisory Commission on Intergovernmental Relations (1969), the New York State Fleischmann Commission (1973), and the President's Commission on School Finance (1972).

There is some dispute as to whether the fiscal neutrality model applies to level of expenditure, level of tax effort, or one as a function of the other. That is to say, it is unclear whether adherence to this model would allow for the possibility of adopting power equalizing plans as suggested by Coons, Clune, and Sugarman (1970). Hickrod (1972) suggests that one interpretation of the principle would lead to the view that the "tax rate may not be a function of wealth, but it may be a function of the expenditure level" (p. 18). Except for Utah, no states currently operate within the parameters of such a plan, and its legal justification has not been tested. The Fleischmann Commission states the case against power equalizing in noting, "The quality of a child's education should, in our view, be no more a function of how highly his neighbors value education than how wealthy they are" (p. 89).

The fourth model, that of fiscal intervention, is based on the sociopolitical supposition that those with the greatest need should receive the greatest allocation of resources. Such an approach, Hickrod notes, would in effect rule "that the level of educational achievement may not be a function of wealth other than the wealth of the state" (p. 20). This is the only model which is stated in terms of output rather than input. It is a marked departure from current thought and even farther from current practice.

The ambiguity over whether our focus should be fixed on inputs or outputs has been noted by many writers. Berke, Campbell, and Goettel (1972) state:

There are, for example, those whose concern with equity focuses on the fairness of how we raise revenues for education. Others concentrate on the way we distribute resources for learning. To still others the touchstone of equity is the output of the educational system, measured either by achievement levels or ideally by some longitudinal evaluation of career patterns and personal development (p. 2).

2. This is inconsistent with an interpretation of the term in its economic jargon—which would imply that the relative financial position of all districts would remain unchanged after aid is given. Using the economic jargon, fiscal neutrality would imply such plans as a collection-based revenue sharing (what some prefer to term "shared taxes"), where each district receives state aid in proportion to revenues that the state collects from the district. Full state funding or flat grants would certainly *not* be fiscally neutral.

In a recent study for the National Education Finance Project, Hickrod states that "the goal of fiscal neutrality is simply a state of affairs in which local district wealth will no longer determine the level of goods and services that are provided to students in an area as crucial to their life chances and upward social mobility as is K-12 education." He then provides an alternative definition of absolute fiscal neutrality "as .000 on a Gini index where enrollments ranked by wealth are one dimension and total state and local expenditures are the second dimension" (Hickrod, [1973]).

**Implementation of the Equalization
Concept**

This section will review existing research which has been undertaken to study the effects of financial inputs in the form of various state equalization plans. It is first necessary to describe the types of plans which are currently in use.

Johns and Salmon (1971) describe state plans for educational finance in terms of the categories developed for the National Educational Finance Project as follows:

1. Flat grants
   a. uniform flat grants
   b. variable flat grants

2. Equalization grants
   a. Strayer-Haig-Mort [foundation] programs
   b. percentage equalization or state aid ratio program
   c. guaranteed valuation program

3. Nonequalizing matching grants

Flat grants are funds which are channeled to school districts on a per student or classroom basis. In the case of uniform flat grants, account is taken of neither variation in educational needs nor community financial capacity. Variable flat grants similarly take no account of financial capacity; however, they do attempt to compensate for differing classroom needs. Most commonly, instructional units are thus weighted for secondary versus elementary instruction. Weights for other factors are found occasionally. Flat grants are often used in conjunction with other plans discussed below.

A majority of the states use equalizing plans to distribute the major portion of general (noncategorical, special purpose) funds, and of these, the foundation program or a variation of it is most popular.

The basic foundation approach is to set a level for a minimum educational package and, within that level, set limits for the state to provide whatever funds are required to bring local revenue at a mandated tax rate up to the foundation level per student. Foundation programs may be either weighted or unweighted with regard to educational level or other factors.

A second type of equalizing plan is the percentage equalizing program. State aid increases with per pupil expenditures on education and is an inverse function of the relative wealth of the district. In a third equalizing approach, guaranteed valuation, the state guarantees a fixed yield from a mandated tax rate. The state pays the difference between what the tax produces and the guaranteed amount. The guaranteed valuation approach is, in effect, equivalent to the basic foundation approach.

In addition to flat grants and the various equalization grants, certain additional state (and federal) monies are available on a matching basis, wherein the district must match dollar for dollar, or in some other proportion, all funds supplied by the subventor. Such grants are not equalizing with regard to financial capacity. However, since many of these grants are for special educational purposes, to that extent they could be described as differentially supplying funds for special educational needs.

Although it will be shown in Chapter 4 that the aid formulas within each type of plan vary among the states, it might be useful to provide fairly rigorous definitions of the plans in terms of their *general* characteristics.

The Foundation Plan

Equalization aid is typically computed according to the formula

$$EA_i = WADA_i (F - rV_i) \qquad (3.1)$$

where

EA_i = equalization aid to the ith district
$WADA_i$ = weighted average daily attendance
F = foundation level
r = mandated tax rate
V_i = assessed valuation per pupil in the ith district.

If EA_i in Equation (3.1) is negative, equalization aid is zero.

The mandated tax rate, r, may be calculated on the basis of the tax levy that would yield the foundation level of support (F) in the wealthiest district. Then,

$$r = F/V_h \qquad (3.2)$$

where V_h is the per pupil valuation in the wealthiest district. Then Equation (3.1) becomes

$$EA_i = WADA_i \cdot F(1 - V_i/V_h). \qquad (3.3)$$

One could also compute r on the basis of the necessary tax levy to yield F when *average* per pupil valuation in the state (V_s) is substituted for V_h. Then Equation (3.3) becomes

$$EA_i = WADA_i \cdot F(1 - V_i/V_s). \qquad (3.4)$$

When Equation (3.3) is used, all but the wealthiest districts would receive some equalization aid. When Equation (3.4) is used, only districts with per pupil valuations under the state average would receive equalization aid. In both cases, aid is given in inverse relation to the relative wealth of the districts.

The Guaranteed Valuation Plan

As noted previously, this plan is algebraically equivalent to the foundation plan. The guaranteed valuation plan specifies a given level of valuation, V_g, which all districts may use to compute the level of property tax revenues per pupil that the state will guarantee. Thus rV_g—where r is the mandatory tax rate—defines the guaranteed yield, which in the foundation plan has been called the minimum foundation support level, F. The guaranteed valuation plan provides for equalization aid on the basis of the following formula:

$$EA_i = WADA_i (rV_g - rV_i).$$ (3.5)

Since rV_g, in effect, is equal to F, Equation (3.5) reduces to Equation (3.1), proving that the two plans are algebraically equivalent.

The equivalence of Equations (3.4) and (3.1) is contingent on the use of r as a *mandated* tax rate. If r is allowed to vary between districts, then the equivalence is no longer true. Moreover, the algebraic equivalence holds only to the extent that $F = rV_g$. Obviously, a change from one system to another, accompanied by changes in the implicit foundation level and/or other parameters in the formula would result in changes in state aid. A good example of this is the very recent change in the state aid distribution system in Illinois which permits districts to use either the old foundation approach or a new guaranteed valuation program (which is called a "resource equalization approach") (Illinois State Department of Education, 1973).[3]

It should be noted, further, that the practical application of the two formulas could result in some differences in equalization aid. For example, V_g in Wisconsin varies according to school organization and school classification (see Riew [1970] and Cohn [1972], pp. 329-31). If such a variation is justifiable— and it may not be—it might be politically easier to effect such a variation in the guaranteed valuation plan than in the foundation plan—in which case one would have to vary the value of F among school organizations and classifications.

The Percentage Equalizing Plan

Equalization aid is distributed according to the following formula:

3. We are indebted to G. Alan Hickrod for raising this point.

$$EA_i = WADA_i\,(1 - xV_i/V_s)\,EXP_i \qquad (3.6)$$

where EXP_i is local per pupil expenditures in the ith district, and x is a scalar between 0 and 1 indicating the extent to which the state is willing to share in educational expenditures. (A higher value of x indicates a *smaller* state share.)

For example, if $V_i/V_s = 1/2$ for district i, and if $x = 0.25$, the state will then pay a proportion $1 - 1/2(0.25) = 0.875$ (87.5 percent) of local expenditures. If, however, $x = 0.5$, the state will pay only $0.75 per dollar of expenditures.

It can also be shown that as the ratio V_i/V_s increases, state aid per dollar of expenditures decreases. For example, if $x = 0.25$ and $V_i/V_s = 2$, the state will pay $0.50 per dollar of local expenditures. If $x = 0.50$, the state will pay no equalization aid to that district.

As noted earlier, many states have combined such equalization plans with flat grants and other types of categorical grants. Also, states using the percentage equalization plan have stipulated maximum levels of EXP_i for the purpose of equalization aid, thus limiting the extent to which equalization could be achieved.

The Power Equalizing Plan

In both the foundation and the percentage equalizing plans, per pupil expenditures in the individual districts remain a function of the district's wealth, measured by assessed valuation of property. Even if some wealthy districts receive no state aid whatever, they may still be able to raise more educational revenues for a given tax effort than other districts receiving state aid. If follows that the quality of the schools in a district (measured by per pupil expenditures) remains a function of wealth.

The power equalizing scheme, proposed by Coons and his colleagues (1970), calls for equal state aid to districts based on equal tax *effort*. That is, school districts that impose a given tax *rate* should be entitled to spend a given sum on education (per pupil) *and no more*. Any discrepancy between the amount the district can raise and that to which it is entitled will be filled by the state. Moreover, if a district can raise educational funds, for a given tax effort, in excess of the stipulated amount set by the state, the excess must be transferred to the state. In sum, any two school districts that impose the same property tax rate will have identical educational funds per pupil at their disposal, no matter how wealthy or poor the community is.

One method by which the concept may be implemented is to define state aid—both positive and negative—on the basis of the following formula:

$$EA_i = WADA_i\,[\,r_iV_s - r_iV_i\,] = WADA_i\,[\,r_i\,(V_s - V_i)\,] \qquad (3.7)$$

where r_i is the tax rate that residents of district i are willing to impose on themselves.

For example, if V_s = \$5,000, and V_i = \$3,000, aid will be given to the districts on the basis of the formula $EA_i = r(\$2,000)\ WADA_i$. If the district chooses a low tax rate, say 10 mills ($r = 0.01$), then per pupil aid is \$20. If it chooses a very high rate, say 100 mills ($r = 0.1$), per pupil aid would be \$200. For each additional mill, the district will get additional aid of \$2.00 per pupil in $WADA$.

On the other hand, if a district has a per pupil valuation (V_i) of \$6,000, it will pay the state negative aid based on the formula $EA_i = r_i(-\$1,000)$. For each mill levied (yielding \$6.00 per pupil), the district will pay the state \$1.00. Hence if the district chose to levy a tax of 10 mills, it will raise \$60 per pupil, pay the state \$10 per pupil, and retain \$50 per pupil. For the district in the preceding paragraph, local revenue for the 10-mill levy would be \$30 per pupil. Add to that the \$20 per pupil in state aid, and it is clear that both districts are left with \$50 per pupil despite the wide disparity in wealth between the two.

Instead of Equation (3.7), it is possible to formulate a specific schedule indicating the amount of educational revenues to which a district is entitled within a given range of tax levies. If revenue entitlement is denoted by RE, then state aid, positive or negative, is given by

$$EA_i = [RE - r_iV_i]\ WADA_i. \tag{3.8}$$

Note that RE in Equation (3.7) is simply r_iV_s, representing tax yield when the average property value in the state is taxed at the rate r_i.

The power equalizing plan has been implemented to date only in Kansas and Utah—and there only partially. Variations of the plan could incorporate a different measure of wealth in Equations (3.7) or (3.8) and perhaps permit a certain amount of variation among districts in per pupil expenditures not based entirely on tax effort. Examples of this would be categorical grants for special purposes or separate transportation and capital aid distribution formulas.[4]

A General Description of Current Aid Programs

States vary not only in the means by which they provide financial assistance to local school districts but also in regard to the percentage of total funds provided by the state and the actual equalizing effect derived from the particular subvention programs. On the other side of the ledger, states also vary considerably in their source of revenues for the schools—whether by legislative appropri-

---

4. The (hypothetical) effect of a variant of the power equalizing plan on total educational revenues for a sample of Pennsylvania districts is illustrated in Summers (1973).

ation or special taxes earmarked for education. The authority and extent to which localities can levy nonproperty taxes is similarly variable in the different states, as is state-wide participation in capital costs, transporation, and the purchase of textbooks, to mention only a few special areas.

The general types of subvention programs currently in use in the states are shown in Table 3-1. It can be seen that a majority of the states currently operate with some variation of the Strayer-Haig-Mort Minimum Foundation Plan. If there is indeed a change from past years, it would appear to be away from flat grants (and in some cases, away from foundation plans) toward increased use of percentage equalizing or guaranteed valuation programs. Although, as indicated in the previous chapter, considerable interest and support has been given to a full state funding approach to education, Hawaii is still the only state with such a plan in operation.

More specifically, thirty-three of the contiguous states operate on a Strayer-Haig-Mort Foundation Plan, including most of the southern, border, midwestern, and western states. A widely dispersed group of ten states at least partially relies on flat grants to school districts. The two more recent types of programs—percentage equalizing and guaranteed valuation—seem to have gained a rather substantial foothold in New England and the Middle Atlantic Region.

This regionality in funding plans is shown in Figure 3-4. The fact that basically similar programs have become clustered in readily identifiable regions of the country would appear to indicate that some particular mix of practical politics and educational philosophy that is distinct in each region leads to specific approaches to educational finance. This view is intensified by the regional variation in state funding of transportation, textbook purchase, and other special services to be discussed shortly.

The variation in percentage of educational costs underwritten by the state as a whole provides perhaps the greatest range of difference of any of the potent factors. It should be recalled that irrespective of the particular formula used for state disbursement of funds, all other things being equal, the larger the state contribution, the more equalizing the system is. This is true even if flat grants are used extensively. The reason for this is simply that most state revenues are collected on some state-wide "per wealth" basis but are returned on some "per student" or "per capita" basis.

Table 3-2 presents data for the percentage of total nonfederal educational funds provided for the schools by the states. The figures shown in this table range from approximately 6 percent in New Hampshire to 83 percent in New Mexico. Some regional patterns regarding this variable may be observed in Figure 3-5. The southern states appear to have the highest percentage of funds provided by the states, while the Plains states have the lowest percentage.

The type of financial plan used and the percentage of state funds relative to total educational costs are the two most important variables in determining the equalizing effect of the state program. This is not to say, however, that all other

Table 3-1
Classification of the States' Basic Multi-Program by Type of Plan Used for Its Calculation, 1971-72

Flat Grants		Strayer-Haig-Mort	Percentage Equalizing	Guaranteed Valuation or Tax Yield Plan	Complete State and Federal Support
Uniform	Variable				
Arizona[a]	Arkansas[b]	Alabama	Iowa[c]	New Jersey[d,e]	Hawaii
California[f,g]	Delaware	California[f,g]	Massachusetts	Utah[h]	
Connecticut	Nebraska[i]	Colorado	New York[d]	Wisconsin	
Oregon[j]	New Mexico	Florida	Pennsylvania		
	North Carolina	Georgia	Rhode Island		
	South Carolina	Idaho	Vermont		
		Illinois			
		Indiana			
		Kansas			
		Kentucky			
		Louisiana			
		Maine			
		Maryland			
		Michigan			
		Minnesota[d]			
		Mississippi			
		Missouri			
		Montana[i]			
		Nebraska[i]			
		Nevada			
		New Hampshire			

New Jersey[d,e]
North Dakota
Ohio[d]
Oregon[j]
South Dakota[f]
Tennessee
Texas
Washington
West Virginia
Wyoming[f]
Oklahoma
Virginia[d]
Alaska[k]

[a]Arizona distributes $15,069,000 in equalization aid; however, the state's primary school funds are distributed on a flat-grant basis.

[b]While local wealth is not taken directly into account in the major portion of the primary school fund, the distribution does equalize to some degree.

[c]Iowa will operate under a Strayer-Haig-Mort Program in 1972-73.

[d]1972-73 school year reported.

[e]While New Jersey operates under a guaranteed valuation program, the law guarantees the levels of funding under the previous Strayer-Hait-Mort type program, and so both classifications apply.

[f]1970-71 school year reported.

[g]California operates under a combination Flat-Grant Plan and Strayer-Haig-Mort Program.

[h]The Utah program could also be classified as a variation of the Strayer-Haig-Mort Program.

[i]Nebraska operates under a combination Flat Grant Plan and Strayer-Haig-Mort Program.

[j]Oregon operates under a combination Flat Grant Plan and Strayer-Haig-Mort Program.

[k]The Alaska plan combines the Strayer-Haig-Mort foundation approach with the percentage equalizing method of determining the local share of the calculation.

Source: Reproduced from Johns (1972), Table 3.

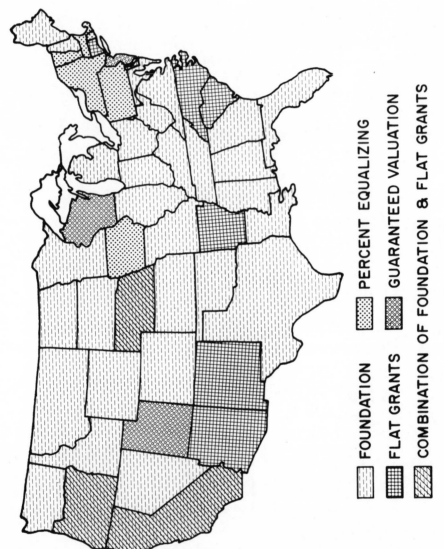

Figure 3-4. State Funding Programs by Aid Plan

FOUNDATION   PERCENT EQUALIZING

FLAT GRANTS   GUARANTEED VALUATION

COMBINATION OF FOUNDATION & FLAT GRANTS

Table 3-2
Percentage of Total Nonfederal Funds Provided by Individual States[a]

Less than 29%	30 to 39%	40 to 49%	50 to 59%	60 to 69%	Over 70%
New Hampshire 6%	Kansas 30%	Massachusetts 40%	Oklahoma 50%	Florida 60%[b]	Minnesota 70%
Iowa 14%	Maine 30%	Illinois 41%[b]	New Jersey 51%	Louisiana 60%	Alabama 73%
South Dakota 15%	Colorado 31%	Michigan 42%	Washington 54%	Kentucky 61%	North Carolina 76%
Nebraska 18%	North Dakota 31%	Arizona 44%[b]	Utah 55%	Georgia 64%	Delaware 80%
Oregon 21%[b]	Wisconsin 31%	New York 44%	Tennessee 56%	West Virginia 65%	New Mexico 83%
Montana 25%	Connecticut 32%	Idaho 47%		Texas 66%	
	Maryland 32%	Pennsylvania 49%		South Carolina 67%[b]	
	Rhode Island 32%			Mississippi 69%	
	Missouri 34%				
	Ohio 36%				
	Vermont 36%				
	California 38%				
	Virginia 38%				
	Indiana 39%				
	Wyoming 39%				

[a]States are listed by percentage category. Within categories, they are listed in ascending percentage contribution. Within the same percentage, they are listed alphabetically.

[b]Percentages for these states were computed from data in National Education Association, Research Division, *Estimates of School Statistics, 1972-73* (Washington, D.C.: The Association, 1972).

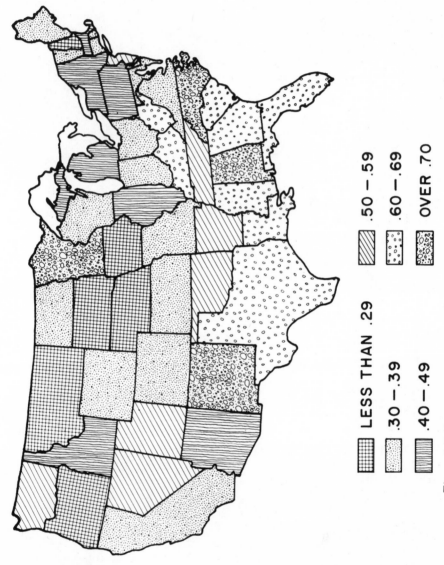

Figure 3-5. Percent of Total Non-Federal Funds Provided by Individual States

things are equal. The remainder of this section will be devoted to a discussion of these other factors.

State participation in school district capital costs provides an interesting case in point. While the modal state pattern is to provide loans or, alternatively, to guarantee loans undertaken within certain limits by the individual school districts, some states are more directly involved in capital construction. In at least two states, a state authority absorbs full cost of construction, builds the facilities, and holds title to them until the buildings are fully amortized.

Most states impose statutory or executive limits in regard to type, use, and functionality of specific school buildings. In the Commonwealth of Pennsylvania, for example, the governor's 1973-74 budget message (Shapp [1973]) indicates strong support for limitations "to control the construction of 'Taj Majal' schools by local school districts." The governor goes on to indicate his belief that "unnecessarily lavish school construction is a chief factor in the rising cost of education at both local and state levels" (p. 10). Pennsylvania would thus seem ready to join many other states in limiting the options of school districts in terms of school construction.

Many states provide subsidies for the cost of textbook purchases. Most typically, the southern states pay the full cost of textbooks with the provision that the books be purchased through the state in accordance with an approved textbook list. This practice has come about partly in response to the fact that many of these states previously required students to purchase books on an individual basis. While it provides the potential for some economies of scale, such centralized control of textual school material would appear to be less palatable to the populace in other regions of the country.

Most states also provide a reimbursement for transportation costs necessary to bring children to school. While all have dollar limitations, various states consider factors such as the quality of the roads, steepness of the terrain, number of miles traveled, availability of commercial or municipal common carriers, and sparsity and/or density of population in the district. Some states go even further with regard to transportation. In both of the Carolinas, for example, the state owns and operates the school buses. In Ohio, the state pays the full cost of bus operation but not their purchase.

In regard to all three of these miscellaneous program areas—buildings, textbooks, and transportation—the majority of the states operate on a flat-grant basis. Significantly, however, a number of states provide these subsidies on an equalizing basis. That is, these programs are either included within the confines of the total program for "general educational costs" or are funded at the same percentage level at which the individual districts receive reimbursement for general educational programs.

In addition to these programs, every state has some program for vocational education, either within the confines of the same school buildings or in separate facilites. These special purpose educational programs go by various names and are occasionally linked with the junior or community college network. Programs of vocational-technical education appear to be most highly developed in the southern states, although other states have shown much recent interest. In New York State, vocational education is only one component of regional "boards of cooperative education" through which neighboring districts provide services which would not be financially feasible to enter into as single units. These services include vocational and distributional education as well as certain compensatory and remedial services. In Pennsylvania, intermediate units operate to provide some of these same support services. In other states, school districts are organized on a county basis (Maryland and Illinois, for example) and are able to provide services on a wider scale with less unnecessary duplication.

Evaluation of Equalization Efforts
in the States

A complete analysis of the degree of equalization achieved in each of the fifty states is beyond the scope of this volume. Such an analysis is indeed difficult and requires information not only about the provisions of the specific enabling legislation in each state, but also knowledge of actual appropriations as well as local costs and local options. A program which appears very equalizing on paper may have no such effect because of inadequate funding, extent of participation, encumbering provisions, or other extrinsic factors.

Instead of attempting a new analysis with a limited data base, it seems most appropriate here to report a recent study of equalization impact undertaken by Johns and Salmon (1971). These investigators studied school funding plans in the fifty states, making use of a typology developed for the National Educational Finance Project. The NEFP evaluation typology is presented in abstracted form below. Equalization levels are arranged from 0 to 14 as follows.

LEVEL 0: State funds are allocated in such a manner as to leave districts with the same or greater differences in financial capacity to support education as they were before receiving state allocations. . . .

LEVEL 1: State funds are allocated on the basis of a flat amount per unweighted pupil or unadjusted classroom unit basis, or some other method which ignores unit cost variations, . . . and a required local share in proportion to the taxpaying ability of the local districts is *not* deducted before the apportionment is made. . . .

LEVEL 2: State funds are allocated on a weighted unit basis, . . . and a required local share in proportion to the tax-paying ability of the local district is *not* deducted before the apportionment is made. . . .

LEVEL 3: State funds . . . are allocated on the basis of *un*weighted [units], . . . *but* a required local share in proportion to the taxpaying ability of the local districts *is* deducted before the apportionment is made. . . .

LEVEL 4: State funds are allocated on a weighted [unit] basis, . . . *and* a required local share in proportion to the taxpaying ability of the local districts *is* deducted before the apportionment is made. . . . [5] [Emphasis added.]

Using the above typology, the levels are scored from 0 (for Level 1) to 8.40 (for Level 4). Local funds are considered in a fashion similar to the method used for rating state finance programs. Dollars which are considered in the state equalization program to be deducted from the basic program are considered Level 3 or 4, depending on whether unit costs are taken into account. Additional local funds are categorized Level 0.

Using this scheme to evaluate school finance programs during the academic year 1968-69, Johns and Salmon found the impact of these programs to vary greatly in the several states. In order of descending equalization effect, in terms of their definitions above, ranking of the states is shown in Table 3-3.

As can be seen, Hawaii (because of its unitary school system) is the only state to manifest a "perfect" equalization score. Of the contiguous states, Utah—the only state with a variation of the power equalizing approach—ranks highest. Connecticut, with a straight flat-grant program of limited proportions, comes out last. In contrast to other states, however, Connecticut puts 34.3 percent of its state education funds into district capital costs. If this were considered, Connecticut's rating would undoubtedly improve considerably.

As in previous sections of this chapter, it is interesting to ask whether any regional pattern emerges from this information. The Johns and Salmon data are divided into the eight geographical regions used by the National Education Association. Information on the matter of regionality is shown in Figure 3-6.

It should be made clear that in this pictorial representation, the unit of analysis is the regional mean. Therefore, each of the states in each region may not be higher or lower in itself than states in other regions, but the means for the regions are in order of magnitude of equalization scores.

Generally, the Rocky Mountain states most nearly equalize the cost of education within their individual borders, followed closely by the Southeast states. The Plains states have the least equalization by a sizeable margin. While the Far Western states sit squarely on the national norm (5.131), the Great Lakes, Southwest, New England, and Plains states are all below the national mean. States above the mean are in the Rocky Mountain, Southeast, and Mideast areas. This information is summarized in Table 3-4.

The fact that the type of plan used is not necessarily indicative of the equalization score would tend to give credence to the hypothesis expressed by many educational finance spokesmen that, short of full state funding such as in Hawaii, no particular type of plan can be said, in and of itself, to be a better equalizing agent than others. Johns and Salmon point out that the equalization score has a significantly positive simple correlation with percentage of funds

5. Abridged from Johns and Salmon (1971), pp. 125-27.

Table 3-3

Ranking and Equalization Scores of the States Based on the NEFP Typology for the School Year, 1968-69

Rank	State	Score	Rank	State	Score
1	Hawaii	8.400	26	Maryland	5.092
2	Utah	7.143	27	Virginia	5.085
3	Rhode Island	6.862	28	Texas	4.963
4	Alaska	6.628	29	California	4.841
5	Wyoming	6.543	30	Montana	4.810
6	Washington	6.368	31	Maine	4.804
7	Idaho	6.318	32	Nevada	4.779
8	Alabama	6.220	33	Massachusetts	4.536
9	Delaware	6.202	34	Oregon	4.535
10	North Carolina	6.148	35	Tennessee	4.521
11	Georgia	6.103	36	Minnesota	4.433
12	Kentucky	6.042	37	Arizona	4.355
13	Florida	5.995	38	Iowa	4.042
14	New York	5.957	39	North Dakota	3.931
15	Louisiana	5.929	40	Missouri	3.852
16	New Mexico	5.915	41	Michigan	3.844
17	Ohio	5.882	42	Kansas	3.820
18	Pennsylvania	5.870	43	New Jersey	3.754
19	Vermont	5.834	44	Indiana	3.704
20	Wisconsin	5.781	45	Oklahoma	3.691
21	Mississippi	5.744	46	Arkansas	3.647
22	West Virginia	5.578	47	Colorado	3.571
23	Illinois	5.398	48	South Dakota	3.420
24	Nebraska	5.378	49	New Hampshire	3.091
25	South Carolina	5.235	50	Connecticut	2.295

Source: Reproduced from Johns and Salmon (1971), p. 137.

supplied by the state and a significantly negative correlation with number of separate state education program funds.

All other things being equal, it appears, then, that the larger the relative amount of state funds and the fewer the number of categorical programs, the more equalizing the total finance program will be. This can be confirmed by reviewing the data presented in Figures 3-4 and 3-6. It can be seen that the regions having above average equalizing impact come from the ranks of those with all of the various funding plans. However, it can be seen from Figures 3-5 and 3-6 that there is some relationship between percent of state funds involved and degree of equalization.

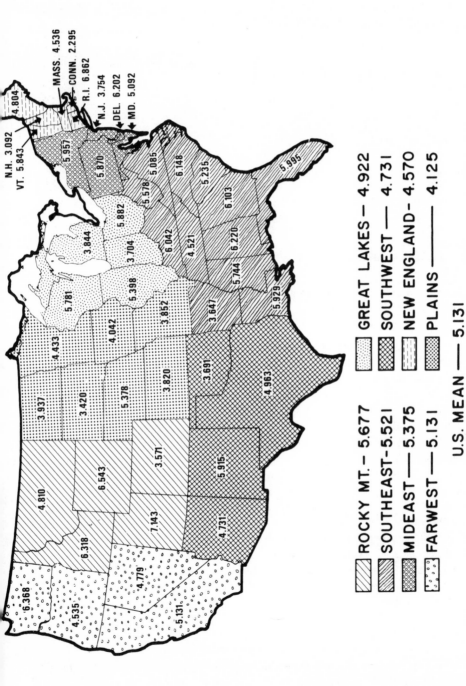

Figure 3-6. Mean National Education Finance Project Equalization Scores by Geographical Regions

ROCKY MT. — 5.677   GREAT LAKES — 4.922

SOUTHEAST — 5.521   SOUTHWEST — 4.731

MIDEAST — 5.375   NEW ENGLAND — 4.570

FARWEST — 5.131   PLAINS — 4.125

U.S. MEAN — 5.131

N.H. 3.092
VT. 5.843
MASS. 4.536
CONN. 2.295
R.I. 6.862
N.J. 3.754
DEL. 6.202
MD. 5.092
4.804

5.957
5.870
5.995
5.085
5.578
6.148
5.235
6.103
3.844
5.882
6.042
4.521
6.220
5.744
5.929
3.704
5.398
3.852
3.647
5.781
4.042
3.820
3.691
4.433
3.937
3.420
5.378
4.963
4.810
6.543
3.571
5.915
4.731
6.318
7.143
4.779
6.368
4.535
5.131

Table 3-4

Mean Equalization Scores in Major Geographical Regions Based on the NEFP
Typology for the Academic Year, 1968-69

Region	Mean Score
Rocky Mountains (Colo., Idaho, Mont., Utah, and Wyo.)	5.677
Southeast (Ala., Ark., Fla., Ga., Ky., La., Miss., N.C., S.C., Tenn., Va., and W.Va.)	5.521
Mideast (Del., Md., N.J., N.Y., and Pa.)	5.375
Far West (Calif., Nev., Oreg., and Wash.)	5.131
Great Lakes (Ill., Ind., Mich., Ohio, and Wis.)	4.922
Southwest (Ariz., N.Mex., Okla., and Texas)	4.731
New England (Conn., Maine, Mass., N.H., R.I., and Vt.)	4.570
Plains (Iowa, Kans., Minn., Mo., Nebr., N.Dak., and S.Dak.)	4.125
All States	5.131

Source: Adapted from Johns and Salmon (1971), p. 139.

Studying the effect of equalization efforts under widely different statutory
conditions is a very difficult task. Nevertheless, in terms of the current research,
it would appear that the Johns and Salmon method leaves something to be
desired. Surely, there are other more important keystones of "student need"
than the simon-pure weightings most states attach to disbursements for elementary and secondary education.

If the two-pronged NEFP definition, stressing taxpaying ability *and* student
educational needs, is to be meaningful, we must speak in terms of individual
student abilities, needs, required compensatory programs, and requisite additional costs involved. In point of fact, there is some fragmentary evidence (see, for
example, Fleischmann Commission [1973]; and Berke, Campbell, Goettel
[1972]) that elementary/secondary funding differentials work to the detriment
of the poorest schools because of the extremely large number of dropouts and
the earliness with which individuals do drop out in blighted areas. Therefore, the
Johns and Salmon schema is not dealing well with the "need" component of
equalization and may in fact be imposing an inverse measure.

Concluding Comments

In addition to defining and discussing the concept of equalization, this chapter
has provided basic information about various state plans for educational finance.
The following chapter carries this discussion further by presenting more detailed
information about current programs for educational finance in the states.

4

Current Status of Educational Finance Programs

This chapter provides additional information about school finance programs which currently operate in the different states. Salient aspects of these programs, along with schemata for categorizations, have been presented in previous parts of this volume. The task here is to fill in more of the detail in terms of operating procedures and formulas, as well as amounts, sources, and uses of funds involved.

The order of presentation in this chapter is as follows. The first five sections will successively describe the operation of (1) flat-grant programs, (2) foundation programs, (3) percentage equalizing programs, (4) guaranteed valuation programs, and (5) modified power equalizing plans. In each case, a group of states using the respective approaches will provide illustration. The chapter concludes with an examination of the various encumbering provisions of state plans and a discussion of sources and specific uses of school revenues.

Flat Grant Programs

Ten states at least partially disburse general (basic) funds for the schools by use of a flat grant procedure. These states are Arizona, California, Connecticut, Oregon, Arkansas, Delaware, Nebraska, New Mexico, North Carolina, and South Carolina. The first four base assistance on a uniform flat grant, the latter six upon variable flat grants. The uniform flat grants take no account of cost variations; variable grants are weighted in accordance with program level or other factor(s). Of these ten states, five (Connecticut, Delaware, New Mexico, North and South Carolina) rely exclusively on flat grant disbursements; the remaining five states use a flat grant in combination with some other equalizing program. Of the states that rely exclusively on flat grants, the level of grant per student is shown in Table 4-1.

States using a combination flat and equalizing grant approach, as might be expected, have flat-grant levels considerably below those which can be observed above. Arizona has a flat grant of $182.50, California $125.00, and Nebraska $35.00 to $49.00 (depending on the qualifications of teachers).

While flat grants are not, by definition, equalization plans in intent, they do, as indicated in Chapter 3, equalize to the extent that they are underwritten by taxes collected in accordance with wealth and are distributed on the basis of attendance units. This degree of equalization occurs if the plans are adequately

Table 4-1
Levels of Per Pupil Flat Grants in Five States, 1971-72

State	Flat Grant Per Pupil in ADA
Connecticut	$205.00
Delaware	(274.00 to 481.00, approximately)[a]
New Mexico	346.95[b]
North Carolina	(243.00 to 542.00, approximately)[a]
South Carolina	(202.00 to 344.00, approximately)[c]

[a]Based on education and experience of teachers.
[b]Per Average Daily Membership (ADM) rather than ADA.
[c]Based on teacher education, experience, and score on National Teachers Examination.
Source: Adapted from Johns (1972).

funded. As can be seen by the figures cited in Table 4-1, none of the flat-grant programs in operation provides anything near the cost of what is considered to be an adequate educational program. Yet in four of the five states described in Table 4-1, state aid is large relative to total nonfederal educational funds. The proportions state aid is of total nonfederal funds are as follows (see Table 3-2): Delaware — 0.80; New Mexico — 0.83; North Carolina — 0.76; and South Carolina — 0.67.

Foundation Plans

Variations of the Strayer-Haig-Mort Minimum Foundation Plan are still the most popular form of state assistance to the schools. Thirty-three of the contiguous states (plus Alaska) use a foundation program. As with the flat grants, there are two types of units upon which to base the foundation level—student or classroom (teacher) units.

The foundation programs based upon students in attendance will be discussed first. There is a great deal of variation in foundation levels among the states. New Hampshire sets its foundation level at $200 (elementary education foundation), while Oregon funds its elementary program at the foundation level of $593.58. Ohio, the only state with a higher figure, pegs its foundation level at $600. The foundation level in the majority of states using student units ranges from $300 to $500 per pupil.

Wyoming has established a foundation level of $11,800 per classroom unit. All other states using a classroom foundation unit allot funds in accordance with the education and experience of the particular classroom teachers. Again, there is a great deal of variation among states, as shown in Table 4-2.

The greatest amount of variation can be seen in the extremes of the degree structure. For beginning teachers with less than a bachelor's degree, the range is

Table 4-2

Minimum and Maximum Stipulated Teachers' Salary Levels, by Educational Attainment, to Determine State Aid in Nine States, 1971-72[a]

State	Less than Baccalaureate	Baccalaureate	Master's	Master's Plus[b]	Doctorate
Florida	$3,000[c]	$5,300[c]	$6,300[c]	$7,000[c]	$7,700[c]
Georgia	[d]	$5,600 to 7,560	$6,328 to 8,650	$7,644 to 9,800[e]	$8,645 to 10,920[f]
Kentucky	$2,600 to 2,900	$5,530 to 6,950	$5,980 to 7,400	$6,430 to 7,850	[d]
Louisiana	$4,000 to 6,600	$6,000 to 8,200	$6,200 to 9,100	$6,200 to 9,800	$6,900 to 10,300
Mississippi	$1,800 to 3,836	$5,400 to 6,000	$5,700 to 6,300	[d]	[d]
Tennessee	$4,160 to 5,170	$5,500 to 6,550	$6,000 to 7,125	$6,500 to 7,625	$7,000 to 8,125
Texas	[d]	$6,000 to 8,050	$6,600 to 9,310	[d]	[d]
Virginia	$3,800 to 5,000	$5,900 to 7,700	$6,400 to 8,100	[d]	[d]
West Virginia[g]	[d]	$5,719[h]	$6,257	$6,794[i]	$7,063

[a]Within each degree level, there are generally from six to fifteen steps. Steps most commonly consist of one year's service. Compensation is for a nine-month contract.

[b]Master's plus refers to attainment of the first professional degree and thirty additional advanced graduate semester hours (or forty-five quarter hours), unless noted otherwise.

[c]For all degree levels in Florida, an additional $400 is added to the base for "each instructional unit sustained by a certificated degree teacher"; additional $400 for seven years Florida teaching experience; additional $400 for ten years; additional $600 for fifteen years.

[d]Salaries for these levels are not reported in these states.

[e]Compensation listed is for attainment of "Sixth Year Certificate."

[f]Compensation listed is for attainment of "Seventh Year Certificate."

[g]West Virginia awards $129 for each additional year of teaching service.

[h]Compensation for bachelor's degree plus fifteen hours of graduate work is $5,888.

[i]Compensation for master's degree plus fifteen additional graduate hours is $6,525.

Source: Data extrapolated from Johns (1972).

from $1,800 in Mississippi to $4,160 in Tennessee. At the doctoral level, the range is from $7,000 in Tennessee to $8,645 in Georgia. At the bachelor's degree level, the variation is only from $5,300 in Florida[1] to $6,000 in Texas and Louisiana. Allotments for master's degree starting salaries are $300 to $600 higher than the respective baccalaureate salaries.

1. Beginning with the school year 1973-74, Florida will operate on a new system taking into account student membership, program costs, and cost of living in the district. The new law does not include variations in aid based upon teacher experience and training.

While foundation plans based on classroom units may at first appear to be closer to actual incurred costs than those based on student units, it must be remembered that the classroom allotments must go toward paying more than just the teachers' salaries. Other direct and indirect instructional costs must also be borne.

One must conclude that such foundation plans, at best, only equalize that portion of the educational costs within the specified levels. All additional nonreimbursible costs fall on the district alone. Unless realistic foundation levels are established, the equalizing effect of these plans is minimal and, perhaps more importantly, deceptive.

Percentage Equalizing Plans

The percentage equalizing approach is currently in operation in the states of Iowa, Massachusetts, New York, Pennsylvania, Rhode Island, and Vermont. While this plan, at the time of its introduction, was seen in some quarters as a panacea, it operates much like a foundation program. The generalized formula for a percentage equalizing plan has been discussed in Chapter 3 (see Equation 3.6). Unlike the foundation-type plan, state aid is a function of the level of expenditures in the percentage equalizing approach. The state shares a portion of total reimbursible expenditures depending on the ratio of local assessed property valuation to total state valuation.

One positive aspect of many percentage equalizing plans is the addition of measures of wealth other than property valuations. The states of Iowa, Rhode Island, and (apparently) Vermont add various measures of district per capita income to property valuation to determine "district wealth."[2]

The exact constituent elements of the various state percentage equalizing plans differ somewhat from one another. Iowa, for example, in developing a composite wealth measure, weights equalized property valuation at 0.70 and district gross income at 0.30. In addition, the pupil counting unit is also a hybrid; it consists of the arithmetic average of ADM and the school census (SC). The formula thus reads:

$$\frac{\text{State Aid}}{\text{Per Pupil}} = \left[1.00 - \left(0.25 \frac{\dfrac{(V_i)(0.7) + (I_i)(0.3)}{(ADM_i + SC_i)/2}}{\dfrac{(V_s)(0.7) + (I_s)(0.3)}{(ADM_s + SC_s)/2}} \right) \right] [EXP_i - BSTR] \quad (4.1)$$

2. Use of wealth measures other than property valuation is not limited to states using percentage equalization plans. Nonproperty measures of wealth are used, among others, in Kansas and Mississippi.

where V_i and V_s are, respectively, total property valuation in the ith district and the state

$$(V_s = \sum_{j=1}^{N} V_j, N \text{ being the number of districts in the state});$$

ADM_i and ADM_s are, respectively, average daily membership in the ith district and the state

$$(ADM_s = \sum_{j=1}^{N} ADM_j);$$

SC_i and SC_s are, respectively, school census in the ith district and the state

$$(SC_s = \sum_{j=1}^{N} SC_j);$$

I_i and I_s are, respectively, personal income in the ith district and the state

$$(I_s = \sum_{j=1}^{N} I_j);$$

and where district revenues from state basic school funds (flat grants) ($BSTR$) are subtracted from reimbursible expense (EXP_i) before computing equalization aid.

To add one more complexity to the Iowa plan, public school *and* nonpublic school students are included in the computation of student units upon which to fund the public schools. By comparison, the Massachusetts formula is very streamlined. On a per pupil basis, the formula is as follows:

$$\text{State Aid Per Pupil} = [1.00 - 0.65 \frac{V_i/ADA_i}{V_s/ADA_s}] EXP_i \qquad (4.2)$$

where EXP_i is reimbursible expenditure per pupil in the ith district.

Except for a difference in the actual weights used, the Massachusetts formula is identical to the New York and Pennsylvania formulas. Rhode Island, however, is slightly different, using a standard (mandated) tax rate times the "equalized weighted assessed valuation of real and tangible property modified by the ratio district median family income bears to state median family income

[*MEWAV*]" (Johns [1972], p. 292). The formula looks somewhat less foreboding than the verbage:

$$\text{State Aid Per Pupil} = [1.00 - \frac{(\text{Mandated tax rate})(MEWAV)}{(\$500)(ADM)}]EXP_i \quad (4.3)$$

where the mandated tax rate is established by the state, and *MEWAV* is as defined above.

Many believe that these plans would equalize to a greater degree if there were not minima and maxima for state aid. In New York, for example, no district can receive more than 90 percent of reimbursible costs or less than $274 or $310 (depending on local options). While Berke et al. (1972) indicate that the maximum aid is not a problem at present (since all districts can afford to expend 10 percent of costs), the minimum provisions provide a disequalizing influence.

Since the entire impetus for percentage equalizing is that equalizable expenditures are not limited to a predetermined level (as in the foundation-type plan), it appears self-defeating to place unrealistic minima and maxima on the program. What is needed is the imposition of rather minimal structural safeguards against unnecessary extravagance and/or fiscal mismanagement.

Guaranteed Valuation Programs

Another recent variant of the foundation plan is the guaranteed valuation program. Currently operating in the states of New Jersey and Wisconsin, the intent is to guarantee to each district, irrespective of wealth, an identical yield from a comparable tax. In New Jersey, for example, valuation in each district is guaranteed at the level of $30,000 per pupil. Those districts above this figure receive the minimum (flat) grant of $110. Those below the $30,000 valuation level receive from the state the difference between what they can actually raise at a mandated tax rate and what they would have received from a levy on the guaranteed level of property valuation. However, in New Jersey, as in other places where marked departures from past programs have been attempted, an encumbering provision provides that no school district will receive less than it did before implementation of the new plan. Therefore, the effectiveness of the guaranteed valuation plan in that state can not be truly measured.

Wisconsin was the first state to implement a guaranteed valuation plan for educational finance, and it is of some interest to examine its current program. Somewhat more complicated than the New Jersey plan, it contains nuances which deserve separate attention.

While the New Jersey plan, as developed by that state's legislature, contains provisions for differing guaranteed valuation levels for different types of districts, lack of full funding of the act has precluded the use of these distinctions at present. In New Jersey, all districts are—at least for the time being—considered "basic" districts. In Wisconsin, on the other hand, the distinction is made between "integrated" and "basic" districts—with the integrated districts being ones with enriched programs and the basic districts having only a standard program. For the three levels of school districts (elementary only, secondary only, or combined), the guaranteed valuation levels per pupil are indicated in Table 4-3.

Wisconsin places approximately 47 percent of total state education funds in the guaranteed valuation plan described. However, an additional 21 percent of the total goes into flat grants distributed to the districts. The flat grants are also based on level and type of district as shown in Table 4-4.

It should be pointed out as shown in Chapter 3, that the generalized formula for guaranteed valuation plans is algebraically equivalent to the formula for foundation programs. It follows, then, that with the relative weights held constant for the two types of programs, they will alternatively equalize or fail to equalize to the same degree.

Table 4-3
Guaranteed Valuation Levels, by Type of District: Wisconsin, 1971-72

	Basic	Integrated
Elementary Districts	$24,500	$45,900
Union High Districts	55,000	114,600
Twelve-Grade Districts	35,925[a]	47,900

[a]Aid for basic twelve-grade districts is computed on the same basis as for integrated districts; however, only 75 percent of the amount is payable. Therefore, although the basic guarantee is officially also $47,900, this amount has been reduced above to 75 percent of guarantee in order to reflect true relationships among types and levels of districts.

Source: Adapted from Johns (1972), p. 366.

Table 4-4
Flat Grants Per Pupil, by Type of District: Wisconsin, 1971-72

	Basic	Integrated
Elementary Districts	$30	$66
Secondary Districts	40	48

Note: Also included in the total Wisconsin program are six types of categorical grants (all flat) for specific purposes. None of the categorical grants distinguish between basic and integrated districts.

Source: Adapted from Johns (1972), p. 366.

Power Equalizing Plans

Although Johns (1972) categorizes Utah as a state operating with a guaranteed valuation plan, the Utah program has the rudiments of a power equalizing format. At the least, it is the closest to a power equalizing approach currently in operation. In 1972-73 the basic Utah plan guaranteed to each district $9,120 per "distribution unit" (which, for practical purposes, is a classroom unit). Districts had to levy a sixteen-mill property tax for education. If the district could not raise the stated amount at this millage, the state would contribute the remainder. If the district raised more than $9,120, the district had to *refund this to the state* for redistribution to other districts.

The refund of excess revenues is only one unique aspect of the Utah plan. In addition, districts voluntarily incrementing their tax rate by another twelve mills were entitled to receive an additional $212 per distribution unit. Further, any district in which the voters approved a higher millage than the above board leeway increment were entitled to $110 per additional mill. These amounts were guaranteed by the state; however, in contrast to the provisions of the original power equalizing plan, excess revenues did not have to be returned to the state.

In 1973 the Utah legislature enacted several basic changes in the plan. First, each district is now required to levy a minimum basic tax rate of 28 mills (with the exception that San Juan District, with only a 17.6-mill levy in 1972-73, which is permitted to approach the 28-mill levy over a three-year period). Excess revenues over the "cost of the basic program" must be paid to the state. Second, the state guarantees $4 per weighted pupil unit for each mill, not to exceed ten mills, over the 28 basic tax levy. This is termed the "State-supported voted leeway program." Voters in the district must approve any levy over 28 mills. Third, instead of classroom units, the plan makes use of "weighted pupil units" (*WPU*). The *basic* number of weighted pupil units is an arithmetic average of average daily membership and average daily attendance. To the basic *WPU*, a number of *WPU* "add-ons" are applied. These include the number of handicapped children, attendance in vocational programs, "necessarily existent small schools," grade distribution, and educational attainment and years of experience of professional staff. Fourth, instead of a fixed guarantee of $X per pupil unit, the legislature authorized a fixed sum of total aid for 1973-74—$155.7 million. Based on enrollment estimates, this would translate into a per weighted pupil aid of $510.

The amounts districts can spend per *weighted* student in 1973-74 will vary according to the willingness of the voters to adopt part or all of the voluntary 10-mill levy. But expenditures per pupil in *ADA* would vary even if all districts chose the same tax rate because of the manner by which the number of weighted pupils is calculated. The plan provides handsome benefits to "necessarily existent small districts." In contrast with the new Kansas plan, which provides a considerable bonus to *all* small districts, the Utah plan acknowledges a distinction between those districts that are small because of sparsity of population, and other small districts. The Utah Act apparently recognizes the disincentive effects that a small-district bonus might create.[3]

Another modified district power equalizing plan has been enacted in 1973 in Kansas. The basic plan may be described as follows:

1. Compute *LER*, the local effort rate, according to Equation (4.4):

$$LER = (BPP_i/BPP_i^n)0.015 \qquad (4.4)$$

where BPP_i is the legally permitted budget per pupil in district i, and BPP_i^n is the per pupil budget norm for the district's enrollment category. For the 1973-74 school year, the enrollment categories and the norm BPPs are:

Enrollment in District (E)	Budgetary Norm per Pupil (BPP^n)
Under 400	$936
400-1,299	$936 − $0.23111(E − 400)
1300 and over	$728

2. District wealth (W_i) is the sum of adjusted property value and taxable income.

3. State aid is, then, computed as the difference between a district's legal budget and its local share. The formula to compute is:

Total state aid for = (enrollment)(BPP_i) − (W_i)(LER) − other receipts   (4.5)
  ith district

Other receipts include district receipts (if any) in the preceding school year under PL 874; district's share of the 2-mill county school foundation tax levy; and district's share of the intangible tax (school districts receive 25 percent of this tax).

4. Although the plan allows each district the power to set its own budget, irrespective of its wealth, the plan falls short of the original power equalization scheme for two main reasons:

   a. The legally authorized budget (BPP_i) is severely restricted. For example, "no district may budget or expend for operating expenses per pupil more than 115% of its *BPP* in the preceding school year *or* 105% of the median *BPP* in the preceding school year of districts within the same enrollment category, *whichever is less*" (Dennis [1973], p. 9; italics in original). Also, a minimum *BPP* of $600 is required.

---

3. For descriptions of the new Utah plan, see *Analysis of Senate Bill 72* (1973), and Cummins (1973).

b. There is no "payback" provision; thus wealthier districts could spend more on education at any given tax rate, or spend the same amount as poorer districts but at lower tax rates. For example, if District A has total wealth per pupil of $100,000, and District B only $50,000, then a tax of 15 mills would raise $1,500 in District A and $750 in B. The two districts will have the same tax burden only when both choose the budget norm for their size category. For example, if BPP^n = $936 for both districts, and if BPP for both districts is $936, then both must levy a 15-mill tax rate. However, if District A were to choose a BPP somewhere between $936 and $1,500, its local effort rate (LER) would, indeed, increase over the minimum 15-mill rate, but it does not necessarily follow that its tax levy must also increase. On the other hand, if District B were to choose any budget over $936, it would almost certainly have to raise its tax rate above the 15-mill levy.

Overall, the Kansas plan appears to be a step in the right direction. But as Hickrod so cogently points out, such plans "can, of course, suffer the same fate as the foundation level formulas and one needs to be ever on the alert against those forces that would emasculate equalization formulas no matter what they look like" (Hickrod [1973], p. 105).[4]

Finally, it should be also mentioned that variants of the power equalizing scheme have recently been enacted by Maine and Montana. The new Maine plan, effective 1974-75, will include the following basic elements:

1. Only 40 percent of educational costs are to be financed by property taxes.

2. All districts will be required to levy a 14-mill tax.

3. "Local add-ons will be limited to 2.5 mills per year . . . For each of these mills, the State will guarantee $50 per pupil with any local yield above this amount reverting to the State Treasury."

4. State support will be determined on the basis of *average* expenditures during the preceding year. For 1974-75, the state will guarantee $600 and $915, respectively, per pupil in elementary and secondary schools.

5. Additional amounts are given to schools with "excess" costs.

6. Additional revenues may be raised upon voter approval in order to maintain the 1973-74 expenditure level.

7. The new Maine law provides equalization not only of operating expenditures but also of special education, vocational education, transportation, capital outlays, and debt service.

The Montana plan is distinguished by the following:

1. A minimum levy of 40 mills.

2. Revenues in excess of "those required for the foundation program and transportation charges" will be transferred to the state.

4. For more on the Kansas Plan, see Dennis (1973).

3. A "permissive levy" of up to 6 and 9 mills, respectively, for secondary and elementary school districts, may be imposed. "If the maximum permissive levies do not yield an amount equal to 25% of the guaranteed foundation program, then the state will reimburse the difference." No voter approval is necessary.

4. Capital outlays may be financed through additional levies.

Although neither the Maine nor the Montana programs follow the original power equalization concept, they nevertheless indicate a tendency to accept the major premises of power equalization, or at least to achieve a reduction in the variations among school districts in per pupil expenditures.[5]

The Impact of Encumbering Provisions

This chapter cannot be closed without a few words about the encumbering legislation which accompanies many of the state educational finance programs. Sometimes it is innocuous enough, but all too often the intent is to sap, in the name of practical politics, any strength the program might have.

Most bothersome of these provisions are the minimum, maximum, and save-harmless aspects of the various programs. Many states have maximum amounts or percentages of total funds that districts can receive from the state, and even more have minimums—amounting to a flat grant. A large number of states have provisions in enabling legislation similar to the case of New Jersey cited earlier. Minnesota requires that any district will receive "not less from those same sources [than] for the immediately preceding school year" (Johns [1972], p. 169).

In regard to the New York provisions, Berke et al. (1972) conclude that:

The 'save-harmless' provision is probably the most limiting factor to equalization. It guarantees that when a change occurs in some component of the formula no district will receive less than it received before the change. Thus aid is not related to fiscal or educational need, as defined in the formula, but rather to the aid previously received. Most important, the save-harmless provision places restraints on making any fundamental changes in the formula because it automatically predetermines where a considerable proportion of the monies will be placed (pp. 23-24).

Sources of School Revenues

Most typically, taxes for the schools are derived at the state level from legislative appropriations of funds collected from broadbased income and other taxes, and at the local level from taxes on real and personal property. However, here as elsewhere, there are variations, some of which deserve special mention.

5. The information concerning Maine and Montana is based on School Finance Study Unit (1973).

According to information presented in Johns (1972), approximately 30 percent of the states provide educational funds, at least in part, from special earmarked tax sources in contrast to general revenues. These monies might come from specific state fees, licenses, or profits from auxiliary enterprises such as state alcoholic beverage control. All or some of the revenue from these specific activities or programs may, by statute, be assigned to the schools. Additionally, many states have established various size endowments for the schools.

Many states allow districts the local option of imposing taxes other than property taxes. While these are typically sales and user taxes and/or payroll taxes, other local taxes authorized for school district collection run the gamut from taxes on raw fish or grain handling to taxes on rural electrification or games of golf. A list of the states allowing miscellaneous local taxes is contained in Table 4-5.

Table 4-5
Local Nonproperty School Taxes Authorized by States

State	Type of Taxes Authorized
Alabama	sales, gasoline, mineral release, amusement, tobacco and alcohol, business licenses, raw fish
Arizona	auto lien, aircraft lien, educational excise, cigarette
Delaware	per capita
Kentucky	poll, whiskey, corporation franchise, utilities, occupation, excise
Louisiana	sales
Maryland	income
Minnesota	grain handling, mortgage registry
Mississippi	severance
Nebraska	license, retail power sales
Nevada	sales, motor vehicle licenses
New Mexico	motor vehicle, business licenses, occupation
New York	sales, income
North Carolina	poll, dog, beer, wine
Oklahoma	rural electrification, severance, auto license, intangibles
Pennsylvania	per capita, income, amusement, sales, occupational, real estate transfer, general business, mechanical devices (vending), golf, pari-mutuel
South Carolina	poll, dog
Tennessee	motor vehicle, sales, tobacco, beer, business privilege
Vermont	poll
Virginia	sales
Wyoming	poll, motor vehicle

Source: Adapted from Moore (1972), pp. 210-211.

These special taxes notwithstanding, the lion's share of local school revenues is derived from property taxes. Moore (1972) estimates 97 to 98 percent of local school revenues are property-based. Furthermore, for independent districts (that is, those districts which are fiscally autonomous from their municipalities), the percentage reliance on property tax rises to 99 percent.

Uses of State School Funds

Revenues from the state available for the schools are funneled to the districts within the context of a number of different programs. Funds may be disbursed for general (basic) educational programs as well as other specialized (categorical) activities. These include transportation, textbooks (and other library and instructional media), vocational education, and capital expenditures (construction). In addition, there are various other activities, at least partially supported by states, which are not discussed here because they are generally funded out of specially generated federal and state accounts. Included in this category are funds for special and compensatory education, school lunches (and breakfasts), driver education, adult community or continuing education, and/or health services. To illustrate, in many states, funds for driver education are provided from a certain percentage of driver's license and vehicle registration fees. Similarly, school meals are, in part, financed through U.S. Department of Agriculture subsidy programs and/or Title I funds.

In terms of the special programs which will be discussed, great variation is noted among states. Not all programs are directly comparable; for example, vocational education programs in some states are aligned with the community/junior college structure, and in other states the entire two-year college program (including other than occupational programs) is attached to the elementary and secondary school systems. Some states fund special purpose programs through the general program, while others separate the monies.

Typically, states place the greatest share of total funds into the general fund for instructional programs and support. There remains a great deal of variation, however, between the states in this regard. Information on the amount of state funds for specific purposes is given in Table 4-6. Some readers may find the absolute number of dollars expended to be of interest and value, but since states vary so greatly in size, composition, wealth, and population, a better means of comparison becomes necessary.

Table 4-7 presents expenditures for particular functions as a percentage of total state education expenditures. This table also indicates total state expenditures per pupil as an additional means of comparison between states.

The absolute number of total dollars expended by states for education ranges from $2.58 billion in New York to $9.2 million in Vermont. When standardized by number of pupils served, however, the gap narrows. With the exception of the

Table 4-6

Amount of State Funds by Specific Purpose, 1971-72 (In Millions of Dollars)

	Total	Basic	Transportation	Texts	Vocational Education	Capital	Other
Alabama	258.6	228.7	a	2.0	12.7	a	15.2
Alaska	112.5	67.1	5.2		0.7[b]	8.6	30.9
Arizona	182.9	75.9			2.1		104.9
Arkansas	116.0	100.5	9.6	1.9	1.0		3.0
California	1,418.7	1,092.3	26.1	19.3	0.6	40.9	239.5
Colorado	159.6	137.1	5.5		7.0		10.0
Connecticut	273.9	131.6	7.4	0.2	12.4	93.9	28.4
Delaware	104.3	77.5	5.8		1.3	15.8	3.9
Florida	712.7	601.0	a	9.0	3.2[b]	31.4	68.1
Georgia	425.7	340.3	a	a	14.9	27.2	43.3
Hawaii	222.9	113.6	3.2	7.4		47.2	51.5
Idaho	48.3	47.9	a		0.4		0.4
Illinois	969.7	766.9	32.9		16.0	70.9	83.0
Indiana	333.1	256.7	18.1		2.1	19.0	37.2
Iowa	211.4	115.0			19.6		76.8
Kansas	126.3	109.6	a		0.4	a	16.3
Kentucky	243.6	240.7	a	2.9	a		
Louisiana	417.7	360.6	a	7.8	3.0[b]		46.3
Maine	65.6	50.3	a		2.3	7.5	5.5
Maryland	467.7	176.7	32.4			217.9	40.7
Massachusetts	312.1	225.0	17.5			43.0	26.6
Michigan	847.4	722.6	32.6			18.6	73.6
Minnesota	644.1	529.3	33.3		34.9		46.6
Mississippi	179.7	142.1	a	3.7	9.8[b]	7.2	16.9
Missouri	325.1	264.8	25.2		6.9	12.4	15.8
Montana	38.4	29.3	1.3		0.5		7.3
Nebraska	43.6	35.0	a		0.1		8.5
Nevada	50.0	50.0	a				0.0
New Hampshire	9.2	2.6			0.2	2.0	4.4
New Jersey	551.1	278.5	35.5		4.7[b]	36.6	195.8
New Mexico	145.2	96.1	8.8	2.7	0.8		36.8
New York	2,582.3	2,345.0	a	17.0		a	220.3
North Carolina	497.7	450.6	4.8[b]	7.7	25.5[b]		9.1
North Dakota	32.0	27.1	a		0.9	0.0	4.0
Ohio	786.9	642.0	49.8		19.3[b]		75.8
Oklahoma	147.6	73.9	a	4.2	2.1[b]		67.4
Oregon	107.1	97.8	a				9.3
Pennsylvania	1,241.1	953.0	46.0		32.7	95.4	114.0
Rhode Island	65.9	55.3				6.1	4.5
South Carolina	216.6	149.2	14.3	3.1	7.1	19.7	23.2

Table 4-6 (cont.)

	Total	Basic	Transportation	Texts	Vocational Education	Capital	Other
South Dakota	18.9	14.8	a		0.5		3.6
Tennessee	246.1	224.5	a	4.7	3.2	10.5	3.2
Texas	979.5	642.1	a	24.0	a		313.4
Utah	128.8	105.4	a	0.5	0.3[b]	3.4	19.2
Vermont	39.1	28.2			1.4	6.8	2.7
Virginia	410.0	267.8	12.5	2.2	12.2		115.3
Washington	356.6	230.1	21.7		5.7[b]	21.0	78.1
West Virginia	153.7	145.2	a		2.8		5.7
Wisconsin	327.1	153.0	13.4	1.3	a		159.4
Wyoming	20.6	19.9	a			0.0	0.7

[a]Indicates that this function is served by general (basic) fund disbursement; no dollar breakdown is available.

[b]Indicates that the amount shown is from categorical grants but is supplemented by disbursements from general (basic) fund.

Source: Adapted from Johns (1972), p. 4.

Table 4-7
State Expenditure Per Student and Percentage of State Funds for Specific Purposes, 1971-72

	State Expenditures per Pupil	Percentage of Total State Funds For:[b]					
		Basic	Transportation	Texts	Vocational Education	Capital	Other
Alabama	321	88.4	—	0.8	4.9	—	5.9
Alaska	1,333	59.6	4.6	—	0.6	7.6	27.5
Arizona	a	41.5	—	—	1.1	—	57.4
Arkansas	251	86.6	8.3	1.6	0.9	—	2.6
California	a	77.0	1.8	1.4	—	2.9	16.9
Colorado	283	85.9	3.4	—	4.4	—	6.2
Connecticut	411	48.0	2.7	0.1	4.5	34.2	10.3
Delaware	773	74.3	5.5	—	1.2	15.1	3.7
Florida	482	84.3	—	1.2	0.4	4.4	9.5
Georgia	389	79.9	—	—	3.5	6.3	10.1
Hawaii	1,214	50.9	1.4	3.3	—	21.1	23.1
Idaho	a	99.1	—	—	0.8	—	0.8
Illinois	a	79.0	3.3	—	1.6	7.3	8.6
Indiana	271	77.0	5.4	—	0.6	5.7	11.2
Iowa	324	54.3	—	—	9.3	—	36.3
Kansas	251	86.7	—	—	0.3	—	12.9
Kentucky	338	98.8	—	1.2	—	—	—
Louisiana	491	86.3	—	1.9	0.7	—	11.1

Table 4-7 (cont.)

	State Expenditures per Pupil	Percentage of Total State Funds For:[b]					
		Basic	Transportation	Texts	Vocational Education	Capital	Other
Maine	a	76.6	–	–	3.5	11.4	8.4
Maryland	a	37.7	6.9	–	–	46.6	8.7
Massachusetts	262	72.0	5.6	–	–	13.8	8.5
Michigan	383	85.2	3.8	–	–	2.2	8.7
Minnesota	a	82.1	5.2	–	5.4	–	7.2
Mississippi	339	79.0	–	2.1	5.5	4.0	9.4
Missouri	318	81.5	7.8	–	2.1	3.8	4.9
Montana	a	76.3	3.4	–	1.3	–	19.0
Nebraska	132	80.3	–	–	0.2	–	19.5
Nevada	384	100.0	–	–	–	–	–
New Hampshire	56	28.2	–	–	2.2	21.7	47.8
New Jersey	a	50.5	6.4	–	0.9	6.6	35.5
New Mexico	510	66.1	6.1	1.9	0.6	–	25.3
New York	a	90.8	–	0.7	–	–	8.5
North Carolina	423	90.5	1.0	1.5	5.1	–	1.8
North Dakota	222	84.7	–	–	2.8	–	12.5
Ohio	323	81.5	6.3	–	2.5	–	9.6
Oklahoma	a	50.0	–	2.8	1.4	–	45.7
Oregon	224	91.3	–	–	–	–	8.7
Pennsylvania	524	76.6	3.7	–	2.6	7.7	9.2
Rhode Island	346	83.9	–	–	–	9.3	6.8
South Carolina	334	68.8	6.6	1.4	3.3	9.1	10.7
South Dakota	114	78.3	–	–	2.6	–	19.0
Tennessee	274	91.2	–	1.9	1.3	4.3	1.3
Texas	348	65.5	–	2.5	–	–	32.0
Utah	421	81.8	–	0.4	0.2	2.6	14.9
Vermont	371	72.1	–	–	3.6	17.4	6.9
Virginia	382	65.3	3.0	0.5	13.0	–	28.1
Washington	443	64.5	6.1	–	1.6	5.9	21.9
West Virginia	381	94.5	–	–	1.8	–	3.7
Wisconsin	327	46.7	4.1	0.4	–	–	48.7
Wyoming	238	96.6	–	–	–	–	3.4

[a]Enrollment data not reported.

[b]Dashes indicate no dollar amount reported for this category in Table 4-6.

Source: Columns 2 thru 5 taken from data in Table 4-6. Column 1 is derived from column 1 in Table 4-6 divided by number of students in membership in that state as reported by Foster and Barr (1972), p. 4.

two noncontiguous states, the remaining states fall within a surprisingly narrow range of one another.

In terms of specific use of funds, the states vary from 100 percent expenditure on the general fund in Nevada to just over 28 percent for this purpose in New Hampshire. Sixteen states place over 85 percent of their educational funds in the general program. Only four states place less than half of their money in the general fund.

Attention should also be drawn to notes *a* and *b* appearing in Table 4-6. These indicate, respectively, that all or some of the state funds for this purpose are furnished to districts *within* the confines of the general program. Additionally, certain other states such as Pennsylvania distribute categorical funds separately, but in the same proportion to the programs' reimbursible costs as the district's subsidy for general purposes bears to general fund reimbursible costs. The importance of this fact is that, to the extent that these funds are distributed in this fashion, they are also equalizing in impact. While funds listed as categorical in the table may or may not be equalizing (depending on legislative mandate), funds emanating from the general fund (in all but flat-grant states) are equalizing—and to the same extent in these special purpose areas as in the primary instructional area.

It should be pointed out that an attempt by a state to place funds in separate categories of school operations may not achieve the implicit purpose of encouraging districts to spend funds in one manner or another because of the fact that "money mixes."[6] For example, state categorical grants for transportation services may supplant local or state general aid funds which otherwise would have been used to pay for such services. Categorical grants only insure that a district spends at least the amount of the categorical grant on the particular service for which a grant is provided. There is no assurance—indeed, it is unlikely—that districts would spend an extra dollar for a specific purpose when an extra dollar of categorical grant for that purpose is provided.

Concluding Comments

This chapter has provided more detailed information about the various state programs of educational finance. Combined with the information presented in the preceding chapter about the mechanics and scope of existing programs, a comprehensive picture of the current situation emerges.

Our study of the 1971-72 state of affairs in state aid to education revealed the following. The Stayer-Haig-Mort Minimum Foundation Plan is clearly the most popular approach to school finance, with thirty-two of the contiguous states currently using variations of this model. Ten states still use flat grants, at least partially, as the core of financial support for the schools. If states which do

6. For an excellent exposition of this issue, consult Goetz (1972), esp. pp. 11-12.

not officially use flat grants but which have minimum guarantees in their equalization plans are added to the flat grant states, most states could also be considered to fall within this group.

Nine states currently operate within the context of the more recent plans—percentage equalizing, guaranteed valuation, or power equalizing. With few exceptions, these states are clustered in the Northeast.

A variety of local nonproperty sources of revenue in states allowing these special taxes were discussed briefly in this chapter, as were the amounts and percentages of funds being used for various school purposes. The great diversity in allocating funds for specific purposes shows that states still attempt to develop their own individual paths to amelioration of educational problems.

The recently enacted plans in Utah, Kansas, Maine, and Montana indicate a hopeful trend toward greater equalization in school finance. It remains to be seen whether such plans are going to work well in these states and whether other states are going to follow suit.[7]

At the same time, the emphasis on *equalization* has resulted in relative laxity regarding matters of *efficiency*. The Kansas plan, for example, clearly eliminates incentives for small districts to reorganize to achieve greater economies of scale. Moreover, it may even encourage districts now operating efficiently (in terms of scale) to reduce their size (e.g., split into two or more districts, if legally feasible) without any financial consequences. Therefore, considerable space is devoted in subsequent chapters to the issue of efficiency and to the manner by which efficiency incentives may be incorporated into the state aid formulas.

---

7. For a discussion of the political difficulties that might arise as a result of drastic changes in school support, see Dimond (1972).

5

Economic Effects of State Aid

The variation in school support systems and amounts of state aid per pupil among the states has been documented in detail in the preceding chapters. But the major assumption behind the drive to reform school support systems is that state aid influences educational outcomes in one form or another. Since educational quality has almost universally been equated to per pupil expenditures, the ultimate test of a good state aid program is its influence on per pupil expenditures.[1] An analysis of such a test is provided in this chapter.

But it is likely that state aid influences other educational parameters. For example, state aid could influence incentives for achieving greater scale economies. Or, nonpublic enrollment rates may be affected. Likewise, state aid could affect the degree to which people are willing to raise revenues from *local* sources and to approve school bonds. An examination of these issues will also be provided in this chapter.

The empirical analysis presented below consists of two main parts. First, a cross-sectional study of the forty-nine states (Hawaii is excluded) is presented. Second, a more disaggregated approach is employed by examining the relationship between state aid and expenditures for counties in Pennsylvania. But before the empirical analysis is presented, a brief review of previous research in this area is provided.

Review of Previous Studies

The earliest study that we could find (Freeman [1953]) shows a negative correlation between state aid and current expenditures per pupil in ADA. Also, the study shows a negative correlation between state aid and local tax burden. (The results are for the late 1940s and early 1950s.) Another study, employing school districts rather than states as the observational unit (Miner [1963]), also demonstrates a negative correlation between state aid and current expenditures per pupil or per capita. The negative correlation remains after other variables are entered into a regression equation. However, only *local* expenditures per pupil are significantly related to state aid (in a negative manner), when other variables are held constant (Miner [1963], Table 4, pp. 98-99). (Miner's results are for 1127 school districts in twenty-three states during 1959-60.)

---

1. Another desirable outcome may be the extent to which the program reduces property tax burden.

A study by Brazer (1959) indicates a positive relationship between state aid and per capita expenditures on education in forty large cities during 1953. The regression coefficient of 0.286 indicates an increase in per capita expenditures of $0.286 for each additional dollar of state aid for education per capita (Brazer [1959], Table 19, pp. 54-55). (The coefficient is statistically significant at the 5 percent level.)

Renshaw's work (1960), employing a cross-section of the states for 1949-50, provides results similar to those of Brazer. But it is shown that the size of the aid coefficient varies with the specification of the regression equation. For example, when per pupil expenditures are determined by state aid, per capita income, and proportion of nonwhites, the coefficient of state aid is 0.1647. When 1953-54 data are employed, with a different set of explanatory variables (including per capita income, "James's estimate of mandated local revenues per pupil in ADA," per pupil state aid, and population density), the coefficient of state aid rises to 0.378. When the nature of the equation (for 1953-54) is changed again, the state aid coefficient rises further to 0.511 (Renshaw [1960], Equations (1), (2), and (3), pp. 171, 172, and 173). Another equation is presented employing changes in variables over the period 1945-49. The results indicate that a change in state aid of one dollar is associated with a change in per pupil expenditures of $0.401. This is similar to the results obtained in the second equation.

The studies mentioned above indicate that state aid is to some extent "substitutive." That is, of a dollar of state aid, at least a portion is diverted from educational expenditures toward other areas or a reduction in tax burden. When the regression coefficient of state aid is *negative*, state aid is said to be *dilutive*. If the coefficient is between 0 and 1, it is both substitutive and stimulative: it stimulates *total* expenditures but substitutes state funds for local funds. A coefficient which is significantly greater than 1 indicates a purely stimulative role for state aid.

The conclusion reached by both Brazer's and Renshaw's analyses (that state aid is both stimulative and substitutive) is also corroborated by Bishop's work (1964). Data for New England school districts for the year 1961-62 indicate, with the exception of New Hampshire, a positive, and statistically significant correlation between state aid and per pupil expenditures. The coefficient for New Hampshire is 0.06, which is not significantly different from zero. For the other states, the coefficient ranges from a low of 0.39 for Maine to a high of 0.80 for Massachusetts.

Bishop argues that use of unweighted data in which large districts are weighted equally with small ones is appropriate when the question to be asked is, "What is likely to be the effect on expenditures *of a school district* of additional state aid?" (p. 139, emphasis supplied). However, if it is desired to assess the impact of state aid on "the state-wide average expenditures per pupil," then it is necessary to make use of weighted data. Bishop employs two variants of weighted data, one in which variables are weighted by the number of pupils, the other in which data are weighted by expenditures. Results of analyses employing weighted data indicate that state aid is generally unrelated to expenditures. Although some coefficients are significantly negative, Bishop argues that they indicate not a dilutive but a substitutive effect: when aid per pupil is associated with lower expenditures per pupil, it is not to be presumed that state aid causes a reduction in educational expenditures but rather that some poor districts receive equalization grants enabling them to reduce their tax burden (p. 135).

The results of the analysis employing weighted data are interpreted by Bishop to indicate that state aid does not have a perceptible effect on expenditures in large districts.

The substitutive-stimulative role of state aid is also confirmed by a study conducted by Sacks and Harris (1964). Using data for the forty-eight contiguous states in 1960, they find a regression coefficient of 0.517 for per capita state aid to local schools. Other explanatory variables are population density, percent urban, and per capita income.

Data for cities and suburbs were utilized by Sacks (1972) to analyze the impact of state aid on educational expenditures. In general, the regression coefficients of state aid indicate, once more, a substitutive-stimulative role for state aid. However, the coefficients in central cities are typically smaller than in the suburbs. When state aid per pupil is combined with income and enrollment ratio to "explain" variations in per pupil expenditures, the state aid coefficient is 0.2253 (not significantly different from zero at the 5 percent level) for central cities and 0.6095 (significant at the 5 percent level) for suburbs. Similar results are obtained when per capita aid and expenditures are examined (Sacks [1972], Table 35, p. 153, and pp. 160-61).

In all of the previously mentioned works (excepting Freeman's) the major statistical technique used to examine the relationship between state aid and expenditure has been single-equation multiple regression. Various variables have been combined to explain variations in per capita or per pupil educational expenditures. It has been argued by several authors that such a technique may produce biased results. If educational expenditures are determined by the interplay of supply and demand forces, then the use of a single-equation approach, combining both demand and supply variables, could lead to a simultaneous-equation bias. In addition, it has been argued that formulation of *ad hoc* equations designed to explain variations in this or that variable without a firm theoretical foundation both as to the choice of variables and the manner by which they are entered into the model is less than satisfactory (Brazer [1970a]).

Two attempts have been made to overcome this problem. One is the work of McMahon (1970), employing demand-for-education and production-of-education functions. The structural equations are transformed into a reduced-form equation, where the ratio of educational expenditures to personal income (by state) becomes a function of demand influences (proportion of persons aged

5-17 and percentage of persons 5-17 not attending school), production costs (pupil/teacher ratio, density, and number of pupils per school district), as well as other variables (such as property values, state and federal aid, percentage of pupils attending high school, and percentage of nonwhites).

McMahon's results with respect to state aid vary with the type of data employed. State aid is not a statistically significant determinant of the ratio expenditures/income in his cross-sectional analysis for 1955-56. On the other hand, the coefficient of the ratio state aid/income is positive, and statistically significant, when time-series data of the ratio expenditures/income for the period 1946-68 are examined. The state aid coefficients in the various versions of the model range from a low of 0.821 to a high of 1.057. These coefficients are substantially higher than the results reported earlier for the various cross-sectional studies.

The final study to be discussed here is a simultaneous-equation model developed by Hu and Booms (1971). The study provides a theoretical foundation to expenditure determination by employing a community welfare analysis.[2] The analysis takes into account competing uses of public funds, factors likely to affect a community's desire for public services (income, social and demographic characteristics, and intergovernmental aid), and the community income constraint (income = private expenditures plus taxes). The model is reduced into a system of equations involving expenditures on each group of local government functions and taxes as endogenous variables (variables to be determined by the model) and income, intergovernmental aids, and a host of sociodemographic factors as exogenous variables (variables which are assumed to be determined outside the model).

The coefficient for state aid to education is 1.027, employing a sample of thirty-one cities with population over 250,000 for the year 1962. The authors are quick to note that the results do not indicate a purely stimulative role for state aid, because the coefficient is not (statistically) significantly different from 1. The results conform to McMahon's time-series findings, but are substantially greater than those reported in earlier studies.

It is quite obvious by now that the body of empirical studies points to a strong link between state aid and educational expenditures. Yet the exact magnitude of the relationship is not clear. Changes in the underlying models and the data base are likely to change the results. At the same time, it is clear that changes in the state aid systems which result in changes in the amount of state aid are likely to have a profound influence on educational expenditures.

The foregoing review included only studies in which state aid to education is included as an explanatory variable in the expenditure equation. There are, in addition, numerous studies that explore the determinants of educational (and other government) expenditures. These studies provide insights regarding the

2. The first to employ a social welfare analysis in studying government expenditures was Henderson (1968).

choice of explanatory variables in the expenditure equation. A study by Booms and Hu (1971) provided the basis for the county model reported below. Among the expenditure-determinants studies, mention should be made of the following (in alphabetical order): Davis (1965), Fabricant (1952), Fisher (1964), Henderson (1968), Hickrod and Sabulao (1969), Hirsch (1960), Horowitz (1968), Morss, Fredland and Hymans (1967), Shapiro (1962), and Sharkansky (1967). Literature reviews have been prepared by Miner (1963), Hickrod (1971), and Hickrod and Sabulao (1969). The most common approach to studying the determinants of government expenditures—the single-equation, least squares method—has been criticized by Morss (1966) and Brazer (1970a).

An Interstate Model

The empirical model presented here provides additional insights regarding the effect of state aid on educational expenditures, employing both a new structure and more recent data. The model also provides a first attempt to study the effect of state aid on three variables: average school size, nonpublic enrollment rates, and bond sales. A fifth variable to be studied is local revenues.

In addition to the state aid variables, each of the variables to be investigated here is also a function of other factors. First, some of the (endogenous) variables mentioned above might influence one another. For instance, per pupil expenditures in a given state are likely to be a function of school size, as several studies (to be discussed in Chapter 6) have indicated. Or, local revenues may be a function of the percentage of enrollment in nonpublic schools. Furthermore, other (exogenous) factors may influence the variables under investigation. For example, the degree of urbanization in the state is likely to affect average school size, local revenues, and per pupil expenditures. Local revenues and expenditures may also be affected by the perceived "quality" of the public schools. Two measures of quality are average teachers' salaries and the student/teacher ratio.

The Model

Denote the five (endogenous) variables which are to be investigated by Y_1, Y_2 ..., Y_5, the variable measuring state aid by $STAID$, and the remaining (exogenous) factors influencing the Y's by X_1, X_2, ..., X_k. The generalized version of the model is then given in a set of five equations:

$$Y_1 = f_1(Y_2, Y_3, \ldots, Y_5; STAID; X_1, X_2, \ldots, X_k) \qquad (5.1)$$
$$Y_2 = f_2(Y_1, Y_3, \ldots, Y_5; STAID; X_1, X_2, \ldots, X_k)$$

.
.
.

$$Y_5 = f_5(Y_1, Y_2, \ldots, Y_4; STAID; X_1, X_2, \ldots, X_k)$$

Since we are interested in the effect of state aid on each of the Y's, regression analysis will be employed to compute a coefficient for *STAID*. But because of the simultaneity in Equation Set (5.1), ordinary-least-squares analysis is likely to provide biased coefficients. Therefore, an attempt is made to modify the equation system so that the two-state least squares (TSLS) technique could be utilized.

The variables chosen for the study have been divided into two categories: endogenous variables (those factors which we seek to explain within the confines of the model) and exogenous variables (those factors which are considered as fixed for the purposes of the model). The five endogenous variables are those under investigation. The exogenous variables include, in addition to *STAID*, such variables as per capita or per pupil personal income, an equalization score, percentage of Negro enrollment in public schools, percentage of urban population, incidence of poverty, and the two school "quality" variables. Both sets of variables are defined in Table 5-1.

In order that the TSLS technique could be applied, it was necessary to modify Equation Set (5.1) so that the equation set would be identifiable. On the basis of a priori reasoning, the Equation Set (5.1) was modified as shown in Equations (5.2) through (5.6):

$$RELSIZE = a_0 + a_1 \%ENNP + a_2 BOND + a_3 REV$$
$$+ a_4 \%TPOPENP + a_5 NEGRO + a_6 URBAN \qquad (5.2)$$
$$+ a_7 INCPOV + a_8 STAID + u_1$$

$$EXP = b_0 + b_1 RELSIZE + b_2 \%ENNP + b_3 BOND$$
$$+ b_4 PPI + b_5 EQUALIZ + b_6 NEGRO \qquad (5.3)$$
$$+ b_7 URBAN + b_8 STAID + b_9 S/T + u_2$$

$$\%ENNP = c_0 + c_1 RELSIZE + c_2 EXP + c_3 REV + c_4 PCI$$
$$+ c_5 EQUALIZ + c_6 NEGRO + c_7 URBAN \qquad (5.4)$$
$$+ c_8 SALARY + c_9 STAID + c_{10} S/T + u_3$$

$$BOND = d_0 + d_1 EXP + d_2 \%ENNP + d_3 REV$$
$$+ d_4 PCI + d_5 EQUALIZ + d_6 NEGRO \qquad (5.5)$$
$$+ d_7 URBAN + d_8 STAID + d_9 S/T + u_4$$

Table 5-1

Means, Standard Deviations, Definitions, and Sources of Variables: Interstate Model

Variable Acronym	Mean	Standard Deviation	Definitions of Variables
Endogenous			
RELSIZE	392.59	144.18	Relative size of schools (pupils in ADA per school), 1967-68
EXP	$625.48	125.83	Current expenditures per pupil in ADA (Average Daily Attendance), 1967-68
%ENNP	0.10	0.061	Percentage of pupils enrolled in nonpublic schools, 1967-68
BOND	$465.99	364.64	Total approved par value of bond issues, 1962-71, per pupil enrolled in public elementary and secondary schools
REV	$379.60	152.26	Local revenue per pupil, 1967-68
Exogenous			
%TPOPENP	23.09	2.12	Percentage of total population enrolled in public schools, 1967-68
PCI	$2,955.10	506.12	Personal income per capita, 1967
PPI	$13,999.59	3,348.94	Personal income per pupil in ADA, 1967
EQUALIZ	5.07	1.12	Equalization score of state, 1968-69
NEGRO	11.74	12.21	Negro enrollment in public schools as a percentage of total enrollment, 1968
URBAN	65.42	14.44	Urban population as a percentage of total population, 1970
INCPOV	13.36	5.57	Incidence of poverty, 1969 (percentage points)
SALARY	$7,161.59	1,025.38	Average teachers' salary, 1967-68
STAID	$275.41	111.42	State aid per pupil in ADA, 1967-68
S/T	0.023	0.0019	Number of students per 1,000 teachers, 1967-68

Sources:

1. Richard H. Barr and Geraldine J. Scott, *Statistics of State School Systems, 1967-68* (Washington, D.C.: U.S. Office of Education, 1970)—for the following variables: *RELSIZE, EXP, REV, %TPOPENP, PCI, PPI, SALARY, STAID,* and *S/T.*

2. Roe L. Johns and Richard G. Salmon, "The Financial Equalization of Public Support Programs in the United States for the Year 1968-69," in *Status and Impact of Educational Finance Programs,* vol. 4, ed. by Roe L. Johns et al. (Gainesville, Florida: National Educational Finance Project, 1971), p. 137—for *EQUALIZ.*

3. U.S. Bureau of the Census, *Statistical Abstract of the United States:* 1969, 1970, and 1971 Editions (Washington, D.C.: Government Printing Office, 1969, 1970, and 1971)—for *NEGRO, URBAN,* and *INCPOV.*

4. Irene A. King, *Bond Sales for Public School Purposes* (Washington, D.C.: U.S. Office of Education, 1972)—for *BOND.*

$$REV = e_0 + e_1 RELSIZE + e_2 \%ENNP + e_3 BOND$$
$$+ e_4 PPI + e_5 EQUALIZ + e_6 NEGRO \qquad (5.6)$$
$$+ e_7 URBAN + e_8 STAID + e_9 S/T + u_5$$

where the lowercase letters, a, b, c, d, and e, are the coefficients which we seek to estimate, whereas the u's represent stochastic error terms.

It is hypothesized in Equation (5.2) that the larger the percentage of pupils enrolled in nonpublic schools, the smaller would the average public school size be, other things equal. It also appears plausible that the variable $BOND$ should be related to school size, but there are two conflicting forces; on the one hand, if proceeds from bond elections are used to build larger schools, the effect on relative size would be positive; on the other hand, if such proceeds are used to reduce crowding by building additional schools (not necessarily of larger average size), then the effect on average school size might be negative. For the same reason, it is not clear a priori how REV and $RELSIZE$ are related.

Among the exogenous variables in the set, five were included in the equation. for $STAID$, a negative coefficient is expected, as additional state aid might reduce incentives for school reorganization.[3] The variable $\%TPOPENP$ (percentage of population enrolled in public schools) indicates the relative demand for public educational facilities in the state. The greater the demand, the greater the average school size is expected to be, other things equal. It is further expected that school size will be directly related to the percentage of black enrollment because of the observed overcrowding in areas where large concentrations of blacks exist. Also, because urban areas are likely to have far greater population densities, greater urbanization should be positively related to school size, other factors remaining the same. Finally, the variable $INCPOV$ has been added to the equation to account for the expected negative relationship between $RELSIZE$ and poverty in states where considerable rural poverty exists.

Concerning Equation (5.3), the determinants of EXP include three endogenous and six exogenous variables. Because scale economies are expected to occur in public school operations, the hypothesized relationship between $RELSIZE$ and EXP is negative. (A parabolic relationship, indicating a U-shaped relation between the two variables, was found to be nonsignificant; hence, only the linear term has been left in the equation.) It is also hypothesized that the greater the percentage of pupils enrolled in nonpublic schools, the higher would EXP be because local educational revenues collected from all citizens without regard to school enrollment would be distributed over a relatively smaller student population. Furthermore, it is expected that higher values of $BOND$ would be directly correlated with EXP because the variable $BOND$ is indicative

---

3. An examination of recent aid systems shows both incentives and disincentives for reorganization. The trend appears to be in favor of more disincentives—rewards for maintaining small schools.

of the citizens' attitude toward education. If they are willing to approve bond issues, they would probably also desire higher per pupil expenditures.

The variable *PPI* is included in the equation to account for differences in wealth per pupil among states. It would also be interesting to compare the results of this study with those of other studies concerning the income elasticity of educational expenditures. It is hypothesized that a higher equalization score would be commensurate with higher per pupil expenditures, that expenditures are lower in states with large black enrollments but higher in urban areas, and that greater school quality requires more expenditures, so that *S/T* and *EXP* should be negatively correlated. A positive coefficient for *STAID* is expected.

Three endogenous and seven exogenous variables are included in Equation (5.4). It is hypothesized that as school size increases, especially because of overcrowding, more parents will send their children to private schools. But if per pupil expenditures are greater, fewer parents will seek private education for their children. The effect of *REV* on *%ENNP* is not unambiguously clear. On the one hand, more local revenues imply more local expenditures, with the likelihood that greater quality in public schools would encourage parents to send their children to public schools. However, if *REV* is directly related to community wealth, the relationship between *REV* and *%ENNP* might be positive. It is possible, of course, that *REV* might be greater not because of greater wealth but because of greater tax effort, implying a more favorable attitude toward—and therefore greater rates of attendance in—public education.

Since *PCI* provides a measure of average wealth, it is expected to be directly related to nonpublic enrollment rates. It is also hypothesized that greater equalization would lead to greater nonpublic enrollments, as would be the case for greater levels of the variables *NEGRO* and *URBAN*. On the other hand, greater school "quality" in the form of higher salaries or *lower S/T* rates should be negatively related to private enrollment rates. The a priori effect of state aid is not clear: on the one hand, if more state aid is synonymous with greater *equalization*, the effect on *%ENNP* might be positive. On the other hand, if more state aid is synonymous with greater educational *quality*, the coefficient might be negative. Hence, no a priori expectations are stated in this case.

Three endogenous and six exogenous variables form the specification of Equation (5.5). It is hypothesized that *EXP* is indicative of a community's attitude toward support of public education; hence a direct relationship between *EXP* and *BOND* is anticipated. Conversely, if a greater proportion of pupils attend nonpublic schools, parents would be more reluctant to support the public schools. It also appears that greater local revenues imply less need for bond financing. However, since *REV* could also be a proxy for local capacity to absorb the financing of the bond as well as community's attitude, it is not clear what sort of relationship one should expect between *REV* and *BOND*.

If per capita income (*PCI*) is indicative of a community's attitudes, a positive correlation between *PCI* and *BOND* would be expected. Such a relationship would be strengthened when it is recognized that wealthier communities are likely to be able to absorb the cost of bond financing with relatively greater ease than is the case in poorer districts. On the other hand, it is expected that a higher value of *EQUALIZ* would result in a lower *BOND* value since incentives for long-term indebtedness by local governments are reduced. Moreover, because of the general deterioration of the urban areas in the United States, especially in cities where the percentage of nonwhite population is relatively large, it is expected that a negative correlation between *NEGRO* and *BOND*, as well as between *URBAN* and *BOND*, will be found. Since a smaller *S/T* requires more facilities, a negative relationship between *S/T* and *BOND* is expected. Finally, since state aid could be substituted for local financing, a negative coefficient for *STAID* is hypothesized.

Three endogenous and six exogenous variables have been included in Equation (5.6). The first hypothesis is that because of anticipated scale economies, greater school size would be negatively related to local revenue requirements, other things equal. The effect of *%ENNP* on *REV* is not unambiguously clear. On the one hand, higher private enrollment rates indicate unfavorable attitudes toward the public schools, pointing to a smaller level of *REV*. On the other hand, states with higher private enrollment rates may also be associated with relatively wealthier districts, in which case *REV* for an equal tax effort should be greater. A positive sign is expected for the *BOND* variable for two reasons. First, the variable is indicative of community attitudes. Second, a greater value for *BOND* is also indicative of greater debt service requirement, which should increase the demand for local revenues.

Per pupil income, as a measure of wealth, should be positively correlated with *REV*. But *EQUALIZ* is hypothesized to be negatively correlated with *REV* because greater equalization is expected to reduce the incentives of many school districts to raise revenues from local sources. It is also hypothesized that local revenues in areas with higher levels of the *NEGRO* and *URBAN* variables would be smaller and that greater school "quality," measured by *S/T*, would require greater local revenues; hence, *S/T* and *REV* should be negatively correlated. Finally, since the literature review produced both positive and negative coefficients for the effect of state aid on local expenditures, no a priori hypothesis is advanced in this case.

A summary of the hypotheses regarding the expected signs of the regression coefficients of Equations (5.2) through (5.6) is provided in Table 5-2.

Data

To implement the model, data have been assembled from various sources, principally publications of the United States Office of Education. The unit of observation is the state, and data are available for forty-nine states. (Hawaii has

Table 5-2
Expected Signs of Coefficients of Equations (5.2) through (5.6)

Equation	Dependent Variable	RELSIZE	EXP	%ENNP	BOND	REV	%TPOPENP	PCI	PPI	EQUALIZ	NEGRO	URBAN	INCPOV	SALARY	STAID	S/T
(5.2)	RELSIZE			−	?	?	+				+	+	−		−	
(5.3)	EXP	−		+	+		+	+		+	−	+			+	−
(5.4)	%ENNP	+	−		?	?		+	+	+	+	+	−	−	?	+
(5.5)	BOND		+			+	?	+	+	−	−	−	−			
(5.6)	REV	−		?			+	+	+	−	−	−	−		?	−

Note: For definition of acronyms, see Table 5-1. The symbol "?" indicates that an expected sign is not unambiguously clear, a priori. A blank space indicates that the independent variable was not included in the equation.

been excluded because it is essentially one large school district and therefore is not suitable for the present analysis.) The definitions of the variables used in this study—along with some descriptive statistics—are provided in Table 5-1. A complete zero-order correlation matrix is provided in Table 5-3.

Although the data are (with exceptions) for the year 1967-68 and hence do not portray the *current* state of affairs in public education, the relationships which we seek to derive are probably as relevant today as they were during the 1967-68 period—and this despite the tremendous changes that have occurred since that period in educational finance and administration.

Regression Results

The regression results are reported in Table 5-4. For each of the Equations (5.2) through (5.6), the table reports the coefficients obtained when the ordinary-least-squares (OLS) estimation procedure was employed—that is, considering each equation independent of the others—as well as the coefficients derived when the two-stage-least-squares (TSLS) estimation procedure was employed—that is, when Equations (5.2) through (5.6) are considered as a system of equations, and the coefficients derived from the TSLS procedure account for the interdependence among the equations.

Average School Size. The interstate data explain almost 80 percent of the variations in average school size. Contrary to hypothesis, state aid appears to contribute positively to that variable. Since our study of the state aid formulas showed little, if any, incentives for attaining optimal school size, it is difficult to conclude that more state aid is the *cause* of larger school size. A possible explanation of the positive correlation is that states that happen to have larger schools are the ones that also happen to give more aid to local districts. Nevertheless, the negative correlation that we expected was definitely refuted by the data in both the OLS and TSLS versions of the model.

Concerning the other explanatory variables, the data provide different results for the OLS and TSLS versions. When the OLS version is employed, three variables are statistically significant at the 0.01 level: *NEGRO, URBAN*, and *INCPOV*. As hypothesized, the sign of the coefficients of both *URBAN* and *NEGRO* is positive, and the sign of *INCPOV* is negative. This is also the case when the TSLS version is used.

When the TSLS technique is employed, two other variables become statistically significant: *%ENNP* and *%TPOPENP*. The results suggest that, as expected, when enrollments in nonpublic schools are greater, average public school size is likely to be smaller. On the other hand, contrary to expectations, the data indicate that a greater relative demand for education, measured by the percentage of total population enrolled in public schools, is associated with smaller school size.

Table 5-3
Zero-Order Correlation Matrix for Endogenous and Exogenous Variables: Interstate Model

	Endogenous Variables					Exogenous Variables									
	RELSIZE	EXP	%ENNP	BOND	REV	%TPOPENP	PCI	PPI	EQUALIZ	NEGRO	URBAN	INCPOV	SALARY	STAID	S/T
Endogenous															
RELSIZE	1.000														
EXP	0.210	1.000													
%ENNP	0.086	0.550	1.000												
BOND	−0.170	0.516	0.041	1.000											
REV	−0.087	0.646	0.662	0.255	1.000										
Exogenous															
%TPOPENP	−0.259	−0.364	−0.729	0.142	−0.408	1.000									
PCI	0.301	0.857	0.567	0.499	0.700	−0.412	1.000								
PPI	0.354	0.800	0.765	0.267	0.698	−0.745	0.896	1.000							
EQUALIZ	0.174	−0.022	−0.154	0.076	−0.425	0.154	−0.141	−0.138	1.000						
NEGRO	0.489	−0.377	−0.261	−0.360	−0.561	−0.097	−0.358	−0.209	0.177	1.000					
URBAN	0.645	0.479	0.368	0.146	0.400	−0.257	0.650	0.624	−0.039	−0.072	1.000				
INCPOV	−0.010	−0.585	−0.503	−0.292	−0.680	0.240	−0.704	−0.619	0.158	0.666	−0.421	1.000			
SALARY	0.480	0.815	0.369	0.524	0.468	−0.227	0.868	0.714	0.064	−0.259	0.668	−0.581	1.000		
STAID	0.532	0.419	−0.031	0.135	−0.333	0.021	0.252	0.187	0.440	0.238	0.230	0.057	0.475	1.000	
S/T	0.374	−0.594	−0.441	−0.294	−0.578	0.213	−0.435	−0.420	0.218	0.452	−0.041	0.417	−0.209	0.090	1.000

Table 5-4

Regression Coefficients and *t*-Ratios (in Parentheses) for Single-Equation (OLS) and Simultaneous-Equation (TSLS) Systems: Interstate Model

Equation	Dependent Variable	Endogenous					Independent Variables		
		RELSIZE	EXP	%ENNP	BOND	REV	%TPOPENP	PCI	PPI
1a (OLS)	RELSIZE			−456.47 (1.69)	206.36 (1.03)	0.29c (1.73)	−9.48 (1.28)		
1b (TSLS)				−2018.28b (2.23)	−0.018 (0.34)	0.22 (0.56)	−41.91a (19.47)		
2a (OLS)	EXP	0.19c (1.98)		−44.51 (0.25)	0.074a (3.47)				0.018a (4.38)
2b (TSLS)		0.28 (0.70)		1347.14 (0.90)	0.23c (1.87)				−0.006 (0.24)
3a (OLS)	%ENNP	0.000093 (0.78)	0.0003c (1.78)			300.38 (1.08)	0.000065 (1.61)		
3b (TSLS)		0.00089b (2.18)	0.00077c (1.95)			17.86 (0.012)	0.000035 (0.55)		
4a (OLS)	BOND		0.96 (0.92)	−2284.13b (2.48)		0.028 (0.85)	0.24 (1.00)		
4b (TSLS)			2.70 (1.24)	−4791.11b (2.94)		0.10 (0.84)	0.32 (1.23)		
5a (OLS)	REV	0.29c (1.73)		300.38 (1.08)	0.028 (0.85)				0.018a (2.80)
5b (TSLS)		0.22 (0.56)		17.86 (0.012)	0.10 (0.84)				0.022 (0.92)

[a]Statistically significant at the 0.01 level, two-tailed test.

[b]Statistically significant at the 0.05 level, two-tailed test.

[c]Statistically significant at the 0.10 level, two-tailed test.

[d]R^2 = coefficient of determination adjusted for degrees of freedom. R^2 is taken from the OLS runs; its meaning for the TSLS runs is not theoretically clear.

[e]SEE = standard error of estimate; also taken only from the OLS runs.

Expenditures Per Pupil. The data confirm the expected relationship between state aid and *EXP*. For each $1.00 of state aid, expenditures per pupil are likely to increase between $0.34 (OLS) and $0.36 (TSLS). The coefficients are statistically significant at the 0.01 and 0.10 levels for the OLS and TSLS versions, respectively. These results suggest that state aid is likely to be both stimulative and substitutive: on the one hand, more state aid implies higher expenditures (stimulative); on the other, the results suggest that *local* expenditures are reduced by $0.66 (OLS) or $0.64 (TSLS) for each $1.00 of state aid.

The coefficients of the other explanatory variables differ in size and significance depending on whether the OLS or TSLS methods are used. Beginning with the OLS estimates, five other variables are found to be statistically significant: *RELSIZE, BOND, PPI, NEGRO,* and *S/T*. Except for *RELSIZE*, the signs of the coefficients confirm the expectations depicted in Table 5-2. The positive sign for *RELSIZE* is surprising; it indicates that, other things the same, larger school size is associated with higher per pupil expendi-

| Independent Variables | | | | | | | | | | |
EQUALIZ	NEGRO	URBAN	INCPOV	SALARY	STAID	S/T	INTERCEPT	$\bar{R}^2$ [d]	SEE [e]	F
	5.62ᵃ	5.75ᵃ	−5.55ᵃ		0.41ᵃ		206.86			
	(4.44)	(7.20)	(2.84)		(4.38)			0.79	65.86	27.00ᵃ
	4.20ᶜ	6.40	−7.60ᵇ		0.40ᵃ		1097.66			
	(1.87)	(5.97)	(2.02)		(3.33)					
−3.83	−2.38ᵃ	−0.80			0.34ᵃ	−2175.12ᵃ	790.45			
(0.59)	(3.22)	(1.01)			(4.29)	(4.75)		0.88	42.69	41.99ᵃ
−13.38	−1.03	−0.56			0.36ᶜ	−16420.16	765.15			
(0.97)	(0.40)	(0.23)			(1.70)	(1.20)				
0.0041	−0.00020	0.00033		−0.00089ᶜ	−0.00015	−0.65	−0.02			
(0.55)	(0.21)	(0.35)		(1.98)	(1.44)	(0.10)		0.35	0.04	3.90ᵃ
0.0091	−0.0040	−0.0034		−0.000088ᵇ	−0.00048ᵇ	−2.95	0.22			
(0.85)	(1.71)	(1.49)		(2.66)	(2.57)	(0.21)				
56.84	−2.78	−7.09			−0.87	−4853.46	−1012.44			
(1.30)	(0.65)	(1.67)			(1.46)	(0.13)		0.38	286.74	4.29ᵃ
66.31	−1.60	−4.62			−1.43ᶜ	19830.68	−1780.68			
(1.54)	(0.37)	(1.02)			(1.86)	(0.38)				
−16.31	−4.23ᵃ	−0.27			−0.54ᵃ	−17999.77ᵇ	690.49			
(1.63)	(3.69)	(0.22)			(4.41)	(2.48)		0.81	66.18	23.90ᵃ
−18.46	−3.25	−0.067			−0.58ᵃ	−15034.51	593.44			
(1.39)	(1.31)	(0.028)			(2.79)	(1.20)				

tures. This result is in sharp contrast to numerous studies indicating just the opposite. It is possible, however, that the measure of school size used here is inadequate and that the unit of observation—the state—may not be the appropriate one for discerning scale effects.

The coefficient for per pupil income (0.018) suggests that for a $1.00 increment in *PPI*, expenditures would rise by only $0.018. At the mean levels of *EXP* and *PPI*, this would imply an income elasticity of 0.399.[4] This is higher than Miner's estimate of 0.23 (Miner [1963], Table 5, p. 107) but lower than either the supply or demand elasticities found by Booms and Hu (1971) (between 0.7 and 0.8) and much lower than the unit elasticity found by Sacks ([1972], p. 165).

The results also confirm the hypotheses that lower levels of expenditures are

---

4. The income elasticity of educational expenditures is defined by $(\partial EXP/\partial PPI)$ · (PPI/EXP). Since $\partial EXP/\partial PPI$ is given by the coefficient of *PPI* in Equation (5.3), the income elasticity at the mean of *EXP* and *PPI* is given by $0.018(14,000/625) = 0.3996$.

associated with higher levels of the *NEGRO* variable and that higher educational "quality" (in terms of the variable *S/T*) requires higher per pupil expenditures, other things being the same. It should also be pointed out that the sign of the coefficient of *EQUALIZ* was negative, contrary to expectations—as is the case for *URBAN*—but neither coefficient is statistically significant.

When the TSLS estimates are considered, none of the explanatory variables is significant at the 0.05 level. The only variables that have relatively large *t*-ratios (significant at the 0.10 level) are *BOND* and *STAID*.

Nonpublic Enrollment Rates. A single-equation model to predict nonpublic enrollment rates (*%ENNP*) does not appear to perform well when the interstate data are applied to it. The overall predictive power, measured by $\overline{R}^2$, is relatively weak (only 0.35), and in addition, none of the coefficients is significant at the 0.05 level. The two variables with highest *t*-ratios (significant at the 0.10 level) are *EXP* and *SALARY*. The positive sign for the coefficient of *EXP* is contrary to expectation, but the negative sign for *SALARY* confirms our hypothesis. Concerning the *STAID* variable, it is found that state aid is negatively related to nonpublic enrollment rates; however, the coefficient is not statistically significant.

When the TSLS estimates are reviewed, the results appear to be more encouraging. Three variables are significant at the 0.05 level: *RELSIZE*, *SALARY*, and *STAID*. The coefficient of *EXP* is significant at the 0.10 level. The coefficient of *STAID* is, again, negative, and the signs of the coefficients of *RELSIZE* and *SALARY* are consistent with a priori expectations. The negative sign of *STAID* provides a measure of credence to the hypothesis that state aid has a lesser impact on equalization than an overall improvement in the quality of education.

Approved Value of Bond Issues. The results for this equation are also less than satisfactory. Only 0.38 percent of the variation in *BOND* is explained by the equation, and only one variable, *%ENNP*, has a statistically significant coefficient. The results suggest that the only significant determinant of bond sales is the percentage of the population enrolled in nonpublic schools. This is consistent with recent reports of school bond election results in Detroit and other areas with large nonpublic enrollments. The small value of $\overline{R}^2$ is probably due to the fact that the equation does not include legal-institutional factors which influence the process by which bond sales are determined.

When the TSLS estimates are used, the coefficient of *STAID* is significantly negative at the 0.10 level, indicating lower bond sales in states where higher state aid is given. This is consistent with our a priori expectations.

Local Revenue. The OLS estimates produce three significant estimators of *REV*: *NEGRO, STAID,* and *S/T.* As expected, states with greater black enrollments are likely to produce less local revenues. Also, the more state aid, the less local revenues will be raised, confirming our earlier results indicating that some substitution of state for local funds takes place. Finally, the data confirm that greater school "quality" (measured by S/T) requires more local revenues.

Although the signs of the coefficients remain the same, their statistical significance is altered when the TSLS estimates are used. The only variable to retain statistical significance is $STAID$; all of the other variables have nonsignificant coefficients.

The model provides several insights into the economic effects of state aid. With the exception of average school size, our a priori expectations of such effects were confirmed by the analysis. The results indicate that a greater level of state aid is associated with greater per pupil expenditures, lower local revenues for education, lower rates of nonpublic enrollments, and lower bond sales. A surprising result is that school size is positively associated with the amount of state aid.

An interesting aspect of the results presented in Table 5-4 is the difference between the OLS and TSLS estimates. One cannot say which of the methods provides more satisfactory results. What can be said is that the TSLS estimates clearly differ from the OLS estimates—and sometimes the differences are quite large—indicating that the OLS method is likely to produce biased estimates.[5]

The only adverse effect of state aid that the data reveal is its impact on local incentives to raise revenue on a short- or long-term basis (REV and $BOND$, respectively). It appears to have a favorable effect on school size, expenditures, and public enrollments. Nevertheless, the state aid distribution formulas do not explicitly provide for incentives for scale and quality effects. Possible courses of action to provide for such incentives are discussed in Chapters 6 and 7.

An Intrastate Model: Pennsylvania Counties

An important limitation of the study is the lack of a measure indicating the manner by which state aid is distributed. The inclusion of the variable $EQUALIZ$ was an attempt to remedy this problem, but both the results and an examination of the method used to obtain the scores indicate the shortcomings of that variable. An analysis devoted exclusively to a single state (Pennsylvania, in our case) would overcome this difficulty.

Another important limitation of the interstate model is that it is too aggregative. Decisions about expenditures, enrollments, school size, and so forth, are made locally. To understand the underlying behavioral patterns of local education organizations one would have to analyze data concerning such units.

---

5. It is beyond the scope of this report to discuss the advantages and disadvantages of each method. For an excellent summary, see Johnston (1972), pp. 408-420.

In what follows, we present an analysis of sixty-seven Pennsylvania counties for 1970. The model was developed by Clyde (1973) and the information presented here is based on his analysis.

The principle objective of Clyde's study was to obtain supply and demand. schedules for local educational expenditures in Pennsylvania counties. Although the school district—the primary decision unit in public education—is not always synonymous with the county, data availability restricted the application of the model to counties. A parallel analysis of school districts would, of course, be highly desirable.

The Model

One interesting aspect of the model is that state aid is included as an endogenous variable (determined *within* the model). The reason for this is that the state aid formula for Pennsylvania is of the percentage equalizing type, so that state aid is both a determinant of, and is determined (to some extent) by, school expenditures. The complete model is presented in Equations (5.7) through (5.11), and the variable acronyms are defined in Table 5-5.

$$EXPPC \text{ (demand)} = a_0 + a_1 PEO + a_2 PTR + a_3 PI$$
$$+ a_4 PPO-17 + a_5 PPO-17E + a_6 ME \qquad (5.7)$$
$$+ a_7 PHSGAC + a_8 MIGR + U_1$$

$$EXPPC \text{ (supply)} = \beta_0 + \beta_1 AIDPC + \beta_2 PTR + \beta_3 PI \qquad (5.8)$$
$$+ \beta_4 DEBT + \beta_5 RELW + U_2$$

$$AIDPC = \gamma_0 + \gamma_1 EXPPC + \gamma_2 SEC + \gamma_3 POOR \qquad (5.9)$$
$$+ \gamma_4 TRANS + \gamma_5 RELW + U_3$$

$$PEO = \delta_0 + \delta_1 URBAN + U_4 \qquad (5.10)$$

$$EXPPC \text{ (demand)} = EXPPC \text{ (supply)} \qquad (5.11)$$

The lowercase (Greek) letters are the coefficients to be estimated by the two-stage-least squares (TSLS) method, and U_1, U_2, U_3, and U_4 are stochastic error terms.

The model contains five endogenous and twelve exogenous variables. The endogenous variables are: expenditures per capita demanded, expenditure per capita supplied, per capita state aid, percentage of local employees in jobs other than education, and the nominal property tax rate. The tax rate serves as a price variable in the demand and supply equations for public funds, following the model presented by Booms and Hu (1971). The fifth equation (Equation [5.11]) is an equilibrium condition needed to close the model and will be ignored in subsequent discussions.

Equation (5.7) specifies the expected relationship between a community's demand for educational services and other factors. It is hypothesized that a greater local effort in noneducational areas competes with educational goals, and hence a negative coefficient for PEO is expected. If PTR is a good proxy for the price a community must pay for educational expenditures, then a negative coefficient for PTR would be hypothesized. Since the variables PI, PPO-17, PPO-17E, and ME are proxies for a community's perceived attitude toward education, the pool of persons seeking public education, and a measure of educational "quality" (PHSGAC), it appears reasonable to hypothesize positive relationships between each of these variables and demand for expenditures. Finally, when a community experiences net out-migration, chances are that it will continue to expect further out-migration, resulting in a measure of reluctance to invest in public education (Weisbrod [1964], pp. 104-107). Hence a negative coefficient for MIGR is anticipated.

The following hypotheses are made with respect to Equation (5.8). Regarding the state aid variable, our review of the literature and results of the interstate model indicate the likelihood of a negative coefficient because the dependent variable is *local* expenditures. However, it is possible that state aid in Pennsylvania is purely stimulative (implying a positive coefficient), hence no a priori hypothesis about AIDPC is made here. A positive coefficient is expected for PTR (on the basis of simple economic theory regarding the relationship between price and supply). The coefficient of PI should also be positive, indicating the ability of the community to supply funds for public purposes. Also, the DEBT variable indicates the extent of borrowing and hence the availability of local funds for education from nontax sources. Finally, because most educational funds in Pennsylvania are raised through property taxation, it is expected that the greater a community's relative wealth (RELW), the greater would be the supply of educational funds.

The state aid equation (Equation [5.9]) embodies some of the major features of the Pennsylvania aid system. A positive coefficient for EXPPC is expected because of the provision rewarding local effort. Positive coefficients are also hypothesized for SEC, POOR, and TRANS, because secondary students are weighted higher than elementary students, a provision is made for extra aid to areas with greater incidence of poverty, and transportation aid is an important element of the aid plan. Finally, the equalizing portion of the formula indicates a negative correlation between RELW and state aid.

The final equation is for the percentage of employees in jobs other than education. Only one explanatory variable is included here—URBAN—and a positive correlation between URBAN and PEO is hypothesized.

Table 5-5
Means, Standard Deviations, Definitions, and Sources of Variables for County Model

Acronym	Unit of Measurement	Mean	Standard Deviation	Definition of Variable
Endogenous				
EXPPC	dollars	50.67	20.36	local current educational expenditures per capita
AIDPC	dollars	101.36	29.21	state aid per capita
PEO	whole pct. points	28.79	8.39	percentage of local government employees in jobs other than education
PTR	percent	0.043	0.0144	nominal property tax rate
Exogenous				
PI	whole pct. points	38.65	9.80	percentage of families with annual income of $10,000 or more
PPO-17	whole pct. points	32.17	3.83	percentage of population 0-17 years of age
PPO-17E	whole pct. points	70.28	7.39	percentage of population 0-17 years of age enrolled in public schools
ME	years	23.22	1.21	median school years completed by the adult population (sum of male and female averages)

PHSGAC	whole pct. points	39.30	7.06	percentage of 1969 high school graduates attending college in 1970
DEBT	dollars	20.48	5.43	debt service for public schools per capita
SEC	whole pct. points	46.54	1.95	percentage of public school enrollment in secondary schools
POOR	whole pct. points	11.52	3.92	percentage of population 0-17 years of age living in families with annual income of $2,000 or less
TRANS	dollars	9.44	4.64	educational transportation costs per capita
RELW	percent	0.91	0.27	market valuation of real property per capita divided by state average
URBAN	whole pct. points	42.01	26.66	percentage population in urban areas
MIGR	whole pct. points	5.01	4.58	percentage change in population (1960-70) due to net out-migration

Sources: The data were obtained from the following sources: Bureau of the Census, *Current Population Reports*, Series P-25, no. 461, "Population Estimates and Projections," June 28, 1971; Bureau of Statistics, *1972 Penna. Statistical Abstract* (14th edition): Bureau of the Census, Census of Pop. 1970, *General Social and Economic Characteristics*, Final Report PC (1)-C40 (Penna.); *Statistical Report of the Secretary of Education* (Pa.), Series No. 17 for the school year ending June 30, 1970; Bureau of the Census, General Population the school year ending June 30, 1970; *Bureau of the Census, General Population Census of Pennsylvania*. The table is based on Clyde (1973), Table 1.

Data

Data for the county model have been obtained for sixty-seven Pennsylvania counties for the year 1970. Definitions of variables, summary statistics, and data sources are documented in Table 5-5. The complete zero-order correlation matrix for the data is presented in Table 5-6.

Results

The TSLS technique has been utilized to obtain estimates for the parameters of Equations (5.7) through (5.10). The model appears to provide good statistical fit for Equations (5.8) and (5.9), a reasonably good fit for Equation (5.10)—considering the fact that only one explanatory variable is included—and a disappointing fit for Equation (5.7). The complete results are given in Table 5-7.

Some of the hypotheses regarding the demand equation for educational expenditures are not supported by the data. In particular, the positive coefficient for *PTR* is puzzling. Also, the positive coefficient for *PEO* is contrary to hypothesis. It could be that the demand for noneducational public services, while creating a measure of competition for educational funds, is also a proxy for a community's ability and willingness to buy educational services. Also, the coefficient of *ME* is negative, contrary to hypothesis, but it is not significantly different from zero.

An interesting finding is the negative coefficient for *MIGR*, corroborating Weisbrod's theory and results. However ,the coefficient is not statistically significant at the 5 percent level.

Of particular interest to this volume is the negative coefficient for *AIDPC* in the supply for expenditure equation. It indicates a substitution of $0.12 out of each dollar of state aid. This is a far smaller level of substitution than the average amount for all states that was found in the interstate model. The figure is also very close to McMahon's results discussed earlier. In addition, all of the hypotheses regarding Equation (5.8) receive a measure of support in the results (Equation 2 of Table 5-7), although only the coefficients of *PI* and *RELW* are statistically significant at the 5 percent level.

Two surprising results are shown in Equation 3 of Table 5-7: the coefficients of *SEC* and *POOR* are negative. However, neither of these coefficients are statistically different from zero at the 5 percent level. Also, the coefficient of *EXPPC* indicates that for each dollar of local effort state aid rises by almost one-half of one dollar. Again, the coefficient is not statistically significant at the 5 percent level. In addition, the results indicate handsome benefits for transportation expenses: for each dollar of transportation costs per capita, aid rises by $5.57 per capita. Obviously, the transportation costs variable must have captured the effect of other, unspecified factors, for it is highly unlikely that the

Table 5-6
Zero-Order Correlation Matrix for County Variables

	Endogenous Variables								Exogenous Variables							
	EXPPC	AIDPC	PEO	PTR	PI	PPO-17	PPO-17E	ME	PHSGAC	DEBT	SEC	POOR	TRANS	RELW	URBAN	MIGR
Endogenous																
EXPPC	1.00	-0.62	0.23	0.41	0.77	0.00	-0.29	0.41	0.65	0.20	-0.57	-0.61	-0.32	0.82	0.47	-0.35
AIDPC		1.00	-0.46	-0.13	-0.54	0.50	0.52	-0.18	-0.47	0.32	-0.00	0.44	0.75	-0.47	-0.60	0.39
PEO			1.00	-0.25	0.19	-0.19	-0.56	0.04	0.32	-0.30	0.00	0.03	-0.42	0.11	0.67	0.21
PTR				1.00	0.43	0.07	-0.04	0.31	0.29	0.19	0.12	-0.29	-0.01	0.31	0.08	-0.15
Exogenous																
PI					1.00	-0.00	-0.39	0.50	0.73	0.31	-0.05	-0.68	-0.47	0.55	0.62	-0.45
PPO-17						1.00	-0.24	-0.04	0.02	0.40	0.04	-0.16	0.27	-0.06	0.00	0.34
PPO-17E							1.00	-0.05	-0.43	0.22	-0.13	0.33	0.58	-0.02	-0.74	-0.13
ME								1.00	0.53	0.24	0.18	-0.48	-0.17	0.30	0.32	-0.27
PHSGAC									1.00	0.15	0.07	-0.51	-0.37	0.41	0.65	-0.30
DEBT										1.00	-0.17	-0.14	0.25	0.17	-0.05	-0.01
SEC											1.00	-0.18	-0.11	-0.22	0.12	0.28
POOR												1.00	0.40	-0.47	-0.47	0.50
TRANS													1.00	-0.00	0.15	-0.76
RELW														1.00	0.14	-0.43
URBAN															1.00	-0.02
MIGR																1.00

Source: Clyde (1973), Table 3.

Table 5-7

Regression Coefficients and t-Ratios (in Parentheses) for County TSLS Model

Equation	Dependent Variable	EXPPC	AIDPC	PEO	PTR	PI	PPO-17	PPO-17E	ME	PHSGAC	DEBT	SEC	POOR	TRANS	RELW	URBAN	MIGR	Intercept	R^2	F
															Independent Variables					
1.	EXPPC (demand)			1.28[a] (2.24)	1187.50[a] (2.06)	0.48 (0.86)	0.92 (1.22)	0.52 (1.15)	-1.76 (0.82)	0.37 (0.79)							-1.14 (1.54)	-90.72	.36	4.06
2.	EXPPC (supply)		-0.12[b] (1.82)		143.97 (0.59)	0.70[a] (2.79)					0.18 (0.69)				39.07[a] (7.60)			-9.34	.85	66.92
3.	AIDPC	0.49 (1.61)										-1.21 (1.24)	-0.72 (1.15)	5.57[a] (10.30)	-87.72[a] (4.54)			168.75	.77	40.07
4.	PEO															0.21[a] (7.37)		19.94	.45	52.73

[a]Significant at the 5 percent level, two-tailed test
[b]Significant at the 10 percent level, two-tailed test
Source: Clyde (1973), Table 2.

state will pay more than $5 in aid per dollar of transportation costs. Finally, the results indicate a good measure of equalization: for each 1 percent in property valuation over the average state valuation, aid decreases by about $0.88 per capita. For example, a district with a relative wealth ratio of 1:2 would get $43.86 more aid per capita than a district with a relative wealth ratio of unity. This is a difference in aid amounting to more than 40 percent of the average per capita state aid ($101.36).

The results for Equation (5.10), reported in Equation 4 of Table 5-7, confirm the hypothesis that a higher proportion of people living in urban areas is associated with higher efforts in noneducational local government services. The coefficient is highly significant.

Summary and Conclusions

The empirical models presented in this chapter were designed for three major purposes: (1) to provide more recent data on the relationship between expenditures and state aid for a cross section of states; (2) to investigate other influences of state aid; and (3) to study the relationship between state aid and educational expenditures within a single state, employing a more disaggregated approach as well as overcoming the problem of distinguishing among the various state aid schemes.

Results from both the empirical models presented in the foregoing pages and much of the previous literature indicate that state aid is likely to have a combined substitutive-stimulative effect on educational expenditures. Whereas *total* expenditures are almost certain to rise as a result of an increase in state aid, *local* expenditures on education are almost certain to decrease. Since an important function of state aid is to reduce the local tax burden, the results indicate that a measure of success has been attained in that regard.

A comparison of the interstate and intrastate (county) models suggests— though it does not prove—that utilization of the percentage equalizing procedure is likely to result in greater local incentives to increase educational spending than is the case for states using the foundation approach. This conclusion is based on our results indicating a substitution of approximately $0.65 for each dollar of state aid when the average of the forty-nine states is considered, as opposed to a substitution of only $0.12 per dollar of state aid in Pennsylvania (a state using the percentage equalizing formula). Clearly more research is needed to conclusively demonstrate this relationship, and the task is far from simple.

Our results also indicate that, on the average, state aid is negatively related to nonpublic enrollments, local revenue, and bond sales, and positively related to average school size (ignoring interdistrict variations in size within states).

Although the empirical study did not reveal any allocative disincentives of state aid (with the exception of local expenditures and revenues), our investigation of the individual states' educational aid programs did not reveal any serious attempt to use state aid as a means to achieve greater efficiency in the allocation of educational resources. The next two chapters are therefore addressed to some models that may be employed to achieve greater efficiency in school operations.

6   Incentive Features—Scale Effects

Considerable evidence demonstrating the existence of substantial scale economies in public (especially secondary) schools has been presented in recent years. Although there are differences in methodology and ultimate results, most of the studies indicate a U-shaped relationship between per pupil costs and school size, measured by enrollment. It follows that most schools are either too large or too small, resulting in considerable waste of resources to society. Yet the state aid formulas provide virtually no incentive to schools to reorganize along lines that will increase efficiency. Certainly, organizational improvement would bolster a school's financial position, but educators are frequently unaware of such possibilities or do not have strong incentives to precipitate change. An explicit incentive structure in the state aid process would not only provide a certain degree of stimulus to change school organization but would also serve to focus attention on the scale issue.

Economies of Scale

The typical approach to determine the extent of scale economies has been to regress school cost data on a quadratic function of school size (enrollment) and a number of other variables which are included in the regression equation in order that interdistrict cost differences due to variations in input or output quality could be taken into account. Let C and S represent current operating costs per pupil and school size, respectively, and let the vector of other school and nonschool factors be denoted by $X_1, X_2, \ldots, X_n$. Then Equation (6.1) is estimated using cross-sectional data for schools in a given state (or other sampling base), employing the familiar technique of ordinary-least-squares estimation.

$$C = b_o + b_1 S + b_2 S^2 + \sum_{j=1}^{n} b_{j+2} X_j \qquad (6.1)$$

where b_o is the intercept, and $b_1, b_2, \ldots, b_{n+2}$ are the $n+2$ (slope) coefficients that we wish to estimate.

To obtain an estimate of the effect of scale on per pupil costs, it is necessary to compute the joint effect of S and S^2 on C. Mathematically, this is achieved by computing the partial derivative of C with respect to S. This is defined in Equation (6.2):

$$\partial C/\partial S = b_1 + 2b_2 S. \tag{6.2}$$

For example, in a study of Iowa high schools for the year 1961-62, the estimated coefficients of b_1 and b_2 were -0.1775 and 0.0000537, respectively (see Cohn [1968], Table 4, Equation IV). Thus, $\partial C/\partial S = -0.1775 + 2(0.0000537)S = -0.1775 + 0.0001074 S$. If $S = 100$, $\partial C/\partial S = -0.16686$. On the other hand, if $S = 2,000$, $\partial C/\partial S = +0.0373$. This implies that an increase in enrollment of one pupil would *reduce* per pupil costs by approximately $0.17 when enrollment is 100, but that per pupil costs would *increase* by nearly $0.04 when another pupil is added to a school in which 2,000 students are already enrolled. Intuitively, it is obvious that the optimal school size is somewhere between 100 and 2,000. To find the optimal school size, we must determine the school enrollment where per pupil costs are at a minimum. That point is found by computing the ratio $-b_1/2b_2$. In the Iowa case, optimal school size is found to be 1,653 (pupils in ADA).[1]

There are a number of problems with this approach. First, it is assumed that the relationship between per pupil costs and school size is U-shaped, so that a parabolic functional form is appropriate. But an investigation of Iowa and Michigan data lends some support to an alternative hypothesis, namely, that a rectangular hyperbola describes the cost-size relationship more accurately. This implies that costs might decrease indefinitely as school size increases, reaching no discernible optimum point.

A second difficulty concerns the use of the school as the unit for which scale effects are measured. On the one hand, it may be argued that certain types of scale economies are more likely to be realized on a district-wide basis—such as the use of specialized personnel (experts in reading difficulty, psychologists, school health officials, district-wide administrative personnel, etc.) and the large-scale purchasing associated with large-size districts. On the other hand, it is possible—and some data are available to confirm this—that economies of scale are likely to accrue in some programs within a school but not in others. Hence, a mere change in enrollments may not achieve the desired reduction in per pupil costs. It follows that a careful analysis of scale economies must be undertaken at several hierarchical levels to ascertain the potential for cost savings through administrative reorganization (Cohn and Hu [1973]).

Last, but certainly not least, is the distinction one should make between expenditure and cost functions. Although the relationship between C and S in Equation (6.1) accounts for other factors, providing a "net" scale effect in Equation (6.2), Equation (6.1) is still far from being a true *cost* function in the

1. The derivation of optimal school size is explained in Cohn (1968), p. 432, and Cohn (1972), pp. 267-69.

economic sense of the term. To obtain a true cost function it is necessary to find the *least-cost* combination of inputs associated with each prespecified level of educational output. (The derivation of the cost function is described in Appendix 6A.)

The cost function which is based on least-cost input combinations is quite difficult to construct for two primary reasons. First, it is necessary to provide a comprehensive index of school output. Although some progress in the direction of providing such a measure is reported in Chapter 7, there is still a need to observe the output index over time and space so that a test of its reliability and consistency can be made. Second, the prices of inputs must be specified. This is relatively simple in the case of some inputs but extremely difficult in other instances. For example, what is the unit price of such inputs as the teacher's verbal ability, number of different subject matter assignments per teacher, teaching load, or curriculum breadth and/or depth? In addition, the derivation of the economic cost function requires the utilization of an educational production function, the shape of which has not been yet determined with any degree of certainty.

So, despite the conceptual difficulties associated with the cost function embodied in Equation (6.1), it appears to be the most promising approach at this time. Further developments along the lines discussed in the preceding paragraphs would be highly desirable.[2]

Proposals for Scale Incentives

A legislature may adopt a number of possible courses of action to encourage districts operating excessively large or small schools to take administrative action to remedy the situation. Three possibilities are discussed here: (1) a penalty factor, (2) incentive payment for schools which take actions to improve their cost posture, and (3) a combination of (1) and (2).

Penalty Factor

Consider a state where aid to education is distributed on the basis of any of the schemes discussed earlier. If each school district is denoted by the subscript i, then the penalty factor for each district would be determined by computing

$$(C_i^* - C_m^*)p = \text{penalty factor} \tag{6.3}$$

2. Other studies on scale economies in public schools include Cohn, Hu, and Kaufman (1972), Hettich (1968), Katzman (1971), Osborn (1970), Riew (1966), and Sabulao and Hickrod (1971).

where C_m^* is the minimum cost per pupil in the state associated with the optimal school size, p is a scalar between 0 and 1 determined by the legislature, and C_i^* is adjusted cost per pupil. C_m^* and C_i^* are derived from Equation (6.4):

$$C_i^* = [b_o + \sum_{j=1}^{n} b_{j+2} \overline{X_j}] + b_1 S_i + b_2 S_i^2 \qquad (6.4)$$

where $\overline{X_j}$ is the mean of the jth factor included in the equation; C_m^* is the cost associated with the optimal scale level, $S^* = - b_1/2 b_2$; and C_i^* is the adjusted cost level associated with the scale S_i of the ith school.

For example, the study of Iowa high schools (Cohn [1968]) included an equation consistent with Equation (6.1), as may be seen in Equation (6.5):

$$C = 263.456 + 1.422 X_1 + 20.2010 X_2 + 0.004 X_3 + 1.3573 X_4$$
$$+ 0.00534 X_5 - 0.0610 X_6 - 0.6398 X_7 - 0.1775 S \qquad (6.5)$$
$$+ 0.0000537 S^2$$

where

X_1 = average number of college semester hours per teaching assignment,
X_2 = average number of different subject matter assignments per high school teacher,
X_3 = median high school teachers' salaries,
X_4 = number of credit-units offered (a unit is one course offered for a full school year),
X_5 = building value per pupil in ADA,
X_6 = bonded indebtedness per pupil in ADA,
X_7 = number of pupils in ADA/number of teachers = class size.

When the means of X_1 through X_7 are utilized, as in Equation (6.4), Equation (6.5) reduces to

$$C_i^* = 390.05 - 0.1775 S_i + 0.0000537 S_i^2. \qquad (6.6)$$

Since S^* (optimal school size) is equal to $0.1775/[2(0.0000537)] = 1,653$, the minimum unit cost, C_m (computed from Equation [6.6]), is approximately $238.

In Table 6-1 adjusted unit costs, based on Equation (6.6), are given for a number of scale levels, ranging from 100 to 3,000 pupils in ADA. The table shows that adjusted unit costs in schools with enrollments of 100 are about $135 higher than in schools with optimal enrollments. Similarly, schools with

Table 6-1
Adjusted Costs and Penalty Factors for Selected School Sizes

School Size (S_i)	Adjusted Unit Costs (C_i^*)	Penalty Factors		
		$C_i^* - C_m^*$	$0.10(C_i^* - C_m^*)$	$0.5(C_i^* - C_m^*)$
100	$372.84	$134.75	$13.47	$67.37
500	314.73	76.64	7.66	38.32
1,000	266.25	28.15	2.81	19.07
1,500	244.63	6.54	0.65	3.27
1,653	238.09	0.00	0.00	0.00
1,750	242.88	5.79	0.58	2.89
2,000	249.90	11.81	1.18	5.90
3,000	340.90	102.81	10.28	51.40

Source: Adjusted costs have been calculated from Equation (6.6), which is based on data for 378 Iowa secondary schools, 1961-62. See Cohn (1968).

enrollments of 3,000 have adjusted unit costs about $100 in excess of schools with optimal enrollments. The extent of cost savings that could have been achieved by capitalizing on scale economies is considerable.

The penalty factor, based on Equation (6.3), is given in Table 6-1 for eight schools with enrollments varying from 100 to 3,000, based upon the Iowa data. The penalties are given for $p = 0.10$ and $p = 0.5$. In the former case ($p = 0.10$), the penalty factor would be as low as $0.58 per pupil for schools with enrollments of 1,750 and as high as $13.47 per pupil in schools with enrollments of 100. If $p = 0.5$, the penalties vary from $2.89 to $67.37 per pupil for schools with respective enrollments of 1,750 and 100. Of course, other values of p may be chosen.

If total state aid for district i is given by A_i, then adjusted aid, A_i^*, would be the difference between A_i and the penalty factors. In symbols, adjusted aid is given in Equation (6.7):

$$A_i^* = A_i - p(C_i^* - C_m^*)S_i \tag{6.7}$$

where S_i is school size in district i.

The analysis could become slightly more complicated when scale economies are computed on a school-by-school basis (where districts operate more than one school). On the one hand, it is probably necessary to distinguish between elementary and secondary schools. On the other hand, a district might operate some schools that are more nearly optimal with regard to size than others. What should be done is twofold. First, cost functions, and hence optimal school sizes, should be estimated for each type of school that ought to be distinguished from any other. Second, the calculation of the penalty factor should be computed for each school, so that the penalty factor for the *district* would be the sum of the penalty factors for all of its schools.

Incentive Payments

An alternative measure for achieving greater efficiency through scale effects would be to reward schools with *additional* aid payments for past cost reductions that are related to scale effects. The legislature could set aside a fixed sum for such incentive payments, let us say an amount equal to $ *IF* (*IF* = Incentive Fund). The share of a school in the incentive fund would depend on the success it had in reducing adjusted costs relative to the reduction in adjusted costs that was achieved by all districts.

Let $(C_i^*)_t$ and $(C_i^*)_{t-1}$ denote adjusted costs of district i during the periods t and $t-1$ (for example, if t is school year 1972-73, $t-1$ is the school year 1971-72). Let $(C_m^*)_t$, $(C_m^*)_{t-1}$, and S_{it} be defined in a similar manner. Then we compute ΔC_i^*, as defined in Equation (6.8), for each school:

$$\Delta C_i^* = S_{it} [(C_i^* - C_m^*)_{t-1} - (C_i^* - C_m^*)_t] . \qquad (6.8)$$

If there are N districts in the state, then we calculate the sum of the cost savings between period t and period $t-1$ due to changes in school size, given by $\sum_{i=1}^{N} \Delta C_i^*$. Then the relative savings by district i, denoted by g_i, is given by

$$g_i = \Delta C_i^* / \sum_{i=1}^{N} \Delta C_i^*. \qquad (6.9)$$

Incentive aid to district i would then be $g_i IF$, and hence total aid to the district would be given by

$$A_i^* = A_i + g_i IF. \qquad (6.10)$$

An illustration of the incentive-payments plan is described in Table 6-2. Consider a state with three school districts, I, II, and III. Adjusted costs, C_i^*, are given in the table for each school for the periods t and $t-1$. Also, the adjusted costs associated with the optimal school size in each of the periods under study are given (C_m^*). In this example, it is assumed that C_m^* is higher in period t than in $t-1$, perhaps because of mandatory increases in teachers' salaries and other cost increases due to price inflation. It is also possible that technological conditions change from year to year, resulting in changes in the level of minimum adjusted unit costs.

Table 6-2
Incentive Payment for Cost Saving through Scale Adjustment: An Illustration

	I	II	III	Total
			Districts	
(1) $C^*_{i\,(t-1)}$	475	450	375	1,300
(2) $C^*_{m\,(t-1)}$	250	250	250	750
(3) (1) − (2)	225	200	125	550
(4) C^*_{it}	450	400	350	1,200
(5) C^*_{mt}	300	300	300	900
(6) (4) − (5)	150	100	50	300
(7) (3) − (6)	75	100	75	250
(8) S_{it}	100	500	1,000	1,600
(9) (8) x (7)	7,500	50,000	75,000	132,500
(10) $g_i = \dfrac{(9)}{132,500}$	0.0566	0.3774	0.5660	1.0000
(11) $S_{it}/1,600$	0.0625	0.3125	0.6250	1.0000

Note: The symbols used in the left-hand column are defined in the text and the Glossary.

When the allocation of incentive payments is based on Equations (6.8), (6.9), and (6.10), the two factors that determine the share of each school in the incentive fund are (1) scale level (enrollment) at year t and (2) cost savings per pupil due to scale effects during the period $t-1$ to t. Of course, only districts with positive cost savings per pupil (row 7 in Table 6-2) are eligible to receive such payments. Whereas the illustration in Table 6-2 is concerned only with payment from the state to a district, one could also use it to *reduce* aid to districts showing a negative amount in row 7, indicating a unit cost increase during the time period.

It is seen in Table 6-2 that District III receives about 57 percent of the incentive aid, whereas the district accounts for almost 63 percent of total enrollment in the hypothetical state. The same proportion (percentage of payment to percentage of total enrollment) is also observed for District I—the two districts having the same per pupil reduction in adjusted unit costs. District II, with the highest cost reduction, gets a relatively larger proportion of the incentive fund.

If the state set aside $10,000 for the incentive fund, District I would receive $566 ($5.66 per pupil), District II would receive $3,774 ($7.55 per pupil), and District III would receive $5,660 ($5.66 per pupil).

As discussed in the previous section, further complications may enter the incentive payment mechanism. For example, it would be desirable to consider adjusted costs by school or programs, so that the calculation of row 7 in Table 6-2 would have to be carried out several times for each district. Row 9 would then be calculated for each school and summed for all schools in the district to obtain g_i. But what if some schools had cost reductions while others had cost increases? Should one sum only the positive amounts (row 9) or also the negative ones? If administrative control rests entirely with the district and not with the schools of which it is composed, why should districts be rewarded for cost savings in some schools which are offset to a greater or lesser extent by cost increases in other schools? On the other hand, if financial reward could be given to *schools*, and if the schools have some control over budgetary matters, then it seems appropriate to apply the formula to schools and not districts.

Penalty Factor and Incentive
Payment Combined

A legislature may wish to penalize districts with excessive current adjusted unit costs and, at the same time, reward those districts (some of which are subject to the penalty factor) which have taken action to reduce adjusted unit cost between the preceding and current periods. If A_i denotes total state aid in the absence of any scale incentive features, then the combination of the two plans would determine adjusted aid according to Equation (6.11):

$$A_i^* = A_i - p\,(\,C_i^* - C_m^*\,)\,S_i + g_i I F. \tag{6.11}$$

Table 6-3 provides an illustration of how Equation (6.11) might work for the school systems described in Table 6-2. If $p = 0.10$, and if the incentive fund (IF) is \$10,000, only District III receives a net incentive payment from the state. The penalties levied on the other districts exceed the incentive payments so A_i^* is lower than A_i. If $p = 0.05$, both Districts II and III receive net incentive payments, whereas District I has a net penalty of \$184. When $p = 0.10$, total penalties amount to \$11,500. If the incentive fund is set equal to the total penalties levied, then, again, only District III receives a net incentive payment. If all districts are to receive a nonnegative net incentive payment (i.e., the incentive payment is at least as large as the penalty factor), the total incentive fund would have to be at least \$13,251 when $p = 0.05$ and \$26,502 when $p = 0.10$.

Equity Considerations of Scale
Incentive Features

In the discussion of the penalty factor and incentive payments, the fiscal capacity of districts has been disregarded. It is, however, plausible to argue that

Table 6-3

Penalty Factors and Incentive Payments Combined: An Illustration

	Districts			
	I	II	III	Total
(1) S_{it}	100	500	1,000	1,600
(2) $(C_i^* - C_m^*)_t$	$ 150	$ 100	$ 50	$ 300
(3) (1) x (2)	$15,000	$50,000	$50,000	$115,000
(4) 0.05(3)	$750	$2,500	$2,500	$ 5,750
(5) 0.10(3)	$1,500	$5,000	$5,000	$ 11,500
(6) g_i	0.0566	0.3774	0.5660	1.0000
(7) g_i ($10,000)	$ 566	$3,774	$5,660	$ 10,000
(8) (7) − (4)	−$184	$1,274	$3,160	$ 4,250
(9) (7) − (5)	−$934	−$1,226	$ 660	−$ 1,500
(10) g_i ($11,500)	$ 650.90	$4,340.10	$6,509.00	$ 11,500
(11) (10) − (4)	−$ 99.10	$1,840.10	$4,009	$ 5,750
(12) (10) − (5)	−$849.10	−$ 659.90	$1,509.00	$ 0.00

Note: For definition of symbols, see text or Glossary.

the penalty factor is inequitable. If there are two districts with identical adjusted costs and enrollments but with different fiscal capacities—abstracting, for the moment, from the problem of defining fiscal capacity—then the penalty would be more burdensome to the poorer district. Of course, if the power equalizing or full state funding schemes are in operation so that educational revenues are entirely unrelated to community wealth, then the equity problem does not exist. However, so long as states use the foundation or percentage equalizing schemes, the penalty factor would seem to result in a greater burden to poorer districts.

The incentive payment, on the other hand, does not appear to have adverse equity problems. If two districts have the same per pupil cost saving, but one is wealthier than the other, the wealthier district would, in fact, receive incentive payment which is a smaller proportion of per pupil wealth than is the case in the poorer school. Just as flat grants *are* equalizing to some extent, so are the incentive payments.

One method that could be used to correct the apparent inequity of the penalty factor would be to multiply the penalty factor by the ratio W_i/W_h, where W_i is per pupil wealth in the ith district, and W_h is per pupil wealth in the wealthiest district in the state. The meaning of "wealth" could vary from one jurisdiction to another, but a combination of personal income and net worth appears to provide an attractive solution to the problem.

When equity considerations are taken into account, the penalty factor would be given by

$$\text{penalty factor} = p\ (\ W_i/W_h\ )\ (\ C_i^* - C_m^*\ )\ S_i. \qquad (6.12)$$

An illustration of the manner by which the penalty factor might be computed is given in Table 6-4 for a hypothetical state composed of only three school districts. The data are consistent with the illustration given in Table 6-3.

The penalty factor of the wealthiest district (III) remains unchanged. In the other two districts, the penalty is reduced in proportion to relative wealth. The major beneficiary is District II, which is forgiven half of its penalty factor. In light of the reduction in total penalties, the state may wish to increase the proportion p if it desires to maintain total penalties at a prespecified level.

One could also vary the incentive payment by a factor related to community wealth in order to increase its equalizing impact. One possibility would be to redefine g_i as follows:

$$g_i^* = [\Delta C_i^* (1 - W_i/W_h)] / [\sum_{i=1}^{N} \Delta C_i^* (1 - W_i/W_h)]. \qquad (6.13)$$

An illustration of how such a scheme could operate is described in Table 6-4 (rows 8-10). Since District III is considered to be the wealthiest district in the state, it will receive *no* incentive payments. If \$10,000 are earmarked for *IF*, then District I shall receive \$1,667 and District II, \$8,333.

Table 6-4

Equity Considerations Applied to Penalty Factor and/or Incentive Payment: An Illustration

		Districts		
	I	II	III	Total
(1) S_{it}	100	500	1,000	1,600
(2) $(C_i^* - C_m^*)_t$	\$150	\$100	\$50	\$300
(3) (1) x (2)	15,000	50,000	50,000	115,000
(4) W_i	20,000	15,000	30,000	65,000
(5) W_i/W_h	0.67	0.5	1.0	—
(6) 0.05 x (5) x (3)	502.50	1,250	2,500	4,252.50
(7) 0.10 x (5) x (3)	1,005.00	2,500	5,000	8,505
(8) ΔC_i^*	7,500	50,000	75,000	132,500
(9) $\Delta C_i^*(1 - W_i/W_h)$	5,000	25,000	0	30,000
(10) $g^* = \dfrac{(9)}{30,000}$	0.167	0.833	0	1.000

Note: For definition of symbols, see text or Glossary.

In summary, there are at least two possible modifications of the scale incentive effects. The first would define total aid as follows:

$$A_i^* = A_i - p\,(\,W_i/W_h\,)\,(\,C_i^* - C_m^*)\,S_i + g_i/F. \tag{6.14}$$

The second modification would substitute g_i^*, as defined in Equation (6.13), for g_i in Equation (6.14).

Summary and Conclusions

The principal objective of this chapter has been to suggest the possibility of introducing incentive features into state aid formulas to encourage schools to organize along lines that would minimize adjusted unit costs. Three plans were developed: a penalty factor for excessively high adjusted unit costs in a given period; incentive payment for cost savings between the preceding and current time periods; and a combination of the two plans. The chapter also examined the possibility of introducing equity considerations into the analysis, and possible modifications of the incentive features have been presented.

It would be presumptuous to claim that these plans constitute the only course of action regarding incentive effects of scale economies. Rather, the proposed schemes provide a point of departure for legislative enactment and scholarly analysis. Whatever the merits of the specific formulas, it appears that the magnitude of cost savings from proper scale adjustments are so vast that at least an experimental program of scale incentive features should be inaugurated.

Appendix 6A: Derivation of an Economic Cost Function to Determine Scale Effects

Suppose that enrollment in a given school is denoted by S, a composite index of per pupil school quality by Q, and the vectors of relevant school and nonschooling inputs by $X_1, \ldots, X_k$ and $Z_1, \ldots, Z_n$, respectively. The production function of educational services can, therefore, be specified (implicitly) as

$$Q = f(S, X_1, \ldots, X_k/Z_1, \ldots, Z_n). \tag{6A.1}$$

Function (6A.1) assumes that nonschooling factors cannot be directly manipulated by the school administrators.

Let $p_1, \ldots, p_k$ denote the prices of inputs $X_1, \ldots, X_k$. Then if we wish to minimize accounting costs, given by

$$C = \sum_{i=1}^{k} p_i X_i,$$

subject to the attainment of a given quality per pupil, Q_o, then we can write the constrained minimum as a Lagrangian expression:

$$L = \sum_{i=1}^{k} p_i X_i - \lambda[f(S, X_1, \ldots, X_k/Z_1, \ldots, Z_n) - Q_o]. \tag{6A.2}$$

Next, we compute the k partial derivatives, $\partial L/\partial X_i$, and set them equal to 0. We then obtain the following k equations:

$$p_1 - \lambda \partial f/\partial X_1 = 0$$

$$\vdots \tag{6A.3}$$

$$p_k - \lambda \partial f/\partial X_k = 0$$

From the set of Equations (6A.3), we can derive a set of $k-1$ independent equations in the form of

This appendix is based on Cohn and Riew (1974).

$$p_i/p_j = (\partial f/\partial X_i)/(\partial f/\partial X_j), i \neq j. \qquad (6A.4)$$

The $k-1$ equations in (6A.4) define X_1 through X_k on the basis of the input prices and their marginal productivities (the partial derivatives) which are functions of school size (S), the X-vector, and the Z-vector (known magnitudes). Thus we obtain a set of $k-1$ equations in k unknowns (the X's). It is possible to solve for the X's when one additional (independent) equation is added to the system. The equation we add is the production function (6A.1) which expresses the X's in terms of Q, S, and the Z-vector. When the system of k equations is solved for the k X's we should get

$$X_1^* = g_1(S, Q; Z_1, \ldots, Z_n; p_1, \ldots, p_k)$$
$$\vdots \qquad (6A.5)$$
$$X_k^* = g_k(S, Q; Z_1, \ldots, Z_n; p_1, \ldots, p_k).$$

The X^*'s are the input levels that reflect minimum cost for quality Q_o. The economic cost function therefore becomes:

$$C^* = \sum_{i=1}^{k} p_i X_i^*. \qquad (6A.6)$$

Since the p_i's are presumed to be known and constant, and the Z-vector is regarded as exogenous, economic costs (C^*) are seen to be a function of quality and school size, that is,

$$C^* = h(S, Q, \text{ and other constant or exogenous quantities}) \qquad (6A.7)$$

Equation (6A.7) may be used to determine the effect of size on economic costs.

The derivation of economic cost functions becomes more complicated when we add other constraints to the model (factor availability, legal factors, etc.), when it is recognized that a composite index of school quality may be extremely difficult to construct, and when the oligopsonistic nature of the factor market for teachers is considered.

7

Incentive Effects—Outputs

The incentive effects considered in Chapter 6 concern *inputs* only. They are designed to encourage school districts to operate at optimal enrollment levels, but they do not provide incentives for districts to obtain the maximum output from available inputs. Several suggestions are provided in this chapter for incorporating incentive features into state aid plans to encourage schools to increase educational output or output per dollar of costs.

Production in Secondary Schools

An operational scheme designed to induce schools to produce more—or to produce at a greater level of efficiency—cannot be formulated unless one is able to specify what is meant by "output" in secondary schools, measure that output, and specify a production function describing the process by which educational inputs are transformed into educational outputs.

The task is clearly formidable; some, if not many, would argue that it is totally impossible. Yet so much progress has been made in this area in recent years that there is much reason to be optimistic. Although the state of the art is far from satisfactory, there is already mounting evidence which provides a starting point for input-output analysis in secondary education.[1]

The output receiving the most attention in recent studies has been achievement in verbal and/or mathematical skills. Other outputs mentioned include holding power (the inverse of the dropout rate), and, for secondary schools, enrollment in postsecondary educational institutions.

A comprehensive list of educational outputs has been developed by the Bureau of Educational Quality Assessment (BEQA) of the Pennsylvania Department of Education as part of its Pennsylvania Plan. The plan spells out ten educational goals, and twelve measures (outputs) have been developed to implement them[2] (see Table 7-1).

On the basis of its experience with the Pennsylvania Plan, the BEQA has been able to test the reliability and content validity of the output measures. The reliability coefficients for the ten goals are reproduced in Table 7-2, which

---

1. Examples of such studies include Bowles (1970); Burkhead, Fox, and Holland (1967); Cohn (1968); Fox (1971); Hanushek (1972); Katzman (1971); Kiesling (1967); Levin (1970); and Raymond (1968). A summary of some of these studies appears in Cohn (1972), Chapter 8.
2. See Campbell and Beers (1970), and Kuhns (1972).

Table 7-1
Goals and Outputs of the Pennsylvania Plan

Goal	Variable Number	Description Quality education should help every child:	Dimensions
I Self-concept	(1)	acquire the greatest possible understanding of himself and an appreciation of his worthiness as a member of society	Control of environment Personal attributes Achieving in school Relating to others
II Understanding others	(2)	acquire understanding and appreciation of persons belonging to social, cultural, and ethnic groups different from his own	Appreciating others who differ
III Basic skills		acquire to the fullest extent possible for him the mastery of the basic skills in the	
	(3)	use of words	Words
	(4)	use of numbers	Numbers
IV Learning attitude	(5)	acquire a positive attitude toward school and the learning process	Attitude toward school assignments Perception of the learning process Perception of the school climate
V Citizenship	(6)	acquire the habits and attitudes associated with responsible citizenship	Personal responsibility attitudes Initiative in advocating change Personal responsibility applications Concern for democratic principles
VI Health habits	(7)	acquire good health habits and an understanding of the conditions necessary for maintenance of physical and emotional well-being	Health knowledge
VII Creativity		by giving opportunity and encouragement to be creative in one or more fields of endeavor	Self-ratings of creative tendencies Tolerance of ambiguity Inner directedness
	(8)	(i) potential	
	(9)	(ii) output	Creative output
VIII Vocational development	(10)	to understand the opportunities open to him for preparing himself for a productive life and should	Perception of work and choice process Involvement in the

Table 7-1 (cont.)

Goal	Variable Number	Description Quality education should help every child:	Dimensions
		enable him to take full advantage of these opportunities	choice process Judgment and independence in decision-making Preference for particular vocational aspects
IX Knowledge of human achievement	(11)	to understand and appreciate as much as he can of human achievement in the natural sciences, the humanities, and the arts	Theater and arts Sports, politics; and science Music
X Readiness for change	(12)	to prepare for a world of rapid change and unforeseeable demands in which continuing education throughout life should be a normal expectation	Importance of education Change in regulations Change in school climate Change in educational processes

Source: Kuhns (1972), pp. 50-51, taken from Beers (1970).

Table 7-2
Reliability Coefficients of Educational Goals in Pennsylvania

Goal		Reliability	
		Grade 5	Grade 11
I	Self-understanding	0.87	0.90
II	Understanding others	0.77	0.88
III	Basic skills	0.90+[a]	0.90+[b]
IV	Interest in school	0.75	0.85
V	Citizenship	0.90	0.91
VI	Health habits	0.82	0.91
VII	Creative potential	0.82	0.78
VII	Creative output	—[c]	0.93
VIII	Vocational development	0.77	0.89
IX	Appreciation of human accomplishments	0.79	0.92
X	Preparation for change	0.79	0.81

[a]Measured by the Stanford Achievement Battery or the Iowa Test of Basic Skills.

[b]Measured by the Stanford Achievement Battery or the Iowa Tests of Educational Development.

[c]Not measured.

Source: Toole, Campbell, and Beers (1970), p. 2.

indicates that the output measures representing the ten goals are, in general, highly reliable. Studies by the BEQA have also demonstrated a highly statistically significant content validity for the output measures.

The Educational Production Function

Suppose there are n educational objectives (outputs $Q_1, Q_2, \ldots, Q_n$)–such as verbal and mathematical skills, vocational development, creative output, and others–k school-related inputs ($X_1, X_2, \ldots, X_k$), and m nonschooling factors ($Z_1, Z_2, \ldots, Z_m$). A generalized educational production function may be described as in Equation (7.1):

$$F(Q_1, Q_2, \ldots, Q_n; X_1, X_2 \ldots, X_k/Z_1, Z_2, \ldots, Z_m) = 0. \qquad (7.1)$$

The function states that educational production is determined by the interaction of the school inputs and outputs, given the level of nonschooling factors.

If each of the n outputs were independent of the other outputs, it would be possible to estimate a production function for each output separately. For the ith output, Q_i, the function would be

$$Q_i = F_i(X_1, X_2 \ldots, X_k/Z_1, Z_2 \ldots, Z_m) \qquad (7.2)$$

where F_i is the functional form expressing the manner by which the input sets combine to produce the output.

If, on the other hand, the outputs are not independent, so that the production of one output is a function of not only the inputs but also some of the remaining $n-1$ outputs, then it would be desirable to utilize a simultaneous-equation technique to avoid the possibility of a simultaneous-equation bias when equations of type (7.2) are estimated independently for the n outputs. A general system of equations, given the above input and output sets, is given in Equation Set (7.3):

$$Q_1 = F_1(Q_2, Q_3, \ldots, Q_n; X_1, X_2, \ldots, X_k/Z_1, Z_2, \ldots, Z_m)$$

$$Q_2 = F_2(Q_1, Q_3, \ldots, Q_n; X_1 X_2, \ldots, X_k/Z_1, Z_2, \ldots, Z_m)$$

$$\vdots \qquad (7.3)$$

$$Q_n = F_n(Q_1, Q_2, \ldots, Q_{n-1}; X_1, X_2, \ldots, X_k/Z_1, Z_2, \ldots, Z_m).$$

There exist several statistical methods, such as the widely used two-stage-least squares technique, to estimate the parameters of Equation Set (7.3), provided a linear functional form is specified.[3]

Of particular interest is the *shape* of the production functions. The most convenient specification for Equation (7.2) would be a linear function given by

$$Q_i = a + \sum_{j=1}^{k} b_j X_j + \sum_{h=1}^{m} c_h Z_h + e_i \tag{7.4}$$

where a, b_j, and c_h are the coefficients (constants) which we seek to estimate, whereas e_i is a stochastic error term.

Equation (7.4) conflicts, however, with accepted economic theory which asserts that each factor of production is subject to diminishing marginal returns (that is, $\partial^2 Q_i / \partial X_j^2 < 0$, at least for some region in the production surface), and the marginal rate of technical substitution between any two inputs should be diminishing—where the marginal rate of technical substitutions between, say, inputs 1 and 2 is given by the ratio $(\partial Q_i / \partial X_1) / (\partial Q_i / \partial X_2)$.

Diminishing marginal returns implies that total output increases at a decreasing rate beyond a given point as each of the inputs is increased, other inputs and technological conditions remaining constant. This is consistent with a total product curve as depicted in Figure 7-1. Note that the curve is nonlinear throughout, indicating a specification different from that in Equation (7.4). If, however, the range of observations regarding inputs and outputs encompasses a relatively short segment of the total product curve, then the linear approximation (7.4) could provide a very good statistical fit to the data. This is shown in Figure 7-1 for the arcs *AB* or *BC*, where a straight line provides an excellent approximation to the true curve. On the other hand, it is possible that the range of observation is greater, such as the arc *AC* in Figure 7-1, indicating the desirability of choosing a nonlinear specification for Equation (7.2). It should also be emphasized that when linear approximations are used, there exists a considerable danger in extrapolating the statistical functions beyond the range of the data.

Diminishing marginal rate of technical substitution explains the substitutability of any two inputs in production. If the linear form (7.4) is used, the marginal rate of substitution is constant (b_1/b_2 is the marginal rate of substituting input 2 for input 1). This implies that the marginal rate of substitution does not depend on the magnitude of the inputs used. Also, the linear function implies that output could be obtained by using any one of the inputs alone.

But once again, when we have data that encompass only a relatively small portion of the input substitution range, a linear function may be satisfactory. In

---

3. See, for example, Johnston (1972), Chs. 12 and 13, for a thorough discussion of identification and estimation of simultaneous-equation systems.

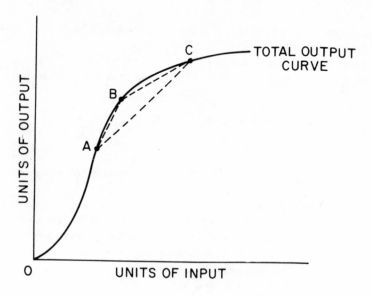

Figure 7-1. Total Product Curve and Linear Approximations

Figure 7-2 an equal product curve is presented. That curve satisfies the requirement of diminishing marginal rate of technical substitution; yet, if we are only interested in a short segment of the curve, say the arc segments *AB* or *BC*, then a linear approximation would provide an excellent fit to the data. Again, one must be careful not to use the estimated coefficients to render recommenda-

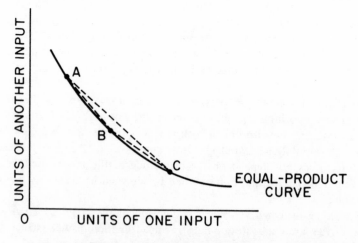

Figure 7-2. Equal Product Curve and Linear Approximations

tions concerning areas of production outside the range of the data. Also, one should test for nonlinearity to avoid misspecification, such as when the segment AC in Figure 7-2 is exhibited by the data.[4]

Composite Output Index

In the absence of a price system that could be used to combine the various outputs into a single total educational product, some composite index of the n outputs must be developed in order that the application of the tool for state aid incentives may become operational. Such a composite index would also be of great value to school administrators who seek to evaluate their total performance rather than approach decision making on an output-by-output basis.

It would be possible to obtain a subjective index of the outputs by resorting to panels of experts or questionnaires which would provide weights to be applied to each of the outputs. An alternative method, used here, is to find the weights, $w_1, w_2, \ldots, w_n$, which would maximize the correlation between the output index,

$$Q = \sum_{i=1}^{n} w_i Q_i,$$

and a composite input index,

$$Y = \sum_{j=1}^{k} v_j X_j + \sum_{h=1}^{m} u_h Z_h,$$

where v_i and u_i are the corresponding input weights.

The technique used to obtain the output and input weights is known as canonical correlations.[5] Given the input and output sets, the technique would assign weights to the inputs and outputs and compute the correlation between Q and Y In each successive step, the technique would recompute the correlation as changes in the weights are effected. The procedure would terminate when it is no longer feasible to achieve a significant increase in the correlation between Q and Y through changes in the weights.

The manner by which the technique may be used is illustrated here using Kuhns's data (1972) for fifty-three Pennsylvania secondary schools (for the academic year 1970-71). Table 7-3 provides the definitions of the input set (of

4. For an excellent treatment of production and input substitution, consult Ferguson (1972). Chs. 5 and 6.

5. A description of the canonical correlation technique is given in Johnston (1972), pp. 331-34. Other studies involving canonical correlations include Chow (1964), Hooper (1959), Hu (1972), Tintner (1946), and Waugh (1942).

Table 7-3

Input Variables for Fifty-Three Pennsylvania Secondary Schools, 1970-71

Symbol	Definition of Variable[a]
FAMASES	Family socioeconomic status: composite of mother's and father's occupational levels
TSALARY	Mean faculty salary in the school
PROC	Number of different subject matter preparations per week per academic teacher
TLOD	Average academic teacher instructional hours per week
CSIZ	Average class size
AEE	Total amount (in dollars) spent in the *school district* for extracurricular activities per secondary student
BRAT	Ratio of building enrollment to actual state-rated capacity
AMAN	Total number of secondary school personnel with administrative responsibilities (e.g., principals, assistant principals, department heads, etc.) per student
AXMAN	Total number of counselors, librarians, and audio-visual personnel per student
FSRAT	Student/academic faculty ratio
PSUP	Sum of the hours worked per week by all nonprofessional teacher aides, including secretaries whose primary function is to aid classroom teachers
ENROL	Enrollment
CUG	Total number of different subject matters available for student registration per secondary grade.

[a]All variables are for the secondary school except as noted.

Source: Kuhns (1972), pp. 55-57.

thirteen variables) used in this exercise. (The Pennsylvania data include many more school and nonschool input factors, but for the purposes at hand the results were computed only on the basis of the thirteen variables in Table 7-3. A more detailed analysis of Kuhns's data will appear in Cohn (1975). The outputs for the analysis have already been described in Table 7-1.)

The normalized weights for the canonical correlation between the weighted input and output sets are given in Table 7-4. On the input side, these weights provide a measure of the importance of each of the inputs in explaining the correlation between the inputs and outputs. Similarly, for the outputs, the weights indicate the relative contribution of each output to the canonical correlation.

The canonical correlation technique, then, provides output weights which indicate the extent to which each of the outputs contributes to the correlation between the output and input sets. The weights, therefore, could be construed to describe the relative "importance" of each output as exhibited by the data for

Table 7-4

Normalized Weights for Canonical Correlation—Fifty-Three Pennsylvania Secondary Schools, 1970-71

Inputs			Outputs	
Symbol	Normalized Weight	Goal	Variable Number	Normalized Weight
FAMASES	0.512656	I	1	0.011236
TSALARY	0.077284	II	2	0.170569
PROC	0.070756	III	3	0.150544
TLOD	0.005625	III	4	0.023409
CSIZ	0.077841	IV	5	0.071289
AEE	0.002500	V	6	0.323761
BRAT	0.000081	VI	7	0.020449
AMAN	0.000144	VII	8	0.011664
AXMAN	0.025281	VII	9	0.021025
FSRAT	0.192721	VIII	10	0.133225
PSUP	0.124649	IX	11	0.002601
ENROL	0.100000	X	12	0.060516
CUG	0.000784			

Notes: Canonical correlation coefficient = 0.866
Number of observations = 53
Chi-square = 233, with 156 degrees of freedom.
Source: Data for computing the weights were taken from Kuhns (1972).

the schools chosen for the particular study. They are likely, therefore, to be inconsistent with one's a priori judgment about the various outputs. Also, it should be pointed out that the weights vary a great deal between iterations of the canonical correlation estimation procedure. Nevertheless, whatever the limitations of the approach, it offers one method to estimate a single output index.

Given the output weights (w's) as presented here in the rightmost column of Table 7-4, one could construct for each school a single output measure, Q. This is achieved by calculating

$$Q = \sum_{i=1}^{n} w_i Q_i$$

(where Q is the output index and the Q_i's are the n output measures—twelve outputs in the Pennsylvania case).

Proposals for Output Incentives

Once it is agreed that a meaningful set of educational outcomes could be measured, that an output index could be formulated, and that a production function of the type (7.2) could be specified to study the relationship between the composite output index and the input factors, the door would then be open for an analysis in which schools could be encouraged to increase output, or output per unit of cost, through incentive provisions in the state aid formula.

The state may wish to consider one of two goals: (1) to achieve greater total output, no matter how efficient (or inefficient) schools are; (2) to achieve greater efficiency in school operations—that is, increase the *ratio* of output to cost. An alternative goal might be to achieve greater output subject to the constraint that the output/cost ratio remains within acceptable limits. In this section, only the first two alternatives will be discussed.

In what follows, the term *cost* would be interpreted as costs adjusted for scale effects. Since scale effects were already discussed in the preceding chapter, the measurement of efficiency here will be based on a cost per pupil basis from which the scale effect has been netted out. The method for obtaining such a net cost figure may be explained on the basis of the material introduced in Chapter 6.

Consider, for example, Equation (6.1) describing a cost function with a parabolic relation between costs and size. If one wishes to obtain per pupil cost for a district which is net of scale effects, the procedure would be to calculate net costs, NC_i, for the ith district, by

$$NC_i = C_i - (C_i^* - C_m^*) \tag{7.5}$$

where C_i^* and C_m^* are per pupil costs associated with enrollment in the ith district and in a district with an optimal enrollment level, respectively. An illustration of the manner by which NC_i might be computed in reference to Iowa high school data (Cohn [1968]) is provided in Table 7-5.

As in the preceding chapter, the incentive features will include a penalty factor, an incentive payment, a combination of the penalty factor and the incentive payment, and adjustments in the incentive systems to account for equity considerations.

Penalty Factor

Suppose there are N districts in a state. Consider a set of n educational outputs, $Q_1, Q_2, \ldots, Q_n$, which may be consolidated into a single output index,

$$Q = \sum_{i=1}^{n} w_i Q_i$$

Table 7-5
Calculation of Per Pupil School Costs in which Scale Effects Are Netted Out

School (1)	School Size (S_i) (2)	Scale Effect $(C_i^* - C_m^*)$ (3)	Per Pupil Costs (C_i) (4)	$NC_i = C_i - (C_i^* - C_m^*)$ (5) = (4) − (3)
A	100	$134.75	$500	$365.25
B	500	76.64	500	423.36
C	1,000	28.15	750	721.85
D	1,500	6.54	350	343.46
E	1,653	0.00	400	400.00
F	1,750	5.79	1,000	994.21
G	2,000	11.81	600	588.19
H	3,000	102.81	700	579.19

Note: For definition of symbols, see text or Glossary.
Source: Column (3) is taken from Table 6-1, which is based on Cohn (1968), Table 4.

where the weights (w_i) are obtained by the canonical correlation or any other acceptable method. The state could then set up an output norm, Q^n, which could be based on the highest current output level in the state, the average state level, or any other level which the state wishes to consider.

If it is desired to achieve increments in output without regard to cost of inputs, then each district will pay a penalty equal to some proportion of the difference between the output norm and its output level. Districts achieving or exceeding the norm would pay no penalty.

It should be recognized, however, that many of the outputs depend quite critically on factors that are not directly under the control of the school district. For example, socioeconomic conditions have been shown to influence student achievement in basic skills. It follows that the output measure that should be used to calculate the penalty factor must be adjusted to take into account such nonschooling factors.

The adjusted output measure, Q^*, would depend on the underlying production function. If the production function is of type (7.4), then adjusted output for each district is given by

$$Q_i^* = Q_i - \sum_{h=1}^{m} c_h Z_{hi} \qquad (7.6)$$

where Z_{hi} is the level of the hth nonschooling factor in district i.

If the state chooses a sum of $\$q_1$ for the penalty factor, total penalties for district i would amount to

$$\text{penalty for district } i = q_1(Q^n - Q_i^*)S_i \qquad (7.7)$$

where S_i is enrollment in district i. Therefore, adjusted state aid—ignoring any scale effects—would be

$$A_i^* = A_i - q_1(Q^n - Q_i^*)S_i. \tag{7.8}$$

For example, if maximum Q is 100, and the norm is set at 70, the penalty factor would be $q_1(70 - Q_i^*)S_i$. A district achieving an adjusted Q-level of 40 would pay a penalty of $30q_1$ per pupil. If q_1 is set at \$1, the district would pay a penalty of \$30 per pupil.

The formula could be used for both a penalty and payment (negative penalty) for schools where Q_i^* exceeds Q^n. The problem with such a program would be that as a school approaches the maximum output level, it becomes much more difficult to attain higher output levels. Also, given scarce funds, most states would probably wish to encourage increased production at districts with low output levels.

Suppose that the state wishes to increase efficiency, measured by output per unit of costs, rather than output. Since scale effects have already been discussed earlier, the concept of "costs" should be net of scale effects, as explained previously. For each district, the output/cost ratio is thus given by Q_i^*/NC_i. Again, the state sets a norm for the output/cost ratio, denoted by $(Q/NC)^n$, based on best practice, the state average, or any other method which the state finds acceptable. If q_2 is the penalty amount set by the state, then the penalty for each district for which $Q_i^*/NC_i < (Q/NC)^n$ is given by

$$\text{penalty for district } i = q_2\left[(Q/NC)^n - (Q_i^*/NC_i)\right]S_i. \tag{7.9}$$

For example, if the output/cost norm is 1/5 (representing, for example, an output norm of 70 and (net) per pupil cost of \$350)—indicating that it takes \$5 to produce a unit of output—then the per pupil penalty for district i would be $q_2(1/5 - Q_i^*/NC_i)$. If district i could manage only an output/cost ratio of 1/10, its penalty would be $q_2(1/10)$ per pupil. If q_2 is set equal to \$50, then the district would pay a penalty of \$5 per pupil.

Adjusted state aid would, in this case, be

$$A_i^* = A_i - q_2\left[(Q/NC)^n - (Q_i^*/NC_i)\right]S_i. \tag{7.10}$$

Incentive Payments

Instead of a penalty levy associated with unsatisfactory output or output/cost levels, a state may wish to allocate a certain sum, say \$IF, for incentive payments to districts showing improvement in their output or output/cost posture over a prespecified time period (from $t-1$ to t).

Let $(Q_i^* - Q^n)_t$ denote the difference between a district's adjusted output and the state's output norm at time period t. Then the improvement in a district's output level during the period from $t-1$ to t is given by

$$\Delta Q_i^* = [(Q_i^* - Q^n)_t - (Q_i^* - Q^n)_{t-1}] S_{it}. \qquad (7.11)$$

If the output norm does not change between the two time periods, i.e., $Q_t^n = Q_{t-1}^n$, then Equation (7.11) reduces to

$$\Delta Q_i^* = [Q_{it}^* - Q_{i(t-1)}^*] S_{it}. \qquad (7.12)$$

If there are N districts in the state, we calculate the sum of the output improvements for all districts, given by

$$\sum_{i=1}^{N} \Delta Q_i^*.$$

The improvement by the ith district relative to total improvement by all districts, denoted by h_{1_i}, is given by

$$h_{1_i} = \Delta Q_i^* / \sum_{i=1}^{N} \Delta Q_i^*. \qquad (7.13)$$

Incentive aid to district i would then be $h_{1_i} IF$, and adjusted state aid would be computed by the formula

$$A_i^* = A_i + h_{1_i} IF. \qquad (7.14)$$

If the state wishes to encourage greater efficiency rather than output per se, we would substitute the following for Equation (7.11):

$$\Delta(Q_i^*/NC_i) = \left\{ [(Q_i^*/NC_i)_t - (Q/NC)_t^n] - [(Q_i^*/NC_i)_{t-1} - (Q/NC)_{t-1}^n] \right\} S_{it} \qquad (7.15)$$

If the output/cost norm does not change between the two periods, Equation (7.15) simplifies to

$$\Delta(Q_i^*/NC_i) = [(Q_i^*/NC_i)_t - (Q_i^*/NC_i)_{t-1}] S_{it}. \qquad (7.16)$$

The relative improvement in the output/cost ratio, h_{2_i}, is defined by

$$h_{2i} = \Delta(Q_i^*/NC_i)/ \sum_{i=1}^{N} \Delta(Q_i^*/NC_i) \tag{7.17}$$

and the share of the ith district in the incentive fund is given by $h_{2i}IF$. Adjusted state aid for district i is therefore given by

$$A_i^* = A_i + h_{2i}IF. \tag{7.18}$$

Combination of the Penalty Factor and Incentive Payment Programs

A state may wish to penalize districts with substandard output or output/cost levels yet also seek to encourage greater output or productivity by rewarding districts showing improvement over a prespecified time period.

If increased output is the state's goal, the adjusted aid formula would be given by

$$A_i^* = A_i - q_1(Q^n - Q_i^*)S_i + h_{1i}IF. \tag{7.19}$$

On the other hand, if the state wishes to encourage greater productivity, adjusted state aid would be given by

$$A_i^* = A_i - q_2[(Q/NC)^n - (Q_i^*/NC_i)]S_i + h_{2i}IF. \tag{7.20}$$

It is, or course, possible to combine the two programs in such a way that one part of the scheme (say the penalty factor) would be related to total output while the other part (the incentive payment) would be related to the improvement in productivity or vice versa.

Equity Aspects of Incentive Formulas

As noted in Chapter 6, it is evident that a dollar of penalty would be more burdensome to poor than to rich districts. One could, therefore, modify Equations (7.8) and (7.10) to take account of a community's fiscal capacity.

If a district's wealth is denoted by W_i and the wealth of the richest district is W_h, then one method which would incorporate equity considerations into the incentive formulas would be to multiply the penalty factor by the ratio W_i/W_h. The penalty factor would remain unchanged for the wealthiest district and would be nill for a very poor district. The modified aid formulas are given in Equations (7.21) and (7.22):

$$A_i^* = A_i - q_1(W_i/W_h)(Q^n - Q_i^*)S_i \qquad (7.21)$$

and

$$A_i^* = A_i - q_2(W_i/W_h)[(Q/NC)^n - (Q_i^*/NC_i)] S_i. \qquad (7.22)$$

One could also modify the incentive payment formulas to provide greater equalization of community wealth. The procedure would be identical to the one described in Equation (6.13) for the scale incentive scheme.

Summary

It has been argued that at least some educational outputs can be measured. Given data on educational inputs and outputs in a given state for certain time periods, it would be possible to develop the output index and calculate an adjusted output for each district. Using such data, it would also be possible to devise incentive features in the state aid formulas to provide for a penalty factor, incentive payments, or both. Such schemes could be applied to encourage greater output levels, greater efficiency (in terms of the output/cost ratio), or both. Modification of the formulas to take account of equity factors has also been described.

It is recognized that the enactment of such incentive features is subject to both practical and theoretical limitations. The nature of the educational outputs and the form and shape of the educational production function need a great deal more study. In addition, it would be desirable to study the proposed formulas in relation to actual information for individual states. Nevertheless, the analysis opens the door to further study in this area, may provide stimulus to researchers to improve the state of the art concerning educational production, and ultimately may result in such schemes being incorporated into state aid formulas.

8   The Finance of Higher Education

Patterns for the financing of higher education—particularly those involving intergovernmental transfers—have not received the degree or kind of systematic study and analysis which elementary and secondary education have undergone. While a literature is beginning to coalesce around higher education finance issues, the emphasis is quite different from the framework thus far introduced here.

The intent of this chapter, then, is to discuss current issues in higher education finance, and where possible, to build bridges between financial concerns of tertiary education and those of the lower branches. However, it is first necessary to devote some attention to the salient differences which distinguish the higher learning in America.

Distinguishing Characteristics of Higher Education

A number of factors combine to make higher education's functions so different from elementary and secondary education that direct comparisons can be made only in a very tenuous fashion. Some of these are discussed below.

It is of primary importance to recognize the implications of the fact that in contrast to earlier schooling higher education is voluntary, at least in a *de facto* sense. While the pressures to attend are variously great, the option to attend is not legally compulsory. In this country, higher education has successively progressed from education for the elite to mass education, and some suggest that it is entering the period of universal education. Nonetheless, current figures indicate that nationally slightly more than half the college-age population are entering college, and the number is expected to peak at approximately 60 percent. Clearly, despite the criticized lockstep in progression through the education process, the transition between high school and college involves a major societal rite of passage during which substantially irreversible decisions must be made.

The noncompulsory quality of higher education has in turn spawned additional differences from the lower schools. Because of voluntary participation, the amount of diversity—in types of programs as well as types of institutions—has been greatly increased. In contrast to the lower schools, there exists in higher education a strong private sector (both sectarian and independent). In point of fact, private institutions predate public colleges and universities

123

in this country, and many high quality programs continue to exist without direct public support.

Even within a given sector, disciplinary offerings in the same field vary greatly in content and focus. The differences in offerings indicate the variation in basic institutional philosophies and purposes. Such magnitude of differences would be difficult to visualize in the elementary and secondary setting.

In addition, because higher education is not compulsory, there is no overriding public compunction to finance this level of education exclusively from the public purse. Rather it is felt that those who voluntarily choose to partake of higher education should personally provide at least a portion of the funds necessary. The amount one must individually contribute depends on the institutional sector selected, and more recently (as for example, in the State University of New York), in terms of the level of education sought.[1]

While it has been demonstrated that there are sizable differences in unit costs of various programs in the secondary schools,[2] differences between costs of alternative higher education programs would appear to be much greater. The monetary differences are less clear than might otherwise be the case because of the great differences in human inputs (faculty and students) in different programs and different types of institutions.

Also, because of the voluntary nature of higher education, we must be more concerned with the cost associated with foregone income. While foregone income must be considered a *social* cost of education so long as the individual has the capacity to be deployed productively, compulsory attendance statutes remove foregone earnings from the *private* domain of decision making with respect to educational attendance. (It is still possible, however, that foregone earnings affect rates of school dropouts and the type and extent of educational activities (homework, for instance) pursued outside the schools. In a regime of voluntary attendance, however, private decisions concerning attendance (both whether to attend at all and where to attend) are greatly influenced by the existence of foregone earnings).[3]

For all these reasons, a discussion of the finance of higher education must proceed along different lines from those which guided earlier discussions. We must raise different questions and seek different answers.

**Intensity of Current
Financial Difficulties**

Higher education currently stands at the threshold of increasing financial uncertainty as it faces the future. An increasing gap between direct costs of

---

1. See, for example, Carnegie Commission on Higher Education (1973).

2. Comparison of the different unit costs of selected vocational and nonvocational programs in the state of Michigan is contained in Cohn, Hu, and Kaufman (1972).

3. For a discussion of foregone earnings, consult Cohn (1972), pp. 94-99, and Solmon (1970).

public and private institutions, a downturn in both college-going rates and the eighteen-year-advanced moving birth rate, and an apparent disaffection with education in general have combined to provide new impetus for the study of how higher education is financed, and who benefits therefrom.

In order to portray the range of sources upon which higher education depends for its support, and also to indicate the current instability in regard to many of these sources, a brief chronology of events occurring during one academic year will be presented here. The year in question is academic year 1970-71; while this is not the most recent year for which information is available, it serves as an ideal model because of the number of reports issued concerning financial support for higher education.

After detailed study for the Carnegie Commission on Higher Education, Cheit (1971) concludes that 1,540 institutions of higher education either are in, or are headed for, serious financial difficulties. The figure represents fully two-thirds of all U.S. colleges and universities. Included among those considered deeply in trouble are the University of California at Berkeley, Stanford, New York University, and seven of the eight Ivy League institutions.

The Cheit volume, issued by the Carnegie Commission in December of 1970, is aptly titled *The New Depression in Higher Education.* The report was not to stand alone as an isolated instance, but rather as an indication of more glum news to come. In this sense, the Cheit volume was only the first indication of what was to be a sustained pattern for the academic year.

In January (*Chronicle of Higher Education*, January 11, 1971), the Association of American Colleges projected that the total deficit at private colleges and universities has reached $370 million. This is in sharp contrast to the surpluses private institutions had reported as a whole up to 1967-68. The study states bleakly, "Taken collectively, private colleges will not long be able to serve higher education and the nation unless significant aid is soon forthcoming."

During March (*Chronicle of Higher Education*, March 29, 1971), Governor John J. Gilligan of Ohio, recognizing that "rapidly rising costs and expanding enrollments in our state colleges and universities have placed a tremendous burden on the state treasury," proposed his Ohio Plan. This plan would require students to pay back to the state over a period of years the cost of their education. While being ultimately unsuccessful in the Ohio legislature, the Gilligan plan served to highlight the fact that not only private institutions were faced with hard times.

In April (*Chronicle of Higher Education*, April 5, 1971), the Council for Financial Aid to Education reported that private gifts to higher education decreased (by $20 million) during 1970-71 for the first time in over a decade.

Also in April (*Chronicle of Higher Education*, April 19, 1971), Theodore M. Hesburgh, president of Notre Dame, told the National Catholic Education Association that Catholic colleges face "the serious possibility of going broke." Others at the meeting expressed similar feelings.

A year which had seen little other than sour financial news for higher education closed out in true style. In July (*Chronicle of Higher Education*, July 5, 1971), a report by the National Association of State Universities and Land Grant Colleges demonstrated that the major public institutions were in about the same shape as everybody else. The study indicated that more than half of the nation's public institutions were losing ground with less than "stand-still budgets."

Very few institutions—public or private, small or large, independent or church-related—could find much to be happy about financially. New approaches would be needed in the quest for learning how to live on less.

The Costs of Higher Education

By broad categories, what are the types of costs involved in higher education? According to Hansen and Weisbrod (1969), the total costs can be broken down into (1) instructional and capital costs, (2) books and supplies, (3) foregone income of students, and (4) room, board, and transportation. These costs do not include institutional expenditures not directly related to instruction of students (i.e., departmental or organized research, extension or community service, or auxiliary enterprises).

What might the dimensions of these costs be? As part of a comprehensive study undertaken in California of the costs of public higher education during the academic year 1964-65, Hansen and Weisbrod report the costs borne by the state of California and by students and parents. These data for the University of California are presented in Table 8-1. Contrary to the expectation that the state bears the lion's share of costs in public institutions, it is found that students and/or their parents contribute in excess of 70 percent of the total costs. And it must be remembered that this is in a state renowned for its highly articulated systems of low-tuition public institutions. Too frequently in determining the proportion contributed by the state, analysts consider only direct instructional costs—which though important, are among the smallest costs involved.

Since the data in Table 8-1 deal only with California, and exclusively with 1964-65, it is important to ask how these figures compare with national costs in more recent years. Information on costs at public institutions during the academic year 1972-73, as determined by individual surveys of the National Association of State Universities and Land-Grant Colleges and the American Association of State Colleges (and reported by the *Chronicle of Higher Education*), is shown in Table 8-2. While the surveys produced data on tuition and fees and room and board, information was not available on books, supplies, and student transportation. Nor do studies of this kind even attempt to estimate foregone income.

As would be expected, current year figures for all states are considerably higher than those reported earlier for California. However, the direct instruction-

Table 8-1
Average Annual Costs: The University of California, 1964-65

Type of Cost	Cost to Student and/or Parents	Cost to State of California
	First Two Years	
Instructional & capital	$ 250	$1214
Books and supplies	150	0
Foregone income	2000	0
Room, board, transportation	500	0
Total	$2900 (71%)	$1214 (29%)
	Second Two Years	
Instructional & capital	$ 250	$1860
Books and supplies	150	0
Foregone income	3980	20
Room, board, transportation	500	0
Total	$4880 (72%)	$1880 (28%)

Source: Hansen and Weisbrod (1969), Table III-1, p. 42.

Table 8-2
Average Student Charges at Public Institutions, 1972-73 (Annual Costs)

Item	State Universities and Land-Grant Colleges[a]	
	Resident	Nonresident
Tuition and fees	$ 518	$1320
Room and board	975	975
Total	$1467	$2328

Item	State Colleges and Regional Universities[b]	
	Resident	Nonresident
Tuition and fees	$ 435	$1264
Room and board	920	920
Total	$1304	$2087

[a]This group, members of the NASULGC, represents the major state universities and/or land-grant institutions in the respective states.

[b]This group, members of AASCU, represents the former state teachers colleges, now state colleges and regional universities.

Source: Annual surveys of the National Association of State Universities and Land-Grant Colleges and the American Association of State Colleges and Universities, as reported in the *Chronicle of Higher Education* (October 2, 1973), p. 4.

al costs and room and board figures appear to maintain the same approximate ratio to each other (1:2).

Table 8-3 illustrates the variations in state appropriations per capita and per pupil enrolled in public institutions of higher education. Appropriations per capita range from as low as $16.79 in New Hampshire to as high as $84.95 in Hawaii. Appropriations per student vary from $745 in New Hampshire to as high as $2,362 in Alaska. It is interesting, however, that the ranks of the states in appropriations per capita differ significantly from the ranks in appropriations per student. For example, New Jersey ranks 43rd in per capita appropriations and 13th in per student appropriations.

The difference between the two rankings is probably due to a number of factors. They include: (1) different age distributions (for example, Florida, a haven for pensioners, ranks only 26th on the per capita column compared to its high rank—9th—on the per student column); (2) some states are net exporters of students, others are net importers (for example, New Jersey is a leading student exporter, which reflects a low per capita and high per student ranking); (3) some states provide aid to nonpublic schools while others do not; and (4) the computation of enrollment in fall 1972 does not distinguish between degree-credit and nondegree-credit enrollment, nor does it differentiate between full-time and part-time enrollments.[4]

It should be pointed out that state appropriations include funds which may or may not have been fully expended during the fiscal year. Also, the appropriations include funds directed to state scholarship and/or loan agencies, state-wide higher education coordination, and in some cases (such as Pennsylvania), grants to private institutions. In addition, for some states, particularly the noncontiguous states, some perturbations create widely divergent figures.[5]

Finally, the procedure employed to estimate the number of students enrolled in public institutions of higher learning in fall 1972 provides only a rough measure of enrollments. The procedure was as follows. First, the ratio (R) of public to total enrollment in fall 1970 was computed for each state. Then estimated public enrollment in fall 1971 was derived by multiplying the ratio (R) by total enrollment in fall 1971. Public enrollment in fall 1972 was estimated by multiplying the fall 1971 estimated public enrollment by 1.062, reflecting the overall projected increase in higher education enrollment between 1971 and 1972.[6]

The procedure is based on two assumptions. (1) It is assumed that the ratio of

4. Detailed information about the finance of higher education on a state-by-state and institution-by-instituion basis is contained in Chambers (1970).

5. The *Chronicle of Higher Education* (November 13, 1972) acknowledges that, "Although the figures provide a reasonably good guide to the relative 'tax effort' of most states, some may be skewed by demographic, organizational, or other idiosyncrasies" (p. 7).

6. Enrollment levels for 1970 and 1971 were obtained from Simon and Grant (1972), Tables 82, 83; projections of enrollments to the year 1972 were obtained from Simon and Frankel (1972), Table 5.

Table 8-3
Total, Per Capita, and Per Student State Appropriations for Higher Education, 1972-73

State	Appropriations, 1972-73 Amount ($) (1)	Rank (2)	2-Yr. Change, 1970-71 to 1972-73 % (3)	Appropriation Per Capita, 1972-73 Amount ($) (4)	Rank (5)	Estimated Enrollment in Public Institutions of Higher Education, Fall 1972 (6)	Appropriations per Student, 1972-73 Amount ($) (1) ÷ (6) (7)	Rank (8)
Alabama	106,444,000	28	42	30.54	46	94,114	1,131	35
Alaska	21,978,000	46	29	73.75	2	9,303	2,362	1
Arizona	112,712,000	26	35	58.86	3	106,158	1,062	41
Arkansas	56,371,000	37	3	28.63	48	48,230	1,169	33
California	1,009,272,000	1	24	50.41	8	1,058,126	954	45
Colorado	115,243,000	24	4	49.80	9	114,016	1,011	43
Connecticut	113,724,000	25	17	37.10	37	78,146	1,455	15
Delaware	25,887,000	44	28	46.31	13	21,282	1,216	28
Florida	302,112,000	8	25	43.18	26	189,083	1,598	9
Georgia	117,819,000	15	20	38.12	35	113,128	1,572	11
Hawaii	64,478,000	34	17	84.95	1	31,647	2,037	3
Idaho	36,785,000	40	17	48.98	11	28,453	1,293	22
Illinois	516,726,000	3	9	46.09	14	320,331	1,613	8
Indiana	210,595,000	12	21	39.86	31	150,704	1,397	20
Iowa	125,505,000	23	16	43.55	22	72,580	1,729	5
Kansas	93,087,000	31	14	41.80	27	97,612	953	46
Kentucky	139,485,000	20	28	45.35	16	84,601	1,649	6
Louisiana	146,664,000	21	21	39.80	33	112,134	1,308	21
Maine	33,612,000	41	21	33.05	41	26,688	1,259	25

Table 8-3 (cont.)

State	Appropriations, 1972-73 Amount ($)	Rank	2-Yr. Change, 1970-71 to 1972-73 %	Appropriation Per Capita, 1972-73 Amount ($)	Rank	Estimated Enrollment in Public Institutions of Higher Education, Fall 1972	Appropriations per Student, 1972-73 Amount ($) (1) ÷ (6)	Rank
	(1)	(2)	(3)	(4)	(5)	(6)	(7)	(8)
Maryland	159,156,000	18	32	39.84	32	130,021	1,224	27
Massachusetts	154,451,000	19	33	26.79	49	122,189	1,264	24
Michigan	417,825,000	5	22	46.08	15	333,697	1,252	26
Minnesota	174,040,000	16	21	44.71	18	145,557	1,196	30
Mississippi	97,008,000	30	35	43.29	23	69,000	1,406	17
Missouri	161,464,000	17	23	34.18	39	143,186	1,127	37
Montana	30,798,000	42	6	43.20	24	29,827	1,033	42
Nebraska	56,780,000	36	17	37.53	36	57,909	981	44
Nevada	20,656,000	47	30	39.80	33	14,764	1,399	19
New Hampshire	12,880,000	50	18	16.79	50	17,300	745	50
New Jersey	236,380,000	10	53	32.28	43	154,404	1,530	13
New Mexico	50,968,000	38	23	48.54	12	45,188	1,128	36
New York	822,425,000	2	10	44.85	17	507,622	1,620	7
North Carolina	223,486,000	11	27	43.64	21	114,980	1,944	4
North Dakota	27,476,000	43	18	44.32	19	30,522	900	47
Ohio	325,105,000	7	25	30.19	47	298,679	1,088	39
Oklahoma	81,720,000	32	18	31.35	44	101,979	801	49
Oregon	106,990,000	27	11	49.10	10	97,415	1,098	38
Pennsylvania	388,874,000	6	26	32.64	42	246,281	1,579	10
Rhode Island	40,029,000	39	28	42.72	25	27,752	1,442	16

South Carolina	104,980,000	29	36	40.42	28	44,971	2,334	2
South Dakota	22,736,000	45	7	33.78	40	26,372	862	48
Tennessee	127,994,000	22	30	31.90	45	108,056	1,185	32
Texas	463,528,000	4	35	40.32	30	388,197	1,194	31
Utah	57,195,000	35	26	51.02	7	52,604	1,087	40
Vermont	16,743,000	49	14	36.24	38	13,224	1,266	23
Virginia	185,756,000	14	37	40.35	29	125,592	1,479	14
Washington	190,467,000	13	**	55.92	5	158,433	1,202	29
West Virginia	77,922,000	33	33	43.78	20	55,530	1,403	18
Wisconsin	257,243,000	9	42	56.94	4	165,428	1,555	12
Wyoming	18,316,000	48	25	53.71	6	15,930	1,150	34

Sources: Columns 1-5:   *Chronicle of Higher Education 7* (November 13, 1972), pp. 6-7.

Column 6:   Derived from *Digest of Educational Statistics* (Washington: U.S. Government Printing Office, 1972), Tables 82 and 83; and *Projections of Educational Statistics to 1980-81* (Washington: U.S. Government Printing Office, 1972), Table 5. The derivation is explained in the text.

public to total enrollments in fall 1970 remained unchanged both in fall 1971 and 1972. (2) It is also assumed that the overall projected growth in higher education enrollments between 1971 and 1972 also applies to public institutions.

A recent report by the Carnegie Commission on Higher Education (1973) also provides information on the total outlay for higher education and its source. In all data presentations, the commission clearly distinguishes between two different approaches to analysis of the financial impact of higher education operations and programs. They consider *monetary outlays* to include all transactions in which actual "real" dollars pass between individuals, governments, and institutions. An analysis of monetary outlays would consider all services provided by the institution regardless of who pays the charges.

In contrast, the total *economic costs* are meant to include all costs, including the opportunity cost of college attendance and other implicit economic considerations. While these may include the effect of exemptions in lieu of property taxes, the deductability of gifts to higher education, and the favored tax status of foundations supporting higher education, the commission considers foregone income of students to serve as the exclusive entry in this portion of the ledger.

Estimates of the total national monetary outlay and economic cost of higher education during academic year 1970-71 by the Carnegie Commission staff are shown in Table 8-4. Monetary outlays were approximately $22 billion in this time period, and total economic costs were approximately $39 billion. If we consider only monetary outlays, students and/or their parents contributed one-third, the remainder coming from the various levels of government and private philanthropy. In considering total economic costs, the figures are reversed, with students and parents contributing two-thirds. This information helps to clarify the confusion resulting from different analyses of college costs and will be important in later discussions of higher education benefits.[7]

The Benefits of Higher Education

In order to make any decisions about the equity or efficiency of the distribution of higher education costs presented in the previous section, one is forced to inquire as to who benefits from investment in colleges and universities. Aside from its consumption function, higher education is believed to provide many pecuniary and nonpecuniary benefits at some future date, thus justifying the term investment.

There are two polar positions on the question of who benefits. Leslie (1972) discusses these two views as follows:

7. Additional information on higher education costs and benefits can be found in Harris (1962, 1972) and Joint Economic Committee (1969).

Table 8-4

The Costs of Higher Education, 1970-71: Monetary Outlays and Economic Costs
(Amounts in Millions of Dollars)

Income or Expense Category	Total Amount	Students/ Parents	Amount Contributed by: Local, State or Fed. Govt.	Philan- thropy
State and local funds	7,604 [a](7,494; 110)		7,604	
Federal funds	1,945 [a](1,295; 650)		1,945	
Tuition and fees	4,850 [a](1,887; 2,963)	4,850		
Endowments	500 [a](701; 430)			500
Gifts	1,160 [a](330; 830)			1,160
Total Educational Funds of Institutions	16,059 [a](11,076; 4,983)	4,850	9,549	1,660
(Percentage of total)		(30.2%)	(59.5%)	(10.3%)
Student subsistence	6,299	6,299		
Student aid		−3,084	+2,383	+321
Total Monetary Outlay	21,978	8,065	11,932	1,981
(Percentage of total)	(100%)	(36.7%)	(54.3%)	(9.0%)
Foregone income	16,859	16,859		
Total Economic Cost	38,837	24,924	11,932	1,981
(Percentage of total)	(100%)	(64.2%)	(30.7%)	(5.1%)

[a]Figures in parentheses indicate relative division of total figure by public and private institutions, respectively.

Source: Adapted from Carnegie Commission for Higher Education (1973), Table 4, p. 24.

Again there is a dichotomy. Some argue that it is the individual who benefits. Others argue that it is society.... Exponents of the individual benefits theory list as evidence: significantly greater lifetime income, greater productivity and thus attractiveness to employers, and the improved life-style of college graduates as opposed to non-graduates. . . .

The second viewpoint is that society is the real beneficiary of higher education because college educated persons are more open-minded, critical and socially responsive. . . . Proponents of this philosophy point out that the individual's economic productivity is shared by society in the form of taxes. They also point out that the college educated occupy fewer jail cells, have fewer auto accidents, are healthier, and have lower absentee rates from their jobs (pp. 11, 16).

Attempting to disentangle the positions, one encounters a host of methodological and conceptual difficulties.[8] Foremost among these, because of the ability selectivity involved, it becomes problematic to determine which of the

8. For a further treatment of these difficulties, consult Cohn (1972), esp. Ch. 5.

ascribed benefits would have accrued to these college-educated individuals purely on the basis of greater talents, had they not attended college. Furthermore, even the definition of benefits, no less their quantification, is particularly difficult. This is especially true of the nonpecuniary benefits, many of which fall disproportionately on the societal side of the account. Methodologically, there is concern about how to weight monetary benefits in terms of native ability, future dollar values, and whether to employ cross-sectional or cohort analysis.

As part of one study devoted principally to assess the distribution of costs and benefits of higher education, Hansen and Weisbrod (1969) computed the additional lifetime earnings of college graduates in California. From previous research evidence, these investigators felt it most appropriate to reduce income by 25 percent as an ability correction and to discount future earnings at a 5 percent rate—which many believe to be quite modest.[9] Using this approach, they estimated that the average male college graduate would earn an additional discounted lifetime income equal to $20,900 due to their college attendance. For females, the amount was considerably less—$3,900. They are forced to conclude: "Viewed in this light—the light in which, incidentally, an ordinary investment is viewed in the business capital markets—higher education is a good deal less valuable than is commonly believed" (p. 27).

In contrast to these results, both Becker (1964) and Taubman and Wales (1972) independently found the rates of return from college to slightly exceed rates applicable in the commercial sector. It would need to be concluded, therefore, that investment in college may lead to some pecuniary gain (variously depending on survey methodology and sample composition), but seldom is it the bonanza that has been so frequently portrayed.

This has caused many to look more toward the consumptive and non-pecuniary investment functions of the college experience. The Carnegie Commission believes that an increasing number of families is providing higher education for their children as a form of consumption for them. Further, the commission feels that funds used to pay for college education are diverted from other consumption alternatives rather than from savings.

Although elementary and secondary education provide benefits to pupils and their parents, there are few who would question a serious role for government (whatever the *level* of government involved). The reason for this is the assumption of large external benefits (i.e., the difference between social and private benefits). In higher education, however, there is a lack of consensus regarding the magnitude and importance of such externalities. In consequence, government's role is not unambiguous.

On the other hand, it has been recognized that whatever externalities that higher education creates are likely to spread over a wider geographical region than is the case for elementary and secondary education. Therefore, there is a stronger case for involving higher levels of government such as the state and

9. The rate of discount currently in use for federal projects is 10 percent.

federal agencies in the regulation and/or support of higher education. Addition-ally, there has been a greater inclination to gloss over the distinction between private and public institutions of higher learning than is the case in lower educational levels.[10]

At the same time, the complexity of higher education in terms of variation of educational costs by program or year of study, the interwoven costs of teaching, research, administration, extension, and so forth, and the lack of knowledge concerning societal benefits has mitigated the development of state aid formulas of the type and degree of sophistication that were developed for elementary and secondary education. Although a description of state aid programs would certainly be of interest, it is beyond the scope of this volume. What could be said at this point is that issues of equity and efficiency, much like those discussed earlier in the volume (for example, Figure 3-1) are also relevant in the case of higher education. The material in Chapters 6 and 7 is likewise relevant, although its application to higher education would require considerable adaptations to the circumstances prevailing in that domain.[11]

Lingering Issues

In adidtion to some of the methodological and substantive concerns mentioned earlier, other general issues exist to which there is no clear resolution. Some of these will be discussed briefly here.

A great deal of interest has been focused on the equity of public finance of higher education in terms of the distribution of costs and benefits of educational subsidies by family income.

Hansen and Weisbrod (1969) noted that in California, to the extent that the lowest income groups availed themselves to higher education opportunities, they tended to be most clustered in the junior and community colleges, where the extent of state subsidies were lowest. This condition is made more salient by the fact that state programs of taxation are known to be at best proportional in the middle-income brackets and regressive at the lower extreme. Hansen and Weisbrod note:

In short, there is a highly unequal distribution in the amounts of public subsidies actually received, even though California prides itself on the wide access to higher education it provides and on the high enrollment ratios which are

10. One example of this attitude is the G.I. Bill of Rights which permits veterans to attend any accredited institution, whether private or public. Another example of this is the recent decision by the U.S. Supreme Court upholding state assistance for construction of facilities at church-related colleges. See *Chronicle of Higher Education* 7 (July 2, 1973): 1, 5.

11. One study on economies of scale in higher education is Maynard (1971). An attempt to measure the relationship between inputs and outputs in higher education was made by Astin (1968).

presumably a reflection of this. Moreover, there is little reason to believe that the distribution of public subsidies through higher education is less unequal in other states than it is in California (p. 68).

Some low income persons have benefited handsomely from the availability of publicly-subsidized higher education. But on the whole, the effect of these subsidies is to promote greater rather than less inequality among people of various social and economic backgrounds by making available substantial subsidies that lower income families are either not eligible for or cannot make use of because of other conditions or constraints associated with their income position. To overcome the effects of the present system would require a substantial overhaul of the pricing system in public higher education, a realignment of the tax structure, and/or a broadening or the eligibility base for public expenditure programs (p. 78).[12]

The Carnegie Commission looked at the same issue on a national basis and arrived at an ambivalent conclusion:

If it is judged merely in relation to estimated tax contributions, the distribution of institutional subsidies by family income appears to contribute to greater social equity. But if one contrasts the distribution of these subsidies with the family income distribution of the college-age population, one might arrive at the opposite conclusion (Carnegie Commission on Higher Education, 1973, p. 46).

The commission was not unaware of the Hansen-Weisbrod finding or the controversy generated by alternative analyses (see, for example, Pechman [1970]). Apparently, this is an issue of importance which has not yet been resolved.

Concern has also been voiced about whether higher education should in the future be financed through institutions or through individual students. Many of the sources cited in regard to "educational vouchers" in Chapter 2 are clearly relevant here too. Leslie (1973) has recently questioned whether the market model can truly be applied to higher education, as proponents of the voucher plans have suggested. While many of these issues were discussed frequently in reference to development and passage of the "Education Amendments of 1972" (Public Law 92-318), again the conclusion must be that the jury is still out on this issue.

Others feel that increased attention needs to be paid to the possibility of weighted tuition and subsidies based on the level of education undertaken. The state of New York has recently initiated such a procedure both in grants to private institutions and in tuition charges at the State University of New York.

There is no question that upper-division undergraduate instruction is currently more costly than lower-division work. And graduate study is currently much more costly than upper-division programs. By charging the same tuition for all levels, one is in effect subsidizing the higher branches out of tuition, fees, or public subsidies derived from the lower levels.

---

12. For another view concerning the policy suggestions, see Cohn (1970).

In addition, because the levels of instruction are often skewed in terms of income distribution of students, a number of critics are quick to point out that this serves to further attenuate the lack of equity in the system.

It is not surprising, therefore, that a variety of solutions have been advanced in recent years for the finance of higher education. They range from full-costs tuition, coupled with scholarships or loans to capable but poor students, to free universal higher education.[13] One position that appears to be gaining strength both academically and politically is a wider use of guaranteed student loans. The Educational Opportunity Bank and other contingency-repayment mechanisms or state loan programs are likely to gain in popularity in the years to come.[14]

Concluding Comments

This chapter has briefly portrayed the nature of higher education finance, presented a data base on the monetary outlays and economic costs of tertiary education, and discussed the relationship of costs to benefits and other related issues. Higher education finance is just now beginning to receive the quantity of study which has been devoted to other branches of education, but much remains to be done.

Higher education is distinguished by its diversity in terms of instructional levels, types of programs, and types of institutions. A large private sector provides much of the educational service. While public subsidies have traditionally supported public institutions, increasingly private institutions are receiving public funds for general operating purposes as well as special programs.

While both society and the individual stand to gain many nonpecuniary benefits from the availability of institutions of higher education, the dimensions of the monetary benefits to both, while considerable, are less amenable to consistent quantification than might be expected. Similarly, the income redistributional aspects of higher education still engender controversy.

Few states have yet dealt effectively with economies of scale, differential costs of alternative programs, or with equitable allocation of resources in their higher education systems. Where formulas exist for distributing higher education funds on a state-wide level, seldom are these formulas specific in detail. Much more work is needed in order to allow the application of procedures specified earlier in chapters to the amelioration of higher education finance. Nonetheless, the case of higher education provides an excellent counterpoint to the previous discussion of the elementary and secondary schools.

---

13. For a defense of full-cost pricing, see Tollison and Willett (1973). For another view consult Hansen and Weisbrod (1971a).

14. See for example, Bowen (1969), Danière (1969), Shell et al. (1970), Van Den Haag (1956), Vickrey (1962), and Zacharias (1969).

Summary and Conclusion

Despite sharp differences among practitioners and scholars regarding the proper sphere for, and mode of, involvement by state governments in educational finance, few would dispute an increasing role for state aid to public education. The early chapters of this volume have attempted to describe in detail some of the major proposals for state aid as well as the current status of state aid in the various states. (Since existing aid formulas have been put under increasing pressure by reformers, what is current at this writing may be obsolete a short time later. Nevertheless, a current description is necessary to put matters in a proper perspective.) Also, the concept of "equalization" has been carefully scrutinized, and some of the problems associated with the goal of achieving a measure of equalization have been noted.

Although the foundation program is still the modal state-aid plan, there are several indications of its demise in future years. Likely successors are variants of the percentage equalizing approach, the guaranteed valuation (resource equalizer) plan, and the district power equalizing plan. In addition, some form of a voucher system has already been put into effect in New Hampshire, and further experiments with the system are continuing in California.

Several interesting insights concerning the effects of state aid are provided in the empirical analysis of Chapter 5. First, support was found for the hypothesis that state aid is both stimulative and substitutive. But results of the interstate model differ from those of the county model, suggesting that the *form* of the state aid formula may influence the incentives local schools have to increase educational spending from local revenues. The results also indicate that state aid is positively associated with average state school size, and negatively associated with nonpublic enrollment rates, bond sales, and local revenues.

Proposals for allocative incentives to be included in the state aid formulas were discussed in Chapters 6 and 7. Several options were discussed in regard to scale effects. One method would be to levy a penalty on schools which have enrollments below or above optimum scale. The penalty would be in proportion to the cost savings that would be realized had the district operated schools with optimal enrollment levels. Another method would be to calculate past improvements in a district's enrollment relative to optimal scale levels and to provide districts with incentive payment which would be in proportion to a district's improvement in school size relative to the improvement experienced by all districts in a state. A further possibility that may be considered is a combination of the penalty factor and the incentive payment. Together, the two methods would penalize schools that have inoptimal enrollment levels yet reward districts that have shown an improvement over past periods. As a final suggestion, the analysis considered the employment of a relative wealth factor in the incentive formulas to increase their equalizing impact.

A number of options concerning the use of incentive features to increase output and/or output per dollar of cost have been discussed. In each instance, penalty factors and incentive payments, along the lines suggested for the scale effects, have been proposed. Combinations of the penalty factor and the incentive payment and/or the output and output-per-dollar-of-cost plans have also been discussed, as have equity considerations.

One could, of course, include the scale effect in the incentive feature for the output-per-dollar-of-cost plan. In that case, variations in costs per unit of output would reflect inefficient management as well as inefficient school size. In order that the school size effect will receive explicit attention, however, the two effects have been separated. Thus the discussion in Chapter 7 (of output per dollar of cost) employed a cost concept from which the scale effect has been netted out.

A brief discussion of the financing of higher education has been presented in Chapter 8. Although rules concerning the distribution of state aid to institutions of higher education have been proposed (for example, basing state aid on student credit-hours), one finds a surprising lack of sophistication and rigor in the analysis of aid to higher education. Although there are numerous factors distinguishing elementary and secondary education from higher learning, some of the *fundamental concepts* involving equalization and allocative incentives which were discussed in the context of the lower levels of education could also be applied to higher levels of education.

Although we believe that the information and ideas provided in this volume should be valuable to students, scholars, and government officials, it is recognized that both the empirical and theoretical components of the study are subject to various limitations. For example, the empirical study could have benefited from additional analysis of less aggregative data, more recent data, and additional variables that were not included in the present study. The development of the incentive features is limited by the nature of the knowledge we possess about scale effects and the educational production process. Moreover, a simulation of the incentive formulas—using actual data for a number of states—would have been highly desirable.

Further development of the empirical model, along the lines suggested above, would appear to be highly advantageous, and a test of the impact of the incentive features on a district's behavior would form a most interesting scholarly investigation. It is hoped that the present study will stimulate further research in this area and generate the enactment of incentive features in state aid formulas so that schools will be provided the incentive to produce more per dollar of cost.

Glossary

A_i	Total state aid to district i
A_i^*	Adjusted state aid to district i
ADA	Average daily attendance
ADM	Average daily membership
$BOND$	Total approved par value of bond issues (1962-71), per pupil enrolled in public elementary and secondary schools
$BSTR$	Basic school funds
C_i	Cost per pupil in district i
C_i^*	Adjusted cost per pupil in district i
C_m^*	The minimum cost per pupil in the state, associated with the optimal school size
Δ	A change in the variable following this symbol
EA_i	Equalization aid to the ith district
$EQUALIZ$	Equalization score of state
EXP_i	Per pupil expenditures in the ith district
F	Foundation level of support
g_i	Relative savings due to improvement in scale by district i
g_i^*	Adjusted relative savings due to improvement in scale by district i
h_{1i}	Relative improvement in output by the ith district
h_{2i}	Relative improvement in output/cost ratio in the ith district
I_i	Personal income in the ith district
I_s	Personal income in the state
IF	Incentive fund
$INCPOV$	Incidence of poverty
$MEWAV$	The equalized weighted assessed valuation of real and tangible property, modified by the ratio of district median family income to state median family income
N	Number of districts in the state
NC_i	Costs net of scale effects for the ith district
$NEGRO$	Negro enrollment in public schools as a percentage of total enrollment

141

p	A scalar between 0 and 1
PCI	Personal income per capita
PPI	Personal income per pupil in ADA
$\%ENNP$	Percentage of pupils enrolled in nonpublic schools
$\%TPOPENP$	Percentage of total population enrolled in public schools
q_1	A sum chosen for the output penalty
q_2	A sum chosen for the output/cost penalty
Q	A composite index of per pupil output
Q^n	An output norm (based on the highest current output level, the average level, or some other level the state wishes to consider)
r	Mandated tax rate
RE	Revenue entitlement, i.e., the amount of educational revenues to which a district is entitled within a given range of tax levies
$RELSIZE$	Relative size of schools
REV	Local revenue per pupil
S	School size, measured by enrollment
$S*$	Optimal school size
$SALARY$	Average teachers' salary
SC	School census
S/T	Student/teacher ratio
$STAID$	State aid
t	A time period (if t = school year 1972-73, then $t-1$ is the school year 1971-72)
$URBAN$	Urban population as a percentage of total population
V_g	A given level of property valuation which all districts may use to compute the level of property tax revenues per pupil that the state will guarantee
V_h	Assessed valuation per pupil in the wealthiest district
V_i	Assessed valuation per pupil in the ith district
V_s	Average per pupil valuation in the state
W_h	Per pupil wealth in the wealthiest district
W_i	Per pupil wealth in the ith district
$WADA$	Weighted average daily attendance
x	A scalar between 0 and 1

Bibliography

Bibliography

Advisory Commission on Intergovernmental Relations (1969). *State Aid to Local Government*. Washington, D.C.: U.S. Government Printing Office.

Alexander, K.; Hamilton, O.; and Forth, D. (1971). "Classification of State School Funds." In *Status and Impact of Educational Finance Programs*, Vol. 4, edited by R.L. Johns, K. Alexander, and D.H. Stollar. Gainesville, Fla.: National Educational Finance Project, 1971, pp. 29-112.

"Analysis of Senate Bill 72: School Finance Program in Utah" (1973). Unpublished memorandum.

Astin, A.W. (1968). "Undergraduate Achievement and Institutional 'Excellence.'" *Science* 161 (August 16, 1968): 661-68.

Bator, F.M. (1958). "The Anatomy of Market Failure." *Quarterly Journal of Economics* 72 (1958): 351-79.

Becker, G.S. (1960). "Underinvestment in College Education?" *American Economic Review (Papers and Proceedings)* 50 (May 1960): 345-54.

_____ (1964). *Human Capital: A Theoretical and Empirical Analysis, with Special Reference to Education*. New York: National Bureau of Economic Research.

Beers, Joan S. (1970). *Educational Quality Assessment Phase II Findings, Section 4: The Ten Goals of Quality Education*. Harrisburg, Pa.: Pennsylvania Department of Education.

Benson, C.S., ed. (1963). *Perspectives on the Economics of Education*. Boston: Houghton Mifflin Co.

_____ (1968). *The Economics of Public Education*. 2nd ed. New York: Houghton Mifflin Co.

Berke, J.S.; Campbell, A.K.; and Goettel, R.J. (1972). *Financing Equal Educational Opportunity*. Berkeley, Calif.: McCutchan Publishing Co.

Bishop, George A. (1964). "Stimulative versus Substitutive Effects of State School Aid in New England." *National Tax Journal* 17 (June 1964): 133-43.

Booms, Bernard H., and Hu, Teh-wei (1971). "Toward a Positive Theory of State and Local Public Expenditures: An Empirical Example." *Public Finance* 26:419-36.

Bowen, H.R. (1969). "Tuitions and Student Loans in the Finance of Higher Education." In Joint Economic Committee (1969): 618-31.

Bowman, M.J. (1970). "Education and Economic Growth." In Johns et al. (1970): 83-120.

Brazer, H.E. (1959). *City Expenditure in the United States*. Occasional Paper 66. New York: National Bureau of Economic Research.

_____ (1970). "Federal, State, and Local Responsibility for Financing Education." In Johns et al. (1970): 235-64.

_____ (1970a). "The Variable Cost Burdens of State and Local Governments." In *Financing State and Local Governments*, pp. 93-106. Boston: Federal Reserve Bank of Boston.

Buchanan, J.M. (1965). *The Public Finances*, rev. ed. Homewood, Illinois: Richard D. Irwin, Inc.

_____, and Stubblebine, W.C. (1962). "Externality," *Economica* (N.S.) 29:371-84.

Bowles, Samuel (1970). "Towards an Educational Production Function." In *Education, Income, and Human Capital*, edited by W. Lee Hansen. New York: Columbia University Press for National Bureau of Economic Research, pp. 11-61.

Burkhead, J., with Fox, T.G., and Holland, J.W. (1967). *Input and Output in Large-City High Schools*. Syracuse, N.Y.: Syracuse University Press.

Campbell, P.B., and Beers, J.S. (1970). *Educational Quality Assessment Phase II Findings, Section I: The Pennsylvania Plan*. Harrisburg, Pa.: Pennsylvania Department of Education.

Carnegie Commission on Higher Education (1973). *Higher Education: Who Pays? Who Benefits? Who Should Pay?* New York: McGraw-Hill.

Carr, R.H., and Hayward, G.C. (1970). "Education by Chit: An Examination." *Education and Urban Society* 2:179-192.

Chambers, M.M. (1970). *Higher Education in the Fifty States*. Danville, Ill.: Interstate Printers and Publishers.

Cheit, E.F. (1971). *The New Depression in Higher Education*. New York: Carnegie Commission on Higher Education (McGraw-Hill).

Chow, G.C. (1964). "A Comparison of Alternative Estimates for Simultaneous Equations." *Econometrica* 32 (October 1964): 532-33.

Chronicle of Higher Education. "Average College Deficit Increases Five-Fold in Year." 5 (January 11, 1971).

_____. "Catholic Colleges, Facing 'Possibility of Going Broke,' Are Urged to Adopt More Humanistic Education." 5 (April 19, 1971).

_____. "Forty-one State Institutions Said to Be in Financial Straits; Ten Expect to Finish Current Fiscal Year in Red." 5 (July 5, 1971).

_____. "Gifts to Colleges Dip, First Time in Ten Years." 5 (April 5, 1971): 1.

_____. " 'Ohio Plan' Creates a Storm; Would Require Students to Repay State for Education in Public Colleges." 5 (March 29, 1971).

_____. "State Tax Funds to Operate Colleges and Universities: 50 Legislatures Appropriate $8.5-Billion for 1972-73." 7 (November 13, 1972): 6-7.

_____. "Student Charges at 327 State Institutions." 7 (October 2, 1972): 4.

Clune, W.H. III. "Law and Economics in Hobson v. Hansen: An Introductory Note." *Journal of Human Resources* 7 (Summer 1972): 275-82.

Clyde, R.W. (1973). "Educational Expenditure Determination Study: A Supply and Demand Approach." Unpublished Masters Essay. University Park, Pa.: The Pennsylvania State University, Department of Economics.

Cohn, Elchanan (1968). "Economies of Scale in Iowa High School Operations." *Journal of Human Resources* 3 (Fall 1968): 422-34.

_____ (1970). "Benefits and Costs of Higher Education and Income Redistribution: A Comment." *Journal of Human Resources* 5 (Spring 1970): 222-26.

_____ (1972). *The Economics of Education*. Lexington, Mass.: D.C. Heath and Company.

_____ (1975). *Input-Output Analysis in Public Education*. Cambridge, Mass.: Ballinger Publishing Company (forthcoming).

Cohn, Elchanan, and Hu, Teh-wei (1973). "Economies of Scale, by Program, in Secondary Schools." *Journal of Educational Administration* 11 (October 1973).

Cohn, Elchanan; Hu, Teh-wei; and Kaufman, Jacob J. (1972). *The Costs of Vocational and Nonvocational Programs: A Study of Michigan Secondary Schools*. University Park, Pa.: Institute for Research on Human Resources, The Pennsylvania State University.

Cohn, Elchanan, and Riew, John (1974). "Cost Functions in Public Schools." *Journal of Human Resources* 9 (forthcoming).

Coleman, J.S. (1970). Foreward to *Private Wealth and Public Education*, by J.E. Coons, W.H. Clune III, and S.D. Sugarman. Cambridge, Mass.: Belknap Press of Harvard University.

Commission on Alternative Design for Funding Education (1973). *Financing the Public Schools: A Search for Equality*. Bloomington, Indiana: Phi Delta Kappa.

Conant, J.B. (1972). "Full State Funding." in *Financing Public Schools* (1972), pp. 111-18.

Coons, J.E.; Clune, W.H. III; and Sugarman, S.D. (1970). *Private Wealth and Public Education*. Cambridge, Mass.: Belknap Press of Harvard University.

Cowle, I.M. (1968). *School Aid in New York State*. New York: Teachers College Press.

Cubberley, E.P. (1905). *School Funds and Their Apportionment*. Contributions to Education, no. 2. New York: Columbia University Teachers College.

_____ (1919). *Public Education in the United States*. Boston: Houghton Mifflin Co.

Cummins, J. (1973). "Utah's Schools Get $216 Million, New Methods to Spend." *The Salt Lake Tribune* (March 11, 1973): A5.

Danière, A. (1969). "The Benefits and Costs of Alternative Federal Programs of Financial Aid to College Students." In Joint Economic Committee (1969): 556-98.

Davis, J.R. (1970). "The Social and Economic Externalities of Education." In Johns et al. (1970): 59-82.

Davis, O.A. (1965). "Empirical Evidence of Political Influence Upon the Expenditure Policies of Public Schools." In Margolis (1965): 92-111.

Denison, E.F. (1962). *The Sources of Economic Growth in the United States*. New York: Committee for Economic Development.

_____ (1964). "Measuring the Contribution of Education (and the Residual) to Economic Growth." In *The Residual Factor and Economic Growth*. Paris: Organization for Economic Co-operation and Development.

Dennis, D.M. (1973). *The School District Equalization Act*. Topeka, Kansas: Legislative Research Department, Department of Education, April 10, 1973.

Dimond, P.R. (1972). "The Art of the Possible." In *Financing Public Schools* (1972), pp. 69-80.

Due, J.F., and Friedlaender, A.F. (1973). *Government Finance: Economics of the Public Sector*, 5th ed. Homewood, Ill.: Richard D. Irwin, Inc.

Ebel, R.L. (1972). "What Are the Schools for?" *Phi Delta Kappan* 54:3-7.

Eckstein, O. (1961). "A Survey of the Theory of Public Expenditure Criteria." In *Public Finances: Needs, Sources and Utilization*, edited by J.M. Buchanan, pp. 439-94. Princeton: Princeton University Press.

Effective Use of Resources in State Higher Education (1970). Atlanta: Southern Regional Educational Board.

Erickson, Donald A. (1970). "Education Vouchers: Nature and Funding." *Theory into Practice* 9:108-116.

Fabricant, S. (1952). *The Trend of Government Activity in the United States Since 1900*. New York: National Bureau of Economic Research.

Ferguson, C.E. (1972). *Microeconomic Theory*, 3rd ed. Homewood, Ill.: Richard D. Irwin.

Fleischmann Commission (1973). *Report on the Quality, Cost, and Financing of Elementary and Secondary Education in New York State*. New York: Viking Press.

Financing Public Schools (1972). Boston: Federal Reserve Bank of Boston.

Fisher, Glenn W. (1964). "Interstate Variation in State and Local Government Expenditure." *National Tax Journal* 17 (March 1964): 57-74.

Foster, B.J., and Barr, R.H. (1972). *Fall 1971 Statistics of Public Schools, Advance Report*. Washington, D.C.: National Center for Educational Statistics, May 1972.

Fox, T.G. (1971). "The Use of Mutually Interdependent vs. Mutually Independent School System Outputs in Estimating Education Production Functions." *Proceedings of the Social Statistics Section, American Statistical Association*.

Freeman, Rodger A. (1953). "State Aid and Support of Our Public Schools." *State Government* 26 (October 1953): 237-40, 252-53.

Friedman, M. (1955). "The Role of Government in Education." In *Economics and the Public Interest*, edited by R.A. Solo. New Brunswick, N.J.: Rutgers University Press, pp. 123-53.

_____ (1962). *Capitalism and Freedom*. Chicago: University of Chicago Press.

Glennan, T.K. (1971). "OEO Experiments in Education." *Compact* 5:3-5.

Goetz, Charles J. (1972). *What is Revenue Sharing?* Washington, D.C.: The Urban Institute.

Hansen, W.L., and Weisbrod, B.A. (1969). *Benefits, Costs, and Finance of Public Higher Education*. Chicago: Markham Publishing Co.

_____ (1971). "On the Distribution of Costs and Benefits of Public Higher education: Reply." *Journal of Human Resources* 6 (Summer 1971): 363-74.

_____ (1971a). "A New Approach to Higher Education Finance." In *Financing Higher Education: Alternatives for the Federal Government*, edited by Mel Orwig, pp. 117-42. Iowa City, Iowa: American College Testing Program.

Hanushek, Eric A. (1972). *Education and Race*. Lexington, Mass.: Heath Lexington Books.

Harris, S.E. (1962). *Higher Education: Resources and Finance*. New York: McGraw-Hill.

_____ (1972). *A Statistical Portrait of Higher Education*. New York: Carnegie Commission on Higher Education (McGraw-Hill).

Haveman, R.H. (1970). *The Economics of the Public Sector*. New York: John Wiley and Sons, Inc.

Henderson, J.M. (1968). "Local Government Expenditures: A Social Welfare Analysis." *Review of Economics and Statistics* 50 (March 1968): 156-63.

Henderson, P.D. (1968). "Investment Criteria for Public Enterprises." In *Public Enterprise*, edited by R. Turvey, pp. 86-169. Baltimore: Penguin Books, Inc.

Herber, B.P. (1971). *Modern Public Finance*, rev. ed. Homewood, Illinois: Richard D. Irwin, Inc.

Hettich, Walter (1968). "Equalization Grants, Minimum Standards, and Unit Cost Differences In Education." *Yale Economic Essays* 8 (Fall 1968): 5-55.

Hickrod, G. Alan (1971). "Local Demand for Education: A Critique of School Finance and Economic Research Circa 1959-1969." *Review of Educational Research* 41:35-49.

_____ (1972). *Definition, Measurement, and Application of the Concept of Equalization in School Finance*. Illinois State Superintendent's Advisory Committee on School Finance (Occasional Paper), February 1972.

_____ (1973). *Alternative Fiscal Solutions to Equity Problems in Public Schools*. Gainesville, Fla.: National Education Finance Project, 1973. Cited in personal letter from G. Alan Hickrod, July 26, 1973.

_____ (1973a). "Demur on Full State Funding." In Hickrod et al. (1973), p. 105.

_____ , and Sabulao, Cesar M. (1969). *Increasing Social and Economic Inequalities among Suburban Schools*. Danville, Ill.: The Interstate Printers & Publishers, Inc.

Hickrod, G.A. et al. (1973). *Final Report of the Superintendent's Advisory Committee on School Finance*. Springfield, Illinois: Office of the Superintendent of Public Instruction, State of Illinois, April 1973.

Hirsch, W.Z. (1960). "Determinants of Public Education Expenditures." *National Tax Journal* 13 (March 1960): 29-40.

_____ , and Marcus, M.J. (1969). "Intercommunity Spillovers and the Provision of Public Education." *Kyklos* 22:641-660.

_____ , Segelhorst, E.W., and Marcus, M.J. (1964). *Spillover of Public Edu-*

cation Costs and Benefits. Los Angeles: Institute of Government and Public Affairs, University of California.

Hooper, J.W. (1959). "Simultaneous Equations and Canonical Correlation Theory." *Econometrica* 27 (April 1959): 245-56.

Horowitz, Ann R. (1968). "A Simultaneous Equation Approach to the Problem of Explaining Interstate Differences in State and Local Government Expenditures." *Southern Economic Journal* 34 (April 1968): 459-76.

Hu, Teh-wei (1972). "Canonical Correlation Analysis vs. Simultaneous Equation Approach: An Empirical Example Evaluating Child Health and Welfare Programs." Paper presented at the European Econometric Society Meeting, September 1972, Budapest, Hungary.

_____, and Booms, Bernard H. (1971). "A Simultaneous Equation Model of Public Expenditure Decisions in Large Cities." *Annals of Regional Science* 5 (December 1971): 73-85.

Illinois State Department of Education (1973). "General State Aid Formulas, 1973-1974." Memo describing House Bill 1484, as amended. Springfield, Illinois.

Jencks, C. (1971). "Giving Parents Money for Schooling." *Compact* 5:25-27.

Johns, R.L. (1971). "The Development of State Support for the Public Schools." In *Status and Impact of Educational Finance Programs*, vol. 4, edited by R.L. Johns, K. Alexander, and D.H. Stollar. Gainesville, Fla.: National Educational Finance Project, pp. 1-27.

_____, and Morphet, E.L. (1969). *The Economics and Financing of Education: A Systems Approach*, 2nd ed. Englewood Cliffs, N.J.: Prentice-Hall.

_____, and Salmon, R.G. (1971). "The Financial Equalization of School Support Programs in the United States for the School Year, 1968-69." In *Status and Impact of Educational Finance Programs*, vol. 4, edited by R.L. Johns, K. Alexander, and D.H. Stollar. Gainesville, Fla.: National Educational Finance Project, pp. 119-91.

_____ et al., eds. (1970). *Economic Factors Affecting the Financing of Education*. Gainesville, Fla.: National Education Finance Project.

Johns, T.L., ed. (1969). *Public School Finance Programs, 1968-69*. Washington, D.C.: U.S. Government Printing Office.

_____, ed. (1972). *Public School Finance Programs, 1971-72*. Washington, D.C.: U.S. Government Printing Office.

Johnston, J. (1972). *Econometric Methods*, rev. ed. New York: McGraw-Hill.

Joint Economic Committee, United States Congress (1969). *The Economics and Financing of Higher Education in the United States*. Washington, D.C.: U.S. Government Printing Office.

Jones, T.H. (1971). *Review of Existing State School Finance Programs* vol. 1. Washington, D.C.: President's Commission on School Finance.

Katzman, Martin T. (1971). *The Political Economy of Urban Schools*. Cambridge, Mass.: Harvard University Press.

Kiesling, Herbert J. (1967). "Measuring a Local Government Service: A Study of School Districts in New York State." *Review of Economics and Statistics* 49 (August 1967): 356-67.

Kuhns, Rodney J. (1972). "Input-Output Analysis of Secondary Schools in Pennsylvania." Unpublished doctoral dissertation, The Pennsylvania State University, Division of Educational Policy Studies.

Leslie, L.L. (1972). *The Rationale for Various Plans for Funding American Higher Education*. University Park, Pa.: Center for the Study of Higher Education, The Pennsylvania State University, Report No. 18.

_____ (1973). *The Trend Toward Government Financing of Higher Education through Students: Can the Market Model Be Applied?* University Park, Pa.: Center for the Study of Higher Education, The Pennsylvania State University, Report No. 19.

Levin, H.M. (1970). "A New Model of School Effectiveness." In *Do Teachers Make a Difference?* pp. 55-78. Washington, D.C.: Government Printing Office.

McKean, R.N. (1958). *Efficiency in Government through Systems Analysis*. New York: John Wiley and Sons, Inc.

McMahon, Walter, W. (1970). "An Economic Analysis of Major Determinants of Expenditures on Public Education." *Review of Economics and Statistics* 52 (August 1970): 242-52.

Margolis, J., ed. (1965). *The Public Economy of Urban Communities*. Washington, D.C.: Resources for the Future, Inc.

Maynard, J. (1971). *Some Microeconomics of Higher Education: Economies of Scale*. Lincoln, Neb.: University of Nebraska Press.

Meyer, A.A. (1967). *An Educational History of the American People*, 2nd ed. New York: McGraw-Hill.

Miner, Jerry (1963). *Social and Economic Factors in Spending for Public Education*. Syracuse, N.Y.: Syracuse University Press.

Mishan, E.J. (1970). *Technology and Growth: The Price We Pay*. New York: Praeger Publishers, Inc.

Moore, D. (1971). "Local Nonproperty Taxes for Schools." In *Status and Impact of Educational Finance Programs*, edited by R.L. Johns, K. Alexander, and D.H. Stollar. Gainesville, Fla.: National Educational Finance Project, pp. 209-221.

Morrison, H.C. (1924). *The Financing of Public Schools in the State of Illinois*. New York: The Macmillan Co.

_____ (1930). *School Revenue*. Chicago: University of Chicago Press.

Morss, E.R. (1966). "Some Thoughts on the Determinants of State and Local Expenditures." *National Tax Journal* 19 (March 1966): 95-103.

_____, Fredland, J.E., and Hymans, S.H. (1967). "Fluctuations in State Expenditures: An Econometric Analysis." *Southern Economic Journal* 33 (April 1967): 496-517.

Mort, P.R. (1933). *State Support for Public Education*. Washington, D.C.: The American Council on Education.

_____; Reusser, W.C.; and Polley, J.W. (1960). *Public School Finance: Its Background, Structure, and Operation*. New York: McGraw-Hill.

Musgrave, R.A. (1959). *The Theory of Public Finance*. New York: McGraw Hill Book Co.

National Education Association, Committee on Educational Finance (1972). *Financial Status of the Public Schools, 1972*. Washington, D.C.: National Education Association.

Netzer, Dick (1966). *Economics of the Property Tax*. Washington, D.C.: The Brookings Institution.

_____(1970). "Impact of the Property Tax: Its Economic Implications for Urban Problems." In *State and Local Finance*, edited by W.E. Mitchell and I. Walter. New York: Ronald Press, pp. 138-74.

O'Brien, Thomas (1971). "Grants-in-Aid: Some Further Answers." *National Tax Journal* 24 (March 1971): 65-77.

Osborn, Donald D. (1970). "Economies of Size Associated with Public High Schools." *Review of Economics and Statistics* 52 (February 1970): 113-15.

Pechman, J.A. (1970). "The Distributional Effects of Public Higher Education in California." *Journal of Human Resources* 5 (Summer 1970): 361-70.

Phi Delta Kappan (1970). Special Issue on Educational Vouchers. Vol. 52 (September 1970).

Pigou, A.C. (1920). *The Economics of Welfare*. London: Macmillan and Co.

President's Commission on School Finance (1972). *Schools, People, and Money*. Washington, D.C.: U.S. Government Printing Office.

Raymond, Richard (1968). "Determinants of the Quality of Primary and Secondary Public Education in West Virginia." *Journal of Human Resources* 3 (Fall 1968): 450-470.

Renshaw, Edward F. (1960). "A Note on the Expenditure Effect of State Aid to Education." *Journal of Political Economy* 68 (April 1960): 170-174.

Ribich, T.I. (1968). *Education and Poverty*. Washington, D.C.: The Brookings Institution.

_____(1970). "The Effect of Educational Spending on Poverty Reduction." In Johns et al. (1970): 207-234.

Riew, John (1966). "Economies of Scale in High School Operations." *Review of Economics and Statistics* 48 (August 1966): 280-87.

_____(1970). "State Aids for Public Schools and Metropolitan Finance." *Land Economics* 46 (August 1970): 297-304.

_____(1971). "The Case for a Federal Tax Credit of Municipal Income Tax." *Public Policy* 19 (Summer 1971): 379-88.

_____(1973). "Assigning Collections of a Statewide Uniform Rate Land Tax to Finance Local Education." In *Property Taxation and the Finance of Education*, edited by Richard W. Lindholm. Madison, Wisconsin: The University of Wisconsin Press.

Rockefeller Brothers Fund (1958). *The Pursuit of Excellence: Education and the Future of America*. New York: Doubleday and Co.

Sabulao, C.M., and Hickrod, G.A. (1971). "Optimum Size of School District Relative to Selected Costs." *Journal of Educational Administration* 9 (October 1971): 178-91.

Sacks, Seymour (1972). *City School, Suburban School: A History of Conflict*. Syracuse, N.Y.: Syracuse University Press.

_____, and Harris, R. (1964). "The Determinants of State and Local Government Expenditures and Intergovernmental Flow of Funds." *National Tax Journal* 17 (March 1964): 75-85.

School Finance Study Unit (1973). "New School Finance Laws in Maine and Montana." Washington: Department of Health, Education and Welfare (August 23, 1973), mimeographed.

Schultz, T.W. (1961). "Education and Economic Growth." In *Social Forces Influencing American Education*, edited by N.B. Henry, pp. 46-88. Chicago: University of Chicago Press.

Scitovsky, T. (1971). *Welfare and Competition*, rev. ed. Homewood, Illinois: Richard D. Irwin, Inc.

Shannon, Thomas A. (1973). "Rodrigues: A Dream Shattered or a Call for Finance Reform?" *Phi Delta Kappan* 55 (May 1973): 587-88, 640-41.

Shapiro, S. (1962). "Some Socioeconomic Determinants of Expenditures for Education: Southern and Other States Compared." *Comparative Education Review* 6 (October 1962): 160-66.

Shapp, Milton J. (1973). *1973-74 Budget Message*. Harrisburg, Pa., February 6, 1973.

Sharkansky, Ira (1967). "Some More Thoughts about the Determinants of Government Expenditure." *National Tax Journal* 20 (June 1967): 171-79.

_____ (1970). "Benefits and Costs of Higher Education and Income Redistribution: Comment." *Journal of Human Resources* 5 (Spring 1970): 230-36.

Sharp, A.M., and Sliger, B.F. (1970). *Public Finance*, rev. ed. Austin Texas: Business Publications, Inc.

Shell, K. (1970). "Notes on the Educational Opportunity Bank." *National Tax Journal* 23 (June 1970): 214-20.

_____ et al. (1968). "The Educational Opportunity Bank: An Economic Analysis of a Contingent Repayment Loan Program for Higher Education." *National Tax Journal* 21 (March 1968): 2-45.

Simon, Kenneth A., and Frankel, M.M. (1972). *Projections of Educational Statistics to 1980-81*. Washington: Government Printing Office.

_____, and Fullam, Marie G. (1968). *Projections of Educational Statistics to 1976-77*. Washington, D.C.: U.S. Office of Education.

_____, and Fullam, Marie G. (1969). *Projections of Educational Statistics to 1977-78*. Washington, D.C.: U.S. Office of Education.

_____, and Grant, W.V. (1972). *Digest of Educational Statistics*. Washington, D.C.: U.S. Office of Education.

Solmon, L.C. (1970). "A Note on Equality of Educational Opportunity," *American Economic Review* 60 (September 1970): 768-71.

Spiegleman, R.G. (1968). "A Benefit/Cost Model to Evaluate Educational Programs." *Socio-Economic Planning Sciences* 1:443-60.

Stigler, G.J. (1966). *The Theory of Price*, 3rd ed. New York: The Macmillan Co.

Strayer, G.D., and Haig, R.M. (1923). *The Financing of Education in the State of New York*. New York: The Macmillan Co.

Summers, Anita A. (1973). "Equity in School Financing: The Courts Move in." *Business Review*, Federal Reserve Bank of Philadelphia (March 1971): 3-13.

Taubman, P., and Wales, T. (1972). *Education as an Investment and a Screening Device*. New York: National Bureau of Economic Research.

Thomas, J. Alan (1970). "Full State Funding of Education." *Administrator's Handbook* 18 (May 1970): 1-4.

Tintner, G. (1946). "Some Applications of Multivariable Analysis in Economic Data." *Journal of the American Statistical Association* 41:472-500.

Tollison, R.D., and Willett, T.D. (1973). "The University and the Price System." *Journal of Economics and Business* 25 (Spring-Summer 1973): 191-97.

Toole, P.F.; Campbell, P.B.; and Beers, J.S. (1970). *Educational Quality Assessment Phase II Findings, Section 3: Reliability and Validity*. Harrisburg, Pa.: Pennsylvania Department of Education.

Van Den Haag, E. (1956). *Education as an Industry*. New York: Augustus M. Kelley.

Vickrey, W. (1962). "A Proposal for Student Loans." In *Economics of Higher Education*, edited by S.J. Mushkin, pp. 268-80. Washington, D.C.: U.S. Office of Education.

Walsh, L.C., and Walsh, M.T. (1930). *The History and Organization of Education in Pennsylvania*. Indiana, Pa.: R.S. Grose Printing Shop.

Waugh, F.V. (1942). "Regressions between Two Sets of Variables." *Econometrica* 10:290-310.

Weisbrod, B.A. (1962). "Education and Investment in Human Capital." *Journal of Political Economy* (Supplement) 70:106-123.

_____ (1964). *External Benefits of Public Education: An Economic Analysis*. Princeton: Industrial Relations Section, Princeton University.

Wise, A.E., and Thomas, J.A. (1973). "Full State Funding." In Hickrod et al. (1973), pp. 67-76.

Weiss, S.J., and Driscoll, D. (1972). "Comparative School Finance Data, New England States vs. California." In *Financing Public Schools* (1972), pp. 16-43.

Zacharias, J.R. (1969). "Educational Opportunity through Student Loans: An Approach to Higher Education Financing." In Joint Economic Committee (1969): 652-663.

Indexes

Author Index

157

Subject Index

About the Authors

Elchanan Cohn is associate professor of economics at The Pennsylvania State University. He received the B.A. and the M.A. from the University of Minnesota and the Ph.D. from Iowa State University. He is the author of *The Economics of Education* and *Public Expenditure Analysis* (Lexington Books, 1972). He has contributed articles, notes, and reviews to professional journals in economics, business, and education, and is the author or coauthor of several research reports submitted to state and federal government agencies. He is preparing a report to the National Institute of Education on management-oriented approaches to study input-output relationships in public education, and a book manuscript, *Input-Output Analysis in Public Education.*

Stephen D. Millman is Staff Specialist for Student Affairs and Services with the Maryland State Board for Community Colleges. He received the Ph.D. from The Pennsylvania State University, where he also served in various research capacities with the University's Institute for Research on Human Resources and Center for the Study of Higher Education. His past research interests have included the impact of educational environments on students, the job-search behavior of college graduates, and the development of state systems of public higher education. He has also served as assistant to the Dean, Student Affairs at The Pennsylvania State University and as resident counselor at the University of Georgia.